Parga, a small port in a typically rugged Greek setting, nestles on pine-covered slopes between the mountains of Epirus and the Ionian Sea. Tiny islands dot its harbor.

R. G. Everts–Rapho-Photo Researchers, Inc.

Funk & Wagnalls New Encyclopedia

VOLUME 11

FRANCE, ANATOLE to GLOVE

LEON L. BRAM
Vice-President and Editorial Director

NORMA H. DICKEY
Editor-in-Chief

Funk & Wagnalls Corporation

Publishers since 1876

Funk & Wagnalls New Encyclopedia is liberally provided with **finding devices** that aid in the search for information. The brief descriptions and suggestions that follow are intended to encourage the proper use of these devices so that full use is made of the information resources within these pages.

The **index** in volume 29 should be the starting point in a search for information. If a search is made *without* the use of the index, the following suggestions should be kept in mind:

- If the search is *unsuccessful*, the index should be used to search again. The topic may be discussed in an article that was overlooked. Only after use of the index can a search be considered thorough or completed.

- If the search is initially *successful*, the index should be used to find additional information. A topic may be discussed in several articles; the index can locate the less-obvious ones.

The use and structure of the index is explained in the Guide to the Index, volume 29, pages 6–8.

Cross-references of several types are used frequently within most articles in Funk & Wagnalls New Encyclopedia. Each cross-reference directs the search for information to other articles that contain additional or related information. The types of cross-references and their specific uses are explained in the Guide to Funk & Wagnalls New Encyclopedia, volume 1, pages 60–63, under the subhead, Cross-references.

Bibliography cross-references follow all the major articles in Funk & Wagnalls New Encyclopedia. They direct the search for further information from the articles to appropriate **reading lists** of books and periodicals in the **bibliography** in volume 28. The reading lists may also be used for independent study. A full description of bibliography cross-references and reading lists is found in the Preface and Guide to the Bibliography, volume 28, pages 186–87.

SELECTED ABBREVIATIONS USED IN TEXT*

AC	alternating current	F	Fahrenheit	Nor.	Norwegian
AD	*anno Domini* (Lat., "in the year of the Lord")	Finn.	Finnish	O.E.	Old English
		fl.	flourished	O.Fr.	Old French
		FM	frequency modulation	O.H.G.	Old High German
alt.	altitude			O.N.	Old Norse
AM	*ante meridiem* (Lat., "before noon")	Fr.	French	Op.	*Opus* (Lat., "work")
		ft	foot, feet	oz	ounce(s)
		g	gram(s)	Pers.	Persian
AM	amplitude modulation	gal	gallon(s)	PM	*post meridiem* (Lat., "after noon")
		Ger.	German		
amu	atomic mass unit(s)	GeV	billion electron volts	Pol.	Polish
Arab.	Arabic			pop.	population
Arm.	Armenian	Gr.	Greek	Port.	Portuguese
A.S.	Anglo-Saxon	ha	hectare(s)	q.v.	*quod vide* (Lat., "which see")
ASSR	Autonomous Soviet Socialist Republic	Heb.	Hebrew		
		hp	horsepower	r.	reigned
atm.	atmosphere	hr	hour	R.	River
at.no.	atomic number	Hung.	Hungarian	repr.	reprinted
at.wt.	atomic weight	Hz	hertz or cycle(s) per second	rev.	revised
b.	born			Rom.	Romanian
BC	before Christ	Icel.	Icelandic	Rus.	Russian
b.p.	boiling point	i.e.	*id est* (Lat., "that is")	S	south; southern
Btu	British Thermal Unit			sec.	second(s); secant
		in	inch(es)	SFSR	Soviet Federated Socialist Republic
bu	bushel(s)	inc.	incorporated		
Bulg.	Bulgarian	Ital.	Italian	Skt.	Sanskrit
C	Celsius	Jap.	Japanese	Span.	Spanish
c.	*circa* (Lat., "about")	K	Kelvin	sp.gr.	specific gravity
cent.	century	kg	kilogram(s)	sq	square
Chin.	Chinese	km	kilometer(s)	sq km	square kilometer(s)
cm	centimeter(s)	kw	kilowatt(s)	sq mi	square mile(s)
Co.	Company, County	kwh	kilowatt hour(s)	SSR	Soviet Socialist Republic
cu	cubic	Lat.	Latin		
Czech.	Czechoslovakian	lat	latitude	St.	Saint, Street
d.	died	lb	pound(s)	Sum.	Sumerian
Dan.	Danish	long	longitude	Swed.	Swedish
DC	direct current	m	meter(s)	trans.	translated, translation, translator(s)
Du.	Dutch	mass no.	mass number		
E	east; eastern	MeV	million electron volts		
ed.	edited, edition, editors			Turk.	Turkish
		mg	milligram(s)	Ukr.	Ukrainian
e.g.	*exempli gratia* (Lat., "for example")	mi	mile(s)	UN	United Nations
		min	minute(s)	U.S.	United States
Egypt.	Egyptian	ml	milliliter(s)	USSR	Union of Soviet Socialist Republics
Eng.	English	mm	millimeter(s)		
est.	established; estimated	m.p.	melting point	v.	versus; verse
		mph	miles per hour	Ved.	Vedic
et al.	*et alii* (Lat., "and others")	Mt(s).	Mount, Mountain(s)	vol.	Volume(s)
				W	west; western
EV	electron volt(s)	N	north; northern	yd	yard(s)

* For a more extensive listing, see ABBREVIATIONS AND ACRONYMS. Charts of pertinent abbreviations also accompany the articles DEGREE, ACADEMIC; ELEMENTS, CHEMICAL; MATHEMATICAL SYMBOLS; and WEIGHTS AND MEASURES.

FUNK & WAGNALLS NEW ENCYCLOPEDIA

FRANCE, Anatole, pseudonym of JACQUES ANA-TOLE FRANÇOIS THIBAULT (1844–1924), French novelist and Nobel laureate, who is frequently regarded as the greatest French writer of the late 19th and early 20th centuries.

France was born on April 16, 1844, in Paris. He attended the Stanislas School in Paris, but was mostly self-educated. From early youth he was an insatiable reader. His first published books were the volume of verse *Les poèmes dorés* (Golden Tales, 1873) and the verse drama *The Bride of Corinth* (1876; trans. 1920). It was not, however, until the publication of his first novel, *The Crime of Sylvestre Bonnard* (1881; trans. 1906), that he exhibited the stylistic grace, subtle, biting irony, and genuine compassion that later became the distinguishing characteristics of his work. He produced a large body of writings, including novels, drama, verse, critical and philosophical essays, and historical works. He was elected to the French Academy in 1896 and was awarded the 1921 Nobel Prize in literature.

In 1883 France formed a liaison with Madame Arman de Caillavet (1844–1910), who inspired France to arduous creative labors and promoted his works through her social connections. His writings of those middle years include the critical essays *La vie littéraire* (The Literary Life, 4 vol., 1888–92); the novels *Thaïs* (1890; trans. 1909) and *The Red Lily* (1894; trans. 1908); and the tetralogy of novels *L'histoire contemporaine* (A Contemporary Tale, 1897–1901), a harsh analysis of the corrosive effects on French life of the Dreyfus affair. France was among the French intellectuals who fought successfully for the exoneration of Alfred Dreyfus (1859–1935), an army captain convicted of treason (*see* DREYFUS AFFAIR).

In his later works France became an advocate of humanitarian causes. He made eloquent pleas in his writings for civil liberties, popular education, and the rights of labor, and he attacked with bitter, brilliant satire the political, economic, and social abuses of his time. Despite his polemics, however, the elegant, sweeping cadences and masterly language of France's works testified to his devotion to classical forms. Outstanding among the writings that demonstrate both his powerful social consciousness and his classical eloquence are the allegorical novels *Penguin Island* (1908; trans. 1909) and *The Revolt of the Angels* (1914; trans. 1914) and an account of the Reign of Terror during the French Revolution, *The Gods Are Athirst* (1912; trans. 1913). France died at Tours on Oct. 13, 1924.

FRANCESCA, Piero della. *See* PIERO DELLA FRANCESCA.

FRANCESCA DA RIMINI (d. 1285?), Italian noblewoman and romantic heroine, daughter of Guido da Polenta (ruled Ravenna, 1275–90), probably born in Ravenna. Most likely because the alliance was important to her father for political reasons, Francesca married (1275) Giovanni Malatesta da Rimini (d. 1304), who was allegedly very unattractive. She was drawn to Giovanni's younger brother Paolo Malatesta da Rimini (d. 1285?), who became her lover. When her husband discovered the relationship, he murdered the couple. This tragic love affair provides the theme of one of the most famous episodes of *The Divine Comedy,* by Dante, in which Paolo and Francesca are depicted with great compassion. The story has inspired other works of literature, including the poem *Story of Rimini* (1816), by the English author Leigh Hunt, and the drama *Francesca da Rimini* (1902), by the Italian writer Gabriele D'Annunzio. The story of Francesca has also been the subject of works by the 19th-century French painters J. A. D. Ingres and Alexandre Cabanel (1823–89), and of the orchestral fantasy "Francesca da Rimini" (1876), by the Russian composer Peter Ilich Tchaikovsky.

FRANCESCO (MAURIZIO) DI GIORGIO MARTINI (1439–c. 1501), Italian artist, whose versatile output—paintings, sculpture, architecture, and military fortifications—made him a dominant figure of the late 15th-century north Italian school. His most important work (aside from unsubstantiated contributions to the Ducal Palace of Urbino) is the octagonal-domed Church of Santa Maria del Calcinaio (1485), near Cortona, one of the most perfect of 15th-century churches; its proportions are strongly indebted to the dome of Florence Cathedral, by the earlier Florentine master Filippo Brunelleschi. Later artists were influenced by Francesco's paintings and sculptures as well as by his *Treatise on Civil and Military Architecture* (1492).

FRANCHISE, in government and economics, a special right or privilege granted to an individual or a group to carry on a particular activity. The term is used in several ways. A municipality, for example, awards franchises to corporations to operate public utilities, such as electric and telephone services, in a given area. Rates to be charged and services to be provided to the public, as well as tenure and labor regulations, are stipulated in a contract between the parties. If the terms of the contract are violated, the grantor may institute proceedings in order to revoke the agreement.

In business, the term *franchise* refers to the exclusive right given to someone to market a company's goods or services in a designated territory. In return for a specified fee and usually a share of the profits, the franchisor provides the product, the name, and sometimes the physical plant and the advertising. One well-known example of a franchised business is McDonald's, the fast-food restaurant chain.

In politics, the franchise is the right of an individual to vote.

See SUFFRAGE; WOMAN SUFFRAGE.

FRANCIA, José Gaspar Rodríguez (1766-1840), Paraguayan dictator, born in Asunción, and educated at the University of Córdoba, Argentina. Although trained in theology, he maintained a legal practice in Asunción. When Paraguay gained its independence from Spain in 1811, he was appointed to the junta, or administrative council. In 1814 he was made dictator of Paraguay for three years and in 1817 was chosen dictator for life. Francia's rule was tyrannical, and he kept the country in semiisolation from the outside world, but he also fostered new developments in industry, trade, and agriculture.

FRANCIS, Saint. *See* FRANCIS OF ASSISI, SAINT.

FRANCIS I (1494-1547), king of France (1515-47), remembered for his rivalry with the Habsburg Holy Roman emperor Charles V, for his patronage of arts and letters, and for his governmental reforms.

A portrait of Francis I, king of France, by the 16th-century Flemish artist Joos van Cleve.

Born at Cognac on Sept. 12, 1494, Francis represented the Angoulême branch of the Valois dynasty, succeeding Louis XII, the last of the Orleanist branch, in 1515. His mother, Louise of Savoy (1476-1531), and his elder sister, Margaret of Navarre, influenced his upbringing and remained close to him during his reign. His first wife was Louis XII's daughter Claude (1499-1524).

The Valois-Habsburg Wars. In 1515 Francis personally won a spectacular victory over the Swiss at Marignano, which enabled him to seize the Italian duchy of Milan. In 1519 he was a candidate for the throne of the Holy Roman Empire, but the imperial electors chose Charles of Habsburg instead. He then embarked on a war against Charles in Italy, but was defeated and captured at Pavia in 1525. Imprisoned in Spain, he was ransomed and returned to France in 1527. After another round of fighting, the two monarchs made peace in 1529, and Francis married the emperor's sister, Eleanor.

Further inconclusive wars were fought against the Habsburgs in 1536-38 and 1542-44. In this period the Catholic Francis did not hesitate to ally himself with German Protestant princes and even with the Muslim Turks.

Religious and Financial Policies. Under his sister's influence Francis was sympathetic to Protestantism, especially in its humanist form, when it appeared in France in the 1520s. In the 1530s, however, he abandoned his earlier tolerance and became a persecutor of the French Protestants. The king had concluded a concordat with the papacy at Bologna in 1516, thereby gaining greater control of the French Catholic church.

The cost of war obliged Francis to undertake extensive reforms. He floated government bonds, punished royal fiscal agents who misappropriated funds, and twice reorganized the treasury. He began openly to sell judicial and financial offices, creating a new class of ennobled magistrates, which remained an important element in French governmental and social structures until the French Revolution. The traditional nobility served in his armies and flocked to court to secure the patronage of the king or his favorites among the magnates. In this way factions arose, and when the king died at Rambouillet on March 31, 1547, his reign had lost much of its glamour.

Patronage of Art and Learning. Francis adopted the pose of a chivalric king, the first gentleman of his kingdom, although his autocratic statecraft was informed by a shrewd realism. His patronage of the arts was intended to augment the splendor of his court. He brought Leonardo da Vinci and other great Italian artists to France to design and ornament his châteaux. He employed the scholar Guillaume Budé in creating a royal library and in founding professorships of Greek, Latin, and Hebrew, which formed the nucleus of the later Collège de France. J.H.M.S.

FRANCIS II (1544–60), king of France (1559–60), born in Fontainebleau, the eldest son of Henry II. In 1558 Francis married Mary, queen of Scots. Francis was a mental and physical weakling and was dominated by François, duke of Guise, and Cardinal Charles of Lorraine, the uncles of his wife. These two men, who in effect were the rulers during Francis's brief reign, tried to repress the growing political power of the Protestants in France. His death ended the ascendancy of the Guises at court.

FRANCIS I, originally Francis Stephen (1708–65), Holy Roman emperor (1745–65), born in Nancy in the duchy of Lorraine, and educated in Vienna. The son of Leopold, duke of Lorraine (r. 1697–1729), Francis succeeded his father in 1729, but ceded Lorraine in 1737 to Stanislas I Leszczyński, king of Poland, in exchange for the Grand Duchy of Tuscany. Francis married Maria Theresa, archduchess of Austria, in 1736 and with her ruled (1740–45) the Habsburg hereditary dominions. In 1745, through the influence of his wife, he became Holy Roman emperor. Francis took little active part, however, in government, leaving that to Maria Theresa. From the time of their marriage, the Austrian dynasty became known as the house of Habsburg-Lorraine.

FRANCIS II (1768–1835), last Holy Roman emperor (1792–1806) and, as Francis I, first emperor of Austria (1804–35). Born in Florence, Italy, and educated in Vienna, he succeeded his father Leopold II as Holy Roman emperor. From the start of his reign until 1815 Francis was involved in the wars of the French Revolution and in the Napoleonic Wars. After the extension of French control over western Germany and the reorganization of the German states by Napoleon Bonaparte in 1803, Francis consolidated his power in Austria, Hungary, Bohemia, and northern Italy and proclaimed himself emperor of Austria in 1804. Two years later he formally dissolved the old Holy Roman Empire. As emperor of Austria, Francis gave Prince Klemens von Metternich almost complete control of foreign affairs after 1809 and devoted himself to the internal administration of the empire. The marriage of his daughter Marie Louise (1791–1847) to Napoleon in 1810 earned for Francis three peaceful years in which to re-create Austrian strength for participation in the campaign that would bring about (1814–15) Napoleon's downfall. By the decisions of the Congress of Vienna in 1815, Francis recovered most of the territory Austria had lost to Napoleon. The last 20 years of his reign were marked by paternalistic measures, reactionary tendencies, and repression of liberalism.

FRANCIS I (1777–1830), king of the Two Sicilies (1825–30), the son of King Ferdinand I. Francis was viceroy of Sicily from 1812 to 1816 and duke of Calabria from 1817 to 1825. In the former post he granted the Sicilians a constitution, but when he became king, he renounced his former liberalism.

FRANCIS II (1836–94), king of Naples (1859–61). Son of Ferdinand II, king of the Two Sicilies, and grandson of Francis I, he was the last Bourbon ruler of the Two Sicilies. He tried to continue the autocratic policies of his father, but his kingdom was lost in the unification of Italy. In 1860 the kingdom was invaded by revolutionary troops under the Italian nationalist leader Giuseppe Garibaldi, and it was forced to capitulate the following year. Compelled to abdicate in 1861, Francis lived thereafter in various European countries, from which he occasionally organized abortive conspiracies against the new kingdom of Italy.

FRANCIS OF ASSISI, Saint (1182–1226), Italian mystic and preacher, who founded the Franciscans. Born in Assisi, Italy and originally named Giovanni Francesco Bernardone, he appears to have received little formal education, even though his father was a wealthy merchant. As a young man, Francis led a worldly, carefree life.

St. Francis Speaking to the Birds *(from a 13th-cent. illuminated manuscript).*   Pierpont Morgan Library

Following a battle between Assisi and Perugia, he was held captive in Perugia for over a year. While imprisoned, he suffered a severe illness during which he resolved to alter his way of life. Back in Assisi in 1205, he performed charities among the lepers and began working on the restoration of dilapidated churches. Francis's change of character and his expenditures for charity angered his father, who legally disinherited him. Francis then discarded his rich garments for a bishop's cloak and devoted the next three years to the care of outcasts and lepers in the woods of Mount Subasio.

For his devotions on Mount Subasio, Francis restored the ruined chapel of Santa Maria degli Angeli. In 1208, one day during Mass, he heard a call telling him to go out into the world and, according to the text of Matt. 10:5–14, to possess nothing, but to do good everywhere.

Upon returning to Assisi that same year, Francis began preaching. He gathered round him the 12 disciples who became the original brothers of his order, later called the First Order; they elected Francis superior. In 1212 he received a young, well-born nun of Assisi, Clare, into Franciscan fellowship; through her was established the Order of the Poor Ladies (the Poor Clares), later the Second Order of Franciscans. It was probably later in 1212 that Francis set out for the

Holy Land, but shipwreck forced him to return. Other difficulties prevented him from accomplishing much missionary work when he went to Spain to preach to the Moors. In 1219 he was in Egypt, where he succeeded in preaching to, but not in converting, the sultan. Francis then went on to the Holy Land, staying there until 1220. He wished to be martyred and rejoiced upon hearing that five Franciscan friars had been killed in Morocco while carrying out their duties. On his return home he found dissension in the ranks of the friars and resigned as superior, spending the next few years in planning what became the Third Order of Franciscans, the tertiaries.

In September 1224, after 40 days of fasting, Francis was praying upon Monte Alverno when he felt pain mingled with joy, and the marks of the crucifixion of Christ, the stigmata, appeared on his body. Accounts of the appearance of these marks differ, but it seems probable that they were knobby protuberances of the flesh, resembling the heads of nails. Francis was carried back to Assisi, where his remaining years were marked by physical pain and almost total blindness. He was canonized in 1228. In 1980, Pope John Paul II proclaimed him the patron saint of ecologists. In art, the emblems of St. Francis are the wolf, the lamb, the fish, birds, and the stigmata. His feast day is October 4.   T.M.H.

FRANCISCANS *or* **ORDER OF FRIARS MINOR,** religious order founded, probably in 1208, by St. Francis of Assisi and approved by Pope Innocent III in 1209. After devoting himself to a life of preaching, service, and poverty, Francis gathered around him a band of 12 disciples. He led them from Assisi to Rome to ask for the blessing of the pope, who expressed doubt about the practicability of the way of life that the group proposed to adopt. Pope Innocent gave them his blessing, however, on condition that they become clerics and elect a superior. Francis was elected superior and the group returned to Assisi, where they obtained from the Benedictine abbey on Mount Subasio the use of the little chapel of Santa Maria degli Angeli, around which they constructed huts of branches. Then, in imitation of Christ, they began a life of itinerant preaching and voluntary poverty.

At this time the brotherhood lacked formal organization and a novitiate, but as the disciples increased and their teaching spread, it became obvious that the personal example of Francis would not suffice to enforce discipline among the friars. In 1223 Pope Honorius III (d. 1227) issued a bull that constituted the Friars Minor a formal order and instituted a one-year novitiate.

Following the death of Francis in 1226, the

convent and basilica at Assisi were built. Their magnificence disturbed some, who believed it inconsistent with Francis's ideals of poverty. After much dissension, Pope Gregory IX decreed that moneys could be held by elected trustees of the order and that the building of convents was not contrary to the intentions of the founder.

As time passed, the order grew, the only body of equal power being the Dominicans. The Franciscans, however, became fractionalized, and in 1517 Pope Leo X divided the order into two bodies, the Conventuals, who were allowed corporate property, as were other monastic orders, and the Observants, who sought to follow the precepts of Francis as closely as possible. The Observants have ever since been the larger branch, and early in the 16th century a third body, the Capuchins, was organized out of it and made independent. At the end of the 19th century Leo XIII grouped these three bodies together as the First Order of Friars Minor, designating the nuns known as Poor Clares as the Second Order, and the tertiaries, men and women living in secular society without celibacy, as the Third Order.

In addition to their preaching and charitable work, the Franciscans have been noted for their devotion to learning. Before the Reformation in England they held many positions in the universities, prominent among the professors being John Duns Scotus, William of Ockham, and Roger Bacon. The order has produced four popes—Sixtus IV, Julius II, Sixtus V, and Clement XIV—and one antipope, Alexander V (c. 1340-1410).

On his first voyage of discovery to America, Christopher Columbus was accompanied by a group of Franciscans. The first convents in America were established by them, at Santo Domingo and La Vega in what is now the Dominican Republic. The rapid conversion of the Indians and the consequent enthusiasm of the missionary-minded in Spain led to the further spread of the order in the West Indies; before 1505, Ferdinand V, king of Castile, found it necessary to issue a decree that new convents should be placed at least five leagues apart. While the Spanish Franciscans gradually spread through the southern part of the New World as far as the Pacific Ocean, the French friars, who had arrived in Canada in 1615, at the behest of the French explorer Samuel de Champlain, set up missions throughout the north. Today the Franciscans conduct a university and five colleges in the U.S., and a seminary, in Allegany, N.Y. They also engage in regular parish work, as well as mission work among the Indians.

The supreme government of the order is vested in an elective general, resident at the General Motherhouse, in Rome. Subordinate are the provincials, who preside over all the brethen in a province, and the *custodes,* or guardians (never called abbots, as are their counterparts in other orders), at the head of a single community or convent. These officers are elected for a period of two years.

In the eary 20th century a number of Franciscan communities for both men and women were established by various Anglican churches. The most prominent of these is the Society of Saint Francis in Cerne Abbas, Dorset, England, which maintains several houses in the British Isles and in New Guinea. In 1967 a similar group in the U.S. was united with these English friars.

FRANCIS FERDINAND, in German, Franz Ferdinand (1863-1914), archduke of Austria, born in Graz, son of Archduke Charles Louis (1833-96) and nephew of Emperor Francis Joseph. In 1875 he inherited the title archduke of Austria-Este. After the deaths of his cousin, Crown Prince Rudolf, in 1889, and of his father, in 1896, Francis became heir to the Austro-Hungarian crown. Because of his morganatic marriage in 1900 to Countess Sophie Chotek, duchess of Hohenberg (1868-1914), Francis relinquished all claim to the throne for his children. Although he was favorably inclined toward the aspirations of the Slavs, he and his wife were assassinated in Sarajevo, Bosnia (now in Yugoslavia), on June 28, 1914, by Serbian nationalists. The incident precipitated World War I.

FRANCIS JOSEPH I, in German, Franz Josef (1830-1916), emperor of Austria (1848-1916) and king of Hungary (1867-1916), the last important ruler of the Habsburg dynasty; his policies played a major role in the events that led to World War I.

Francis Joseph was born in Vienna on Aug. 18, 1830, the eldest son of Archduke Francis Charles (1802-78), brother and heir of Austrian Emperor Ferdinand I. Francis Charles having renounced his right to the throne, Francis Joseph became emperor when Ferdinand abdicated during the revolution of 1848. With Russian help, he and his prime minister, Felix, prince zu Schwarzenberg (1800-52), restored order in the empire and reestablished Austrian dominance in the German confederation (1849-50). In 1854 he married Elizabeth (1837-98), daughter of Duke Maximilian of Bavaria, with whom he had one son and three daughters. Francis Joseph's failure to support Russia in the Crimean War (1854-56) permanently damaged Austro-Russian relations, and in the decade that followed, Austria lost most of its Italian possessions, as well as its position of lead-

11

ership in Germany. Weakened by these reverses, Francis Joseph was forced to agree to Hungarian demands for autonomy in 1867, when he and Elizabeth were formally crowned in Budapest as king and queen of Hungary. He also planned to grant some form of self-government to the Austrian Slavs but backed down because of opposition from the German and Hungarian elite that controlled the new monarchy of Austria-Hungary. The resulting dissatisfaction among Francis Joseph's Czechoslovakian and Serbian subjects further weakened the Habsburg realms and caused increased friction with Russia, which championed the cause of Europe's Slavic peoples. Beginning in the 1870s, Austria-Hungary gradually became subservient to its powerful neighbor and ally, the Prussian-dominated German Empire.

Francis Joseph's later years were marked by a series of tragedies in his family. In 1889 his only son and heir to the throne, Archduke Rudolf, committed suicide; in 1898 his wife, the empress Elizabeth, was assassinated by an Italian anarchist; and in 1914 his nephew, Francis Ferdinand, who had replaced Rudolf as heir to the throne, was assassinated by a Serbian nationalist. The murder of Francis Ferdinand precipitated the crisis between Austria-Hungary and Germany on the one hand, and Serbia and Russia on the other, that led to World War I. Francis Joseph did not live to see Austria's defeat in the war and the extinction of the Habsburg monarchy. He died on Nov. 21, 1916.

FRANCIS OF SALES, Saint (1567–1622), French Roman Catholic prelate and writer, born in Thorens, of a noble Savoyard family, and educated at the Jesuit College of Clermont in Paris and at the University of Padua. He received the degree of doctor of laws at the latter institution in 1591 and was ordained a priest two years later. In 1594 he was sent to Chablais, a former region in the duchy of Savoy, to convert the Calvinists. In 1602 he was appointed bishop of Geneva. In 1610 he helped found the Order of the Visitation of Our Lady specifically for persons debarred by physical handicaps from entry into other orders. Francis is chiefly remembered, however, for his insistence—contrary to the popular belief of his time—that it is possible for an ordinary person to lead a wholly pious and saintly life while remaining in worldly society, instead of withdrawing into a monastic order. He was canonized in 1665, and in 1877 Pope Pius IX declared him a Doctor of the Church. Since 1922 he has been regarded as the patron saint of Roman Catholic writers. His works include the widely read religious classic *Introduction to the Devout Life,*

Treatise on the Love of God, and letters and sermons. His feast day is January 29.

FRANCIS XAVIER, Saint. *See* XAVIER, SAINT FRANCIS.

FRANCIUM, radioactive metallic element, symbol Fr, one of the alkali metals (q.v.) in group 1 (or Ia) of the periodic table (*see* PERIODIC LAW); at.no. 87, at.wt. (most stable isotope) 223. Marguerite Perey (1909–75) of the Curie Laboratory of the Radium Institute of Paris discovered this element in 1939 and studied its physical and chemical properties.

Actinium disintegrates into francium. Francium is naturally radioactive; its longest-lived isotope, francium-223, or actinium-K, has a half-life of 22 minutes. It emits a beta particle of 1,100,000 electron volts (EV) energy. Isotopes ranging in mass from 204 to 224 are known.

Francium is the heaviest of the alkali metals and closely resembles cesium in its chemical properties. It is the most electropositive element. All its isotopes are radioactive and short-lived; they have been studied only by tracer chemistry. *See* RADIOACTIVITY.

FRANCK, César Auguste (1822–90), Belgian-born French composer and organist, whose work during the late 19th century significantly influenced the direction of French music.

Franck was born in Liège. A precocious musician, he made a piano concert tour of Belgium at the age of 11. He studied music in Liège and, from 1837 to 1842, at the Paris Conservatoire,

César Auguste Franck

where he revealed great ability as an organist and composer. From 1844 he taught music privately in Paris. In 1872 he became professor of organ at the conservatory, and from 1858 to 1890 he was organist at the Church of Sainte Clotilde, Paris. Among his pupils at the conservatory were the French composers Vincent d'Indy and Ernest Chausson. Franck became a French citizen in 1873. He died on Nov. 8, 1890, following a street accident in Paris.

Franck's work is characterized by the use of classical forms, including the symphony and sonata, which he imbued with a romantic spirit. He alternated between themes of a mystical and brooding nature and those of a dramatic and emotional type. He was one of the outstanding practitioners of the modern cyclical form, in which themes recur in modified form throughout a work.

Although Franck's work was neglected during his lifetime, his compositions are now part of the standard repertoire of instrumentalists and orchestras. His Symphony in D minor (1886-88) ranks among the most popular of all symphonies and has served as the model for many important French symphonic works.

Among Franck's other compositions are the oratorio *Les béatitudes* (1869-79); orchestral works, including three symphonic poems; *Variations symphoniques* for piano and orchestra (1885); the Sonata for Piano and Violin (1886); and organ works, including *Six pièces pour grand orgue* (1860-62) and *Trois chorals* (1890).

FRANCK, James (1882-1964), German-American physicist, chemist, and Nobel laureate, born in Hamburg, and educated at the universities of Heidelberg and Berlin. He was professor of physics at several universities in Germany and the U.S. In collaboration with the German physicist Gustav Hertz, Franck conducted notable experiments on the effects produced by bombarding atoms with electrons. For that research, which provided experimental verification of the quantum theory, he shared the 1925 Nobel Prize in physics with Hertz. Franck is also noted for his important contributions to the study of photosynthesis.

FRANCO, Francisco (1892-1975), general and authoritarian leader (caudillo), who governed Spain from 1939 to 1975.

Franco was born on Dec. 4, 1892, in El Ferrol, Spain. After graduating from the infantry academy in 1910, he rose rapidly in the army, earning a reputation for efficiency, honesty, and complete professional dedication. He was named commander of the Spanish foreign legion in 1923. Franco became a national hero for his role

Francisco Franco

in suppressing revolts in Morocco, and at the age of 33 he was made brigadier general. Having quelled a miners' revolt in Asturias in 1934, he became army chief of staff in 1935.

The Spanish Civil War. In February 1936 the leftist government of the Spanish republic exiled Franco to an obscure command in the Canary Islands. The following July he joined other right-wing officers in a revolt against the republic. In October they made him commander in chief and head of state of their new Nationalist regime. During the three years of the ensuing civil war against the republic, Franco proved an unimaginative but careful and competent leader, whose forces advanced slowly but steadily to complete victory on April 1, 1939. The war was bloody, with numerous atrocities on both sides.

During the civil war, Franco established his control over Nationalist political life and expanded the Falange (q.v.) into an official political party at the service of his government. Tens of thousands of executions during the war and in the years immediately following it guaranteed the stability of Franco's authoritarian regime.

Franco as Ruler of Spain. Franco kept Spain out of World War II, but after the Axis defeat he was labeled the "last of the Fascist dictators" and ostracized by the UN. As the cold war gained in intensity, however, foreign opposition to Franco lessened. In 1953 the signing of a military assistance pact with the U.S. marked the return of Spain to international society.

Franco's regime became somewhat more liberal during the 1950s and '60s. It depended for support not on the Falange, renamed the National Movement, but on a range of "political families," running from those on the center right to extreme reactionaries. Franco balanced off these groups against one another, retaining for himself a position as arbiter above the affairs of day-to-day politics. Helped along by the general prosperity of Europe, Spain enjoyed rapid economic growth in the 1960s. By the end of the decade its previously agricultural economy had been industrialized.

In 1947 Franco declared Spain a monarchy, with himself as a sort of regent for life. In 1969 he designated Prince Juan Carlos, grandson of Spain's former king, Alfonso XIII, as his official successor. In 1973 Franco relinquished his position as premier but continued to be head of state. At Franco's death in Madrid on Nov. 20, 1975, Juan Carlos became king.

No consensus has been reached on Franco's role in Spanish history. His partisans point to the prolonged peace following the civil war and to the economic boom of the 1960s. His detractors stress the repressive politics of the regime and suggest that economic growth would have taken place even without Franco.   J.F.C.

FRANCONIA (Ger. *Franken*), duchy of medieval Germany, extending along both sides of the Main River, from the Rhine River on the west to the Fichtelgebirge range on the east. It also included the territory containing the cities of Mainz, Speyer, and Worms, on the western bank of the Rhine. Franconia was conquered by the Franks for whom the region was named in the late 5th century and soon afterward became part of the kingdom of Austrasia. The Treaty of Verdun (843) made Franconia the center of the newly formed East Frankish, later German, kingdom consisting of the duchies of Saxony, Swabia, Bavaria, Lorraine, and Franconia. Lacking political unity, however, the duchy declined in importance, and it was soon divided into Rhenish Franconia and Eastern Franconia. In the 10th century Conrad the Red, duke of Lorraine (fl. 944–55), the son-in-law of Holy Roman Emperor Otto I, established the Salian family as dominant in the area. The political power of this family was first felt in 1024, when Conrad, duke of Franconia, was elected Emperor Conrad II, thus founding an imperial house, which by its direct and collateral branches gave rulers to the

Holy Roman Empire for more than two centuries. During this period, Eastern Franconia increased in political influence. Rhenish Franconia, however, lost its identity, and a large portion was divided among the count palatine of the Rhine, the archbishop of Mainz, and the bishops of Speyer and Worms. The remainder gradually became a land of lesser nobles and free towns. By the 13th century the name Franconia fell into disuse. It was revived in 1512, however, when Emperor Maximilian I established the province of Franconia. With the dissolution of the Holy Roman Empire in 1806, the name Franconia disappeared from the political divisions of Germany. In 1837 King Louis I of Bavaria revived the name of the old duchy, naming the three northern portions of his kingdom Upper Franconia, Middle Franconia, and Lower Franconia. The territory comprising the old duchy of Franconia is now included in the German states of Baden-Württemberg, Hesse, and Bavaria.

FRANCONIA MOUNTAINS. *See* WHITE MOUNTAINS.

FRANCO-PRUSSIAN WAR, war in 1870–71 lost by France to the German states under the leadership of Prussia. The underlying causes of the conflict were the determination of the Prussian statesman Prince Otto von Bismarck to unify Germany under Prussian control and, as a step toward this goal, to eliminate French influence over Germany. On the other hand, Napoleon III, emperor of France, sought to regain both in France and abroad the prestige lost as a result of numerous diplomatic reverses, particularly those suffered at the hands of Prussia in the Austro-Prussian War of 1866. In addition, the military strength of Prussia, as revealed in the war with Austria, constituted a threat to French dominance on the Continent. *See also* FRANCE; GERMANY.

Initiating Incidents. The event directly precipitating the Franco-Prussian War was the candidacy of Leopold, prince of Hohenzollern-Sigmaringen (1835–1905), for the throne of Spain, rendered vacant by the Spanish revolution of 1868. Leopold had accepted the candidacy under persuasion from Bismarck. The French government, alarmed at the possibility of a Prusso-Spanish alliance resulting from the occupancy of the Spanish throne by a member of the Hohenzollern dynastic family, threatened Prussia with war if Leopold's candidacy was not withdrawn. The French ambassador to the Prussian court, Comte Vincente Benedetti (1817–1900), was dispatched to Ems, a spa in northwestern Germany being visited by William I of Prussia, with instructions to demand that the Prussian monarch order Prince

Leopold to withdraw his candidacy. William, although angered, gave Benedetti permission to communicate directly with Leopold by telegraph. Leopold could not be reached, but his father, Prince Charles Anthony (1811–85), wired a retraction of the candidacy in the name of his son.

The government of Napoleon III, still not content, was determined to humiliate Prussia, even at the cost of war. Antoine Agénor Alfred, duc de Gramont (1819–80), the French foreign minister, demanded that William submit a personal letter of apology to Napoleon III and a guarantee that the Hohenzollern candidacy would never be renewed. In an interview with Benedetti at Ems, the Prussian king rejected the French demands. The same day, Bismarck obtained William's authorization to publish the French demands and the Prussian rejection contained in the Ems Dispatch. Bismarck edited the document in a manner calculated to aggravate the resentment of the French and the Germans. The Prussian statesman realized that this move would in all probability precipitate war, but he knew that Prussia was prepared, and he counted on the psychological effect of a French declaration of war to rally the south German states to Prussia's cause, thus accomplishing the final phase in the unification of Germany.

The War Begins. On July 19, 1870, France declared war on Prussia. The south German states, in fulfillment of their treaties with Prussia, immediately joined King William in a common front against France. The French were only able to mobilize about 200,000 troops; the Germans, however, quickly marshaled an army of about 400,000 men. All German forces were under the supreme command of William, with the great strategist Count Helmuth von Moltke as his chief of staff. Three German armies drove into France, led, respectively, by Gen. Karl Friedrich von Steinmetz (1796–1877), Prince Frederick Charles (1828–85), and Crown Prince Frederick William, later Frederick III of Prussia and emperor of Germany. The first engagement, a minor skirmish, was won by the French on August 2, when they drove a small Prussian detachment from the city of Saarbrücken, near the border between France and Germany. In the major battles at Weissenburg (August 4), at Wörth (August 6), and at Spichern (August 6), however, the French under Marie Edmé Patrice Maurice, comte de MacMahon were defeated. MacMahon was ordered to fall back on Châlons. Marshal Achille Bazaine (1811–88), in command of all French troops east of Metz, was directed to maintain his positions. Metz itself was to be held at all costs. These orders split the French forces, which were unable thereafter

to regain their unity or freedom of action. On August 12 the French emperor handed the supreme command over to Bazaine, who was badly beaten in the great battles of Vionville (August 15) and Gravelotte (August 18), and forced into Metz. There he was besieged by two German armies. MacMahon then was ordered to relieve Metz. The Germans surprised and defeated (August 30) his leading corps at Beaumont, whereupon he decided to withdraw his army to Sedan.

Battle of Sedan and Capture of Napoleon III. The decisive battle of the war opened in Sedan on the morning of September 1 (*see* SEDAN, BATTLE OF). At about 7:00 AM MacMahon was severely wounded, and an hour and a half later Gen. Emmanuel Félix de Wimpffen (1811–84) received the chief command. The battle continued until 4:15 PM, when Napoleon, who meanwhile had arrived in Sedan, resumed command. Recognizing the hopelessness of the situation, he ordered the white flag to be hoisted. Terms of surrender were negotiated during the night, and on the following day Napoleon, together with 83,000 troops, surrendered to the Germans.

Upon receiving intelligence of the capture of the French emperor, Paris rose in rebellion, the Legislative Assembly was dissolved, and France was proclaimed a republic. Before the close of September, Strasbourg, one of the last points at which the French had hoped to stem the German advance, capitulated, and Paris was completely surrounded. On October 7 the minister of the new French government, Léon Gambetta, made a dramatic escape from Paris by balloon, and with his chief assistant, Charles Louis de Saulces de Freycinet (1828–1923), carried on from Tours the organization and equipment of 36 military divisions. The efforts of these troops proved unavailing, however, and they were at length driven into Switzerland, where they were disarmed and interned.

Siege of Paris, French Capitulation, and German Occupation. On October 27 Marshal Bazaine surrendered at Metz with 173,000 men. Paris, meanwhile, was subjected to siege and bombardment. Its citizens, attempting to stave off the enemy with crude and makeshift weapons, and reduced to eating cats, dogs, and even rats, were at length compelled, on Jan. 19, 1871, to open negotiations for surrender.

A day earlier, January 18, an event had occurred that represented the culmination of Bismarck's unremitting efforts for the unification of Germany. The Prussian king was crowned William I, emperor of Germany, in the Hall of Mirrors at Versailles. The formal capitulation of Paris took place on January 28, following which an ar-

A contemporary woodcut of Prussian artillery employed in the siege of Paris. Bettmann Archive

mistice of three weeks was arranged. A French national assembly, elected to negotiate the peace, convened at Bordeaux on February 13 and chose Louis Adolphe Thiers as the first president of the Third Republic. On March 1 the preliminaries of peace were ratified at Bordeaux. The final treaty, signed on May 10, 1871, at Frankfurt am Main, provided that the French province of Alsace (excepting Belfort) and part of Lorraine, including Metz, were to be ceded to the German Empire, and that France was to pay a war indemnity of 5 billion francs, submitting to occupation by German troops until the amount was rendered in full. This heavy obligation was discharged in September 1873, and during the same month, after an occupation of almost three years, France was at last freed of German soldiers.

For further information on this topic, see the Bibliography in volume 28, section 939.

FRANK, Anne (1929–45), German diarist, born in Frankfurt am Main. In 1933 she and her family, who were Jewish, left Nazi Germany and settled in Amsterdam. In July 1942 they and four other exiles went into hiding in the sealed-off back rooms of an Amsterdam office building in order to avoid arrest by German occupation forces. In August 1944 their hiding place was revealed, and they were taken into custody. Anne died in the

German concentration camp at Belsen less than one year later. Her Dutch diary, describing with humor and tenderness her two arduous years in seclusion, was found in the hiding place. Published in 1947 as *Het Achterhuis* (The House Behind), it appeared (1952) in the U.S. as *Anne Frank: The Diary of a Young Girl*. It was dramatized for the stage under the title *The Diary of Anne Frank* in 1956 and filmed in 1959.

FRANK, Jacob, real name Jankiew Liebowicz (1726–91), Polish theologian and mystic, born in Podolia (now a region of Ukraine). He was the son of a rabbi and as a young man traveled in the Middle East, where the Turks called him Frank, their customary designation for a European; he retained that surname through life. At Thessaloníki, Greece, he became a member of the religious sect founded by the Smyrnean-Jewish mystic and self-styled messiah, Sabbatai Zevi. On his return to Poland in 1755, Frank became the center of a secret semireligious society of Jews, against which charges of immorality were leveled. Subsequently, he claimed to be the recipient of direct revelations from heaven and exhorted his followers to espouse Christianity as an intermediate stage in the transition to a future messianic religion.

In 1759 the Frankists underwent a spectacular

mass baptism at Lvov, Poland (now Lviv, Ukraine), at which members of the Polish nobility served as godparents. Almost at once, however, Frank's sincerity was impugned, and the church brought charges of heresy against him, which resulted in his imprisonment in 1760. Upon his release 13 years later, Frank, assuming the role of messiah, selected 12 apostles and settled at Brünn, Austria (now Brno, Czechoslovakia). There he attracted the favorable notice of Maria Theresa, archduchess of Austria, who patronized him as an apologist of Christianity to the Jews. After 1786 Frank moved to the small German town of Offenbach, where he spent the rest of his life, maintained in luxury by the donations of his worshipful followers. After the death of Frank, leadership of the sect was assumed by his daughter Eve Frank (d. 1816), but the Frankists lost their identity as a group and became communicants of the Roman Catholic church.

FRANKEL, Zacharias (1801–75), Bohemian rabbi and scholar, best known as a founder of the conservative position in the debate over Jewish religious reform. Frankel was born in Prague. He received a secular as well as a traditional Jewish education, earning a doctorate in classical languages at Budapest in 1831. He held rabbinical posts in Leitmeritz, Teplitz, and Dresden before becoming, in 1854, director of the first modern rabbinical school, the Jüdisch-Theologisches Seminar in Breslau, which he headed until his death. In opposition to more radical reformers, Frankel endorsed only those changes in Jewish thought and practice that would accord with the spirit of the tradition as it developed historically—the so-called positivist-historical approach, to which the Conservative movement in American Judaism would later appeal. As a scholar, Frankel is best known for his work on the rabbinic legal tradition, particularly his *Darkhé ha-Mishnah* (The Methods of the Mishnah, 1859). R.S.S.

FRANKENTHALER, Helen (1928–), American abstract expressionist painter, who has pioneered new methods of using color. Born in New York City, she studied art at Bennington College. Her early work shows a variety of influences, but after 1951, under the influence of Jackson Pollock, she developed her own unique style. Inspired by Pollock's method of dripping paint onto canvas, Frankenthaler used thinned-down paint to soak or stain unprimed canvas, creating diaphanous silky pools of color in such works as the delicately pink and blue *Mountains and Sea* (1952, Metropolitan Museum, New York City). This and some later works, although completely abstract, contain strong evocations of landscape.

In the 1960s Frankenthaler began leaving large areas of blank canvas in many of her works, in order—in her words—to allow the pictures to "breathe." In 1962 she first used acrylic paints, which were both brighter and less dense than oils, and the coloration of her canvases became correspondingly stronger. Her work has been an important influence on the American color-field artists Morris Louis and Kenneth Noland.

FRANKFORT, city, capital of Kentucky and seat of Franklin Co., on the Kentucky R., in the N central part of the state; inc. 1839. Situated in the heart of the state's Bluegrass Region, the city is a distribution center for corn, tobacco, and Thoroughbred horses; manufactures include clothing, electrical equipment, air brakes, and bourbon whiskey. Of interest are the State Capitol (1910), modeled after the U.S. Capitol; a floral clock on the capitol grounds, with more than 22,000 plants; the Greek Revival-style old capitol (originally completed 1830, now restored), housing the Kentucky Historical Society; Liberty Hall (1796); and the graves of the pioneer Daniel Boone and his wife, Rebecca (1739–1813), in the Frankfort Cemetery. The city is the site of Kentucky State University (1886). A game reserve is nearby.

Frankfort was established in 1786 by the Vir-

A front view of the old capitol of Kentucky, completed in 1830. Kentucky Historical Society

ginia Assembly on land owned by the American Revolution general James Wilkinson. The site had first been known as Frank's Ford in honor of Stephen Frank, a frontiersman killed (1780) in a skirmish with Indians at a ford in the river here. The present name was officially adopted in 1786, but Frank's Ford was in popular use until about 1830. Frankfort was chosen as the state capital in 1792, when Kentucky was admitted to the Union. After the old capitol burned on two occasions during its early history, the larger Kentucky cities of Louisville and Lexington sought to become the seat of the state government. Frankfort was retained, however, because of its more central location. During the American Civil War, Confederate Gen. Braxton Bragg camped in Frankfort briefly (1862) before being expelled by Union Gen. Don Carlos Buell (1818–98). The first Boy Scout troop in the U.S. was organized in Frankfort in 1909. The city suffered heavy flood damage in 1937. Pop. (1980) 25,973; (1990) 25,968.

FRANKFURT or **FRANKFURT AM MAIN** (Eng. *Frankfort*), city, W central Germany, in Hesse, a port on the Main R. It is a major manufacturing, financial, commercial, and transportation center, served by rail lines and the busy Rhine-Main Airport. Manufactures include machinery, electrical equipment, chemicals (notably in the Höchst district), pharmaceuticals, motor vehicles, clothing, and printed materials. International trade fairs, including a yearly book fair, are held here.

Frankfurt is divided into an old town, or Altstadt, bordering the river, and a new town, or Neustadt, N of the older section. The new town contains the business quarter and the most important public buildings. The home of the Rothschild family, the famous Jewish financiers, is the only reminder of the Juden-Gasse, or Jewish sector. A cluster of Gothic houses, the Römer, was used as the town hall for nearly 500 years. It forms the nucleus of the Römerberg, a square flanked by medieval houses of various dates. Other places of interest are the Leinwand-Haus, or linen drapers' hall, of the 14th century; the Eschenheim Turm, a 15th-century tower; the palace of the princes of Thurn and Taxis, which was (1816–66) the meeting place of the diet of the Germanic Confederation; and the house (now a museum) where the German poet and writer Johann Wolfgang von Goethe spent his youth.

The outstanding church of Frankfurt is the Cathedral of Saint Bartholomew. It was constructed in the 13th century on the site of a 9th-century church and was the seat of the elections of Holy Roman emperors and, after 1562, of the imperial coronations. Also notable are Saint Paul's Church (18th–19th cent.), where the Frankfurt Parliament, the first German national assembly, met (1848–49); Saint Leonard's Church (15th–16th cent.); and Saint Michael's Church (1953). Major museums include Senckenberg Museum, with a large collection on natural history, especially paleontology; the Städel Museum, with rich displays of painting, notably by 16th-century German masters; the Liebieg Museum of Sculpture; the Postal Museum; and museums of applied art, ethnography, and local history. The city also has a large zoo and a botanical garden and is the seat of a university (1914).

Frankfurt was probably established as a Roman settlement about the 1st century AD. In the late 8th century, it was referred to as Frankonovurd by Einhard, the biographer of Charlemagne. During Charlemagne's reign (800–14), imperial councils were held here. The Golden Bull of 1356 established Frankfurt as the seat of the imperial elections, and it was made a free imperial city in 1372. About 1530 it became an important stronghold of Protestantism. Upon the formation of the Confederation of the Rhine in 1806, Frankfurt became subordinate to the confederation. It regained the status of a free city in 1815, and it was the unofficial capital of the Germanic Confederation until 1866. In the same year, during the Seven Weeks' War, Frankfurt was seized by Prussia. During World War II, the city was heavily damaged. Pop. (1987 est.) 592,400.

FRANKFURT or **FRANKFURT AN DER ODER** (Eng. *Frankfort*), city, NE Germany, in Brandenburg, on the Oder R., near Berlin. The city lies on one of the principal road and railway routes between eastern Germany and Poland. The leading products manufactured here include iron castings, agricultural machinery, hardware, chemicals, textiles, and foodstuffs. The site upon which the city stands was settled by a group of Franconian merchants in the 13th century. It was granted a charter in 1253, and it was (1368–1450) a flourishing member of the Hanseatic League. The University of Frankfurt (1506) was transferred to Breslau (now Wrocław, Poland) in 1811. In the spring of 1945, during World War II, Frankfurt was captured by Soviet troops, and following the war the city was included in the Soviet Zone of Occupation. Pop. (1989 est.) 87,900.

FRANKFURTER, Felix (1882–1965), American jurist and associate justice of the U.S. Supreme Court.

Born in Vienna and brought to the U.S. in 1894, Frankfurter was educated at the College of the City of New York (now City College) and Harvard University. He served as assistant U.S. attorney in New York City (1906–10) and in the War Department (1910–14). As a teacher at Harvard

Law School (1914–39), he became known as a leading authority on constitutional law. A long-time adviser to President Franklin D. Roosevelt, he recommended to the president many of the executives who were selected to administer the agencies established under the New Deal; he was instrumental in writing the Securities Act (1933), Securities Exchange Act (1934), Public Utility Holding Company Act (1935), and other New Deal legislation affecting the railroads and labor.

In 1939 Roosevelt nominated Frankfurter as an associate justice of the Supreme Court; he served on the Court until 1962, when he retired because of illness. Legal and political observers expected Frankfurter to join the liberal wing of the Court; instead, he became known as the leader of the conservative members of that body. His philosophy was one of judicial restraint. He believed that the Court should not interfere with the rulings of state legislatures and Congress, which represent the will of the electorate. His opinions often supported the right of the state and federal governments to self-protection, as in the ruling of 1951 upholding the conviction of 11 leaders of the Communist party for conspiring to overthrow the U.S. government by force. Frankfurter's concern for states' rights is evidenced by his dissent from a Court decision in 1962 requiring reapportionment of state legislatures.

He wrote many books and articles on legal matters, including *The Case of Sacco and Vanzetti* (1927) and *Of Law and Men; Papers and Addresses, 1939–56* (1956). *Felix Frankfurter Reminisces* (1960) is an autobiography, and *Roosevelt and Frankfurter* (1968) is a collection of letters exchanged by the two men between 1928 and 1945.

FRANKINCENSE, name applied to various gum resins, containing volatile oils, that diffuse a strong fragrance in burning. Oriental frankincense, also known as olibanum, was esteemed by ancient peoples for use in embalming and as incense (q.v.) and is still the most important incense resin. It is obtained from several Oriental trees of the genus *Boswellia,* growing in northeastern Africa and Arabia. The hardened, semitransparent yellowish material is still used widely as ceremonial incense. Common frankincense is obtained from the bark of *Picea abies,* the Norway spruce. When boiled in water and strained, the resin becomes Burgundy pitch, formerly used in making medicinal plasters. *See* RESINS.

FRANKL, Victor E. (1905–   ), Austrian psychotherapist, who developed the concept of logotherapy, the theory that the underlying need of human existence is to find meaning in life. Born in Vienna, Frankl was educated at the University of Vienna. In 1947 he joined the university as a professor of neurology and psychiatry. He was imprisoned (1942–45) in Nazi concentration camps, and wrote of this in *From Death Camp to Existentialism* (1959). Perhaps his best-known work is *Man's Search for Meaning: An Introduction to Logotherapy* (1962; trans. 1970).

FRANKLAND, Sir Edward (1825–99), British chemist, who determined that the atom of one element can combine only with specific numbers of atoms of another element. This valence (q.v.) theory became a cornerstone of modern chemistry. Born in Churchtown, Lancashire, England, Frankland started as an apprentice to a druggist and then became a professor of chemistry at several British institutions. He also discovered zinc methyl, the first organometallic compound—an organic compound containing a metal—thus identified. With the British astronomer Sir Joseph Norman Lockyer he identified helium—previously observed as a line in the solar spectrum—as an element, and gave it its name. Frankland was knighted for his work in 1897.

FRANKLIN, city, seat of Williamson Co., central Tennessee, on the Harpeth R. It is a suburb of Nashville with some light industry. O'More College of Design (1970) and a community college are here. Officially founded as the county seat in 1799, the community was the site of two American Civil War battles, including the important Battle of Franklin (Nov. 30, 1864). Pop. (1980) 12,407; (1990) 20,098.

FRANKLIN, BATTLES OF, engagements in the American Civil War, the most important of which was fought on Nov. 30, 1864, near Franklin, a town in central Tennessee. The Union general John McAllister Schofield was under orders to retreat before the Confederate general John Bell Hood (1831–79), until the main body of the Union army under Gen. George Henry Thomas could be reinforced. Schofield retreated from Pulaski, Tenn., to Franklin, where he was temporarily immobilized by the absence of bridges across the Harpeth River. Hood, with a force of 27,000 troops, immediately attacked the Union army of 28,000. The nine-hour battle was indecisive. Confederate casualties totaled 6500, and Union casualties, 2326. An indecisive engagement occurred in the same vicinity in March 1863 between Union forces and troops under the Confederate general Nathan Bedford Forrest.

FRANKLIN, Benjamin (1706–90), American printer, author, diplomat, philosopher, and scientist, whose many contributions to the cause of the American Revolution, and the newly formed federal government that followed, rank him among the country's greatest statesmen.

Franklin was born on Jan. 17, 1706, in Boston. His father, Josiah Franklin (1658–1745), a tallow chandler by trade, had 17 children; Benjamin was the 15th child and the 10th son. His mother, Abiah Folger (1667–1752), was his father's second wife. The Franklin family lived modestly, like most New Englanders of the time. After his attendance at grammar school from age eight to ten, Benjamin was taken into his father's business. Finding the work uncongenial, he entered the employ of a cutler. At age 13 he was apprenticed to his brother James (1697–1735), who had recently returned from England with a new printing press. Benjamin learned the printing trade, devoting his spare time to the advancement of his education. His reading included *Pilgrim's Progress* by the British preacher John Bunyan, *Parallel Lives,* the work of the Greek essayist and biographer Plutarch, *Essay on Projects* by the English journalist and novelist Daniel Defoe, and the *Essays to Do Good* by Cotton Mather, the American Congregational clergyman. When he acquired a copy of the third volume of the *Spectator* by the British statesmen and essayists Sir Richard Steele and Joseph Addison, he set himself the goal of mastering its prose style.

In 1721 his brother James Franklin established the *New England Courant,* and Benjamin, at the age of 15, was busily occupied in delivering the newspaper by day and in composing articles for it at night. These articles, published anonymously, won wide notice and acclaim for their pithy observations on the current scene. Because of its liberal bias, the *New England Courant* frequently incurred the displeasure of the colonial authorities. In 1722, as a consequence of an article considered particularly offensive, James Franklin was imprisoned for a month and forbidden to publish his paper, and for a while it appeared under Benjamin's name.

Philadelphia and London. As a result of disagreements with James, Benjamin left Boston and made his way to Philadelphia, arriving in October 1723. There he worked at his trade and made numerous friends, among whom was Sir William Keith (1680–1749), the provincial governor of Pennsylvania. He persuaded Franklin to go to London to complete his training as a printer and to purchase the equipment needed to start his own printing establishment in Philadelphia. Young Franklin took this advice, arriving in London in December 1724. Not having received from Keith certain promised letters of introduction and credit, Franklin found himself, at age 18, without means in a strange city. With characteristic resourcefulness, he obtained employment at two of the foremost printing houses in London, Palmer's and Watt's. His appearance, bearing, and accomplishments soon won him the recog-

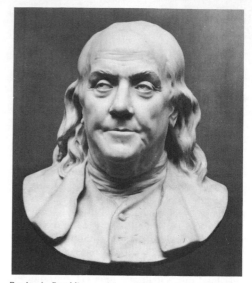

Benjamin Franklin, *marble sculpture dated 1778 by Jean Antoine Houdon.* Metropolitan Museum of Art–Gift of John Bard

nition of a number of the most distinguished figures in the literary and publishing world.

In October 1726, Franklin returned to Philadelphia and resumed his trade. The following year, with a number of his acquaintances, he organized a discussion group known as the Junto, which later became the American Philosophical Society. In September 1729, he bought the *Pennsylvania Gazette,* a dull, poorly edited weekly newspaper, which he made, by his witty style and judicious selection of news, both entertaining and informative. In 1730 he married Deborah Read (1705–74), a Philadelphia woman whom he had known before his trip to England.

Projects and Experiments. Franklin engaged in many public projects. In 1731 he founded what was probably the first public library in America, chartered in 1742 as the Philadelphia Library. He first published *Poor Richard's Almanack* in 1732, under the pen name Richard Saunders. This modest volume quickly gained a wide and appreciative audience, and its homespun, practical wisdom exerted a pervasive influence upon the American character. In 1736 Franklin became clerk of the Pennsylvania General Assembly and the next year was appointed deputy postmaster of Philadelphia. About this time, he organized the first fire company in that city and introduced methods for the improvement of street paving and lighting. Always interested in scientific studies, he devised means to correct the excessive smoking of chimneys and invented, around 1744, the Franklin stove, which furnished greater heat with a reduced consumption of fuel.

In 1747 Franklin began his electrical experiments with a simple apparatus that he received from Peter Collinson (1694–1768) in England. He advanced a tenable theory of the Leyden jar, supported the hypothesis that lightning is an electrical phenomenon, and proposed an effective method of demonstrating this fact. His plan was published in London and carried out in England and France before he himself performed his celebrated experiment with the kite in 1752. He invented the lightning rod and offered what is called the "one-fluid" theory in explanation of the two kinds of electricity, positive and negative. In recognition of his impressive scientific accomplishments, Franklin received honorary degrees from the University of Saint Andrews and the University of Oxford. He also became a fellow of the Royal Society of London for Improving Natural Knowledge and, in 1753, was awarded its Copley Medal for distinguished contributions to experimental science. Franklin also exerted a great influence on education in Pennsylvania. In 1749 he wrote *Proposals Relating to the Education of Youth in Pennsylvania;* its publication led to the establishment in 1751 of the Philadelphia Academy, later to become the University of Pennsylvania. The curriculum he suggested was a considerable departure from the program of classical studies then in vogue. English and modern foreign languages were to be emphasized as well as mathematics and science.

Public Office. In 1748 Franklin sold his printing business and, in 1750, was elected to the Pennsylvania Assembly, in which he served until 1764. He was appointed deputy postmaster general for the colonies in 1753, and in 1754 he was the delegate from Pennsylvania to the intercolonial congress that met at Albany to consider methods of dealing with the threatened French and Indian War. His Albany Plan, in many ways prophetic of the 1787 U.S. Constitution, provided for local independence within a framework of colonial union, but was too far in advance of public thinking to obtain ratification. It was his staunch belief that the adoption of this plan would have averted the American Revolution.

When the French and Indian War broke out, Franklin procured horses, wagons, and supplies for the British commander Gen. Edward Braddock by pledging his own credit to the Pennsylvania farmers, who thereupon furnished the necessary equipment. The proprietors of Pennsylvania Colony, descendants of the Quaker leader William Penn, in conformity with their religious opposition to war, refused to allow their landholdings to be taxed for the prosecution of the war. Thus, in 1757, Franklin was sent to England by the Pennsylvania Assembly to petition

the king for the right to levy taxes on proprietary lands. After completing his mission, he remained in England for five years as the chief representative of the American colonies. During this period he made friends with many prominent Englishmen, including the chemist and clergyman Joseph Priestley, the philosopher and historian David Hume, and the philosopher and economist Adam Smith.

Franklin returned to Philadelphia in 1762, where he remained until 1764, when he was once again dispatched to England as the agent of Pennsylvania. In 1766 he was interrogated before the House of Commons regarding the effects of the Stamp Act upon the colonies; his testimony was largely influential in securing the repeal of the act. Soon, however, new plans for taxing the colonies were introduced in Parliament, and Franklin was increasingly divided between his devotion to his native land and his loyalty as a subject of George III of Great Britain. Finally, in 1775, his powers of conciliation exhausted, Franklin sorrowfully acknowledged the inevitability of war. Sailing for America after an absence of 11 years, he reached Philadelphia on May 5, 1775, to find that the opening engagements of the Revolution—the battles of Lexington and Concord—had already been fought. He was chosen a member of the Second Continental Congress, serving on ten of its committees, and was made postmaster general, an office he held for one year.

Diplomat of the Revolution. In 1775 Franklin traveled to Canada, suffering great hardship along the way, in a vain effort to enlist the cooperation and support of Canada in the Revolution. Upon his return, he became one of the committee of five chosen to draft the Declaration of Independence. He was also one of the signers of that historic document, addressing the assembly with the characteristic statement: "We must all hang together, or assuredly we shall all hang separately." In September of the same year, he was chosen, with two other Americans, Arthur Lee and Silas Deane, to seek economic assistance in France. His scientific reputation, his integrity of character, and his wit and gracious manner made him extremely popular in French political, literary, and social circles, and his wisdom and ingenuity secured for the U.S. aid and concessions that perhaps no other man could have obtained. Against the vigorous opposition of the French minister of finance, Jacques Necker, and despite the jealous antagonism of his coldly formal American colleagues, he managed to obtain liberal grants and loans from Louis XVI of France. Franklin encouraged and materially assisted

American privateers operating against the British navy, especially John Paul Jones. On Feb. 6, 1778, Franklin negotiated the treaty of commerce and defensive alliance with France that represented, in effect, the turning point of the American Revolution. Seven months later, he was appointed by Congress as the first minister plenipotentiary from the U.S. to France.

In 1781 Franklin, John Adams, and John Jay were appointed to conclude a treaty of peace with Great Britain. The final treaty was signed at Versailles on Sept. 3, 1783 (see PARIS, TREATY OF). During the remainder of his stay in France, Franklin was accorded a number of honorary distinctions. His scientific standing won him an appointment from the French king as one of the commissioners investigating the Austrian physician Franz Anton Mesmer and the phenomenon of animal magnetism. As a dignitary of one of the most distinguished Freemason lodges in France, Franklin met some of the philosophers and leading figures of the French Revolution, upon whose political thinking he exerted a profound influence. Although he favored a liberalization of the French government, he opposed change through violent revolution.

A Framer of the Constitution. In March 1785, Franklin, at his own request, left his duties in France and returned to Philadelphia, where he served (1785–87) as president of the Pennsylvania executive council. In 1787 he was elected a delegate to the convention that drew up the U.S. Constitution. Franklin was deeply interested in philanthropic projects, and one of his last public acts was to sign a petition to the U.S. Congress, on Feb. 12, 1790, as president of the Pennsylvania Abolition Society, urging the abolition of slavery and the suppression of the slave trade. Two months later, on April 17, Franklin died in his Philadelphia home at 84 years of age.

Franklin's most notable service to his country was the result of his great skill in diplomacy. To his common sense, wisdom, wit, and industry, he joined great firmness of purpose, matchless tact, and broad tolerance. Both as a brilliant conversationalist and a sympathetic listener, Franklin had a wide and appreciative following in the intellectual salons of the day. For the most part, his literary reputation rests on his unfinished *Autobiography,* which is considered by many the epitome of his life and character.

For further information on this person, see the section Biographies in the Bibliography in volume 28.

FRANKLIN, Sir John (1786–1847), British rear admiral, explorer of the Arctic, and discoverer of the Northwest Passage.

Franklin was born in Spilsby, Lincolnshire, England. He participated in the battles of Copenhagen in 1801 and Trafalgar in 1805 during the Napoleonic Wars. In 1818 he commanded the *Trent* in an unsuccessful voyage to the Arctic, and from 1819 to 1822 he commanded an overland expedition commissioned to explore the northern coast of Canada east from the mouth of the Coppermine River. In a subsequent Arctic expedition (1825–27), he traced the North American coastline from the mouth of the Mackenzie River on the Beaufort Sea in northwestern Canada to about the 150th meridian in northeastern Alaska. In 1829 he was knighted and awarded the gold medal of the Geographical Society of Paris. From 1836 to 1843 he was lieutenant governor of Van Diemen's Land (now Tasmania), where he established a college and scientific society. In 1845 he was appointed commander of an expedition to discover the Northwest Passage. The expedition, consisting of the *Erebus* and the *Terror,* with 129 officers and men, was last seen by a whaling vessel on July 26, 1845, in Baffin Bay.

Subsequently, many searching expeditions were dispatched to the Arctic. In July 1857 Lady Jane Franklin (1792–1875), Franklin's second wife, outfitted the *Fox,* which succeeded in discovering the history of the ill-fated expedition. The search party obtained from the Inuit (Eskimo) in Boothia Peninsula many remains of the expedition. A record found at Victory Point related details of Franklin's expedition up to April 25, 1848. According to this record, in 1846 the *Erebus* and *Terror* had navigated Peel Sound and Franklin Strait in a southerly direction, but had been stopped by ice between Victoria Island and King William Island. The two ships, icebound from September 1846, had been deserted on April 22, 1848. At that time the total casualties had been 9 officers and 15 men; Franklin had died on June 11, 1847. The survivors left the ships on April 26, 1848, but apparently perished some days later.

A U.S. expedition (1878–80) discovered the wreckage of one of Franklin's ships and skeletons of members of his party. A monument commemorating Franklin was erected in 1875 in Westminster Abbey. In the 1980s a Canadian anthropologist, through studies of tissue remains of the crew, determined that they had most likely succumbed to the effects of lead poisoning.

FRANKLIN, Rosalind Elsie (1920–58), British biophysicist. Born in London, she was educated in physical chemistry at Newnham College, Cambridge. Franklin conducted X-ray diffraction studies on the structure of the DNA molecule, the carrier of hereditary information, while working in the laboratory of British biophysicist Maurice

Wilkins. This work enabled American biochemist James Dewey Watson and the British Francis Crick to determine the helical structure of the DNA molecule.

FRANKLIN, STATE OF, autonomous state, now included in the eastern part of Tennessee, formed in 1784 and dissolved in 1788. In 1784 North Carolina ceded to the U.S. government the western lands, a portion of which had originally been governed by the self-constituted Watauga Association. The cession was to be accepted within one year, but North Carolina repealed the cession before the year expired. Before learning of the repeal, however, the settlers in the eastern counties had organized the state of Franklin, named in honor of Benjamin Franklin, and elected John Sevier (1745–1815) as governor. North Carolina attempted to conciliate the westerners by creating a Washington District with Sevier as brigadier general and David Campbell (1750–1812) as judge, thus removing the necessity of taking court cases across the mountains for trial; the settlers, however, decided to continue the separate-state movement. The U.S. Congress failed by two votes to gain the two-thirds majority necessary for passage of a resolution to accept the North Carolina cession. North Carolina refused, until 1789, to remake the cession and encouraged opponents of Sevier, led by John Tipton (1730–1813), to maintain North Carolina government in the Franklin area. For three years the governments of North Carolina and Franklin attempted to govern the same people and region. The government of Franklin had a constitution providing for the payment of taxes and salaries in the produce of the country. An even more democratic constitution, which would have renamed the state Frankland, was rejected through the influence of Sevier. The feud between Sevier and Tipton reached the point of hostilities, and Sevier was arrested by North Carolina on a charge of high treason. The charge was later dropped, and Sevier was seated in the North Carolina legislature and in Congress. The legislature ceded the region a second time; Congress accepted the cession in 1790 and created the Territory South of the River Ohio, which became the state of Tennessee in 1796.

FRANKLIN, William (1731–1813), American colonial administrator, illegitimate son of Benjamin Franklin, born in Philadelphia. Before he was 21 years old, he was commissioned as a captain to serve with the Pennsylvania forces on the Canadian frontier during King George's War. In 1754 his father, then postmaster general, appointed him comptroller of the Philadelphia post office. Franklin held the post until 1756, also serving as clerk of the Pennsylvania Provincial Assembly during part of that period. In 1757 he accompanied his father to London, studied law, and was admitted to the bar in London in 1758. He was appointed governor of New Jersey in 1763 and as a defender of royal authority was in constant conflict with the colonists. He remained a Loyalist during the American Revolution. Arrested by order of the Provincial Congress of New Jersey in 1776, he was detained until 1778. In 1782 he went to England, where he lived until his death.

FRANKLIN INSTITUTE SCIENCE MUSEUM, institution organized in Philadelphia in 1824 for the

An engraving of the first expedition of Sir John Franklin to the northern coast of Canada, 1819–22.

promotion and study of applied science and the mechanic arts. It is the oldest institution of its kind in the U.S. In 1933, through the joint efforts of the institute and the Benjamin Franklin Memorial Foundation, a building was erected as a permanent memorial to Benjamin Franklin. The building houses a memorial hall, the Fels Planetarium, and a museum containing nine hands-on exhibits (on astronomy, aviation, bioscience, communications, electricity, mathematics, mechanics, and trains) that demonstrate the fundamentals and applications of science. The *Journal of the Franklin Institute*, published continuously since 1826, issues papers on the latest scientific developments and their applications to industry. The institute annually awards the Franklin Medal for distinctive contributions to the advancement of science. The Futures Center addition, open in 1990, contains eight state-of-the-art exhibits that highlight the advances and implications of future technology, including FutureSpace, FutureEarth, FutureHealth, FutureChemistry, FutureComputer, and FutureEnergy.

FRANKLINITE, mineral containing the oxides of iron, manganese, and zinc, with the formula $(Fe, Zn, Mn)(Fe, Mn)_2O_4$. It crystallizes in the cubic system (*see* CRYSTAL) and occurs chiefly as octahedral crystals. It also occurs as rounded grains and compact masses. It is slightly magnetic, opaque, iron black in color, and has a metallic luster. Its sp.gr. ranges from 5.07 to 5.22 and its hardness (q.v.) from 5.5 to 6.5. In the U.S. it occurs in considerable quantity in Franklin and Ogdensburg, N.J.

FRANKLIN STOVE. *See* FRANKLIN, BENJAMIN.

FRANKS, group of Germanic tribes that, about the middle of the 3d century AD, dwelt along the middle and lower Rhine River. The Franks appeared in the Roman provinces around 253 and soon thereafter established themselves in two principal groups, the Salian and the Ripuarian. The Salian Franks inhabited the territory along the lower stretches of the Rhine, and the Ripuarian Franks lived along the middle course of the river. The Salians were conquered by the Roman emperor Julian in 358 and became allies of Rome. During the early 5th century, when the Romans retired from the Rhine, the Salians established themselves in most of the territory north of the Loire River.

Under the Salian king Clovis I, founder of the Merovingian dynasty, the power and extent of the Frankish kingdom grew considerably. In 486 Clovis overthrew Syagrius (430?–86), the last Roman governor in Gaul, and then successively subjugated the Alamanni, the Burgundians, the Visigoths of Aquitania, and the Ripuarian Franks.

Ultimately, the borders of his kingdom extended from the Pyrenees Mountains to Friesland and from the Atlantic Ocean to the Main River. Clovis was converted to Christianity in 496, and thus began the close connection between the Frankish monarchy and the papacy.

After the death of Clovis, the kingdom was divided among his four sons, and for the following century it went through several divisions and reunifications until finally consolidated by Clotaire II (c. 584–629) in 613. Shortly after his death, however, the kings ceased to exercise any influence, and authority passed into the hands of the great officers of state, most notably the major of the palace (*major domus*). The office of *major domus* existed in all of the Frankish kingdoms. In the eastern part, Austrasia, however, arose a powerful family, the Carolingian, which retained exclusive possession of the palace mayoralty for more than 100 years, ruling as monarchs in fact if not in name. In 687 Pepin of Herstal, the Austrasian mayor of the palace, overthrew the forces of Neustria (the western part) and Burgundy, setting himself up as *major domus* of a united Frankish kingdom. His son, Charles Martel, extended the frontiers of the kingdom in the east and in 732 repelled the Moors in a decisive battle fought at a site between Tours and Poitiers. Frankish power attained its greatest development under Charles Martel's grandson, Charlemagne, who in his time was the most powerful monarch in Europe. On Dec. 25, 800, he was crowned Carolus Augustus, emperor of the Romans, by Pope Leo III. Charlemagne's imperial title was later borne by the Holy Roman emperors until the early 19th century. His Frankish lands, more specifically, developed into the kingdom of France, which is named for the Franks.

See also CAROLINGIAN; HOLY ROMAN EMPIRE; MEROVINGIAN.

For further information on this topic, see the Bibliography in volume 28, sections 937, 954.

FRANZ JOSEF LAND (Russ. *Zemlya Frantsa-Iosifa*), archipelago, NW Russia, in the Arctic Ocean, E of the Norwegian archipelago Svalbard and N of Novaya Zemlya Archipelago. The archipelago, of volcanic origin, has ice-covered mountains of basalt formation that attain heights of about 730 m (about 2400 ft) above sea level. Franz Josef Land comprises about 100 small islands that are separated by bays, fjords, and straits. The principal islands of the archipelago are Alexandra Land, Graham Bell (Greem-Bell) Island, Wilczek (Vilcheka) Land, George Land, Rudolf Island, and Hooker (Gukera) Island.

Because most of the land area is covered by ice, vegetation is limited to lichens, mosses, and some flowering plants. Animal life includes the polar bear, fox, walrus, ringed seal, and a number of species of seabird. Insects are rare, with only about six species being found. The climate is arctic, the temperature ranging from −28.3° C (−19° F) in winter to 1.7° C (35° F) in summer. Dense fog and violent gales are frequent. At other times, however, the sky is clear, and displays of the aurora borealis may be seen.

During an Austro-Hungarian expedition in 1873, Julius von Payer (1842–1915) and Karl Weyprecht (1838–81) made an initial exploration of the islands, naming them after Francis Joseph I, the emperor of Austria. The complete exploration of the archipelago was accomplished by various expeditions between 1880 and 1905. The Soviet Union annexed Franz Josef Land in 1926 and subsequently established government observation stations here.

FRASER, river, S British Columbia. It rises in the Rocky Mts., in Mt. Robson Provincial Park near the Alberta border, and flows 1368 km (850 mi) before emptying, through a delta, into Georgia Strait, near Vancouver.

The Fraser initially flows NW through a section of the Rocky Mt. Trench. It then turns S near the city of Prince George, where it receives its major W tributary, the Nechako R. In its central section, the volume of the river increases, and below Quesnel its banks gradually take on a canyonlike aspect. Important tributaries in this section include the West Road and Chilcotin rivers, from the W, and the Thompson R., from the E. From Lytton to Yale the river flows through a canyon of great scenic beauty as it traverses a part of the Coast Mts. A little below Yale, at Hope, the Fraser turns sharply W, and the fertile lower Fraser Valley begins. The Fraser empties into Georgia Strait through three main channels. The river is used by commercial vessels for a short distance upstream. From May to July the Fraser Valley is subject to flooding; a series of dikes helps protect the delta.

The Fraser drains an area of about 238,000 sq km (about 91,890 sq mi). Much of the river basin is heavily wooded, and forest-products industries dominate the economy of the settlements along the river. The lower Fraser Valley, including the delta, has highly productive farms. Various species of salmon spawn in the Fraser, and salmon fisheries are located near the river's mouth. The river has great hydroelectric potential, but it remains undeveloped for fear of detrimental effects on the migratory habits of the salmon.

The first European to visit the river was Sir Alexander Mackenzie in 1793. It is named for the fur trader Simon Fraser (1776–1862), who explored much of it in 1808. In 1858 gold was found in alluvial gravels N of Yale, and a major gold rush ensued.

FRASER, Malcolm (1930–   ), prime minister of Australia (1975–83), born in Melbourne. He was first elected to the Australian Parliament in 1955 and joined the cabinet as minister for the army in 1966; he later held the portfolios of education and science (1968–69 and 1971–72) and defense (1969–71). Chosen leader of the Liberal party in March 1975, he became prime minister after a constitutional crisis in November of that year and a month later led his coalition government to victory in national elections. He was returned to office, but with a substantially reduced majority, in the elections of 1980. The Liberal coalition was defeated in the general elections of March 1983 by the Labor party under Bob Hawke.

FRATERNAL ORDERS, in the U.S. as generally defined in law, voluntary nonprofit associations established for the mutual aid and sociability of their members. They are also called fraternal societies or benefit associations. These orders generally provide for the payment of death and other benefits, mainly through a form of insurance known as fraternal insurance. In this respect fraternal orders are the American counterpart of the English friendly societies that originated in the 16th century. Most U.S. fraternal orders, however, were patterned after certain European benevolent secret societies modeled on the order established by the Freemasons. These prototypes included such organizations as the Independent Order of Odd Fellows, the Ancient Order of Druids, and the Ancient Order of Foresters, which were introduced into the U.S. in 1819, about 1830, and 1832, respectively. From these and similar associations fraternal orders of the U.S. derived their lodge system of organization and democratic form of representative self-government, their practice of doing business in confidential meetings, and their ritualism and social characteristics.

The first fraternal order of American origin was the Improved Order of Red Men, established in 1833, which included in its ritual many American Indian customs. During the latter half of the 19th century the number and size of fraternal orders in the U.S. greatly increased. A mark of their influence was the adoption of the lodge form of organization by a number of trade unions. A notable fraternal association of the time, organized in behalf of workers, was the Jefferson Lodge Number 1 of the Ancient Order of United Workmen, organized in Meadville, Pa., in 1868. Many other fraternal associations were modeled on the Jefferson Lodge, but subsequently workingmen

Members of the Ancient Order of Druids meet annually in London to participate in a ceremonial celebration of the autumnal equinox.   UPI

intent on improving conditions tended to join trade unions rather than fraternal associations. The scope of fraternal orders was further limited by the increasing urbanization of American life that became especially marked during the first decades of the 20th century. As cities and towns grew, they offered a multitude of social activities with a consequent decline in the need for the social functions performed by the fraternal orders. Nonetheless, fraternal orders are still numerous and have millions of members. Among the large orders, in addition to the Freemasons and the Odd Fellows, are the Order of the Eastern Star, the Modern Woodmen of America, the Benevolent and Protective Order of Elks, the Knights of Pythias, and the Knights of Columbus.

FRATERNITIES AND SORORITIES, associations, mainly of college and university students in the U.S., established to further the social, scholastic, and professional interests of the members. Because they are almost always designated by letters of the Greek alphabet, they are frequently called Greek-letter societies.

Social fraternities and sororities are organized primarily for social purposes. Membership in these associations is by invitation. Kappa Alpha Society, the oldest social fraternity in continuous existence, was founded in 1825; Alpha Delta Pi, the oldest sorority was established in 1851.

Professional fraternities and sororities invite the membership of students and faculty involved in a specific professional or vocational field, for example, journalism, law, medicine, or music. One of the oldest professional societies is Phi Delta Phi, a legal fraternity founded in 1869.

Honor societies are composed mostly of students who achieve distinction in scholarship and meet with the standards of character and other requirements established by the societies. A number of honor societies are limited to those fulfilling high standards of scholarship in a single field of study, for example, engineering, or to those who display outstanding qualities of leadership. The oldest, largest, and most distinguished of such honor societies is Phi Beta Kappa (q.v.), the oldest association of college students in the country, which was founded as a social fraternity in 1776 and reorganized as an honor society in 1883. The second oldest honor society is Tau Beta Phi, established in 1885 for students who achieve distinction in the study of engineering.

FRATICELLI (Ital., "little brothers"), in a general sense, members of the religious orders founded in Italy in the 13th century, especially the Franciscans. The name also refers to members of the groups that separated from the Franciscans in the 14th and 15th centuries, charging the order with improper views regarding poverty. One of the earliest of these divergent groups, known as the Franciscan Celestines, or Spirituals, practiced severe asceticism. This group was declared heretical and ordered suppressed by Pope John XXII in 1317. In reply, the Celestines declared themselves not only the sole rightful Franciscan order, but the only true Catholics as well, condemning the entire church as heretical and declaring the papal decrees invalid. Small groups of Fraticelli continued their activities for more than a century. The church took strong measures against them in the 15th century, however, and their popular support diminishing, the Fraticelli eventually disappeared.

FRAUD, in law, general term for any instance in which one party deceives or takes unfair advantage of another. Any means used by one person to deceive another may be defined as fraud. For example, if a person represents himself or herself as the agent of a business with which he or she is unconnected and causes another to make a contract to the other party's disadvantage or injury, the first party is guilty of fraud. Furthermore, if, in making a contract, a person obtains an unjust advantage because of the youth, defective mental capacity, or intoxicated condition of the other party to the contract, he or she is guilty of fraud. In a court of law, it is necessary to prove that a representation was made as a statement of fact; that it was untrue and known to be untrue; that it was made with intent to deceive and to induce the other party to act upon it; and that the other party relied on it and was induced to act or not to act, to his or her injury or damage.

In equity, fraud includes any act, omission, or concealment, involving a breach of legal or equitable duty or trust, which results in disadvantage or injury to another. An example of fraud in this sense is the act of an insolvent who contrives to give one creditor an advantage over the others. Fraud can also be constructive, that is, deemed fraud by interpretation. The sole difference in the case of constructive fraud is that no dishonest intent need be adduced. It arises from a breach of duty, such as the breach of a fiduciary relationship in which a trust or confidence has been betrayed.

FRAUNHOFER, Joseph von (1787–1826), German optician and physicist, born in Straubing. Fraunhofer instituted many improvements in the manufacture of optical glass, the grinding and polishing of lenses, and the construction of telescopes and other optical instruments. He also invented a number of scientific instruments. His name is associated with the fixed, dark lines in the solar spectrum, called Fraunhofer lines, which he was the first to describe in detail. His investigations in the refraction and dispersion of light led to the invention of the spectroscope and the science of spectroscopy. In 1823 Fraunhofer became a member of the Academy of Science at Munich and its conservator of physics.

FRAUNHOFER LINES, dark lines identifiable in the absorption spectrum of the sun, which were first observed by the English physicist W. H.

Wollaston in 1802 and later described in detail by Joseph von Fraunhofer. Of the 25,000 lines in the solar spectrum, von Fraunhofer mapped 576, assigning letters to identify the most prominent ones. Some of these are as follows:

A	(extreme red)	made by terrestrial oxygen
B	(red)	made by terrestrial oxygen
C	(red)	made by solar hydrogen
D_1	(yellow)	made by solar sodium
D_2	(yellow)	made by solar sodium
E	(green)	made by solar iron
F	(blue)	made by solar hydrogen
G	(violet)	made by solar iron and calcium group
H	(extreme violet)	made by solar calcium

The lines are the result of absorption of selected wavelengths of light by atoms of gas in the atmosphere of the sun and earth.

FRAZER, Sir James George (1854–1941), British anthropologist, born in Glasgow, Scotland, and educated at the universities of Glasgow and Cambridge. He was elected a fellow of Trinity College, Cambridge, in 1879, and was made a professor of social anthropology at the University of Liverpool in 1907. Frazer's work covered a wide area of anthropological research, but he was especially interested in the study of myth and religion. He is best known for his book *The Golden Bough* (1890), a study of ancient cults, rites, and myths and their parallels with early Christianity. This book, which established Frazer's reputation as a distinguished scholar, was expanded to 13 volumes in 1915. Frazer was knighted in 1914. He wrote many other works, including *Totemism and Exogamy* (1910), *Man, God, and Immortality* (1927), and *Creation and Evolution in Primitive Cosmogonies* (1935).

FRÉCHETTE, Louis Honoré (1839–1908), French-Canadian poet and politician, born in Lévis, Que. Working as a journalist in Chicago, Fréchette wrote *La voix d'un exilé* (The Voice of an Exile, 1866–68), a poem attacking Québec conservatism. On his return to Canada in 1871, Fréchette entered politics, serving in the provincial Legislative Council. In 1880 his poems *Les fleurs boreales* (The Northern Flowers) and *Les oiseaux de neige* (Snow Birds) were awarded a prize by the French Academy, the first time a Canadian had been so honored. Notable among Fréchette's later poetry is a cycle of historical poems, *La légende d'un peuple* (Story of a People, 1887), which reflects his liberal, nationalist view. Fréchette's other writing includes several short stories and plays.

FRECKLES, flat, round, brown spots on the skin that contain an excess of melanin, the human skin pigment (q.v.). Freckles appear in genetically predisposed individuals following exposure to sunlight or any other ultraviolent light source. Light stimulates the proliferation of melanocytes, the cells that synthesize melanin; in persons who develop freckles, the melanocytes grow faster. Freckles are not considered dangerous and do not develop into skin cancer.

FREDERICK. Numbered rulers named Frederick are entered below by their countries, in alphabetical order, and by regnal numbers.

Denmark	Prussia
Frederick I	Frederick I
Frederick II	Frederick II
Frederick III	Frederick III
Frederick IV	
Frederick V	**Sicily**
Frederick VI	
Frederick VII	Frederick I (*see* Holy
Frederick VIII	Roman Empire,
Frederick IX	Frederick II)
	Frederick II
	Frederick III
Germany	
	Sweden
Frederick I (*see* Holy	
Roman Empire,	Frederick I
Frederick I)	
Frederick II (*see* Holy	**Württemberg**
Roman Empire,	
Frederick II)	Frederick I
Frederick III	
Frederick IV (*see*	
Holy Roman	
Empire, Frederick	
III)	
Holy Roman Empire	
Frederick I	
Frederick II	
Frederick III	

FREDERICK I (1471–1533), king of Denmark and Norway (1523–33), son of Christian I and brother of King Hans (1455–1513). He was elected to succeed his deposed nephew, Christian II. Owing his throne to the nobles, Frederick granted them many privileges, thereby diminishing the royal power. A sympathizer of Lutheranism, he facilitated the spread of that faith in his dominions.

FREDERICK II (1534–88), king of Denmark and Norway (1559–88), son of Christian III. He began his reign by conquering the independent republic of Dithmarschen (now a region of Germany) in the western part of the duchy of Holstein. Encouraged by his success, he began a war with Sweden in 1563; it was, however, settled under the Peace of Stettin (1570) with little gain for Denmark. During the latter part of his reign, which was peaceful, he suppressed piracy on the North and Baltic seas and built the fortress-castle of Kronborg in Helsingør (Elsinore). The castle is the setting of Shakespeare's *Hamlet.*

FREDERICK III (1609–70), king of Denmark and Norway (1648–70), born in Haderslev, Denmark, the second son of King Christian IV. He became king in 1648 after he signed a charter greatly restricting the royal authority. But the power of the nobles was soon undermined by charges of improper self-enrichment against their leaders, many of whom were forced to leave the country. In 1657 Frederick began a war against Sweden to regain provinces lost by his father. He was defeated and in 1658 signed the Treaty of Roskilde, ceding a portion of Norway and some Danish islands to Sweden. Shortly after the conclusion of peace the Swedes reopened the war and besieged Copenhagen. With aid from the German region of Brandenburg, the Danes expelled the Swedes from the Jylland (Jutland) Peninsula. In 1660, however, deserted by his allies, Frederick was obliged to make peace, relinquishing all claims to the territories possessed by Denmark in southern Sweden. In that year both the commons and the clergy agreed to the transformation of the kingship from an elective to an absolute and hereditary monarchy.

FREDERICK IV (1671–1730), king of Denmark and Norway (1699–1730), son of Christian V (1646–99). In 1700 Frederick allied himself with Russia and Poland in the Great Northern War against Sweden, but he was soon compelled by Charles XII, king of Sweden, to withdraw from the conflict and to promise not to reenter it. After the defeat of Charles at Poltava (now in Ukraine) in 1709, however, Frederick again declared war on Sweden, subsequently taking the German duchy of Schleswig and participating with the Poles in the invasion of the Swedish portion of Pomerania. By treaty in 1720 Frederick agreed to return to Sweden all conquests made in the war, except for Schleswig. Among the accomplishments of his reign was the freeing of the peasants from serfdom in 1702.

FREDERICK V (1723–66), king of Denmark and Norway (1746–66), son and successor of Christian VI. Little interested in the affairs of state, he left control of the government largely to his foreign minister, Count Johann Hartwig Ernst von Bernstorff (1712–72), who served Frederick in that capacity from 1751 until 1770. Frederick was a patron of learning. He founded a military academy in Sorø, Denmark, and established schools in Bergen and Trondheim, Norway, for the education of Laplanders. In Copenhagen he established academies of printing and sculpture. During Frederick's reign, trade in Asia and the Americas was stimulated and the national wealth was increased.

FREDERICK VI (1768–1839), king of Denmark (1808–39) and of Norway (1808–14), born in Copenhagen, the son and successor of Christian VII. He was made head of the state council in 1784, when his father became insane, and acted as regent until Christian's death in 1808. Aided by Count Andreas Peter Bernstorff (1735–97), Frederick instituted such reforms as civil rights for Jews, the abolition of the slave trade, and freedom of the press. In 1800, because of British failure to respect the rights of free ships during the French Revolution, Frederick joined the armed neutrality of the northern European states formed against Great Britain by Russia, Sweden, and Prussia. As a result, all Danish vessels in British ports were seized; in the next year, when Frederick refused to withdraw from the neutrality convention, the Danish fleet was virtually destroyed by the British navy under Lord Horatio Nelson. Although Denmark remained neutral, Frederick continued to stand firm against the British during the Napoleonic Wars, and the British bombarded Copenhagen in 1807. In that year Frederick became an ally of Napoleon. When Napoleon was defeated in 1814, Frederick was compelled to cede Norway to Sweden under the Treaty of Kiel. The war left his country bankrupt, and Frederick devoted several years to the restoration of financial order. Toward the end of his reign he yielded to the demand for constitutional government and consented to the establishment of provincial councils.

FREDERICK VII (1808–63), king of Denmark (1848–63), son of Christian VIII. In 1849 Frederick promulgated the Unionist constitution abolishing the principle of absolute royal power. During most of his reign Denmark was involved in the Schleswig-Holstein disputes with Germany and Austria.

FREDERICK VIII (1843–1912), king of Denmark (1906–12), born in Copenhagen, and educated at the University of Oxford. He succeeded to the throne on the death of his father, Christian IX. His son, Prince Charles, became Håkon VII, king of Norway, in 1905. Frederick was a brother of Alexandra (1844–1925), queen consort of Great Britain, and of George I, king of Greece.

FREDERICK IX (1899–1972), king of Denmark (1947–72), son and successor of King Christian X,

born near Copenhagen. Frederick was educated at the Danish Naval Academy and the University of Copenhagen. He broke the Danish royal tradition by choosing a naval instead of an army career. During the German occupation of Denmark in World War II, Frederick was virtually interned in the palace. Because he had no male heir, Denmark's succession law was changed during his reign, and he was succeeded by his eldest daughter, Margaret II.

FREDERICK I, called Frederick Barbarossa (1123?–90), Holy Roman emperor and king of Germany (1152–90), king of Italy (1155–90), and as Frederick III, duke of Swabia (1147–52, 1167–68). He was born in Waiblingen, the son of Frederick II of Hohenstaufen, duke of Swabia (1090–1147), and the nephew of Conrad III, king of Germany. Conrad III, favoring Frederick over his own son, on his deathbed recommended to the German princes that Frederick be chosen for the German kingship and the imperial throne. Accordingly, after the death of his uncle in 1152, Frederick Barbarossa was made German king and elected Holy Roman emperor. He conceived of his imperial title as a grant from God, through the German princes, and wished to restore the glory of the Roman Empire. He consequently decided to consolidate the imperial position in Germany and Italy and began by issuing a general order for peace among the princes of Germany, at the same time granting them extensive concessions. In 1154 he proceeded to Italy, where he received the Lombard crown at Pavia. The following year he was crowned Holy Roman emperor by Pope Adrian IV, whose authority Frederick had reinstated before his coronation.

In 1156 Pope Adrian aroused Frederick against the papacy by implying in a letter to him that the emperor held lands only as a fief from the pope. Two years later Frederick incurred the hostility of the Lombards by demanding recognition of all his royal rights, including his power to appoint the imperial podesta, or governor, in every town. Such cities as Milan, Piacenza, Brescia, and Crema considered that demand a denial of their communal liberties and in 1158 began a struggle that lasted until 1183 and required Frederick to lead five expeditions to Italy. Between 1158 and 1162 Frederick warred with Milan and its allies, subduing that city and confirming claims to other Italian cities. Meanwhile Frederick had set up a series of antipopes in opposition to the reigning pope, Alexander III, who espoused the cause of the Milanese and their allies and who, in 1165, excommunicated Frederick. By attacking the Leonine City in Rome in 1167–68, Frederick was able to install one of the antipopes, Paschal III

FREDERICK II

Emperor Frederick I, called Frederick Barbarossa.

(d. 1168), on the papal throne. The Lombard League, consisting of the cities of Milan, Parma, Padua, Verona, Piacenza, Bologna, Cremona, Mantua, Bergamo, and Brescia, was formed in 1167 and eventually acknowledged Pope Alexander as leader. During the next seven years the league acquired military strength, rebuilt Milan, constructed the fortress city of Alessandria, and organized a federal system of administration. The fifth expedition (1174–76) of Frederick to Italy terminated in defeat by the Lombard League at Legnano. The defeat was significant in military history, because it was the first major triumph of infantry over a mounted army of feudal knights. Frederick was forced in 1177 to acknowledge Alexander III as pope and in 1183 to sign the Peace of Constance, acceding to the demands of the Lombards for autonomy but retaining imperial suzerainty over the towns.

Although imperial control in Italy was virtually ended by his defeat at Legnano, Frederick managed to enhance his prestige in central Europe. He made Poland tributary to the empire, raised Bohemia to the rank of a kingdom, and erected the margravate of Austria into an independent hereditary duchy. His own power as emperor in Germany was firmly established in 1180, when he ended his long struggle with the Welfs by putting down a revolt led by the Welf Henry the Lion and depriving him of most of his lands.

Frederick initiated the Third Crusade in 1189, and in the next year, having resigned the government of the empire to his son Henry, later Holy Roman Emperor Henry VI, set out for Asia Minor. After gaining two great victories over the Muslims at Philomelion (now Akşehir) and Iconium (now Konya), he was drowned in the Calycadnus (now

Göksu) River in Cilicia (now in Turkey) on June 10, 1190.

For further information on this person, see the section Biographies in the Bibliography in volume 28.

FREDERICK II (1194–1250), Holy Roman emperor (1215–50) and as Frederick I, king of Sicily (1198–1212).

Born in Lesi, Italy, on Dec. 26, 1194, Frederick was the son of Henry VI and grandson of Frederick I, Holy Roman emperor. He was made German king in 1196 and on the death of his father two years later became king of Sicily. When his mother, Constance of Sicily (1146–98), acting as regent, died several months later, the four-year-old prince was placed under the guardianship of Pope Innocent III, the new regent of Sicily. Emperor Otto IV was deposed in 1211, and the German princes selected Frederick to replace him. A contest for the imperial throne ensued, because Otto was unwilling to relinquish the crown. Supported by the papacy, to which he promised many concessions, and aided by the French, Frederick was eventually secure in his title. He was crowned king of Germany at Aix-la-Chapelle (now Aachen, Germany) in 1215 and Holy Roman emperor at Rome in 1220.

On his coronation Frederick made a number of elaborate promises to the church, including a

Frederick II, Holy Roman emperor, an illustration from his work on the art of falconry. **Bettmann Archive**

vow that he would go on a Crusade. He postponed the Crusade, however, because of an outbreak of anarchy in Sicily and because of the resistance of the Lombard cities, which in 1226 renewed the Lombard League, originally formed against his grandfather, Frederick I. The following year Frederick annulled the Treaty of Constance and put the Lombard cities under the ban of the empire. Threatened several times with excommunication if he did not fulfill his coronation pledge, Frederick determined to sail for Jerusalem in 1227. An epidemic forced him to return three days after his departure, whereupon Pope Gregory IX declared him excommunicated. In 1228 Frederick led the Fifth Crusade to the Holy Land, where he took Jerusalem and concluded a 10-year truce with the sultan of Egypt. Having married Yolande (1212–1228?), the young daughter of the titular king of Jerusalem, John of Brienne, and having assumed his title upon her death, Frederick was crowned king of Jerusalem in that city in 1229.

He returned to Europe and spent many of his remaining years attempting to bring the Lombards under subjection. During intermittent struggles with the papacy he was excommunicated twice again, by Pope Gregory IX in 1239 and in 1245 by Pope Innocent IV. His participation in costly wars in Italy caused him to neglect the welfare of his German subjects. Frederick managed to establish peace, prosperity, and order in Sicily, however, promulgating there in 1231 a comprehensive code of laws, described as the best issued by any Western ruler since the reign of Charlemagne. Frederick also made worthy contributions to learning in Italy. Because he was a man of culture, he gathered scholars and men of letters at his Sicilian court, which Dante called the birthplace of Italian poetry. The University of Naples was founded by Frederick in 1224. For about a century after his death, on Dec. 13, 1250, the belief persisted that Frederick was still alive. According to one famous legend, Frederick resides in a cave in the Kyffhäuser Mountains, in the region of Thuringia, awaiting the summons of the German people to return and restore peace in the empire. The legend was later interpreted to refer to Frederick I.

FREDERICK III, called Frederick the Fair (1286?–1330), Habsburg king of Germany (1314–22). The son of the German king Albert I (1250?–1308), Frederick became duke of Austria in 1306 and was elected king of Germany by a minority of electors in 1314; the majority favored Louis IV, duke of Bavaria. After eight years of conflict, Louis defeated and imprisoned (1322) Frederick, but later released (1325) him and recognized him

as coruler. His authority, however, was limited to Austria.

FREDERICK III (1415–93), Holy Roman emperor (1440–93), and as Frederick IV, king of Germany (1440–86). The son of Ernest of Habsburg, duke of Styria and Carinthia (1377–1424), Frederick was elected Holy Roman emperor and king of Germany in 1440 and crowned by the pope in Rome in 1452, the last time an emperor was crowned in that city. Because he had sacrificed the liberty of the German church in order to secure papal support, he incurred the disfavor of the German princes. Frederick was a disinterested and an incapable ruler who ignored revolts and failed to defend the Habsburg domains against invasion. Nevertheless, by marrying his son and successor, Maximilian, to Mary of Burgundy (1457–82) in 1477, he increased the wealth and power of his dynasty. In 1486, when Maximilian was elected German king, Frederick turned the government over to his son and settled in Linz, where he devoted himself to the study of sciences.

FREDERICK I (1657–1713), first king of Prussia (1701–13), and as Frederick III, elector of Brandenburg (1688–1701), son of Frederick William, the Great Elector, born in Königsberg, Prussia (now Kaliningrad, Russia). Frederick endeavored to establish a court modeled on that of Louis XIV of France. He wished to secure a royal title for himself, but could not do so as ruler of Brandenburg, as the title *king* was forbidden to princes of the Holy Roman Empire. Prussia, however, which was part of Frederick's domain, lay outside the empire, and in 1701 Emperor Leopold I recognized Frederick as king of Prussia in return for his military support in the War of the Spanish Succession. Frederick crowned himself at Königsberg, expending vast sums of money on his coronation. Although he depleted the public treasury during his reign, he undertook some projects beneficial to the welfare of Prussia, such as the establishment in 1694 of the University of Halle and the founding in 1707 of the Academy of Sciences, Berlin. He patronized scholars, including the German philosopher and mathematician Gottfried Wilhelm Leibniz, and encouraged persecuted Protestants from other countries to settle in Prussia.

FREDERICK II, called The Great (1712–86), king of Prussia (1740–86), son of King Frederick William I and grandson of Frederick I. During his reign, he was considered among the most notable of enlightened despots in 18th-century Europe.

Frederick was born in Berlin on Jan. 24, 1712. As crown prince he was trained, under his father's supervision, to become a soldier and a thrifty administrator. Frederick, however, encouraged by his mother, Sophia Dorothea of Hannover (1666–1726), and his tutors, showed a preference for courtly life, music, and French literature. Frederick William, failing to understand the tastes of his son, developed an open dislike for him. At the age of 18, Frederick decided to escape to England; his proposed plan was discovered, and he was arrested, imprisoned, temporarily deprived of his status as crown prince, and forced to witness the execution of one of his two confederates. After he had subsequently applied himself diligently to fiscal and military affairs and had consented to a marriage in 1733 with Elizabeth Christine (1715–97), daughter of Ferdinand Albert II of Brunswick (1680–1735), Frederick was reinstated to his position as crown prince. He then went to live for seven years on his estate at Rheinsburg, where, in his leisure time, he studied philosophy, history, and poetry and corresponded with the French philosophers, notably Voltaire. In his *Antimachiavell,* written during that period and published by Voltaire in 1740, Frederick idealistically opposed the political doctrines of the Italian statesman and philosopher Niccolò Machiavelli, favoring peaceful and enlightened rule.

King and Military Leader. On the death of his father in 1740 Frederick became king and embarked almost immediately on a policy of Prussian aggrandizement. When Maria Theresa became archduchess of Austria in that same year, Frederick demanded the cession of duchies of Silesia in return for Prussian recognition of the Pragmatic Sanction, which gave the Austrian Habsburg dominions to Maria Theresa. Refused by Austria, Frederick invaded Silesia, commencing the War of the Austrian Succession. He led his forces to victory at Mollwitz in 1741 and at Chotusitz in 1742; in the latter year, by the Treaty of Breslau, Maria Theresa was obliged to yield the Silesian territory demanded by Prussia. Frederick acquired East Friesland (now a region of Germany) in 1744, on the death of the last ruler without heirs of that principality, and in 1745 he fought and won a second war with Austria, terminated by the Peace of Dresden, which assured Prussia the possession of Silesia.

By this time Frederick was recognized as an able military leader, and the position of Prussia in Europe had risen considerably. The military greatness of Frederick was demonstrated during the Seven Years' War, fought from 1756 to 1763. Frederick and his forces, aided only by financial assistance from Great Britain, which was at war with France, opposed the armies of Austria, Russia, Sweden, Saxony, and France. The Peace of Hubertusburg in 1763 awarded Prussia no new terri-

Frederick the Great, a rendering by Adolph Friedrich Erdmann von Menzel. German Information Center

tory, as it merely confirmed the boundaries that had existed before the war; at the end of the war, however, Prussia was established as a rival to Austria for domination of the German states. Frederick made an alliance with Catherine II of Russia, in 1764, and by the first partition of Poland in 1772 he received Polish Prussia, exclusive of Gdańsk (Danzig) and Toruń (Thorn), thus uniting the regions of Brandenburg and Pomerania. By the Treaty of Teschen in 1779, after the War of the Bavarian Succession, a short conflict with Austria, Prussia was awarded the Franconian principalities of Bavaria; Austria retained only a part of Lower Bavaria. A further step was made toward destroying Austrian dominance in 1785, when Frederick gathered the German princes into a union of princes, the Fürstenbund, to preserve the constitution of the Holy Roman Empire.

Administrator. Frederick was extremely sympathetic to the American Revolution and was an admirer of George Washington. He was one of the first sovereigns to conclude a commercial treaty with the U.S. He did not, however, limit his activities to the international scene; internal affairs flourished during his reign. His rule was absolute; he was a ubiquitous administrator, constantly checking the work of his officials, from whom he exacted the utmost in conscientiousness. Under his rule new methods of agriculture and manufacturing were introduced. Marshes were drained, providing new lands for cultivation and colonization and the institution of serfdom, while not abolished, was somewhat liberalized. Under Frederick's personal supervision the efficiency and size of the army were increased. He reviewed the troops frequently, concerned himself with the discipline of his officers and men, and wrote works for his generals on the science of warfare. In 1747 Frederick, who was particularly interested in the equitable distribution of justice to all classes, issued a new codification of Prussian law, the *Codex Fridericianus*.

Patron of Culture. Frederick continued to patronize the arts and sciences throughout his life. The Academy of Sciences again became an important center of learning during his reign, and elementary education progressed as under no previous Prussian sovereign. In his favorite residence, the palace of Sans Souci, Frederick held court, but always entertained with judicious economy. Contemptuous of the German language and culture, Frederick spoke French at court and patronized French writers, many of whom, including Voltaire, paid him visits in Berlin. Frederick himself was a musician, spending many hours with his flute. He was also a prolific writer; his complete works were published in 30 volumes between 1846 and 1857. He died at Sans Souci on Aug. 17, 1786.

For further information on this person, see the section Biographies in the Bibliography in volume 28.

FREDERICK III (1831–88), king of Prussia and emperor of Germany (March 9–June 15, 1888), son of Emperor William I, born in Potsdam. When his father succeeded to the throne of Prussia in 1861, Frederick became Frederick William, crown prince of Prussia. Liberal in his political views, he opposed Prince Otto von Bismarck throughout the ministry of the latter. Although opposed to war with Austria in 1866, Frederick became commander of an army and led the Prussian forces to victory at the Battle of Sadowa (Königgratz), which terminated the Seven Weeks' War. During the Franco-Prussian War of 1870–71 he commanded the armies of the southern German states, participating in the battles of Wörth and Sedan and the siege of Paris.

A man of learning and culture, Frederick patronized art and literature and encouraged the work of the royal museums. As Crown Prince Frederick William, he was genially called "Our Fritz" by the German people, most of whom anticipated with pleasure his accession to the throne. Frederick became ill, however, in 1887 and lived only three months after succeeding to the throne on his father's death in 1888. He was in turn succeeded by his son, William II.

FREDERICK II (1272–1337), king of Sicily (1296–1337), who established an independent dynasty on the island. The third son of King Pedro III of Aragón (1239–85), Frederick became regent of Sicily, a possession of Aragón, in 1291. Four years later, when Aragón surrendered the island to the papacy, the Sicilians revolted, choosing Frederick as their leader and crowning him king in 1296. As the pope's administrator, King Charles II of Naples (c. 1254–1309) then tried to conquer Sicily. The war was inconclusive, but by the Treaty of Caltabelotta (1302) Frederick was given possession of the island until his death, at which time it would revert to Neapolitan control. Frederick later made another war on Naples. Despite the treaty, Frederick's son, Peter (r. 1337–42), acquired Sicily on the death of his father. His successors ruled the island as a separate kingdom until 1412.

FREDERICK III, called The Simple (1341–77), king of Sicily (1355–77); he was a member of the Sicilian branch of the Aragonese dynasty. To preserve the independence of his kingdom he continued the war against Naples begun during the reign of King Frederick II of Sicily. The war was ended in 1372 by agreement with Joanna I, queen of Naples (1326–82). Frederick retained control of Sicily until his death.

FREDERICK I (1676–1751), king of Sweden (1720–51), born in Kassel, Germany. He was a landgrave, or count, of Hesse-Kassel in 1715, when he married Princess Ulrika Eleonora (1688–1741), the sister of King Charles XII. In 1718 Ulrika succeeded to the throne, and two years later she abdicated in favor of Frederick. His royal powers were sharply limited by a new constitution that granted increased legislative powers to the Riksdag, or Parliament, and vested executive power in a committee of aristocrats. The aristocracy was, however, divided into two factions: the Caps, who sought a conciliatory foreign policy, and the Hats, who wanted to regain territory lost to Russia during the reign of Charles. In 1738 the Hats gained a political majority, and from 1741 to 1743 Sweden was at war with Russia. Sweden lost additional territory in Finland, and Russian influence reached into Sweden. Frederick was succeeded by Adolph Frederick of Holstein-Gottorp (1710–71), who was the choice of Empress Elizabeth Petrovna of Russia.

FREDERICK I (1754–1816), king of Württemberg (1806–16). As Frederick II he was duke of Württemberg from 1797 to 1805. He fought against France during the early phase of the Napoleonic Wars and lost part of his duchy in 1801. Frederick later supported Napoleon, who by 1805 restored to Frederick the lost territory and increased the size of his dukedom. With Napoleon's permission, Frederick proclaimed himself King Frederick I in 1806. After Napoleon's defeat at the Battle of Leipzig in 1813, Frederick shifted sides again and joined the allied coalition against France.

FREDERICK, city, seat of Frederick Co., NW Maryland, on a tributary of the Monocacy R.; settled by 1745, inc. 1817. It is a trade and shipping center of a rich dairy-farming and corn- and wheat-growing region; manufactures include electrical and electronic equipment, control devices, biomedical products, hardware, and pumps. Hood College (1893), Maryland School for the Deaf (1867), and a U.S. Army research laboratory are here. The city has several churches dating from the 18th and early 19th centuries. Francis Scott Key, author of "The Star-Spangled Banner," Chief Justice Roger B. Taney, and Barbara Fritchie, a devoted Unionist during the American Civil War, are buried in Frederick. In 1864, during the Civil War, Confederate Gen. Jubal A. Early extracted a $200,000 ransom from the city before defeating Union forces at the Battle of Monocacy, which was fought nearby. Frederick probably is named for Frederick Calvert, 6th baron Baltimore (1731–71). Pop. (1980) 28,086; (1990) 40,148.

FREDERICK AUGUSTUS I, called The Just (1750–1827), first king of Saxony (1806–27), and, as Frederick Augustus III, elector of Saxony (1763–1806), born in Dresden. He aided Frederick II, the Great, king of Prussia, against Austria in 1778–79 during the bloodless War of the Bavarian Succession. Attempting to establish his neutrality, Frederick Augustus declined the Polish throne in 1791 but cooperated with the other European powers in their wars with revolutionary and Napoleonic France. Following Napoleon's victory at Jena in 1806, Frederick Augustus made peace with France. Under terms of the treaty, signed at Posen (now Poznań, Poland), Frederick Augustus became king of Saxony and joined the French-sponsored Confederation of the Rhine. His alliance with Napoleon, to which he adhered to the end, proved costly to him. The Congress of Vienna, meeting in 1814–15 after the Napoleonic Wars, awarded the northern portion of his kingdom to Prussia. In 1815 Frederick Augustus led Saxony into the newly formed German Confederation, and Saxony was then largely eclipsed by Prussia. Frederick Augustus was succeeded as king by his brother Anthony (1755–1836).

FREDERICK AUGUSTUS II (1797–1854), king of Saxony (1836–54), nephew of King Frederick Augustus I and King Anthony (1755–1836), born in Dresden. As joint regent (1830–36) with Anthony (r. 1827–36), he was partly responsible for the

reforms in the Saxony constitution of 1831. After he became king in 1836, however, his reign was disturbed by demands for additional political and social reforms. In 1849 he refused to accept the liberal German constitution written in Frankfurt, and ensuing riots in Dresden had to be quelled by Prussian troops. Thereafter, the king largely withdrew from the affairs of state. He was succeeded as king by his brother John (1801–73).

FREDERICK HENRY (1584–1647), prince of Orange and stadtholder (chief executive and military commander) of the Dutch Republic (1625–47), son of William I, The Silent, born in Delft. He was given strict military training by his brother, Maurice of Nassau (1567–1625), whom he succeeded as stadtholder of five of the seven provinces of the United Provinces of the Netherlands in 1625. As stadtholder he prosecuted the war against Spain, making alliances successively with Denmark, Sweden, and France. Under his generalship many cities were taken from the Spanish, among them 's Hertogenbosch (1629), Maastricht (1632), Breda (1637), and Hulst (1645). Finally, in 1646, he started peace negotiations with Spain. The resulting treaty, concluded in 1648 after his death, accorded the United Provinces all the advantages for which they had been fighting during the preceding 80 years.

Frederick Henry reigned during the Golden Age of the Dutch Republic. The republic was at the height of its powers and suffered little political or religious conflict. Culture flourished, and such painters as Rembrandt and Frans Hals emerged. Amsterdam was the financial center of Europe, and commerce expanded with the establishment of colonies in the Far East and the conquest of territory in South America.

FREDERICKSBURG, city, in (but administratively independent of) Spotsylvania Co., N Virginia, on the Rappahannock R.; settled 1728, inc. as a city 1879. It is a commercial hub of a livestock-raising and corn-growing area; manufactures include chemicals, motor vehicles, clothing, and wood products. Mary Washington College (1908) and several museums are here. Fredericksburg is also a tourist center, with many historic sites in and near the city. George Washington was born nearby, at Wakefield, the family estate, and many buildings associated with him have been preserved here. These include the lodge where he became a Mason; the home of his mother, Mary Washington (1708–89); and Kenmore, the plantation house of his sister. Also of interest is the house of the naval hero John Paul Jones.

During the American Civil War, the Fredericksburg region, strategically located between Wash-

The Union army assault on Fredericksburg, Va., depicted in a contemporary engraving.   Clarence Homung

ington and Richmond, was the scene of fierce fighting. The Battle of Fredericksburg was fought here in December 1862, and the battles of Chancellorsville, the Wilderness, and Spotsylvania Courthouse occurred nearby. Parts of these major battlefields are now in Fredericksburg and Spotsylvania National Military Park. The city is named for Frederick Louis (1707–51), prince of Wales, father of George III of Great Britain. Pop. (1980) 15,322; (1990) 19,027.

FREDERICKSBURG, BATTLE OF, one of the early important battles of the American Civil War, fought in and near Fredericksburg, Va., Dec. 13–15, 1862. The contending forces were the Union Army of the Potomac with 122,000 troops and 312 guns, under Ambrose Everett Burnside, and the Confederate Army of Northern Virginia with 78,500 men and 270 guns, under Robert E. Lee.

After the Battle of Antietam in September 1862, Lee withdrew from Maryland to Virginia, and the federal government decided that a counteroffensive was strategically in order. Burnside intended to cross the Rappahannock River at several points and encircle and capture Fredericksburg as a preliminary to launching the general offensive against the Confederate army. The Union crossing of the Rappahannock was held up, however, because of a delay in shipment of the pontoon train necessary to the crossing. In the interim, Lee, who had at first decided to await the Union forces at a point 58 km (36 mi) south of Fredericksburg, moved to the Rappahannock and fortified the heights commanding the river. The Union army crossed the Rappahannock directly opposite Fredericksburg and launched frontal assaults

against the Confederate troops. The attacks were repulsed by the Confederates, and the defeated Union army was compelled to withdraw to Falmouth, Va. Union losses were 1284 killed, 9600 wounded, and 1769 missing; Confederate losses were 595 killed, 4061 wounded, and 653 missing.

For further information on this topic, see the Bibliography in volume 28, section 1155.

FREDERICK WILLIAM (1620–88), elector of Brandenburg (1640–88), called the Great Elector, who laid the foundations for the strong Prussian state of the 18th century.

The son of Elector George William (1595–1640), Frederick William was born on Feb. 12, 1620, in Berlin. He succeeded to the electorate during the Thirty Years' War, when Swedish forces were occupying Brandenburg. Concluding an armistice with Sweden, he was able to repair some of the war's damage to the country. He remained neutral until the Peace of Westphalia ended the war in 1648; by that treaty he received eastern Pomerania, along the Baltic Sea, and some smaller territories. Over the next 30 years, by alliances and wars and systematic strengthening of his army, Frederick William acquired more lands and power for Brandenburg. In 1656, during the war between Sweden and Poland, he switched his allegiance from Poland to Sweden and back to Poland in return for the latter's recognition of his suzerainty over East Prussia, until then a Polish dependency. In 1675 he defeated invading Swedish forces at Fehrbellin and conquered western Pomerania, long coveted for its important seaports, but at the insistence of France, Sweden's ally, he relinquished the territory at the Peace of Saint-Germain-en-Laye in 1679.

FREDERICK WILLIAM I

Frederick William centralized government administration and improved almost every area of public affairs, especially industry and commerce. After the Edict of Nantes in 1685 he admitted large numbers of Huguenots, who, with the technological skills they had acquired in France, aided in the development of Prussian industry. He also created the Prussian navy, founded colonies in western Africa, and established the Royal Library in Berlin. He died in Potsdam on May 9, 1688.

FREDERICK WILLIAM I (1688-1740), king of Prussia (1713-40), who during his reign made his kingdom into a major European state.

Frederick William was born on Aug. 15, 1688, in Berlin, the son of King Frederick I. He succeeded his father in 1713 and for the next seven years was involved in a dispute with Sweden over Pomerania, a part of which he finally received by the Treaty of Stockholm in 1720. In return for recognizing (1726) the Pragmatic Sanction, by which Maria Theresa, archduchess of Austria, was given the Austrian Habsburg dominions, he hoped to gain support for his claim to the Lower Rhine duchies of Jülich and Berg, but his expectations were dashed.

Frederick William's greatest accomplishment was in the internal development of Prussia. Contemptuous of the luxury of his father's reign, he instituted a system of rigid and efficient economy at court and transferred public financial administration from local governments to the central royal authority. He was thus able to repay the debts incurred by his father and greatly improve the financial condition of Prussia. He built up industry by forbidding the importation of finished goods and the exportation of raw materials, and directed the colonization of nonpopulous areas, especially in East Prussia. He also instituted compulsory elementary education in Prussia. The development of the army was his fondest achievement; he was particularly proud of the Potsdam Guard, composed of exceptionally tall men hired, and sometimes kidnapped, from all parts of Europe. Under his supervision the number of soldiers in the army was increased from about 38,000 to some 83,500 and Prussia became the third ranking military power in Europe. Frederick William died at Potsdam on May 31, 1740, and was succeeded by his son, Frederick II, the Great.

FREDERICK WILLIAM II (1744-97), king of Prussia (1786-97), grandson of Frederick William I and nephew of Frederick II, born in Berlin. He succeeded to the throne in 1786 upon the death of his uncle. In 1792 he made an alliance with Leopold II, Holy Roman emperor, to support Louis XVI of France in the French Revolution. As a result of Frederick's participation in the ensuing wars, he was forced in 1795 by the Treaty of Basel to cede to France Prussian territories west of the Rhine River. He secured territory from Poland, however, by participating in the Polish partitions of 1793 and 1795. Influenced during his reign by the Rosicrucian order, of which he was a member, he suppressed the ideas of the Enlightenment, imposing censorship on religion, education, and the press. He lacked interest in military affairs and allowed a supreme college of war to supervise the army, which declined markedly during his reign. Through his own ineptitude and that of the favorites he appointed to administrative positions, the treasury of Prussia was bankrupted and the reputation of the country diminished by the end of his reign.

FREDERICK WILLIAM III (1770-1840), king of Prussia (1797-1840), son of Frederick William II, born in Potsdam. He was given military training in his youth and from 1792 to 1794 fought against France during the French Revolution. In 1797 he succeeded to the throne and set about rebuilding the economy and the army, which had suffered during the reign of his father. He kept Prussia neutral in the Napoleonic Wars until 1805, when persuaded by Russia and the aroused spirit of his people, he joined the allies against France. Prussia was defeated at Jena and Auerstädt in 1806. By the Treaty of Tilsit in 1807, various Prussian territories were ceded to France. Through the efforts of the administrators Baron H. F. K. vom Stein, Count A. N. von Gneisenau, Prince K. A. von Hardenberg, and G. J. D. von Scharnhorst (1755-1813), the Prussian army was reconstituted between 1807 and 1812 and participated in the victorious campaigns against Napoleon from 1813 until 1815. In this period Frederick William promised the Prussian people a constitution. At the close of the war in 1815, however, he joined the Holy Alliance and participated in the alliance's repression of liberal movements in Europe. Within Prussia, he accomplished the reorganization of parts of the adminstrative system and consented to formation of the Zollverein, or customs union.

FREDERICK WILLIAM IV (1795-1861), king of Prussia (1840-61). The son of Frederick William III, he was born in Berlin on Oct. 15, 1795. He gave indications of becoming a liberal monarch by increasing freedom of religion and relieving press censorship on his accession to the throne in 1840. In 1847 he convened the United Diet, which, although limited, was a step toward a popular representative assembly. When revolution broke out in Prussia in March 1848, he at first acceded to the demands of his people, promising a constitution and agreeing to become the leader of a united Germany. In 1849 he refused the imperial crown offered to him by the Frankfurt Parliament, opting instead for a union of German states under Prussian leadership (the Erfurt Union), proposed by his foreign minister, Joseph von Radowitz (1797–1853). Under Austrian pressure, he abandoned this project by the Treaty of Olmütz (November 1850). In the constitution granted the same year, most of the governing power was vested in the king, suffrage was restricted, and membership in the parliament was considerably limited. After suffering two paralytic strokes in 1857, Frederick William became mentally unfit to rule. In 1858 a regency was established under his brother William, who, as William I, succeeded to the throne when Frederick William died on Jan. 2, 1861.

FREDERICTON, city, capital of New Brunswick, and seat of York Co., on the Saint John R., in the S central part of the province; inc. as a city 1848. It is a commercial and distribution center for the surrounding farming, lumbering, mining, and quarrying region. Major manufactures include building materials, shoes, processed food, and wood products. Government activities, educational institutions, and tourism are of prime importance to the city's economy.

In Fredericton are the University of New Brunswick (1785), Saint Thomas University (1910), a community college, and the Maritime Forest Research Centre. Points of interest in the city include the Beaverbrook Art Gallery, the York-Sunbury Historical Society Museum, the New Brunswick Sports Hall of Fame, Christ Church Cathedral (dedicated 1853), and the buildings of the provincial legislature. Nearby attractions are a military museum at the Canadian Forces Base, Gagetown; Kings Landing Historical Settlement, a restoration of a pre-1870 Loyalist village; and Woolastook Wildlife Park.

Fredericton is located on the site of Fort Nashawaak, built by the French in 1692, and the Acadian settlement of Saint Anne's Point, established in 1731 and later abandoned. A group of United Empire Loyalists from the U.S. platted the community in 1785 and named it for Frederick Augustus (1763–1827), a son of George III of England. In 1973 the city annexed several adjoining communities, thereby increasing its area from about 60 sq km (about 23 sq mi) to 132 sq km (51 sq mi). Pop. (1986) 44,352; (1991) 46,466.

FREDERIKSBERG, borough, E Denmark, a suburb of Copenhagen. Frederiksberg is the site of an imposing palace, built by King Frederick IV in the first half of the 18th century. Industrial establishments in the borough include the Royal Porcelain Works, a faience factory, and breweries. Pop. (1988 est.) 85,800.

FREE CHURCH OF SCOTLAND, name commonly applied to the church established by a group of about 450 ministers who seceded from the Church of Scotland in 1843, thereby effecting a schism that came to be known as the Disruption. The basic issue in the split was the jurisdiction of the civil powers over the doctrines, discipline, and government of the church; it was brought to a head in 1838 by a decision of the civil courts that forbade any congregation to reject a pastor who had been appointed to serve it. This decision was upheld by the House of Commons in March 1843. Known as nonintrusionists, the ministers who opposed acceptance of this decision were led by Thomas Chalmers. At the meeting of the General Assembly of the Church of Scotland, held in May 1843, they declared their intention of separating from the church and immediately establishing a new one. They then withdrew and organized the first Assembly of the Free Church of Scotland, of which Chalmers was elected moderator, or presiding officer.

Except for its independent attitude toward the civil authorities and its voluntary renunciation of all claim to the parent church's properties and benefices, the seceding group retained all the doctrines and practices of the Church of Scotland. The Free Church received such active and financial support from its adherents, who included about one-third of the former members of the Church of Scotland, that by the end of 1847 more than 700 churches had been erected, and the New College had been built in Edinburgh as an institution for theological studies. Similar institutions were later established in Aberdeen and Glasgow.

Between 1863 and 1873 unsuccessful efforts were made to create a union of the Free Church and the United Presbyterian Church; such a union was finally brought about in 1900; the new church was known as the United Free Church of Scotland. A small group within the Free Church refused to participate in the union and declared itself the true Free Church. In October 1929 the United Free Church and the Church of Scotland were reunited, under the latter name.

FREEDMEN'S BUREAU, agency established as part of the U.S. War Department by an act of Congress in March 1865. The full title of the agency was Bureau of Refugees, Freedmen, and Abandoned Lands. Its principal aim was to provide assistance to the newly emancipated blacks of the South after the American Civil War. Originally created for one year, the bureau was con-

A primary school for former slaves in Vicksburg, Miss., after the American Civil War (from a contemporary magazine).   Library of Congress

tinued in 1866 by Congress overriding the veto of President Andrew Johnson and was thereafter repeatedly extended. The bureau was headed by a commissioner, Gen. Oliver Otis Howard, who was assisted by one assistant commissioner for each Southern state.

The bureau took responsibility for furnishing food and medical supplies to blacks, most of whom were destitute, and to needy whites as well. It was also concerned with the regulation of wages and working conditions of blacks, the establishment and maintenance of schools for illiterate former slaves, and the control and distribution of lands abandoned by or confiscated from Southern proprietors. In addition, the bureau handled legal trials involving blacks. The lands controlled by the bureau, totaling about 325,000 ha (about 800,000 acres), were originally intended to be distributed to former slaves and to persons of proved loyalty to the Union, in lots not exceeding 16 ha (40 acres). For various reasons this plan was abandoned, and much of the land was returned to the former owners, causing severe disappointment to blacks, who had hoped thereby to establish themselves as independent farmers. Most of the activities of the bureau were ended in 1869, except for the edu-

cational program, which continued in effect until 1872 and effected the most significant achievements of the agency. Although it was denounced as an instrument of Northern politicians for economic and political advantage, accomplishments of the bureau included the establishment of a system of free public schools for blacks and of such higher educational institutions as Howard, Fisk, and Atlanta universities and the Hampton Institute; the expenditure of about $20 million in various types of relief and assistance; and some improvements in the social, economic, and political status of Southern blacks.

For further information on this topic, see the Bibliography in volume 28, section 1157.

FREEDOM. *See* LIBERTY.

FREEDOM OF INFORMATION ACT, U.S. law that provides public access to U.S. government files. The act, which went into effect on July 4, 1967, is based on the principle that every person should have clear access to identifiable records without having to state a reason for wanting the information. In 1974, in the wake of the Watergate (q.v.) conspiracy, amendments were added to strengthen the statute.

The act provides that each government agency will publish in the *Federal Register* descriptions of its organization, operations, and procedures; further, that each agency will make available opinions, orders, and statements of policy, including manuals and instructions, that affect the public. Agencies are permitted to delete identifying details in order to avoid clearly unwarranted invasions of personal privacy. Individuals who request government records generally must pay standard fees for document search and duplication. Agencies have ten working days to comply with a request, but this time may be extended if collecting records from field facilities, examining voluminous files, or consulting with another agency having a substantial interest is necessary. The requester must be notified of the reason for the time extension.

Under the act, nine categories of records may be withheld, including national defense information, matters under litigation, and medical files. District courts, however, may enjoin the withholding of records, and the Civil Service Commission may take disciplinary action against officials who illegally withhold information.

Federal agencies estimated the cost of complying with the act to be about $48 million a year. It has been criticized on the grounds that it diverts government personnel from their principal work, that the information obtained often is used for commercial purposes, and that it discourages prospective informants from supplying information to the government for fear that their names will be made public.   L.B.K.

FREEDOM OF THE PRESS. *See* PRESS, FREEDOM OF THE.

FREEDOM OF RELIGION. *See* RELIGIOUS LIBERTY.

FREEDOM OF THE SEAS. *See* SEAS, FREEDOM OF THE.

FREEDOM OF SPEECH. *See* SPEECH, FREEDOM OF.

FREE ENTERPRISE SYSTEM. *See* CAPITALISM.

FREE FALL, common term for any motion that, in theory, is determined solely by gravitational forces (*see* GRAVITATION). Examples are the moon's motion around the earth, and an object dropping to the earth's surface. A person in free fall experiences weightlessness (*see* SKY DIVING; SPACE EXPLORATION). In fact, influences besides gravitation are unavoidable. Air resistance in the earth's atmosphere, for instance, slows down an object's rate of descent, while less-obvious attritional forces affect the speed of orbiting objects.

FREE FRENCH, designation popularly applied to the armed forces of the French National Committee of Liberation, an organization founded in London on June 28, 1940, following the capitulation of France to Germany in World War II. The committee was established, on the initiative of Gen. Charles de Gaulle—who had refused to accept France's surrender—for the purpose of carrying on the war against Germany. The Free French took part in the North African invasion in 1942 and later in the invasion of southern France. They were the first to enter Paris in 1944.

FREEMAN, Mary E(leanor) Wilkins (1852-1930), American writer, born in Randolph, Mass. Her earliest and finest writings, contained in the two collections of short stories *A Humble Romance* (1887) and *A New England Nun* (1891), reflect her keen observation of the spiritual frustrations caused by the changing social structure of rural New England.

FREEMASONRY, largest and most widely established fraternal order in the world. The masons' guilds were originally restricted to stonecutters, but with the completion of the building of the cathedrals in the 17th century, and especially in England during the Reformation, they admitted as members men of wealth or social status. The guilds thus became societies devoted to general ideals, such as fraternity, equality, and peace, and their meetings became social rather than business occasions. Four or more such guilds, called lodges, united in London on June 24, 1717, to form the Grand Lodge of England; all recognized grand lodges have been derived from it. The Grand Lodge of All England was formed at York in 1725, that of Ireland by June of the same year, and of Scotland in 1736. The York body came under the jurisdiction of the Grand Lodge at London later in the century.

As a result of the patronage of the order by members of the nobility, the rising British mercantile class looked upon Freemasonry as an adjunct to social success, and the order became popular. The Masonic ideals of religious toleration and the basic equality of all people were in keeping with the growing spirit of liberalism during the 18th century. One of the basic tenets of the Masonic orders throughout the English-speaking world has been that religion is the concern solely of the individual. Opposition on the part of the Roman Catholic church has been chiefly on the grounds that Freemasonry, with its binding principles and religious nature, has usurped the prerogatives of the church. As a result, the Freemasons have never been permitted in some strictly Roman Catholic countries, such as Spain. In France, however, following the atheistic and Protestant trend of the French Revolution, the order flourished.

Functions. In most English-speaking countries, the charitable and protective features of the fraternity have been responsible for the establishment of Masonic homes for the care of dependent aged Masons and their widows and orphanages and schools for the children of members. The Mason is instructed that his fraternal obligations involving aid to members are to be subordinated to the duty he owes to God, his country, and his family, with full recognition of the duty he owes to humanity. The Masonic fraternity differs radically from the other private benevolent societies, and from the Independent Order of Odd Fellows, the next largest private, international, fraternal association, in that the relief or charity extended among members is purely voluntary, dependent on the need in each individual case. It is in no way part of a contract or other understanding that the distress of a brother shall call for specific financial recognition or care. Freemasonry is essentially an educational society, attempting to teach its members a moral philosophy of life.

Freemasons in America. The earliest of the U.S. lodges, founded by authority of the Grand Lodge of England, were the First Lodge of Boston, established in 1733, and one in Philadelphia, established about the same time. By the time of the American Revolution, about 150 lodges existed in colonial America. American Freemasons today make up about three-fourths of the total number of all members throughout the world; world membership exceeds 6 million.

Major Systems. Scores of Masonic rites have sprung up since the 17th century, but only five of any great consequence survive today. Two Masonic systems are called the York Rite and the Scottish Rite. Neither has any connection, historically or otherwise, with York, England, or Scotland. The York Rite was formed in the late 18th century and is called Capitular and the members Royal Arch Masons (4 degrees); the next step is Cryptic and the members Royal and Select Masons (3 degrees); and the final step is Chivalric and the members Knights Templar (3 orders).The Scottish Rite was formed in Charleston, S.C., in 1801 (33 degrees including three Symbolic Lodge Degrees).

In many other groups, loosely attached in some way to the York Rite, members are usually selected but sometimes are elected. They are interested in special aspects of Masonry, including Masonic research. One might say they are offshoots of the main stem. Among them are the Royal Order of Scotland, the Allied Masonic Degrees, the Red Cross of Constantine, the Masonic Rosicrucian Society (SRICF), the Rite of Strict Observance (CBCS), the Grand College of Rites, Knight Masons, Order of Corks, the York Cross of Honour, the Blue Friars, and the Holy Royal Arch Knights Templar Priests. There are also what might be called "fun degrees," such as the Shrine, the Grotto, and the Tall Cedars of Lebanon, many of which are of considerable size. In addition some very small groups cater to students of special aspects of the Craft.

For other Mason-affiliated organizations, see EASTERN STAR, ORDER OF THE.

Opposition. Anti-Masonic sentiment occurred chiefly in two ways since the founding of the order. The first, religious, is the opposition of the Roman Catholic church, although Freemasonry does not bar Catholics and a great many belong to lodges in Latin America and the Philippines. The second is political. For about a decade following the abduction from Batavia, N.Y., in 1821, of William Morgan (1774?–1826?), a Freemason who had threatened to publish Masonic secrets and who was commonly thought to have been kidnapped by the Masons, a general outcry was that many Masonic lodges had to be abandoned throughout the eastern and middle states. In the northern states the Anti-Masonic party was formed; for a few years it was practically the only opponent to the Democratic party. In 1832 the Anti-Masonic party nominated a lawyer, William Wirt (1772–1834), as its candidate for the presidency, but he was defeated by Andrew Jackson, who supported Masonry. Ironically, Wirt himself was a Mason. After that date the Freemasons encountered little political opposition in the U.S. or elsewhere, until the rise to power of the National Socialists in Germany in 1933. In that year Hitler charged the Masons with responsibility for various subversive activities, including all the incidents leading to World War I, and decreed the dissolution of all Masonic bodies in Germany.

FREE METHODIST CHURCH OF NORTH AMERICA, Protestant denomination organized in Pekin, N.Y., in 1860. The denomination adheres strictly to the doctrines and practices of primitive Methodism, and its polity is substantially the same as that of the Methodist church. The chief policymaking body is a quinquennial general conference. Headquarters is at Winona Lake, Ind. The biweekly *Light and Life* is a widely known denominational periodical. The Free Methodist Church is one of a group of independent denominations known as Holiness bodies because the members attach central importance to the doctrine of Christian perfection, known also as perfect love or holiness.

The denomination originated among ministers and laypeople expelled from the Methodist Episcopal church in the Genesee (N.Y.) Conference and other members who voluntarily joined them.

Their dissatisfaction arose from what they felt to be a less strict observance of Christian teaching as interpreted by the founder of Methodism, John Wesley.

In the late 1980s the church reported about 72,200 members in more than 1000 churches in North America. The denomination supports several institutions of higher education, a theological seminary, a worldwide radio ministry, and an international missionary program.

For further information on this topic, see the Bibliography in volume 28, section 110.

FREEPORT, city, seat of Stephenson Co., N Illinois, on the Pecatonica R.; inc. 1855. It is an agricultural and manufacturing center, producing foodstuffs, electrical equipment, rubber goods, and toiletries. A community college and an art museum and cultural center are here. The community was settled in the 1830s; its name may reflect the generosity of a local trader who, according to his wife, ran a "free port" for travelers. The second Lincoln-Douglas debate, in which Senator Stephen A. Douglas advanced the "Freeport doctrine" that a locality in a U.S. territory could prohibit slavery despite the U.S. Supreme Court's ruling in the Dred Scott case, was held here on Aug. 27, 1858. Pop. (1980) 26,266; (1990) 25,840.

FREEPORT, village, Nassau Co., SE New York, on the S shore of Long Island; settled 1659, inc. 1892. It is a residential suburb of New York City and a boating and fishing center; access to the Atlantic Ocean is through Jones Inlet. Manufactures include marine supplies, plastic goods, and electronic equipment. The name of the community was derived from the practice, in colonial times and the early 19th century, of using the port to avoid paying customs. Pop. (1980) 38,272; (1990) 39,894.

FREE PORT, harbor in which the vessels of all nations may enter and load or unload without payment of import duty. Charges are made for harbor services only. Goods unloaded may be reshipped elsewhere on payment of a transit duty or may be admitted to that country for consumption upon payment of import duty. More common than the free port is the free zone maintained in many ports. New York City port has a free zone on Staten Island in New York Bay.

FREE RADICAL. *See* RADICAL.

FREER GALLERY. *See* SMITHSONIAN INSTITUTION.

FREESIA, genus of plants belonging to the family Iridaceae (*see* IRIS), named in honor of the German physician F. H. Freese (1795?–1876). Freesias are native to the Cape of Good Hope, South Africa. The fragrant tubular flowers of freesias vary in color from white to yellow, orange, lav-

Freesia, Freesia refracta

ender, and pink. Freesias grow from a corm, or thickened underground stem. They are important as commercial cut flowers and are grown for market in southern California. They are not sucessful garden plants in the northern U.S. but may be grown in greenhouses. Freesias that are raised in the U.S. are varieties of two wild species, *Freesia armstrongi* and *F. refracta,* or of their hybrids.

FREE SILVER. *See* MONEY.

FREE-SOIL PARTY, American political party organized in 1848 on a platform opposing the extension of slavery. The growing conflict between proslavery and antislavery forces in the U.S. was intensified by the acquisition of new territories from Mexico and the ensuing argument over whether or not slavery would be permitted in those territories. The defeat of the Wilmot Proviso, which was intended to prevent the extension of slavery, and the struggle over it in Congress brought the conflict to a head; the refusal of both the Whig and Democratic parties to endorse the principles of the proviso convinced opposition groups of the need for a new party. The major groups involved in the organization of the Free-Soil party at a convention in Buffalo, N.Y., in 1848 were the abolitionist Liberty party, the antislavery Whigs, and a radical faction of the New York Democrats, the Barnburners, who had broken with the state party when it came under control of the conservative Hunkers.

The Free-Soil convention nominated Martin Van Buren and Charles Francis Adams as candidates for president and vice-president, respectively, and adopted a platform opposed to the extension of slavery and calling also for a homestead law and a tariff for revenue only. The slogan of the party was "free soil, free speech, free labor, and free men." The party polled 291,263 votes in the election of 1848; it carried no states, but turned the election in New York to the Whigs, and thus played a decisive role in the election of President Zachary Taylor. The party also elected 2 U.S. senators and 14 representatives. The Compromise Measures of 1850 on the extension of slavery caused the return of the Barnburners to the Democratic party and the loss of other allies, but the Free-Soil party continued to function; in 1852, even though it polled fewer votes than four years previously, it increased its representation in Congress. The passage of the Kansas-Nebraska Act in 1854 caused the final breaking of the old party lines and resulted in the formation of the Republican party, into which the Free-Soil party was absorbed.

For further information on this topic, see the Bibliography in volume 28, section 204.

FREETOWN, capital, largest city, and principal port of Sierra Leone, on a peninsula on the S bank of the estuary of the Sierra Leone R. The city lies on sloping ground at the foot of a range of hills and faces one of the best natural harbors on the W coast of Africa. It has exports that include palm products, cacao, coffee, and ginger. Manufacturing is limited to such activities as diamond cutting and the processing of food and tobacco. Fine beaches are located near the city, and tourist facilities are being developed; an international airport is located to the N. Points of interest include the Sierra Leone National Museum, a botanical garden, and the Anglican Saint George's Cathedral (1828). Fourah Bay College (1827) was made a part of the University of Sierra Leone in 1967. Freetown was founded in 1787 by British abolitionists as a home for liberated slaves. Eliminated by disease, the community was reestablished in 1792. The peninsula was declared a British colony in 1808. Freetown became the capital of the independent state of Sierra Leone in 1961. Pop. (1985) 469,776.

FREE TRADE, interchange of commodities across political frontiers without restrictions such as tariffs, quotas, or exchange controls. This economic policy contrasts with protection, or the fostering of domestic industrial or agricultural production by means of import tariffs or other legal obstacles to the movement of goods across frontiers. *See* Tariff; Tariffs, United States.

Early Free Trade Doctrines. Foreign trade doctrines began to develop with the emergence of dynastic nation-states during the 15th century. One early form of economic policy, known as mercantilism, dominated Western Europe from about 1500 to about 1800. Supporters of this policy worked to promote national unity and to increase the strength of the state. They considered wealth a necessary condition of power, and the accumulation of gold and silver specie a necessary condition of wealth. Countries without gold or silver mines acquired specie by maintaining a surplus of exports over imports through strict governmental control of foreign trade.

A reaction against such control occurred in France in the 18th century. This led to the formulation of the first theory of free trade by a group of economic philosophers known as the physiocrats, who were followers of the economist François Quesnay. The physiocrats maintained that the free movement of goods was in accordance with the principles of natural liberty. Although their ideas had little effect in France, they influenced the British economist Adam Smith, whose free trade theories contributed to the later development of trade policy in Great Britain.

Smith decisively refuted the protectionist conclusions of mercantilist thought. He pointed out that wealth consisted not in specie itself but in the material that specie could purchase. Governmental regulation of trade actually reduced the wealth of nations, because it prevented them from purchasing the maximum amount of commodities at the lowest possible price. With free trade, each nation could increase its wealth by exporting the goods it produced most cheaply and importing goods that were produced cheaper elsewhere.

According to Smith, each country would specialize in the production and export of goods in which it had an absolute advantage. Another British economist, David Ricardo, extended the analysis early in the 19th century to encompass the more general case of comparative advantage. Ricardo noted that some nations lack an absolute advantage in the production of any commodity. Even these nations could gain from free trade if they concentrated on those commodities in which they had a relative advantage in production. This principle has remained the theoretical basis of all argument for free trade.

Ricardo assumed that all nations would share in the gains from free trade. The British philosopher and economist John Stuart Mill later demonstrated that such gains depend on the strength of reciprocal demand for imports and exports. The stronger the demand for the exports of a country relative to its demand for imports, the greater its gain from free trade. The gain would be reflected in an improvement in the international terms of trade for the country, as expressed by ratio of its export prices to its import prices.

Modern Trade Theory. The classical theory of trade developed by Smith, Ricardo, and Mill was concerned primarily with the analysis of the gains from trade. Modern trade theory, by contrast, takes the principle of comparative advantage for granted. It is mainly concerned with the analysis of the basis for trade and with accounting for differences in comparative advantage.

Classical theorists assumed that differences in comparative advantage resulted from differences in the productivity of resources, reflecting the unequal distribution of technologies and labor skills among nations. A more complete explanation was offered by several 20th-century economists, who noted that differences in the prices of final goods tend to reflect differences in the prices of productive resources and that the latter are accounted for mainly by differences in the availability of resources. Countries specialize in the production and export of goods requiring relatively large amounts of those resources that they possess in abundance, and they import goods requiring relatively large amounts of resources that are scarce within their borders.

Arguments for Protection. Despite the conclusions of classical theory, few countries have ever actually adopted a policy of free trade. The major exception was Great Britain, which, from the 1840s until the 1930s, levied no import duties of any kind. The historical prevalence of protectionist policies reflects in part the strength of industrial vested interests fearful of foreign competition, and in part the strength of various theoretical arguments for protection. Such arguments can be classified in three groups: those intended to influence the composition of production; those intended to influence the level of employment; and those intended to influence the distribution of income. Under appropriate circumstances all three groups of arguments have theoretical validity as well as limitations.

One of the oldest arguments for protection is the so-called infant-industry argument. According to this theory, when foreign competition is reduced or eliminated by import barriers, domestic industries can develop rapidly. After their development is complete, they should theoretically be able to hold their own in competition with industries of other nations, and protection should no longer be required. In practice, however, protection frequently cannot be removed, because the domestic industries never develop sufficient competitive strength. The limitation of the infant-industry argument is its inability to identify those industries that are capable of growing to genuine maturity.

The national defense argument for protection seeks to avoid dependence on foreign sources for supplies of essential materials or finished products that might be denied in time of war. The limitation of this argument is that identification of those industries indispensable for national defense is difficult.

A third instance in which protection is advocated is to counter dumping from abroad. Dumping occurs when products are made available as imports at prices lower than the prices prevailing in the exporting country. Protection may be justified in these circumstances, but only if the clear intention of foreign suppliers is to establish a permanent monopolistic position by driving domestic suppliers out of business.

During periods of unemployment, protection is often urged as a means of increasing employment. With imports reduced, demand for domestic substitutes will be stimulated, expanding production at home. Economists call this a "beggar-my-neighbor" policy: The improvement of employment at home is achieved entirely at the expense of employment elsewhere. The limitation of such a practice is that it invites retaliation from other nations suffering from similar problems of unemployment.

Protection can be used to redistribute income either within nations or between nations. For example, if a nation finds that the demand for its exports is relatively strong, it can gain income at the expense of other countries by imposing tariffs or other import barriers. Foreigners will then find it more difficult to earn the income to pay for the exports they desire. Consequently, they will be forced to reduce their prices, thus improving the terms of trade for the protectionist nation. Like the employment argument, this method invites retaliation from abroad.

Recent Developments. Although most countries officially favor freer trade and deny protectionism, the achievement of this goal is somewhat difficult, even among highly industrialized countries. Since World War II the leading trading nations have generally made a concerted effort to promote freer trade and remove protection barriers. When economies are booming and jobs seem secure, most people tend to support free trade. When recessions occur, however, many nations become more protectionist because of national interest and pressure from organized labor and other interest groups that are adversely affected by prolonged recessions.

The integration of the world's economies has proceeded so far that domestic economic policies now have distinct international effects. This has raised new arguments in favor of protection on the grounds that the economic policies of some foreign nations are unfair. Existing rules governing trade under the auspices of the General Agreement on Tariffs and Trade (q.v.) do not cover domestic policies, thus accusations of unfairness, often followed by retaliation or protective measures, have become widespread.

See also COMMERCIAL TREATIES; ECONOMICS; EUROPEAN COMMUNITY; EUROPEAN FREE TRADE ASSOCIATION; MONOPOLY.   B.J.C.; REV. BY C.M.A.

For further information on this topic, see the Bibliography in volume 28, sections 328–30.

FREE VERSE, rhymed or unrhymed poetry composed without attention to rules of meter. Free verse was first written and labeled *vers libre* (Fr., "free verse") by a group of French poets of the late 19th century, including Gustave Kahn (1859–1936) and other symbolists. Their purpose was to deliver French poetry from the restrictions of formal metrical patterns and to re-create instead the free rhythms of natural speech. Pointing to the American poet Walt Whitman as their precursor, they wrote lines of varying length and cadence, usually not rhymed. The emotional content or meaning of the work was expressed through its rhythm. Free verse has been characteristic of the work of many modern American poets, including Amy Lowell, Ezra Pound, and Carl Sandburg.

FREE WILL, power or ability of the human mind to choose a course of action or make a decision without being subject to restraints imposed by antecedent causes, by necessity, or by divine predetermination. A completely freewill act is itself a cause and not an effect; it is beyond causal sequence or the law of causality. The question of human beings' ability to determine their actions is important in philosophy, particularly in metaphysics and ethics, and in theology. Generally, the extreme doctrine in which freedom of the will is affirmed is termed libertarianism; its opposite, determinism, is the doctrine that human action is not willed freely, but is rather the result of such influences as passions, desires, physical conditions, and external circumstances beyond the control of the individual.

Philosophical Views. Freedom of the will has necessarily been a concern of metaphysicians, who attempt to formulate theories explaining the nature of ultimate, universal reality and the relationship of human beings to the universe. Some metaphysicians hold that if the universe is rational it must be based on a sequence of cause and effect: Every action, or effect, must be preceded by a cause and must form a part of the unbroken chain of causation extending back to the First Cause, that is, God, or the Divine. An act of absolute free will on the part of a person or an animal is, however, an uncaused act outside the causal chain; to accept the possibility of an uncaused act negates such divine, rational order and makes the universe seem irrational. Viewed in this manner, this question has never been satisfactorily resolved. During the Middle Ages, the inexplicability of free will led to intense argument among religious philosophers and to the famous dilemma known as "Buridan's Ass" (*see* BURIDAN, JEAN).

The validity of free will has also been a subject of considerable debate among ethical philosophers. It would appear that a system of ethics must imply free will, for the denial of the ability to choose a course of action would seem to negate the possibility of moral judgment. A person without moral judgment is not responsible for his or her actions. In an attempt to resolve this problem, ethical philosophers have taken a great variety of positions, ranging from absolute determinism to absolute libertarianism. Socrates and Plato maintained that people could will their own actions, but that those actions alone were truly free that accorded with the good or harmony of the whole. Thus, only a wise action is free. Baruch Spinoza, the Dutch philosopher, reinterpreted free will as self-determination, that is, insofar as a person fits into God's nature and the world's own nature. Immanuel Kant, the German philosopher, believed that a person must be free because freedom is a necessary postulate of the moral consciousness; the Kantian categorical imperative is beyond any theoretical analysis. The prevailing philosophical opinion has been that partial self-determination exists, and that, although many considerations other than will are involved in the formation of moral judgments, in certain circumstances a core remains, however small, of creative decision.

Theological Views. Free will is important in theology. One of the basic tenets of traditional Christian theology is that God is omniscient and omnipotent, and that every human action is foreordained by God. The doctrine of predestination, the theological counterpart of determinism, seemingly precludes the existence of free will. Because morality, duty, and the avoidance of sin are also basic elements in Christian teaching, how, it is asked, can people be morally responsible once predestination is accepted? Many attempts have been made by theologians to explain this paradox. St. Augustine, the great Father and Doctor of the Church, firmly believed in predestination, holding that only those elected by God would attain salvation; no one, however, knows who is among the elect, and therefore all should lead God-fearing, religious lives. Freedom, for him, was the gift of divine grace. This doctrine was opposed by the British monk Pelagius (c. 355–c. 425; see PELAGIANISM) and particularly by his followers, who maintained that Adam's sin concerned only Adam and not the whole human race, and that everyone, although helped by divine grace to attain salvation, has complete freedom of will to choose or reject the way to God. Eventually, Roman Catholic theologians stated the doctrine of prevenient grace to explain free will; according to this doctrine, God bestows on individuals the grace to will themselves into a state of grace.

During the Reformation, the question of free will became a religious battleground. Many Protestant sects, notably the Calvinists, emphasized the Augustinian doctrine of predestination and the complete exclusion of free will. Calvinistic predestination was considered a paramount heresy by the Roman Catholic church; and the Council of Trent in the 16th century condemned all who denied free will. Still the problem was not resolved. The French Roman Catholic prelate Jacques Bossuet offered yet another approach, which became widely held; he stated that free will and divine foreknowledge are certain truths that must be accepted even though they are not logically connected.

Current Attitudes. Psychologists have found it difficult to explain free will; their method of scientific causality predicates determinism. The rational philosophers of the 17th and 18th centuries, who were, in a sense, psychologists, attempted to state mechanistic laws that would include mental phenomena as they did physical phenomena, such as gravity; free will, being anarchistic by definition, could not be patterned into law. In the 20th century, certain psychologists—including the Americans Rollo May (1909–), Gordon Allport (1897–1967), and Abraham Maslow and especially the advocates of existentialism—have recognized the element of spontaneity in the human mind that is admitted to lie outside any possible scientific law. This spontaneity can be interpreted to be free will, or at least a measure of self-determination that people feel themselves to possess and by which they make moral judgments.

FREEZING POINT, temperature at which a liquid congeals into the solid state at a given pressure (see PRESSURE; TEMPERATURE).

The freezing point of a pure (unmixed) liquid is essentially the same as the melting point of the same substance in its solid form and may be regarded as the temperature at which the solid and liquid states of the substance are in equilibrium. If heat is applied to a mixture of liquid and solid substance at its freezing point, the temperature of the substance remains constant until it has become completely liquefied, because the heat is absorbed not in warming the substance but in providing the latent heat of fusion. Similarly, if heat is abstracted from a mixture of liquid and solid substance at its freezing point, the substance will remain at the same temperature until it has become completely solid, because heat is given off by the substance in its change from the liquid to the solid state. Hence, the freezing point or melting point of a pure substance may also be defined as the temperature at which freezing or melting continues once it has commenced.

All solids melt when heated to their melting points, but most liquids can remain liquid even though cooled below their freezing points. A liquid may remain in this supercooled state for some time. This phenomenon is explained by molecular theory, which conceives the molecules of a solid as being well ordered and the molecules of a liquid as being disordered. To solidify, a liquid must have a nucleus (a point of molecular orderliness) around which the disordered molecules can crystallize. The formation of a nucleus is a matter of chance, but once a nucleus forms, the supercooled liquid will solidify rapidly. The freezing point of a solution is lower than the freezing point of the pure solvent before introduction of the solute (substance dissolved).

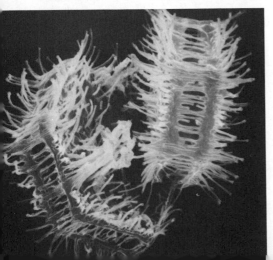

Magnified details of the growth of airborne ice crystals below the freezing point in air that contains a trace of ammonia. The application of a plastic coating allows the crystals to last long enough to be photographed.
Naval Weapons Center, California

The amount that the freezing point is lowered depends on the molecular concentration of the solute and on whether the solution is an electrolyte. Nonelectrolytic solutions have higher freezing points for a given concentration of solute than do electrolytes. The molecular weight of an unknown or unidentified substance may be determined by measuring the amount by which the freezing point of a solvent is lowered when a known amount of the unidentified substance is dissolved in it. This process of determining molecular weights is called cryoscopy.

In mixed substances and alloys, the freezing point of the mixture may be much lower than the freezing points of any of its individual components.

The freezing point of most substances is increased by increase of pressure. In substances, however, that expand on freezing (for example, water) pressure lowers the freezing point. An example of this effect can be observed if a heavy object is placed on a block of ice (q.v.). The area immediately underneath the object will begin to turn to liquid and will refreeze, without any change in temperature, when the object is removed. This process is known as regulation.

See also CRYOGENICS; CRYSTAL.

For further information on this topic, see the Bibliography in volume 28, section 399.

FREGE, Gottlob (1848–1925), German mathematician and philosopher, the founder of modern mathematical logic. Frege was born in Wismar, in Mecklenburg-West Pomerania. He studied at the universities of Jena and Göttingen, later joining the mathematics faculty at Jena. Frege sought to derive the principles of arithmetic from the principles of logic. Faced with the ambiguity of ordinary language and the inadequacy of available logical systems, he invented many symbolic notations, such as quantifiers and variables, thus providing the foundation for modern mathematical logic. His work greatly influenced the British philosopher Bertrand Russell. *Conceptual Notation* (1879; trans. 1972) is regarded as the most important of his publications, which also include *The Foundations of Arithmetic* (1884; trans. 1950) and *Grundgesetze der Arithmetik* (2 vol.; 1893–1903), portions of which have been translated as *The Basic Laws of Arithmetic: An Exposition of the System* (1965).   R.M.B.

FREIBERG, city, E central Germany, in Saxony, on the Freiberger Mulde R., near Dresden and Chemnitz. It lies on the N slopes of the Erzgebirge about 404 m (about 1325 ft) above sea level. Freiberg has long been the center of the state's important lead- and silver-mining industry. Manufactures include gold and silver articles, woolen cloth, leather, china, machinery, chemicals, scientific and optical instruments, and cigars. The Mining Academy (1765) and a radium research facility are located here.

The area was settled about 1180, after the discovery of silver deposits nearby. Freiberg contains a cathedral originally dating from the 12th century, rebuilt in Gothic style after its destruction by fire in the late 15th century, and restored in 1893. A doorway, known as the Golden Gate, remains from the original structure. Henry the Pious, duke of Saxony (1473–1541), and a number of his successors are buried in the cathedral. Pop. (1989 est.) 51,300.

FREIBURG, in full Freiburg im Breisgau, city, SW Germany, in Baden-Württemberg, at the foot of Schlossberg Mt., in the Breisgau Valley of the Dreisam R. Manufactures include machinery, scientific and musical instruments, chemicals, paper, and textiles. The city is the site of the famous Albert Ludwig University (1457). The Freiburg Münster, or cathedral, built between the 13th and 16th centuries, is one of the finest Gothic ecclesiastical structures in Germany. It is surmounted by a tower 118 m (386 ft) tall and contains paintings by the artists Hans Holbein the Younger and Hans Baldung-Grien.

Freiburg was founded and chartered as a free town in 1120. It quickly attained considerable commercial prosperity. In 1219 it came under the control of the counts of Urach. In 1366 it purchased its freedom for 20,000 silver marks. Unable, however, to repay the creditors, Freiburg came under the control of the Habsburg family. In 1644, during the Thirty Years' War, Freiburg and the surrounding area was the site of several major military engagements between the French and Austrian-Bavarian forces. For a short period in the late 17th century the city belonged to the French, and in 1806 became part of Baden. Since the 1820s it has been an archbishopric. Most of the old section of Freiburg was destroyed during World War II. Pop. (1987 est.) 186,200.

FREI MONTALVA, Eduardo (1911–82), president of Chile (1964–70), born in Santiago, and educated there. As a young man he was active in the National Falange, a student organization associated with the Conservative party. In 1938, however, he broke with the Conservatives and in the following years earned a reputation as a publicist and writer. In 1946–47 he served briefly as minister of public works.

Elected to the Chilean Senate in 1949 and 1957, Frei was the first presidential candidate of the new Christian Democratic party in 1958. Although he lost, he doubled the party's vote, and he won handily when he ran again in 1964. During his presidency, Frei introduced sweeping reforms of Chilean society, aimed at the democratic equalization of economic opportunities. Barred from succeeding himself, he was again elected to the Senate in 1973, shortly before it was dissolved by the army coup of that year. He remained head of his party until it was suspended by the military junta in 1977.

FREMANTLE, city, SW Australia, in Western Australia State, on the Indian Ocean, at the mouth of the Swan R., part of the Perth metropolitan area. Fremantle is the chief seaport of Western Australia, and its extensive harbor facilities make it an important port of call on the European and South African trade routes. The principal industrial establishments are shipyards, iron foundries, furniture factories, flour mills, sawmills, soap factories, tanneries, and breweries. The leading items of export are timber, wheat, wool, and fruit. Founded in 1829, the city is one of the oldest settlements in Australia. Pop. (1986) 22,790.

FREMONT, city, Alameda Co., W California, on San Francisco Bay, near San Jose; inc. 1956 with the consolidation of five communities. It is a major commercial and agricultural center; vegetable and flower farms, vineyards, and a noted winery are in the area. The chief manufactures include motor vehicles, toys, electronic equipment, and salt. The city has a junior college. In 1797 Mission San José de Guadalupe (partly preserved as a museum) was founded here; a group of Mormons settled on the site of the city in 1846. The city is named for the army officer and explorer John C. Frémont. Pop. (1980) 131,945; (1990) 173,339.

FREMONT, city, seat of Dodge Co., E Nebraska, on the Platte R.; inc. 1871. It is a regional agricultural processing and health-care center. Manufactures include processed poultry, soybeans, and flour and building materials. Midland Lutheran College (1883) is here. Founded by homesteaders in 1856 and named for the army officer and explorer John C. Frémont, a presidential candidate that year, it grew as a stopping place on the California and Mormon trails. It became an agricultural market center with the arrival of the railroad in 1866. Pop. (1980) 23,979; (1990) 23,680.

FREMONT, city, seat of Sandusky Co., N Ohio, on the Sandusky R.; inc. 1866. It is a commercial and manufacturing center located in a fertile agricultural region. Products include cutlery, batteries, aluminum items, tools, motor-vehicle seat covers, and beet sugar and other processed food. The home and grave of President Rutherford B. Hayes are here. Fort Stephenson was established on the site in 1812 and was the scene (1813) of a U.S. victory in the War of 1812. The settlement that grew around the fort was known as Lower Sandusky until 1849, when it was renamed for the army officer and explorer John C. Frémont. Pop. (1980) 17,834; (1990) 17,648.

FRÉMONT, John Charles (1813–90), American explorer, army officer, and politician, noted for his explorations of the Far West.

John Charles Frémont

Frémont was born on Jan. 31, 1813, in Savannah, Ga., and was educated at the College of Charleston, S.C. In 1838 he was commissioned second lieutenant in the Corps of Engineers, U.S. Army. During the following year Frémont was a member of the expedition of the French explorer Joseph Nicolas Nicollet (1786–1843) that surveyed and mapped the region between the upper Mississippi and Missouri rivers. Between 1842 and 1845 Frémont led three expeditions into Oregon Territory. During the first, in 1842, he mapped most of the Oregon Trail (q.v.) and ascended, in present-day Wyoming, the second highest peak in the Wind River Mountains, afterward called Fremont Peak (4185 m/13,730 ft). In 1843 he completed the survey of the Oregon Trail to the mouth of the Columbia River on the Pacific coast. The party, guided by the famous scout Kit Carson, turned south and then east, making a midwinter crossing of the Sierra Nevada Mountains. Frémont made his third expedition in 1845, further exploring both the area known as the Great Basin (q.v.) and the Pacific coast.

During the Mexican War (1846–48), Frémont attained the rank of major and assisted greatly in the annexation of California. He was appointed civil governor of California by the U.S. Navy commodore Robert Field Stockton (1795–1866), but in a conflict of authority between Stockton and the U.S. Army brigadier general Stephen Watts Kearny, Frémont refused to obey Kearny's orders. He was arrested for mutiny and insubordination and was subsequently court-martialed. He resigned his commission after President James Polk remitted his sentence of dismissal from the service. In the winter of 1848 and 1849 Frémont led an expedition to locate passes for a proposed railway line from the upper Rio Grande to California. In 1850 he was elected one of the first two senators from California, serving until 1851. In 1856 he was the presidential candidate of the newly formed Republican party, but was defeated by James Buchanan. During the American Civil War Frémont was appointed a major general in the Union Army and held several important but brief commands; he resigned his commission in 1862 rather than serve under Gen. John Pope (1822–92). In 1864 Frémont was again a presidential nominee; he withdrew, however, in favor of President Abraham Lincoln. He served as governor of the territory of Arizona from 1878 to 1883. In 1890 he was restored to the rank of major general and retired with full pay. He died in New York City on July 13, 1890.

Frémont wrote *Report of the Exploring Expedition to the Rocky Mountains in the Year 1842, and to Oregon and North California in the Years 1843–44* (1845) and *Memories of My Life* (1887).

FRENCH, Daniel Chester (1850–1931), one of the best-known American sculptors of his time. Born in Exeter, N.H., he studied sculpture in New York City and Florence, Italy. His bronze statues of American historical and allegorical figures are characterized by grace, poetic feeling, dignified emotion, and masterful technique. He established his reputation with his first major work, the *Minute Man* (1875, Concord, Mass.), commemorating the American Revolution. Other works include the famous seated *Lincoln* (1919, Lincoln Memorial, Washington, D.C.), the equestrian statues *General Grant* (1899, Philadelphia) and *General Washington* (1900, Paris), the *Four Continents* (1907, Customs House, New York City), and portrait busts.

FRENCH, John Denton Pinkstone, 1st Earl of Ypres (1852–1925), British supreme commander during the opening phase of World War I. He served as commander of a cavalry division in the Boer War in South Africa, distinguishing himself by relieving Kimberley and occupying Bloemfontein. In 1912 he was made chief of the imperial general staff, but he resigned in 1914 because he was unwilling to use force against opponents of home rule in northern Ireland. After the outbreak of World War I he was made supreme commander of the British armies on the western front; at the First Battle of Ypres he prevented the Germans from breaking through to Calais. In December 1915 he resigned under criticism over the cost in soldiers and matériel. After his return to England, French was made a viscount and was commander in chief in the United Kingdom until 1918, when he was appointed lord lieutenant of Ireland. On his resignation in 1921 he was made an earl.

FRENCH ACADEMY, usual designation (in English) of the Académie Française, the oldest of the five learned societies that make up the Institut de France (q.v.).

FRENCH BROAD, river, W North Carolina and E Tennessee, rising near the foot of the Blue Ridge Mts. It flows N past Asheville and then NW into Tennessee, where it joins the Holston R. near Knoxville to form the Tennessee R. Its total length is about 400 km (about 250 mi).

FRENCH BULLDOG, breed of dog developed in France, probably from a small type of English bulldog (*see* BULLDOG) that was then crossed with other breeds. The French bulldog is small, standing only about 30 cm (about 12 in) at the shoulder, but it is relatively heavy, weighing up to about 13 kg (about 28 lb). It has high, batlike ears and a naturally short tail. The skull is flat between the ears and curves directly above the eyes. The smooth coat is usually brindle, brindle and white, fawn, or white in color. The heavy-jawed face is blunt and wrinkled, creating a comical more than a pugnacious appearance. The breed was recognized by the American Kennel Club in 1947.

FRENCH CAMEROONS. *See* CAMEROON, UNITED REPUBLIC OF.

FRENCH COMMUNITY. *See* COMMUNITY, THE.

FRENCH EAST INDIA COMPANY. *See* EAST INDIA COMPANY.

FRENCH EQUATORIAL AFRICA, former French possession in Africa, encompassing what are now the Central African Republic (q.v.), Chad, Congo (*see* CHAD, REPUBLIC OF; CONGO, PEOPLE'S REPUBLIC OF THE), and Gabon (q.v.). The administrative capital and chief city was Brazzaville.

FRENCH GUIANA, overseas department of France, situated on the NE coast of South America. It is bounded on the N by the Atlantic Ocean, on the E and S by Brazil, and on the W by Suriname. Among other offshore islands it includes the Îles du Salut, or Safety Islands, of which Devil's Island (q.v.) is the best known. French Guiana is the oldest of the overseas possessions of France and the only French territory

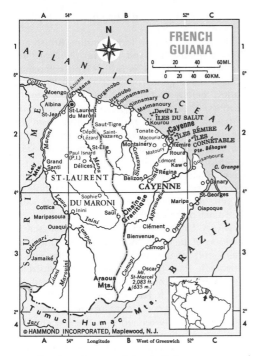

on the American mainland. It has an area of 91,000 sq km (35,135 sq mi). The capital, chief town, and main port is Cayenne (q.v.), which had a population (1982) of 38,135.

Land and Population. French Guiana lies in the equatorial forest zone of South America. It is separated from Brazil by the Tumuc-Humac mountain range on the S and by the Oyapock R. on the E. The Maroni, Litani (Itany), and Lawa rivers mark its boundary with Suriname on the W. The land rises from the low marshy coastal areas in the N, called the *terres basses,* through the broad central plateau, covered by dense tropical forest, to the *terres hautes,* or highlands, which ascend from foothills to the Eureupoucigne and Oroye ranges in the extreme S. The territory is well watered by numerous rivers that rise in the mountains and course northward to the Atlantic. The climate of French Guiana is tropical, with a mean annual temperature of 26.7° C (80° F). Cool, onshore breezes in the coastal zone fail to mitigate the effects of the high humidity. The dry season from June to November is succeeded by torrential rains achieving maximum intensity in April and May. The average annual rainfall at Cayenne is about 3200 mm (about 126 in).

French Guiana had a 1982 census population of 73,022; the estimated population in 1989 was 94,700, giving an average density of 1 person per sq km (2.7 persons per sq mi). Most of the residents are Creoles, people of mixed white, Indian, and black African descent. Indians, descended from the aboriginal Arawak, Carib (qq.v.) and Tupí-Guaraní groups, inhabit the remote interior of French Guiana. Virtually untouched by Western civilization, they have preserved their traditional customs. Along the waterways are the settlements of the Saramancas, Boeschs, and Bonis, whose forebears were fugitive black slaves.

Economy and Government. The extensive forests of French Guiana, covering more than four-fifths of the entire land surface, are rich in timber of commercial importance. Less than 1% of the land is devoted to agriculture. The principal food crops are corn, rice, cassava, pineapples, yams, and bananas. Sugarcane is the only significant cash crop. Fishing is of growing importance; the catch is largely shrimp, which is exported. Placer mining for gold is undertaken, and commercial reserves of bauxite, clay, and cinnabar also exist. Industrial establishments are small and include sawmills, rum distilleries, potteries, and brick and dye works. A satellite launching base (est. 1968) is located at Kourou. The chief imports are foodstuffs, refined petroleum, cement, metals, and machinery. Articles of export include commercial woods, rosewood essence, gold, shrimp, rice, bananas, cacao, rum, and mounted butterflies. The unit of currency is the French franc (5.728 francs equal U.S.$1; 1990).

French Guiana is administered by a prefect, who is assisted by a 19-member general council and a 31-member regional council, each elected by universal adult suffrage. The department is represented in both houses of the French National Assembly.

History. The first French settlement on the Guiana coast was established early in the 17th century. Captured by the Portuguese and the British in 1809, the colony was restored to France between 1814 and 1817. In 1852 it was made the site of a penal colony. Because of the unsavory reputation French Guiana thus acquired, attempts at colonization were generally unsuccessful. In 1938 penal servitude in French Guiana was abolished. After the fall of France in World War II (June 1940), the local administration of the territory, despite strong popular sentiment in favor of the Free French movement under Gen. Charles de Gaulle, proclaimed its allegiance to the pro-German Vichy regime of Marshal Henri Pétain. On March 18, 1943, however, the Vichy-oriented authorities in French Guiana were expelled by a pro-Allied committee that had the support of the French military forces and the majority of the population of the colony. Vichy decrees aimed at the suppression of democratic rights were revoked, political prisoners were liberated, and minor pro-Vichy officials were removed from the administration. The Allied blockade of French Guiana was lifted, and trade was resumed with the U.S., Brazil, and the British and Dutch possessions in America. The area became an overseas department of France on March 19, 1946.

FRENCH HORN. See HORN.

FRENCH INDIA, former overseas territory of France, comprising four enclaves on the Indian subcontinent known officially as Établissements Français de l'Inde (French Establishments in India). In descending order of size the enclaves, called *villes libres* ("free cities"), were Pondicherry, Karikal, and Yanaon, all on the southeast coast, and Mahé on the southwest coast. Pondicherry Commune was the territorial capital. The territory was ceded to India in 1956.

FRENCH AND INDIAN WAR (1754–63), contest between France and Great Britain with their respective Indian and colonial allies for the domination of North America. Britain's eventual victory stripped France of its North American empire and thus concluded the four Anglo-French conflicts that had been fought since 1689 (see KING GEORGE'S WAR; KING WILLIAM'S WAR; QUEEN ANNE'S WAR). Before the war ended, it expanded into Europe, where it was known as the Seven Years' War (1756–63), and into Asia, where it was called the Third Carnatic War (1756–63); its American name reflects the prominence of France's Indian allies in the minds of the British colonists, although

the powerful Iroquoian Confederacy was allied with the British forces.

The war arose from long-standing British and French rivalry for land and fur. Tensions increased in the 1750s as British land companies secured large grants of wilderness in the Ohio Valley, thereby threatening French claims to the territory. The French sought to protect their control with a string of forts extending from the mouth of the Saint Lawrence River westward to the Great Lakes region and southward to Saint Louis and New Orleans. In the process, the French encroached on land claimed by Virginia since 1609. In 1753 Gov. Robert Dinwiddie of Virginia dispatched George Washington to warn the French of their alleged invasion of English territory. In 1754 Dinwiddie ordered Washington to the forks of the Ohio, the confluence of the Allegheny and Monongahela rivers (later the site of Pittsburgh, Pa.), to protect workmen constructing a fort. The French had already captured the fort and named it Fort Duquesne. Washington then built Fort Necessity, at Great Meadows near Pittsburgh, but surrendered to the French. The French and Indian War had begun.

The Opening Campaigns. In 1755 the British general Edward Braddock arrived in America to retake Fort Duquesne. In July, however, near the fort, a small band of French and Indians ambushed and badly defeated Braddock's British regulars and colonial troops. In September the British repulsed a French and Indian attack at the Battle of Lake George but were unable to take Crown Point on Lake Champlain in New York. The English faltered in 1757 in their plans to assault the French fortress at Louisbourg, which guarded the entrance to the St. Lawrence River, and also lost Fort Oswego on Lake Ontario and Fort George and Fort William Henry, both on the Lake Champlain waterway.

The British Victory. England's dismal performance ended when William Pitt the Elder rose to political power in 1757. Pitt initiated a series of well-coordinated campaigns designed to win control of France's American strongholds and appointed able commanders to lead them. In 1758 British forces were repulsed at Fort Ticonderoga, but succeeded in taking Louisbourg, Fort Duquesne (which they renamed Fort Pitt), and Fort Frontenac on Lake Ontario.

The following year British strategy focused on cutting off the Great Lakes and the West from the St. Lawrence; taking Fort Ticonderoga and Crown Point while advancing up the Lake Champlain waterway to the St. Lawrence Valley; and launching an amphibious assault on Québec, capital of France's North American empire. This

Indian allies of the French participating in the defeat of Gen. Edward Braddock at Fort Duquesne in July 1755 (from Ballou's Pictorial Drawing-Room Companion, *1855).*

strategy succeeded, climaxing in Gen. James Wolfe's victory at Québec in September 1759. The following year British forces converged up river from Québec at Montréal, where they compelled the governor of Canada to surrender the entire province.

The Treaty of Paris (1763) awarded all French territory east of the Mississippi to the British; the area west of the Mississippi was given to France's ally, Spain, which in turn ceded Florida to Britain. The war concluded three-quarters of a century of conflict and determined that English rather than French institutions and ideas would dominate North America. Hence, in terms of importance, the French and Indian War rivals the American Revolution and the American Civil War.

Results of the War. Despite the common culture uniting all those of English descent, the war's end precipitated divisions between Britain and its 13 North American colonies. The elimination of a French threat to the West reduced colonial dependence on British military aid. Moreover, in order to pay part of the enormous war debts, Parliament began to tax the colonies for the first time (1765). In the eyes of the colonials, however, taxation and concomitant regulations not only violated traditional self-government but also denied their rights as English people. In sum, the defeat and removal of French rule encouraged the colonials to think about their problems, institutions, and interests in terms of an American nationality instead of an English one.   R.S.

For further information on this topic, see the Bibliography in volume 28, section 1148.

FRENCH LANGUAGE, language of the people of France. It is also spoken in parts of Belgium and Switzerland, and in present and former French colonies, including French Guiana, northwestern Africa, Indochina, Haiti, Madagascar, and parts of Canada. (For Breton, a Celtic language also spoken in parts of France, *see* CELTIC LANGUAGES). French belongs to the Romance language group of the Italic subfamily of the Indo-European languages (q.v.).

Origins. The ancient Gauls, or Celts, the earliest inhabitants of Gaul, or present-day France, spoke a primitive Celtic language from which Irish, Welsh, Breton, and other modern Celtic languages were derived. Celtic gave way, after the conquest of Gaul in the 1st century BC by the Roman general and statesman Gaius Julius Caesar, to the form of Latin used by the uneducated classes in Rome and known as the *lingua vulgaris* in contrast to the *sermo urbanus* used by writers and orators. By the end of the 4th century AD Latin had entirely replaced Celtic in Gaul. The Celtic tongue spoken in the modern French region of Bittany is not a survival of the pre-Roman native culture; it is believed to have been brought there by Celtic inhabitants of the British Isles who took refuge in Brittany from the invasions of Britain by the Angles, Jutes, and Saxons in the 5th to the 7th century AD. Several words of purely Celtic origin, about 50 in all, have passed into modern French, including Celtic-Latin, *alauda,* modern French, *alouette* ("lark"); and Celtic, *carruca,* Celtic-Latin, *carrus,* modern French, *char* ("car").

The *lingua vulgaris* was so firmly established in Gaul that the succeeding conquerors of the country, the German tribes, Visigoths, Burgundians, and Franks, did not impose their language upon the conquered territory; instead they adopted the language that they found there. In modern French only about 400 words are of Germanic origin, for example, *franc* ("free") and *français* ("French"), both from the Germanic word *Franko* ("freeman"); *fauteuil* ("armchair") from the Germanic *faldastol;* and *auberge* ("inn"), from the Germanic *heriberga.* Greek words were also introduced into the *lingua vulgaris* at various times, beginning in the 6th century, through Greek colonies along the Mediterranean Sea, notably those at Marseille and Nice. By the 7th century the *lingua vulgaris* had been greatly modified by the people of France; the language spoken by them at that time was known as the Roman, or Romanic, language and was spoken by the upper classes as well as common people. As early as the 6th century, the homilies of the church councils that took place in France were translated into Romanic, and in the 8th century the Frankish leader Charlemagne by royal edict ordered church dignitaries to deliver their sermons in the popular tongue.

Evolution. In early medieval times the spoken languages north and south of the Loire River began to develop separately. By the end of the 13th century they had become two distinct languages, the *langue d'oïl* of the north and the *langue d'oc* of the south; the terms were derived from *oïl* and *oc,* the words for "yes" in each of the languages. The chief phonetic difference in the two languages was their treatment of the free unaccented vowel *a* of Latin. The vowel became *e* in the *langue d'oïl* but remained unchanged in Provençal, the principal dialect of the *langue d'oc;* thus, the Latin word *mare* ("sea") became *mer* in the *langue d'oïl* and *mar* in Provençal. In each language several dialects developed. In addition

to Provençal, the principal dialects of the *langue d'oc* were the Gascon, Languedocien, Auvergnat, Limousin, and Béarnais. A great deal of poetry and other literary work was written in the *langue d'oc;* for a time, particularly in the 12th century, it seemed that it would establish supremacy over the *langue d'oïl,* but after the 12th century the *langue d'oc* rapidly became less important. In the 19th century efforts were made by a literary school known as *félibrige,* the chief members of which were the poets Frédéric Mistral and Joseph Roumanille (1818–91), to revive the use of modern Provençal and other dialects of the *langue d'oc* that are still spoken; they were not successful, however, and the language today is seldom used as a literary dialect. The *langue d'oc* has contributed about 500 words to modern French, including *bague* ("ring"), *cadeau* ("gift"), and *velours* ("velvet") (*see also* PROVENÇAL LANGUAGE). The principal dialects of the *langue d'oïl* were named for the five northern provinces in which they were spoken: Île de France, Normandy, Picardy, Poitou, and Burgundy. After the accession of Hugh Capet as king of France in 987, Paris became the seat of government, and the language spoken there began to dominate other French dialects, as the court at Paris became politically important to the provincial nobility. Modern French has developed directly from the dialect of the Île de France, which gradually superseded other French dialects during the late Middle Ages.

In the 12th and 13th centuries the *langue d'oïl* was popular throughout Europe. It was the court language of Naples; German princes and barons maintained French-born tutors who taught it to their children, and in England for the two centuries following the Norman Conquest in 1066, French strongly rivaled English as the spoken language of the land and almost supplanted it as the literary language. *See* NORMAN FRENCH LANGUAGE AND LITERATURE. In the Middle Ages a considerable number of Arabic words were added to the language, because of the prestige among French scholars of Arabic science and because the French brought the words back from Arabic lands that they had invaded during the Crusades. Among the words of Arabic derivation in French are *chiffre* ("number"), *cimetière* ("cemetery"), *girafe* ("giraffe"), *épinard* ("spinach"), and *jupe* ("skirt").

The 14th and 15th centuries, the period of the Hundred Years' War between France and England, which devastated French territory, gave popular impetus to French nationalism and to acceptance of the court dialect as a national linguistic standard. The 16th century brought a great advance in linguistic development. In accordance with the Ordinance of Villers-Cotterêts (1539) of Francis I, king of France, French as spoken in Île de France, especially in Paris, became the official language throughout the kingdom. In the second half of the 16th century, especially during the reign (1574–89) of Henry III, a group of French poets known as the Pléiade, which included Joachim du Bellay and Pierre de Ronsard, declared that French was the proper language for prose and poetry. The group conceded that the language required improvement, which they urged be brought about by modeling French writings on masterpieces of Greek and Latin literature. The principles of the Pléiade were embodied by du Bellay in *La défense et illustration de la langue française* (The Defense and Glorification of the French Language, 1549).

An International Language. In the early 17th century the poet François de Malherbe, through his poetic and critical works, succeeded in establishing a standard of exactness in the use of French words. That standard shaped the language into a sophisicated instrument for the clear, concise expression of thought. One of the most important steps toward standardizing and otherwise improving the French language was the compilation, in the 17th century, of a dictionary by the French Academy, a literary society formed in 1635 by the statesman and cardinal Richelieu. The Academy began the compilation of an official French dictionary in 1639; the first edition appeared in 1694 and was followed by seven others; the eighth appeared in 1932–35. During the reign of Louis XIV, the French language reached the highest point of importance in its history, becoming an international language in Europe, especially for diplomats and scientists.

By the 17th century the French language had developed into what is essentially its present form. Inflectional endings inherited from Latin had been for the most part dropped, and the language depended instead on prepositional phrases and word order to indicate syntactical relationships between words. Publication of the dictionary, widespread literacy, and the extensive use of printing all contributed to the stabilization of the language. Changes occurring later in French were virtually limited to the slow modification of pronunciation and to the addition of new words. The wars with Italy in the first half of the 16th century had resulted in the introduction of about 800 words, for the most part of two types: those derived from the arts, such as *fugue* and *opéra;* and military terms, such as *colonel* and *soldat.* French wars with Spain in the early part of the 17th century enriched the French language with about 200 words, including *cigare* and *nègre.* French wars with Germany in the 17th century resulted in the introduction of a small number of words from German, such as *blocus* ("blockage") and *cible* ("target"). A section of the newly founded (1795) Institut de France, successor of the old French Academy, issued an edition of the dictionary in 1798; the appendix of the work included a number of words that had been coined since the outbreak of the French Revolution. Among those that survive in the French language are *divorcer* ("to divorce"), *guillotiner* ("to behead with a guillotine"), and *bureaucrate* ("bureaucrat").

Modern Influences. In the early part of the 19th century, the exponents of French literary romanticism inaugurated a movement to restore many archaic words to the language. That and a similar movement led by the symbolist poets later in the century had little permanent effect on the language, however. On the contrary, the whole tendency since the late 18th century has been to enrich the language with words dealing with new objects and concepts. Most additions to French since the late 19th century have come from one of two sources, the English language and technological or scientific terms. Among French words that have been taken from English and are spelled the same in both languages are *sandwich, square, ticket, toast,* and *weekend;* others given new spellings are *boxe* ("boxing"), *bouledogue* ("bulldog"), and *rosbif* ("roast beef"). Terms taken from technology include *automobile, jet, photographie,* and *télégraphe.*

In the 16th and 17th centuries French replaced Latin as a common language for international, especially diplomatic, communication in Europe, and it continues to be used for that purpose. It is one of the working languages of the Secretariat of the UN.

For further information on this topic, see the Bibliography in volume 28, section 844.

FRENCH LITERATURE, literature written in the language of France from about the end of the 11th century to the present day. Before the 9th century, Latin was the literary language of France.

PRECLASSICAL LITERATURE

In the 11th century the first notable works written in French, the *chansons de geste,* appeared. These works narrated heroic exploits and are early forms of poetry.

The Medieval Period. The *chansons de geste* were long poems relating the deeds of Christian knights and were composed possibly by wandering minstrels, known as jongleurs, to entertain pilgrims or the feudal courts. The authors of the chansons drew their inspiration from three main sources; accordingly their poems are classified as belonging to one of three groups: the French, Breton, or Classical cycles.

The *Cycle de France* is primarily concerned with the French heroes who put their arms at the service of religion. The central figure is Charlemagne, who is made the champion of Christianity. The most famous epic of this group, composed at the beginning of the 12th century, is the *Chanson de Roland.*

The *Cycle de Bretagne* (Brittany) is based largely on Celtic folklore. Its principal poet was Chrétien de Troyes, who lived during the latter part of the 12th century.

The *Cycle antique* is the least original and therefore the least important group. Turning to classical antiquity for their material, the authors Christianized Agamemnon, Achilles, Ulysses, and the heroes of Thebes, Troy, and Rome. The best-known work of the *Cycle antique* is the *Roman d'Alexandre.*

Concurrently a more popular literature of short stories in verse existed. At first these stories were concerned only with religious subjects, indicating the Roman Catholic church's domination of literature. Later the church monopoly of

culture was broken when lay authors began to write secular works. The fabliau flourished during the 12th and 13th centuries, and in this period appeared the satires *Le roman de Renart* and *Le roman de la rose.*

Le roman de Renart is an animal allegory of about 32,000 verses (later increased to 100,000), in which certain classes of medieval society, including the clergy and nobility, are cautiously criticized. The way for this type of literature had been prepared by collections of ancient animal fables, particularly by a verse translation of selected fables by Marie de France during the 12th century.

Allegory is carried still further in the 13th-century *Roman de la rose,* a work of more than 21,000 lines in which the rose symbolizes love and abstract ideas are personified. The first 4058 lines were composed by Guillaume de Lorris, and Jean de Meun (or Meung; c. 1240–1305) later added the remainder of the poem. The influence of this poem persisted throughout Europe well into the 17th century.

Encouraged by the academies that organized contests and awarded prizes, lyric poetry became increasingly popular, especially in the south of France. Unquestionably the greatest lyric poet of

The stories of Reynard the fox, from the 12th-century satirical poem Le roman de Renart, *became the basis for several other European literary works in the centuries that followed.*

A miniature depicts Narcissus at the fountain, a scene from the medieval allegory Le roman de la rose *(14th-cent. manuscript).*   In the Library of Ambroise Firmin-Didot, Paris

medieval France was François Villon. His two major works, *Le petit testament* (1456) and *Le grand testament* (1461), were composed in the form of burlesque wills. *Le grand testament* was interspersed with ballads. Those works, which together contain fewer than 2500 lines, introduced a vigorous self-expression into French poetry. They are self-revelations of a man with a lusty appetite for life, yet sharing the medieval sense of sin and preoccupation with death. Because of their expressiveness and individuality, Villon's poems have exerted a continuous influence over lyric poetry even into the 20th century.

The evolution of French medieval literature from religious to secular forms emerges most clearly in the theater. The *drames liturgiques* of the 11th century were composed, in Latin prose, of sentences from the Bible. As a rule, they concerned the nativity and passion of Christ. With the appearance of lay actors during the 12th century, the French language was adopted in the *drame profane* or *drame sécularisé,* which still employed biblical episodes. The scope was extended in the 13th century to include miracle plays about the saints and the Virgin Mary. This period also contains the first pastoral play and comic opera, *Le jeu de Robin et de Marion* (The Play of Robin and Marion). The miracle of the Virgin Mary remained the favorite subject during the 14th century, and scenes from the chansons were further adapted for use in religious plays. In the succeeding century, popular interest in the theater increased, and theater production was freed from ecclesiastical influence.

Except for its historical interest, prose is of lit-

tle importance in French literature before the 16th century. The long *Romans d'aventure* (Romances of Adventure) consisted merely of prose versions of the chansons.

Only a few historians need be mentioned, among them Geoffroi de Villehardouin (c. 1150–1213) and Jean de Joinville, chroniclers of the Crusades; Christine de Pisan, author of graceful verse chronicles of the court; and Alain Chartier, verse chronicler of the disastrous Battle of Agincourt. All were overshadowed by Jean Froissart, whose *Chroniques* vividly pictured the age of chivalry. The *Mémoires* (1524) of Philippe de Comines, whose ideas are similar to those of his Italian contemporary, Niccolò Machiavelli, provide the first connected French account of political events from the point of view of a statesman.

The Renaissance. In the 16th century French literature came under the sweeping influence of the Italian Renaissance. Petrarchan verse forms and classical concepts, particularly those of Platonic philosophy, were enthusiastically accepted. They were espoused at the court of Margaret, queen of Navarre, which became the center of French culture of that period. Chief among the early French Renaissance poets was the 16th-century writer Maurice Scève (c. 1510–64), whose work reflects the intellectuality of the Renaissance. Instead of the intimate emotional expressiveness of Villon and of the later Pléiade poets, Scève's verse is characterized by a formalized expression of perception and knowledge. In this regard and in his obscure allusiveness he has a certain kinship with a major mode of 20th-century poetry.

In the poets of the next generation the Renaissance came to its full flowering. Seven poets, forming a group known as the Pléiade, under the leadership of Pierre de Ronsard, brought about a new literary era. Ronsard's widely imitated odes and sonnets, in *Amours de Cassandre* (Loves of Cassandra, 1552), and his unfinished epic, *La Franciade* (1572), made him the most famous poet of the century. Ronsard used the ancients as models, in accord with the poetic theories of Joachim du Bellay, second in importance among the Pléiade poets. In the perfection of his poetic forms, Ronsard helped prepare the advent of classicism.

The new ideas of the Renaissance and especially the new concept of humanism made their first strong appearance in the writings of François Rabelais. Of his five books, the most celebrated are *Pantagruel* (1532) and *Gargantua* (1534), epic comic stories of giants. Rabelais used the latter to personify the freedom and potentialities of humanism, which called for the full development

The feeding of Gargantua, the giant hero of Les grandes et inestimables cronicques du grand et énorme géant Gargantua by François Rabelais, a 19th-century engraving by Gustave Doré.

of the body and mind. He urged a broad morality, called Pantagruelism, dedicated to satisfying all the demands of human nature, as a rational acceptance of reality. Rabelais projects a realism, germs of which are to be found in the medieval allegory Le roman de la rose, which was to reappear in the comedies of the 17th-century playwright Molière. One of the most powerful prose writers of France, Rabelais is remarkable for his vitality and inventiveness and for his boundless faith in the capacities of the human spirit.

Michel de Montaigne represents the supreme type of French humanist and scholar. He de-

scribed his Essais (1571–88) as a self-portrait, an expression of his personal philosophy on all subjects that engaged his attention. He recommended a mild but universal skepticism as the philosophic means for escaping frustration and disillusion and achieving contentment in life. His pedagogical system stresses an open-minded spirit of inquiry rather than an accumulation of facts. In politics and religion Montaigne was a conservative, seeking social as well as individual serenity. The Essais offer the first model of the honnête homme, that is, the cultivated gentleman of the 17th century.

THE CLASSICAL PERIOD AND THE ENLIGHTENMENT

The 17th century, known as *Le Grand Siècle,* is the classical period of French literature. It was marked by the long reign of Louis XIV, during which France reached the apex of its power and influence in European politics and culture. This period was followed by the Age of Enlightenment in the 18th century, during which French power declined and the intellectual energies of the nation turned toward change and reform.

The Classical Period. A leading figure of the classical period was François de Malherbe, who, although a mediocre poet himself, fixed the literary criteria of the century: pure reason, common sense, and perfection of manner. Two influences contributed to the acceptance of these standards, the salon of the marquise de Rambouillet (1588–1665) and the French Academy.

The marquise de Rambouillet is regarded as the founder of preciosity, a reform in language, manners, and wit. For all its affectation and exaggeration, later satirized by Molière in his *Les précieuses ridicules* (The Affected Young Ladies, 1659), it promoted refinements in language, feelings, and social relations. The marquise de Rambouillet brought together in her salon the majority of contemporary literary figures. The question of content and form was the subject of the most notable literary controversy of the period. It was evoked by a critical discussion of two sonnets, "Job," by Isaac de Benserade (1612–91), and "Uranie," by Vincent Voiture (1598–1648). Other women influenced literary trends in that period, notably the marquise de Maintenon.

Originally a private society of scholars, the French Academy was transformed in 1635 into a state corporation at the insistence of the statesman Cardinal Richelieu. It was proposed that the academicians prepare a dictionary, a grammar, and a work on rhetoric. Of these, the dictionary alone was completed and published. Much of the work on this lexicon was done by Claude Favre Vaugelas (1585–1650), whose *Remarques sur la langue française* (Remarks on the French Language, 1647) did much to establish standards of usage. Among the other original members of the Academy were Valentin Conrart (1603–75), its first secretary, and the poets Jean Chapelain, François Maynard (1582–1646), the marquis de Racan (1589–1670), and Vincent Voiture. Antoine Furetière (1619–88), who became a member in 1662, was expelled in 1685 for having compiled a dictionary (not published until 1690) upon what is now recognized to have been a more logical plan than that adopted by the Academy.

Nicolas Boileau-Despréaux was the principal literary theorist and critic of the classical age; his influence spread throughout Europe, affecting the work of such English masters as John Dryden and Alexander Pope. Believing in reason and natural law and fond of exact definitions, he sought to establish rules by which literature could be made a discipline as precise as science. His chief works, written in verse, are *Satires* (begun in 1660), *Épîtres* (Epistles, begun 1669), and *L'art poétique* (1674; *The Art of Poetry,* 1683).

A powerful literary influence was exerted also by Jacques Bénigne Bossuet, the most celebrated preacher of the age of Louis XIV. He was tutor to the dauphin and held a succession of high church offices, becoming the principal spokesman for the church in France. His sermons and his funeral orations (*Oraisons funèbres,* 1689) are models of classical rhetoric.

Pierre Corneille was the first of the French masters of classical tragedy. His initial and greatest success was *Le Cid* (1636 or 1637). Corneille sought to realize the Aristotelian unities of place, time, and action, but the dramatic tension in his tragedies is psychological, deriving from the aspirations and frustrations of his characters in their efforts to achieve greatness by supreme exercise of the will. Jean Baptiste Racine, who followed Corneille, is even more highly regarded. Less rhetorical and less formal, his work gained in naturalness; his later dramas were enlivened by lyrical passages, by the use of choruses and spectacular settings, and by the turn from classical subjects, for example, *Bérénice* (1670) and *Phèdre* (1677), to biblical subjects in *Esther* (1689) and *Athalie* (1691). In all his dramas women are the chief protagonists, and the dramatic tensions derive chiefly from the vicissitudes of love.

Molière, third of the famous 17th-century playwrights, is the French master of comedy. His fine sense of theater, which makes his work playable even to modern audiences, may be attributed, at least in part, to his having been an actor and a director. Among his best-known comedies are *Les précieuses ridicules, Tartuffe* (1664), *Le misanthrope* (1666), and *Le bourgeois gentilhomme* (The Would-Be Gentleman, 1670). Molière satirized contemporary foibles, such as the affectations of the literary salons, and common human failings such as hypocrisy, gullibility, avarice, and hypochondria. Philosophically, he was akin to Rabelais and Montaigne in maintaining the right of individuals to develop according to their own inclinations.

Notable contributions were made in this period by the Jansenists, a puritanical Catholic sect opposed to the Jesuits. Some of the most forceful and original French writers and thinkers of the

Members of a 17th-century literary salon listen to a reading of a new work.

age were Jansenists, among them the theological polemicists Antoine Arnauld and Pierre Nicole (1625–95) and above all the philosopher, physicist, mathematician, and mystic Blaise Pascal. In the *Pensées* (1670), Pascal sought to confute skepticism by the use of skepticism and concluded that certain spiritual realities were beyond the range of human reason.

Among other notable writers of the period were the two moralists François de la Rochefoucauld and Jean de La Bruyère. La Rochefoucauld is regarded as one of the most brilliant epigrammatists of all time. In his *Réflexions ou sentences et maximes morales* (Reflections or Moral Thoughts and Maxims, 1665), he combines psychological insight with a concision that gives each of his epigrams a gemlike finish and compactness. His social standing as an aristocrat lent authority to his judgment of court life. Because the essence of his maxims is the vanity of human pretension and striving, he was enlisted as an ally by the Jansenists.

The moral judgment that La Bruyère made upon his time was harsher and more comprehensive than La Rochefoucauld's. His major work, *Les "caractères" de Théophraste, traduits du grec, avec les caractères ou les moeurs de ce siècle* (The "Characters" of Theophrastus, Translated from the Greek, with Characters or Customs of This Century, 1688), is a collection of epigrams interspersed with character studies portraying and satirizing personalities who embodied the vices and frailties of the time.

The best novelist of the period was Comtesse Marie Madeleine de La Fayette. Because of its psychological insight, her *La princesse de Clèves* (1678) is valued as an early example of the modern novel. Written with charming art, it is distinguished for its economy, having only two characters, the lovers whose relationship takes up the entire action.

Jean de La Fontaine, who must be ranked with Racine as a poet and with the great moralists, is one of the masters of the age. In his *Fables* (1668–94) he used the framework of the moral fable of Aesop. He brought to each fable, however, the ease and narrative interest of the short story. The use of animals as characters in an age of censorship enabled him to give free reign to his wit, fancy, humor, and observation on human weaknesses.

The Age of Enlightenment. The 18th century Age of Enlightenment was so named because much of the intellectual effort expended at the time went into dissipating superstition and the obscurantism of church and other institutional doctrines. Among its precursors were François de Salignac de la Mothe Fénelon, Bernard le Bovier de Fontenelle, and Pierre Bayle. In his *Histoire des oracles* (History of the Oracles, 1686) Fontenelle attacked the miraculous basis of Christianity and the church under the pretext of exposing the credulity of the Greeks and the Romans. Fénelon's *Télémaque* (Telemachus, 1699) advocated religious tolerance and was written as a guide to his royal pupil, the Duc de Bourgogne (1682–1712). Both writers were distinguished for the charm of their style.

Bayle's *Pensées diverses sur la comète de 1680* (Diverse Thoughts on the Comet of 1680; 1682) and, in particular, his *Dictionnaire historique et critique* (Historical and Critical Dictionary, 1697) served the writers and thinkers who followed him as an intellectual armory. Imbedded in this mass of learning was an uncompromising religious skepticism that was supported by argument and examples.

The incarnation of the spirit of the Enlightenment was Voltaire. In his *Lettres anglaises ou philosophiques* (English or Philosophical Letters, 1734) he attacked the methods by which, in his view, the church exploited human weakness. He also attacked the theistic and optimistic systems of philosophers, theologians, and reformists, particularly those of the German philosopher Gottfried von Leibniz and the English philanthropist Anthony Cooper, 7th earl of Shaftesbury. In his own day Voltaire was regarded primarily as a phi-

Voltaire   Bettmann Archive

losopher, and his philosophical works overshadowed, until a later day, his satirical classics, such as the novel *Candide* (1759).

The English empiricism of Sir Francis Bacon and John Locke had its French disciples, principally Étienne Bonnot de Condillac. Calling themselves *le parti des philosophes*, the French rationalists rejected scholasticism and expounded the new mechanistic concepts. The latter were also embodied in the *Encyclopédie*, a work designed to comprehend and systematize all human knowledge. This vast undertaking was directed by Denis Diderot, whose witty *Le neveu de Rameau* (1761, or later; *Rameau's Nephew*, 1964) and other works entitle him to separate distinction as a creative writer. On the *Encyclopédie* he had the collaboration of many distinguished contemporaries, including naturalists, ethnologists, philosophers, economists, and statesmen.

A notable book of this period, *L'esprit des lois* (1748; *The Spirit of Laws*, 1750) by Charles de Secondat, baron de Montesquieu, remains an important influence on modern political thought.

Eighteenth-century fiction, when it was not philosophical fantasy, like Voltaire's, was written in the spirit of *La princesse de Clèves*. Like that novel, *Manon Lescaut* (1731), by Abbé Prévost, and *La vie de Marianne* (The Life of Marianne, 1731–41), by Pierre de Marivaux, were limited to two characters and the crises of their love. More elaborate was the witty, scandalous novel of society intrigue, *Les liaisons dangereuses* (1782), by Pierre Choderlos de Laclos (1741–1803).

The naturalist Georges Leclerc de Buffon devoted his life to the compilation of the monumental *Histoire naturelle* (44 vol., 1749–1804), a part of the vast reclassification of flora and fauna that preoccupied the 18th-century naturalists.

Although Jean Jacques Rousseau is now remembered mostly for his *Confessions* (1782; trans. 1783, 1790), he had a revolutionary effect on political thinking in his own time through his *Du contrat social* (1762; *The Social Contract*, 1797), in which the relations of the individual to society are conceived as a contract by which the individual surrenders some personal rights in return for equality of status and mutual assistance. The leaders of the French Revolution regarded themselves as his disciples. He also had a revolutionary influence on educational thinking, through his *Émile* (1762; trans. 1763), and on fiction, in which he inaugurated the romantic trend with his *Julie, ou la nouvelle Héloïse* (1760; *Julie, or the New Eloise*, 1773).

Finally, the work of André Chénier, who was guillotined at the age of 31, deserves mention.

FRENCH LITERATURE

Although he completed an amazing number of remarkable poems, he was, like the English poet John Keats, only at the beginning of his mature powers when he died. Like Keats, too, his poetry is distinguished for its pure beauty. Chénier is regarded by some authorities as the greatest French poet of the 18th century.

In the period of reaction that followed the French Revolution, the principal creative writers were Comte Joseph de Maistre (1754–1821), who dwelt nostalgically on the glories of the *ancien régime,* and Vicomte François René de Chateaubriand, who promoted a revival of religion. Chateaubriand's Byronic individualism, dithyrambic celebration of nature, and emphasis on the esthetic values of religion helped usher in the romantic movement.

THE 19TH CENTURY

Numerous literary groups emerged in France in the 19th century. First came the romantics, followed by the realists, Parnassians, symbolists, and naturalists.

The Romantic Movement. Madame de Staël, despite her radical politics, anticipated in her novels the preoccupations and methods of the romantics of the following generation. *Corinne, ou l'Italie* (1807; *Corinna, or Italy,* 1807) is regarded as her masterpiece.

Chief of the early romantics was Alphonse de Lamartine, a sentimental writer and an accomplished craftsman. The romantics ventured to break rules and to replace classical restraint with ebullient emotion. The most productive and the most militant member of the movement was Victor Hugo, who, in *Hernani* (1830), used the stage as a forum from which to expound romantic ideas. He was supported by the novelists Alexander Dumas *père* and Théophile Gautier, and the poets Alfred de Vigny, Alfred de Musset, and Charles Nodier (1780–1844). The writings of the romantics influenced, and were influenced by, similar currents in painting and music, as in the works of the artist Eugène Delacroix and the composer Ambroise Thomas.

The conflict between revolutionary and reactionary thinking after the restoration of the French monarchy in 1815 was reflected in literature. The major writers on the conservative side have been cited above. The radical writers included the poet Pierre Jean de Béranger, twice imprisoned for the republican views expressed in his later verses; the novelist and early feminist George Sand, some of whose works were pioneer social novels; the historian Jules Michelet (1798–1874), who exalted the French Revolution; and such forerunners of socialism as Saint-Simon, Charles Fourier, Pierre Proudhon, and

Honoré de Balzac   Bettmann Archive

Louis Blanc. A middle view appeared in the work of the historians F. P. G. Guizot, Adolphe Thiers, and Augustin Thierry (1795–1856), and in the writing of Benjamin Constant. Constant's novel *Adolphe* (1816; trans. 1959), however, for which he is chiefly known and in which he portrays his stormy affair with Madame de Staël, has no political overtones.

The Realists. Honoré de Balzac may be said to bridge the romantic movement and the realist movement that followed it. In his vast force, variety, and comparative formlessness, he resembles the romantic writers. His materialistic cast of mind, minute observation, and preoccupation with factual detail, on the other hand, make him the first of the realists. His ambitious *La comédie humaine* (47 vol., 1829–50; *The Human Comedy,* 40 vol., 1895–98), composed over a period of 20 years, consists of related novels and short stories. The characters of this work include almost every class and profession and reproduce the social scene of 19th-century France.

Other great French realists include Stendhal, Gustave Flaubert, and Prosper Mérimée. Stendhal's keen psychological perception, anticipating that of modern psychological novelists, was recognized and praised by Balzac. Stendhal's principal novels are *La chartreuse de Parme* (1839; *The Charterhouse of Parma,* 1925) and *Le rouge et le noir* (1830; *The Red and the Black,* 1926). Flaubert's meticulous realism was best exemplified in his *Madame Bovary* (1857). The effects of his method are subtle, for a growing sense of character and situation is constructed from a gradual accumulation of carefully observed details. Mérimée, in spite of certain romantic qualities, may be included among the realists because of the psychological truth in his characterizations. His best works are lengthy short stories, among them *Carmen* (1846; trans. 1881) and *Colomba* (1852; trans. 1853).

The greatest French critic, Charles Augustin Sainte-Beuve, may also be included among the realists. He started as a partisan of the romantics but broke with them and became an advocate of realism. Believing that the critic's chief duty is not to judge but to understand, he explored biographical and environmental factors affecting an author's work. His essays are virtually the first and perhaps the best examples of sociological and psychological criticism. Among his chief works are *Causeries du lundi* (15 vol., 1851–62; *Monday Chats,* 1877); *Portraits des femmes* (Portraits of Women, 1844); *Portraits contemporains* (1846); and *L'histoire de Port-Royal* (1840–59).

Parnassians and Symbolists. In poetry, the reaction against romanticism began with *Émaux et camées* (Enamels and Cameos, 1852; enlarged ed., 1872), by Théophile Gautier, who in his youth had been a leader of the romantic school. It was carried further in the work of the group known as the Parnassians, outstanding among whom were Charles Marie René Leconte de Lisle, Sully Prudhomme, and José de Heredia. These poets sought and achieved a restrained, impersonal, and chiseled beauty, but their work may be regarded more as a return to classicism than as an advance from romanticism. Charles Baudelaire's work was different. Although the technical polish of his

Charles Baudelaire   Bettmann Archive

verse is as marked as that of the Parnassians, he is intensely personal in the expression of his bitterness, agony, and despair. His great work is *Fleurs du mal* (Flowers of Evil, 1857), the publication of which was suppressed until certain offending stanzas were removed.

Baudelaire was followed by the symbolists, sometimes derogatorily termed the decadents, whom he influenced. Their work was marked by experimentation, notably in free verse. Among the symbolists were Paul Verlaine, Henri de Régnier (1864–1936), Stéphane Mallarmé, le Comte de Lautréamont (1846–70), Tristan Corbière (1845–75), Charles Cros (1842–82), Jules Laforgue, and the American expatriate writers Francis Viélé-Griffin (1864–1937) and Stuart Merrill (1863–1915). Lautréamont's work *Les chants de Maldoror* (The Songs of Maldoror, 1868) subsequently influenced the surrealists. A number of Belgian writers were associated with the symbolists, among them Georges Rodenbach (1855–98), Émile Verhaeren (1855–1916), and Maurice Maeterlinck. The most influential of the symbolists was, however, Arthur Rimbaud, most of whose powerful and vivid poems were written before the age of 19. Symbolist poetry has a suggestive, veiled quality that links it to the impressionist paintings of artists such as Claude Monet and the works of impressionist composers such as Claude Debussy.

In prose, several writers sought symbolist effects. Among them were Rémy de Gourmont, the literary critic; Édouard Dujardin (1861–1949), whose novel *Les lauriers sont coupés* (1888; *We'll to the Woods No More,* 1938) is an early example of stream-of-consciousness writing; and Henri de Régnier, a noted symbolist poet.

The Naturalists. During the late 19th century some of the realistic tendencies exemplified by the work of Flaubert led toward the movement known as naturalism, which stressed environment and heredity as the principal determinants of human action. The movement was given direction by the historian and critic Hippolyte Taine, whose best-known work is *Histoire de la littérature anglaise* (1863–64; *History of English Literature,* 1871–72). Taine believed that human values such as virtue and vice are products like sugar and acids, and that human culture is the result of such formative influences as race and climate. The brothers and literary collaborators Edmond and Jules de Goncourt were the precursors of naturalism in the novel, notably in *Germinie Lacerteux* (1864; trans. 1891). After his brother's death, Edmond de Goncourt (who endowed the prestigious French literary award, the Prix Goncourt) wrote several novels indepen-

Émile Zola   Bettmann Archive

dently. He influenced the work of Alphonse Daudet, a realist novelist—best known for his sketches of Provence, *Letters from My Mill* (1869; trans. 1900)—whose work is lightened by humor in the manner of Charles Dickens.

Naturalism was adopted as a fundamental principle and literary method by Émile Zola, the most famous writer of the movement. He used the term particularly to describe the content and purpose of his novels, which were characterized by the type of historical determinism formulated by Taine. Zola's literary method is best seen in *L'assommoir* (The Dram Shop, 1877), *Nana* (1880), and *Germinal* (1885; trans. 1901). The influence of this method was so extreme that in 1887 Edmond de Goncourt and Daudet, as well as five of Zola's own disciples, formed an opposition group responsible for a manifesto against Zola's novel *La terre* (Earth, 1888). Another counterforce is expressed in the work of Paul Bourget (1852–1935), best known for his novel *Le disciple* (1889). He stressed psychological rather than environmental motivation, an aspect of naturalism ignored by Zola. In the field of the short story, the most important naturalist writer is Guy de Maupassant, whose works include the collections *Mademoiselle Fifi* (1882) and *Contes des jours et de la nuit* (Tales of the Days and the Night, 1885), as well as several novels; as a short-story writer, de Maupassant, whose literary master was Flaubert, has no peers.

Opposed to the materialism of Taine and also to the romantic individualism of Michelet is the work of the influential historian and critic Ernest Renan. His principal work is *Histoire des origines du Christianisme* (8 vol., 1863–83; *The History of the Origins of Christianity*, 5 vol., 1888–90), deal-

ing with the foundations of Christianity. Renan influenced the novelists Pierre Loti, Maurice Barrès, and Anatole France.

Anatole France had social views somewhat akin to Zola's, but he used irony for their expression. His books are a commentary on the irrational forces of society. They are filled with pity for the weak and anger against the abuses of power. Most characteristic of his works, perhaps, are his realistic short novel, *Crainquebille* (1901), and his satirical fantasies *L'île des pingouins* (1908; *Penguin Island*, 1909) and *La révolte des anges* (1914; *The Revolt of the Angels*, 1914).

Another great 19th-century writer was the naturalist Jean Henri Fabre. His delightfully readable studies of insect life have become a model for popularized scientific writing abroad as well as in France.

THE 20TH CENTURY

Literature in 20th-century France has been strongly affected by the ferment and change that have marked the entire cultural life of the nation. To the impulses supplied by the symbolist innovations were added strong foreign impulses, such as the modern dance introduced by the American dancer Isadora Duncan and the modern ballet introduced by Russian ballet; the music of the Russian composer Igor Stravinsky; primitive art; and, in literature, the impact of the Russian novelist Fyodor Mikhaylovich Dostoyevsky and, a little later, of the Irish novelist James Joyce. The trends are so interpenetrating and the changes so rapid that time will be necessary to set them in perspective.

Some Individualists. *Du côté de chez Swann* (1913; *Swann's Way*, 1928), by Marcel Proust, volume 1 of his *À la recherche du temps perdu* (16 vol., 1913–27; *Remembrance of Things Past*, 1922–32), is generally recognized as one of the greatest psychological novels of all time. Romain Rolland, whose most famous novel, *Jean Christophe*, appeared in ten volumes between 1904 and 1913, spent World War I in Switzerland, writing pacifist appeals to the combatants. His ideas on war were embodied in his novel *Clérambault: histoire d'une conscience libre pendant la guerre* (Clérambault: History of a Free Conscience During the War, 1920). *L'immoraliste* (1902; *The Immoralist*, 1930) by André Gide expressed the conviction that, while freedom in itself is admirable, acceptance of the responsibilities demanded by that freedom is difficult, a theme which Gide carried further in *La porte étroite* (1909; *Strait Is the Gate*, 1924). Gide's work was distinguished by his independence of thought and expression. The widely read novel *Jean Barois* (1913; trans. 1949), by Roger Martin du Gard (1881–1958), is a study of the conflict between a mystical background and the scientific mind in the 1880s. Among outstanding Catholic writers were the mystical poet and novelist Francis Jammes (1868–1938) and François Mauriac. Mauriac's work, completely innocent of didacticism or proselytism, is devoted to the study of evil, sin, weakness, and suffering. His novels, plays, and poetry show the influence, not of novelists, but of Pascal, Racine, and Baudelaire, in all of whom a sense of tragedy fosters a certain aloofness of attitude and starkness of style.

Jean Cocteau, active in many different fields, was the author, among other works, of the book of poems *Plain-Chant* (1923), of the novel *Les enfants terribles* (1929; *Children of the Game,* 1955), of the play *La machine infernale* (1934; *The Infernal Machine,* 1936), of the film *Le sang d'un poète* (Blood of a Poet, 1930), of criticism, as well as of ballets.

Jean Giraudoux first won attention by his realistic accounts of French provincial life (*Les Provinciales,* 1909). The impression he then made as a forceful and original writer was strengthened by the realism of his war books, one of which was awarded the Grand Prix Balzac. Later he established a comparable position as a dramatist, two of his plays, *Amphitryon 38* (1929; trans. 1938) and *La folle de Chaillot* (1945; *The Madwoman of Chaillot,* 1947), having achieved international success. Most of Giraudoux's work exhibits inventive fantasy and graces of style that some critics have condemned as preciosity, although others have acclaimed him one of the great stylists of literature.

After writing first for the theater, Jules Romains turned to the novel. In *Les hommes de bonne volonté* (27 vol., 1932–46; *Men of Good Will,* 1933–46), he attempted to compress the whole of modern French life into a work of 27 volumes. The conception of the work draws upon the doctrine of unanimism, that is, that the individual and the society in which the individual lives are one. Jules Romains's novel portrays the collective soul of a society.

Guillaume Apollinaire was a poet and writer of cultural manifestos. His *Cubist Painters* (1913; trans. 1949) was instrumental in establishing the cubist school of painting. His volumes of poems *Alcools* (1913; trans. 1964) and *Calligrammes* (1918) were popular among the young surrealists, upon whom he had much influence.

The Catholic poet, playwright, and apologist Paul Claudel remained outside all literary coteries. Religious feeling dominates his work and is the inspiration for his lyric poetry, such as *Cinq grandes odes* (1910; *Five Great Odes,* 1967) and

La cantate à trois voix (The Cantata in Three Voices, 1931), and plays such as *Le livre de Christophe Colombe* (The Book of Christopher Columbus, 1930).

The Théâtre du Vieux-Colombier, founded in 1913 by the actor and drama critic Jacques Copeau, did much to encourage young playwrights such as Claudel. It produced, during its first season, plays by him and by Martin du Gard, among others.

Beginning as a symbolist, Paul Valéry became one of the greatest philosophical poets of the time. Intent upon technique, he strove to express his abstract ideas within the strictest formal framework. Mallarmé and Valéry continued a tendency in modern French poetry introduced by Baudelaire, through his translations of works by the 19th-century American writer Edgar Allan Poe, and his own subsequent work. It is characterized, in part, by a special concern with significant sound. In his definition of symbolism, Valéry observes that the new poetry seeks to recapture from music what belongs to poetry. In practice, however, Valéry revived the classical rules of prosody. He believed that the act of writing poetry is a bending of the will to useful constraints.

The themes of the novels of Henry de Montherlant range from sports (*Les olympiques,* 1924) and bullfighting (*Les bestiaires,* 1926; *The Bullfighters,* 1927), to the place of woman in modern life (*Les jeunes filles,* 4 vol., 1936–39; *Pity for Women,* 1937, and *Costals & the Hippogriff,* 1940). Like Mauriac and Giraudoux, Montherlant turned to the theater, writing historical tragedies such as *La reine morte* (The Queen Dies, 1942) and a few dramas set and costumed in the modern period.

Because of her great popular success and her extraordinary productivity (her published works total more than 80 volumes), Colette (Sidonie Gabrielle Colette) was slow to win recognition as a serious writer. The literary value of her writing was eventually recognized in France by Marcel Proust and André Gide and in England by Somerset Maugham. The style of novels such as *Chéri* (1920; trans. 1929) and *Gigi* (1945; trans. 1952) has effortless grace, and their keen perceptions link Colette with the great psychological realists of world literature.

World War I. The realistic account of World War I in *Le feu* (1916; *Under Fire,* 1917) by Henri Barbusse inspired *Les croix de bois* (1919; *Wooden Crosses,* 1921) by Roland Dorgelès (1886–1973), forerunners of the antiwar books of the late 1920s that appeared not only in France but also in Germany, England, and the U.S. The essayist

*Madame Sidonie Gabrielle Claudine Colette, pictured
with other members of the Goncourt Academy in 1945.*
French Embassy Press & Information Div.

André Maurois found war a subject for humor in
his *Les silences du Colonel Bramble* (1918; *The
Silence of Colonel Bramble,* 1920). Later he became one of the initiators of the novelized biography in his *Ariel, ou la vie de Shelley* (1923;
Ariel, the Life of Shelley, 1924). The gentle irony
with which the surgeon Georges Duhamel
treated war in his *Vie des martyrs* (1917; *The New
Book of Martyrs,* 1918) sets him apart both from
those who looked upon war as a glorious experience and from others who found horror in everything connected with it. In his later novels
Duhamel became a chronicler of bourgeois
France. The full horrors of World War I found
their expression in *Le grand troupeau* (The Great
Herd, 1931) by Jean Giono, all of whose works
express militant pacifism and antipathy to the
machine age.

Dada and Surrealism. The later years of World
War I were notable for the growth (in France,
Germany, Switzerland, and the U.S.) of the
movement of young poets and painters known
as Dadaism. In revolt against all traditional artistic forms, they set out with the declared intention of destroying art. About 1923, certain
members of the group, under the leadership of
André Breton, broke away and formed a new
movement which, using a word invented by
Guillaume Apollinaire, they called surrealism.
Breton, the leader and expositor of the movement, began his career as a medical student. In
1916 he fell under the influence of Jacques
Vaché, whose proclaimed desire was to live in a
continual state of mental aberration. The impres-

sion made by this almost legendary character, together with Breton's enthusiasm for the poems
of Rimbaud, produced a philosophy of art and
life in which the most important values were
those dictated by the subconscious. Despite the
attacks that were leveled at surrealism, the
movement had its sources deep in the literature
of France. Lautréamont, Baudelaire, Cros, Rimbaud, and the symbolists in general were its direct ancestors.

Because of Breton's dictatorial nature, which
was matched by the independence of its other
members, the group always had a shifting membership. Some of those who have, at one time or
another, been important surrealists are mentioned below.

Beginning as a Dadaist, Louis Aragon became a
surrealist in 1924 and produced several books of
poems, including *Le libertinage* (Libertinism,
1924). In 1928, however, in *Traité du style* (Treatise on Style), he attacked the motives behind
their works. Becoming a Communist in 1930, he
was expelled from the surrealist movement. His
novels *Les cloches de Bâle* (1934; *The Bells of
Basel,* 1936) and *Les beaux quartiers* (1936; *Residential Quarter,* 1938) brought him acclaim at
home and abroad. During the German occupation of France in World War II, he once more
turned to poetry, in *Le crève-coeur* (1941; *Heart-
break,* 1943) and *Les yeux d'Elsa* (1942; *The Eyes
of Elsa,* 1944), to lament the defeat of his country.

In Paul Éluard the movement found, perhaps,
its greatest poet. After a Dadaist start, his poems,
in *Le necéssité de la vie et la conséquence des*

rêves (The Necessity of Life and the Consequences of Dreams, 1921), were patterns of images viewed in detachment. With his adherence to the surrealist movement, in about 1923, Éluard wove his images into a contemplation of love as a part of the universal spirit, particularly in *Mourir de ne pas mourir* (To Die of Not Dying, 1924) and *Capitale de la douleur* (Sorrow's Capital, 1926). In such works the images exist as a pure emanation of the poet himself, and have no connection with nature as a separate entity. Although no longer closely connected with surrealism, Éluard's poems of World War II, *Poésie et vérité* (Poetry and Truth, 1942) and *Au rendezvous Allemand* (At the German Rendezvous, 1945), employ the same technique of imagery to lament the fall of France and extol its subsequent resistance.

Philippe Soupault (1897–1990), founder of the surrealist movement with Breton, was disowned in 1930 for his failure to adhere to its principles in his studies *Henri Rousseau, le Douanier* (1927) and *William Blake* (1928; trans. 1928). Since then his important books have been *Charlot* (1931), an examination of the American comedian Charles Chaplin, and *Souvenirs de James Joyce* (Remembrances of James Joyce, 1944), in which Soupault recalls his experiences as one of the translators of Joyce's novel *Ulysses*.

Other Modes and Themes. Certain novelists strove in a different, nonsurrealist way to express the spirit of the times. André Malraux, having lived in the presence of revolution and counterrevolution, mirrored a life always in the shadow of death in his novels *La condition humaine* (1933; *Man's Fate*, 1934), dealing with the revolution in China; *Les temps du mépris* (1935; *Days of Wrath*, 1936), dealing with the anti-Nazi underground in Germany; and *L'espoir* (1938; *Man's Hope*, 1938), dealing with the Spanish civil war. The American émigré novelist Julien Green, who wrote in French, depicted a strange hallucinatory world in which an atmosphere of terror is unrelieved by humor. He treated French provincial life in such novels as *Adrienne Mésurat* (1927; *The Closed Garden*, 1928) and *Léviathan* (1929; *The Dark Journey*, 1929) and American life in *Mont cinère* (1926; *Avarice House*, 1927) and *Moira* (1950; trans. 1951). Green's first play, *Sud* (South, performed in Paris in 1953), is a classical tragedy.

The aviator Antoine de Saint-Exupéry became known as the greatest writer of his generation on the conquest of the air with such works as *Vol de nuit* (1931; *Night Flight*, 1932) and *Terre des hommes* (1939; *Wind, Sand and Stars*, 1939). His humanistic approach is found also in *Le petit prince* (1943; *The Little Prince*, 1943), a gentle fable that has become a universal favorite with children and adults alike. For sheer misanthropy, on the other hand, the novels of Louis Ferdinand Céline have seldom been surpassed; *Voyage au bout de la nuit* (1932; *Journey to the End of Night*, 1934) depicts catastrophe without hope of relief, and in *Mort à crédit* (1936; *Death on the Installment Plan*, 1938) all human aspirations are subjected to contemptuous irony. Marguerite Yourcenar (1903–87), born in Brussels and holder of dual French and U.S. citizenship, is acclaimed for the classical purity of her style and her intellectual breadth. Writer of historical novels such as *Mémoires d'Hadrien* (1951; *Hadrian's Memoirs*, 1954) and her family biography *Souvenirs pieux* (Pious Memories, 1973), she became, in 1980, the first women ever elected to the French Academy. In distinct contrast are the popular semiautobiographical stories of modern love by Françoise Sagan (1935–), one of the first novelists published after World War II. Sagan's first novel, *Bonjour triestesse* (1954; trans. 1955), which won the Prix des Critiques, established her celebrity.

Among the most distinguished poets of this century is Saint-John Perse. His *Anabase* (1924; *Anabasis*, 1930) paradoxically depicts the poet as both detached from human activity and deeply involved in it. The official attitude of the symbolists was aloofness; that of the surrealists was aggressiveness. Perse represents a more balanced, classical attitude in which the poet both contemplates life and participates in it. This atti-

Jean Jacques Servan-Schreiber   Christian Taillandler

Jean Paul Sartre, founder of the existentialist movement, poses with his friend and literary colleague Simone de Beauvoir. French Embassy Press & Information Div.

tude is apparent in *Amers* (1957; *Seamarks*, 1958), his longest poem. René Char (1907–88) was one of the outstanding poets of his generation. His adherence to surrealism during the 1930s was modified in the early 1940s by his participation in the Resistance movement. His best poems, written between 1940 and 1944 and collected in *Feuillets d'hypnos* (Leaves of Hypnosis), transcend the theme of war.

Jean Jacques Servan-Schreiber (1924–), founder of the left-wing weekly *L'Express* (1953) and a member of the cabinet of President Valéry Giscard d'Estaing in 1970, is now credited with having turned opinion against the war in Algeria with his controversial exposé of French atrocities, *Lieutenent en Algérie* (1957). His *Le défi américain* (1968; *The American Challenge,* 1968) warns against U.S. influence in Europe.

Existentialism. In the 1940s, under the leadership of the philosopher, dramatist, and novelist Jean Paul Sartre, the negative, pessimistic dimension of the philosophical and literary movement called existentialism (q.v.) developed. The general thesis—outlined in Sartre's *L'être et le néant* (1943; *Being and Nothingness,* 1953)—is essentially that human existence is pointless and frustrating, and that the individual is in fact only the sum of personal experiences. In his plays *Les mouches* (1943; *The Flies,* 1946), *Huis-clos* (1944; *No Exit,* 1946), and *Les mains sales* (1948; *Dirty Hands,* 1949), Sartre expanded on problems al-

ready raised before the war in his book of short stories *Le mur* (The Wall, 1939). In his trilogy *Les chemins de la liberté* (The Roads of Liberty, 1945–49), he attempted to show the individual without illusions and aware of the necessity of participating in all functions of society. Sartre's most zealous disciple was his lifelong companion Simone de Beauvoir, who wrote, among many other works, the novel *Les mandarins* (1954; *The Mandarins,* 1956), which deals in a thinly disguised form with the private relationships of some leading French existentialists. Her *La cérémonie des adieux* (1981; *Adieux: A Farewell to Sartre,* 1984) is a memoir of her colleague. At one time Albert Camus might have been described as an existentialist, particularly in his play *Caligula* (1944; trans. 1948); in both his important novels, however, *L'étranger* (1942; *The Stranger,* 1946) and *La peste* (1947; *The Plague,* 1948), he recognized the desirability, and indeed the necessity, of human endeavor.

Recent Trends. During the 1950s, two schools of experimental writing flourished in France. The "theater of the absurd" or "antitheater" is best illustrated in the plays of Romanian-born Eugène Ionesco; Samuel Beckett, an Irishman who began writing in French after World War II; and Jean Genet. The popular *En attendant Godot* (1948; *Waiting for Godot,* 1952) of Beckett, and *Les nègres* (1959; *The Blacks,* 1960) and *Les paravents* (1961; *The Screens,* 1962) of Genet exemplify this school of writing, which is opposed to the psychological analysis and ideological content of existentialism.

Albert Camus UPI

Simultaneously with the "antitheater," the "antinovel" or *nouveau roman* (a term first applied by Sartre to a book by Nathalie Sarraute [1902–]) has attracted considerable attention, chiefly through the novels and theories of Sarraute, Claude Simon (1913–), Alain Robbe-Grillet, and Michel Butor (1926–). Like the playwrights, the new novelists have opposed the traditional forms of the psychological novel; they emphasize the purely objective world of things. Emotions and sentiments are not described as such; rather, the reader has to imagine what they are by following the relationship between characters and the objects they touch and see. Sarraute's *Portrait d'un inconnu* (1947; *Portrait of a Man Unknown,* 1948) led the way, followed by such works as her *Vous les entendez?* (1972; *Do You Hear Them?,* 1973) and, earlier, Robbe-Grillet's *La jalousie* (1957; *Jealousy,* 1959) and Butor's *La modification* (1957). Simon writes densely constructed historical novels, with much use of the stream-of-consciousness device. Most notable of his works is *La route de Flandres* (1960; *The Flanders Road,* 1961).

A new school of literary criticism, structuralism, based in part on the work of French anthropologist Claude Lévi-Strauss, began to flourish in France in the 1960s and '70s. A leading exponent of this school was Roland Barthes (1915–80). His *Elements of Semiology* (1964; trans. 1967) is an introduction to semiotics; his *Critical Essays* and *New Critical Essays* were published in 1964 and 1972 (trans. 1972 and 1980, respectively). More recently, a mode of criticism known as deconstruction was pioneered by the philosopher and critic Jacques Derrida (1930–).

See also CRITICISM, LITERARY. W.F.

For further information on this topic, see the Bibliography in volume 28, sections 834, 844.

FRENCH POLYNESIA (Fr. *Polynésie Française*), overseas territory of France, consisting of several groups of small islands scattered over a wide area of the E South Pacific Ocean. The territory has a total land area of 4000 sq km (1544 sq mi).

French Polynesia is divided into five administrative districts: the Windward Islands and the Leeward Islands, which together form the Society Islands (q.v.) group; the Tuamotu Archipelago, which includes the Gambier Islands (q.v.); the Austral Islands (q.v.); and the Marquesas Islands (q.v.). Clipperton Island, an uninhabited atoll, S of the coast of Mexico, is also part of the territory. The population is primarily Polynesian, with minorities of Chinese and Europeans. French is the official language, but various Polynesian languages are generally spoken. The principal island is Tahiti (q.v.); its chief town, Papeete (pop., 1983,

23,496), is the capital of the territory. Copra, coffee, vanilla, and mother-of-pearl are the leading exports. Subsistence activities include fishing and the culture of tropical fruits. Tourism, a growing business, is very important to the economy. The unit of currency is the CFP franc (103 CFP francs equal U.S.$1; 1990).

The islands were annexed by France beginning in the 1840s. In 1958 a plebiscite was held, the islands voting for the status of an overseas territory within the French Community. The territory is governed by a 41-member territorial assembly, elected by universal adult suffrage, and is represented in both houses of the French National Assembly. The islands were given increased autonomy in 1977. Pop. (1983) 166,753.

FRENCH REVOLUTION, cataclysmic political and social upheaval, extending from 1789 to 1799, which resulted, among other things, in the overthrow of the Bourbon monarchy in France and in the establishment of the First Republic. It was generated by a vast complex of causes, the most important of which were the inability of the ruling classes of nobility, clergy, and bourgeoisie to come to grips with the problems of state, the indecisive nature of the monarch, extortionate taxation of the peasantry, impoverishment of the workers, the intellectual ferment of the Age of Enlightenment, and the example of the American Revolution. Recent scholarship tends to downplay the social class struggle and emphasize political, cultural, ideological, and personality factors in the advent and unfolding of the conflict. The Revolution itself produced an equally vast complex of consequences. This article deals mainly with highlights of the revolutionary period. For an account of many of the important events that preceded and followed the Revolution, *see* FRANCE.

Historical Reasons for the Revolution. For more than a century before the accession of Louis XVI in 1774, the French government had undergone periodic economic crises, resulting from the long wars waged during the reign of Louis XIV, royal mismanagement of national affairs under Louis XV, the losses incurred in the French and Indian War (1756–63), and increased indebtedness arising from loans to the American colonies during the American Revolution (1775–83). The advocates of fiscal, social, and governmental reform became increasingly vocal during the reign of Louis XVI. In August 1774, Louis appointed a liberal comptroller general, the economist Anne Robert Jacques Turgot, baron de L'Aulne, who instituted a policy of strict economy in government expenditures. Within two years, however, most of the reforms had been withdrawn and his dismissal forced by reactionary members of the

The storming of the Bastille by the people of Paris on July 14, 1789.

nobility and clergy, supported by Queen Marie Antoinette. Turgot's successor, the financier and statesman Jacques Necker, similarly accomplished little before his downfall in 1781, also because of opposition from the reactionaries. Nevertheless, he won popular acclaim by publishing an accounting of the royal finances, which revealed the heavy cost of privileges and favoritism. During the next few years the financial crisis steadily worsened. Popular demand for convocation of the Estates-General (an assembly made up of representatives of the clergy, the nobility, and the commoners), which had been in adjournment since 1614, finally compelled Louis XVI in 1788 to authorize national elections. During the ensuing campaign, censorship was suspended, and a flood of pamphlets expressing ideas derived from the Enlightenment circulated throughout France. Necker, who was reinstated as comptroller general by Louis in 1788, supported the king in his decision that the third estate (com-

moners) would have as many representatives in the Estates-General as the first estate (the clergy) and the second estate (the nobility) combined, but both he and Louis failed to make a ruling on the method of voting.

Despite general agreement among the three estates that national salvation required fundamental changes in the status quo, class antagonisms precluded unity of action in the Estates-General, which convened at Versailles on May 5, 1789. The delegations representing the privileged strata of French society immediately challenged the third-estate caucus by rejecting its procedural proposals on methods of voting. The proposals were designed to establish a system of simple majority rule, thereby ensuring domination of the Estates-General by the third estate, numerically the most powerful caucus. The deadlock on procedure persisted for six weeks, but finally, on June 17, the insurgent caucus, led by Emmanuel Joseph Sieyès and Honoré Gabriel

Riqueti, comte de Mirabeau, proclaimed itself the National Assembly. This display of defiance of the royal government, which had given its support to the clergy and nobility, was followed by the passage of a measure vesting the National Assembly with sole power to legislate taxation. In swift retaliation, Louis deprived the National Assembly of its meeting hall. The National Assembly responded, on June 20, by gathering at a Versailles tennis court and swearing, in what is known in history as the Tennis Court Oath, that it would not dissolve until it had drafted a constitution for France. At this juncture, serious divisions split the ranks of the upper two estates, and numerous representatives of the lower clergy and a number of liberal nobles broke off to join forces with the National Assembly.

Open Rebellion. Continued defiance of royal decrees and the mutinous mood of the royal army forced the king to capitulate. On June 27 he ordered the refractory nobility and clergy to join the unicameral legislature, which then designated itself the National Constituent Assembly. Yielding to pressure from the queen and the comte d'Artois, later Charles X, Louis issued orders for the concentration of several loyal foreign regiments in Paris and Versailles. At the same time, Necker, the popular apostle of a regenerated France, was again dismissed from the government. The people of Paris reacted to these provocative acts with open insurrection. Rioting began on July 12, and on July 14 the Bastille, a royal prison that symbolized the despotism of the Bourbons, was stormed and captured.

Even before the Parisian outburst, violence, sporadic local disturbances, and peasant uprisings against oppressive nobles occurred in many parts of France, alarming the propertied bourgeoisie no less than the Royalists. Panic-stricken over these ominous events, the comte d'Artois and other prominent reactionaries, the first of the so-called émigrés, fled the country. The Parisian bourgeoisie, fearful that the lower classes of the city would take further advantage of the collapse of the old administrative machine and resort again to direct action, hastily established a provisional local government and organized a people's militia, officially designated the National Guard. A red, white, and blue tricolor was substituted for the white standard of the Bourbons as the national flag. Provisional local governments and militia units were soon established throughout the nation. The National Guard was placed under the command of the marquis de Lafayette, a hero of the American Revolution. Unable to stem the rising tide of revolt, Louis XVI withdrew his loyal troops. He recalled Necker, and then he formally legal-ized the measures that had been taken by the provisional authorities.

Drafting a Constitution. Provincial unrest and disorder, known as the Great Fear, stimulated the National Constituent Assembly to action. During the night session of Aug. 4, 1789, the clergy, nobles, and bourgeoisie renounced their privileges; a few days later the assembly passed a law abolishing feudal and manorial prerogatives, but guaranteeing compensation in certain cases. Parallel legislation included prohibition of the sale of public offices, of exemption from taxation, and of the right of the Roman Catholic church to levy tithes.

The assembly then proceeded to grapple with its primary task, the drafting of a constitution. In the constitutional preamble, known in history as the Declaration of the Rights of Man and of the Citizen, the delegates formulated the revolutionary ideals later summarized as *Liberté, Égalité, Fraternité* ("Liberty, Equality, Fraternity"). While the Constituent Assembly deliberated, the hungry population of Paris, a hotbed of discontent and of rumors of Royalist conspiracy, clamored for food and agitated for action. Reports of a gala banquet at Versailles stirred the political ferment in Paris to the boiling point. On October 5–6 a large body of Parisians, mostly women, marched on Versailles and laid siege to the royal palace. Louis and his family were rescued by Lafayette, who, on demand of the crowd, escorted them to Paris. After this episode some conservative members of the Constituent Assembly, which followed the king to Paris, handed in their resignations. In Paris, both the court and the assembly became increasingly subject to pressures from its citizens. Radical sentiment became predominant in the assembly, but the original objective, a constitutional monarchy, was retained.

The first draft of the constitution received the approval of the French monarch on July 14, 1790, at elaborate ceremonies in Paris, attended by delegations from all parts of the nation. By the terms of the document, the provinces of France were abolished, and the country was divided into departments, each named for a mountain or stream and provided with a local elective administrative apparatus. Hereditary titles were outlawed, trial by jury in criminal cases was ordained, and fundamental modification of French law was projected. By the institution of property qualifications for the vote, the constitution confined the electorate to the middle and upper classes. The constitution vested legislative authority in a Legislative Assembly, to consist of 745 members elected by an indirect system of voting. Although executive authority was vested

Declaration of the Rights of Man, the constitution of the French Republic as formulated in 1792 by Maximilien Robespierre.

French Embassy Press & Information Div.

in the king, strict limitations were imposed on his powers. His veto power was merely suspensive, and the assembly had effective control of his conduct of foreign affairs. Severe restrictions on the power of the Roman Catholic church were legalized through a series of articles, called the Civil Constitution of the Clergy, the most important of which confiscated all ecclesiastical estates. To relieve financial distress, the state was authorized to issue a new form of paper currency, called assignats, which were secured by the seized lands, constituting a tenth of France. The constitution also provided for the election of priests and bishops by the voters, for remuneration of the clergy by the state, for a clerical oath

of allegiance to the state, and for dissolution of most monastic orders.

During the 15-month interval between Louis's acceptance of the initial draft of the constitution and completion of the final draft, important changes in the relationship of forces within the French revolutionary movement took shape. These changes were dictated, first of all, by the mood of suspicion and discontent among the disfranchised section of the population. Wanting the vote and relief from social and economic misery, the nonpropertied classes steadily gravitated toward radicalism. This process, largely accelerated throughout France by the highly organized Jacobins and, in Paris, by the Cordeliers, acquired further impetus as reports circulated that Marie Antoinette was in constant communication with her brother Leopold II, Holy Roman emperor. Like most other monarchs of Europe, Leopold had afforded sanctuary to the émigrés and had otherwise revealed his hostility to the revolutionary occurrences in France. Popular suspicions regarding the activities of the queen and the complicity of the king were confirmed when, on June 21, the royal family was apprehended at Varennes while attempting to escape from France.

The Growth of Radicalism in the Government.
On July 17, 1791, the Republicans of Paris massed in the Champ de Mars and demanded that the king be deposed. On the order of Lafayette, who was affiliated politically with the Feuillants, a group of moderate monarchists, the National Guard opened fire on the demonstrators and dispersed them. The bloodshed immeasurably widened the cleavage between the republican and bourgeois sections of the population. After suspending Louis for a brief period, the moderate majority of the Constituent Assembly, fearful of the growing disorder, reinstated the king in the hope of stemming the mounting radicalism and of preventing foreign intervention. Louis took the oath to support the revised constitution on September 14. Two weeks later, with the election of the new legislature authorized by the constitution, the Constituent Assembly was dissolved. Meanwhile, on August 27, Leopold II and Frederick William II, king of Prussia, had issued a joint declaration regarding France, which contained a thinly veiled threat of armed intervention against the revolution.

The Legislative Assembly, which began its sessions on Oct. 1, 1791, was composed of 750 members, all of whom were inexperienced, inasmuch as members of the Constituent Assembly had voted themselves ineligible for election to the new body. The new legislature was divided

Major figures in the political struggle during the French Revolution. Top left: Georges Jacques Danton, leader of the Montagnard faction of the Legislative Assembly. Bottom left: Maximilien Robespierre, leader of the Reign of Terror. Right: The painting Death of Marat (1793), by Jacques Louis David, depicts the Jacobin leader Paul Marat after his assassination by Charlotte Corday.

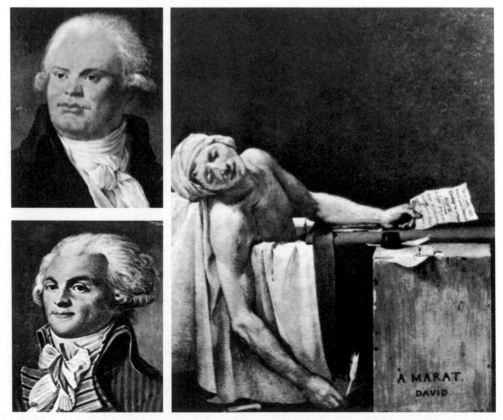

A MARAT.
DAVID

into widely divergent factions, the most moderate of which was the Feuillants, who supported a constitutional monarchy as defined under the Constitution of 1791. In the center was the majority caucus, known as the Plain, which was without well-defined political opinions and consequently without initiative. The Plain, however, uniformly opposed the Republican factors that sat on the left, composed mainly of the Girondists, who advocated transformation of the constitutional monarchy into a federal republic similar to the U.S., and of the Montagnards, consisting of Jacobins and Cordeliers, who favored establishment of a highly centralized, indivisible republic. Before these differences caused a serious split between the Girondists and the Montagnards, the Republican caucus in the assembly secured passage of several important bills, including stringent measures against clergymen who refused to swear allegiance. Louis exercised his veto against these bills, however, creating a cabinet crisis that brought the Girondists to power. Despite the opposition of leading Montagnards, the Girondist ministry, headed by Jean Marie Roland de la Platière (1734–93), adopted a belligerent attitude toward Frederick William II and Francis II, Holy Roman emperor, who had succeeded his father, Leopold II, on March 1, 1792. The two sovereigns openly supported the activities of the émigrés and sustained the opposition of the feudal landlords in Alsace to the revolutionary legislation. Sentiment for war spread rapidly among the monarchists, who hoped for defeat of the revolutionary government and the restoration of the Old Regime, and among the Girondists, who wanted a final triumph over reaction at home and abroad. On April 20, 1792, the Legislative Assembly declared war on the Austrian part of the Holy Roman Empire, beginning the series of conflicts known as the French revolutionary wars.

The Struggle for Freedom. Aided by treasonable errors of omission and commission among the French high command, mostly monarchists, the armies of Austria won several victories in the Austrian Netherlands. The subsequent invasion of France produced major repercussions in the national capital. The Roland ministry fell on June 13, and mass unrest erupted, one week later, into an attack on the Tuileries, the residence of the royal family. On July 11, after Sardinia and Prussia joined the war against France, the Legislative Assembly declared a national emergency. Reserves were dispatched to the hard-pressed armies, and volunteers were summoned to Paris from all parts of the country. When the contingent from Marseille arrived, it was singing the patriotic

hymn thenceforth known as the "Marseillaise." Popular dissatisfaction with the Girondists, who had rallied to the support of the monarchy and had dismissed charges of desertion against Lafayette, increased the agitation. On August 10 the discontent, combined with the threat contained in the manifesto of the allied commander, Charles William Ferdinand, duke of Brunswick (1735–1806), to destroy the capital city if the royal family were mistreated, precipitated a Parisian insurrection. The insurgents, led by radical elements of the capital and national volunteers en route to the front, stormed the Tuileries and massacred the king's Swiss guard. Louis and his family took refuge in the nearby hall of the Legislative Assembly, which promptly suspended the king and placed him in confinement. Simultaneously, the insurrectionists deposed the governing council of Paris, which was replaced by a new provisional executive council. The Montagnards, under the leadership of the lawyer Georges Jacques Danton, dominated the new Parisian government. They swiftly achieved control of the Legislative Assembly. The assembly shortly approved elections, by universal male suffrage, for a new constitutional convention. Between September 2 and 7, more than 1000 Royalists and suspected traitors who had been rounded up in various parts of France, were tried summarily and executed. These "September massacres" were induced by popular fear of the advancing allied armies and of rumored plots to overthrow the revolutionary government. On September 20 a French army, commanded by Gen. Charles François Dumouriez (1739–1823), checked the Prussian advance on Paris at Valmy.

On the day after the victory at Valmy, the newly elected National Convention convened in Paris. In its first official moves that day, the convention proclaimed establishment of the First Republic and abolished the monarchy. Agreement among the principal convention factions, the Girondists and the Montagnards, extended little beyond common approval of these initial measures. No effective opposition developed, however, to the decree sponsored by the Girondists and promulgated on November 19, which promised the help of France to all oppressed peoples of Europe. Encouraging reports arrived almost weekly from the armies, which had assumed the offensive after the battle at Valmy and had successively captured Mainz, Frankfurt am Main, Nice, Savoie, the Austrian Netherlands, and other areas. In the meantime, however, strife steadily intensified in the convention, with the Plain vacillating between support of the conservative Girondists and the radical Montagnards. In the first major test of strength, a majority approved the Montagnard proposal that Louis be brought to trial before the convention for treason. On Jan. 15, 1793, by an almost unanimous vote, the convention found the monarch guilty as charged, but on the following day, when the nature of the penalty was determined, factional lines were sharply drawn. By a vote of 387 to 334, the delegates approved the death penalty. Louis XVI went to the guillotine on January 21.

Girondist influence in the National Convention diminished markedly after the execution of the king. The lack of unity within the party during the trial had irreparably damaged its national prestige, long at low ebb among the Parisian populace, who favored the Jacobins. The Girondists lost influence as a consequence of the military reverses suffered by the French armies after the declaration of war against Great Britain and the United Netherlands (Feb. 1, 1793) and against Spain (March 7), which, with several smaller states, had entered the counterrevolutionary coalition against France. Jacobin proposals designed to strengthen the government for the crucial struggles ahead met fierce resistance from the Girondists. Early in March, however, the convention voted to conscript 300,000 men and dispatched special commissioners to the various departments for the purpose of organizing the levy. Royalists and clerical foes of the Revolution stirred the anticonscription feelings of peasants in the Vendée into open rebellion. Civil war quickly spread to neighboring departments. On March 18, the Austrians defeated the army of Dumouriez at Neerwinden, and Dumouriez deserted to the enemy. The defection of the leader of the army, mounting civil war, and the advance of enemy forces across the French frontiers inevitably forced a crisis in the convention between the Girondists and the Montagnards, with the more radical elements stressing the necessity for bold action in defense of the Revolution.

The Reign of Terror. On April 6 the convention established the Committee of Public Safety (q.v.) as the executive organ of the republic and reorganized the Committee of General Security and the Revolutionary Tribunal. Agents were sent to the departments to supervise local execution of the laws and to requisition men and munitions. During this period rivalry between the Girondists and the Montagnards became increasingly bitter. A new Parisian outburst, organized by the radical journalist Jacques René Hébert (1757–94) and his extremist colleagues, forced the convention to order the arrest of 29 Girondist delegates and the Girondist ministers Pierre Henri Hélène Marie Lebrun-Tondu (1763?–93) and Étienne Clavière

(1735–93) on June 2. Thereafter, the radical faction in control of the government of Paris played a decisive role in the conduct of the Revolution. On June 24 the convention promulgated a new constitution, the terms of which greatly extended the democratic features of the republic. The document was never actually put into effect, however. Leadership of the Committee of Public Safety passed, on July 10, to the Jacobins, who completely reorganized it. Three days later the radical politician Jean Paul Marat, long identified with the Jacobins, was assassinated by the aristocrat Charlotte Corday, a Girondist sympathizer. Public indignation over this crime considerably broadened the Jacobin sphere of influence. On July 27 the Jacobin leader Maximilien Robespierre was added to the Committee of Public Safety and soon became its dominant member. Aided by Louis Saint-Just, Lazare Carnot, Georges Couthon (1755–94), and other prominent Jacobins, Robespierre instituted extreme policies to crush any possibility of counterrevolution. The powers of the committee were renewed monthly by the National Convention from April 1793 to July 1794, a period known in history as the Reign of Terror.

From a military standpoint, the position of the republic was extremely perilous. Enemy powers had resumed the offensive on all fronts. Mainz had been recaptured by the Prussians, Condé-Sur-L'Escaut and Valenciennes had fallen, and Toulon was under siege by the British. Royalist and Roman Catholic insurgents controlled much of the Vendée and Brittany. Caen, Lyons, Marseille, Bordeaux, and other important localities were in the hands of the Girondists. By a new conscription decree, issued on August 23, the entire able-bodied male population of France was made liable to conscription. Fourteen new armies, numbering about 750,000 men, were speedily organized, equipped, and rushed to the fronts. Along with these moves, the committee struck violently at internal opposition.

On October 16 Marie Antoinette was executed, and 21 prominent Girondists were beheaded on October 31. Beginning with these reprisals, thousands of Royalists, nonjuring priests, Girondists, and other elements charged with counterrevolutionary activities or sympathies were brought before revolutionary tribunals, convicted, and sent to the guillotine. Executions in Paris totaled 2639; more than half (1515) the victims perished during June and July, 1794. In many outlying departments, particularly the main centers of Royalist insurrection, even harsher treatment was meted out to traitors, real and suspect. The Nantes tribunal, headed by Jean

Baptiste Carrier (1756–94), which dealt most severely with those who aided the rebels in the Vendée, sent more than 8000 persons to the guillotine within three months. In all of France, revolutionary tribunals and commissions were responsible for the execution of almost 17,000 individuals. Including those who died in overcrowded, disease-ridden prisons and insurgents shot summarily on the field of battle, the victims of the Reign of Terror totaled approximately 40,000. All elements of the opposition suffered from the terror. Of those condemned by the revolutionary tribunals, approximately 8 percent were nobles, 6 percent were members of the clergy, 14 percent belonged to the middle class, and 70 percent were workers or peasants charged with draft dodging, desertion, hoarding, rebellion, and various other crimes. Of these social groupings, the clergy of the Roman Catholic church suffered proportionately the greatest loss. Anticlerical hatred found further expression in the abolition, in October 1793, of the Julian calendar, which was replaced by a Republican calendar. As a part of its revolutionary program, the Committee of Public Safety, under the leadership of Robespierre, attempted to remake France in accordance with its concepts of humanitarianism, social idealism, and patriotism. Striving to establish a "Republic of Virtue," the committee stressed devotion to the republic and to victory and instituted measures against corruption and hoarding. In addition, on Nov. 23, 1793, the Commune of Paris, in a measure soon copied by authorities elsewhere in France, closed all churches in the city and began actively to sponsor the revolutionary religion known as the Cult of Reason. Initiated at the insistence of the radical leader Pierre Gaspard Chaumette (1763–94) and his extremist colleagues (among them Hébert), this act accentuated growing differences between the centrist Jacobins, led by Robespierre, and the fanatical Hébertists, a powerful force in the convention and in the Parisian government.

The tide of battle against the allied coalition had turned, meanwhile, in favor of France. Initiating a succession of important victories, Gen. Jean Baptiste Jourdan (1762–1833) defeated the Austrians at Wattignies-La-Victoi on Oct. 16, 1793. By the end of the year, the invaders in the east had been driven across the Rhine, and Toulon had been liberated. Of equal significance, the Committee of Public Safety had largely crushed the insurrections of the Royalists and the Girondists.

Struggle for Power. The factional struggle between the Committee of Public Safety and the extreme group surrounding Hébert was resolved with the execution, on March 24, 1794, of Hébert and his principal associates. Within two weeks, Robespierre moved against the Dantonists, who had begun to demand peace and an end of the terror. Danton and his principal colleagues were

Louis XVI prepares to mount the steps to the guillotine on Jan. 21, 1793, after being convicted of treason by the National Convention.

beheaded on April 6. As a result of these purges and wholesale reprisals against supporters of the two factions, Robespierre lost the backing of many leading Jacobins, especially those who feared for their own safety. A number of military successes, notably that at Fleurus, Belgium, on June 26, which prepared the way for the second French conquest of the Austrian Netherlands, increased popular confidence in eventual triumph. As a consequence, doubt regarding the necessity of Robespierre's terroristic security measures became widespread. The general dissatisfaction with the leader of the Committee of Public Safety shortly developed into full-fledged conspiracy. Robespierre, Saint-Just, Couthon, and 98 of their followers were seized on July 27, the Ninth Thermidor by the Republican calendar, and beheaded the next day. The Ninth Thermidor is generally regarded as marking the end of the "Republic of Virtue."

Until the end of 1794, the National Convention was dominated by the group, called Thermidoreans, that overthrew Robespierre and ended the Reign of Terror. The Jacobin Clubs were closed throughout France, the revolutionary tribunals were abolished, and various extremist decrees, including one that had fixed wages and commodity prices, were repealed. After the recall to the convention of expelled Girondists and other rightist delegates, Thermidorean conservatism was transformed into sharp reaction. During the spring of 1795, bread riots and protest demonstrations spread from Paris to many sections of France. The outbreaks were suppressed, and severe reprisals were exacted against the Montagnards.

The morale of the French armies was undamaged by these events on the home front. During the winter of 1794-95, French forces, commanded by Gen. Charles Pichegru (1761-1804), overran the Austrian Netherlands, occupied the United Netherlands, which the victors reorganized as the Batavian Republic, and routed the allied armies of the Rhine. This sequence of reversals resulted in the disintegration of the anti-French coalition. On April 5, 1795, by the Treaty of Basel, Prussia and a number of allied Germanic states concluded peace with the French government. On July 22 Spain also withdrew from the war, leaving Great Britain, Sardinia, and Austria as the sole remaining belligerents. For nearly a year, however, a stalemate prevailed between France and these powers. The next phase of the struggle opened the Napoleonic Wars.

Peace was restored to the frontiers, and in July an invading army of émigrés was defeated in Brittany. The National Convention then quickly completed the draft of a new constitution. Formally approved on Aug. 22, 1795, the new basic law of France vested executive authority in a Directory, composed of five members. Legislative power was delegated to a bicameral legislature, consisting of the Council of Ancients, with 250 members, and the Council of the Five Hundred. The terms of one member of the Directory and a third of the legislature were renewable annually, beginning in May 1797, and the franchise was limited to taxpayers who could establish proof of one-year residence in their voting district. The new constitution contained additional evidence of retreat from Jacobin democracy. In its failure to provide a means of breaking deadlocks between the executive and legislative bodies, it laid the basis for constant intragovernmental rivalry for power, successive coups d'etat, and ineffectual administration of national affairs. The National Convention, however, still anticlerical and anti-Royalist despite its opposition to Jacobinism, created safeguards against the restoration of the monarchy. By a special decree, the first directors and two-thirds of the legislature were to be chosen from among the convention membership. Parisian Royalists, reacting violently to this decree, organized, on Oct. 5, 1795, an insurrection against the convention. The uprising was promptly quelled by troops under the command of Gen. Napoleon Bonaparte, a little-known leader of the revolutionary armies who later became Napoleon I, emperor of France. On October 26 the powers of the National Convention were terminated; on November 2 it was replaced by the government provided for under the new constitution.

Although a number of capable statesmen, including Charles Maurice de Talleyrand-Périgord and Joseph Fouché, gave distinguished service to the Directory, from the outset the government encountered a variety of difficulties. Many of these problems arose from the inherent structural faults of the governmental apparatus; others grew out of the economic and political dislocations brought on by the triumph of conservatism. The Directory inherited an acute financial crisis, which was aggravated by disastrous depreciation (about 99 percent) of the assignats. Although most of the Jacobin leaders were dead, transported, or in hiding, the spirit of Jacobinism still flourished among the lower classes. In the higher circles of society, Royalist agitators boldly campaigned for restoration. The bourgeois political groupings, determined to preserve their hard-won status as the masters of France, soon found it materially and politically profitable to direct the mass energies unleashed by the Revolution into militaristic channels. Old scores remained to be settled with the Holy Roman Empire. In addition, absolutism, by its nature a threat to the Revolution, still held sway over most of Europe.

The Rise of Napoleon. Less than five months after the Directory took office, it launched the initial phase (March 1796 to October 1797) of the Napoleonic Wars. The three coups d'état—on Sept. 4, 1797 (18 Fructidor), on May 11, 1798 (22 Floréal), and on June 18, 1799 (30 Prairial)—which occurred during this period, merely reflected regroupings of the bourgeois political factions. Military setbacks inflicted on the French armies in the summer of 1799, economic difficulties, and social unrest profoundly endangered bourgeois political supremacy in France. Attacks from the left culminated in a plot initiated by the radical agrarian reformer François Noël Babeuf who advocated equal distribution of land and income. This planned insurrection, called the Conspiracy of the Equals, did not materialize, however, as Babeuf was betrayed by an accomplice and executed on May 28, 1797 (8 Prairial). In the opinion of Lucien Bonaparte, president of the Council of the Five Hundred, of Fouché, minister of police, of Sieyès, then a member of the Directory, and of Talleyrand-Périgord and other political leaders, the crisis could be overcome only by drastic action. A coup d'état on Nov. 9–10, 1799 (18–19 Brumaire), destroyed the Directory. In these and subsequent events, which culminated on Dec.

Napoleon Bonaparte (from an 18th-cent. stamp).

24, 1799, in a new constitution and the Consulate, Gen. Napoleon Bonaparte, currently the popular idol of the recent campaigns, was a central figure. Vested with dictatorial power as First Consul, he rapidly shaped the revolutionary zeal and idealism of France to his own ends. The partial reversal of the national Revolution was compensated for, however, by its extension, during the Napoleonic conquests, to almost every corner of Europe.

Changes Resulting from the Revolution. One direct result of the French Revolution was the abolition of the absolute monarchy in France. The Revolution was also responsible for destroying the feudal privileges of the nobles. Serfdom was abolished, feudal dues and tithes were eliminated, the large feudal estates were broken up, and the principle of equal liability to taxation was introduced. With the sweeping redistribution of wealth and landholdings, France became the European nation with the largest proportion of small independent landowners. Other social and economic reforms initiated during this period included eliminating imprisonment for debt, introducing the metric system, and abolishing the rule of primogeniture in the inheritance of land.

During the Consulate, Napoleon Bonaparte carried through a series of reforms that were begun during the Revolution. He established the Bank of France, which has continued to function, more or less unchanged, up to the present time, as a quasi-independent national bank and as the agent of the French government for currency, public loans, and the deposit of public funds. The present highly centralized, uniform, secularly controlled French educational system was begun during the Reign of Terror and completed by Napoleon; the University of France and the Institut de France were organized. Teaching appointments, based on competitive examinations, were opened to all citizens regardless of birth or wealth. The reform and codification of the diverse provincial and local law, which culminated in the Napoleonic Code, reflected many of the principles and changes introduced during the Revolution: equality before the law, right of habeas corpus, and provisions for fair trial. Trial procedure provided for a board of judges and a jury for criminal cases; an accused person was considered innocent until proven guilty and was guaranteed counsel.

An additional area in which the Revolution played an important part was that of religion. Although not always practiced in the revolutionary period, the principles of freedom of religion and the press, as enunciated in the Declaration of the Rights of Man, resulted ultimately in freedom of conscience and in civil status for Protestants and Jews. The Revolution paved the way also for separation of church and state.

The more intangible results of the Revolution were embodied in its watchwords, "Liberty, Equality, Fraternity." These ideals became the platform of liberal reforms in France and Europe in the 19th century and remain the present-day passwords of democracy. Revisionist historians, however, attribute to the Revolution less laudable effects, such as the rise of the highly centralized (often totalitarian) state and mass warfare involving total wars of nations-in-arms.

For further information on historical figures, see biographies of those whose names are not followed by dates. REV. BY D.J.H.

For further information on this topic, see the Bibliography in volume 28, sections 906, 957.

FRENCH REVOLUTIONARY CALENDAR. *See* REPUBLICAN CALENDAR, FRENCH.

FRENCH SOMALILAND. *See* DJIBOUTI.

FRENCH SOUTHERN AND ANTARCTIC TERRITORIES, overseas territory of France (since 1955), comprising the Kerguelen and Crozet archipelagoes (*see* KERGUELEN ISLANDS) and the islands of Saint Paul and Amsterdam, all located in the S Indian Ocean, and Adélie Coast (or Adélie Land), a narrow segment of the Antarctic continent.

The Crozet Islands (area about 300 sq km/116 sq mi) is a group of 20 small mountainous islands. Little plant life occurs; animal life consists mainly of elephant seals and various species of birds. Amsterdam (60 sq km/23 sq mi) and St. Paul (7 sq km/3 sq mi) are both islands of volcanic origin, and the center of St. Paul is occupied by a large crater with hot springs. The climate is extremely humid and windy, but temperate. Vegetation is relatively abundant. Adélie Coast (area about 432,000 sq km/166,800 sq mi) lies on the Antarctic continent S of lat 66° S. The terrain consists of a glacier-covered plateau.

The only inhabitants of the territory are personnel of the permanent scientific stations located on Kerguelen, the Crozets, Amsterdam, and Adélie Coast. The territory is governed by an administrator and a consultative council, both appointed by the French government; the council meets in Paris twice a year.

Amsterdam and St. Paul islands were sighted in 1522 by the Magellan expedition. Kerguelen and the Crozets were discovered in 1772. An expedition under Capt. Jules Dumont d'Urville discovered Adélie Coast in 1840. Pop. (1989 est.) 210.

FRENCH SPOLIATION CLAIMS, demands made upon the U.S. government by American merchants for shipping losses incurred at the hands of the French between 1793 and 1800. The Amer-

ican merchant vessels were sunk by the French, after the U.S. had been charged by France with violating the terms of a commercial treaty concluded between the two countries in 1778, during the American Revolution. The spoliation claims were settled when the U.S. government effectuated the Louisiana Purchase in 1803 and, in addition, assumed the claims of the American merchants against the French to the amount of $3,750,000. Between 1800 and 1850, approximately 50 legislative bills to reimburse the claimants or their descendants came before Congress. Appropriations were voted on two occasions but were vetoed by Presidents James Polk and Franklin Pierce. Finally, in 1885, the claims were adjudicated and the descendants of the original claimants were awarded $4.8 million.

FRENCH SUDAN. *See* MALI, REPUBLIC OF.

FRENCH WEST AFRICA, former French possession in Africa, encompassing what are now the republics of Benin, Guinea, Ivory Coast, Mali, Mauritania, Niger, Senegal, and Upper Volta (qq.v.). The administrative capital was Dakar.

FRENCH WEST INDIES, also French Antilles, islands of the West Indies, in the Caribbean Sea, belonging to France. These islands, all of which are in the Lesser Antilles, are Martinique and Guadeloupe and the five small island dependencies of Guadeloupe: Marie-Galante, Îles des Saintes, Désirade, Saint-Barthelemy, and part of Saint Martin. During the 17th century the French, in competition with the Spanish, English, Dutch, and Danes, colonized several of the West Indian islands, including Saint Christopher, Saint Eustatius, Grenada, Dominica, Martinique, Guade-

A war memorial in Basse-Terre, Guadeloupe, in the French West Indies, is dedicated to the soldiers who died for France during the two world wars.
British West Indian Airways

loupe, St.-Barthélemy, St. Martin, and Hispaniola. Only Martinique, Guadeloupe, and the nearby small islands, settled in 1635, survived as the French West Indies. In 1775 they were established as separate colonies. In 1946 Guadeloupe and dependencies and Martinique were established as separate overseas departments of the Fourth French Republic. The two departments retained this status following the establishment of the Fifth French Republic late in 1958.

For further information on this topic, see the Bibliography in volume 28, section 1137.

FRENEAU, Philip Morin (1752–1832), American poet and journalist, known as the poet of the American Revolution, born in New York City, and educated at the College of New Jersey (now Princeton University). His reputation as a satirist was first achieved with a series of vitriolic poems attacking the British, written shortly after the outbreak of the Revolution. Early in 1780, Freneau took part in a privateering expedition to the West Indies. He was captured by the British and imprisoned aboard a ship in New York Harbor. The harsh treatment he received during his confinement provided him with material for *The British Prison-Ship, a Poem in Four Cantoes* (1781). While working in the post office at Philadelphia (1781–84), he continued to produce brilliant, satiric verse in the same patriotic vein.

Freneau spent the next six years at sea, and in 1791 Secretary of State Thomas Jefferson appointed him a translator. While serving in that capacity, Freneau founded and was editor of the *National Gazette,* a newspaper that gave forceful expression to the libertarian ideals of Jeffersonian democracy and that attacked the American statesman Alexander Hamilton and the Federalist party. Freneau retired in 1793 to his farm in New Jersey. Among his most famous individual poems are "The Wild Honeysuckle," "The House of Night," and "The Indian Burying Ground."

FREON. *See* FLUORINE.

FREQUENCY, term used in the physical sciences to denote the number of times that any regular recurring phenomenon occurs in a given period of time. The term has wide usage in mechanics, in the study of sound waves, and in all studies of radiation.

Oscillation (q.v.) may be of many kinds, ranging from the slow tremors of earthquakes, which may reach a maximum frequency of one every several seconds, to the rapid electromagnetic oscillations of gamma rays. In all forms of mechanical vibration a primary relationship exists between frequency and the physical dimensions of the vibrating object. Thus, the time required by a pendulum to make one complete swing is par-

FREQUENCY AND WAVELENGTH TABLE

Type of Oscillation	Approximate *f* or λ
Ocean tides	1 cycle in 12.5 hr
Tidal wave	1 cycle in 15 min
Earthquake wave in rock	1 cycle in 20 sec
Lowest note of organ	16 Hz
Lower limit of normal human ear	25 Hz
A above middle C	440 Hz
Upper limit of normal human ear	20 kHz
Ultrasonic range	20 kHz–1000 MHz
Long-wave radio stations	50–550 kHz
Broadcast stations	550–1700 kHz
High-frequency (HF) stations	10–100 m or 3000 kHz–30 MHz
Very-high-frequency (VHF) stations (FM and television bands)	1–10 m or 30–300 MHz
Ultrahigh-frequency band (microwave radar)	1–10 cm or 3000–30,000 MHz
Infrared rays	less than 1 mm to 7500 A
Visible red light	6500 A
Visible violet light	4000 A
Ultraviolet rays	3500–100 A
Soft (1250-V) X ray	10 A
Hard (125,000-V) X ray	0.1 A
Million-V gamma ray	0.0125 A
Billion-V cosmic ray	0.0000125 A

tially determined by the length of the pendulum; the frequency or speed of vibration of a string of a musical instrument is partially determined by the length of the string. In each instance, the shorter the object the higher is the frequency of vibration.

In wave motion of all kinds, the frequency of the wave usually is given in terms of the number of wave crests reaching a given point in a second. The velocity of the wave and its frequency and wavelength are interrelated. The wavelength (the distance between successive wave crests) is inversely proportional to frequency and directly proportional to velocity. In mathematical terms, this relationship is expressed by the equation $V = f\lambda$, where V is velocity, f is frequency, and λ is wavelength. From this equation any one of the three quantities can be found if the other two are known.

The common term for the expression of frequency is cycles per second (cps). The correct scientific term for 1 cps, however is hertz (Hz), in honor of the German physicist Heinrich Rudolf Hertz, who first demonstrated the nature of electromagnetic wave propagation. Kilohertz (kHz), or thousands of cycles per second, megahertz (MHz), or millions of cycles per second, and gigahertz (GHz), or billions of cycles per second, are employed in describing the frequencies of radio waves, for example, or the limits of response of an audio amplifier or other audio component. Radio waves and other types of electromagnetic radiation (q.v.) may be characterized by their wavelengths rather than their frequencies. Electromagnetic waves of extremely high frequencies, such as light and X rays, are usually described in terms of wavelength expressed in angstrom units (A; hundred-millionths of a cm). An electromagnetic wave of 1 A length has a frequency of about 3 billion GHz.

See SOUND; ULTRASONICS; WAVE MOTION.

For further information on this topic, see the Bibliography in volume 28, section 394.

FREQUENCY MODULATION, system of radio transmission in which the carrier wave is modulated so that its frequency varies with the modulating signal. Colloquially it is often called FM.

Electronic engineers knew for many years that a carrier wave could be frequency modulated; however, the first workable system for radio communication was described by the American inventor Edwin H. Armstrong in 1936. *See* RADIO.

Frequency modulation has several advantages over the system of amplitude modulation (AM) used in the alternate form of radio broadcasting. The most important of these advantages is that an FM system has greater freedom from interference and static. Various electrical disturbances, such as those caused by thunderstorms and automobile-ignition systems, are all amplitude modulated in character and are received as noise by AM receivers. A well-designed FM receiver is not sensitive to such disturbances when it is tuned to an FM signal of sufficient strength. FM broad-casting stations can be operated in the very-high-frequency bands at which AM interference is frequently severe. These bands, being relatively much wider than the standard broadcast band, have room for a greater number of broadcasting stations in a given area. The range of transmission on these bands is also limited so that stations operating on the same frequency can be located within a few hundred miles of one another without mutual interference.

These features, coupled with the comparatively low cost of equipment for an FM broadcasting station resulted in rapid growth in the years following World War II. Within three years after the close of the war 600 licensed FM stations were broadcasting in the U.S. By the end of the 1980s there were over 4000. Because of the crowding in the standard broadcast band and the inability of standard AM receivers to eliminate noise, the tonal fidelity of standard stations is purposely limited. FM does not have these drawbacks and therefore can be used to transmit musical programs that reproduce the original performance with a degree of fidelity that cannot be reached on AM bands. In 1961 the Federal Communications Commission authorized FM stereophonic broadcasting. A second sound channel is transmitted by a 38-kHz AM subcarrier signal added to the normal FM sig-

nal. Thereafter the FM band drew increasing numbers of listeners to popular as well as classical music, and commercial FM stations began to draw higher audience ratings than AM stations.

For further information on this topic, see the Bibliography in volume 28, section 547.

FRESCO (Ital., "fresh"), method, or art, of painting with watercolors on plaster, while the plaster is still wet, or fresh. The term is also applied to the painting executed in this manner. In the Renaissance this process was termed *true fresco* or *buon fresco* to differentiate it from *fresco secco*, the process of painting on dry plaster. The term *fresco* is also sometimes used, improperly, for tempera painting (q.v.), or distemper, in which watercolor is mixed with egg or other glutinous substances and applied directly on masonry.

Fresco Techniques. In executing fresco, the painter applies to the wet plaster surface a sketch, or cartoon (q.v.), of the painting. The outlines of the various figures and forms of the cartoon are then indented on the plaster surface with a pointed implement. After removal of the cartoon, color is applied, often aided by another sketch of the color scheme. As the plaster dries, the lime in the plaster reacts chemically with the carbon dioxide in the air to form calcium carbonate; this compound forms a film over the colors, which binds them to the plaster. This makes them part of its actual surface and also gives the colors an unusual clarity. The colors of a fresco are usually thin, transparent, and light, often with a chalky look. In the Renaissance, methods were found to give the colors somewhat more opacity.

In buon fresco, the painting must be done quickly and confined to essentials. The artist must know precisely how much watercolor the plaster will absorb. Too much paint causes the surface to become "rotten." Cutting away the defective portion, laying on fresh plaster, and repainting is then necessary.

In fresco secco, the dry plaster is rubbed with pumice stone to remove the crust, then washed with a thin mixture of water and lime. The colors are applied on this surface. The effect of fresco secco is inferior to true fresco; the colors are not as clear, and the painting is less durable.

History. Fresco painting was known to the ancient Egyptians, Cretans, and Greeks. The Romans also practiced fresco painting; extant examples have been found in Herculaneum and Pompeii. The early Christians (2d cent. AD) used frescoes to decorate the walls of catacombs, or underground burial vaults. Fresco painting was neglected until the late 13th century, when the art experienced a great revival in Italy, begun by the Florentine painters Cimabue and Giotto, who

A detail from The Tribute Money *(c. 1427), a famous fresco by Masaccio in the Brancacci Chapel of Santa Maria del Carmine, Florence.*   Scala Fine Arts

painted numerous fine examples in churches in Assisi, Florence, and Pisa. In the 15th century the art flourished in Florence, notably in the work of Masaccio, Benozzo Gozzoli, Pinturicchio, and Ghirlandaio. Fresco painting reached its peak in the 16th century, with the supreme achievements of Raphael in the Vatican Palace and with Michelangelo's *Last Judgment* and *Genesis* frescoes in the Vatican's Sistine Chapel.

Fresco painting was widely practiced in Europe in the 18th century, with nobility of style replaced by elegance and illusionistic effects. The outstanding fresco painters in this period were Giovanni Battista Tiepolo in Italy and Germany and Jean Honoré Fragonard and François Boucher in France. In the 19th century the art was revived, largely for the embellishment of public buildings. The most important center for fresco painting in the 20th century has been Mexico. Two Mexican painters in particular, Diego Rivera and José Clemente Orozco, created outstanding frescoes in Mexican government buildings.

See also PAINTING and individual biographies of all artists mentioned.

For further information on this topic, see the Bibliography in volume 28, sections 652, 656.

FRESCOBALDI, Girolamo (1583–1643), Italian organist and composer of the late Renaissance, who greatly influenced the development of baroque music. Born and trained in Ferrara, he was organist at Saint Peter's in Rome from 1608 until his death, except for six years as court organist in Florence. His importance can be noted in the shifting harmonies, daring chromaticism, and subtle dissonances of his toccatas, fantasias, ricercari, and other keyboard forms and in his ingenious variations. His liturgical collection *Fiori musicale* (Musical Flowers, 1635) so deeply impressed J. S. Bach that he copied it out in full.

FRESHWATER LIFE, the plants, animals, and other life forms adapted to live and reproduce in the flowing waters of streams and rivers and in the still waters of lakes and ponds.

Lotic Habitats. Flowing-water (lotic) habitats include rapid headwater streams and brooks, slower midvalley streams with pools and riffles, slow-moving rivers of the floodplain zone, and the estuaries where rivers flow into the sea (*see* ESTUARY).

Species inhabiting fast-flowing streams possess adaptations that enable them to maintain their position in the current. Some, such as the brook trout and certain mayfly nymphs, are streamlined, reducing resistance to the current. Other organisms, such as mayfly and stone fly nymphs, have flattened bodies, enabling them to hide beneath and cling to the undersurfaces of stone. Still others, such as blackfly larvae, attach themselves to rocks with hooks and suckers; certain caddis fly larvae build cases of small pebbles, which they anchor to rocks. Among plants, water moss clings to rocks by strong holdfasts and aligns with the current. Some algae grow tightly to rocks and are covered with a gelatinous coating to reduce water friction.

As the current slows downstream, organisms of fast water are replaced by bass, sunfish, and free-swimming aquatic insects, which are adapted to slower water and warmer temperatures. Plant plankton may develop, and rooted aquatics appear along shore.

Most streams depend upon adjoining terrestrial ecosystems (see ECOLOGY) for their primary energy source. Leaves and wood from streamside vegetation, once they have been softened by bacteria and fungi, are consumed by a feeding group of aquatic insects called shredders. Particles of organic matter, along with bits of algae loosened from rocks by another feeding group, the grazers or scrapers, are picked up from the current by collectors. One collector is the caddis fly, *Hydropsyche,* which spins an underwater web. Feeding on all of these are predaceous fishes and insects.

Lentic Habitats. Still-water (lentic) ecosystems consist of a shallow-water zone along the shore; an upper open-water zone that extends to the depth at which light is insufficient for photosyn-

thesis; a deep-water zone on which the warmer, less dense water floats; and a bottom zone of soft mud and silt, where decomposition takes place.

The shallow-water zone is dominated by submerged, floating, and emergent vegetation (*see* MARSHLAND), among which life is abundant. Living on the underside of a green blanket of floating duckweed are desmids, protozoans, minute crustaceans, hydras, and snails. Dragonfly larvae, diving beetles, pickerel, and sunfish find food and protection in the beds of vegetation. Nesting and feeding in cattails and other emergent vegetation are red-winged and yellow-headed blackbirds, marsh wrens, muskrats, and water voles.

In open-water zones, plant plankton and filamentous green algae supply most of the energy for lentic ecosystems. In this food-rich layer, animal plankton—rotifers, copepods, and cladocerans—graze on plant plankton. Large-mouthed bass and pike also inhabit this zone.

In the deep-water zone, life is influenced by temperature and the amount of dissolved oxygen. In cold lakes where oxygen is sufficient, lake trout and plankton inhabit deep water. In the bottom zone, mud and overlying water often lack oxygen due to decomposing organic matter. Life on the bottom includes burrowing mayflies, midge larvae, and protozoans, all feeding on organic matter and able to exist with little oxygen.

R.L.S.

For further information on this topic, see the Bibliography in volume 28, section 445.

FRESNEL, Augustin Jean (1788–1827), French physicist, born in Broglie, Eure-et-Loir, and educated at Caen and at the École Polytechnique in Paris. As an adherent of the wave theory of light,

A fishing spider, Dolomedes triton, *walks on the surface of a pool but submerges to hunt prey.* Joe McDonald–Bruce Coleman, Inc.

he made numerous experiments in the interference of light. Fresnel was the first to demonstrate that two beams of light polarized in different planes do not exhibit interference effects. From this experiment he correctly deduced that the wave motion of light is transverse, rather than longitudinal (like that of sound) as had been previously believed. The first to produce circularly polarized light, he also worked out a number of basic optical formulas, including those for reflection, refraction, double refraction, and the polarization of light reflected from a transparent substance. Fresnel's work on optical effects caused by the motion of objects was important in the later development of the theory of relativity. In the field of applied optics, Fresnel designed the type of compound lens, often called a Fresnel lens, that is used to produce parallel beams of light from lighthouses and in a type of spotlight frequently used in theatrical lighting. Fresnel's scientific work was known only to a small group of scientists during his lifetime, and some of his papers were not published until after his death. He was a member of the French Academy of Sciences and of the Royal Society of London.

FRESNO, city, seat of Fresno Co., central California; inc. 1885. It is a major marketing, shipping, and processing center of the irrigated San Joaquin Valley, one of the country's richest farming areas. Cotton, cattle, poultry, dairy items, and a wide variety of fruits and vegetables are produced nearby. Manufactures of the city include raisins and other dried fruits, wine, cotton goods, glass, carpets, forest products, and machinery. Government service jobs have increased the economic stability of the city. Fresno Pacific College (1944), California State University-Fresno (1911), and a junior college are here. The city, which also has a symphony orchestra, several museums, and a zoo, is a gateway to Sierra National Forest and Yosemite, Sequoia, and Kings Canyon national parks. Fresno was founded in 1872 on the site of a railroad telegraph office. The community was laid out in 1873 and was settled by much of the population of adjacent Millerton, which had been bypassed by the railroad. The city's name, Spanish for "ash tree," refers to the white ash trees in the area. Pop. (1980) 218,202; (1990) 354,202.

FREUD, Anna (1895–1982), Austrian-British psychoanalyst and daughter of Sigmund Freud, noted especially for her work in the psychoanalysis of children. Born in Vienna, she became a children's teacher and also worked closely with her father in the development of psychoanalytic theory. She and her father escaped to London from the Nazis in 1938. Anna Freud's work stressed the function of the ego in personality development and emphasized the use of defense mechanisms such as repression. She founded the Hampstead Child Therapy Course and Clinic in London in 1947 and served as its director after 1952. The author of numerous scientific books and papers, she also helped found the annual periodical *Psychoanalytic Study of the Child,* in 1945.

FREUD, Sigmund (1856–1939), Austrian physician, neurologist, and founder of psychoanalysis.

Freud was born in Freiberg (now Příbor, Czechoslovakia), on May 6, 1856, and educated at the University of Vienna. When he was three years old his family, fleeing from the anti-Semitic riots then raging in Freiberg, moved to Leipzig. Shortly thereafter, the family settled in Vienna, where Freud remained for most of his life.

Although Freud's ambition from childhood had been a career in law, he decided to become a medical student shortly before he entered the University of Vienna in 1873. Inspired by the scientific investigations of the German poet Goethe, Freud was driven by an intense desire to study natural science and to solve some of the challenging problems confronting contemporary scientists.

In his third year at the university Freud began research work on the central nervous system in

Sigmund Freud　　　　**Wide World Photos**

The consulting room of Sigmund Freud in Vienna.
Edmund Engelman

the physiological laboratory under the direction of the German physician Ernst Wilhelm von Brücke (1819–92). Neurological research was so engrossing that Freud neglected the prescribed courses and as a result remained in medical school three years longer than was required normally to qualify as a physician. In 1881, after completing a year of compulsory military service, he received his medical degree. Unwilling to give up his experimental work, however, he remained at the university as a demonstrator in the physiological laboratory. In 1883, at Brücke's urging, he reluctantly abandoned theoretical research to gain practical experience.

Freud spent three years at the General Hospital of Vienna, devoting himself successively to psychiatry, dermatology, and nervous diseases. In 1885, following his appointment as a lecturer in neuropathology at the University of Vienna, he left his post at the hospital. Later the same year he was awarded a government grant enabling him to spend 19 weeks in Paris as a student of the French neurologist Jean Charcot. Charcot, who was the director of the clinic at the mental hospital, the Salpêtrière, was then treating nervous disorders by the use of hypnotic suggestion. Freud's studies under Charcot, which centered largely on hysteria, influenced him greatly in channeling his interests to psychopathology.

In 1886 Freud established a private practice in Vienna specializing in nervous disease. He met with violent opposition from the Viennese medical profession because of his strong support of Charcot's unorthodox views on hysteria and hypnotherapy. The resentment he incurred was to delay any acceptance of his subsequent findings on the origin of neurosis.

The Beginning of Psychoanalysis. Freud's first published work, *On Aphasia,* appeared in 1891; it was a study of the neurological disorder in which the ability to pronounce words or to name common objects is lost as a result of organic brain disease. His final work in neurology, an article, "Infantile Cerebral Paralysis," was written in 1897 for an encyclopedia only at the insistence of the editor, since by this time Freud was occupied largely with psychological rather than physiological explanations for mental disorders. His subsequent writings were devoted entirely to that field, which he had named *psychoanalysis* in 1896.

Freud's new orientation was heralded by his collaborative work on hysteria with the Viennese physician Josef Breuer (1842–1925). The work was presented in 1893 in a preliminary paper and two years later in an expanded form under the title *Studies on Hysteria.* In this work the symptoms of hysteria were ascribed to manifestations of undischarged emotional energy associated with forgotten psychic traumas. The therapeutic procedure involved the use of a hypnotic state in which the patient was led to recall and reenact the traumatic experience, thus discharging by catharsis the emotions causing the symptoms. The publication of this work marked the beginning of psychoanalytic theory formulated on the basis of clinical observations.

During the period from 1895 to 1900 Freud developed many of the concepts that were later incorporated into psychoanalytic practice and doctrine. Soon after publishing the studies on hysteria he abandoned the use of hypnosis as a cathartic procedure and substituted the investigation of the patient's spontaneous flow of thoughts, called free association, to reveal the unconscious mental processes at the root of the neurotic disturbance.

In his clinical observations Freud found evidence for the mental mechanisms of repression and resistance. He described repression as a device operating unconsciously to make the memory of painful or threatening events inaccessible to the conscious mind. Resistance is defined as the unconscious defense against awareness of repressed experiences in order to avoid the resulting anxiety. He traced the operation of unconscious processes, using the free associations of the patient to guide him in the interpretation of dreams and slips of speech. Dream analysis led to his discoveries of infantile sexuality and of the so-called Oedipus complex, which constitutes the erotic attachment of the child for the parent of the opposite sex, together with hostile feelings toward the other parent. In these years he also developed the theory of transference, the process by which emotional attitudes, established originally toward parental figures in childhood, are transferred in later life to others. The end of this period was marked by the appearance of Freud's most important work, *The Interpretation of Dreams* (1900). Here Freud analyzed many of his own dreams recorded in the 3-year period of his self-analysis, begun in 1897. This work expounds all the fundamental concepts underlying psychoanalytic technique and doctrine.

In 1902 Freud was appointed a full professor at the University of Vienna. This honor was granted not in recognition of his contributions but as a result of the efforts of a highly influential patient. The medical world still regarded his work with hostility, and his next writings, *The Psychopathology of Everyday Life* (1904) and *Three Contributions to the Sexual Theory* (1905), only increased this antagonism. As a result Freud continued to work virtually alone in what he termed "splendid isolation."

By 1906, however, a small number of pupils and followers had gathered around Freud, including the Austrian psychiatrists William Stekel

(1868–1940) and Alfred Adler, the Austrian psychologist Otto Rank, the American psychiatrist Abraham Brill, and the Swiss psychiatrists Eugen Bleuler and Carl Jung. Other notable associates, who joined the circle in 1908, were the Hungarian psychiatrist Sándor Ferenczi (1873–1933) and the British psychiatrist Ernest Jones (1879–1958). **International Acceptance.** Increasing recognition of the psychoanalytic movement made possible the formation in 1910 of a worldwide organization called the International Psychoanalytic Association. As the movement spread, gaining new adherents through Europe and the U.S., Freud was troubled by the dissension that arose among members of his original circle. Most disturbing were the defections from the group of Adler and Jung, each of whom developed a different theoretical basis for disagreement with Freud's emphasis on the sexual origin of neurosis. Freud met these setbacks by developing further his basic concepts and by elaborating his own views in many publications and lectures.

After the onset of World War I Freud devoted little time to clinical observation and concentrated on the application of his theories to the interpretation of religion, mythology, art, and literature. In 1923 he was stricken with cancer of the jaw, which necessitated constant, painful treatment in addition to many surgical operations. Despite his physical suffering he continued his literary activity for the next 16 years, writing mostly on cultural and philosophical problems.

When the Germans occupied Austria in 1938, Freud, a Jew, was persuaded by friends to escape with his family to England. He died in London on Sept. 23, 1939.

Freud created an entirely new approach to the understanding of human personality by his demonstration of the existence and force of the unconscious. In addition, he founded a new medical discipline and formulated basic therapeutic procedures that in modified form are applied widely in the present-day treatment of neuroses and psychoses. Although never accorded full recognition during his lifetime, Freud is generally acknowledged as one of the great creative minds of modern times.

Among his other works are *Totem and Taboo* (1913), *Ego and the Id* (1923), *New Introductory Lectures on Psychoanalysis* (1933), and *Moses and Monotheism* (1939).

See also PSYCHOANALYSIS; PSYCHOTHERAPY.

W.C.M. & P.G.U.

For further information on this person, see the section Biographies in the Bibliography in volume 28.

FREY *or* **FREYR,** in Norse mythology, son of the fertility god Njord. Frey was the god of fruitfulness, prosperity, and peace and the bestower of sunlight and rain. He wakened the earth from the long sleep of winter, and prayers for a bountiful harvest were addressed to him. His sister was Freya, and his wife, Gerd. Frey was the patron god of Sweden; his chief shrine was at Uppsala.

FREYA *or* **FREYJA,** in Norse mythology, goddess of love, fertility, and beauty, sometimes identified as the goddess of battle and death. Her father was Njord, a fertility god. Blond, blue-eyed, and beautiful, Freya traveled on a golden-bristled boar or in a chariot drawn by cats. She resided in the celestial realm of Folkvang, where it was her privilege to receive half of all the warriors slain in battle; the god Odin received the other half at Valhalla. In Germany, Freya was sometimes identified with Frigg, the wife of Odin.

FRIAR (Lat. *frater,* "brother"), term applied to members of certain religious orders who practice the principles of monastic life and devote themselves to the service of humanity in the secular world. Originally, their regulations forbade the holding either of community or personal property, and the resulting dependence of friars on voluntary contributions in order to live caused them to be known as mendicant orders. The founders of the orders used the term *friar* to designate members; St. Francis of Assisi called his followers Friars Minor, and St. Dominic used the name Friars Preachers. The larger orders were given popular names, derived usually from the color or other distinguishing marks of their habits, such as Black Friars (Dominicans), Gray Friars

Henry Clay Frick

(Franciscans), and White Friars (Carmelites). Friars differed from monks in that the monk was attached to a specific community within which he led a cloistered life, having no direct contact with the secular world. The friar, on the other hand, belonged to no particular monastic house but to a general order, and worked as an individual in the secular world. Thus, friar and monk are not synonymous terms, even though in popular usage monk is often used as a generic term for all members of religious orders.

FRIBOURG (Ger. *Freiburg*), city, W Switzerland, capital of Fribourg Canton, near Bern. Located on a rocky peninsula bounded by the Sarine R., it is known for the medieval appearance of the old part of the city. Major manufactures include processed food (especially Gruyère cheese and chocolate), metals, machinery, electrical equipment, and chemicals. Landmarks include a 12th-century church and a 13th-century cathedral. The University of Fribourg (1889) is also here. The city was founded in 1157. It became part of the Swiss Confederation in 1481 and was a stronghold of Roman Catholicism during the Counter Reformation (16th cent.). Pop. (1986 est.) 34,422.

FRICK, Henry Clay (1849–1919), American industrialist and philanthropist, born in Westmoreland Co., Pa. In 1871 he organized the H. C. Frick Coke Co., which became one of the largest coke-producing firms in the world. The financial panic of 1873 enabled Frick to acquire the properties of his rivals and so to arrange an alliance, on very favorable terms, with the steel firm of Carnegie Brothers. He was chairman of the board of directors of the Carnegie firm from 1889 to 1900, and during this period his actions in handling the Homestead (Pa.) strike of 1892 led to an attempt at his assassination by the anarchist Alexander Berkman (1870–1936). Frick was a director of many companies, and in 1901 he took a prominent part in the negotiations that resulted in the formation of the United States Steel Corp. On his death he left land and an endowment to provide a park in Pittsburgh, Pa., and bequeathed his house, with its notable collection of paintings, to the city of New York. The bequest, now known as the Frick Collection, is associated with the Frick Art Reference Library.

FRICTION, in mechanics, resistance to the sliding, rolling, or flowing motion of a body in relation to another body with which it is in contact (*see* MECHANICS).

In any solid the molecules display internal friction. This form of friction is the force that causes any oscillating object, such as a piano string or a tuning fork, to stop oscillating. Internal friction in liquids and gases is called viscosity.

External friction is of two kinds, sliding friction and rolling friction. In sliding friction, the resistance is caused by the interference of irregularities on the two surfaces. In rolling friction the resistance is caused by the interference of small deformations or indentations formed as one surface rolls over another. In both forms of friction molecular attraction between the two surfaces causes some resistance. The frictional resistance in either case is directly proportional to the force pressing the two objects against each other. Friction between any two surfaces is measured in terms of the coefficient of friction, the ratio between the force required to move two surfaces in contact with each other and the force holding the two surfaces together. If a 50-lb (23-kg) weight is resting on a flat surface and it requires a force of 10 lb (5 kg) to move the weight along the surface, the coefficient of friction between the weight and the surface is 10 divided by 50, or 0.2. The coefficient of friction between well-oiled metallic surfaces is about 0.01 to 0.05, and between ball bearings and a bearing face in rolling contact about 0.002. The friction between two objects is at maximum just before they begin to move in relation to each other and less when the objects are in motion. The maximum value of friction is called static friction, or friction of rest, and the value of friction between moving objects, kinetic friction or friction of motion. Motion between two bodies is discontinuous, and kinetic friction may be regarded as a series of static frictions.

The angle of friction is the angle to which a surface must be tilted before an object placed on the surface will slide steadily down the surface. This angle measures the effectiveness of friction in overcoming the force of gravity that tends to make the object slide down the tilted surface.

For further information on this topic, see the Bibliography in volume 28, section 392.

FRIDAY (A.S. *frīgedaeg;* from O.H.G. *Frīa,* a goddess; O.E. *daeg,* "day"), English name of the sixth day of the week. The day was held sacred to Venus, the goddess of love, by the Romans, who called it *dies veneris* ("day of Venus"). In the Romance languages the name of the day is derived from the Latin, as in the French *vendredi,* the Italian *venerdi,* and the Spanish *viernes.* Germanic peoples held the day sacred to the Norse goddess of love, Frigg, or Frija. The Germanic languages, like English, use variations of the Old High German *frīatag* ("day of Frija") to designate the day. The Hebrew name for Friday, *yom shishi,* means "sixth day." Among many Slavic peoples, however, Friday is not regarded as the sixth day of the week, as evidenced by its Russian name,

pyatneetza, or "fifth day." Friday is the Muslim Sabbath and is the day for religious gatherings. The day was chosen by the Prophet Muhammad in commemoration of the creation of man on the "sixth day" of creation and to differentiate his followers from Christians and Jews.

In the Christian religion the day is consecrated to the memory of the crucifixion of Christ. The Greek theologian Clement of Alexandria and other early writers indicate that from the early days of Christianity, Friday was observed by fasting and prayer. In the Greek Orthodox church, as was formerly the practice in the Roman Catholic church, Friday is a day of abstinence from the eating of meat, except when it coincides with a major feast day, such as Christmas.

Friday has long been regarded as an unlucky day. This superstition may be due to the occurrence of the crucifixion of Christ on that day, and may have been strengthened by the fact that Friday was for many years the day of execution of criminals, commonly called "hangman's day."

FRIDLEY, city, Anoka Co., E Minnesota, on the Mississippi R., a suburb of Minneapolis; inc. as a city 1957. Major manufactures include naval ordnance, pumps, electrical equipment, machine tools, medical supplies, generators, processed food, and cosmetics. In 1847 the area was settled by Maj. Abram M. Fridley (1817?–88), an agent of the Hudson's Bay Co. Pop. (1980) 30,228; (1990) 28,335.

FRIEDAN, Betty Naomi (1921–), American feminist leader and author, born in Peoria, Ill., and educated at Smith College. Her book *The Feminine Mystique* (1963) challenged several long-established American attitudes, especially the notion that women could find fulfillment only as wives and mothers. She was a founder (1966) and the first president (1966–70) of the National Organization for Women (NOW), devoted to the fight for equal rights for women. Among her other publications are *It Changed My Life* (1976) and *The Second Stage* (1981).

FRIEDLAND, BATTLE OF (June 14, 1807), victory of Napoleon over the Russians in the War of the Third Coalition. On June 13, Napoleon, intending to capture Königsberg (now Kaliningrad, Russia), sent Marshal Jean Lannes (1769–1809) with 12,000 men to occupy the village of Friedland (Pravdinsk) southeast of the city. There Lannes met a Russian force of 46,000 under Gen. L. L. von Bennigsen (1745–1826), which he held off until reinforced by Napoleon on the afternoon of June 14. The French then attacked with 65,000 men, breaking the Russian lines. Nearly 20,000 Russians were cut down by artillery fire in the village, and thousands more drowned trying to escape across the Alle (Lava) River. Napoleon then occupied Königsberg, and Alexander I of Russia made peace at Tilsit in July.

FRIEDMAN, Milton (1912–   ), American economist and Nobel laureate.

Friedman was born in New York City and educated at Rutgers University and the University of Chicago. He worked as an economist with various federal agencies in Washington, D.C., from 1935 to 1940 and from 1941 to 1943. In 1946 he joined the economics department at the University of Chicago. He is considered a leading protagonist of the economic theory that free market forces, rather than increased government intervention, can most effectively produce a balanced and noninflationary rate of economic growth. He is the outstanding exponent of the policy that the Federal Reserve System can best promote economic stability by increasing the supply of money at a fairly fixed rate instead of sharply expanding or contracting it.

Friedman was awarded the 1976 Nobel Prize in economics for "his achievements in the fields of consumption analysis, monetary history and theory, and for his demonstration of the complexity of stabilization policy." Among his books are *Capitalism and Freedom* (1962), *A Monetary History of the United States, 1867–1960* (1963), *Dollars and Deficits* (1968), *A Theoretical Framework for Monetary Analysis* (1971), and *Free to Choose* (1980), the latter written with his wife, Rose Friedman.

FRIEDRICH, Caspar David (1774–1840), outstanding 19th-century German romantic painter, whose awesome landscapes and seascapes are not only meticulous observations of nature but are also allegories.

Friedrich was born on Sept. 5, 1774, in Greifswald and was largely self-taught. In 1798 he settled in Dresden, where he became a member of an artistic and literary circle imbued with the ideals of the romantic movement. His early drawings—precisely outlined in pencil or sepia—explored motifs recurrent throughout his work: rocky beaches, flat, barren plains, infinite mountain ranges, and trees reaching toward the sky. Later, his work began to reflect more of his emotional response to natural scenery. He began to paint in oils in 1807; one of his first canvases, *The Cross in the Mountains* (c. 1807, Gemäldegalerie, Dresden), is representative of his mature style. A bold break from traditional religious painting, this work is almost pure landscape; the figure of the crucified Christ, seen from behind and silhouetted against a mountain sunset, is almost lost in the natural setting. According to Friedrich's own writings, all the elements in the composition have symbolic meanings. The mountains are allegories of faith; the rays of the setting sun symbolize the end of the pre-Christian world; and the fir trees stand for hope. Friedrich's cold, acid colors, clear lighting, and his sharp contours heighten the feeling of melancholy, isolation, and human powerlessness against the ominous forces of nature expressed in his paintings. As a faculty member of the Dresden Academy, Friedrich influenced later German romantic painters. Although his reputation declined after his death—on May 7, 1840, in Dresden—20th-century viewers are fascinated by his imagery. *See also* ROMANTICISM: *Art*.

FRIEDRICHSHAFEN, city, SW Germany, in Baden-Württemberg, on the Lake of Constance (Bodensee). It is a rail junction and port, a resort, and an industrial center. Manufactures include aircraft, electrical equipment, and furniture. Friedrichshafen was formed in 1811 with the merger of Buchhorn (founded in the 9th cent. and declared a free city of the Holy Roman Empire in 1275) and the monastery and village of Hofen. The city is the site of the former Zeppelin airship works and was the starting point of several famous flights of the *Graf Zeppelin* airship under the command of Hugo Eckener (1868–1954). The city was badly damaged during World War II. Pop. (1989 est.) 52,300.

FRIENDS, SOCIETY OF, in full Religious Society of Friends, designation of a body of Christians more commonly known as Quakers. Their fundamental belief is that divine revelation is immediate and individual; all persons may perceive the word of God in their soul, and Friends endeavor to heed it. Terming such revelation the "inward light," the "Christ within," or the "inner light," the first Friends identified this spirit with the Christ of history. They rejected a formal creed, worshiped on the basis of silence, and regarded every participant as a potential vessel for the word of God, instead of relying upon a special, paid clergy set apart from the rest.

Beliefs. Quakerism emphasizes human goodness because of a belief that something of God exists in everyone. At the same time, however, it recognizes the presence of human evil and works to eradicate as much of it as possible. Quakerism is a way of life; Friends place great emphasis upon living in accord with Christian principles. Truth and sincerity are Quaker bywords; thus, Quaker merchants refuse to bargain, for bargaining implies that truth is flexible. Emulating Christ, the Friends attempt to avoid luxury and emphasize simplicity in dress, manners, and speech. Until late in the 19th century, they retained certain forms of speech known as plain speech, which employed "thee" as opposed to the more formal "you"; this usage indicated the leveling of social classes and the spirit of fellowship integral to Quaker teaching.

In the administration and privileges of the society, no distinction between the sexes is made. Membership qualifications are based on moral and religious grounds and on the readiness of the candidate to realize and accept the obligations of membership. Meetings for worship are held regularly, usually once or twice a week, and are intended to help members to feel God's presence as a guiding spirit in their lives. In these meetings the members measure their insights and beliefs against those of the meeting as a whole. Because the religion of the Quakers was founded as a completely spiritual belief requiring no physical manifestation, the meetings have traditionally had no prearranged program, sermon, liturgy, or outward rites. Today, however, more than half of the Friends in the U.S. use paid ministers and conduct meetings for worship in a programmed or semiprogrammed manner.

In both the unprogrammed and programmed meetings members accept a great deal of responsibility. A group called Worship and Ministry, or Ministry and Oversight, accepts considerable responsibility for the spiritual life of the meeting.

Overseers undertake to provide pastoral care for the member or share in that care when a regular pastor is employed. The religious discipline and administration of the society are regulated by periodic meetings known as Meetings for Business. One or more congregations constitute a Monthly Meeting, one or more Monthly Meetings form a Quarterly Meeting, and the Quarterly Meetings within a stated geographical area form a Yearly Meeting of the Religious Society of Friends. The decisions of the Yearly Meeting are the highest authority for all doctrinal or administrative questions raised in any subsidiary meeting within its jurisdiction. Usually no voting takes place in Quaker meetings; members seek to discover the will of God by deliberation concerning any matter at hand. As an integral part of Quaker doctrine, at meetings members are regularly and formally queried on their adherence to Quaker principles. These queries relate to such matters as the proper education of their children, the use of intoxicants, care of the needy, and, on a broader scale, racial and religious toleration and the treatment of all offenders in a spirit of love rather than with the object of punishment. Most American groups of Friends are represented by the American Friends Service Committee (AFSC), founded in 1917. Originally established to handle

The Bradford Friends meetinghouse (built 1765) in Marshallton, Chester Co., Pa.

many of their philanthropic activities, the organization today is primarily concerned with creating a society in which violence need not exist.

Origins. The Society of Friends may be traced to the many Protestant bodies that appeared in Europe during the Reformation. These groups, stressing an individual approach to religion, strict discipline, and the rejection of an authoritarian church, formed one expression of the religious temper of 17th-century England. Many doctrines of the Society of Friends were taken from those of earlier religious groups, particularly those of the Anabaptists and Independents, who believed in lay leadership, independent congregations, and complete separation of church and state. The society, however, unlike many of its predecessors, did not begin as a formal religious organization. Originally, the Friends were the followers of George Fox, an English lay preacher who, about 1647, began to preach the doctrine of "Christ within"; this concept later developed as the idea of the "inner light." Although Fox did not intend to establish a separate religious body, his followers soon began to group together into the semblance of an organization, calling themselves by such names as Children of Light, Friends of Truth, and, eventually, Society of Friends. In reference to their agitated movements before moments of divine revelation, they were popularly called Quakers. The first complete exposition of the doctrine of "inner light" was written by the Scottish Quaker Robert Barclay in *An Apology for the True Christian Divinity, as the Same Is Held Forth and Preached by the People Called in Scorn Quakers* (1678), considered the greatest Quaker theological work.

The Friends were persecuted from the time of their inception as a group. They interpreted the words of Christ in the Scriptures literally, particularly, "Do not swear at all" (Matt. 5:34), and "Do not resist one who is evil" (Matt. 5:39). They refused, therefore, to take oaths; they preached against war, even to resist attack; and they often found it necessary to oppose the authority of church or state. Because they rejected any organized church, they would not pay tithes to the Church of England. Moreover, they met publicly for worship, a contravention of the Conventicle Act of 1664, which forbade meetings for worship other than that of the Church of England. Nevertheless, thousands of people, some on the continent of Europe and in America as well as in the British Isles, were attracted by teachings of the Friends.

Friends began to immigrate to the American colonies in the 1660s. They settled particularly in New Jersey, where they purchased land in 1675,

George Fox formulated in his Paper of Advice *(1668) ideas that led to the organization of the Society of Friends.*　　　Bettmann Archive

and in the Pennsylvania colony, which was granted to William Penn in 1681. By 1684, approximately 7000 Friends had settled in Pennsylvania. By the early 18th century, Quaker meetings were being held in every colony except Connecticut and South Carolina. The Quakers were at first continuously persecuted, especially in Massachusetts, but not in Rhode Island, which had been founded in a spirit of religious toleration. Later, they became prominent in colonial life, particularly in Pennsylvania and Rhode Island. During the 18th century the American Friends were pioneers in social reform; they were friends of the Indians, and as early as 1688 some protested officially against slavery in the colonies. By 1787 no member of the society was a slave owner. Many of the Quakers who had immigrated to southern colonies joined the westward migrations into the Northwest Territory because they would not live in a slave-owning society.

During the 19th century differences of opinion arose among the Friends over doctrine. About 1827, the American Quaker minister Elias Hicks became involved in a schism by questioning the authenticity and divine authority of the Bible and the historical Christ; many Friends seceded with Hicks and were known as Hicksites. This schism alarmed the rest of the society, who became known as Orthodox Friends, and a countermovement was begun to relax the formality and discipline of the society, with a view to making Quakerism more evangelical. The evangelical movement, led by the British Quaker philanthropist Joseph John Gurney (1788–1847), aroused considerable opposition, particularly in the U.S., and another schism resulted among the Orthodox Friends. A new sect, the orthodox conservative Friends, called Wilburites after their leader John Wilbur (1774–1856), was founded to emphasize the strict Quakerism of the 17th century. It is very small today. The general result of these modifications, both those dealing with doctrine and those pertaining to the relations of Quakers to the world in general, was a new spirit among all the Friends. Most abandoned their strange dress and speech and their hostility to such worldly pursuits as the arts and literature.

Numerically, the Friends have always been a relatively small group. In the early 1980s world membership totaled about 200,000, distributed in about 30 countries. The greatest number of Friends is in the U.S., where, according to the latest available statistics, the society had about 1100 congregations with about 117,000 members. The Yearly Meetings in Africa, with about 39,000 members, and in Great Britain and Ireland, with about 21,000 members, are the next largest groups. Other groups are located in Central America, Australia, Canada, and New Zealand. The Friends World Committee for Consultation is the international organization of the society.

E.B.B.

For further information on this topic, see the Bibliography in volume 28, sections 105, 110.

FRIES, John (1750?–1818), American insurgent leader, born in Montgomery Co., Pa. He fought in the American Revolution and later became an auctioneer. In 1798 a federal property tax was voted by Congress in anticipation of a possible war with France. The following year, after the quota for Pennsylvania had been fixed and federal officers began to collect the tax, Fries led many Pennsylvania Germans in armed rebellion against the assessors and collectors. Although no shot was fired and no one was hurt, President John Adams eventually called out the militia, and Fries was captured along with several others; he was convicted of treason and condemned to death. In 1800, however, the president pardoned him and issued a general amnesty to all concerned in Fries's Rebellion.

FRIGATE BIRD, common name for large ocean birds of the family Fregatidae, order Pelecaniformes, noted for possessing a larger wingspan in proportion to their weight than any other bird. Frigate birds, also called man-o'-war birds, live on fish that they steal from other birds; they also catch flying fish and snatch dead fish from the surface of the ocean. Only five living species are known. The magnificent frigate bird, *Fregata magnificens,* which has a wingspan of about 1.8 to 2.1 m (about 6 to 7 ft), breeds on coastal shores and islets in warm areas of the Atlantic Ocean and Caribbean Sea, and in the eastern Pacific from Mexico to Ecuador. The adult male is glossy black on its back and duller black on its lower parts. During the mating season the male develops a deep red or brilliant orange color on its expansible throat pouch. The female differs in having the sides and breast white; immature birds have a white head. The average length of *F. magnificens* is 102 cm (40 in), of which 43 cm (17 in) is tail. A slightly smaller but similar frigate bird is *F. aquila,* which is found

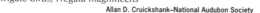

A group of magnificent frigate birds, Fregata magnificens

only on Ascension Island in the South Atlantic Ocean; *F. minor* is found in tropical areas around the world; *F. andrewsii* is found on several islands in the Indian Ocean; and *F. ariel,* the smallest species of frigate bird, is found in the Atlantic, Pacific, and Indian oceans, in the southern hemisphere.

FRIGG or **FRIGGA,** in Norse mythology, goddess of the sky and wife of Odin, the chief of the gods. She was worshiped as the protector of married love and housewives. A bunch of keys was her symbol. Frigg had two sons, Balder (q.v.), the god of light, and Hoder, the blind god of darkness, who killed Balder with a mistletoe sprig. Frigg's name survives in the English word *Friday* (Frigg's day). In German mythology, Frigg was sometimes identified with Freya, the goddess of love.

FRIML, (Charles) Rudolf (1879–1972), American composer, born in Prague. He studied at the Prague Conservatory under the Czech composers Josef Jiránek (1855–1940) and Antonín Dvořák. Friml became the accompanist for the noted violinist Jan Kubelik (1880–1940), with whom he toured Europe and the U.S. After 1906 Friml resided permanently in the U.S., becoming a citizen in 1924. He was one of the leading composers of operettas (a total of 33), musical comedies, and revues of his time. Among his more successful works are *The Firefly* (1912), *High Jinks* (1913), *Katinka* (1916), the *Ziegfeld Follies* (1921, 1923, 1924, 1925), *Rose Marie* (1923), *The Vagabond King* (1925), *The Three Musketeers* (1928), and *Annina* (1934). Among his well-known songs are "Rose Marie," "Indian Love Call," and "Song of the Vagabonds." Friml composed chamber music and music for films.

FRISCH, Frankie, real name FRANCIS FRISCH (1898–1973), American baseball player, born in New York City, and educated at Fordham University, where he was a noted athlete. He played baseball for Fordham and other amateur teams, and in 1919, without minor league experience, became a second baseman for the New York Giants. In 1926 he became second baseman for the Saint Louis Cardinals. Frisch, known as the "Fordham Flash," remained with the Cardinals until 1939, serving part of that period as manager of the team; from 1940 to 1946 he was manager of the Pittsburgh Pirates. In 1947–48 he was a radiobroadcaster for the games of the New York Giants, and in 1948 he joined the Giants again as coach. He also managed the Chicago Cubs from 1949 to 1951. Frisch played in more than 2300 games, had more than 2800 hits, and his lifetime batting average was .316. In 1947 Frisch was inducted into the Baseball Hall of Fame.

FRISCH, Karl von (1886–1982), Austrian zoologist and Nobel laureate, whose pioneering work on the chemical and visual perception of fish and bees led him to discover how honeybees orient and communicate. Born in Vienna on Nov. 20, 1886, Frisch received a Ph.D. in 1910 from the University of Munich. In his early work, Frisch demonstrated that fishes, thought to be unable to see colors, not only could distinguish many different colors but were also highly sensitive to sounds. After 1919, when he began his research on honeybees, he found that their sense of smell was close to that of humans, and that they could distinguish all flower colors except red.

After World War II, when Frisch returned from the University of Graz in Austria to the University of Munich, he discovered that bees, through their perception of polarized light, were able to use the sun as a compass, and that even on overcast days they did not lose their sense of orientation. Using marked bees, he discovered that on returning to the hive a bee would perform a circling dance if it had found food less than a certain distance away. If the bee found food at a greater distance, it would perform a waggle dance (*see* HONEYBEE).

In 1958 Frisch retired from the University of Munich, and in 1973 he shared the Nobel Prize in physiology or medicine with the Dutchman Nikolaas Tinbergen and the Austrian Konrad Lorenz, who were both cited for their individual studies in animal behavior. He died in Munich, June 12, 1982.

FRISCH, Max Rudolf (1911–1991), Swiss playwright and novelist, one of the most prominent contemporary German-language writers. Born May 15, 1911, in Zürich, Frisch studied at the University of Zürich and then worked as a journalist and an architect.

Among Frisch's more notable plays is *The Chinese Wall* (1946; trans. 1961), an experimental farce that mixes ancient with modern settings and characters and addresses the problem of human self-destructiveness. Next appeared *Als der Krieg zu Ende war* (When the War Was Over, 1949). Perhaps his best-known plays are *Andorra* (1961; trans. 1962), a tragic parable on the effects of anti-Semitism, and the farce *The Firebugs* (1958; trans. 1962).

I'm Not Stiller (1954; trans. 1958), a novel about an intellectual struggling with his identity, is regarded by some as Frisch's finest work. His other novels include *Homo Faber* (1957; trans. 1959), *A Wilderness of Mirrors* (1964; trans. 1965), *Man in the Holocene* (1979; trans. 1980), and *Bluebeard* (1982; trans. 1983). Frisch's diaries have also been published, as *Sketchbook 1946–1949*

(1965; trans. 1977) and *Sketchbook 1966–1971* (1972; trans. 1974).

Frisch died in Zurich, April 4, 1991.

FRISCH, Ragnar (1895–1973), Norwegian economist and Nobel laureate, born in Oslo, and educated at the University of Oslo. From 1931 to 1965 Frisch was a professor of social economy and statistics and director of the Institute for Social Economy at Oslo. In the 1930s, he was a pioneer in the new science of econometrics, the use of mathematical formulas based on statistics in solving economic problems. In 1930, as visiting professor at Yale University, he founded the Econometrics Society, and he was the editor of the society journal *Econometrica* until 1955. For this work Frisch shared the first Nobel Prize in economics (1969) with the Dutch economist Jan Tinbergen.

FRISCHES HAFF (Low Ger., "freshwater bay"), also Vistula Lagoon (Pol. *Wiślany Zalew*), large inlet of the Gulf of Danzig (an arm of the Baltic Sea), N Poland and SW Kaliningrad Oblast, Russia. In 1946, following World War II and the liquidation of the state of Prussia, part of the coastline contiguous to Frisches Haff was ceded to Poland and the remainder was included in the USSR. Frisches Haff is 84 km (52 mi) long, varies from 6 to 19 km (4 to 12 mi) in width, and has an area of about 860 sq km (about 330 sq mi).

FRISIA, low-lying region, NW Europe, encompassing the Frisian Islands, most of Friesland Province of the Netherlands, and adjacent coastal areas of Germany. The region, which was settled by the Frisians in prehistoric times, has historically shared a common culture and language. The area is known for its dairy farming.

FRISIAN ISLANDS, group of islands, North Sea, off the coasts of the Netherlands and Germany, and extending N from the mouth of the Elbe R. along the Jutland Peninsula to Denmark. The group comprises the West, East, and North Frisian Islands. The islands are low-lying and are separated from the mainland by shallows. They mark the outer edge of the former continental coastline. Dikes and artificial embankments have been erected to protect the islands against incursions of the sea. Despite these efforts, parts of the Frisian Islands are slowly disappearing because of the constant marine erosion. The chief occupations of the Frisians are fishing, raising sheep and cattle, and farming (mainly potatoes). Summer resort activity is important on many of the islands.

The West Frisian islands belong to the Netherlands and include Texel (q.v.), Terschelling, Vlieland, Ameland, Schiermonnikoog, Rottumerplaat, and Rottumeroog.

The East Frisian Islands belong to Germany and include Borkum, Baltrum, Langeoog, Norderney, Spiekeroog, Memmert, Juist, and Wangerooge.

The North Frisian Islands, with the exception of the Danish islands of Fanø and Rømø, also belong to Germany. The group includes Sylt, Nordstrand, Pellworm, Föhr, and Helgoland (q.v.), as well as Fanø and Rømø.

FRISIAN LANGUAGE, language of the historical Frisian people, now an official language in the Dutch province of Friesland, with dialects still spoken on the Frisian Islands, and in a few German villages. Frisian, most closely related to English, belongs to the Anglo-Frisian group in the western branch of the Germanic languages (q.v.). Similar Frisian and English words include *boi* (boy), *tolve* (twelve), and *hy* (he). Frisian was once the prominent tongue along the North Sea coast and on nearby islands, from the present Dutch-Belgian border to the modern German-Danish border. Since the 16th century, Frisian has gradually been replaced by Dutch and Low German, but it was revived in the 20th century. *See also* FRISIA; FRISIAN LITERATURE.

FRISIAN LITERATURE, writings in the Frisian language (q.v.), spoken in the Dutch province of Friesland and the Frisian Islands. No document in Frisian can be dated earlier than the 13th century, and little was written in the language between the 18th and 20th centuries. The oldest writings extant are collections of laws, Germanic sagas, and verses. New West Frisian literature dates from the 17th century; the first notable work in that language was a comic dialogue, *Wouter en Tialle* (1609). The two greatest figures in Frisian literature are the poet Gijsbert Japiks (1603–66) and the writer Jan Althuysen (1715–63).

FRITCHIE, Barbara (also Frietchie), legendary American heroine, who reputedly defied the Confederate troops under Stonewall Jackson as they advanced through Frederick, Md., by waving the Stars and Stripes from an upper window of her home. This story, now considered apocryphal, is the subject of a popular patriotic poem, "Barbara Frietchie" (1864), by John Greenleaf Whittier, and a play, *Barbara Frietchie* (1899), by Clyde Fitch.

FRIULI-VENEZIA GIULIA, region, NE Italy, bordered on the N by Austria, on the E by Yugoslavia, on the S by the Gulf of Venice (an arm of the Adriatic Sea), and on the W by the Italian region of Veneto. The region is divided into Gorizia, Pordenone, Trieste, and Udine provinces. The N portion of the region is mountainous, with some elevations exceeding 2740 m (8990 ft); it receives the highest rainfall in Italy. This area, the Friuli section, is known for its trade in ham and dairy products. Other industries include livestock raising, lead and zinc mining, and some lumbering. The Tagliamento R. runs in a N-S direction through the center of the region into the Adriatic Sea. In the S a low fertile coastal plain supports subsistence agriculture. The chief products are wheat, corn and other vegetables, and fruits, particularly grapes for wine. Along the coast fishing is important. Tobacco is produced in the SE around Trieste, the regional capital and one of Italy's chief ports. Both Trieste and Monfalcone contain shipyards. Other leading cities are Udine and Gorizia. Industries include the manufacture of textiles, chemicals, cutlery, and machinery.

In the 2d century BC the area that is now Friuli-Venezia Giulia was occupied by the Romans, who called it the Julian region. Later it came under the control of the Byzantines, the Venetians, and the Habsburgs. In the 18th century the Habsburgs made Trieste a free port. In 1866 Udine, or the W portion of Friuli, became part of the kingdom of Italy; E Friuli was joined to Italy after World War I, becoming part of the province of Venezia Giulia. After World War II Udine Province and Gorizia, a portion of Venezia Giulia, were combined to form the modern region of Friuli-Venezia Giulia. In 1954 the N half of the former Free Territory of Trieste, including the city of Trieste, was assigned to Italy by the UN and incorporated into the region of Friuli-Venezia Giulia. Pordenone Province was established in 1968. Area, 7846 sq km (3029 sq mi); pop. (1988 est.) 1,210,200.

FROBISHER, Sir Martin (1535?–94), English navigator, one of the earliest explorers to seek the Northwest Passage to the Orient, and among the greatest of Elizabethan seamen.

Frobisher was born about 1535 in Altofts, Yorkshire, and spent his early years in London after his father's death. He was apprenticed as a cabin boy in 1544, his skills and daring as a seaman brought him a steady rise in rank, and by 1565 he had become a captain.

In 1576 Frobisher was placed in command of an expedition to the New World, the first attempt by an Englishman to search for the Northwest Passage. On June 7, 1576, he set sail with three small ships, the *Gabriel,* the *Michael,* and a pinnace that was lost in a storm. The *Michael* deserted soon afterward and the *Gabriel* continued alone, sighting the mouth of what is now known as Frobisher Bay on Baffin Island—and mistaking it for the entrance to the Northwest Passage—a little more than a month after starting out on the voyage. On his return to England Frobisher brought back a few pieces of "black earth," which were rumored to contain gold. In 1577 he returned to Canada with another fleet outfitted

by Queen Elizabeth I of England. Both this expedition and a subsequent voyage were unsuccessful in finding valuable ore or in establishing colonies, but Frobisher continued in the favor of the queen.

In 1585, as vice admiral on the *Primrose,* he participated in an expedition to the West Indies to raid its Spanish colonies, led by the English seaman and adventurer Sir Francis Drake. In 1588 Frobisher was knighted for his valiant role in the defeat of the Spanish Armada. In 1591 he settled in Yorkshire, but soon tired of country life, and in 1592 he commanded a fleet outfitted by Sir Walter Raleigh to harry Spanish merchant ships bringing gold from Panama. In November 1594, engaged in the relief of Fort Crozon near Brest, France, against Spanish forces, Frobisher was mortally wounded and died on Nov. 22, 1594, in Plymouth, England.

FROBISHER BAY, inlet, North Atlantic Ocean, cutting deeply into SE Baffin Island, Northwest Territories. The bay is about 240 km (about 149 mi) long and up to 64 km (40 mi) wide and has exceptionally high tides. The town of Frobisher Bay (pop., 1981, 2333) is near the head of the bay. Discovered (1576) by Sir Martin Frobisher, the bay is named for him.

FRÖDING, Gustaf (1860–1911), Swedish poet, whose work lent vigor to a late 19th-century renaissance of Swedish poetry and exerted a strong influence on Swedish poets. He was born in Värmland and educated at the University of Uppsala. In his first collection of poetry, *Guitar and Concertina* (1891; trans. 1925), which contains many droll poems about provincial life in Värmland, he made frequent use of the local dialect and often captured the rhythm of its folk songs and dances. This book was followed by *New Poems* (1894; trans. 1925) and other collections.

Fröding suffered several nervous breakdowns early in his career. After 1894, although he was either insane or on the verge of insanity, he wrote his finest work. The masterly use of language, the lyricism, and the irony that he had displayed even before his illness were enriched by a more somber tone and a new prophetic quality. Fröding's later collections of poetry deal with profound religious and moral questions and are pervaded by his belief that all things on earth serve a divine purpose. From 1898 to 1905 Fröding was confined to a mental hospital in Uppsala, but he continued to write.

FROEBEL, Friedrich (1782–1852), German educator, the originator of the kindergarten.

Born April 21, 1782, in Oberweissbach, Froebel was largely self-educated, but was able to study for a few years at the universities of Jena,

Göttingen, and Berlin. Froebel tried a number of vocations, including forestry, surveying, and architecture, before discovering his true vocation, teaching. He became an instructor at the Frankfurt Model School in Frankfurt am Main, and from 1806 to 1810 he worked and studied with the noted Swiss educational reformer Johann Pestalozzi at Yverdon, Switzerland. Froebel's teaching career was interrupted from 1813 to 1815 by service in the Prussian army and by work as an assistant in the Mineralogical Museum of the University of Berlin.

In 1816 Froebel founded at Griesheim a school called the Universal German Educational Institute, and in 1817 he moved the school to Keilhau near Rudolstadt. At the institute, Froebel developed ideas for the education of preschool children aged three to seven. These ideas culminated in his establishing at Blankenburg, Thuringia, in 1837, the first institution exclusively for the education of such children; for this school he coined the term *Kindergarten,* meaning "children's garden."

In spite of interest in Froebel's work by progressive educators, his ideas, which stressed encouraging the natural growth of a child through action or play, were too novel to be readily accepted by the public, and for a time he found it financially difficult to carry on his school. In addition, he was suspected of sharing the radical political and social views of his nephew Julius Froebel (1805–93), a professor at Zürich, and in 1851 the Prussian government banned all kindergartens in Prussia; the ban was not removed until 1860. Froebel lived and worked in Marienthal from 1850 until his death on June 21, 1852. His disciples, especially the Baroness von Marenholtz-Bülow (1810–93), caused kindergartens to be established throughout western Europe and the U.S. in the 1850s and in Germany after 1860.

Froebel is considered one of the greatest contributors of the 19th-century to the science of education. The institution of the kindergarten has spread over the entire world. Among his principal writings are *The Education of Man* (1826; trans. 1885) and *Mother Play and Nursery Songs* (1843; trans. 1906).

See also KINDERGARTEN.

FROG, amphibian (q.v.) of the order Anura or Salientia, usually characterized by absence of a tail in the adult, smooth skin, external eardrums situated behind the eyes, long hind-legs, and, in most species, partly or completely webbed feet.

Physiology and Behavior. The frog's skeleton is characterized by a meeting and joining of the two halves of the shoulder girdle in a line along the middle of the underside. During the course of its growth, a frog characteristically goes through a true metamorphosis (q.v.), starting with a fishlike larval stage and ending with the adult frog stage.

The eggs hatch in water into short-bodied larvae during early spring or summer. At this stage they are called tadpoles and have gills and a tail. The tadpole feeds on algae and other vegetation; as it matures, the tail is absorbed, the gills disappear, lungs develop, the limbs appear as buds and grow to their final size, and the adult emerges from the water onto the land.

Various frog species frequent a variety of habitats, but most prefer moist regions. Although they are air breathers, frogs can stay under water for long periods, and they absorb water through the skin. Some frogs are adapted for tree living (*see* TREE FROG). Others are permanently aquatic and have fully webbed toes; still others spend most of their lives in underground burrows, coming up only to feed or to breed. The frog hibernates after burrowing deep in mud. Some kinds, such as Australian frogs, estivate (*see* HIBERNATION) after burying themselves in sand and clay.

Frogs subsist principally on insects, worms, spiders, and centipedes. The capture of prey is facilitated by the frog's tongue, which is covered with a sticky substance, and which is attached at its base to the front of the mouth instead of the rear, leaving the end of the organ free to dart out and seize its prey. Aquatic frogs sometimes eat other frogs, tadpoles, and small fish. The bullfrog (q.v.) eats objects as large as mice or newborn water snakes. Occasionally a frog, like some snakes and birds, seizes living food too large to swallow all at once and will leave the prey sticking partly out of its mouth, ingesting it gradually or even choking on it or regurgitating the food.

Classification. The scientific classification of frogs is complex, having changed over the centuries. The Greek word for frog, *batrachus,* was given originally to all amphibia, which were known as batrachia. Amphibia replaced batrachia as a term for the class, and the latter came to designate an order of the class. Batrachia, however, was subsequently replaced by the current name for the order.

Most herpetologists subdivide the order into 16 families, based primarily on skeleton and tooth differences. Toads belong to the family Bufonidae, a nearly cosmopolitan family native to all continents except Australia and Antarctica. One large species, the marine toad, *Bufo marinus,* is native to tropical America, but has been introduced successfully into many warm areas of the world, including Australia, to help control in-

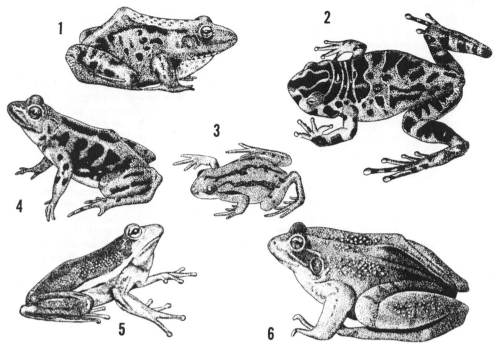

Various frogs: (1) gopher frog; (2) barking frog; (3) swamp cricket frog; (4) mink frog; (5) green tree frog; (6) Oregon red-legged frog.

sect pests. It secretes, however, a substance poisonous to small animals.

Another large and nearly cosmopolitan family is Ranidae, comprising the true frogs, many species of which are well known. This family includes the largest of all frogs, the African giant frog, *Rana goliath*, which grows as long as 66 cm (26 in) and weighs as much as 4.5 kg (10 lb). The largest true frog in the U.S. is the bullfrog, *R. catesbeiana*, which weighs up to 0.5 kg (1.2 lb) and has a total length of 46 cm (18 in) from the snout to the tip of the toes. One of the commonest North American species is the leopard frog, *R. pipiens*, which is easily recognized by the numerous black, often light-edged spots on the back and legs. Another North American species, the wood frog, *R. sylvatica*, is small and reddish-brown, with two black bands on the head giving it the appearance of a mask. Unlike most other true frogs, the wood frog wanders considerable distances away from water. The green frog, *R. clamitans*, is another common species in North America; it has a wide color range, some being predominantly brown. The pickerel frog, *R. palustris*, looks much like the leopard frog but has squarish, dark marks arranged in two defined rows down the back. This frog inhabits cool, woodland streams or bogs. Two well-known European frogs of this group are the common frog, *R. temporaria*, which resembles the North American wood frog, and the edible frog, *R. esculenta*.

A large and interesting family of frogs with world-wide distribution is the Hylidae. This family includes the tree frogs, which have expanded, adhesive disks at the ends of the toes, permitting them to climb the smooth surfaces of trees. Some members of the Asian family Rhacophoridae have even more specialized structures for arboreal life; their feet are webbed with fanlike structures that enable them to jump safely to the ground from considerable heights; they are sometimes known as flying frogs, although they do not actually fly. One of the most unusual frogs is *Astylosternus robustus*, called the hairy frog because of the hairlike dermal projections that develop on the side of the body and legs of the male during the breeding season.

The frog aids humans in many ways. It controls insect pests in the woods, farm, and garden, and several species have been introduced to various parts of the world to aid humans in their struggle with undesirable insects. From earliest times the frog has been widely used as food. Many efforts have been made to rear frogs for the market, but all frogs eaten today are taken from their natural habitat. The frog is an important experimental animal in research and medical laboratories, the males of many species being used in present-day diagnostic tests for human pregnancy.

For further information on this topic, see the Bibliography in volume 28, sections 445, 470.

FROGMOUTH, common name for any of 12 species of wide-mouthed birds constituting the family Podargidae, of the goatsucker (q.v.) order, Caprimulgiformes. Frogmouths are found in southern India, Indonesia, the Philippines, and Australia. They range from 23 to 58 cm (from 9 to 23 in) long and have large heads, large eyes, and broad, hooked bills. Frogmouths feed on large insects and small vertebrates at night. During the day they sit quietly in an erect position, and, with their mottled plumage in various shades of brown and gray, they resemble a tree stump or broken branch. One or two eggs are laid, and both parents take care of the young.

FROHMAN, name of two American theatrical managers and producers who were brothers.

Daniel Frohman (1851–1940), born in Sandusky, Ohio. He entered the theatrical business about 1871 as a road-company manager. Starting his career as a theater manager in 1879, he supervised various theaters in New York City, including the Madison Square Theater, the Fifth Avenue Theater, and the Lyceum Theater. At the Lyceum he organized the Daniel Frohman Stock Company and presented the popular team of E. H. Sothern (1859–1933) and Julia Marlowe (1866–1950) in Shakespearian productions. Frohman was often involved in theatrical enterprises with his brother Charles and was a member of the "theatrical trust," organized by the latter.

Charles Frohman (1860–1915), born in Sandusky, Ohio. His first theatrical experience was as a box-office clerk in a theater in Brooklyn, N.Y.; later he became a road-company manager. His first successful production was *Shenandoah* by the American playwright Bronson Crocker Howard (1842–1908) in 1889. The following year he assembled the Charles Frohman Stock Company at the Empire Theatre, New York City, which included the playwright David Belasco as stage manager. In 1895–96 Frohman organized the syndicate, sometimes known as the "theatrical trust," that owned or controlled a large number of theaters in the U.S. Among the actors who were at one time under his management were John Drew, Ethel Barrymore, Maude Adams, Otis Skinner (1858–1942), and Billie Burke (1886–1970). He produced the plays of many of the leading dramatists of the day, including several by James Matthew Barrie in London (1903–8) and those by John Galsworthy, George Bernard Shaw, and Harley Granville-Barker. Frohman died in the

sinking of the liner *Lusitania* by German torpedoes during World War I.

FROISSART, Jean (1333?–1410?), French chronicler, born in Valenciennes. In 1361 he went to England, where he was appointed secretary to Philippa, queen consort of England (1314?–69), the wife of King Edward III. Froissart visited Scotland in 1365, later journeying to Brussels and traveling widely in France and Italy. Throughout his travels he devoted himself to gathering information about contemporary events. About 1372 he entered the church and was appointed priest of the village of Lestines in the diocese of Liège.

During the next 12 years Froissart composed a verse romance entitled *Méliador* and worked on the *Chronique de France, d'Angleterre, d'Ecosse et d'Espagne,* which was translated by the English diplomat and man of letters John Bourchier, 2d Baron Berners (1467–1533), as *Chronicle of France, England, Scotland, and Spain* (1523–25). Resuming his travels about 1386, Froissart visited England and many parts of the Continent, continuing to expand the *Chronicle.* The death of Richard II, king of England, is the last notable event recorded in the work.

In the *Chronicle,* Froissart described many of the significant events of the last three-quarters of the 14th century; he is especially noted for his accounts of the Hundred Years' War between England and France. Imbued with the ideals of chivalry, he concerned himself exclusively with the activities of the nobility and the military.

FROMM, Erich (1900–80), American psychoanalyst, best known for his application of psychoanalytic theory to social and cultural problems. He was born in Frankfurt am Main, Germany, and educated at the universities of Heidelberg and Munich and at the Psychoanalytic Institute in

Erich Fromm　　　　　　　　　　　Harper & Row

Berlin. He immigrated to the U.S. in 1934 and subsequently became a citizen.

Fromm was recognized as an important leader of contemporary psychoanalytic thought (*see* PSYCHOANALYSIS). According to his views, specific personality types are related to specific socioeconomic patterns. He broke away from biologically oriented theories to see humans as products of their culture. He also felt that attempts should be made to create harmony between the drives of the individual and the society in which the individual lives. Fromm's many publications include *Escape from Freedom* (1941), *Man for Himself* (1947), *The Forgotten Language* (1951), *The Sane Society* (1955), *The Art of Loving* (1956), *Sigmund Freud's Mission* (1956), *Beyond the Chains of Illusion* (1962), *The Heart of Man* (1964), and *The Anatomy of Human Destructiveness* (1973).

FRONDE, series of revolts against the French government between 1648 and 1653, during the minority of King Louis XIV. Begun as a protest by the Parlement of Paris and its supporters against the heavy taxation policies of the king's chief minister, Cardinal Jules Mazarin, the Fronde evolved into armed insurrection. Order was restored, but a second phase began with a struggle for power by the nobles against the Crown. Their unsuccessful venture marked the last insurrection of the French nobility against the monarchy and a strengthening of the royal power.

FRONT. *See* METEOROLOGY.

FRONTENAC, Louis de Buade, Comte de Palluau et de (1620–98), French soldier and colonial governor of New France (Canada). Between 1635 and 1672 he was intermittently engaged in military service in the Low Countries and in Italy. He was appointed governor of the French possessions in North America in 1672. In the first years of his administration he attempted to give the people of Québec greater political freedom by establishing a municipal government of three estates — clergy, nobility, and people. This measure ran counter to the French policy of strict royal autocracy; consequently, the powers of the sovereign council were extended and the office of intendant was reinstated to limit the authority of the governor. Frontenac subsequently disagreed with the intendant, who claimed precedence, and with the clergy, who tried to subordinate the state to the church. Despite the restrictions placed on him, the governor was able to open additional North American territory to France by encouraging the explorations of Louis Jolliet, Jacques Marquette, and Robert Cavalier, sieur de La Salle and by establishing forts and trading posts in the new areas. He was notably skilled and tactful in his relations with the Indians and managed to maintain peace and amity with the powerful Iroquois. In 1682 strife between the governor and the sovereign council, which continually supported the clergy, caused both the intendant and Frontenac to be recalled to France. In 1689, however, when the Iroquois were menacing the inhabitants of New France, Frontenac, then aged 69, was again sent to North America. He was able to subdue the Indians and successfully governed until his death.

FROST. *See* DEW.

FROST, Robert Lee (1874–1963), American poet, who was one of the major American poets of the 20th century.

Frost was born March 26, 1874, in San Francisco and educated at Dartmouth College and Harvard University. In 1885 his father died, and his mother moved with the family to Lawrence, Mass. After graduation from high school, Frost sporadically attended college and earned his living by working variously as a bobbin boy in a wool mill, a shoemaker, a country schoolteacher, the editor of a rural newspaper, and a farmer. He also wrote poetry, but he had little success in having his poems published.

In 1912 Frost sold his farm, gave up a teaching post at the New Hampshire State Normal School, and went to live in England. There he met such

Robert Frost   UPI

established poets as Edward Thomas (1878–1917), Rupert Brooke, and Lascelles Abercrombie (1881–1938), who became his friends and did much to aid his literary career. With their help, Frost published his first two volumes of poetry, a group of lyrics entitled *A Boy's Will* (1913) and a series of dramatic monologues called *North of Boston* (1914). These works won him immediate recognition, and in 1915 Frost returned to the U.S. to find that his fame had preceded him. Thereafter he continued to write poetry with increasing success, while living on farms in Vermont and New Hampshire and teaching literature at Amherst College, the University of Michigan, Harvard University, and Dartmouth College. Among the volumes of poetry he produced are *Mountain Interval* (1916), *West-Running Brook* (1928), *A Further Range* (1936), *A Masque of Reason* (1945), and *In the Clearing* (1962). Frost was awarded the Pulitzer Prize for poetry four times (1924, 1931, 1937, 1943); in 1961, at the inauguration of John F. Kennedy, he became the first poet to read a poem at a presidential inauguration. He died Jan. 29, 1963, in Boston.

Frost's poetry is based mainly upon the life and scenery of rural New England, and the language of his verse reflects the compact idiom of that region. Although he concentrates on ordinary subject matter, his emotional range is wide and deep, and he is capable of shifting in the same poem from a tone of humorous banter to the passionate expression of tragic experience. The underlying philosophy of Frost's poetry is rooted in traditional New England individualism, and his work shows his strong sympathy for the values of early American society.

FROSTBITE, injury to the skin and sometimes the deeper tissues of the body due to freezing or formation of ice crystals in the tissue cells. Frostbite usually develops when the air temperature is below $-12°$ C (10° F), but may occur at a temperature nearer the freezing point (0° C/32° F) when other elements, such as high winds, dampness, or general chilling of the body, are present. The onset of frostbite causes little discomfort and may not be noticed by the victim because the cold has an anesthetic effect on the tissues.

Frostbite develops in three stages: a reddening of the skin, formation of blisters, and finally death of some of the skin cells and the underlying tissues. Clots often form in the blood vessels. Mild cases of frostbite often result in chilblain; more severe cases may result in a dangerous gangrene. Free circulation of the blood inhibits the onset of frostbite.

The parts of the body most often affected are the hands, feet (especially the heels and toes), ears, cheeks, chin, and nose. The recommended first-aid treatment for frostbite is the immediate application of warmth to the injured parts; if possible the affected areas should be soaked in warm water. Vigorous massage should be avoided as it would cause further harm to the damaged tissues. Heparin or some other agent that prevents clotting of the blood is administered in severe cases.

FROUDE, James Anthony (1818–94), British historian, born in Dartington, England, and educated at Westminster School, London, and Oriel College, University of Oxford. He was elected a fellow of Exeter College in 1842 and two or three years later was ordained a deacon. After meeting the Scottish writer Thomas Carlyle, who strongly influenced him and whose literary executor he later became, Froude's religious views began to change; he subsequently manifested a strong anticlerical attitude that culminated in his withdrawal from the ministry in 1872. In 1892, in recognition of his brilliant historical writings, which, like Carlyle's, emphasized the role of the individual in history, Froude was appointed professor of modern history at Oxford. As literary executor for Carlyle, Froude prepared for publication Carlyle's *Reminiscences* (1881) and *Letters and Memorials of Jane Welsh Carlyle* (1883). Froude was the author of two important biographies of his friend: *Thomas Carlyle, a History of the First Forty Years of His Life* (1882) and *Thomas Carlyle, a History of His Life in London* (1884). His great work, however, is his *History of England from the Fall of Wolsey to the Defeat of the Spanish Armada* (12 vol., 1856–70).

FRUCTOSE, also levulose or fruit sugar, monosaccharide with the formula $C_6H_{12}O_6$ that occurs with glucose (q.v.) in sweet fruits and fruit juices. It is formed along with glucose in the splitting of sucrose (q.v.) and is produced in the hydrolysis of various carbohydrates, but it is best prepared by treating inulin with dilute acid. Fructose is crystallized with difficulty; the crystals melt in the range from 102° to 104° C (216° to 219° F). It is levorotatory; that is, solutions of fructose rotate the plane of polarized light to the left. Fructose is fermented by yeast to yield ethyl alcohol and carbon dioxide. *See* SUGAR; SUGAR METABOLISM.

FRUIT, mature ovary in flowering plants, together with all inseparably connected parts of the flower (q.v.). In strict botanical usage, the meaning may be restricted to the ovary alone. Commonly the term *fruit* is often restricted to succulent, edible fruits of woody plants, to melons, and to such small fruits as strawberries and blueberries. In nature, fruit is normally produced

coconut is the complete pericarp, and the edible part inside, including the "milk," is the seed.

In typical cases, the fruit is confined to the ripened ovary, as in the pea pod; but in apples it includes ovary plus receptacle (other fused floral parts), in strawberries it is an aggregation of small individual fruits on a fleshy receptacle, called achenes, and in pineapples it is a development of an entire inflorescence, or cluster of flowers.

Types of Fruit. Fruit is classified by several characteristics, the most significant being the number of ovaries included. A simple fruit is a single ovary, developed from the pistil of a single flower, which may be single or compound; an aggregate fruit is composed of many ovaries attached to a single receptacle; a multiple, or collective, fruit is formed from the coalesced ovaries of an entire inflorescence. Simple fruits are further subdivided into two categories, dry or fleshy. Ovary walls that develop into simple fruits are succulent when young, but as they mature, those of dry fruits lose most of their moisture, whereas those of fleshy fruits increase in size and moisture capacity. Dry fruits that dehisce, or split, when ripe are called dry dehiscent fruits; those that do not are known as indehiscent fruits.

The bracts of a banana blossom are rolled back to reveal the flowers, the ovaries of which will develop into tiny green bananas. UPI

only after fertilization of ovules has taken place, but in many plants, largely cultivated varieties such as seedless citrus fruits, bananas, and cucumbers, fruit matures without fertilization, a process known as parthenocarpy. In either case, the maturation of the ovary results in the withering of stigmas and anthers and enlargement of the ovary or ovaries. Ovules within fertilized ovaries develop to produce seeds. In unfertilized varieties, seeds fail to develop, and the ovules remain their original size. The major service performed by fruit is the protection of developing seeds. In many plants, fruit also aids in seed distribution. *See* SEED.

Structure of Fruit. As the ovary matures, its wall develops to form the pericarp, divided into three layers. The outermost, exocarp, is usually a single epidermal layer. The extent of the middle layer, mesocarp, and the inner layer, endocarp, varies widely, but in any single type of fruit one of the layers may be thick, the others thin. In fleshy fruits the pulpy layer is usually the mesocarp, as in peaches or grapes. The seed or seeds, which lie immediately within the pericarp, in some cases constitute the entire edible portion of the fruit. For example, the hard outer husk of a

The pineapple is a multiple fruit, made up of an entire inflorescence, or cluster of flowers. UPI

FRUIT

Among the dry dehiscent fruits, a pod, or legume, characterizes most of the legumes. The shell of the pod is the pericarp, and the beans or peas inside it are the seeds. Dehiscence occurs along the sutures of the two edges, the seeds being attached to the ventral suture. A few leguminous plants have pods that do not dehisce but break at maturity; a pod of this type is termed a loment. A follicle, found in the peony and in milkweed, has two sutures like the pod but opens only along one of them. A capsule, unlike a follicle, contains more than one seed chamber, or fused carpels. When capsules split down the middle of each chamber, as in lilies, their dehiscence is termed loculicidal. When the dehiscence occurs at the lines of fusion of the chambers, as in the azalea, it is called septicidal. Poppy capsules open by pores, the dehiscence known as poricidal. Capsules of plantain split along a circular horizontal line, so that a "lid" comes off the top; this type of dehiscence is termed circumscissile. A silique, characteristic of the mustards, is a two-chambered dry fruit that dehisces along two sutures, leaving the exposed seeds clinging to a thin, membranous partition. Most siliques are at least as long as they are broad; when broader than long, as in delphinium, they are usually called silicles.

Most indehiscent fruits develop a single seed for each ovary. The pericarp of these fruits is so closely invested around the seed that the entire fruit assumes the appearance of a seed. The true grain, or caryopsis, characteristic of grasses, is little more than a seed with a thin, membranous pericarp inseparable from it. The achene, such as the "grain" of buckwheat, is sometimes called a naked seed because of its thin, separable pericarp. The samara, or key fruit, typified by the fruits of elms, maples, and ashes, has a winglike outgrowth of the ovary wall that aids in dispersal by wind. The typical fruit of the Apiaceae, the schizocarp, has more than one seed, unlike other dry indehiscent fruits, but the fruit splits into single-seeded portions at maturity. The nut (q.v.), exemplified by acorns, chestnuts, and hazelnuts, is a single-ovaried fruit with an extremely hard pericarp.

All fleshy fruits are indehiscent, the pulpy parts remaining attached to the seeds during dispersal. The true berry, typified by the tomato, blueberry, and gooseberry, possesses seeds dispersed throughout the fleshy mesocarp and endocarp. The exocarp is thin and skinlike. Many fruits, such as strawberries and raspberries, are commonly, but incorrectly, called berries. Two specialized types of berry, the hesperidium and the pepo, include valuable commercial fruits. All cit-

The grape is a berry grown in temperate climates. Grapes are used to make wine, juice, jelly, and raisins; their seeds are used to produce grape-seed oil, and a purple dye is made from the skins of purple grapes.

UPI

rus fruits, including oranges, lemons, and grapefruits, are hesperidia, having leathery rinds composed of exocarp and mesocarp, and juicy sections of endocarp. The pepo is the characteristic fruit of the cucumber family, Cucurbitaceae, including cucumbers, pumpkins, melons, and gourds. The outer layer of the pepo is receptacle tissue covering the exocarp; the pulpy portion of the fruit is mostly endocarp and mesocarp. The remaining type of fleshy fruit, the pome, has a pericarp limited to the so-called core and the inner fleshy portion of the fruit, as in apples, pears, and quinces. The other portion of the fleshy part of a pome is tissue developed from the fusion of the other floral parts and the ovary. The drupe is the stone fruit of such plants as plum, cherry, olive, peach, and almond. (The familiar, edible, almond, incorrectly called a nut, is the dried stone of a large drupe.) The single seed is surrounded by a stony endocarp; the fleshy portion is mesocarp. A small drupe occurring as part of a larger cluster is usually called a drupelet.

The constituent fruitlets of most aggregate and multiple fruits can be recognized as belonging to the same classification as simple fruits. The aggregate fruitlets of blackberries, raspberries, and dewberries, for example, are drupelets, and those of strawberries are achenes. It is not the fruit, that is, achenes, of strawberries that are eaten, but the fleshy receptacle. In the pineapple, on the other hand, the separate fruitlets cannot be classified as types of simple fruit; the multiple fruit is a mass of fused ovaries growing from the central axis of the pineapple.

Food Value. Fruits are eaten raw or cooked, dried, canned, or preserved. Carbohydrates, including starches and sugars, constitute the principal nutritional material. Citrus fruits, tomatoes, and strawberries are primary sources of vitamin C, and most fruits contain considerable quantities of vitamin A and vitamin B. Vitamin content is sharply reduced in storage and shipping of fresh fruits, but is maintained efficiently in frozen fruit (*see* VITAMIN). The jelly-making quality of many fruits is due to pectin, an important carbohydrate constituent. In general, fruits contain little protein or fat. Exceptions are avocados, nuts, and olives, which contain large quantities of fat, and grains and legumes, which contain considerable protein. Although the edible portions of fruits have a small ash content, fruits supply an important part of the mineral matter necessary in human diet. Dried or evaporated fruits contain much more nutritional material in proportion to their bulk than do fresh fruits, due to concentration

Blueberries, the fruit of a shrub in the heath family, are true berries, having small seeds dispersed throughout the fleshy mesocarp and endocarp. UPI

by evaporation. *See* NUTRITION, HUMAN.

See also CROP FARMING: *Fruit Crops;* HORTICULTURE; ORCHARD; PLANT BREEDING; PRUNING; and articles on the various fruits mentioned.

For further information on this topic, see the Bibliography in volume 28, sections 451, 453, 584, 592–93.

FRUIT FLY, common name for two families of true (two-winged) flies, order Diptera (*see* FLY), the larvae of which feed on fresh or decaying vegetable matter. True fruit flies, such as the housefly-sized apple maggot, belong to the family Tephritidae. They have intricate, often colorful wing patterns by which females recognize males of their species, and are sometimes called peacock flies because of the way they wave and display their wings in courtship. The term fruit fly is also applied to the much smaller vinegar flies of the family Drosophilidae.

Among the tephritids, adults of the apple maggot, *Rhagoletis pomonella,* are found in orchards throughout the summer months. The female punctures the apple skins with its sharp ovipositor and lays one or more eggs in each apple. The maggots bore through the pulp and grow to about 6 mm (about 0.25 in) in length. After the apple has fallen, the larvae burrow about 3 cm (about 1 in) underground, where they spend the winter and spring as pupae. The cherry maggots, *R. cingulata* and *R. fausta;* the currant fruit fly, *Epochra canadensis;* the melon fly, *Dacus cucurbitae;* and the olive fruit fly, *D. oleae,* have similar life cycles. The Mediterranean fruit fly, *Ceratitis capitata,* spoils fruits grown in Mediterranean climates. Brought under control in Florida in 1930, it reappeared in other countries in 1956, causing worldwide quarantines on imported fruit; it reoccurred in California in the 1980s.

The small drosophilids, or vinegar flies, the study of which has provided much of the current information on heredity, proliferate on yeast produced from rotting fruit and similar fermenting substances. The most important drosophilid is the red-eyed pomace fly, *Drosophila melanogaster.* It has exceptionally large chromosomes in the salivary gland and can produce a large new generation in only two weeks, making it an ideal subject for genetic experiments.

For further information on this topic, see the Bibliography in volume 28, sections 466, 590.

FRUNZE, from 1926 to 1991 the name of BISHKEK (originally BISHBEK, or PISHPEK), city, capital of Kyrgyzstan, N Kyrgyzstan. Located in the irrigated Chu R. valley, it is a transportation and industrial center. Manufactures include farm machinery, processed food, textiles, and construction materials. Kirgiz State University (1951), the

Kirgiz Academy of Sciences, a symphony orchestra, and several museums and theaters are in the city. In the mid-19th century the Uzbek khan of Kokand built a fortress here. The stronghold was taken in 1862 by the Russians, who named it (and the surrounding community) Pishpek, a corruption of the original Bishbek. In 1926 the city was renamed Frunze to honor the Soviet army commander M. V. Frunze (1885–1925). Pop. (1989) 616,000.

FRY, Christopher (1907–   ), English dramatist, born in Bristol. His original name was Christopher Harris. Fry's first major success, *The Lady's Not for Burning* (1948), a tragicomic fantasy in verse, was enthusiastically received both in London and New York City. In the same genre are *Venus Observed* (1950) and *Ring Round the Moon* (1950), a translation of *L'invitation au chateau* (Invitation to the Castle) by the French playwright Jean Anouilh. Among Fry's other works are the religious drama in verse *A Sleep of Prisoners* (1951) and the historical drama *The Dark Is Light Enough* (1955). *Tiger at the Gates* (1955), *Duel of Angels* (1960), and *Judith* (1962) are translations of plays by the French dramatist Jean Giraudoux.

FUAD I (1868–1936), sultan (1917–22) and king (1922–36) of Egypt. Son of Ismail Pasha, Fuad was born in Cairo and originally named Ahmed Fuad Pasha; he was educated in Italy. Fuad was a general in the Egyptian army from 1892 until 1895. In 1908 he played an important role in the founding of the Egyptian University (now named Cairo University) at Giza, serving for a time as its president. Fuad succeeded his brother, Hussein Kamil (1853–1917), to the sultanate. He became king of Egypt in 1922, on the nominal termination of the British protectorate, and proclaimed an Egyptian constitution the next year. Although opposed to British domination, Fuad was an adversary of the powerful Wafd, or Nationalist, party, with which he waged a struggle for power throughout his reign, succeeding temporarily in imposing his personal rule on the country by dissolution of Parliament in 1928–29 and from 1930 to 1935. Fuad was succeeded by his son, Faruk I.

FUCHS, Sir Vivian Ernest (1908–   ), British geologist and explorer of the Antarctic, born on the Isle of Wight. He received an M.A. degree from the University of Cambridge in 1929 and in the same year served as geologist with the Cambridge East Greenland Expedition. During the 1930s, Fuchs was a geologist with two expeditions engaged in geological and survey work in east Africa. He was commissioned a second lieutenant in the British army in World War II and rose to the rank of major. In November 1957,

Fuchs set out as head of the 12-member British team of the Commonwealth Trans-Antarctic Expedition, on the first crossing of Antarctica, about a 3473-km (about 2158-mi), 99-day journey from the Weddell Sea, across the South Pole to the Ross Sea. Equipped with snow tractors, the Fuchs party traversed much of the previously unexplored area of the Antarctic landmass and gathered important scientific information. The expedition is considered one of the outstanding accomplishments undertaken in connection with the International Geophysical Year and earned Fuchs a knighthood in 1958. With Sir Edmund Hillary, Fuchs wrote *The Crossing of Antarctica* (1960).

FUCHSIA, genus of tropical and subtropical plants of the family Onagraceae (*see* EVENING PRIMROSE), named after the German botanist and physician Leonhard Fuchs (1501–66). Except for a few Australasian species, fuchsias are found in forests and shady mountain habitats in Central and South America. A few are climbing plants, and others are small trees, but most wild fuchsias are shrubs. Fuchsias cultivated in the U.S. are grown in green-houses and as houseplants in colder regions of the country; in the summer, and in milder regions, they may be grown in windowboxes or as bedding plants. The graceful pendulous flowers, often called lady's eardrops because of their shape, may be solitary or arranged in clusters in leaf axils. Each flower has a colored, funnel-shaped, four-part calyx and a corolla

Fuchsia, Fuchsia magellanica   New York Botanical Garden

composed of four petals. In many fuchsias, the color of the calyx contrasts sharply with the color of the corolla. Fuchsia fruits are small berries, which, in several species, are edible.

Most cultivated fuchsias are hybrids of wild species or varieties. One of the most attractive cultivated varieties, *Fuchsia hybridia*, has crimson sepals and purple, rose, or white petals.

For further information on this topic, see the Bibliography in volume 28, sections 452, 592–93.

FUEL, substance that reacts chemically with another to produce heat, or that produces heat by nuclear processes. The term *fuel* is generally limited to those substances that burn readily in air or oxygen, emitting large quantities of heat. Fuels are used for heating, for the production of steam for heating and power purposes, for powering internal-combustion engines (*see* INTERNAL-COMBUSTION ENGINE), and for a direct source of power in jet and rocket propulsion. In cases where a fuel must supply its own oxygen, as in many rockets and torpedoes, an oxidizing agent such as hydrogen peroxide or nitric acid is added to the fuel mixture (*see* JET PROPULSION; ROCKET).

Chemical reactions in the combustion of all ordinary fuels involve the combination of oxygen with any carbon, hydrogen, or sulfur present in the fuels. The end products are carbon dioxide, water, and sulfur dioxide. Other substances present in fuels do not contribute to the combustion but either are driven off in the form of vapor or remain after combustion in the form of ash.

Fuel efficiency or heating value of a fuel is usually measured in terms of the number of Btu (*see* BRITISH THERMAL UNIT) that are produced when a given amount of the fuel is burned under standard conditions. Heating values for solid and liquid fuels are stated in terms of Btu per lb, and values for gases in Btu per cu ft. A distinction is sometimes made between higher heating value, the entire heat evolved during combustion, and lower heating value, the net heat evolved, with allowance for the heat lost in the vaporization of the water produced by combustion. Approximate higher heating values of common fuels are: Solid fuels (Btu per lb): coal 12,000 to 15,000; lignite 6000 to 7400; coke 12,400; dry wood 8500. Liquid fuels: alcohol 11,000; fuel oil 19,000; gasoline 20,750; kerosene 19,800. Gaseous fuels (Btu per cu ft): acetylene 1480; blast-furnace gas 93; carbon monoxide 317; coke-oven gas or coal gas about 600; hydrogen 319; natural gas 1050 to 2220; oil gas 516; producer gas 136. See separate articles on most of these fuels.

See also ENERGY SUPPLY, WORLD; GASES, FUEL; GASOHOL; NUCLEAR ENERGY; PETROLEUM; SOLAR ENERGY.

For further information on this topic, see the Bibliography in volume 28, section 540.

FUEL CELL, electrochemical device in which the energy of a chemical reaction is converted directly into electricity. Unlike an electric cell or battery (q.v.), a fuel cell does not run down or require recharging; it operates as long as the fuel and an oxidizer are supplied continuously from outside the cell.

A fuel cell consists of an anode—to which fuel, commonly hydrogen, ammonia, or hydrazine, is supplied—and a cathode—to which an oxidant, commonly air or oxygen, is supplied. The two electrodes of a fuel cell are separated by an ionic conductor electrolyte. In the case of a hydrogen-oxygen fuel cell with an alkali metal hydroxide electrolyte, the anode reaction is $2H_2 + 4OH^- \rightarrow 4H_2O + 4e$ and the cathode reaction is $O_2 + 2H_2O + 4e \rightarrow 4OH^-$. The electrons generated at the anode move through an external circuit containing the load and pass to the cathode. The OH^- ions generated at the cathode are conducted by the electrolyte to the anode, where they form water by combining with hydrogen. The fuel cell voltage in this case is about 1.2V but decreases as the load is increased. The water produced at the anode has to be removed continuously in order to avoid flooding the cell. Hydrogen-oxygen fuel cells using ion exchange membranes or immobilized phosphoric acid electrolytes found early use in the Gemini and Apollo space programs, respectively. Phosphoric acid fuel cells are in limited use by electric utilities for power generation.

Fuel cells with molten carbonate electrolytes are also under development. The electrolyte is solid at room temperature but is a liquid and a carbonate ion conductor at the fuel cell operating temperatures (650° to 800° C/1200° to 1470° F).

Diagram of the operation of a hydrogen-oxygen fuel cell. The water produced by an H-O cell can be used for drinking on a spaceship.

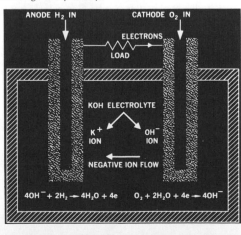

ANODE H₂ IN   CATHODE O₂ IN

ELECTRONS

LOAD

KOH ELECTROLYTE

K⁺ ION   OH⁻ ION

NEGATIVE ION FLOW

$4OH^- + 2H_2 \rightarrow 4H_2O + 4e$ $O_2 + 2H_2O + 4e \rightarrow 4OH^-$

This system has the advantage of utilizing carbon monoxide as a fuel; therefore, mixtures of carbon monoxide and hydrogen, such as are produced in a coal gasifier, may be used as a fuel.

Also being developed are fuel cells that employ solid zirconium dioxide as the electrolyte. These are called solid oxide fuel cells. Zirconium dioxide becomes an oxide ion conductor at about 1000° C (about 1800° F). Suitable fuels include hydrogen, carbon monoxide, and methane, with air or oxygen being supplied to the cathode. The high operating temperature of the solid oxide fuel cell permits the direct use of methane, a fuel that does not require expensive platinum catalysts on the anode. Solid oxide fuel cells have the advantage of being relatively insensitive to fuel contaminants, such as sulfur and nitrogen compounds, that impair the performance of the other fuel systems.

The relatively high operating temperature of both molten carbonate and solid oxide fuel cells facilitates the removal of water produced in the reaction in the form of steam. In low-temperature fuel cells, provision must be made for the removal of liquid water from the anode chamber.

FUELS, SYNTHETIC, gaseous or liquid fuels produced from coal, shale formations, tar sands, or renewable biomass resources such as crops or animal wastes, and used as substitutes for petroleum (q.v.) or natural gas (*see* GASES, FUEL). For example, four methods may be used to convert coal (q.v.) to gas or oil: (1) synthesis, developed in the 1870s to produce gas, in which coal is pulverized and mixed with oxygen and steam at high temperatures, then purified; (2) carbonization, heating coal in the absence of air; (3) extraction, dissolving coal with an organic liquid, then exposing it to hydrogen; and (4) hydrogenation, reacting coal with hydrogen at high pressures, usually in the presence of a catalyst. By the synthesis method, a ton of coal can produce 340 cu m (12,000 cu ft) of gas; by the other methods, three barrels of oil. Oil may be extracted from certain types of shale (q.v.) by heating the rock in the absence of air or oxygen—a chemical process called pyrolysis; oil may also be extracted from tar sands by mixing the sands with hot water and steam. Gasohol (q.v.) is a mixture of gasoline with ethanol or methanol; the latter alcohols may be distilled from waste-wood products or crop plants. These processes remain too expensive to compete commercially, but may be needed to meet future energy demands.

For further information on this topic, see the Bibliography in volume 28, section 540.

FUGARD, Athol (1932–   ), South African playwright, director, and actor, born Harold Athol Lannigan Fugard in Middleburg, Cape Province. His experimental theater group in Port Elizabeth produced his first play *No Good Friday*, in 1959. International recognition came with the production of *The Blood Knot* (1961). By focusing on conflict between characters from different backgrounds, Fugard's plays explore the racism and repression of apartheid in particular and of civilization in general, and celebrate the strength of the human spirit. Many of his plays have been produced in Britain and the U.S., including *Boesman and Lena* (1969), *Sizwe Bansi Is Dead* (1972), *The Island* (1973), and *Master Harold and the Boys* (1982). Fugard wrote about his work and his life in the theater in *Notebooks 1960–1977* (1984).

FUGITIVE SLAVE LAWS, acts passed by the U.S. Congress in 1793 and 1850, intended to facilitate the recapture and extradition of runaway slaves and to commit the federal government to the legitimacy of holding property in slaves. Both laws ultimately provoked dissatisfaction and rancor throughout the country. Northerners questioned the laws' infringements on civil liberty and deplored the national character they lent to the South's institution. Southerners complained that the laws were circumvented both because of legal deficiencies (especially the law of 1793) and growing popular hostility to enforcement. The controversy grew with the Republic itself.

The Constitution and the Law of 1793. Aware that the northern states might become havens of refuge for escaped slaves, South Carolina's delegates at the Constitutional Convention (1787) sought the return of slaves on the same basis as the extradition of common criminals. They were unsuccessful. Article IV, Section 2, merely stated that persons "held to Service or Labour" in one state who escape into another state "shall be delivered up on Claim of the Party to whom such Service or Labour may be due." The ambiguity of the document made necessary the law of 1793 whereby the process of taking custody was first defined. The statute authorized slave owners or their agents to apprehend fugitives in any state or territory and provided that owners could apply to a circuit or district judge for a certificate to take custody of runaways. The law did not, however, grant judges power to issue warrants of arrest, nor did it require federal marshals to assist owners. The law was not uniformly enforced, and its legal defects irritated slaveholders.

Further difficulties arose from free-state legislation defining citizenship, a necessary accompaniment to the gradual emancipation acts (1776–1827) that ultimately abolished northern slavery. These early personal liberty laws were partly designed to protect free blacks from dishonest slave-catchers. Organized antislavery efforts in the 1830s denounced northern complicity in bondage, citing the act of 1793 as a primary example. Southern dissatisfaction, in turn, mounted as slaveholders detected antislavery conspiracies in a growing movement to rescue the fugitives. *See* UNDERGROUND RAILROAD.

The Law of 1850. In an attempt to lay the issue to rest, Congress enacted a law in 1850 that created commissioners under federal court appointment to adjudicate fugitive cases. They had active roles in ensuring retrieval of escaped slaves. Federal marshals also were enjoined to help recapture slaves, under $1000 penal fines for dereliction. If a runaway escaped while in a marshal's custody, the marshal had to forfeit the slave's full value to the owner. Persons guilty of abetting slave escape were subject to fine and a maximum prison sentence of six months. As in southern courts, slaves could not testify against whites, but a master's circumstantial evidence was easily admissible. Federal commissioners received $5 for proslave verdicts, $10 for decisions favorable to masters. If warranted by a threat of interference, federal officers were authorized to accompany the slave out of the area of risk.

Northern Resistance to the Laws. Owing to northern resentments, the acts of 1793 and 1850 faced legal challenges, primarily in the form of jurisdictional disputes over state personal liberty laws. In *Prigg* v. *Pennsylvania* (1842), the U.S. Supreme Court had ruled against a Pennsylvania citizenship statute and upheld the first fugitive slave law's constitutionality. Nevertheless, some states continued to pass laws strengthening the applicability of habeas corpus writs and prohibiting state officials from accepting jurisdiction under federal law. In Ohio, the chief objective was less a desire to expand black rights than to ensure that outright kidnapping was not condoned. (Ohio did not repeal its virulently discriminatory Black Code until 1849.) Southerners objected strenuously to personal liberty laws as a violation of sectional equity and reciprocal trust; but the 1850 act, seen in the North as punitive and tyrannical, only aroused greater sectional animosities. Northern opposition was most dramatically illustrated when an abolitionist Boston mob tried to rescue Anthony Burns, a fugitive from Virginia, in May 1854. The mission failed. Commissioner Edward Loring had Burns remanded to slavery, and U.S. troops escorted him through sullen crowds to a waiting ship. The effort cost the federal government more than $100,000.

The legal conflict that pitted northern personal liberty statutes against federal fugitive slave measures reflected the concepts of double sovereignty that citizens of the federated Union then entertained. Southerners insisted on the sovereignty of the states, but in this controversy northerners "nullified" those federal laws that were unwelcome. Although the constitutionality of the fugitive slave laws was unquestioned, only the force of arms could finally define the nature of the Union, determine its source of authority, and outline the boundaries of liberty. *See also* COMPROMISE MEASURES OF 1850.   B.W.

For further information on this topic, see the Bibliography in volume 28, section 209.

FUGUE (Lat. *fuga*, "flight"), musical composition in which a melodic theme is systematically subjected to melodic imitation; the musical texture of a fugue, therefore, is contrapuntal (based on interwoven melodies), and its most important stylistic feature is its treatment of thematic material by means of imitation. This characteristic is typical also of the *fugato*, a passage employing fugal techniques within another form, for instance, the sonata. The fugue, however, does not necessarily conform in every detail to a fixed form. In the hands of its masters, the fugue depends on the rigorous contrapuntal exploitation of a single idea; thus, any given fugue will adhere essentially to the abstract formula but will deviate from it to some degree.

Fugues may be written for a single instrument, such as the organ or piano, groups of instruments, or groups of voices either accompanied or unaccompanied by instruments. The number of parts or voices, at least two but most commonly four, usually remains constant throughout the piece.

Structure. The principal parts of the fugue are the exposition and the episode. The fugue opens with an exposition in which the subject is stated by one voice. At the conclusion of this statement appears the answer, in which a second voice restates, or imitates, the subject, typically five scale degrees above, or four scale degrees below, the initial statement. The answer may be a literal repetition of the subject or may have minor alterations to adjust the theme to the key.

During the answer the first voice continues with free counterpoint; if the free counterpoint contains a significant melody that makes subsequent appearances, the melody is called a countersubject. A brief period of free counterpoint in both voices may follow the answer, but in a relatively short time a third voice enters with a statement of the subject. These alternate statements of subject and answer continue until all the parts have entered. The voices already active continue in free counterpoint but sometimes remain silent for brief periods.

FUGUE

The first complete exposition is followed by an episode—freely contrapuntal passages constructed of melodic figures derived from the subject, countersubject, or free counterpoint of the exposition. Subsequent expositions sustain the free contrapuntal texture of the preceding episode. The middle expositions also involve modulation from the main key to closely related keys.

The fugue may employ additional contrapuntal devices, such as augmentation, the statement of the subject with the time values lengthened; diminution, the statement of the subject with the time values decreased; inversion, the repetition of the subject melodically turned upside down; stretto, a series of compressed imitative entrances, each voice beginning the subject before the preceding voice has finished stating it; or pedal point, a tone sustained in the bass while the other voices continue in counterpoint.

The polythematic fugue is either a double or triple fugue, which includes expositions on second and third subjects. In another type of double fugue the second subject appears as a countersubject in the first exposition and then is used throughout the piece; an example is found in the Kyrie in the Requiem of Wolfgang Amadeus Mozart. Accompanied fugues are vocal fugues with an instrumental accompaniment melodically independent of the fugue proper.

History. The fundamental stylistic feature of the fugue—imitation of a subject by successively entering voices—crystallized in the Renaissance motet and chanson about 1500. These forms developed into the immediate antecedents of the fugue, namely, the *ricercare* and the *canzona*, or *canzone,* instrumental forms prominent in the 16th and the early 17th centuries. Especially influential in the development of the fugue proper were the *ricercare* of the Italian composer Girolamo Frescobaldi and the organ fantasias by the Dutch composer Jan Pieterszoon Sweelinck.

During the late baroque period (first half of the 18th century) the fugue was highly developed by the north German organist-composers, notably Dietrich Buxtehude. In the next generation Johann Sebastian Bach thoroughly demonstrated all the nuances and artifices of the fugue in two monumental collections, *The Well-Tempered Clavier* and the unfinished *Art of the Fugue.* In England, Bach's German-born contemporary, George Frideric Handel, used accompanied choral fugues as the vehicle for the vivid drama of his oratorios. In the classical era (c. 1750–c. 1800) composers such as Joseph Haydn, Ludwig van Beethoven, and Mozart absorbed the fugal technique in their sonatas, symphonies, choral works, and string quartets. Subsequent notable exponents of fugal tech-

Snowcapped Mt. Fuji.
Japan National Tourist
Organization

nique include Johannes Brahms and César Franck in the 19th century, and in the 20th century, Paul Hindemith.   F.M.S.

For further information on this topic, see the Bibliography in volume 28, section 721.

FUJI *or* **FUJIYAMA,** also Fuji-no-Yama or Fujisan, celebrated sacred volcano of Japan, S Honshu Island, near Tokyo. Fuji, the highest mountain in Japan, rises as a cone to a height of 3776 m (12,389 ft) above sea level, with the apex broken by a cone-shaped crater 610 m (2000 ft) in diameter. The S slopes extend to the shore of Suruga Bay, and the isolated peak can be seen from many of the outlying prefectures. The mountain is part of Fuji-Hakone-Izu National Park. According to legend, Fuji arose from the plain during a single night in 286 BC. The most recent recorded eruption of Fuji lasted from Nov. 24, 1707, until Jan. 22, 1708. As the sacred mountain of Japan, it is visited annually by thousands of pilgrims from all parts of the country, and numerous shrines and temples are on its slopes. Fuji is also revered in Japanese literature and art.

For further information on this topic, see the Bibliography in volume 28, section 867.

FUJIAN, also Fukien, province, SE China, on Taiwan (Formosa) Strait opposite the island of Taiwan. It has an almost entirely mountainous terrain and an irregular coast, indented by numerous bays and harbors. Rice, double-cropped in the humid subtropical climate, is grown in small alluvial valleys; tea and fruit are produced in upland areas. Lumbering and fishing are also important. The capital and largest city is Fuzhou (Fuchou); other urban centers are Amoy (Xi-amen), Zhangzhou (Chang-chou), and Nanping.

Fujian came under Chinese domination in the Ch'in dynasty (221–206 BC), but was not effectively Sinicized before the 7th century AD. Its overseas trade prospered from the 12th to the 17th century and then declined with the rise of the port of Canton to the W. Fuzhou and Amoy, opened to foreign trade in 1842, were important as tea ports in the 19th century. The presence of Nationalist forces on the strategic offshore islands of Matsu and Quemoy since 1949 has adversely affected coastal shipping. The construction of railroads to neighboring provinces since the 1950s has alleviated the region's physical isolation. Area, 120,000 sq km (46,332 sq mi); pop. (1982) 25,870,000.

FUJIWARA, noble family that controlled the Japanese emperors and dominated the imperial court from the 9th to the 12th century. In 858 Fujiwara Yoshifusa (804–72) acquired the office of regent (*sessho*), which then became hereditary in his family. His nephew Mototsune (836–91) became the first *kampaku* (chancellor). The greatest Fujiwara statesman was Michinaga (966–1027), whose daughters married five successive emperors. The Fujiwara period was marked by a great flowering of literature and the arts, but also by a weakening of central authority and the division of the country into large estates ruled by feudal clans. In 1160 the Taira clan ousted the Fujiwara and took control of the imperial court.

FUKUOKA, city, Japan, capital of Fukuoka Prefecture, NW Kyushu Island, on Hakata Bay. The city, divided by the Naka R., includes Fukuoka, on the W bank, an old castle town of a family of feudal barons, and Hakata, on the E bank, the main commercial section. It is the closest large Japanese port to the Asian mainland and is an important manufacturing center for silk products, dolls, porcelain, machinery, paper, and metal goods. Kyushu University (1911) and Fukuoka University (1934) are here. Pop. (1988 est.) 1,517,100.

FUKUYAMA, city, Hiroshima Prefecture, SW Japan, on the S shore of the island of Honshu, on the Inland Sea. An industrial center, it has manufactures that include electronic items, textiles, machinery, and processed foods. After a castle was built here in 1619, Fukuyama developed as a commercial port. Industrial growth was rapid after World War II. Pop. (1988 est.) 363,100.

FUKUZAWA YUKICHI (1835–1901), Japanese educator, who was among the first to disseminate Western ideas and culture in Japan. Born in Nakatsu on Kyushu, a low-ranking samurai, he was sent to Nagasaki to study Dutch and later added English to his studies. By 1862 he had been to Europe and America as an interpreter·of trade and diplomatic missions. Impressed with the West, he became critical of Japan's feudal system and its isolation, and in 1863 he founded the Keio Gijuku school for Western-style studies (merged into Keio University, Tokyo). His impressions, *Seiyo Jijo* (Conditions in the West, 1866), became extremely popular. Following the abolition of feudalism in 1868, Fukuzawa became the Meiji era's leading advocate of Westernization. To that end he founded (1882) the newspaper *Jiji Shimpo* and wrote more than 100 books.

FULANI, cattle-herding people of Africa numbering about 7 million and dispersed in varying, often sizable, concentrations throughout the grassland areas of West Africa from Senegal and Guinea to Nigeria, Cameroon, and Chad.

The dark-skinned Fulani have Caucasoid racial features. Their language is closely related to the languages of Senegal, suggesting the possibility that their ancestors migrated from the Middle East through North Africa to Senegal. By the 10th century, they had adopted a new language in

Senegal and begun to spread eastward, reaching present-day Nigeria by about the 14th century.

Although most Fulani remained cattle herders through the centuries, many settled down and turned to politics, successfully establishing a series of kingdoms between Senegal and Cameroon by the 19th century, and conquering the Hausa by about 1810. The Fulani held much of northern Nigeria in subjection until defeated (1900–06) by the British. The religious beliefs of a large percentage of the cattle-herding Fulani are animistic, although many of the politically oriented Fulani are Muslim and have often justified their conquests on religious grounds.

FULBRIGHT, J(ames) William (1905–   ), American educator and politician, born in Sumner, Mo., and educated at the University of Arkansas, the University of Oxford, and George Washington University Law School. He was admitted to the Washington, D.C., bar in 1934 and served for a year as a special attorney in the U.S. Department of Justice. He taught at George Washington University (1935–36) and at the University of Arkansas (1936–39). He served as president of the latter from 1939 until 1941. A member of the Democratic party, Fulbright was elected to the U.S. House of Representatives in 1942 and to the U.S. Senate in 1944. In the Senate he sponsored the Fulbright Act of 1946, amended in 1961 by the Fulbright-Hays Act, providing for fellowships for Americans to study and teach abroad and for foreigners to study in the U.S. Fulbright gained much influence during his long tenure (1959–74) as chairman of the Senate Committee on Foreign Relations. Running for his sixth term in 1974, however, he was defeated in the Arkansas Democratic primary, and he resigned from the Senate at the end of the year.

FULLER, Loie, full name MARIE LOUISE FULLER (1862–1928), American dancer, actor, producer, and playwright, who achieved sensational fame for her improvisatory dances using billowing fabrics and multicolored electric lighting. Born in Fullersburg, Ill., she acted professionally as a child and was self-taught as a dancer. Performing mainly in Europe, she composed about 130 dances, including the solos *Serpentine Dance* (1890) and *Dance of Fire* and works for her troupe, such as *Bottom of the Sea* (1906) and *Ballet of Light* (1908). The subject of portraits by the French artists Henri de Toulouse-Lautrec and Auguste Rodin, she was honored by French scientists for her theories of artistic lighting.

FULLER, (Sarah) Margaret (1810–50), American social reformer and author, who espoused transcendentalism and fought for equal rights for women.

Fuller was born on May 23, 1810, in Cambridge, Mass., and educated chiefly by her father, the American lawyer and legislator Timothy Fuller (1778–1835). At an early age she displayed remarkable intellectual powers, becoming, while a young woman, a member of the group of distinguished writers and philosophers who met frequently in the Boston area and who espoused the doctrines of transcendentalism. From 1835 to 1837 she taught languages in Boston, and in the latter year she became principal teacher at the Green Street School, Providence, R.I., where she served for two years. In 1839 her translation of *Conversations with Goethe* by the German writer Johann Peter Eckermann was published. In the following year she founded, with the aid of the poet and essayist Ralph Waldo Emerson and the critic and reformer George Ripley (1802–80), the *Dial*, a periodical dedicated to publishing the verse and philosophical writings of the transcendentalists.

For about five years beginning in 1839, Fuller organized gatherings of women in Boston for the intellectual and social development of the participants. These meetings provided her with much of the material used in *Women in the Nineteenth Century* (1845), in which she expounded the doctrine of equal rights for women. From 1844 to 1846 she was literary critic for the *New York Tribune* and gained recognition as one of the foremost critics in the U.S.

In 1846 Fuller journeyed to Europe, where she dispatched letters to the *Tribune* describing her experiences. While visiting Rome, in 1847, she met and married Marquis Giovanni Angelo Ossoli (1820?–50), a follower of the nationalist revolutionary Giuseppe Mazzini. Fuller remained in Rome after the outbreak of the Revolution of 1848, and when the city was besieged by French forces in 1849, she assumed the direction of one of its hospitals while her husband took part in the fighting. They escaped when the city fell and in 1850, with their infant son, embarked for the U.S. Their ship was wrecked off Fire Island, N.Y., on July 19, and all three were drowned.

For further information on this person, see the section Biographies in the Bibliography in volume 28.

FULLER, Melville Weston (1833–1910), American politician and jurist, eighth chief justice of the U.S. Born in Augusta, Maine, on Feb. 11, 1833, he was educated at Bowdoin College and Harvard Law School. He was admitted to the bar in Augusta in 1855 and in the following year he moved to Chicago, where he established a successful law practice. Beginning in 1862, when he was a member of the Illinois State Constitutional Convention, and for the next 18 years, Fuller was active in the Democratic party. He was a delegate from Illinois to the national conventions of the party from 1864 to 1880. Fuller became the eighth chief justice of the U.S. in 1888. During his tenure of 22 years he helped to broaden the powers of the federal courts. In 1899 he served on the commission to arbitrate the Venezuela boundary dispute. From 1900 until his death on July 4, 1910, Fuller also served as a member of the Permanent Court of Arbitration in The Hague.

FULLER, R(ichard) Buckminster (1895–1983), American engineer, inventor, designer, architect, writer, educator, philosopher, and poet, noted for his innovative use of technology to deal with global problems facing humanity in the second half of the 20th century.

Fuller, a great-nephew of the transcendentalist Margaret Fuller, was born in Milton, Mass., July 12, 1895. He attended Harvard University from 1913 to 1915. In the early 1920s he joined his father-in-law in developing the Stockade Building System for producing lightweight, insulated, fireproof, and waterproof housing. When the company failed, Fuller dedicated himself to finding entirely new ways to increase the social benefits accruing from efficient and principled use of the earth's energy and material resources.

Dymaxion Designs. In 1932 Fuller founded the Dymaxion Corp. to produce a variety of his innovative designs. (The name is a play on the words *maximum, dynamic,* and *ion.*) His inexpensive, factory-assembled, and highly portable Dymaxion House was a doughnut-shaped structure hung from a central mast; his Dymaxion Airocean World Map is a flat cartographic projection that can be folded into a rough globe without the usual visible distortions of other world maps. His Dymaxion car was an omnidirectional, three-wheeled, fuel-efficient, versatile automobile, but it was never mass-produced. During World War II Fuller served on the Board of Economic Warfare as head of the mechanical engineering department.

The Geodesic Dome. In 1947 and 1948, Fuller developed what he called a synergetic-energetic system of geometry, an architectural consequence of which is the geodesic dome. The geodesic dome (patented in 1947) comprises a spidery network of interconnected tetrahedrons (four-sided pyramids of equilateral triangles) forming a three-way, hemispherical grid that distributes stress evenly to all members of the entire structure and hence exhibits a high strength-to-weight ratio. This led to his extensive development of geodesics, the mathematical study of economical space-spanning structures. In 1953

the Ford Motor Co. commissioned Fuller to design the Ford Rotunda Dome in Dearborn, Mich. Thereafter he designed domes housing military radar antennas (radomes), the 117-m (384-ft) Union Tank Car Co. dome in Baton Rouge, La. (1958), the 60-m (200-ft) "golden dome" that dominated the U.S. pavilion at the American Exchange Exhibition (1959) in Moscow, and the dome for the American pavilion at Expo '67 in Montréal, among many other structures.

Later Career. In the course of his work, Fuller evolved a philosophy of anticipatory design: "I just invent. Then I wait until man comes around to needing what I've invented." In 1959 he became a research professor at Southern Illinois University, Carbondale, where he established his World Game research team for the application of design theory to the security of humankind and preservation of the earth. In 1972 Fuller was named a World Fellow in residence at the University City Science Center, administered by a consortium of institutions in the Philadelphia area. The same year, the nonprofit Design Science Institute was established in Washington, D.C., to disseminate Fuller's philosophy and work. He died in Los Angeles on July 1, 1983.

Among his many influential published works are *Nine Chains to the Moon* (1938, reissued 1963), *Operating Manual for Spaceship Earth* (1969), *Approaching the Benign Environment* (1970), and *Synergetics: Explorations in the Geometry of Thinking* (1975), written in collaboration with E. J. Applewhite (1919–   ).   J.W.D.

FULLER, Thomas (1608–61), English clergyman, author, and wit. In 1634 he became rector of Broadwinsor, Dorsetshire. His first book of sermons, *Joseph's Party-Coloured Coat* (1640), is distinguished by the conceits and wit characteristic of the sermons of this period. In 1642 Fuller settled in London, where he preached in favor of the signing of articles of peace by both Royalists and Parliamentarians in the Great Rebellion. In 1643 he joined the forces of Charles I, king of England, at Oxford, as chaplain to one of its regiments. During this period he collected the materials for *The Church History of Britain from the Birth of Christ Until the Year 1648* (1655) and for *The Worthies of England,* a valuable source of antiquarian information, published posthumously in 1662.

FULLERTON, city, Orange Co., SW California, near Los Angeles; inc. 1904. Manufactures include electronic and aerospace equipment, medical instruments, paper products, and processed food; petroleum is also produced. California State University-Fullerton (1957), Pacific Christian College (1928), colleges of law and optometry, and a junior college are here. Situated on the old Camino Real, Fullerton was settled in 1887 and is named for George H. Fullerton (1843–1929), a land developer who was instrumental in bringing the railroad here in 1888. In the early 1920s oil was discovered nearby and brought a spurt of growth; rapid growth began in the mid-1950s. Pop. (1980) 102,034; (1990) 114,144.

FULMAR, common name for two species of seabirds constituting the genus *Fulmarus*, of the family Procellariidae, which also includes the petrels and shearwaters. The northern fulmar, *F. glacialis*, breeds on islands and coastal cliffs in the northern Pacific and Atlantic oceans. The Antarctic fulmar, *F. glacialoides*, breeds on the Antarctic mainland and subantarctic islands. In winter northern birds wander as far south as Baja California, and Antarctic birds to within 10 degrees of the equator off western South America. Both are large, heavyset birds with pale gray and dark gray color phases. They feed on fish, other marine animals, and organic garbage discarded from ships.

FULMINATES, salts of fulminic acid, a volatile, poisonous, explosive liquid with the formula HONC, which is isomeric with cyanic acid. Fulminic acid has not been isolated in a pure state because of its instability. The fulminates, although more stable than the acid, are readily explosive when heated or struck. Fulminates were prepared as early as 1798, and their explosive properties were used. *See* EXPLOSIVES.

FULTON, Robert (1765–1815), American inventor and engineer, who designed the first efficient steamboat, thus inaugurating a new era of power-driven navigation.

Fulton was born on a farm on Nov. 14, 1765, in Lancaster Co., Pa. As a young man he worked as a professional artist, and he studied painting in London with Benjamin West from 1786 to 1793. Thereafter he turned to mechanics and engineering, designing canal systems with inclined planes to replace locks, but he found little acceptance. In 1800 he attempted to sell to the French government a submarine to sink British ships. Demonstrated in Rouen with Fulton aboard, the *Nautilus* folded its mast and sails flat on the deck and, with three crew members cranking a screw, dove to a depth of 7.6 m (25 ft). The French and later the British, however, showed no interest.

In 1802, with the help and later the partnership of Robert R. Livingston, then U.S. minister to France, Fulton launched a small, steam-driven paddle-wheel boat that traveled up the Seine River at 4.8 km/hr (3 mph). Fulton then sailed to New York City, where Livingston had obtained a statewide steamboat monopoly on the stipula-

Robert Fulton (self-portrait, c. 1807)
William Rockhill Nelson Gallery of Art and Atkins Museum of Fine Arts, Kansas City, Mo.

tion that he would put in operation a steamboat that traveled 6.4 km/hr (4 mph). On Aug. 18, 1807, Fulton's 45-m (150-ft) *Clermont* made its famous successful run of 240 km (150 mi) from New York City to Albany in 32 hours, or about 7.5 km/hr (about 4.7 mph)—a trip that took four days by sailing sloop—and Fulton received a patent for its construction.

During his remaining years Fulton designed steamboats that sailed on the Raritan, Potomac, and Mississippi rivers, ferryboats for river crossings in New York, Boston, and Philadelphia, and the first steam warship, *Fulton the First* (1814–15). He died in New York City on Feb. 24, 1815.

For further information on this person, see the section Biographies in the Bibliography in volume 28.

FUMITORY, common name for a family, Fumariaceae, of flowering plants, and for its representative genus, *Fumaria*. The family contains about 16 genera and 400 species, mostly north temperate in distribution, with a few genera and species occurring in eastern and southern Africa; the greatest concentration of species is in Eurasia. More than 300 species occur in the genus *Corydalis* and about 60 in *Fumaria*. The remaining genera, including the bleeding heart (q.v.) or Dutchman's-breeches genus, *Dicentra,* contain a few species each. Plants of the fumitory family are herbaceous with watery, alkaloid-containing sap. Many have swollen root-stocks, and the leaves are always much dissected. The flowers have a complicated and distinctive structure, although features of some of the simpler representatives demonstrate that the fumitory family is a member of the poppy (q.v.) order. The flowers have two small sepals and four petals; the variously lobed petals form bleeding-heart-shaped flowers; the six stamens are in two groups, and the ovary is composed of two fused carpels. Some species of *Fumaria* are agricultural weeds.   M.R.C.

FUNABASHI, city, Japan, E Honshu Island, in Chiba Prefecture, on Tokyo Bay, near Tokyo. The city, a road hub and a rail junction on the Sobu line, is a center for the manufacture of wood products, flour, and pens. Funabashi has fish hatcheries and one of the largest fish markets in the area. The Hokekyoji Temple, built in 1260 and sacred to the Nichiren Buddhists, is nearby, at Shimosanakayama. Pop. (1988 est.) 515,300.

FUNCHAL, city, Portugal, on the S shore of the island of Madeira, capital of Madeira District, on Funchal Bay. Industries here include sugar and flour milling, wine production, fruit canning, and the manufacture of tobacco products and soap. Fish, fruit, and the famous Madeira wines, as well as embroideries and laces, are exported. The city, sometimes called the Pearl of the Ocean, is a noted winter resort because of its beaches and mild climate. It is the site of remains of 16th- and 17th-century forts and of the 15th-century Cathedral of Santa Clara, which contains the tomb of João Gonçalves Zarco, discoverer of Madeira and founder of Funchal. Founded in 1421 and chartered in 1508, it was under Spanish rule from 1580 to 1640 and was occupied by the British in 1801 and 1807. Pop. (1981) 44,111.

FUNCTION, in mathematics, term used to indicate the relationship or correspondence between two or more quantities. The term *function* was first used in 1637 by the French mathematician René Descartes to designate a power x^n of a variable x. In 1694 the German mathematician Gottfried Wilhelm Leibniz applied the term to various aspects of a curve, such as its slope. The most widely used meaning until quite recently was defined in 1829 by the German mathematician Peter Dirichlet (1805–59). Dirichlet conceived of a function as a variable y, called the dependent variable, having its values fixed or determined in some definite manner by the values assigned to the independent variable x, or to several independent variables $x_1, x_2, \ldots, x_k$.

The values of both the dependent and independent variables were real or complex numbers. The statement $y = f(x)$, read "y is a function of x," indicated the interdependence between the variables x and y; $f(x)$ was usually given as an explicit formula, such as $f(x) = x^2 - 3x + 5$, or by a rule stated in words, such as $f(x)$ (for real x's) is the first integer larger than x. If a is a number, $f(a)$ is the value of the function for the value $x = a$. Thus, in the first example, $f(3) = 3^2 - 3\cdot3 + 5 = 5$, $f(-4) = (-4)^2 - 3(-4) + 5 = 33$; in the second example, $f(3) = f(3.1) = f(\pi) = 4$.

The emergence of set theory first extended and then altered substantially the concept of a function. The function concept in present-day mathematics may be illustrated as follows. Let $X = [x]$ and $Y = [y]$ be two sets with quite arbitrary elements; in particular, the elements may or may not be numbers, and the elements of X are not necessarily of the same type as those of Y. For example, X might be the set of the 50 states of the U.S. and Y the set of positive integers. Let P be the set of all possible ordered pairs (x, y) and F a subset of P with the property that if (x_1, y_1) and (x_2, y_2) are two elements of F, $Y_1 \neq \frac{1}{2}$ implies that $x_1 \neq x_2$; that is, F contains no more than one ordered pair with a given x as its first member. (If $x_1 \neq x_2$, it may happen that $y_1 = y_2$.) A function is now regarded as the set F of ordered pairs with the stated condition and is written $F: X \to Y$. The set X_1 of x's that actually occurs as first elements in the ordered pairs of F is called the domain of the function F; the set Y_1 of y's that occurs as second elements in the ordered pairs is called the range of the function F. Thus, {(New York, 7), (Ohio, 4), (Utah, 4)} is one function defined by the above example; the domain is the three states named, and the range is 4, 7.

The modern concept of a function is related to the Dirichlet concept. Dirichlet regarded $y = x^2 - 3x + 5$ as a function; today, $y = x^2 - 3x + 5$ is thought of as the rule that determines the correspondent y for a given x of an ordered pair of the function; thus, the preceding rule determines $(3, 5)$, $(-4, 33)$ as two of the infinite number of elements of the function. Although $y = f(x)$ is still used today, it is better to read it as "y is functionally related to x".

A function is also called a transformation or mapping in many branches of mathematics. If the range Y_1 is a proper subset of Y (that is, at least one y is in Y but not in Y_1), F is a function or transformation or mapping of the domain X_1 into Y; if $Y_1 = Y$, F is a function or transformation or mapping of X_1 into Y.   J.Si.; REV. BY J.Le.B.

For further information on this topic, see the Bibliography in volume 28, section 369.

FUNCTIONALISM, in architecture, a movement in the late 19th and 20th centuries that stripped architecture of all ornamentation so that a building's structure plainly expressed its function or purpose. *See* BAUHAUS; CHICAGO SCHOOL; INTERNATIONAL STYLE; MIES VAN DER ROHE, LUDWIG; SULLIVAN, LOUIS HENRI.

FUNCTIONALISM, also functional psychology, school of psychological thinking that stressed the study of the mind as a functioning and useful part of the organism. The functionalist attitude was a natural outcome of the widespread interest in Darwinism and in the doctrine of the "survival of the fittest." Functionalism emphasized such techniques as human intelligence tests and controlled experiments designed to test the ability of animals to learn and solve problems. This type of investigation represented a clear break with the introspective methods favored by other 19th-century psychologists. William James was one of the earliest proponents of the functionalist approach, and John Dewey was the first to teach the doctrine formally. From about 1890 to 1910 functionalism was the most important movement in psychology. In many respects it was the precursor of behaviorism. Functionalism is no longer regarded as a separate psychological doctrine, but its viewpoint has had a lasting influence on such fields of modern applied psychology as intelligence and aptitude testing. L.C.

FUNDAMENTALISM, conservative movement among Protestants in the U.S., which began in the late 19th century. It emphasized as absolutely basic to Christianity the following beliefs: the infallibility of the Bible, the virgin birth and the divinity of Jesus Christ, the sacrifice of Christ on the cross as atonement for the sins of all people, the physical resurrection and second coming of Christ, and the bodily resurrection of believers.

Origins. Fundamentalism is rooted in 18th- and 19th-century American revivalism (see REVIVALS, RELIGIOUS). Until the middle of the 19th century, its principal beliefs were held by almost all orthodox Protestant denominations, particularly by evangelical denominations. Fundamentalism as an organized, conservative movement dates from the early part of the 20th century. It developed out of a series of Bible conferences, the first ones held in 1876. These were called by members of various denominations who strongly objected to the following: the historical-literary study of the Bible, known as the higher criticism (see BIBLICAL SCHOLARSHIP); the attempts (still continuing) to reconcile traditional Christian beliefs and doctrines with contemporary experience and knowledge; and the acceptance of a scientific view of the world, particularly the popularization of the theory of evolution. Such trends and beliefs were opposed by many conservative members of Protestant denominations.

The more conservative members of each denomination at first attempted to exclude from their own institutions persons they considered outspoken or unyielding liberals. As a result a number of ministers and theologians were dismissed for espousing higher criticism. The exceptionally conservative, however, set up various rival bodies and educational institutions to spread their creed.

Fundamentalism began to flourish in 1909 with the publication and distribution of 12 books called *The Fundamentals.* By the time the 12th of the series had been published, about 3 million copies of *The Fundamentals* had been distributed throughout the U.S. and abroad. About this time a number of Bible institutes, such as the Los Angeles Bible Institute and the Moody Bible Institute in Chicago, were established or began to teach Fundamentalist beliefs and doctrines.

Current Status. Fundamentalism spread in the 1920s. It was strongest in rural areas, particularly in California, in the border states, and in the South. In these areas, Fundamentalists sharply delineated the issue of biblical infallibility in historical and scientific matters. The controversy over this issue grew most intense in the secular sphere when Fundamentalists urged many states to pass legislation forbidding the teaching of evolution in public schools. Several southern and border states, among them Tennessee, passed such laws. The Tennessee statute led, in 1925, to the world-famous trial of John Thomas Scopes (1900–70), a high school instructor, who was convicted of teaching evolution in defiance of law. The orator and politician William Jennings Bryan was an associate prosecutor at the trial; the lawyer Clarence Darrow defended Scopes. In 1968 the U.S. Supreme Court ruled that the Tennessee law was unconstitutional.

Fundamentalism lost momentum in the early 1930s. The main reasons were the acceptance by most Americans of modern scientific theories and methods and more liberal religious doctrines and the lack of an effective national organization to lead the Fundamentalist associations. Fundamentalism, along with the related, but more moderate Evangelical movement (see EVANGELICALISM), has since revived, however, primarily in reaction to such contemporary theological movements as ecumenicity (see ECUMENICAL MOVEMENT), neoorthodoxy, and Modernism (q.v.). Since the 1940s Fundamentalists have spent large sums annually to broadcast radio and television programs setting forth their views on the Bible. They established (1941) the American Council of Christian Churches as a conservative alternative to the National Council of Churches. In 1948 an international Fundamentalist group was formed; centered in Amsterdam, the International Council of Christian Churches claims support from 45 denominations in 18 countries. At the founding convention, some members of this group opposed the stated purposes of the World Council of Churches and offered their group as an alternate to the council.

E.C.B.

For further information on this topic, see the Bibliography in volume 28, sections 109–10.

FUNDY, BAY OF, large tidal inlet of the North Atlantic Ocean, separating the provinces of New Brunswick and Nova Scotia, and bordering on SE Maine. It is about 275 km (about 171 mi) long and up to 80 km (about 50 mi) wide. In the E, Fundy divides into two arms, Chignecto Bay on the N and Minas Channel (which leads into Minas Basin) on the S. The funnel effect of these narrowing arms increases the tidal range of the bay, and at times the water in the arms rises by as much as 18 m (about 60 ft), creating one of the world's highest tides. The tidal surge in Chignecto Bay produces a large crested wave, or bore, ranging to 1.8 m (about 6 ft) in height, in the lower Petitcodiac R. The rising tide in Fundy proper creates a "reversing falls" on the lower Saint John R., at Saint John, N.B. Passamaquoddy Bay, a W arm of Fundy, forms part of the boundary between New Brunswick and Maine. Although Fundy is very deep, navigation is difficult because of the rapid rise and fall of the tide. Major deepwater harbors are located at St. John and at Digby and Hantsport, N.S. Fundy National Park borders the bay in New Brunswick. The bay was discovered by the French explorer Pierre du Guast, sieur de Monts, in 1604.

FUNDY NATIONAL PARK, SE New Brunswick, established 1948. The park encompasses a rolling, forested highland containing many streams, waterfalls, and small lakes. Its rugged 13-km (8-mi) shoreline on the Bay of Fundy is characterized by eroded sandstone cliffs. Area, 206 sq km (80 sq mi).

FUNERAL RITES AND CUSTOMS, observances connected with death and burial. Such observances are a distinctive human characteristic. Not only are they deeply associated with religious beliefs about the nature of death and the existence of an afterlife, but they also have important psychological, sociological, and symbolic functions for the survivors. Thus, the study of the ways in which the dead are treated in different cultures leads to a better understanding of the many diverse views about death and dying, as well as of human nature.

Funerary rites and customs are concerned not only with the preparation and disposal of the body, but also with the well-being of the survivors and with the persistence of the spirit or memory of the deceased.

Preparation and Disposal of the Body. In all societies, both advanced and simple, the human body is prepared in some fashion before it is finally laid to rest. The first known deliberate burials were those of early *Homo sapiens* groups. Archaeological evidence indicates that one of these early groups, the Neanderthals, stained their dead with red ocher—a possible indication of some belief in an afterlife. Washing the body, dressing it in special garments, and adorning it with ornaments, religious objects, or amulets are common procedures. Sometimes the feet are tied together—possibly to prevent the ghost of the deceased from wandering about. The most thorough treatment of the body is embalming (q.v.), which probably originated in ancient Egypt. The Egyptians believed that in order for the soul to pass into the next life, the body must remain intact; hence, to preserve it, they developed the procedures of mummification (*see* EGYPTIAN MYTHOLOGY). The purpose of embalming in the U.S. is to prevent mourners from confronting the process of putrefaction.

The various methods used for disposal of the body are linked to religious beliefs, climate and geography, and social status. Burial (q.v.) is associated with ancestor worship or beliefs about the afterlife; cremation (q.v.) is sometimes viewed as liberating the spirit of the deceased. Exposure, another widespread practice, may be a substitute for burial in Arctic regions; among the Parsis it has religious significance. Less common are water burial (such as burial at sea); sending the corpse to sea in a boat (a journey to ancestral regions or to the world of the dead); and cannibalism (q.v.; a ceremonial act to ensure continued unity of the deceased with the tribe).

Funeral and Mourning Rituals. The actual funeral—conveying the deceased to the place of burial, cremation, or exposure—also provides an occasion for ritual. Frequently, transporting the body develops into a procession by detailed prescriptions. In Hinduism, the procession to the place of cremation is led by a man carrying a firebrand. The mourners at one point walk around the bier; in former times among some groups, a widow was expected to throw herself onto the burning pyre of her husband (*see* SUTTEE). Finally, the cremated remains are deposited in a sacred river. In ancient Greece, Egypt, and China, servants were sometimes buried with their masters. This form of human sacrifice was based on the belief that in the afterworld the deceased continued to need their services.

In modern Western societies, funeral rituals include wakes, processions, the tolling of bells, the celebration of a religious rite, and the delivery of

A Balinese cremation ceremony takes place on a sunny beach. In the rear is the traditional cremation tower.   Suzanne J. Engelmann

a eulogy. Military funerals often require special salutes fired by weapons. Jewish tradition prescribes a seven-day period of seclusion (*shibah*) following the funeral of a close relative.

The desire to preserve the memory of the departed has resulted in many kinds of memorial acts. These include preserving a part of the body as a relic, building monuments, reciting elegies, and inscribing an epitaph (q.v.) on a tombstone. *See also* CATACOMBS; CRYPT; DOLMEN; MAUSOLEUM; MEGALITHIC MONUMENTS; SARCOPHAGUS; TOMB.

Symbolism and Social Significance. Contemporary anthropological studies interpret funeral customs as symbolic expressions of the values that prevail in a particular society. This approach is strengthened by the observation that much of what occurs during a funeral is determined by custom. Even the emotions exhibited during death rituals can be dictated by tradition. Mourners who are unrelated to the deceased may be hired to wail and grieve. Also, the time and place where relatives are expected to show emotion may be defined by traditional rules.

Some anthropologists have noted that in spite of the wide variation in funerary practices, four major symbolic elements frequently recur. The first is color symbolism. Although the association of black with death is not universal, the use of black clothes to represent death is widely distributed. A second feature is the treatment of the hair of the mourners, which is often shaved as a sign of grief or, conversely, is allowed to grow to emphasize dishevelment as a symbol of sorrow. Another broad usage is the inclusion of noisy festivities and drumming at funerals. Finally, several mundane techniques for processing the dead body are employed in many cultures. The classical anthropological interpretation of the ceremonies surrounding death (like those accompanying birth, initiation, and marriage) is to view them as a rite of passage.

In terms of the society, the symbolic significance of death is most forcefully depicted in the funerals of rulers. Especially in cultures where the tribe or nation is personified in the ruler, such funerals often reach the proportion of a political drama in which the whole nation is at stake. The ruler's burial is not simply a religious event; it is an occurrence with great political and cosmological consequences. The pyramids (q.v.) of Egypt, for example, became both a symbol and a proof of royal authority. Because the pharaohs were the living embodiment of societal permanence and of spiritual and temporal authority, these elements were all threatened at their demise. The participation of their successors in the funeral rites provided assurance of continuity. In Thailand, after the cremation of the monarch, the new king and members of the royal family searched the ashes for fragments of bone. Some of these relics became the focus of a royal cult that indirectly stressed the continuation of the deceased ruler's presence and authority.

In societies as diverse as those of England, 18th-century France, and the Shilluk people of the Sudan, the funeral rituals for monarchs were related to cultural ideas about the nature of monarchy and the political order and to the maneuvering for power that takes place upon the transfer of authority.

Funeral practices in the U.S. have been interpreted economically, psychologically, and symbolically. Economic explanations interpreted the uniformity of American death customs as a product of ruthless capitalism and the content of these customs as expressing only materialistic values. Psychological theories explained the ritual process as a manifestation of fear and guilt related to the inevitable confrontation with death and as a mechanism to help mourners come to terms with their loss. More recently, symbolic interpretations have centered on the social context of funeral rites, considering them an expression of a core of life values sacred to the society in which they occur. In this view, American death rituals, which present the corpse so that it appears natural and comfortable for its last public appearance, are neither a manifestation of universal revulsion at confronting the decay of the body, nor an example of capitalistic manipulation and exploitation. Rather, they are a somber rite of passage that reflects American social and religious values concerning the nature of the individual and the meaning of life.

For further information on this topic, see the Bibliography in volume 28, section 343.

FUNGI, diverse group of either single-celled or multicellular organisms that obtain food by direct absorption of nutrients. The food is dissolved by enzymes that the fungi excrete, is then absorbed through thin cell walls, and is distributed by simple circulation, or streaming, of the protoplasm (q.v.). Together with bacteria (q.v.), fungi are responsible for the decay and decomposition of all organic matter and are found wherever other forms of life exist. Some are parasitic on living matter and cause serious plant and animal diseases (see PARASITE). The study of fungi is called mycology.

Fungi were traditionally classified as a division

in the kingdom Plantae. They were thought of as plants that have no stems or leaves and that in the course of becoming food absorbers lost the pigment chlorophyll, which is needed for conducting photosynthesis (q.v.). Most scientists today, however, view them as an entirely separate group that evolved from unpigmented flagellates (q.v.) and place them either in the kingdom Protista (q.v.) or the kingdom Fungi, according to their complexity of organization (see Classification below). Approximately 100,000 species of fungi are known. The more complex groups are believed to have derived from the primitive types, which have flagellated cells at some stage in their life cycle.

Structure. Most fungi are composed of delicate protoplasm-containing tubes known as hyphae, which frequently are partitioned by dividing walls called septa. One or two nuclei are found in each hyphal cell, and protoplasm moves through a tiny pore in the center of each septum. In the algaelike fungi of the phylum Zygomycota, however, the hyphae ordinarily do not have septa, and numerous nuclei are scattered throughout the protoplasm. Hyphae grow by elongation at the tips and also by branching. The resulting profusion of hyphae is called the mycelium. Abundant development of mycelium may result in the formation of large fruiting structures such as mushrooms and puffballs. Other types of massive hyphal structures enable some fungi to exist under difficult conditions or to spread to suitable nutritional sources. The cordlike strands of mycelium of the honey mushroom, *Armillaria mellea,* enable it to spread from the roots of one tree to another. Some fungi form resistant, more or less spherical masses of mycelium, called sclerotia, which may be smaller than grains of sand or as large as cantaloupes.

Reproduction. Most fungi reproduce by spores, which are tiny particles of protoplasm enclosed in walls (*see* SPORE). The common mushroom *Agaricus campestris* may form 12 billion or more spores on its fruiting body; the giant puffball *Calvatia gigantea* may produce several trillion. See MUSHROOM.

Spores are usually formed in one of two ways. In one process the spores form after the union of two or more nuclei within a specialized cell or series of cells. These spores typically germinate into hyphae that have different combinations of the hereditary characteristics of the parent nuclei. The four types of spores that are produced in this way—oospores, zygospores, ascospores, and basidiospores—are representative of the four principal groups of fungi. Oospores are formed by sexual union of a male and a female cell, zygospores by conjugation of two similar sex cells. Ascospores are spores (usually eight) that are contained in sacs (asci), and basidiospores (usually four) are contained in clublike structures (basidia).

The other usual method of spore production involves the transformation of hyphae into numerous short segments or into various kinds of more complicated structures. Here, the fusion of two nuclei is not a requirement. The principal reproductive spores formed in this asexual manner include oidia, conidia, and sporangiospores. Sporangiospores are formed inside bladderlike containers called sporangia. Most fungi produce spores both sexually and asexually.

Classification. Although relatively complicated systems of fungus classification are used in various textbooks, mycologists commonly employ a simple system that has the merit of convenience. In this system the four main phyla are the Oomycota, Zygomycota, Ascomycota, and Basidiomycota, which individually produce oospores, zygospores, ascospores, and basidiospores. A large variety of species is loosely placed in a fifth major phylum, Deuteromycota (also called Fungi Imperfecti), because they are not known to produce spores by fusion of nuclei and are therefore difficult to classify. Most, however, seem to be related to Ascomycota.

Several other phyla are considered fungi or closely related to fungi: Actinomycota, Myxomycota, Plasmodiophoromycota, Labyrinthulomycota, and Acrasiomycota. The Actinomycota, with very delicate hyphae and reproduction usually by oidia or conidia, are grouped as intermediate between bacteria and fungi. The Myxomycota, or true slime molds (q.v.), are included among the fungi by some mycologists and placed with the animallike protists by others. In this group the nutritional phase is an unwalled mass of amoebalike protoplasm, called a plasmodium. The reproductive phase includes swimming cells, called swarm cells, which are propelled by two flagella of unequal length. The Plasmodiophoromycota resemble Myxomycota in having swarm cells and a plasmodial stage. The Labyrinthulomycota and Acrasiomycota have some slime mold characteristics, but their nutritional stage (the pseudoplasmodium) is different.

Oomycota. The phylum of oomycetes is composed of algaelike fungi, ranging from a single cell to a complex mass of hyphae that are not walled off by septa (nonseptate mycelium). Besides forming oospores, the oomycetes form zoospores that move about by two flagella. Included in the phylum are water molds, white rusts, and downy mildews. Most water molds live on dead matter, but *Saprolegnia parasitica* invades living fish. The white rusts and downy mildews, belonging to the order Peronosporales, are parasitic on plants. In some downy mildews, including *Phytophthora* and *Peronospora*, the spore cases containing the zoospores may be modified to resemble and function as conidia.

Chytridiomycota. Chytrids are regarded as closely related to the Oomycota. In some classification systems they are considered protists rather than true fungi. *See* CHYTRIDS.

The scarlet cup fungus, Sarcoscypha coccinea, *an ascomycete, has a white exterior and a distinctively colored hymenium, where spores are formed.*

John MacGregor–Peter Arnold, Inc.

Zygomycota. The zygomycetes are characterized by the formation of sexual, thick-walled zygospores and asexual, nonswimming sporangiospores. Black bread mold (*Rhizopus nigricans*), a well-known representative of this group in the order Mucorales, forms a mass of hyphae on stale bread, fruits, and other foodstuffs. Fungi in the order Entomophthorales are parasitic on flies and other insects; they have single sporangiospores in spore cases, and each spore case develops into a structure that becomes detached and functions as a conidium. The order Zoopagales includes fungi parasitic on amoebas, nematodes, and arthropods.

Ascomycota. Ascomycetes, also called sac fungi, bear a definite number of ascospores inside a bladderlike sac called an ascus. Except for some yeasts and a few other types, ascomycetes have well-developed hyphae, usually with a single nucleus in each hyphal cell. Certain cells become binucleate shortly before formation of the spore sacs. Nuclear union occurs in the young ascus; division usually produces eight daughter nuclei, which become centers of ascospore formation. Some ascomycetes have only one ascospore; others may have up to several hundred.

The three main classes of Ascomycota are the Hemiascomycetes, Euascomycetes, and Loculoascomycetes. The Hemiascomycetes include yeasts and similar fungi that do not have asci formed within or on a supporting hyphal mass. Brewer's yeast (*Saccharomyces cerevisiae*), in addition to forming ascospores, reproduces by forming protuberances, or buds, that eventually pinch off from the parent cell. The yeasts of the genus *Schizosaccharomyces* divide by fission. The Taphrinales, such as the parasite causing peach leaf curl, often are included as an order here, but their true relationship is uncertain.

The simplest forms of Euascomycetes are those, as in the order Eurotiales, in which asci are scattered throughout the interior of a ball of hyphae called a cleisthothecium. *Penicillium* and *Aspergillus* are conidial stages of the Eurotiales. The Erysiphales, a group of plant parasites called the powdery mildews, have cleistothecia of specialized form. Some ascomycetes, known usually as Pyrenomycetes, have asci formed inside flask-shaped structures called perithecia. Many perithecia may be borne on a supporting mass of hyphae called an ascocarp. The morels, truffles, and cup fungi are well-known ascocarps, with asci borne at the upper surface. Another Pyrenomycete, the genus *Neurospora*—familiar as a red bread mold—has been used extensively in the study of heredity.

The Loculoascomycetes differ from the groups previously described by having double-walled asci formed within holes in the interior of hyphal masses. Representative orders are the Myriangiales, Dothideales, and Pleosporales.

Basidiomycota. This phylum comprises numerous and varied types of fungi, reproductive structures of which are the basidia, located at the tips of the hyphae and usually bearing four basidiospores on stalklike protrusions. The basidia may be club-shaped, cylindrical, or oval. The two principal classes of Basidiomycota are the Heterobasidiomycetes, which commonly have four-celled basidia, and the Homobasidiomycetes, typically with one-celled basidia.

The Heterobasidiomycetes include some important plant parasites, such as the rusts in the order Uredinales and the smuts in the order Ustilaginales. These groups have basidia that are either deeply cleft or divided into several cells, usually four, each of which produces a spore.

Many rusts, including *Puccinia graminis*, the black stem rust of wheat and other grains, have a complicated life cycle, requiring growth on two different hosts for production of the various spore forms. In the black stem rust, small, flask-shaped structures, known as the spermagonia, bear numerous tiny, sporelike bodies, called spermatia, on the upper surfaces of barberry leaves. On the lower surfaces develop cup-shaped structures called aecia, from the bases of which arise rows of aeciospores. The aeciospores never reinfect barberry, but attack only grain plants, producing clusters of red, spore-containing pustules called uredia, which give a rustlike appearance to the plant stems and leaves. Later in the season another type of spore, known as the teliospore, or winter spore, which is black and thick walled, is produced on the wheat stem. In the following spring the teliospores develop cylindrical projections, each of which divides into four cells bearing individual basidiospores. Rusts that alternate between two hosts are termed heteroecious; those that have all stages of development confined to one host are known as monoecious.

In the smuts the teliospores are known as chlamydospores. These spores may soon reinfect the host plant but usually germinate in the soil the next spring and produce a short filament of approximately four cells, which bear basidiospores called sporidia. The remaining Heterobasidiomycetes include various jelly fungi in the orders Auriculariales, Dacrymycetales, and Tremellales.

The Homobasidiomycetes are subdivided into two main groups: the Hymenomycetes, in which the fruiting surface, or hymenium, is external; and the Gasteromycetes, in which the basidia are

Claviceps purpurea, *an ascomycete, growing on grain heads of rye.*

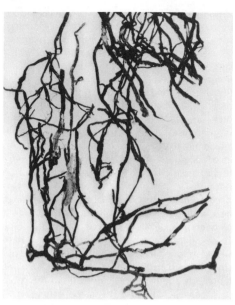

Honey mushroom (Armillaria mellea), *a basidiomycete, with masses of hyphae growing in strands.*

formed inside the fruiting body. These groups may be regarded as subclasses of the Homobasidiomycetes. Most of these fungi are saprophytic, that is, they live on dead or decaying organic matter.

The Hymenomycetes include the families comprising the mushrooms, coral fungi, and the pore, or bracket, fungi, which differ in the type of fruiting body, or basidiocarp. In the mushrooms, which are known as gill fungi, Agaricaceae, the hymenium is formed along the sides of elongated blades, or gills. Coral fungi, Clavariaceae, have a multibranched basidiocarp, with the hymenium on its smooth surface. In the bracket fungi, Polyporaceae, common on rotting logs, the hymenium lines the inside of tubes. Tooth fungi, Hydnaceae, have the hymenium on spiny outgrowths.

The Gasteromycetes include such familiar forms as the puffballs in the order Lycoperdales and stinkhorns in the order Phallales. The basidiocarps of the puffballs often are large, globular structures, containing enormous numbers of spores. The fruiting body of the stinkhorns is a cylindrical structure, and the sporebearing surface at the apex of the structure emanates a foul odor that attracts carrion-feeding insects and ensures dissemination of the spores.

Deuteromycota. The deuteromycotas are conidial stages mostly of ascomycetes and less commonly of zygomycetes or basidiomycetes. In the order Moniliales, represented by such genera as

Aspergillus, Penicillium, Verticillium, Alternaria, and *Fusarium,* oidia or conidia are formed usually on a fluffy down of loosely interlaced hyphae. The Melanconiales, with genera such as *Colletotrichum,* have minute saucerlike fruiting structures (acervuli). The conidia of the Sphaeropsidales are formed inside flask-shaped structures (pycnidia). *See* DEUTEROMYCETES.

Fungus Physiology. Most fungi have hyphal walls consisting primarily of a white, horny substance known as chitin and also containing some hemicelluloses. Cellulose is found in only a few groups of fungi, but is characteristic of the Oomycota. The water content of jelly fungi in the Heterobasidiomycetes often is more than 90 percent. Spores may have less than 50 percent water content, and dormant structures such as sclerotia contain even less. Fungi require free oxygen and large amounts of water and of carbohydrates or other carbon sources for growth. Sugars such as glucose and levulose are usable by most fungi, but the use of other carbon sources depends on the ability of the fungus to produce suitable enzymes. Some of the mycorrhizal fungi may use nitrogen from the atmosphere, but all of the others depend on nitrates, ammonium salts, or other inorganic or organic nitrogen compounds. Other elements necessary for fungus growth include potassium, phosphorus, magnesium, and sulfur. Traces of iron, manganese, copper, molybdenum, zinc, and gallium and small amounts of growth substances also are necessary. Some fungi are at least partially deficient in one or more of these growth substances.

The enzymes of fungi enable them to act upon a variety of substances. A group of enzymes, called the zymase complex, permits yeasts to carry on alcoholic fermentation (q.v.). Other enzymes, including protopectinase, pectase, and pectinase, which are elaborated by such fungi as *Botrytis cinerea* and *Aspergillus oryzae*, hydrolyze pectic substances contained in the middle layers of plant-cell walls. Amylase, cellobiase, cytase, dextrinase, invertase, lactase, maltase, protease, and tannase are among the other enzymes produced by fungi.

Glycogen, a substance related to starch and dextrin, is the most common reserve carbohydrate of fungi. In addition, various fungi form polysaccharides and polyhydroxy alcohol such as mannitol and glycerol (*see* GLYCERIN). Proteins and fats are produced in abundance by some fungi. Oxalic acid and other organic acids such as citric, formic, pyruvic, succinic, malic, and acetic acids are formed by many fungi, but lactic acid production is largely confined to the Mucoraceae. Other fungus products include complex sulfur compounds, chlorine-containing substances, and numerous pigments. A few fungi have the ability to form volatile arsenic compounds when they are growing on arsenic-containing substrates.

Fungus Ecology. Spores and hyphal fragments of fungi are carried for long distances in the atmosphere. Spores of *Cladosporium* are especially abundant in the air.

Water habitats often abound with chytrids and water molds. A number of ascomycetes and deuteromycetes also frequent either fresh or salt water. In recent years many fungi have been discovered in polluted rivers and streams. These fungi participate in the natural decomposition of sewage. Of special interest, because they cause disease in humans, are the species *Aspergillus fumigatus* and *Geotrichum candidum*.

Soil is a natural habitat for saprophytic fungi, which live on organic remains, as well as a reservoir for parasitic fungi, which infect living plants and animals. The water molds, downy mildews, and Mucorales are common soil inhabitants, as are various Eurotiales, other ascomycetes, and many deuteromycetes. Many such fungi decompose cellulose and proteins and thus are active in the formation of humus (q.v.).

Certain fungi live in a symbiotic association with algae (*see* SYMBIOSIS), forming characteristic structures known as lichens (*see* LICHEN). Most lichen fungi are ascomycetes, but the fungus components of *Cora pavonia* and a few other species are basidiomycetes. Fungi that are intimately associated with roots of higher plants form mycorrhiza, a specialized type of hyphal

The zygomycote Rhizopus stolonifer, *a black bread mold, forms a mass of hyphae on a sweet potato.*

Stinkhorns are basidiomycotes that spread their spores by attracting insects with their foul odor.

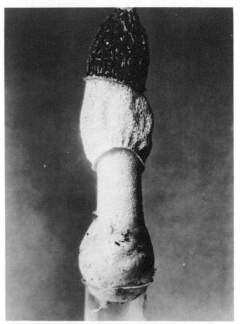

The earthstar fungus, Geastrum triplex, a basidiomycete, grows beneath trees and releases spores when water drops strike its bared spore capsule.

P. A. Hinchliffe–Bruce Coleman, Inc.

growth in which a portion of the mycelium either wraps itself around the tips of roots, forming a velvety white cover, or penetrates into the cortex of the root. A number of plants seem to be dependent on this relationship for satisfactory development. Certain species of mushrooms are prominent in forming mycorrhizae.

Some fungi, which ordinarily grow on dead organic matter, are capable of infecting live plants when given the opportunity. Others cannot exist except as parasites of living plants. Diseases caused by chytrids, oomycetes, and other simple fungi include clubroot of cabbage, powdery scab of potatoes, potato wart, white rusts, potato late blight, and downy mildews. Diseases caused by ascomycetes and their conidial stages include the spot anthracnoses, chestnut blight, Dutch elm disease, oak wilt, ergot, brown rot of stone fruits, and numerous others. The rusts and smuts are basidiomycetes. See DISEASES OF PLANTS; articles on some individual diseases.

Some soil-inhabiting fungi trap microscopic organisms such as amoebas and nematodes. Most of these predacious fungi seem to be deuteromycetes or conidial stages of zygomycetes, but some appear to be conidial stages of basidiomycetes. Nematodes are trapped by networks of hyphae covered by an adhesive substance, by knoblike outgrowths that come into contact with the prey, or by hyphal rings that in some instances swell shut abruptly after the nematodes have entered. After an amoeba or nematode is trapped, special hyphae grow into its body and deplete it of protoplasm.

Many small animals, insects, and millipedes eat fungi and thus are instrumental in spore distribution. Some groups of insects cultivate fungi as food. Notable among these are the ambrosia beetles, tropical leaf-cutting ants, and certain groups of termites. Numerous fungi, including *Entomophthora muscae* and other members of the order Entomophthorales, are parasites of insects. *Septobasidium*, in the Heterobasidiomycetes, has a relationship with scale insects that is partly parasitic, partly symbiotic.

Uses of Fungi. The hydrolytic enzymes of fungi are useful for a number of industrial processes. When grown on steamed wheat bran or rice bran, *Aspergillus oryzae* produces an amylase product useful in alcoholic fermentation. Proteases obtained from *A. flavus* are used in the manufacture of liquid glue. Commercial production of industrial ethyl alcohol is accomplished by fermentation of sugarcane molasses or hydrolyzed starch by means of enzymes formed by *Saccharomyces cerevisiae*. In the process of making bread, yeast is added to dough to produce carbon dioxide.

A. niger is used for the commercial production of citric acid (q.v.) and in the production of gluconic acid and of gallic acid, which is used in the manufacture of inks and dyes. Synthetic resins are manufactured from itaconic acid produced by *A. terreus* and from fumaric acid formed by the black bread mold *Rhizopus stolonifer*. Gibberellic acid, which promotes increased growth of plant cells, is formed by *Gibberella fujikuroi*, a fungus causing disease in rice plants. Commercially usable oils have been obtained from species of *Fusarium, Endomyces,* and other genera, and the species *Torulopsis utilis* is a practical source of edible proteins. Vitamin D is prepared by irradiation of ergosterol, a substance which may be obtained from the waste brewer's yeast. A yeastlike fungus called *Eremothecium ashbyii* is a source of riboflavin, and biotin accumulates during production of fumaric acid by *Rhizopus nigricans. Penicillium roqueforti* is used to produce Roquefort cheese and *P. camemberti* to ripen Camembert cheese.

Fungi have been used medicinally since ancient times. The use of *Polyporus officinalis* as a purgative is no longer prevalent, but the alkaloid in the sclerotium of ergot, *Claviceps purpurea,* still is used to produce uterine contractions in childbirth. Ergot alkaloids are also a source of lysergic acid diethylamide (q.v.), commonly known as LSD, which produces hallucinogenic effects, often of a severe nature. The use of antibiotics (*see* ANTIBIOTIC) in medical practice dates from recognition of the antibiotic properties of penicillin (q.v.). Many antibiotics today are produced by nonfungal microorganisms. Griseofulvin, however, is an antifungal antibiotic formed by several species of *Penicillium.*

See also FUNGICIDES; FUNGUS INFECTIONS. P.L.L.

For further information on this topic, see the Bibliography in volume 28, section 457.

FUNGICIDES, toxic substances applied either to prevent the growth of or to kill fungi detrimental to plants, animals, or humans. Most agricultural fungicides are sprayed or dusted on seeds, leaves, or fruit to prevent the spread of rusts, smuts, molds, or mildew (*see* DISEASES OF PLANTS). Three serious fungus diseases that can now be checked by fungicides are wheat rust, corn smut, and the potato-blight fungus, the last of which caused the potato famine in Ireland in the early 1840s. Bordeaux mixture, developed in 1882 and made of slaked lime and copper sulfate, was the first effective fungicide. For many decades it was applied to a broad range of plants and fruit trees. Now many other fungicides are more selectively applied to specific plants and fungi. Other commonly used fungicides include organic mercury compounds, effective in treating seeds before planting, and dithiocarbamates, sulfur-containing compounds used on a wide variety of plant and tree crops and ornamentals.

For further information on this topic, see the Bibliography in volume 28, sections 453, 590.

FUNGUS INFECTIONS, diseases caused by the growth of fungi (q.v.) in or on the body. In most healthy persons fungal infections are mild, involving only the skin, hair, nails, or other superfi-

cial sites, and they clear up spontaneously. They include the familiar ringworm and athlete's foot (qq.v.). In someone with an impaired immune system (q.v.), however, such infections, called dermatophytoses, can persist for long periods. The organisms causing dermatophytoses belong to the genera *Microsporum, Epidermophyton,* and *Trichophyton.*

Fungi can also invade internal organs of the body, especially the lungs, where the infections resemble pneumonia or pulmonary tuberculosis. These infections usually occur in persons whose immune system has been suppressed by diseases such as AIDS, by anticancer drugs, or by radiation; patients being treated with steroid hormones (*see* HYDROCORTISONE); persons with diabetes; and those being treated with antibiotic drugs for a long time. Two fungi often found in such cases are *Cryptococcus* and *Aspergillus,* which are called opportunistic pathogens.

Systemic infections also occur in healthy persons, involving the fungi *Blastomyces; Histoplasma,* endemic to the midwestern U.S.; or *Coccioides,* endemic to the southwestern U.S. The infectious agents *Nocardia* and *Actinomyces,* formerly classed as fungi, are now considered bacteria.

Fungi belonging to the genus *Candida,* especially *C. albicans,* can infect both internal organs and mucous membranes of the mouth (*see* THRUSH), throat, and genital tract. In persons with impaired immunity, this organism can cause a chronic infection.

Many drugs are available for treating fungal infections. These include both intravenous and oral drugs, and many agents are available for topical (local) application. Persons chronically infected with *Candida, Histoplasma,* or *Cryptococcus* may require long-term therapy with an oral or an intravenous drug.

For further information on this topic, see the Bibliography in volume 28, sections 487, 511, 521.

FUNK, Isaac Kauffman (1839–1912), American editor and publisher, born in Clifton, Ohio, and educated at Wittenberg College and Wittenberg Theological Seminary. An ordained Lutheran minister, he held several pastorates. In 1875 he founded the firm of I. K. Funk & Co. in New York City. The publisher Adam Willis Wagnalls joined him in founding the Funk & Wagnalls Co. in 1877. Funk was the editor of *A Standard Dictionary of the English Language* (1894) and chairman of the editorial board of *The Jewish Encyclopedia* (12 vol., 1901–6). Funk was the author of several books, and he edited periodicals dealing with diverse subjects such as theology, prohibition, psychic phenomena, and simplified spelling.

FUNK & WAGNALLS, publishing company long associated with reference books and other nonfiction. The firm was originally founded in New York City in 1875 by Isaac K. Funk; it became Funk & Wagnalls two years later, after Adam Willis Wagnalls became a partner in the enterprise. Both founders were Lutheran ministers. During its early years the company published periodicals and religious books for the clergy. A major undertaking was the publication in 1894 of *A Standard Dictionary of the English Language.* The *Funk & Wagnalls Standard Encyclopedia* was first published in 1912; the encyclopedia, under various names, has been continuously revised and expanded since that time. During its first 90 years Funk & Wagnalls published many reference works, books in the humanities and sciences, and periodicals such as *The Literary Digest.*

In 1965 Funk & Wagnalls Co. was purchased by the Reader's Digest Association. The rights to publish the encyclopedia had previously been obtained by the Unicorn Press, later known as the Standard Reference Work Publishing Co. By 1953 that firm began to sell the encyclopedia and other educational materials through supermarket continuity promotions, enjoying considerable success with this marketing technique. The company (by this time Funk & Wagnalls, Inc.) was acquired by Dun & Bradstreet in 1971. It retained *Funk & Wagnalls New Encyclopedia,* but all other properties were transferred to other publishers in later corporate mergers. In 1984 the firm was purchased by its senior officers; it was acquired by the Field Corporation in 1988. In 1991 it was purchased by K-III Holdings, Inc.

See also DICTIONARY; ENCYCLOPEDIA.

FUNSTON, Frederick (1865–1917), American army officer, prominent in the U.S. conquest of the Philippine Islands. Col. Funston and his regiment, the Kansas Volunteers, were sent (1898) to the Philippines after the islands had been ceded to the U.S. by Spain. He directed the regiment in operations against the Filipino nationalists led by Emilio Aguinaldo, planning and taking part personally in the expedition that captured Aguinaldo in 1901. For this exploit he was promoted to brigadier general in the regular army.

Funston was in command of the California military department during the San Francisco earthquake and fire of 1906 and rendered valuable assistance to the civil authorities in maintaining order after the disaster. He was promoted to major general in 1914.

FURFURAL, also furfuraldehyde, organic liquid aldehyde, $C_5H_4O_2$, derived by steam distillation from agricultural residues treated with dilute sulfuric acid. The group of compounds related to furfural are called furans. A colorless, oily liquid in the pure state, furfural has a pungent almondlike odor, turns reddish brown upon exposure to air, and boils at 161.7° C (323.1° F). It is widely used industrially as a refining solvent in the manufacture of synthetic rubber and nylon and in the production of resins for molded plastics and metal coatings. It is also a component of insecticide, embalming, and disinfectant fluids, and certain light-sensitive furfurals are used in lithography. *See also* FORMALDEHYDE.

FURIES. *See* ERINYES.

FUR INDUSTRY, area of commerce that encompasses farming or trapping certain furbearing animals, processing their skins for sale to manufacturers of fur garments, and marketing finished garments to retail outlets. The term *fur* refers to any animal skin or part that has hair, fleece, or fur fibers attached, either in a raw or processed state. Skins of furbearing animals are also called peltries or pelts.

From earliest times, fur has been a prized commodity. Exploration in the New World made furs more readily available, and as early as 1530 regular shipments of beaver pelts were sent to Europe from the colonies. The beaver, trapped by American Indians, was a main source of barter at trading posts that later grew into such cities as Chicago; Saint Louis, Mo.; Saint Paul, Minn.; Spokane, Wash.; and Detroit.

Fur Farming. Fur farming, or raising animals in captivity under controlled conditions, started in

Fur nailer. After being wetted, skins are tacked, upside down, with thousands of nails in the position required by the pattern. **Fur Information and Fashion Council**

Canada in 1887 on Prince Edward Island. Animals with unique characteristics of size, color, or texture can pass those characteristics on to their offspring through controlled breeding. Fur farmers customarily cross-breed animals (mate different varieties from the same species) and inbreed animals (mate close relatives) to produce furs with desirable characteristics. The silver fox, which is developed from the red fox, was the first fur produced in this way. Today, so-called mutation minks ranging from white to near black and from bluish to lavender and rosy-tan colors, each with exotic trade names, are raised on thousands of fur farms, as are chinchilla, nutria, and fox. Fur-farmed animals provide a steady supply of fine-quality, well-cared-for peltries.

Marketing Channels for Furs. North American fur trappers and farmers have come under increasing pressure from foreign competition. By the late 1980s, the Scandinavian countries produced 45 percent of the world supply of peltries; the USSR supplied 31 percent, the U.S. 10 percent, and Canada only 3 percent. Retail sales of furs in the U.S. grew from less than $400 million in the early 1970s to $1.5 billion by the mid-1980s, then stagnated at between $1.8 billion and $2 billion annually. The fur industry has also been hurt by protests from animal rights activists and the increasing popularity of artificial fur.

Trappers send peltries to local collecting stations or to dealers who send them on to receiving houses, where they are prepared for auction. Prime furs, those caught during the coldest season (when fur and skin are best for garments), are labeled as firsts. Unprime furs, caught earlier or later, are labeled as seconds, thirds, or fourths. Fur-farmed peltries are often brought to collecting stations; more commonly, the farmer is part of a farming cooperative, such as the Great Lakes Mink Association or the Mutation Mink Breeders Association, whose representatives supervise the assembling and sale of peltries.

At fur auction houses, the furs, bundled in groups according to color, size, quality, and source, are sold to the highest bidders; all sales are for cash. Some furs are sold through brokerage firms. Fur dealers and manufacturers buy at the auctions or through brokers. Factoring, begun in 1935, is a method of financing dealers, brokers, and manufacturers. Factors charge a percentage for the use of their money.

Processing Furs. Furs bought at auction need to be preserved and beautified. Dressing and dyeing firms specialize in certain types of furs and charge a price for each processed skin.

Dressing. Dressing entails carefully scraping the skins to remove fat, washing them, and treating

Fur cutter. Long and narrow skins are needed for fur coats. In the letting-out process, each skin is cut into diagonal strips, which are then sewn together in invisible cross seams.　**Fur Information and Fashion Council**

them with a series of chemicals that soften and preserve, or tan, the skin. Because the fur fiber—the shorter, fluffier fur that keeps the animal warm—and the longer guard hair—the coarser, harsher hair that sheds water and protects the fur fiber—are the beauty marks of most fur, they are given special treatment. Repeated tumblings in sawdust remove remaining grease and clean the furs. A final glazing, ironing or spraying with a chemical and air blowing, puts a sheen on the finished fur. Some furs go through additional beautification steps. Coarse guard hair, for example, from beaver and Alaska fur seal, is removed by plucking. The remaining fur fiber is then sheared with revolving blades to a velvety texture. Nutria, some rabbit, and muskrat, to imitate seal, may also be sheared. Pointing, a process of gluing either badger or monkey guard hair into furs, adds thickness and beauty to the fur by adding contrasting colors. Furs that, after glazing, have a rich coloration, are sold in their natural state.

Dyeing. Less attractive furs may have their color changed by dyeing or bleaching. Both of these processes tend to weaken the skins somewhat and to oxidize the furs, causing them to turn reddish or yellowish upon lengthy exposure to sun and air.

Dye may be applied in a bath of color, by rolling the dye onto the fur, by stroking it on with a feather, or simply by touching up the tips of the guard hair. Some furs, such as rabbit, may be stenciled to resemble leopard or other spotted furs. To brighten furs, a fluorescent dye is used, and some furs have their color altered by the application of a solution of copper or iron salts. The processed skins are then made into fur garments.

Fur Garment Manufacture. Since the mid-1970s furs have been made in more varied, sporty, and exotic ways as designers have created new, dramatic styles. Good-quality garments are made from the choice parts of the skin, which excludes the belly (flanks), paw, and head sections. Less costly garments are made from this waste fur.

Cutting and shaping. Large skins, such as mouton lamb, may have the garment pattern cut from the skin. The garment parts are then joined together. Most animals, however, have smaller skins that must be joined in various ways to create a garment. The skin-on-skin method, commonly used with muskrat, squirrel, rabbit, small lamb, and some chinchilla, joins the trimmed skin lengthwise to other skins. This method leaves a straight, a zigzag, or a rounded joining mark, visible in all but curly-haired furs. Furriers lengthen and narrow the small skins in more costly garments to eliminate these cross markings. Thus, a mink skin that is about 15 cm (about 6 in) wide by about 40 cm (about 16 in) long, after being "let out" can become approximately 5 cm (about 2 in) wide and as much as 100 cm (about 39 in) long. To achieve this, diagonal slices are cut on the skin side in widths ranging from 1.25 cm (about 0.5 in) to 0.16 cm (about 0.06 in) and are then realigned and stitched to produce an elongated peltry. The stitching of thousands of such seams

in a garment compacts the fur, making it richer and fluffier, and enables the furrier to drape the fur in many flowing directions. After sections of the garment are sewn, they are dampened, nailed into permanent shape on large flat boards, and left to dry. Thousands of tiny nails are used to flatten the seams on let-out garments.

Garment parts are then stitched together, linings are inserted, and the garment is tailored for fit and drape. Waste parts of the fur, cut from the skins of these quality garments, are assembled into sections, called plates, that are later cut, as is fabric to make less costly garments.

Retailing of furs. Some manufacturers custom-tailor garments for specific customers. Others have showrooms for customers. Still others sell only to retailers for resale. Some use manufacturers representatives who gather fur garments from many different sources in their showrooms for selection by retailers. Fur storage, cleaning, and remodeling of customers' furs are other services offered by retailers, manufacturers, or firms specializing in such work.

Fur Products Labeling Act. After processing, dyeing, shearing, and construction, furs are often difficult to identify. To protect sellers from others who may falsify their products and to protect consumers against misrepresentation, the Fur Products Labeling Act was passed in the U.S., effective Aug. 9, 1952, with minor amendments added in 1961, 1967, 1969, and 1980. Under this law, furs must be invoiced, advertised, labeled, and sold under their accepted English names. Waste fur and used fur articles must be so labeled. In addition, if any dye, color alteration, or change has been made that affects the fur's appearance, it must be so noted. If furs have been

A fur merchant's storeroom. Fox, mink, squirrel, muskrat, and Persian lamb, all from American fur farms, are inspected by a buyer.
Fur Information and Fashion Council

pointed, that fact must be disclosed on the label.

Furs of one type may not be used to define another, as for example, "sable mink" or "chinchilla rabbit"; nor may dyed furs be labeled by other names, such as "mink-dyed muskrat." Furs originating in countries other than the U.S. must disclose the name of the country of origin. Unprime skins must be so labeled. The accompanying table lists the more commonly known commercially valuable furs.

Carnivora Canidae—fox, raccoon, wolf
Carnivora Felidae—jaguar, leopard, lynx, ocelot, snow
  leopard, spotted cat
Carnivora Mustelidae—badger, ermine, fisher, fitch,
  kolinsky, marten, mink, otter, sable, skunk, spotted
  skunk, weasel, wolverine
Marsupialia—kangaroo, opossum, wallaby
Pinnipedia—fur seal, hair seal, rock seal
Primates—*Colobus* monkey
Rodentia—beaver, burunduk, chinchilla, chipmunk,
  hare, marmot, muskrat, nutria, rabbit, squirrel
Ungulata—antelope, goat, guanaquito, kid, lamb, pony,
  sheep

Endangered Species Conservation Act. Several groups of people, concerned that certain animal species are threatened with extinction or that using furs as wearing apparel represents cruelty to animals, have sought to protect them. Efforts by such organizations as the World Wildlife Fund, Friends of Animals, and the Fur Conservation Institute of America have resulted in the enactment of the Endangered Species Conservation Act of 1973 and its added convention in 1977 by which the U.S. and nearly 80 other nations established procedures to control and monitor the import and export of imperiled species covered by treaty. The act and convention define as endangered any species that is in danger of extinction, and as threatened any species that is likely to become endangered within the foreseeable future. Covered by the act and convention are some seals, many cats, otters, badgers, kangaroos, *Colobus* monkeys, some rabbits, non-fur-farmed chinchilla, flying squirrels, and wolves. The agreement with other countries and within the U.S. is that furs will not move in intercountry or interstate commerce unless proof is provided that the species is not threatened or endangered. K.R.G.

For further information on this topic, see the Bibliography in volume 28, sections 463, 633.

FURLONG. *See* WEIGHTS AND MEASURES.

FURNACE, enclosed apparatus in which heat is produced, either by burning a fuel such as coal, coke, oil, or gas, or by passing current through a resistive electrical conductor. The amount of heat that is produced in a furnace can be controlled.

To minimize the heat lost by radiation, the furnace is usually covered with insulation, such as firebrick.

Building Furnaces. Homes and many public and commercial buildings are heated by hot-air, hot-water, or steam-heating systems. The fuel is burned in a part of the furnace called the firebox, and the heat rises into a combustion chamber. In a hot-air system, hot air then flows directly into insulated ducts and is distributed throughout the building; in a hot-water system, water is heated in a boiler located above the combustion chamber, and pipes then carry the hot water to and from radiators installed in the building; in steam-heating systems, pipes carrying water pass through the combustion chamber, and the water is converted into steam that flows through pipes and into the radiators. *See* HEATING, VENTILATING, AND AIR CONDITIONING.

Industrial Furnaces. Industries make use of a number of different kinds of furnace. In the metallurgical industry, furnaces are used to roast and smelt ores. The blast furnace (q.v.) smelts iron ore; other types of furnace, such as the basic-oxygen furnace and the open-hearth furnace, convert liquid iron into liquid steel. Electric-arc furnaces are used to make high-quality steel. Shaft furnaces (cupolas) remelt iron in foundries. Volatile metals such as mercury are separated from their ores in retort furnaces. The properties of rolled or wrought metals are altered in annealing furnaces, which are also used in toughening sheet glass. Salt-bath furnaces are used to heat steel parts before they are hardened by rapid cooling. The ceramics industry uses a furnace called a kiln to fire products made of clay and to set glazes. Kilns are also used to calcinate limestone and to reduce certain ores.

See also ELECTRIC FURNACE; IRON AND STEEL MANUFACTURE; METALLURGY; SOLAR ENERGY.

FURNITURE, objects that furnish a room or, most succinctly defined, the (usually) movable parts of a room that make it function. The most common forms are beds, chairs, tables, and chests.

MATERIALS AND DESIGN

Historically, the most common material for making furniture is wood, but other materials, such as metal and stone, have also been used. Furniture designs have reflected the fashion of every era from ancient times to today. Whereas in most periods a single style dominated, a diversity of old and new styles influences present-day design. Some of the most highly prized furniture used in contemporary homes, however, are antiques—pieces anywhere from 50 to 300 or more years old. Today the most astute designers are eclectic, and furniture ranges from innovative designs to adaptations of historical models for special needs, including also carefully made reproductions that duplicate early examples.

The basic requirements of a furniture design are complex, for appearance has always been as important as function, and the general tendency has been to design furniture to complement architectural interiors. Indeed, some forms were conceived architecturally, with legs designed as columns; other forms were at least in part anthropomorphic, with legs in animal forms. Furniture design ranges from simple to elaborate, depending on the pieces' intended use rather than on the period in which they were made. The earliest records, such as ancient Mesopotamian inventories, describe richly decorated interiors with gold cloth and gilded furniture. Some surviving ancient Egyptian examples are elaborate and were originally sheathed in gold, but many very plain pieces were also made in ancient times. In the history of furniture, however, the elegant work is emphasized, because in general it has been the best preserved. In addition, elaborate designs reveal the most about a period because the elaborate changes more frequently than other styles to reflect new ideas. The simplest work, made for the farmer or worker, tends to be more purely functional and timeless; tables and chairs used by working people in 1800 BC are surprisingly like tables and chairs in farmhouses of AD 1800. Dutch genre paintings of the 1600s and early 19th-century American paintings depict rural interiors that often look remarkably similar.

HISTORY OF FURNITURE

Reconstruction of the prehistoric house with any certainty is impossible, although all indications are that it contained furniture. A history of furniture must begin with a discussion of the oldest surviving examples, those from the 4th to the 6th Dynasty (c. 2680–2255 BC) of Old Kingdom Egypt.

Egyptian Furniture. The dry Egyptian climate and the elaborate burial procedures are in part responsible for the extant pieces, which include stools, tables, chairs, and couches. In addition, wall paintings give insight into the design of Egyptian furniture. In both design and construction the methods used in ancient Egypt are followed wherever furniture is made today. In large pieces, particularly seating and tables, the mortise-and-tenon construction familiar in ancient Egypt is still in use, although the tenon may be replaced by a dowel to speed up production. The sides of more delicate boxes and chests were put together in ancient Egypt by dovetailing, a technique that persists in contemporary work. One ancient Egyptian stool illustrated on a wooden panel (c. 2800 BC, Egyptian Museum, Cairo) from the tomb of Hesire has animal legs as the supports. It does not differ much from a chair (c. 1325 BC, Egyptian Museum) from the tomb of the New Kingdom pharaoh Tutankhamen.

A chair, table, couch, and canopy (c. 2600 BC, Egyptian Museum) from the 4th Dynasty tomb at Giza of Queen Hetepheres were reconstructed from remnants of their original gold sheathing. They have animal legs, a solid chair back, and arm supports of openwork panels in papyrus patterns. The bed, higher at the head, has a headrest and a footboard. The relief decoration on some of the furniture consists of symbols of gods and scenes of religious significance. Other surviving tables and stools are restrained in design, with legs that are beautifully made but plain. It is conceivable that ornament could have been applied originally in stamped metal sheathing, but wall paintings do illustrate simple, upholstered pieces.

Extant examples and illustrations from wall paintings suggest the broad scope of decoration used on furniture. Gold sheets were applied to legs of chairs and tables; inlays of ivory and other materials were employed on panels of chests and other surfaces. The basic notion of forms with legs as anthropomorphic and of storage pieces as

One of the many pieces of furniture found in the tomb of Tutankhamen, king of Egypt in the 14th century BC.
Metropolitan Museum of Art

buildings in miniature was popular in ancient Egypt, and in succeeding cultures.

Mesopotamian Furniture. Although virtually no examples have survived, inlays and reliefs provide an idea of what furniture from the Tigris-Euphrates Valley looked like. Tables, stools, and thrones are illustrated in works from about 3500 to 800 BC. A Sumerian standard—a box on a pole (c. 3500–3200 BC, Iraq Museum, Baghdad)—has shell inlays that illustrate very simple chairs and thrones. Also surviving, however, is a Sumerian harp (c. 2685 BC, University of Pennsylvania Museum, Philadelphia) that has rich, colorful inlays and a bearded bull's head carved in the round and covered in gold foil. A stele made about 2300 BC shows a backless throne that appears to have been elegantly upholstered but had very plain straight legs. The furniture shown in a relief (9th cent. BC, British Museum, London) of Ashurnasirpal II and his queen is more elaborate, with tables and thrones supported on both trumpet-shaped and animal-form legs and embellished with relief decoration.

Minoan and Mycenaean Furniture. Examples of furniture in the roughly contemporaneous civilizations of the Mycenaeans on mainland Greece and the Minoans in the Aegean Islands are equally difficult to find. Relief representations on Minoan rings and small bronze and terra-cotta representations provide most of the evidence. One splendid exception, the gypsum throne in the Throne Room at Knossos (c. 1600–1400 BC), suggests that function and materials were more important than design in the Aegean, because the basic designs are less stylized on both the throne and the small terra-cotta pieces. The extant examples—stools, chairs, couches, benches, and chests—do not suggest the use of much elaborate decoration. One or two tablets have been discovered, however, that make reference to inlays and gold embellishments on furniture. A single ivory leg from Thebes is also elaborately ornamented.

Greek Furniture. Greek furniture, like Mesopotamian, is best known from paintings and sculpture, as little has survived. Details on vase paintings and grave stelae (tombstones) tell a good part of the story, but the frieze from the Parthenon and a group of miniature seated figures in terra-cotta and in bronze help fill in the gaps. A few marble thrones have survived, as have isolated wooden elements from actual Greek pieces. The evidence available suggests that Greek designers did not follow the free forms of the earlier Aegean examples. The tendency to base furniture ornament on architectural decoration, and the general symmetry and regularity of overall design, appear to follow Egyptian precedent. Nevertheless, although they resemble each other, the Greek couch is quite different in function from the Egyptian bed. Used for eating as well as resting, the Greek couch was made with the horizontal reclining area at table height, rather than low off the ground and at an incline. The headrest was often curved to support pillows; no foot rest was used. Although the animal-form leg is seen occasionally, legs were more often a trumpet form or a rectangular design based on a columnar form. Various stools were used for sitting. Folding stools with X-shaped legs and stationary stools with straight legs were made at least from the 6th century BC to the Hellenistic era.

Functional and plain examples were to be seen as well as the more elaborate. More distinctively an innovation of Greek designers is the chair known as a *Klismos,* a light (or easy) chair with a back. Comfortable and very popular, it was used most in the Archaic and Classical periods. The *Klismos* is essentially plain, with legs curving out from the seat and a back support consisting of a simple rectangular panel curved inward from sides to center. Tables pictured in paintings are generally small. Rectangular tops appear to have been the more popular type; most often the support consists of three legs—mostly simple and curved but sometimes carved in animal forms—that were at times reinforced with stretchers near the top. Literary references and illustrations suggest that typical tables were light. They were moved in to serve individuals at a dinner and removed after the meal, to allow space for entertainers to perform. Round tables of Greek origin were made in the Hellenistic period.

Chests in ancient Greece varied in size from those on a miniature scale to monumental examples, and, in design, from those with plain flat tops to the more architectural style with gabled lids. They were made of wood, of bronze, and of ivory, with architectural decoration. The chest shapes are a long-lived phenomenon; they were first found in ancient Egypt and then became traditional, remaining evident in 19th-century folk examples.

Roman Furniture. At first glance, Roman design appears to have been based on Greek prototypes. In the first century AD opulent Roman design reflected strong Greek influence. The ruins of Pompeii and Herculaneum provide clear evidence of handsome domestic architecture and show the settings that required furniture. Pompeiian frescoes illustrate the use of furniture and suggest that a wider variety of forms was known. The source and date of new storage pieces that had been introduced in Hellenistic Greece are questionable. No secure evidence confirms the theory that cupboards were introduced then. Examples of them on Roman frescoes may be copies of Greek paintings, but a cupboard from the house of Lararium in Herculaneum has survived.

Extant examples indicate that more marble and bronze furniture was made in Roman than in Greek times; also, the designs were more complex, even though they employed the same basic vocabulary of ornament. In addition to the small tables common in Greece, larger, rectangular examples and round tables of various sizes were used. More practical designs were also introduced: tables that could be taken apart and others with folding bases. The richness of elegant inlays and elaborate work in ivory, bronze, marble, and wood are mentioned in Roman literature, and enough fragments exist to prove the accuracy of the early descriptions.

Byzantine and Early Medieval Furniture. Although other surviving artifacts are abundant, there is strangely little evidence of furniture from Early Christian and Byzantine times, either in the East or the West. Byzantine art has been much admired; the richness of imperial churches in Istanbul, Turkey, and in Ravenna, Italy, indicates that there must have been a parallel magnificence in the furnishings of the palatial homes of ruling families. Byzantine mosaics suggest that, although classical ornament may have become stylized, it was still used between about AD 400 and 1000. A single Byzantine monument, the Throne of Bishop Maximian (c. 550, Archiepiscopal Museum, Ravenna), a masterpiece of ivory relief sculpture completely covering a wooden frame, was designed for ecclesiastical use, but the throne reveals the rich, stylized ornament of the period, and it suggests the manner in which secular Byzantine furniture design must have been conceived.

The so-called Throne of Dagobert I (c. 600, Bibliothèque Nationale, Paris), a bronze folding stool, has animal legs familiar from Roman examples but rendered far more boldly. Manuscripts and an occasional mosaic from the 5th to the 9th century provide further evidence that, although Roman influence persisted, changes in taste inspired artisans to render detail more abstractly and simply. Flat patterns replaced the high relief of Roman times. Conservatism, a strong element in the illuminated manuscript illustrations of the period, was also evident in its furniture.

The years 1000 to about 1200—the Romanesque period—are known for the regeneration of spirituality and for the large number of new churches built in western Europe, but little evi-

French 15th-century chair. Like most furniture of the period, it is made of oak.

Metropolitan Museum of Art–Gift of J. Pierpont Morgan

dence exists of the actual furniture of the period. Romanesque furniture design is best known from the assortment of 12th-century representations in French sculpture, in which simplified, schematic interpretations of Greco-Roman ornament are used. A few surviving turned-post (lathe-turned) chairs from 12th-century Scandinavia are Romanesque in spirit. Wooden chests, made somewhat later, are carved in schematic, geometric patterns that carry on the Romanesque style.

Gothic Furniture. Gothic architecture involved new, dramatic conceptions of space through the use of pointed arches, flying buttresses, and other radical innovations, but 12th-century furniture design was not influenced by the new style. The new cathedrals were expressions of affluence, but for their interiors the rich patrons of the church appear to have enjoyed simple, functional oak furniture enriched with tapestries and metalwork. The decorative elements of the Gothic, particularly the pointed arch, were not seen in furniture ornament until about 1400. Then, for more than a century, tracery and arches were carved on the panels of chairs, on chests, and on tables of every size.

In the 15th century a few new forms were introduced. One was a type of sideboard, with a small storage area set on tall legs; it had display space on the top of the enclosure as well as on a shelf below it. Cupboards were made with either one or two tiers of storage areas enclosed with doors. Another important storage piece was the armoire, with tall doors enclosing a 1.5- to 2-m (4- to 6-ft) area. Along with such architectural motifs as arches, columns, and foliate patterns appeared decorative carving based on hanging textiles, a motif known as linenfold. As a primarily northern European style, Gothic remained significant in furniture design into the early 16th century.

Renaissance Furniture. Renaissance painting, sculpture, and architecture developed in Italy before 1425, but Italian furniture design in the 15th century tended to be simple and functional.
Italy. The first innovation in Italian Renaissance furniture was the elaborately decorated chest known as a *cassone*, with its gilt, stucco, and painted decoration based on classical prototypes. *Cassone* forms were to some degree inspired by Roman sarcophagi; some early examples, however, had scenes illustrating the international Gothic romance, *Le Roman de la rose*. Interiors in 15th-century paintings, such as those in the *Dream of St. Ursula* (1490–95, Accademia, Venice) by Vittore Carpaccio and the *Birth of the Virgin* (1485–94, Santa María Novella, Florence) by Domenico Ghirlandaio, suggest the restraint of Italian furniture design before the High Renaissance at the end of the 15th century.

A 16th-century carved walnut cabinet from the Palazzo Davanzati in Florence, Italy, illustrates the use of classical motifs in Renaissance furniture, with its severe architectonic lines, fluted Ionic pilasters, and door panels carved in an austere geometric design of diamonds and triangles. Editorial Photocolor Archives

FURNITURE

Rich marquetry, imaginative carving, and a use of walnut in place of oak (which had been preferred for earlier work) characterized the more flamboyant efforts of the 1500s. A greater variety of forms and richer ornament were employed than in earlier periods. Portable folding chairs were revived, with seats of tapestry or leather. New solid-backed side chairs were developed; these have carved backs and, instead of legs, solid carved panels as supports.

France. Even richer decoration is found on the French furniture of the 1500s that reflected Renaissance influence. The courts of Francis I and his son Henry II employed Italian artists who brought the Renaissance to France. During the reign of Henry II, designs by the architect Jacques du Cerceau were adapted for furniture. His complex juxtapositions of classical motifs were used for decorating furniture panels in the new Renaissance taste. A major figure, the cabinetmaker Hugues Sambin, published an influential folio of designs that featured works richly carved in ingenious designs. Distinctive examples reveal a basic understanding of the new classicism.

The impetus of the designers working in the 16th century carried the style into the 17th century. Characteristic tables with thin columnar legs and chairs with paneled backs, first made in the 1560s and '70s, continued to be made after 1600. In the first decades of the 17th century, changes in design became subtle. During the reign (1610–43) of Louis XIII, furniture forms followed 16th-century models but with greater delicacy and with an increased use of rare ebony and rich tortoiseshell veneers instead of carving.

England. English Renaissance design was essentially simpler than that of France. Characteristic were less elegant carved detail, simpler decoration in turned parts, and flatter, more stylized foliate motifs. Oak continued to be the predominant furniture wood in England in the 16th century. As in France, the interest in Renaissance design persisted until about the mid-17th century in England.

The Netherlands. This general interest is documented in several 17th-century publications. Two books of designs influential in the early 17th century were published in Amsterdam by Jan Vredeman de Vries (1527–1604?) and Crispin van de Passe (c. 1565–1637). Dutch cabinetmakers created furniture closer in spirit to the English efforts than those of the French. The Dutch were conservative, and Renaissance designs were still popular in the 1650s and later. One special form—the armoire, with a bold overhanging cornice crowning it and with doors made three-dimensional by the application of projecting

Oak was a favorite material for furniture and paneling in Elizabethan times. Shown here is the Carved Oak Room from the William Crowe House, Great Yarmouth, Norfolk, England. **Metropolitan Museum of Art**

This mid-18th-century mahogany china cabinet is in the Chinese Chippendale mode, an exotic variant of rococo devised by the English designer Thomas Chippendale; it features straight legs of elaborate fretwork, rectangular glass cases with delicately carved tracery, and fantastic pagoda roofs. © Sotheby Parke-Bernet. Agent: Editorial Photocolor Archives

moldings—is characteristically Dutch and was used over a long period by Dutch settlers in North America. Dutch influence—probably because of the design books—can be seen in other northern European furniture, although each area developed distinctive designs for popular forms. **Spain.** In Spain influences were more varied. The new ideas of the Renaissance affected design, but so did a long local Moorish tradition. Although Spain had long been free of direct connections with the East, the delicate patterns on tiles and leather, and the bold combinations of wood, iron, and gold (or gilding) that remained popular there in the 16th and 17th centuries, proved the continuing Moorish influence.

Chinese Furniture of the Ming Dynasty. The 17th century was a period of growing cosmopolitanism. Trade routes had opened a century earlier and were becoming sources for new ideas and new materials. The 16th and 17th centuries were an ideal time for the West to discover Chinese furniture, for during the Ming dynasty (1368-

1644) Chinese furniture making was at its height. Tall cabinets, graceful tables, chairs, and benches were made in subtle designs. Straight legs on tables and chairs were often finished with delicately curved edges. Brackets and stretchers used as reinforcements added special decorative elements; these were restrained but showed to advantage the cabinetmaker's understanding of the beauty of wood. Oriental decoration was well known in the 17th century and was probably an important influence on later Western design. Lacquer chests were used extensively in Western settings, beginning in the 17th century. A number of examples have gilt stands, which were made in the West to adapt the lacquer chest to Western needs.

Baroque Furniture. Baroque design is most evident in furniture of the late 17th century, decades after the Italian baroque architects Gian Lorenzo Bernini and Francesco Borromini had first introduced their innovative approaches in Rome. In the early part of the century the new style had influenced surfaces but not shapes. In the last quarter, however, a growing number of changes took place. Among these was an increased use of caryatids as supports, along with scroll-shaped and spiral-turned legs that were different from the earlier Renaissance models.

At the very end of the 17th century, curved fronts were first used on large case pieces such as wardrobes and chests of drawers, reflecting the new baroque architecture. In chairs, rich carving on new high-backed forms came into fashion. Both English and Continental examples were made with caned seats and backs as alternate ways of handling areas that had often been upholstered. Simple variations of these chairs were made with turned parts in place of the carved areas, but the same tall backs were used.

French baroque. The most elegant and elaborate furniture of its day was made for the court of Louis XIV in France. The outstanding craftsman André Charles Boulle created unusual forms and embellished them with inlays combining metal (pewter, gilt, bronze, or silver), tortoiseshell, and ebony in designs that were imaginative juxtapositions of classical motifs. These sometimes look as if the basic inspiration was ancient Roman fresco. Columnar legs, handsomely gilded, were used to support tables, chairs, and stands for chests.

English and American colonial baroque. Variations made in other countries limited the gilding and emphasized the new shapes. In England the influence is most easily seen in work from the reign of William and Mary, when marquetry was used most freely. On the North American continent, Renaissance design was still important in the late 17th century. American artisans used Elizabethan and Tudor models as partial inspiration for distinctively American "Pilgrim-style" efforts in oak, updated by being stained a walnut color.

Rococo Furniture. The baroque was popular in many areas until about 1730, when fashions changed, first in Paris and then in the rest of the Western world. The new style, now known as the rococo (see ROCOCO STYLE), called for greater delicacy in the scale of objects and a more intimate connection of furniture and people. Architectural ornament was less relevant, as pieces in Parisian interiors were conceived to be in scale with people rather than with rooms.

French rococo. French sources were of primary importance and influence; their results were the most elegant. Rococo began in the reign of Louis XIV and flourished in that of Louis XV. The French version included ambitious designs in a variety of materials that required great skill to ex-

Painted Venetian secretary-cabinet of the 18th century.
Parke-Bernet Galleries

ecute. These were characterized by complex, sinuous forms that curved in every direction. Fanciful patterns were inlaid on layers of veneer that, in turn, were framed with ormolu (gilded bronze) outlining the legs, edges, and drawer fronts of a piece. Columnar legs were replaced by animal-form legs in a variety of curved forms.

English rococo. In England the rococo was much more restrained. Inlays were used rarely because cabinetmakers favored the use of fine walnut and mahogany, which were handled with great skill to exploit graining. English designers—and those who were inspired by them—introduced cabriole (curved) legs with claw-and-ball feet for chairs, tables, and chests. This foot must have been inspired by the claw and ball known on Chinese bronzes (but not on Chinese furniture prototypes); it represents a popularization of Oriental design. Toward the end of the rococo period in England, the London cabinetmaker

Thomas Chippendale published a book of designs, *The Gentleman and Cabinet Maker's Director* (1754), in which he presented the English interpretation of the rococo style. He was the first to categorize the varieties of rococo as French, Chinese, or Gothic and offered samples of each approach. Innovative French designs of the 1750s were translated by Chippendale into engraved designs of elaborately carved examples without the French use of ormolu or inlays. The element of the rococo emphasized by Chippendale and by most English artisans was its air of whimsy, achieved in French examples by a novel use of classical motifs. In the *Director*, Chinese and Gothic designs were included as additional ways of achieving whimsy; moreover, these designs could be executed more easily than those based on French sources.

English designers of the period (about 1740 to 1760) worked consistently in a small scale; some, however, chose to follow designs that were classical and more in keeping with an architectural style called the Palladian. In it, Renaissance designs of the Italian 16th-century architect Andrea Palladio were scaled to 18th-century taste. The London cabinetmaker William Vile (active 1750–67), who was employed by the Crown in the 1750s and '60s, made some classical furniture along with rococo work. In the American colonies, the lightly scaled classical was as important as the pure rococo in furniture made between 1740 and 1780.

English and American chair designs are the exception to the rule of continuing classical emphasis. Fashionable designers in London developed elegant side and armchairs with wooden backs, a basic form different from the upholstered-back chairs favored on the Continent. At first, the backs were made with solid splats as the central support, framed by curving rails and stiles in a design that was a very free adaptation of Chinese chairs. Later, the frame was yoke-shaped, and the splat was executed in one of a large repertoire, rococo in spirit, of pierced-work designs.

In the English approach to furniture design,

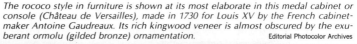

The rococo style in furniture is shown at its most elaborate in this medal cabinet or console (Château de Versailles), made in 1730 for Louis XV by the French cabinetmaker Antoine Gaudreaux. Its rich kingwood veneer is almost obscured by the exuberant ormolu (gilded bronze) ornamentation.   Editorial Photocolor Archives

woods were handLed with a special sense of understanding; American cabinetmakers chose to follow the same path. On the Continent, cabinetmakers were more intent on creating the appropriate rococo fantasies, using paint where inlays and ormolu might prove too expensive. Italian, German, Scandinavian, and even provincial French cabinetmakers followed this Continental manner of executing rococo design.

Neoclassical Furniture. Neoclassicism, a reaction to the rococo and a return to classicism, was a movement that began when the rococo was at its height. The designers who initiated it advocated a return to ancient Greco-Roman sources rather than to the Renaissance. To suit 18th-century taste, however, they adapted the ancient models by scaling down the ornament to a delicacy that appealed to those bored with the rococo.

The question of who was responsible for this revolution in design is a disputed one. Robert Adam, the English architect, introduced the first of his neoclassical designs before 1760. Across the English Channel in Paris, however, an important collector, La Live de Jully (1725–75), had furnished a room "à la grecque," or in the neoclassical style, at about the same time. Artists of English, French, and other nationalities were finding the ruins in Rome and Athens worthy of study and were becoming aware of the place of history in the study of design. Neoclassicism was the first conscious effort to revive a style, rather than to use elements of a past style as inspiration for new designs. The earliest efforts were less Roman than its designers seemed to believe, but the change to purer historicism occurred in a relatively short time.

French neoclassicism. In France the first phase of neoclassicism is called the Louis XVI style, although his reign began in 1774 and prime specimens were made earlier. The classicism of this style manifested itself in a whole vocabulary of motifs derived from Greco-Roman sources, but the overall shapes also reflected the new style. Furniture shapes were simple and geometric; rectangular, circular, and oval forms rested on straight, tapering legs that were either square or round in cross section. Garlands of flowers or drapery, architectural motifs such as paterae (medallions), dentils, Doric, Ionic, or Corinthian moldings, and related details were used as ornaments for neoclassical pieces.

English neoclassicism. In England painted furniture became popular, and interest revived in inlaid decoration, which had all but disappeared in the rococo era. The new high style was appealing to a growing number, and design books communicated suggestions for new furniture forms,

shapes, and decorations. The posthumously published *Cabinet Maker and Upholsterer's Guide* of 1788 by George Hepplewhite (fl. 1760–86) adapted some French and some traditional English designs to the needs of cabinetmakers seeking neoclassical suggestions. The most famous part of the book is the section on chairs that describes a number of shield-shaped backs, but Hepplewhite's repertoire was much broader (*see* HEPPLEWHITE STYLE). Popular neoclassical design in England is generally regarded as being inspired by Hepplewhite or by Thomas Sheraton, whose first book, the *Cabinet Maker and Upholsterer's Drawing Book*, appeared, in part, in 1791. Sheraton's complete work, published in 1802, included designs that were more literally classical, but what is popularly considered Sheraton are the rectangular chair backs shown in his first book.

Empire Furniture. The use of archaeologically inspired design increased in the late 18th century, and it appears to have influenced furniture made on both sides of the English Channel. This new emphasis marks a second phase of neoclassicism, called the Empire style (q.v.) because it was first identified with Napoleon's imperial efforts. Although the tendency to design furniture in ancient Roman style had begun before the French Revolution, Napoleon's designers, Charles Percier (1764–1838) and Pierre François Léonard Fontaine (1762–1853), were the most innovative. The publication, beginning in 1796, of designs inspired by them in the *Journal des Modes* of Pierre de La Mésangère (1761–1831) helped make the style international. The furniture plates in La Mésangère's journals appear to have been appropriated by Rudolph Ackermann (1764–1834) for use in his London-based journal, *Repository of Arts, Literature, and Fashions,* which began in 1809. German-language publications disseminated versions of the Empire style throughout the Continent and Scandinavia.

More careful investigation, however, reveals special distinctive sources in each country. In England—where it was called the Regency style (q.v.)—Henry Holland (1745–1806), architect to the prince of Wales beginning in the 1780s, designed furniture in the Empire spirit for royal residences and major country houses. Thomas Hope (c. 1770–1831), a collector and connoisseur with great enthusiasm for the classical, was the author of *Household Furniture and Interior Decoration* (1807), which illustrates his conception of a classical style in which Greek and Egyptian influences were strong.

Empire became an international style, with Scandinavian, German, Italian, Russian, and American interpretations. The basic concept was constant, with ancient prototypes adapted to 19th-century taste. The major change, besides the increase in archaeological influence, was in scale. Designers were attempting to regain the sense of monumentality that had been lacking since the beginning of the 18th century, when it was dropped to achieve the human scale then desired. In the German-speaking areas the style, recognized as typically middle class, has been called Biedermeier (*see* BIEDERMEIER STYLE), after a comic character who was supposed to satirize middle-class tastes. The name was applied as the style was going out of fashion in about 1850. Whatever it was called, Empire was a lasting style; introduced before 1800, it did not disappear completely until the middle of the 19th century. In the U.S., one cabinetmaker, the New Yorker Duncan Phyfe, who had begun activity in the 1790s, did not close his shop until 1847. His ouput included a grand variety of neoclassical designs, although he is best known for distinctive work made between about 1800 and 1820, in which light proportions and archaeologically correct details were integrated.

Victorian Eclectic Furniture. Concurrent with the neoclassical in the first half of the 19th century were revivals of other styles.

Gothic Revival. The Gothic, which Chippendale had used as a source of ornamental motif, was also of interest to Sheraton and a few later de-

signers. In George Smith's *Collection of Designs for Household Furniture and Interior Decoration* (1808), a few Gothic designs are shown along with the predominantly neoclassical work. By the 1830s interest in the Gothic was more profound. The Gothic was admired by some as a delightful reaction against the classical; others regarded it as a Christian style to be preferred over the pagan. On the one hand, romantic enthusiasm favored ruins and asymmetry; on the other, there was a strong desire for design inspired by faith. Whatever the impetus, the Gothic Revival flourished on both sides of the Atlantic, in England as well as on the Continent. Research into Continental aspects, however, is far behind that of English historians, who have discovered the accomplishments of two generations of Pugins—the father, Augustus Charles Pugin (1762–1832), and his son Augustus Welby Northmore Pugin. Essentially, revival of the Gothic involved the use of Gothic architectural ornament on 19th-century forms. Closely associated with the Gothic Revival is what Americans call the Elizabethan Revival, inspired by 16th- and 17th-century English designs.

Rococo revival. A completely different approach was taken by the designers who strove for a return to elegance. Beginning in the 1820s, the 18th-century rococo was the inspiration for a revival—actually a reinterpretation—of Parisian ro-

The Empire style in its Greek mode is illustrated by this marble-topped console (early 19th-century French, attributed to the firm of Jacob Frères); its massive mahogany forms are decorated with ormolu (gilded bronze) figures in relief (central panel) and in the round (four caryatid pillars). © Sotheby Parke-Bernet. Agent: Editorial Photocolor Archives

This installation of an elegantly curving stairway, moved from a North Carolina residence of the early 19th century, recreates the flavor of the period. The furniture groupings, which all show English influence, include a pier table (front) by the French cabinetmaker Charles Honoré Lannuier, who worked in New York City (1803–09), and other pieces attributed to John Seymour and his son Thomas, cabinetmakers in Boston (c. 1794–1804). Gilbert Ask–Henry Francis du Pont Winterthur Museum

coco design. The rococo revival was popular in England, on the Continent, and in the U.S. The American rococo revival, which flourished between about 1840 and 1860, is possibly responsible for the most distinctive furniture. One New York manufacturer, John Henry Belter (1804–63), obtained four patents for improvements in production that enabled the Belter shop to make flamboyantly carved work curved to the extreme by using laminated wood. Belter and contemporaries in Europe as well as in the U.S. found inspiration in baroque as well as rococo ornament.

Renaissance Revival. By the 1860s the rococo fad had subsided and Renaissance Revival became fashionable. Renaissance was defined very broadly, because the revival style included neoclassical motifs as well as those based on French Renaissance models. A revival of Louis XVI design was favored by some, but in general the new style was characterized by large, straight-lined forms decorated with inlays, low relief, and incised linear decoration. French, English, and Continental examples include a broad range of decoration that is more elegant than that on most American examples.

The Revolt Against Mass Manufacture. The striving for elegance inspired a certain amount of fakery. Veneers covered up cheap woods, and both the carving and inlays that embellished low-priced stylish furniture were poorly executed.

Arts and Crafts furniture. In reaction to mass-produced sham, the Arts and Crafts movement (q.v.) was established in 1861 by the English poet and designer William Morris. Along with such associates as the architect Philip Webb (1831–1915) and the Pre-Raphaelite painters Ford Madox Brown and Edward Burne-Jones, Morris sought a return to medieval handcraft traditions. Together, the group produced designs for every branch of the decorative arts, with the intent of elevating them to the level of the fine arts. Their products, including furniture, were much admired for their beauty and consummate craftsmanship and were widely copied. By the 1890s, the movement had spread to the Continent and North America. The influence of Morris and his followers was enormous; their designs are often considered the wellspring of modern furniture design. Morris's ideas were expressed in popular language by the English architect and writer

Charles Eastlake (1836–1906) in his hugely successful *Hints on Household Taste in Furniture, Upholstery and other Details* (1868). Eastlake advocated a return to simple, straight-lined designs inspired by country work, executed in oak and various fruitwoods. In the U.S., where Eastlake's book became a decorating bible, the simplicity was often embellished with such luxurious additions as ebonized wood, gilding, and inlays.

Art Nouveau furniture. Directly fostered by the Arts and Crafts movement was the style called Art Nouveau (q.v.), which flourished between the 1890s and 1910 in all of the arts. Art Nouveau may be characterized as an organic style derived from natural forms that convey a sense of movement, exemplified by the famous "whiplash" curve found in many Art Nouveau works. In furniture, its early exponents were the Belgian architects Henri van de Velde and Victor Horta, who furnished the interiors of their buildings to complement the sinuous forms of the architectural settings. In France, the architect Hector Guimard, creator in 1900 of the graceful Métro (subway) stations in Paris, also designed similarly asymmetrical, heavily carved free-form furniture. The noted glassmaker Émile Gallé (1846–1904) also designed some of the most opulent Art Nouveau furniture, in which plant and flower motifs predominate. Louis Majorelle (1859–1926) produced luxurious furniture, again inspired by forms from nature, and went on to become a notable Art Deco designer after World War I. The Scottish architect Charles Rennie Mackintosh produced, in his unique interpretation of Art

A carved mahogany desk (c. 1900) by the French designer Louis Majorelle is typical of Art Nouveau furniture, with its use of subtle curves, delicate inlays of stylized floral motifs in the backboard, and ormolu (gilded bronze) mounts to contrast with the highly finished wood.

© Sotheby Parke-Bernet. Agent: Editorial Photocolor Archives

Nouveau, chastely beautiful furniture. Characteristic pieces are of oak painted white, with elegant inlays and appurtenances of metal or stained glass in curvilinear, abstracted plant forms.

20th-Century European Furniture. Reform and revolution in the arts, including furniture design, marked the turn of the century. Prominent among the leaders of the revolt was the Austrian architect and designer Josef Hoffmann, who, with other architects and artists, founded the Vienna Sezession (*see* SEZESSIONSTIL) in 1897 and the Wiener Werkstätte (Vienna Workshop) in 1903. The Werkstätte produced, among other types of decorative arts, furniture in cubicular forms that contrasted radically with the Art Nouveau obsession with curvilinear forms. They are reminiscent of Mackintosh's restrained designs, which were much admired by the group. The right angle was used consistently, and detailing was rigidly austere. *Sezessionstil* was the precursor of two major 20th-century styles, the German Bauhaus and the French Art Deco.

Bauhaus furniture. The Bauhaus (q.v.), founded in 1919 in Weimar, Germany, by the architect Walter Gropius, was an all-encompassing art and architecture school that proved to be one of the most influential forces in the development of 20th-century art. Classic contemporary furniture, still being manufactured, was designed by its most renowned architects, Marcel Breuer and Ludwig Mies van der Rohe. Breuer designed his "Wassily" armchair, of chrome-plated steel tubing and canvas, in 1925, and his much-copied cantilevered side chair, of tubing with wood-framed cane seat and back panels, in 1928. Mies created his world-famous Barcelona chair, a masterpiece consisting of two elegantly curved X-frames of chromed steel strips supporting rectangular leather cushions, in 1929. The aim of both architects was to devise aesthetically pleasing furniture for mass production.

Scandinavian furniture. Some of the most admired contemporary furniture has originated in Scandinavia. To name two of a host of designers, the Finnish architect Alvar Aalto and the Danish designer Arne Jacobsen (1902–71) created laminated wood furniture of exquisite proportions and eminent practicality for mass manufacture.

Art Deco furniture. Art Deco (q.v.), although its name is derived from the 1925 Paris exposition of decorative arts, can be traced back to the first decade of the 20th century, especially to the sharply defined geometric forms of the *Sezessionstil*. The Bauhaus concern with the use of new materials also had its influence. The style persisted through 1939, and has had a revival of

This living room, popular in the mid-1980s, features more eclecticism and softer lines than did the stark interiors of Scandinavian design. R. Embery/FPG

interest and even imitation in the 1970s and '80s. The most accomplished Art Deco designers were French: Louis Majorelle, André Groult (1884–1967), Pierre Chareau (1883–1950), and Jacques Émile Ruhlmann (1879–1933). Their pieces have a streamlined richness that owes as much to superb handcrafting—lustrously finished rare woods with inlays of such exotic materials as ivory in angular, abstracted designs—as to their daring geometric shapes. The style was rapidly debased, however, by shoddy, mass-produced versions.

20th-Century American Furniture. Furniture designers in the U.S. were, until 1946, overshadowed by their European counterparts and were heavily influenced by them, with few exceptions. *American furniture to 1939.* American arts-and-crafts movements led at the turn of the century to the establishment of numerous ateliers and small factories, such as that of Gustav Stickley (1857–1942). Stickley devised the Mission style (q.v.), ostensibly based on old Spanish furniture in the California missions. His furniture, made between 1900 and 1913, was straight-lined, simple, and utilitarian, carefully made of oak, with decoration limited to the handsomely crafted hardware. American mass manufacturers took up the Mission style with a will and produced great quantities of ponderous imitation Stickley. With the exception of Louis Comfort Tiffany, who designed furniture primarily for his own use, the U.S. produced no outstanding Art Nouveau furniture. Art Deco flourished in America, mostly in mass-produced furniture of lesser quality. A no-

table exception is the work of the studio of Donald Deskey (1894–1989), which created in 1932 the palatial Art Deco interiors and the furniture of Radio City Music Hall in New York City. The American architect Frank Lloyd Wright also designed furniture, but its idiosyncratic appearance defies categorization, since the furniture design was entirely subordinated to the design of the building; the same motifs appear in both. He consistently favored built-in furniture, however, because the furniture thus became part of the architecture.

Contemporary American furniture. After World War II, many American furniture designers came to prominence within a decade. Among the best known were the architects Charles Eames and Eero Saarinen. Adapting wartime technology in the use of wood, metals, and plastics, they collaborated on the design of the so-called Eames chair and ottoman, constructed of subtly curved molded plywood with deeply padded leather upholstery, set on a metal pedestal base. In 1956 Saarinen designed an entire range of pedestal furniture in molded plastic and metal; the white chairs, in silhouette resembling a wineglass, have loose cushion seats in bright fabrics; the tables, ranging in size from side tables to conference tables, have tops of either marble or wood. They, like many other well-designed modern pieces, have been copied extensively by mass manufacturers. Other gifted designers included the sculptor Harry Bertoia, who in 1952 produced the lightweight wire mesh chair that bears his name, manufactured by Knoll Associates; Florence S.

Knoll (1917–), like Eero Saarinen and Bertoia a graduate of the Cranbrook Academy of Art in Bloomfield Hills, Mich., and later president of Knoll International, New York City; and Paul McCobb (1917–69), who based his widely marketed Planner group on simple and functional 18th- and 19th-century Shaker furniture.

By the 1980s furniture styles had so proliferated that literally hundreds of examples existed. The positive aspect of this stylistic glut was the enormous range of choice it offered, from classic modern pieces still in manufacture to "high-tech" medical and industrial furnishings, from antiques of any period (or costly reproductions of them) to inexpensive do-it-yourself disassembled furniture in any style desired.

See also BED; CHAIR; CHINOISERIE; FOLK ART; HOUSE; INLAY; INTERIOR DESIGN; LACQUER WORK; RUGS AND CARPETS; TAPESTRY; VENEER; WOOD CARVING. For additional information on individual artists, see biographies of those whose names are not followed by dates.   M.D.S.

For further information on this topic, see the Bibliography in volume 28, sections 661, 710–11.

FÜRTH, city, S central Germany, in Bavaria, at the junction of the Pegnitz and Rednitz rivers, near Nuremberg. Manufactures include toys, clothing, and glass products. Notable buildings in Fürth are Saint Michael's Church, completed during the 14th century, and the 19th-century town hall, with a high tower. Reputedly founded by Charlemagne, Fürth was for a time in the possession of the burgraves of Nuremberg and later of the archbishopric of Bamberg; it was acquired by Bavaria in 1806. In 1835 it became a terminal of the first railroad built in Germany, from Nuremberg to Fürth. The city was badly damaged in World War II. Pop. (1989 est.) 98,800.

FURTWÄNGLER, (Gustav Heinrich Ernst Martin) Wilhelm (1886–1954), German conductor, whose interpretations of the German repertoire won him wide admiration. Born in Berlin and privately educated, he studied for many years during his career with the influential German theorist Heinrich Schenker (1868–1935), analyzing musical scores. Furtwängler's principal conducting post was as director of the Berlin Philharmonic, where he became known for his forceful, expressive approach and for developing the orchestra's rich string sound. Although he remained in Germany through most of World War II, he opposed the Nazi regime and was exonerated of charges of collaboration. After the war he resumed an international career.

FURZE, common name for any plant of the genus Ulex, of the family Fabaceae (see LEGUME), also known as gorse. Common furze, U. europaeus, is native to Great Britain and western Europe. It is a thorny evergreen shrub with sharply pointed leaves and solitary flowers having a two-lipped, shaggy, deep yellow calyx subtended by two small bracts. The fruit is a pod. In mild climates the flower blooms all winter. In its natural state furze provides food for sheep; after the spines are removed, the shoots provide winter fodder for horses and cattle. Furze is sometimes planted as a sand binder; U. europaeus, introduced to the eastern coast of the U.S. from Nantucket to Virginia, serves in this capacity. Seeds of U. europaeus yield a poisonous alkaloid, ulexine, which was formerly used as a local anesthetic and diuretic.

FUSAN. See PUSAN.

FUSE, safety device used to protect an electric circuit from the effect of excessive current. Its essential component is usually a strip of metal that will melt at a given temperature. A fuse is so designed that the strip of metal can easily be placed in the electric circuit. If the current in the circuit exceeds a predetermined value, the fusible metal will melt and thus break, or open, the circuit. Devices used to detonate explosives are also called fuses (see EXPLOSIVES).

Cutaway view of an ordinary one-time fuse.

Two types of fuses are commonly used, cylindrical fuses and plug fuses. A cylindrical fuse consists of a ribbon of fusible metal enclosed in a ceramic or fiber cylinder. Metal end caps fastened over the cylinder make contact with the metal ribbon. This type of fuse is placed in an electric circuit so that the current must flow through the metal strip to complete the circuit. If excess current surges through the circuit, the metal link will heat to its melting point and break. This action will open the circuit, stop the current flow, and thus protect the circuit. The cylindrical type of fuse is used mostly to protect electrical equipment and appliances.

Plug fuses are commonly used to protect electric wiring in homes. This type also consists of a

Left: Ordinary plug fuse. Right: Fusetron dual-element plug fuse.

fusible metal strip through which the current must flow to complete the circuit. The strip is, however, enclosed in a plug that can be screwed into an ordinary electric receptacle or light socket. Plug fuses usually have a mica window at the base of the plug so that the condition of the metal strip can be seen at a glance.

Recent fuse developments include types that will permit a momentary overload without breaking the circuit. These are necessary for circuits that are used to power air conditioners or electric broilers, because initial surges of power can be expected with such appliances. Another recently developed type of fuse contains several links that can be selected by the flip of a switch. If the fuse is blown, another link can be switched in without replacing the fuse.

In high-voltage circuits, subject to frequent interruptions, and increasingly in residential wiring, protection is provided by circuit breakers instead of fuses. See ELECTRIC POWER SYSTEMS.

For further information on this topic, see the Bibliography in volume 28, section 543.

FUSELI, Henry (1741–1825), Swiss-English painter, whose imaginative paintings, emphasizing melodrama, fantasy, and horror, exerted an important influence on the budding romantic movement in England and on the Continent.

Fuseli, originally named Johann Heinrich Füssli, was born in Zürich. Encouraged by the English painter Sir Joshua Reynolds, he spent a decade (1768–78) in Italy studying Michelangelo's work and then settled in England in 1779. Fuseli became well known for his expressive and often melodramatic historical paintings, which led to his election to the Royal Academy in 1799 and his designation as keeper of the academy in 1804.

Fuseli's enduring fame, however, rests on his imaginative fantasy paintings, which abound with apparitions, extravagant poses, and lurid nocturnal effects. One of the best known is *The Nightmare* (1781, Kunsthaus, Zürich), picturing a young woman in the throes of a nightmare, attended by horrific apparitions of a monkey and a glowing horse's head. Fuseli exerted a strong influence on the work of later romantics, especially the English poet and painter William Blake.

FUSHUN, also Fu-shun, locally called Funan, city, NE China, in Liaoning Province, an important industrial center in a region of abundant coal and oil-shale deposits. Manufactures include aluminum, iron and steel, refined petroleum, machinery, cement, rubber, and fertilizers. Local coal seams, overlaid by oil shale, which is exceptionally thick, are mined by opencut methods.

The old walled city of Fushun was built in 1669. Its modern growth dates from the early 20th century when it was developed as a coal-mining center by Russian industrialists. Industrialization accelerated under Japanese control (1905–45), and oil-shale processing began in the 1930s. The city suffered heavy damage during the Sino-Japanese War (1937–45), and during looting in 1945 it lost much industrial equipment. It was rebuilt in the 1950s, and highly mechanized coal mines and other modern industrial facilities were developed here. Pop. (1987 est.) 1,126,400.

FUSION, change of a substance from the solid to the liquid state, usually by the application of heat. The process of fusion is the same as melting, but the term *fusion* is usually applied to substances such as metals that become liquid at high temperatures, and to crystalline solids. When a substance is at its melting or fusing temperature, additional heat is absorbed by the substance in changing its state without raising its temperature. This additional heat is known as the heat of fusion (*see* FREEZING POINT). The term *fusion* applies also to the process of heating a mixture of solids to give a single liquid solution, as in the formation of alloys.

For a discussion of nuclear fusion, *see* ATOM AND ATOMIC THEORY; NUCLEAR ENERGY.

FUST or **FAUST, Johann** (c. 1400–66), German moneylender and printer, born in Mainz. Between 1450 and 1452 Fust lent about 1600 guldens to the printer Johann Gutenberg, with which Gutenberg was supposed to make "tools" for his press, then still in an experimental stage. Failing to recover his money, Fust brought suit, claiming the then-secret machinery of the press against the debt. The disposal of the disputed machinery is unclear, but Fust seems to have obtained a part of the press, as he subsequently published books in his own house, in partnership with his son-in-law Peter Schöffer (1425?–1502?). The psalter they printed on Aug. 14, 1457, a folio of 350 pages, is the first printed book with a date and with a complete colophon, or identifying device of the printer. Fust and Schöffer also printed, in 1462, a Latin Bible, and, in 1465, *De Officiis* (On Moral Obligations) by Marcus Tullius Cicero. This quarto of 88 leaves was the first printed edition of a Latin classic and contained the first printed Greek characters.

FUTURISM, early 20th-century movement in art that pointedly rejected all traditions and attempted instead to glorify contemporary life, mainly by emphasizing its two dominant themes, the machine and motion. The principles of futurism were originated by the Italian poet Filippo Tommaso Marinetti (1876–1944) and published by him in a manifesto in 1909. The following year the Italian artists Giacomo Balla, Umberto Bocci-

The futuristic movement is exemplified by the painting Dog on a Leash, by Giacomo Balla.
Museum of Modern Art–A. Conger Goodyear Collection

oni, Carlo Carrà (1881–1966), Luigi Russolo (1885–1947), and Gino Severini signed the *Technical Manifesto of Futurist Painting*. Futurism was characterized by the attempted depiction of several successive actions of positions of a subject at the same time. The result resembled somewhat a stroboscopic photograph or a high-speed series of photographs printed on a single plate. Interesting examples are Severini's *Dynamic Hieroglyphic of the Bal Tabarin* (1912, Museum of Modern Art, New York City) and his *Armored Train* (1915, Collection Richard S. Zeisler, New York City). Although futurism was short-lived, lasting only until about 1914, its influence can be seen in the works of the painters Marcel Duchamp, Fernand Léger, and Robert Delaunay in Paris and the constructivists in Russia. The futurist worship of the machine survived as a fundamental part of Fascist doctrine.

FUXIN, also Fu-hsin, Fou-hsin, or Fusin, city, NE China, in Liaoning Province, a major coal-mining center in a highly industrialized region. Coal deposits occur here in thick beds suitable for surface (opencut) mining methods. Mining began during the Japanese occupation (1931–45) of NE China, and the mines suffered heavy damage during World War II. The mines were reconstructed and modernized by the Chinese in the early 1950s. Other industries in Fuxin include the generation of electricity and the manufacture of chemicals. Pop. (1987 est.) 593,600.

FUZHOU, also Fu-chou, Fuchow, or Foochow, city, SE China, capital of Fujian (Fukien) Province, an industrial center and seaport on the Min R. Manufactures include chemicals, silk and cotton textiles, iron and steel, and processed food. Among its exports are fine lacquer ware and handcrafted fans and umbrellas. The city's trade is mainly with Chinese coastal ports; exports of timber, food products, and paper move through the harbor at Guantou (Kuan-t'ou). Fuzhou consists of an old walled city, about 3.2 km (2 mi) from the Min R., and a modern riverside quarter, which is connected by bridge to Nantai Island.

A university is in the city, and several noted pagodas and temples are nearby. The strategically located island of Matsu, held by Taiwan, is near Fuzhou, in Taiwan Strait.

Fuzhou, founded in the 2d century BC, was absorbed into China during the 6th century AD. It was opened to foreign trade in 1842, and until the late 19th century was a major port for the export of tea. The city's other trade declined after contacts with nearby Taiwan, a traditional commercial partner, were severed in 1949. Thereafter, Fuzhou was linked (1958) by rail to N China and grew as an industrial center. Pop. (1987 est.) 805,500.

FYN (Ger. *Fünen*), island, S Denmark, separated from the Jutland Peninsula on the W by the Lille Baelt (Little Belt) Channel and from the island of Sjaelland (Zealand) on the E by the Store Baelt (Great Belt) Channel. The surface of Fyn is slightly elevated in the S and in the W, rising to more than 122 m (more than 400 ft) above sea level. The terrain in the N and in the E is level, with notably fertile soil. Cereal grains are raised, considerable amounts being exported, and livestock raising is carried on extensively. Together with several nearby smaller islands, Fyn forms a county of the same name. The principal towns on Fyn are Odense and Svendborg. Area, about 2980 sq km (about 1150 sq mi); pop. (1980 est., Fyn Co.) 452,965.

FYT, Jan (1611–61), Flemish painter and etcher, who was especially skilled at depicting animals and still life. He was born in Antwerp (now in Belgium) and studied principally with Frans Synders, the greatest of Flemish animal and still-life painters. Fyt traveled and worked for ten years in France, Holland, and Italy before returning to Antwerp in 1643. His work is characterized by extreme realism in the depiction of the textures of fur and plumage, as well as by harmonious color and, frequently, bold and dramatic action. His favorite subjects included dogs, as for example, *Wolves Attacked by Dogs* (1652, National Gallery, Oslo), and dead game.

141

G, seventh letter in the English and other alphabets derived from the Latin. The uppercase, or capital *G* is derived from the Latin *C,* which in turn is from the Greek *G, gamma,* rounded in the 7th century BC. Latin *c* represented the sounds of both *g* and *k* until the 3d century BC, when the character was modified to make a distinction of the *g* sound (*see* C). Once established, the new letter took the place in the alphabet of the Greek *Z, zeta,* which was not used in Latin. The modern lowercase *g* developed from a form that appeared in the 7th century.

GABBRO, general name for a large group of granular igneous rocks, the intrusive equivalents of basalt, composed of plagioclase feldspar with a predominance of dark minerals, usually pyroxenes, hornblende, or olivine (qq.v.). The rocks are heavy, often greenish in color. Gabbros occur in the Adirondack Mountains, in the vicinity of Baltimore, Md., and in the highlands along the north shore of Lake Superior.

GABIN, Jean, professional name of JEAN ALEXIS MONCORGE (1904–76), French motion picture actor, born in Paris. The son of a theatrical family, Gabin appeared at the Folies Bergères in Paris and in cabarets, vaudeville, and the legitimate theater before 1930, when he appeared in the first of scores of films. Julien Duvivier (1896–1967), noted French film director, cast Gabin in *Maria Chapdelaine* (1931; U.S. release, 1935), which made him a star. Duvivier also directed Gabin in *Pépé le Moko* (1937; U.S. release, 1941). Gabin's distinctive tough-but-gentle naturalistic characterization was established in this film. Other important films in which Gabin starred include *Grande Illusion* (Grand Illusion, 1937), and *Le Jour Se Lève* (Daybreak, 1939). During the last 25 years of his life, Gabin made about two dozen films, including *Le Clan des Siciliens* (1969; The Sicilian Clan, 1970).

GABIROL. *See* IBN GABIROL, SOLOMON BEN YEHUDA.

GABLE, (William) Clark (1901–60), American film actor, born in Cadiz, Ohio. Before achieving fame, Gable performed a wide variety of jobs, from drilling oil wells to playing minor parts in silent films. He made a successful Broadway appearance in *Machinal* (1928). The first film in which he was featured was *The Painted Desert* (1931). During the 1930s Gable was the outstanding leading man in American films; he played opposite the best-known female stars of the time and was frequently cited as the personality whose films made the most money at the box office. In films such as *It Happened One Night* (1934), for which Gable won an Academy Award, *Mutiny on the Bounty* (1935), and *Gone With the Wind* (1939), he played a role that was the prototype of the virile, adventurous American male. Gable served as a combat gunner in World War II. After the war he returned to the screen in such films as *Command Decision* (1949), *Across the Wide Missouri* (1951), and *Mogambo* (1953). He died a few days after completing his last film, *The Misfits.*

GABO, Naum (1890–1977), Russian-American sculptor, one of the leading practitioners of 20th-century constructivism. Born in Briansk and originally named Naum Pevsner, he changed his name to avoid confusion with his brother, Antoine Pevsner, also an artist. He studied (1910–14) medicine and engineering in Munich, but in 1914 took up sculpture, producing cubist-inspired heads and busts using cutout sheets of metal, cardboard, or celluloid.

In Moscow from 1917 to 1922, Gabo helped found the constructivist movement, which advocated the construction of sculpture from industrial materials rather than from traditional carving in stone or casting in bronze. In 1920 he and his brother issued their Realist Manifesto, calling for new art forms based on space and time; in keeping with this theory, Gabo executed several works with moving parts, called kinetic sculp-

Clark Gable and co-star Claudette Colbert try to thumb a ride in a scene from the 1934 comedy classic It Happened One Night. UPI

ture. He lived in Germany from 1922 to 1932, where he executed works characterized by a monumental architectural quality, as in the glass, metal, and plastic *Column* (1923, Museum of Modern Art, New York City). During World War II, in London, Gabo continued to produce such characteristic works as *Linear Construction, Variation* (1943, Phillips Collection, Washington, D.C.), in which an oval space is outlined in clear plastic forms that, in turn, are delicately webbed with intersecting planes of nylon thread. In 1946 he settled in the U.S. One of Gabo's most notable works is a large-scale, 26-m (85-ft) tree-shaped monument (1957) commissioned for the rebuilt Bijendorf (Beehive) Department Store in Rotterdam, the Netherlands, to commemorate those who perished in 1940 in the Nazi destruction of Rotterdam. His last major work (1976) was a fountain for St. Thomas's Hospital, London.

GABON, officially Gabonese Republic (Fr. République Gabonaise), independent nation, W central Africa, bounded on the NW by Equatorial Guinea, on the N by Cameroon, on the E and S by the Republic of Congo, and on the W by the Atlantic Ocean. The area of Gabon is 267,667 sq km (103,347 sq mi).

LAND AND RESOURCES

A belt of coastal lowlands, generally narrow in width, is found in the W part of Gabon. To the interior is the plateau zone, which extends over the entire N and E sections of Gabon and part of the S. The Crystal Mts. in the N are about 914 m (about 3000 ft) high. The central Chaillu Mts. contain Mt. Iboundji (1575 m/5167 ft), the highest summit in the country. This escarpment is crossed by numerous rivers, notably the Ogooué R., which empties into the Atlantic Ocean. Virtually the entire country is contained in the basin of the Ogooué R., which is navigable to Ndjolé. Three-quarters of the land is covered by a dense equatorial rain forest.

Climate. Gabon has a hot and humid climate. The temperature varies only slightly throughout the year. The average daily temperature is 26.7° C

GABON

(80° F). From June to September virtually no rain falls but humidity is high. In December and January the rainfall is slight, and during the remaining months it is heavy. At Libreville, the capital, the average annual rainfall is 2515 mm (99 in).

Natural Resources. Gabon is rich in mineral resources. The country has deposits of uranium, manganese, and petroleum, all of which are being exploited; large deposits of iron ore, considered among the richest in the world, have also been found, and lead and silver ores have been discovered. Gabon also has valuable forest resources, mainly in its stands of okoumé, mahogany, kevazingo, and ebony.

POPULATION

The ethnic makeup of the Gabonese is diversified, although almost all the inhabitants are Bantu-speaking. Of the country's approximately 40 ethnic groups, the largest are the Fang, the Eshira, and the Adouma. Europeans, mostly French, form a small but prominent minority. Pygmies are believed to have been the original

A group of Gabonese on their way home from market.
United Nations

Aerial view of Lambaréné, palm oil and lumbering center and site of a hospital established by Dr. Albert Schweitzer.

inhabitants of the country, but only a few thousand remain. About 95% of the population is nominally Christian; most of the remainder follow traditional beliefs; and about 1% is Muslim. The official language is French.

Population Characteristics. In 1981 the government of Gabon, revising the 1980 official census, declared the country's population to be about 1,232,000, including 122,000 Gabonese citizens residing abroad. Gabon had an estimated resident population of 1,245,000 in 1989; about three-fifths of the people lived in rural areas, and the overall population density was about 5 per sq km (about 12 per sq mi). Much of the country's interior is uninhabited.

Principal Cities. Libreville, the capital and largest city of Gabon, has (1983 est.) 257,000 inhabitants. Port-Gentil (123,300) is the center of the plywood and petroleum industries. Lambaréné (pop., est., 22,700) is the center for the oil-palm plantations in the region and the site of the hospital established by the French medical missionary Albert Schweitzer.

Education. Schooling is compulsory in Gabon for all children between the ages of 6 and 16. In the mid-1980s about 178,800 pupils were annually attending primary schools, and about 39,300 students were enrolled in secondary schools. The country has technical institutions and teachers colleges, as well as a university, the Université Omar Bongo (1970).

ECONOMY

The economy of Gabon is largely dependent on the exploitation of mineral and forest resources. Gabon's gross domestic product of $2970 per capita in the late 1980s was the highest in sub-Saharan Africa. Estimated annual national budget figures in the late 1980s included revenue of $927 million and expenditure of $1.2 billion.

Agriculture. The economy of Gabon has a large subsistence agriculture sector, occupying two-thirds of the active labor force. Cassava, bananas, plantains, sugarcane, taro, and rice are grown for home consumption, and small amounts of cacao, coffee, palm oil, peanuts, and pepper are grown for export.

Forestry and Fishing. Gabon is the world's largest producer of okoumé, a softwood that is used to make plywood. In the late 1980s the annual cut of roundwood in Gabon was approximately 3.8 million cu m (134.2 million cu ft). The government is engaged in preservation and reforestation programs. The annual fish catch in the late 1980s was about 20,900 metric tons.

Mining. Mining has developed rapidly since Gabon's independence. Annual production of extremely high-grade manganese ore, from Moanda in the SE, was nearly 2.3 million metric tons in the late 1980s. The rich deposits of iron ore located at Mekambo and Bélinga in the NE have reserves estimated at more than 500 million metric tons. Exploitation of the iron ore has been hampered by the lack of transportation facilities, particularly railroads. Uranium production annually totaled about 900 metric tons in the late 1980s. Petroleum is extracted along the coast and offshore. Annual petroleum production, which stood at 56.8 million barrels in the late 1980s, is declining due to depletion of the modest reserves. Oil refineries are located at Port-Gentil and Pointe Clairette. Production of petroleum products is about 833,000 metric tons per year. Some gold also is produced.

Manufacturing. Gabon has a small manufacturing sector, the leading products being refined petroleum and wood items. Other manufactures include processed food, beer, and cement. About 876 million kwh of electricity were generated annually in the late 1980s. About three-fourths of the power was produced in hydroelectric facilities, primarily at an installation at Kinguélé (near Libreville).

Currency and Foreign Trade. The currency of Gabon is the CFA franc (286.4 CFA francs equal U.S.$1; 1990). The value of the country's yearly exports typically is much higher than the cost of its imports; in the late 1980s exports earned $1.2 billion and imports were valued at $791 million. France, the U.S., Italy, Spain, Great Britain, Germany, Japan, and the Netherlands are the principal trading partners.

Transportation and Communications. Gabon has about 7535 km (about 4680 mi) of roads, of which about 8% are paved. An 869-km (540-mi) highway crosses Gabon from N to S, linking the country with Loubomo in the Republic of Congo and Douala in Cameroon. Government planning has stressed road construction. Before the 1970s, the country's only railroad linked Mbinda (Congo) with the Pointe Noire-Brazzaville Line. Construction began in 1974 on the 697-km (433-mi) Trans-Gabon Railroad; a section between Owendo and Booué was completed in 1982, and the extension to Franceville in the SE was inaugurated in 1986. A link to the iron-ore deposits of the NE is also planned. Owendo and Port-Gentil are the principal ports. The Ogooué R. and its tributaries, the Ivindo and Ngounie rivers, provide navigable waterways. The government operates television and radio stations. An estimated 103,300 radios and 37,200 television sets were in use in Gabon in the late 1980s.

GOVERNMENT

Under the 1961 constitution, as amended, the president of Gabon was directly elected for a 7-year term, serving as both chief of state and head of government. The unicameral National Assembly comprised 111 elected and 9 appointed members. The Gabonese Democratic party was the sole legal political party.

The mineral resources of Gabon are among the richest in the world. In this mill, earth containing manganese deposits is transported on modern conveyor belts. **United Nations**

Gabon entered a period of political transition as the 1990s began. The ruling Gabonese Democratic party was reconstituted as the Gabonese Social Democratic Rally, and the ban on multiparty politics was lifted. In legislative elections held during September and October 1990, opposition parties won 55 of the 120 seats at stake. A new constitution was adopted in March 1991.

Gabon consists of nine provinces, each with an appointed governor. The judiciary comprises the supreme court, the high court of justice, a court of appeal, and a court of state security, as well as several courts of first instance. In the early 1990s the armed forces included an army of 3200 personnel, a navy of 500, and an air force of 1000.

HISTORY

Discoveries of tools from the end of the Old Stone Age and the New Stone Age indicate early settlements in what is now Gabon, but little is known about the first inhabitants. By the 13th century AD the Mpongwe people were established in the country. The first contact with Europeans was with the Portuguese in the 1470s. During the following 350 years, first the Portuguese and later the French, Dutch, and English carried on a lucrative trade in slaves. The first permanent European settlement was made by the French, with the agreement of the Mpongwe ruler, in 1839. Libreville was founded a decade later by freed slaves. Over the next several years the French extended their rule inland, and in 1866 they appointed a governor to Gabon, which was then attached to the French Congo; it became part of French Equatorial Africa in 1910.

During World War II Gabon was held by the Free French, and in 1946 it became an overseas territory of France. The first Gabonese cabinet was formed in 1957, with Leon M'Ba (1902–67) as prime minister. The following year Gabon voted to become a semiautonomous republic in the French Community. The country declared its independence on Aug. 17, 1960, and in 1961 M'Ba was elected president.

A military coup overthrew President M'Ba's government in 1964, but French troops, in accordance with a Franco-Gabonese defense agreement, intervened and restored him to power; he was reelected president in 1967. Upon M'Ba's death later that year, Vice-President Albert Bernard Bongo (1935–) succeeded to the presidency. Bongo, who later assumed the Islamic first name Omar, was reelected in 1973. During the mid-1970s Gabon began to loosen its ties with France and the French-speaking regional organizations. With Gabonization, the government became a partner in many foreign firms, and native Gabonese filled management positions once held by foreigners. Favorable markets for Gabonese exports, especially oil, natural gas, uranium, and manganese, contributed to rapid economic expansion during the 1970s, but the economy cooled during the following decade.

Reelected to 7-year terms in December 1979 and November 1986, President Bongo faced rising opposition as the 1990s began. Tentative steps toward a multiparty system were taken in 1990, but the newly legalized opposition parties accused the government of fraud in the legislative elections that were held in September and October. The National Assembly enacted a new constitution in March 1991.

For further information on this topic, see the Bibliography in volume 28, section 1012.

GABOR, Dennis (1900–79), British physicist, engineer, and Nobel laureate, born in Budapest, Hungary, and educated at the Technical University, Budapest, and the Technische Hochschule, Charlottenburg, Germany. He taught and performed research in Germany until 1933, when he immigrated to Great Britain. A naturalized British citizen, in 1949 he joined the faculty of the University of London.

Gabor concentrated his research on electron and plasma physics, electron microscopy, and physical optics. He became prominent for his invention (1947) and the subsequent development of holography, a lensless system of three-dimensional photography. For this work, Gabor was awarded the 1971 Nobel Prize in physics. His publications include *The Electron Microscope* (1946) and *Inventing the Future* (1963).

GABORONE, formerly GABERONES, city, capital of Botswana, SE Botswana, near the Notwani R. It is located on the railroad from South Africa to Zimbabwe. The city is primarily an administrative center with government offices but also has a small manufacturing sector that produces metal and wood items and beer. Located in Gaborone are the National Museum and Art Gallery, the University College of Botswana (1976), and the Botswana Agricultural College (1967). The community was founded by the British South Africa Co. in the 1890s as part of the Gaborone Block, originally reserved for white settlement. Gaborone remained a small town until the administrative seat of Bechuanaland (which became independent as Botswana in 1966) was transferred here in 1965 from Mafeking (Mafikeng). Pop. (1981) 59,657.

GABRIEL, angel of high eminence in Jewish, Christian, and Muslim tradition. He is one of the four most often noted archangels (*see* ARCHANGEL) in Judaism and Christianity, the others being Michael, Raphael, and Uriel. Gabriel is the heavenly messenger who appears in order to reveal God's will. In the Old Testament, Gabriel interprets the prophet's vision of the ram and the he-goat (see Dan. 8:15–26) and explains the prediction of the 70 weeks of years (or 490 years) for the duration of the exile from Jerusalem (see Dan. 9:21–27). In the New Testament, he announces to Zacharias the birth of Zacharias's son (see Luke 1:11–20), who is destined to become known as John the Baptist, and to Mary that she is to be the mother of Jesus Christ (see Luke 1:26–31). Among Muslims, Gabriel is believed to be the spirit who revealed the sacred writings to the Prophet Muhammad.

Gabriel is the prince of fire and the spirit who presides over thunder and the ripening of fruits. He is an accomplished linguist, having taught Joseph the 70 languages spoken at Babel. In art he is generally represented carrying either a lily, Mary's flower, at the annunciation, or the trumpet he will blow to announce the second coming.

For further information on this topic, see the Bibliography in volume 28, section 73.

GABRIEL, Jacques Ange (1698–1782), leading French neoclassical architect of the 18th century. Although not a conspicuous innovator, he revived the ideals of classical architecture in France, producing buildings of a grace, nobility, and chaste simplicity that were described as "Greek" by his contemporaries.

Born in Paris into a famous family of architects, Gabriel succeeded his father as first architect to Louis XV in 1742. He built the superb Opera House of the Palace of Versailles in 1748; it represents a move away from the heavily ornamented French baroque of the first half of the 18th century toward a more subtle neoclassicism. In Paris, Gabriel designed the École Militaire (1751) and the Place de la Concorde (1754), both monumental projects illustrating his sensitive disposition of space and his talent for robust large-scale facades. The culmination of his neoclassical style was the Petit Trianon (1768) at Versailles, a square pavilion outstanding for its harmonious lines and pleasing proportions; its four facades, each subtly different from the others, nevertheless retain a unifying cohesion.

GABRIELI, Andrea (c. 1510–86), Venetian composer influential in the transition from Renaissance to baroque music. Born in Venice, Italy, he was a choirboy at the Cathedral of San Marco, where he studied under the famous Flemish composer Adrian Willaert (c. 1490–1562). Gabrieli worked briefly for Duke Albert V of Bavaria, then became organist at San Marco. He died in Venice. Famed for his madrigals and organ music, as well as for his Venetian style of writing for multi-

ple choirs, he also helped establish instrumental music as a genre in itself.

GABRIELI, Giovanni (c. 1554–1612), influential late Renaissance Venetian composer. Born in Venice, Italy, he studied with his uncle, Andrea Gabrieli, and worked in Munich (1574–79) with the Flemish composer Orlando di Lasso. From 1585 he was organist at the Cathedral of San Marco. He died in Venice.

His multiple ensembles of soloists, choirs, and instrumentalists, with their varying tonal colors and combinations, helped establish the principle contrast that permeated 17th- and 18th-century music. His treatment of harmony also foreshadowed baroque usage. His *Sonata pian' e forte* (1597, in *Sacrae symphoniae*, Vol. 1) was among the earliest printed works to specify loudness, softness, and instrumentation. Gabrieli was also noted for his motets and organ music. His most famous pupil was the German composer Heinrich Schütz.

GAD (Heb., "fortune"), name of two characters in the Old Testament.

The more important was Gad, the son of the patriarch Jacob and of Zilpah, a handmaiden of Leah, Jacob's wife (see Gen. 35:26). He is believed to have been the ancestor of the tribe of Gad, which either conquered or was allotted a strip of land east of the Jordan River, about 40 km (about 25 mi) wide, extending from the southern shore of the Sea of Galilee (now Lake Tiberias) almost to the northern shore of the Dead Sea (see Num. 32). The tribe was warlike and is reported to have given great assistance to King David at one time. The Gadites were conquered in the 8th century BC by the Assyrian King Tiglathpileser III (r. 745–727 BC), according to 1 Chron. 5:26, and are not again mentioned after their transportation as captives to Assyria.

Another Gad was a seer at the court of King David. He wrote a book of the Acts of David (see 1 Chron. 29:29) and also helped arrange the musical services in the "house of God" (see 2 Chron. 29:25).

GADDI, Taddeo (c. 1300–c. 1366), Florentine painter and architect, the most important of the pupils of the Florentine painter Giotto, assisting his master for 24 years, as well as painting independently. After Giotto's death Gaddi became the leading painter of the Florentine school for several decades. Taddeo dutifully followed Giotto's principles in his work, setting his naturalistic figures against somber landscapes. He also experimented with the depiction of individualized human features and with lighting effects, both in his altarpieces and in his numerous frescoes. Among Taddeo's frescoes are the series illustrat-

Virgin and Child with Four Saints, *an altarpiece by Taddeo Gaddi.* Metropolitan Museum of Art–Rogers Fund

ing the life of the Virgin and the ceiling paintings *Eight Virtues* (1338, both Baroncelli Chapel, Santa Croce, Florence); *Last Supper* and *Tree of Life* (both c. 1340, refectory of Santa Croce); and frescoes in the Church of San Francesco, Pisa. Among his altarpieces are *Virgin in Glory* (1355, Uffizi, Florence), and *Virgin and Child with Four Saints* (Metropolitan Museum, New York City). His architectural career, according to the Italian biographer Giorgio Vasari, included the building of the Ponte Vecchio over the Arno River in Florence, and the continuation of work on Giotto's campanile for Florence Cathedral. His son Agnolo Gaddi (1345?–96) studied under him and later worked in Florence, Rome, and Prato.

GADFLY, common name of any of various flies that are parasitic on animals or human beings, particularly the botfly and the horsefly (qq.v.).

GADOLINIUM, metallic element, symbol Gd, one of the rare earth elements (q.v.) in the lanthanide series (q.v.) of the periodic table (*see* PERIODIC LAW); at.no. 64, at.wt. 157.25. Gadolinium melts at about 1313° C (about 2395° F), boils at about 3273° C (about 5923° F), and has a sp.gr. of 7.9. It is named after the Finnish chemist John Gadolin (1760–1852). It occurs with other rare earth elements in many minerals, such as samarskite, gadolinite, monazite, and some varieties of Norwegian ytterspar. It is the 41st element in order of abundance in the crust of the earth. Gadolinium oxide was first separated from other rare earth elements by the Swiss chemist Jean de Marignac (1817–94) in 1880. The oxide and many salts of gadolinium have been prepared. Gadolinium oxide is white and the salts are colorless. Because gadolinium has the largest known cross section, or stopping power, for neutrons of any element, it is used as a component of control rods in nuclear reactors. Like the other rare earth elements, it is used in electronic apparatuses such as vacuum tubes, capacitors, masers, and ferrites; in metal alloys; in high-temperature furnaces; and in apparatuses for magnetic cooling.

GADSDEN, city, seat of Etowah Co., NE Alabama, on the Coosa R.; settled 1840, inc. 1871. It is one of Alabama's major industrial centers. Chief manufactures include steel, motor-vehicle tires, and machine tools. The Gadsden Museum of Fine Arts, a cultural arts center, and a junior college are here. Noccalula Falls (about 27 m/90 ft high), bordered by botanical gardens and a pioneer homestead, is nearby. Industrialization was spurred by the building here of one of the world's first hydroelectric projects in 1906. The city is named for the American diplomat James Gadsden (1788–1858). Pop. (1980) 47,565; (1990) 42,523.

GADSDEN PURCHASE, land purchased by the U.S. from Mexico in 1854 and named for the American railroad entrepreneur and diplomat James Gadsden (1788–1858). Adjoining the Mexican border, it comprises a narrow band of today's southern New Mexico and roughly the southern quarter of Arizona. The area is about 76,735 sq km (about 29,640 sq mi), bounded on the east by the Rio Grande, on the north by the Gila River, and on the west by the Colorado River.

The purchase was necessitated by the misunderstandings arising from the 1848 Treaty of Guadalupe Hidalgo, which ended the Mexican War. Not only had the treaty defined the border between Mexico and the U.S. on the basis of an innaccurate map, but one article of it had also made the U.S. responsible for restraining marauding Indians on the frontier; this article had not been enforced, and Mexico claimed millions of dollars in damages.

The situation was further complicated by the fact that U.S. proponents of a southern transcontinental railroad considered the best route to the Pacific to be in the disputed area, through the Mesilla Valley (now in New Mexico). When Franklin Pierce became president in 1853, he repudiated the compromise achieved under President Millard Fillmore (in which Mexico retained the Mesilla Valley). Pierce sent Gadsden as minister to Mexico with instructions to purchase the needed territory and also Lower California if possible, for up to $50 million. Gadsden and the Mexican president, Antonio López de Santa Anna, whose administration was in financial need, negotiated a treaty on Dec. 30, 1853. Under its terms Mexico was to cede a border strip in exchange for $15 million; the article pertaining to Indians was abrogated; and all claims for damages were cancelled. The U.S. Senate ratified the treaty on April 25, 1854, only after a bitter debate, much of which centered on adding more slave territory to the U.S. The version ratified by the Senate lowered the payment to $10 million and reduced the territory acquired. The Southern Pacific Railroad was eventually built through the region. In Mexico the sale met with great opposition and contributed to the political downfall of Santa Anna.

GADWALL, common name for a large, mainly freshwater duck (q.v.), *Anas strepera,* native to North America, Europe, North Africa, and parts of Asia. Males have brownish heads, grayish bodies, dark bills, and yellow feet. The females are a mottled brown. Both sexes of the gadwall have a white speculum, or wing patch. Although normally a surface-feeding bird and therefore almost entirely herbivorous, the gadwall often dives for its food underwater. In North America it nests mainly in western and central regions and winters principally in the lower Mississippi Valley and Mexico. The gadwall frequently associates with the American wigeon and pintail.

GAEA *or* **GE,** in Greek mythology, the personification of Mother Earth, and the daughter of Chaos. She was the mother and wife of Father Heaven, who was personified as Uranus. They were the parents of the earliest living creatures, the Titans, the Cyclopes, and the Giants—the Hecatoncheires (Hundred-Headed Ones). Fearing and hating the monsters, although they were his sons, Uranus imprisoned them in a secret place in the earth, leaving the Cyclopes and Titans at large. Gaea, enraged at this favoritism, persuaded her son, the Titan Cronus, to overthrow his father. He emasculated Uranus, and from his blood Gaea brought forth another race of monsters, the Giants, and the three avenging goddesses the Erinyes. Her last and most terrifying offspring was Typhon, a 100-headed monster, who, although conquered by the god Zeus, was believed to spew forth the molten lava flows of Mount Etna.

GAELIC FOOTBALL, type of football played principally in Ireland, where it originated and where it became popular in the 16th century. At that time a team consisted of all the able-bodied men of a town or parish; the number of players on each team ranged from 25 to 100. Frequently the game started at a point midway between two towns or parishes and ended when one team had driven the ball across a boundary line into its opponent's town or parish. The rules of the modern game were promulgated in 1884 by the Gaelic Athletic Association; that body still controls and regulates the sport.

Fifteen players constitute a team in Gaelic football. The players may kick, punt, or punch the ball; or they may "hop" or dribble it, that is, keep bouncing it while advancing. Throwing or carrying the ball is not allowed. At each end of the field is a goal consisting of two vertical posts and a horizontal crossbar; behind the goal, under the crossbar, is a net. Kicking or punching the ball over the crossbar counts one point; punching or kicking it into the net counts three points. The game is popular in Ireland today and is also played in large cities in Canada and the U.S., principally in New York City, which has a club that competes in Ireland's National League.

GAELIC LANGUAGE. *See* CELTIC LANGUAGES.

GAELIC LITERATURE, literature, both oral and written, in the Gaelic languages of Ireland and Scotland. Before the development of a distinct Scottish Gaelic language in the 15th century, the literature of both countries may be considered as one.

Early Period. The earliest pre-Christian writings in Ireland are tombstone inscriptions in the ogham alphabet, which date from the 5th to the 8th century. The earliest Christian writings survive in a few manuscripts of the 7th through the 10th century, for example, some material on the life of St. Patrick included in the 9th-century illuminated gospels *The Book of Armagh.* The scarcity of literary works until the 11th century is the result of the Norse invasions of Ireland in the 8th century and the sacking of the monasteries, the centers of learning. While some manuscripts were preserved on the European continent by scholars fleeing the invaders, most of the literary works composed in this period survive, in fragments, in much later manuscripts. A characteristic form was the praise poetry composed by a professional class of bards, the *filidh,* in honor of their kings and chieftains. Freer, more personal poetry was written by anonymous poets, such as the one who addressed his white cat, or the writer who composed *The Old Woman of Beare* (9th cent.), an expression of longing for the pagan past. In the form of a dramatic monologue, it is one of the earliest examples of a genre popular in Gaelic poetry. The hermit monks of the early Irish church, living on intimate terms with their environment, established the tradition of nature poetry that is one of the glories of Irish and, later, Scottish Gaelic verse. Some fine examples of this genre are from the 8th century.

11th–15th Century. The great victory over the Norse in 1014 freed Ireland from their domination and was indirectly a great stimulus to literary production. In two 12th-century manuscripts known as *The Book of the Dun Cow* and *The Book of Leinster* are preserved the earliest Gaelic sagas, part in prose, part in poetry, themselves remnants of a much older oral tradition. These sagas have been divided by modern scholars into two cycles. The Ulster, or Red Branch, Cycle is older, consisting of some 100 tales about the heroes of the kingdom of Ulster in the century before Christ, especially the warrior Cú Chulainn (Cuchulainn). Among the more notable tales are *The Cattle Raid of Cooley* (7th or 8th cent.) and the story of the tragic heroine Deirdre. The later Fenian, or Ossianic, Cycle centers about the hero Finn mac Cumhail or MacCool, a legendary chieftain and bard of the 2d or 3d century. Among his followers was Ossian, also a warrior bard, believed to be his son (*see* OSSIAN AND OSSIANIC BALLADS). The dominant strain of these tales, mostly in ballad form, is nostalgia for the heroic past; tinged with Christianity, they are more romantic than epic. Among the better-known stories are *The Pursuit of Diarmuid and Grainne* and the lengthy *Dialogue of the Old Men.*

Aside from these cycles are groups of mythological tales, including a series of marvelous voyages to the Western Isles, notably *The Voyage of Bran;* king tales, for example *The Madness of Sweeney;* religious prose, with much emphasis on miracles; and visions, the best known of which is *The Vision of Adamnan.*

In the later Middle Ages popular ballads and prose tales began to replace the formal bardic literature, and Gaelic translations made the Arthurian legends and some classical literature accessible. The advent of printing, however, which made literature available to large numbers of people in other countries, had little impact in Ireland. Bards there continued to be supported by patrons, their work copied by hand—a tradition that lasted until the early 19th century.

Irish Gaelic Literature, 17th–20th Century. Their support gone when the nobility was dispossessed during the reign of Elizabeth I, the bards themselves disappeared, and Gaelic gave way to English as the vernacular. Despite this, a good deal of prose, much of it devoted to Ireland's past, was written. Examples are *The Annals of the Four Masters* (1636), the history of Ireland up until 1616, by Michael O'Clery (1575–1643); and the *History of Ireland* (c. 1620) by Geoffrey Keating (1570–c. 1650). At the same time, expressions of defiance of English rule began to appear in the folk poetry that circulated clandestinely. Among the most famed writers of the 17th and 18th centuries were the passionate nationalists Dáibhidh Ó Bruadair (1630–98) and Egan O'Rahilly (fl. 1670–1724), and Brian Merriman (1740–1808), a schoolteacher in county Clare. The latter's *The Midnight Court* (trans. 1945), a broad satire on marriage customs, is considered the best long-sustained poem in Irish Gaelic.

Throughout the 19th century, principally because of the depopulation caused by the potato famine of 1845, the Gaelic language, both written and spoken, fell into disuse; most of the Gaelic speakers were by now illiterate. Toward the end of the century efforts were made not only to restore Gaelic as a spoken language but also to stimulate the writing of literary works in Gaelic. Interest in the language was revived by the work of various societies, particularly the Gaelic League, founded in 1893, and by the works of such scholars and nationalists as Douglas Hyde, Canon Peter O'Leary (1839–1920), Patrick O'Connery (1881–1928), and Padhraic Pearse (1879–1916). In the last decade of the 19th and the first half of the 20th centuries the Gaelic revival resulted in the publication of many collections of Irish folk tales and in the writing of a considerable number of plays, works of fiction, and poetry in Gaelic.

Among the numerous 20th-century lyric poets and novelists writing in Gaelic was Tomás O Crohan (1856–1937), who wrote *The Islandman* (1937; trans. 1951) about a Munster fisherman. Brendan Behan, better known for his works in English, composed *The Hostage* originally in Gaelic (1957; trans. 1958).

Scottish Gaelic Literature, 16th–17th Century.

The first evidence of a distinct Scottish Gaelic literary tradition appears in *The Book of the Dean of Lismore,* compiled between 1512 and 1526 by Sir James MacGregor (fl. 1511–51). It is an anthology of writings by Scottish and Irish authors: heroic sagas; poetry (dating from the 14th century on), including a group of 28 Ossianic ballads; and ecclesiastical texts. Although it is presumed that much other early poetry existed, popular verse as well as the work of professional bards, none of it has survived.

Some 16th-century folk poetry that had survived orally was written down in the mid-18th century; and in the 17th and 18th centuries, work songs, also descendants of an older oral tradition, were set down in writing. Predominant among these are the "waulking" songs that accompany the fulling of cloth. In the 17th century Scottish Gaelic poetry flowered. Much of it was contained in three manuscript collections, *The Black Book of Clanranald* and *The Red Book of Clanranald,* written by the MacMhuirich family, hereditary bards to the MacDonalds of Clanranald. The third anthology was the Fernaig manuscript (1688–93), a compilation of political and religious verse. Among many poets, three stand out. Mary MacLeod (c. 1615–c. 1706), bard of Harris and Skye, employed conventional imagery with a fresh, natural style, using strophic meters rather than the strictly syllabic meters of the bards. Iaian Lom (c. 1620–c. 1707), active in contemporary events, wrote poems about the Battle of Killiecrankie and the restoration of Charles II, and in opposition to the union of the Scottish and English parliaments. Remarkable for their intensity of feeling are the works of Roderick Morison (c. 1656–1713?), known as the Blind Harper, such as "Song to John MacLeod of Dunvegan."

18th-Century Scottish Gaelic Literature.

In the 18th century contact with other literatures brought new vigor to Scottish Gaelic writing. Probably the most significant poet of the century was Alexander Macdonald (c. 1690–c. 1780), whose *Resurrection of the Ancient Scottish Tongue* (1751) was the first book of secular poetry printed in Scotland. His masterpiece is *The Birlinn of Clanranald* (after 1751), a vivid description of a sea voyage from the Hebrides to Ireland. He also wrote nature and love poetry, drinking songs, and bitter satires. The poems of Duncan Macintyre (1724–1812), published in 1768, such as *Praise of Ben Doran* and *The Misty Corrie,* are emotional, finely detailed lyrics inspired by the scenery of Perthshire and Argyllshire. The greatest 18th-century writer of religious verse was Dugald Buchanan (1716–68), whose "Day of Judgment"

and "The Skull" employ impressively somber imagery.

The Scottish Gaelic Renaissance.

Short stories first began to appear in a number of periodicals in the late 19th century. Particularly notable are the works in this genre by Iain Crichton Smith (1928–). Much innovative poetry, still adhering to the old tradition of vivid nature imagery, is written by Smith and by his contemporaries Sorley Maclean (1911–), George Campbell Hay (1915–), and Derick Thomson (1921–).

Since 1760, when James Macpherson's *Fragments of Antient Poetry* (actually forgeries of Ossianic ballads) were published, interest in Gaelic culture has never died. It has, indeed, been encouraged by scholarly anthologies of early texts, such as *Reliquiae Celticae* (2 vol., 1892–94), by Alexander Cameron (1827–88), and the *Carmina Gadelica* (6 vol., 1928–71), edited by Alexander Carmichael (1832–1912), and by the work of An Comunn Gaidhealach (The Gaelic League).

Lively interest in the Gaelic language and culture is also still maintained in Canada among descendants of Highland settlers in Nova Scotia. Notable among poets writing in Gaelic was John (The Bard) Maclean (1787–1848), whose bitterness at the lot of the exile is expressed in his "The Bard in Canada." Others were James MacGregor (1759–1820), who translated the Psalms into Gaelic; Duncan Blair (1815–93), best known for a majestic poem on Niagara Falls; and Malcolm Gillis (1856–1929), whose poetry praises the landscape of Cape Breton.

For further information on this topic, see the Bibliography in volume 28, section 837.

GAGARIN, Yury Alekseyevich (1934–68), Soviet astronaut, born near Smolensk. After graduating from technical and vocational schools, he enrolled at the Soviet air force cadet training center at Orenburg, graduating as a pilot in 1957. On April 12, 1961, Gagarin, then a major in the air force, became the first man to travel in space when he rode aboard the earth satellite *Vostok* (later referred to as *Vostok 1*) on a 27,400 km/hr (17,000 mph) single orbit of the earth. The flight lasted 1 hr 48 min, on an elliptical course having an apogee of 327 km (203 mi) and a perigee of 180 km (112 mi). He was killed in the crash of a test airplane.

GAGE, Thomas (1721–87), British general and colonial governor in America, born in Firle, England. He entered the British army in 1740 with a lieutenancy and, after serving in Scotland and Flanders, was sent to America in 1754 as lieutenant colonel under Gen. Edward Braddock in the French and Indian War. In 1761 Gage was appointed a major general and military governor of

Montréal, where his unyielding character and stern efficiency brought him to the attention of the colonial authorities. From 1763 until his return to England in 1772 he was commander of all British forces in North America; he was promoted to lieutenant general in 1770. In 1774 he returned to America to become governor and military commander of the Massachusetts colony. His rigorous enforcement of unpopular British measures, such as the Boston Port Act, aggravated an already tense situation; on April 18, 1775, he sent an expedition to destroy military stores belonging to colonists at Lexington and Concord, resulting in the Battle of Lexington (April 19) and the beginning of the American Revolution. On June 17 he ordered the attack on the American forces occupying Breed's Hill and was widely criticized for the heavy British casualties that resulted (see BUNKER HILL, BATTLE OF). Appointed commander in chief in North America in August 1775, he resigned two months later and returned to England. In 1782 he was appointed a full general.

GAG RULES, in U.S. history, general designation of a number of procedural rules adopted by the U.S. House of Representatives from 1836 to 1844, designed to exclude from consideration by the House, or by House committees, petitions asking for the abolition of slavery in the District of Columbia. The first such rule was introduced by Congressman Henry Laurens Pinckney (1794–1863) of South Carolina. The rules were supported by southern congressmen and by many northern representatives who regarded the antislavery petitions as inflammatory and inimical to the continued union of the states.

The former president of the U.S., John Quincy Adams, was then a member of the House from Massachusetts and led the long fight to abolish the gag rules. He contended that because the U.S. Constitution forbade Congress to enact laws abridging the right of petition, the refusal of Congress to consider petitions was, in effect, an unconstitutional nullification of the right of petition. At the beginning of each session, when the House adopted its rules of procedure, Adams moved to strike out the offending gag rule. Finally, on Dec. 3, 1844, he was successful, and the gag rule was abolished.

GAILLARDIA, genus of about 28 New World herbs of the family Asteraceae (see COMPOSITE FLOWERS), named for Gaillard de Marentonneau, a French amateur botanist. Gaillardias, commonly called blanketflowers, are annual, biennial, or perennial. Two wild species grow in the western U.S.: *Gaillardia lutea,* with yellow flowers, and *G. aristata,* with bright yellow ray flowers, deep red at the base in some varieties, and brownish-purple disk flowers. Also a perennial garden flower, the latter blooms from early summer to late autumn, growing to 91 cm (36 in) tall. *G. pulchella* is an annual species with purple disks and yellow ray flowers that have rose-purple shading at the base. Native to the central U.S., it grows up to 51 cm (20 in) tall and has two major varieties: var. *lorenziana,* with enlarged, tubular ray flowers, and var. *picta,* with heads larger than those of the typical *G. pulchella* and rays in shades of yellow, red, or white. Popular as cut flowers, gaillardias grow best in open, well-drained spaces.

GAINESVILLE, city, seat of Alachua Co., N Florida; inc. as a city 1907. It is the processing and shipping center for an area producing beef cattle, poultry, and lumber. Its various manufactures include sporting goods, batteries, electronic parts, and plastics. The University of Florida (1853) is here. Points of interest include the Florida Museum of Natural History and the Samuel P. Harn Museum of Art. Seminole Indians lived here when the area was settled about 1830. The city is named for Gen. Edmund P. Gaines (1777–1849), a figure of the War of 1812 and the Second Seminole War. Pop. (1980) 81,371; (1990) 84,770.

GAINSBOROUGH, Thomas (1727–88), English painter, who is considered one of the great masters of portraiture and landscape.

Life. Gainsborough was born in Sudbury, Suffolk, on May 14, 1727. He showed artistic ability at an early age, and when he was 15 years old he studied drawing and etching in London with the French engraver Hubert Gravelot (1699–1773). Later he studied painting with Francis Hayman (1708–76), a painter of historical events. Through Gravelot, who had been a pupil of the great French painter Jean Antoine Watteau, Gainsborough came under Watteau's influence. Later he was also influenced by the painters of the Dutch school and by the Flemish painter Sir Anthony van Dyck. From 1745 to 1760 Gainsborough lived and worked in Ipswich. From 1760 to 1774 he lived in Bath, a fashionable health resort, where he painted numerous portraits and landscapes. In 1768 he was elected one of the original members of the Royal Academy; and in 1774 he painted, by royal invitation, portraits of King George III and the queen consort, Charlotte Sophia (1744–1818). Gainsborough settled in London the same year. He was the favorite painter of the British aristocracy, becoming wealthy through commissions for portraits. Gainsborough died in London on Aug. 2, 1788.

Work. Gainsborough executed more than 500 paintings, of which more than 200 are portraits. His portraits are characterized by the noble and

Master John Heath-cote, *one of about 200 portraits by Thomas Gainsborough.*
National Gallery of Art, London

refined grace of the figures, by poetic charm, and by cool and fresh colors, chiefly greens and blues, thinly applied. Among his world-famous portraits are *Orpin, the Parish Clerk* (Tate Gallery, London); *The Baillie Family* (1784) and *Mrs. Siddons* (1785), both in the National Gallery, London; *Perdita Robinson* (1781, Wallace Collection, London); *The Hon. Francis Duncombe* (c. 1777, Frick Collection, New York City); *Mrs. Tenant* (1786–87, Metropolitan Museum, New York City); and many in private collections, including *The Blue Boy* (c. 1779, Huntington Collection, San Marino, Calif.).

The effect of poetic melancholy induced by faint lighting characterizes Gainsborough's paintings. He was obviously influenced by Dutch 17th-century landscape painting. Forest scenes, or rough and broken country, are the usual subjects of his landscapes, most notably *Cornard Wood* (1748) and *The Watering Place* (1775), both in the National Gallery. Gainsborough also executed many memorable drawings and etchings.

GAISERIC, also Genseric (400?–77), king of the Vandals (428–77) at the time of their greatest power. The illegitimate son of Godigiselus (d. 406), leader of the Vandals during the invasion of Gaul, Gaiseric succeeded his brother Gunderic (r. 406–28) in 428. The next year he led all his people from Spain to Africa. The Roman general in Africa, Bonifacius (d. 432), tried vainly to turn the Vandals back, but was defeated and forced to flee to Italy. After a triumphant progress across northern Africa, the Vandals captured Carthage in 439, and Gaiseric made the city his capital. Vandal fleets raided Sicily, Sardinia, and Corsica. In 455 Gaiseric used the death of the Roman emperor Valentinian III as a pretext for the invasion of Rome. The city was undefended, and the Vandals entered it peacefully, pillaged it for 14 days, and carried away its treasures. When he withdrew, Gaiseric took as hostages Valentinian's widow, the empress Eudoxia (b. 422), and her two daughters, along with Roman citizens, who were treated as slaves. He then led his armies eastward, laying waste to Greece and Dalmatia and threatening Constantinople. Two major attempts to subdue the Vandals, by the Western Roman emperor Majorian (r. 457–61) in 457 and by the Eastern Roman emperor Leo I (400?–74) in 468, were unsuccessful. The Eastern emperor Zeno was forced to recognize and make peace with Gaiseric in 476. Gaiseric was succeeded by his son Hunneric (r. 477–84), under whom the African empire of the Vandals began to disintegrate.

GAITHERSBURG, city, Montgomery Co., central Maryland; platted 1769, inc. 1878. Near Washington, D.C., it is the site of the National Institute of Standards and Technology. Manufactures include electrical and precision equipment. The city is named for Benjamin Gaither (c. 1764–1838), an early settler. The major population growth occurred in the 1970s and '80s due to the many government and high-technology employers nearby. Pop. (1980) 26,424; (1990) 39,542.

GALAGO, common name for any of several African prosimians of the family Lorisidae (*see* LORIS), sometimes called bush babies. They are nocturnal and arboreal in habit, eating fruit and insects. Smaller species build nests in trees. The largest species, *Otolemur crassicaudatus,* found on the east coast of Africa, measures little more than 30 cm (12 in), exclusive of the tail. The smallest species, Demidoff's galago, *Galagoides demidovi,* measures only about 13 cm (about 5 in). The tails are longer than their bodies; their hind legs are longer and stronger than their forelegs, with two of the ankle bones (calcaneum and navicular) very much elongated. Their strong digits, well adapted for grasping branches, are all nail-bearing except the second on the hind foot, which is clawed. Galagos are covered with a soft, fawn-gray or brown, woolly fur. They are distinguished from other prosimians by their dentition and by their habit of folding their large, hairless, thin ears lengthwise close to the head when at rest and while leaping through trees. The head is small and round like that of a cat. The immense eyes are a rich brown color, translucent, and marked with minute lines, with large, oval pupils contracting in daylight to vertical slits. Galagos usually have one to three young per litter.

For further information on this topic, see the Bibliography in volume 28, section 458.

GALAHAD. See ARTHURIAN LEGEND.

GALÁPAGOS ISLANDS *or* **COLÓN ARCHIPELAGO,** group of islands, Ecuador, in the Pacific Ocean, constituting a province of the country, about 1050 km (about 650 mi) off the W coast. The archipelago consists of 15 large and several hundred small islands lying on or near the equator. The principal islands are Isabela (Eng. Albemarle), San Cristóbal (Chatham), San Salvador (James),

Santa María (Charles), and Santa Cruz (Indefatigable). The total land area is 7844 sq km (3029 sq mi).

The Land. The islands are volcanic in origin, with level shorelines and mountainous interiors culminating in high central craters, some of which rise more than 1524 m (5000 ft) above sea level. Several volcanoes are active. The islands are fringed with mangroves; farther inland, although still in coastal regions, where little rain falls, the vegetation consists chiefly of thorn trees, cactus, and mesquite. In the uplands, which are exposed to a heavy mist, the flora is more luxuriant. The climate and the temperature of the waters surrounding the islands are modified by the cold Humboldt Current from the Antarctic.

The Galápagos group is noted for its fauna, which includes numerous animals found only in the archipelago and different subspecies on separate islands. Unique to the archipelago are six species of giant tortoise (Span. *galápago*—thus the islands' name). Other reptiles on the islands include two species of large lizards in the iguana family: a burrowing land lizard and an unusual marine lizard that dives into the ocean for seaweed. The islands contain as many as 85 different species of birds, including flamingos, flightless cormorants, finches, and penguins. Sea lions are numerous, as are many different shore fish. Part of the Galápagos is a wildlife sanctuary.

Population and Economy. The islands have a total population of 9240 (1989 est.), mainly Ecuadorians. The administrative center is Baquerizo Moreno on San Cristóbal. Vegetables, tropical fruits, and coffee are grown. Fishing for tuna, groupers, and spiny lobsters is important.

History. The islands were uninhabited at the time of their exploration by the Spanish in 1535. During the 17th and 18th centuries they were used as a rendezvous by pirates and buccaneers. British and U.S. warships and whaling vessels landed frequently at the Galápagos in the 19th century. The islands were not settled until after they were annexed by Ecuador in 1832. In 1835 Charles Darwin, traveling on the HMS *Beagle,* spent six weeks studying the fauna of the Galápagos. His observations furnished considerable data for his *Origin of Species.* A satellite tracking station has been on the Galápagos since 1967.

For further information on this topic, see the Bibliography in volume 28, sections 1233, 1241.

GALATEA, in Greek mythology, one of the 50 Nereids, the daughters of Nereus, the old man of the sea. The gay, mocking sea nymph was loved by the Cyclops Polyphemus, an ugly giant with one huge eye in the middle of his forehead. Galatea did not return his love, however; she teased and ridiculed him, arousing his hopes with kind words and then rejecting him. In later legends, although her attitude toward the lovelorn Cyclops grew kinder, Polyphemus never won her. Galatea finally fell in love with Acis, a handsome young prince, whom Polyphemus killed in a jealous rage.

In Roman mythology, Galatea was the name of a statue of a beautiful woman that was brought to life by Venus, goddess of love, in response to the prayers of the sculptor Pygmalion, who had fallen in love with his creation.

GALAȚI *or* **GALATZ,** city, E Romania, capital of Galați Region, a port on the Danube R. The city is built on a slight rise in the marshlands formed by the nearby Siret and Prut rivers, both part of the huge Danube estuary. Industrial establishments include large warehouses, grain elevators, sawmills, flour mills, rope factories, petroleum refineries, steel mills, and a shipyard. The city is also a principal port of entry for textiles and metal goods. The principal exports are cereal grains, cattle, and timber. Educational facilities include the University of Galați (1948) and the Pedagogic Institute (1959). Pop. (1986 est.) 295,400.

GALATIA, ancient region of Asia Minor, named for the Galatians, a Gallic people from Europe who settled here in the early 3d century BC. The region lies in the basins of the present-day Kizil Irmak and Delice Irmak (rivers), on the great central plateau of Turkey. Galatia possesses some expanses of fertile soil, but most of the land is suitable only for pasturing the large flocks of sheep and goats raised here. In addition to the Gauls, many Greeks settled in the region, and it eventually became Hellenized; the inhabitants, therefore, were often referred to as Gallo-Graeci. Dominated by Rome through regional rulers from 189 BC, Galatia and adjacent regions became a Roman province in 25 BC. It was conquered by the Seljuks in the 11th century AD. Paul the Apostle visited Galatia and addressed his Epistle to the Galatians to several churches here.

GALATIANS, New Testament Epistle, written by St. Paul to churches he had founded in the Roman province of Galatia. The exact location in Galatia of the churches addressed by Paul is unknown, despite intense research. Scholars generally date the Epistle from the middle of the 1st century, about AD 54.

The occasion for writing the Epistle was the growing influence on the Galatians of Jewish Christians who preached close observance of the Mosaic Law and Jewish rituals. In so doing, the Jewish Christians deemphasized faith in Christ as a fundamental principal of Christianity, thereby challenging Paul's apostleship and authority.

To counteract this teaching, which might have turned Christianity into a sect within Judaism, Paul asserted as the central theme of the Epistle that faith in Christ, not works of the law, is the essential condition for salvation (chap. 3–5). To prove his claim to apostleship and the truth of his gospel, Paul contended that he received both by the revelation of Jesus Christ and that his authority had been accepted by the Judean Christians (chap. 1–2). An epilogue (6:11–18) reiterates the principal contents of the Epistle. This section was apparently written in Paul's own handwriting (6:11), in contrast to the body of the Epistle, which probably was dictated to a scribe.

Primarily because of Paul's exposition of the doctrine of faith, the Epistle to the Galatians has been a continuing source of inspiration for Christian theologians. It is often called the Magna Charta of Christian liberty because in it Paul developed his teaching on the independence of Christianity from Judaism and the total efficacy of the salvation obtained through Christ. The Epistle is also historically valuable because of the autobiographical information it contains in chapters 1 and 2.

GALAUP, Jean François de. *See* LA PÉROUSE, JEAN FRANÇOIS DE GALAUP, COMTE DE.

GALAXY, a massive ensemble of hundreds of millions of stars, all gravitationally interacting, and orbiting about a common center. All the stars visible to the unaided eye from earth belong to the earth's galaxy, the Milky Way. The sun with its associated planets is just one star in this galaxy. Besides stars and planets, galaxies contain clusters of stars; atomic hydrogen gas; molecular hydrogen; complex molecules composed of hydrogen, nitrogen, carbon, and silicon, among others; and cosmic rays.

Early History of the Study of Galaxies. A Persian astronomer, al-Sufi (903–36), is credited with first describing the spiral galaxy seen in the constellation Andromeda. By the middle of the 18th century, only three galaxies had been identified. In 1780, the French astronomer Charles Messier (1730–1817) published a list that included 32 galaxies. These galaxies are now identified by their Messier (M) numbers; the Andromeda galaxy, for example, is known among astronomers as M31.

Thousands of galaxies were identified and cataloged by the British astronomers Sir William and Caroline Herschel and Sir John Herschel, during the early part of the 19th century. Since 1900 galaxies have been discovered in large numbers by photographic searches. Galaxies at enormous distances from earth appear so tiny on a photograph that they can hardly be distinguished from stars. The largest known galaxy has about 13 times as many stars as the Milky Way.

In 1912 the American astronomer Vesto M. Slipher (1875–1969), working at the Lowell Observatory in Arizona, discovered that the lines in the spectrum of all galaxies were shifted toward the red spectral region (see RED SHIFT; SPECTROSCOPY). This was interpreted by the American astronomer Edwin Hubble as evidence that all galaxies are moving away from one another and led to the conclusion that the universe is expanding. It is not known if the universe will continue to expand or if it contains sufficient matter to slow down the galaxies gravitationally so they will eventually begin contracting to the point from which they arose. See COSMOLOGY.

Classification of Galaxies. When viewed or photographed with a large telescope, only the nearest galaxies exhibit individual stars. For most galaxies, only the combined light of all the stars is detected. Galaxies exhibit a variety of forms. Some have an overall globular shape, with a bright nucleus surrounded by a luminous struc-

tureless disk. Such galaxies, called ellipticals, contain a population of old stars, usually with little apparent gas or dust, and few newly formed stars. Elliptical galaxies come in a vast range of sizes, from giant to dwarf.

In contrast, spiral galaxies are flattened disk systems containing not only some old stars but also large populations of young stars, much gas and dust, and molecular clouds that are the birthplace of stars (see STAR). Often the regions containing bright young stars and gas clouds are arranged in long spiral arms that can be observed to wind around the galaxy. Generally a halo of faint older stars surrounds the disk; a smaller nuclear bulge often exists, emitting two jets of energetic matter in opposite directions.

Other disklike galaxies, with no overall spiral form, are classified as irregulars. These galaxies also have large amounts of gas, dust, and young stars, but no arrangement of a spiral form. They are usually located near larger galaxies, and their appearance is probably the result of a tidal encounter with the more massive galaxy. Some extremely peculiar galaxies are located in close

The Great Spiral in the constellation Andromeda, shown with its two satellite elliptical galaxies.

The spiral galaxy in the constellation Pisces.

groups of two or three, and their tidal interactions have caused distortions of spiral arms, producing warped disks and long streamer tails.

Quasars are objects that appear stellar or almost stellar, but their enormous red shifts identify them as objects at very large distances (*see* QUASAR; RADIO ASTRONOMY). Most astronomers now believe that quasars are active galaxies whose nucleii contain enormous black holes. They are probably closely related to radio galaxies and to BL Lacertae objects (q.v.).

Determination of Extragalactic Distances. In viewing a galaxy with a telescope, inferring its distance is impossible, for it may be a gigantic galaxy at a large distance or a smaller one closer to earth. Astronomers estimate distances by comparing the brightness or sizes of objects in the unknown galaxy with those in the earth's galaxy. The brightest stars, supernovas, star clusters, and gas clouds have been used for this purpose. Cepheid variables, stars the brightness of which varies periodically, are especially valuable because the period of pulsation is related to the intrinsic brightness of the star. By observing periodicity, the true brightness can be computed and compared with the apparent brightness; distance can then be inferred. Recently astronomers have learned that the speed of the stars as they orbit the center of their galaxy depends on the intrinsic brightness and mass of that galaxy. Rapidly rotating galaxies are extremely luminous; slowly rotating ones are intrinsically faint. If the orbital velocities of stars in a galaxy can be determined, then the distance of that galaxy can be inferred.

Distribution of Galaxies. Galaxies are generally not isolated in space but are often members of small or moderate-sized groups, which in turn form large clusters of galaxies. The earth's galaxy is one of a small group of about 20 galaxies that astronomers call the Local Group. The earth's galaxy and the Andromeda galaxy are the two largest members, each with a million million stars. The Large, Small, and Mini Magellanic Clouds are nearby satellite galaxies, but each is small and faint, with about 100 million stars.

The nearest cluster is the Virgo cluster; the Local Group is an outlying member of the cluster, which contains thousands of galaxies of many types. They all share a common direction of motion, the cause of which might be a supercluster hidden from view by our own galaxy, since superclusters up to 300 million light-years across are known. Some theorists suggest instead that a cosmic "string"—a one-dimensional flaw in the fabric of space-time—could be the cause.

Overall, the distribution of clusters and superclusters in the universe is not uniform. Instead, superclusters of tens of thousands of galaxies are arranged in long, stringy, lacelike filaments, arranged around large voids. The Great Wall, a galactic filament discovered in 1989, stretches across more than half a billion light-years of space. Cosmologists theorize that "dark matter," a hypothetical material that neither radiates nor reflects light, has sufficient mass to generate the gravitational fields responsible for the heterogeneous structure of the universe.

The most distant galaxies known, near the edge of the observable universe, are faint blue objects called "blue fuzzies" because of their appearance on photographic plates. The images were obtained by aiming a telescope at apparently blank regions of the sky and using a solid-state charge-coupled detector to gather the very faint light, then processing the images by means of a computer. The galaxies, moving away from earth at about 88 percent of the speed of light, may have been formed about 2 billion years after the origin of the universe.

Rotation of Spiral Galaxies. Stars and gas clouds orbit about the center of their galaxy. Orbital periods are more than 100 million years. These motions are studied by measuring the positions of lines in the galaxy spectra. In spiral galaxies, the stars move in circular orbits, with velocities that increase with increasing distances from the center. At the edges of spiral disks, velocities of 300 km/sec (about 185 mi/sec) have been measured at distances as great as 150,000 light-years.

This increase in velocity with increase in distance is unlike planetary velocities in the solar system, for example, where the velocities of planets decrease with increasing distance from the sun. This difference tells astronomers that the mass of a galaxy is not as centrally concentrated as is the mass in the solar system. A significant portion of galaxy mass is located at large distances from the center of the galaxy, but this mass has so little luminosity that it has only been detected by its gravitational attraction.

Radiation from a Galaxy. Knowledge of the appearance of a galaxy is based on optical observations. Knowledge of the composition and motions of the individual stars comes from spectral studies in the optical region also. Because the hydrogen gas in the spiral arms of a galaxy radiates in the radio portion of the electromagnetic spectrum, many details of galactic structure are learned from studies in the radio region. The warm dust in the nucleus and spiral arms of a galaxy radiates in the infrared portion of the spectrum. Some galaxies radiate more energy in the optical region.

Recent X-ray observations have confirmed that galactic halos contain hot gas, gas with temperatures of millions of degrees. X-ray emission is also observed from objects as varied as globular clusters, supernova remnants, and hot gas in clusters of galaxies. Observations in the ultraviolet region also reveal the properties of the gas in the halo, as well as details of the evolution of young stars in galaxies.   V.C.R.

For further information on this topic, see the Bibliography in volume 28, sections 376, 381.

GALBRAITH, John Kenneth (1908–), American economist, born in Ontario. He was educated at the universities of Toronto and California and taught economics from 1934 to 1942, first at Harvard University and later at Princeton University. He served with the National Defense Advisory Committee, the Office of Price Administration, and with several other federal agencies of the U.S. From 1943 to 1948 he was a member of the editorial board of *Fortune* magazine. In 1949 he returned to Harvard as a professor of economics. From 1961 to 1963, on leave from Harvard, he served as U.S. ambassador to India.

A prolific and lucid writer on economics, Galbraith wrote *American Capitalism* (1951), a discussion of the balance of economic power among major U.S. companies, and *The Affluent Society* (1958), in which he held that the U.S. had reached a stage in its economic development that should enable it to direct its resources more toward providing better public services and less to the production of consumer goods. His other books include *The Great Crash: 1929* (1955), *The New Industrial State* (1967), *Ambassador's Journal: A Personal Account of the Kennedy Years* (1969), and *A China Passage* and *Economics and the Public Purpose* (both 1973). Among his novels is *A Tenured Professor* (1990).

GALDÓS, Benito Pérez. *See* PÉREZ GALDÓS, BENITO.

GALE. *See* WIND.

GALEN (c. 130–200), the most outstanding physician of antiquity after Hippocrates. His experiments on animals and observations of how the human body functions dominated medical theory and practice for 1400 years. Born of Greek parents in Pergamum, Asia Minor, he received his formal medical training in nearby Smyrna and then traveled widely, gaining more medical knowledge. About 161 he settled in Rome, where he became a physician to emperors and other notable persons and was renowned for his dissections and public lectures. Most of his later life was probably spent in Rome.

Dissecting both live and dead animals, particularly goats, pigs, and monkeys, Galen demonstrated how different muscles are controlled at different levels of the spinal cord. He noted the functions of the kidney and bladder and identified seven pairs of cranial nerves. By tying off the recurrent laryngeal nerve, he showed that the brain controls the voice. Although he thought that the liver was the central organ of the vascular system and that blood moved to the periphery of the body to form flesh, he nevertheless conceived that the body in some way metabolizes, and he disproved the 400-year-old belief that arteries carry air. Galen also described the valves of the heart and noted the structural differences between arteries and veins, but fell short of conceiving that the blood circulates.

Galen was also highly praised in his time as a philosopher. In his treatise *On the Uses of the Parts of the Body of Man* he closely followed Aristotle's view that nothing in nature is superfluous. His principal contribution to philosophic thought was the concept that God's purposes can be understood by examining nature.

Galen's observations in anatomy remained his most enduring contribution; his medical writings were translated by 9th-century Arab thinkers and became highly esteemed by medical humanists of Renaissance Europe. Galen produced about 500 tracts on medicine, philosophy, and ethics, many of which have survived in translated form.

GALENA, city, seat of Jo Daviess Co., NW Illinois, on the Galena R.; inc. 1835. It is a commercial and tourist center. Noted as a well-preserved 19th-century community, with 85 percent of its buildings in the National Historic Register, the city has among its points of interest the Galena Historical Museum, Dowling House (1826), the Old Market House (1845), and a house that was built in 1859 and presented to Ulysses S. Grant in 1865. Originally called Fever River Settlement, the community was laid out in 1826 and named for the mineral galena, a principal source of lead, which had been mined in the region since about 1700. The community suffered when mining declined after 1860. Pop. (1980) 3876; (1990) 3647.

GALENA, a mineral consisting of lead sulfide (PbS). It crystallizes in the isometric system (*see* CRYSTAL), in well-formed cubes and cuboctahedrons, but it also occurs in large masses with a coarse or granular structure. Galena is characterized by perfect cubic cleavage, softness, heaviness, and the ease with which it is fused. Opaque, gray to black in color, galena has a metallic luster. Its sp.gr. is 7.4 to 7.6 and its hardness (q.v.) 2.5 to 2.75.

Galena is an important lead and silver ore. It usually contains small amounts of silver and is often mined for the silver as well as for the lead. Smaller amounts of other metals, such as copper, gold, arsenic, antimony, and selenium, also occur in galena deposits. It is widely distributed and is frequently found associated with the sulfides of iron, copper, or zinc. In the U.S. the principal deposits are in Idaho, Kansas, Missouri, Montana, Oklahoma, Utah, and Wisconsin.

GALESBURG, city, seat of Knox Co., W Illinois; inc. as a city 1857. The city serves as a commercial and distribution center for the surrounding agricultural and coal-mining region. Major manufactures include household appliances, motor-vehicle accessories, and plastic and steel products. In Galesburg are Knox College (1837), a junior college, and the birthplace and grave of the poet Carl Sandburg. The community was established in 1836 by colonists from New York State led by a Presbyterian minister, George Gale (1789–1861), for whom it is named. In 1858 a debate on slavery between Abraham Lincoln and

Zakopane, in Poland, near the Czechoslovakian border, offers a breathtaking view of the high Tatra Mts., part of the Carpathian mountain system in Galicia. **Polish Travel Office**

Stephen A. Douglas was held at Knox College. Pop. (1980) 35,305; (1990) 33,530.

GALICIA (anc. *Gallaecia* or *Callaecia*), former province in northwest Spain, bounded on the west and north by the Atlantic Ocean and the Bay of Biscay, on the east by León and Asturias, and on the south by Portugal. The region is noted for the production of flax. The most important commodity is cattle. Galicia was a kingdom from 411 to 585, and again in the 11th century after the death of Ferdinand I, king of Castile and León. In 1833 the ancient province was divided into the present provinces of La Coruña, Lugo, Orense, and Pontevedra.

GALICIA, region along the N slopes of the Carpathian Mts., formerly an Austrian crown land, now a part of SE Poland and the W Ukraine. Galicia was an important Slavic principality in the 11th and 12th centuries and later belonged to Poland. In 1772, as a result of the first partition of Poland, Galicia became a part of the Austrian Empire and remained an Austrian crown land until 1918, when it was claimed by the new Polish Republic. In 1919, West Galicia was assigned to Poland by the Treaty of Versailles following World War I, and East Galicia was later given the right of self-determination. That same year East Galicia was granted autonomy under a Polish protectorate that endured for 20 years. This decree was approved in 1923 by the Council of Ambassadors, an agency of the League of Nations. Galicia comprised the Polish provinces of Kraków, Lwów, Stanisławów, and Tarnopol. In the invasion of Poland by Germany and the Soviet Union in 1939, Stanisławów, Tarnopol, and part of Lwów, populated mainly by Ukrainians and White Russians, were included in the Soviet Zone of Occupation. Under a Polish-Soviet agreement in 1945, Galicia was assigned to the USSR and incorporated into the Ukrainian SSR, with Tarnopol changed to Ternopol, Lwów to Lvov, and Stanisławów becoming the Stanislav Oblast, which was renamed the Ivano-Frankovsk Oblast in 1962.

GALILEE (Heb. *galil*, "circle"), region, N Israel. In ancient times the boundaries of the region were vague, but by the beginning of the Christian era, Galilee was a Roman province comprising all of what was then N Palestine W of the Jordan R. and Lake Tiberias. The region is generally mountainous and is divided geographically into Upper Galilee in the N and Lower Galilee in the S. Peaks in Upper Galilee attain heights of about 914 m (about 3000 ft) above sea level, with Mt. Meiron rising 1208 m (3963 ft); the terrain in the S is more level. The entire region is well watered; the mountain slopes are covered with shrubs, and grain is cultivated on the large plains. Upper Galilee was long famous for the cultivation of olives and grapes. During ancient times the area contained numerous towns and villages and was heavily populated with Syrians, Phoenicians, Arabs, Greeks, and Jews.

In AD 70, Tiberias, one of the important cities in Galilee, became a center of rabbinical learning. In 1516, Galilee was included in the area that became the Turkish province of Syria. After World War I, the League of Nations assigned the mandate for Palestine to Great Britain. In 1947, when the General Assembly of the UN partitioned Palestine into an Arab and a Jewish state, Galilee was included in the Jewish sector and subsequently became part of Israel. In 1952 the Beit Natufa Dam, part of an irrigation system, was constructed here.

GALILEE, SEA OF. *See* TIBERIAS, LAKE.

GALILEO, full name GALILEO GALILEI (1564–1642), Italian physicist and astronomer, who, with the German astronomer Johannes (or Johann) Kepler, initiated the scientific revolution that flowered in the work of the English physicist Sir Isaac Newton. Galileo's main contributions were, in astronomy, the use of the telescope in observation and the discovery of sunspots, lunar mountains and valleys, the four largest satellites of Jupiter, and the phases of Venus. In physics, he discovered the laws of falling bodies and the motions of projectiles. In the history of culture, Galileo stands as a symbol of the battle against authority for freedom of inquiry.

Galileo was born near Pisa, on Feb. 15, 1564. His father, Vincenzo Galilei (c. 1520–91), played an important role in the musical revolution from medieval polyphony to harmonic modulation. Just as Vincenzo saw that rigid theory stifled new forms in music, so his eldest son came to see Aristotelian physical theology as limiting scientific inquiry. Galileo was taught by monks at Vallombroso and then entered the University of Pisa in 1581 to study medicine. He soon turned to philosophy and mathematics, leaving the university without a degree in 1585. For a time he tutored privately and wrote on hydrostatics and natural motions, but he did not publish. In 1589 he became professor of mathematics at Pisa, where he is reported to have shown his students the error of Aristotle's belief that speed of fall is proportional to weight, by dropping two objects of different weight simultaneously from the Leaning Tower. His contract was not renewed in 1592, probably because he contradicted Aristotelian professors. The same year, he was appointed to the chair of mathematics at the University of Padua, where he remained until 1610.

At Padua, Galileo invented a calculating "compass" for the practical solution of mathematical problems. He turned from speculative physics to careful measurements, discovered the law of falling bodies and of the parabolic path of projectiles, studied the motions of pendulums, and investigated mechanics and the strength of materials. He showed little interest in astronomy, although beginning in 1595 he preferred the Copernican theory (see ASTRONOMY: *The Copernican Theory*)—that the earth revolves around the sun—to the Aristotelian and Ptolemaic assumption that planets circle a fixed earth. Only the Copernican model supported Galileo's tide theory, which was based on motions of the earth. In 1609 he heard that a spyglass had been invented in Holland. In August of that year he presented a telescope, about as powerful as a modern field glass, to the doge of Venice. Its value for naval and maritime operations resulted in the doubling of his salary and his assurance of lifelong tenure as a professor.

By December 1609, Galileo had built a telescope of 20 times magnification, with which he discovered mountains and craters on the moon. He also saw that the Milky Way was composed of stars, and he discovered the four largest satellites of Jupiter. He published these findings in March 1610 in *The Starry Messenger* (trans. 1880). His new fame gained him appointment as court mathematician at Florence; he was thereby freed from teaching duties and had time for research and writing. By December 1610 he had observed the phases of Venus, which contradicted Ptolemaic astronomy and confirmed his preference for the Copernican system.

Professors of philosophy scorned Galileo's discoveries because Aristotle had held that only perfectly spherical bodies could exist in the heavens and that nothing new could ever appear there. Galileo also disputed with professors at Florence and Pisa over hydrostatics, and he published a book on floating bodies in 1612. Four printed attacks on this book followed, rejecting Galileo's physics. In 1613 he published a work on sunspots and predicted victory for the Copernican theory. A Pisan professor, in Galileo's absence, told the Medici (the ruling family of Florence as well as Galileo's employers) that belief in a moving earth was heretical. In 1614 a Florentine priest denounced Galileists from the pulpit. Galileo wrote a long, open letter on the irrelevance of biblical passages in scientific arguments, holding that interpretation of the Bible should be adapted to increasing knowledge and that no scientific position should ever be made an article of Roman Catholic faith.

Galileo   New York Public Library–Picture Collection

Early in 1616, Copernican books were subjected to censorship by edict, and the Jesuit cardinal Robert Bellarmine instructed Galileo that he must no longer hold or defend the concept that the earth moves. Cardinal Bellarmine had previously advised him to treat this subject only hypothetically and for scientific purposes, without taking Copernican concepts as literally true or attempting to reconcile them with the Bible. Galileo remained silent on the subject for years, working on a method of determining longitudes at sea by using his predictions of the positions of Jupiter's satellites, resuming his earlier studies of falling bodies, and setting forth his views on scientific reasoning in a book on comets, *The Assayer* (1623; trans. 1957).

In 1624 Galileo began a book he wished to call "Dialogue on the Tides," in which he discussed the Ptolemaic and Copernican hypotheses in relation to the physics of tides. In 1630 the book was licensed for printing by Roman Catholic censors at Rome, but they altered the title to *Dialogue on the Two Chief World Systems* (trans. 1661). It was published at Florence in 1632. Despite two official licenses, Galileo was summoned to Rome by the Inquisition to stand trial for "grave suspicion of heresy." This charge was grounded on a report that Galileo had been personally ordered in 1616 not to discuss Copernicanism either orally or in writing. Cardinal Bellarmine had died, but Galileo produced a certificate signed by the cardinal, stating that Galileo had been subjected to no further restriction than applied to any Roman Catholic under the

1616 edict. No signed document contradicting this was ever found, but Galileo was nevertheless compelled in 1633 to abjure and was sentenced to life imprisonment (swiftly commuted to permanent house arrest). The *Dialogue* was ordered to be burned, and the sentence against him was to be read publicly in every university.

Galileo's final book, *Discourses Concerning Two New Sciences* (trans. 1662–65), which was published at Leiden in 1638, reviews and refines his earlier studies of motion and, in general, the principles of mechanics. The book opened a road that was to lead Newton to the law of universal gravitation that linked Kepler's planetary laws with Galileo's mathematical physics. Galileo became blind before it was published, and he died at Arcetri, near Florence, on Jan. 8, 1642.

Galileo's most valuable scientific contribution was his founding of physics on precise measurements rather than on metaphysical principles and formal logic. More widely influential, however, were *The Starry Messenger* and the *Dialogue,* which opened new vistas in astronomy. Galileo's lifelong struggle to free scientific inquiry from restriction by philosophical and theological interference stands beyond science. Since the full publication of Galileo's trial documents in the 1870s, entire responsibility for Galileo's condemnation has customarily been placed on the Roman Catholic church. This conceals the role of the philosophy professors who first persuaded theologians to link Galileo's science with heresy. In 1984 a papal commission acknowledged that the church was wrong.   S.D.

For further information on this person, see the section Biographies in the Bibliography in volume 28.

GALL, also cecidium, swelling or excrescence of plant tissues caused by the action of parasites. Such swellings, which may occur on any part of a plant but are usually found in regions of active cell division and growth, are initiated by the chemical action of secretions of infesting organisms, usually insects or fungi. Galls assume a great variety of forms; each form is characteristic of the parasite that causes it, and usually each species of gall-forming parasite infects a specific organ of a specific plant. The growth of the gall may result either from a tremendous swelling of the individual cells or from the rapid division of cells near the point of attack by the parasite. The gall provides a protective capsule for the parasite while it feeds on the plant.

The most striking galls are caused by insects that begin their invasion by laying eggs in plant tissues. The resultant enlargement of surrounding tissue is caused either by growth-promoting stimulation furnished by the eggs or by secretions of the larvae. The gall wasps, a family of small hymenopterous insects, Cynipidae, include the greatest number of species of gall-forming insects. These species restrict their attacks to about 20 genera of plants included in 6 families, especially the oaks; various species produce galls on roots, trunks, leaves, buds, flowers, or acorns. Several cynipids of the genera *Amphibolips* and *Diplolepis* stimulate production of galls known as oak apples. Specialization of function is so great in the cynipids that reproduction in some has been altered. *Plagiotrochus punctatus,* for example, produces in the summer a normal generation, the larvae of which cause blister galls on oak leaves. A second generation, entirely female, is produced in the spring; its larvae cause irregular swellings on oak twigs. The unfertilized eggs of the second generation produce gall wasps of both sexes, which repeat the cycle.

Several galls caused by members of the genus *Cynips* are important sources of tannic acid (*see* TANNINS). The commercial gallnut, *C. gallaetinctoriae,* which infests several Eurasian oaks, contains about 65 percent tannic acid. These gall nuts may be harvested and sold to leather-tanning or ink-manufacturing industries.

For further information on this topic, see the Bibliography in volume 28, section 453.

Cross-section model of a spongy oak gall, which may form on leaves of red or scarlet oak.
American Museum of Natural History

GALLA, African people of Hamitic origin numbering about 10 million and inhabiting the territory between central Ethiopia and the Sabaki River in Kenya. The name is thought to derive from the Arabic *ghaliz,* "rough" or "wild," although in Shoa Province of Ethiopia it is connected with the Gala River. The Galla, who refer to themselves as Oromoto, are related to the Somali and to the Afars in the Danakil region of northeastern Ethiopia. They speak Galla, or Cushitic language, which is a branch of the Afro-Asian linguistic family. The Galla are tall and long-headed, with brown complexions and regular features. A nomadic pastoral existence is followed by most of the Galla; some, however, live in agricultural settlements. Livestock raising and beekeeping are the primary occupations. Monogamy is generally the rule, but in some areas polygamy is practiced, the number of wives being dependent upon the economic status of the husband. Some of the Galla are Muslims and others are Christians who are adherents of the Coptic church, but the majority are animists. Among the most important of the more than 200 Galla tribes are the warlike Tulama group, consisting of about 35 tribes, with traditions of caste and slaveholding, and the Wallo, consisting of about 25 tribes.

GALLATIN, (Abraham Alfonse) Albert (1761–1849), American statesman and financial expert, born in Geneva, and educated at the Academy of Geneva. He immigrated to the U.S. in 1780 and became successively a merchant, a French tutor at Harvard College, and a land speculator in western Pennsylvania and Virginia. He served in the Pennsylvania state legislature from 1790 to 1792. In 1793 he was elected to the U.S. Senate but in the following year was unseated because he was not a U.S. citizen of nine years' standing. He returned to his home in western Pennsylvania and from 1795 to 1801 served in the U.S. House of Representatives. He was instrumental in establishing the Finance Committee (now the Ways and Means Committee) in the House and became recognized as the financial expert among the Republican minority. He was an advocate of free trade and a severe critic of the Federalist party, opposing its financial policy and its advocacy of commercial treaties of reciprocal advantage with other nations.

In 1801 Gallatin was appointed secretary of the treasury by President Thomas Jefferson and served in that capacity until 1814. Between 1801 and 1807 he managed to reduce the public debt considerably and create a surplus of funds, despite the Louisiana Purchase, which he had strongly supported. He opposed war as detrimental to the national economy and worked to bring a quick end to the War of 1812. At the close of hostilities in 1814, he was prominent in the peace negotiations with Great Britain and in drawing up the Treaty of Ghent. Gallatin served as minister to France from 1816 to 1823 and as minister to Great Britain in 1826–27. In 1827 he retired from politics and settled in New York City, where from 1831 to 1839, he was president of a bank. He was interested in ethnology, and in 1842 he was instrumental in founding the American Ethnological Society in New York City and was elected the first president. From 1843 until his death he was president of the New-York Historical Society.

GALLAUDET, Thomas Hopkins (1787–1851), American educator, who devoted his life to the welfare and education of the deaf.

Gallaudet was born in Philadelphia on Dec. 10, 1787, and educated at Yale College and Andover Theological Seminary. He became interested in the teaching of the deaf and went to Europe to learn the methods, including sign language, used there. After studying at the Institut Royal des Sourds-Muets in Paris, he returned to the U.S. in 1816 with a French teacher, Laurent Clerc (1785–1869). Helped by a land grant from Congress, the two founded the first free public school for the deaf in the U.S., the American Asylum for Deaf-Mutes (now the American School for the Deaf in Hartford, Conn.). Some of the people Gallaudet trained went on to lead similar institutions and gave a strong impetus to the previously neglected education of the deaf.

Gallaudet retired in 1830 and devoted himself to various educational causes; he advocated establishing public schools for teacher training and providing higher education for women. He died in Hartford on Sept. 10, 1851.

His two sons, Thomas Gallaudet (1832–1902) and Edward Miner Gallaudet (1837–1917), continued his work as teachers of the deaf. In 1852 Thomas, an Episcopal priest, opened Saint Ann's Church for Deaf-Mutes in New York City. He also founded the Gallaudet Home for elderly deaf-mutes in Poughkeepsie, N.Y. Edward became head of the Columbia Institute in Washington, D.C., the first American institution of higher education for the deaf. In 1894 its senior division was among the earliest proponents of the teaching of lipreading and speech to the deaf.

GALLBLADDER, muscular organ that serves as a reservoir for bile (q.v.), present in most vertebrates. In humans, it is a pear-shaped membranous sac on the undersurface of the right lobe of the liver just below the lower ribs. It is generally about 7.5 cm (about 3 in) long and 2.5 cm (1 in) in diameter at its thickest part; it has a capacity varying from 1 to 1.5 fluid ounces. The body (corpus) and neck (collum) of the gallbladder extend backward, upward, and to the left. The wide end (fundus) points downward and forward, sometimes extending slightly beyond the edge of the liver. Structurally, the gallbladder consists of an outer peritoneal coat (tunica serosa); a middle coat of fibrous tissue and unstriped muscle (tunica muscularis); and an inner mucous membrane coat (tunica mucosa).

The function of the gallbladder is to store bile, secreted by the liver and transmitted from that organ via the cystic and hepatic ducts, until it is needed in the digestive process. The gallbladder, when functioning normally, empties through the biliary ducts into the duodenum to aid digestion by promoting peristalsis and absorption, preventing putrefaction, and emulsifying fat. See DIGESTIVE SYSTEM.

The major disorder associated with the gallbladder is the presence of gallstones, varying in shape and size from a pea to a small pear. Accreted from the constituent salts in the bile, they are most common in diabetic patients, in blacks, and in women; their presence increases with age. Two of the reasons for the growth of gallstones are believed to be the presence of excessive amounts of substances such as calcium and cholesterol in the bile and the retention of bile in the gallbladder for a long period of time. The usual treatment for gallstones is surgical removal. Two naturally occurring bile salts, chenodeoxycholic acid and ursodeoxycholic acid, taken orally dissolve gallstones in some patients. Ultrasound (see ULTRASONICS) treatment to shatter the stones also eliminates the need for surgery in some cases.

Another common disorder of the gallbladder is cholecystitis, or inflammation of the organ, which is believed to be a result of the presence of highly concentrated bile. Chronic cholecystitis is sometimes aggravated by bacterial infection, leading to perforation and peritonitis (q.v.). Less common is the growth of malignant tumors, which are associated with gallstones and constitute about 3 percent of all cancer in humans.

For further information on this topic, see the Bibliography in volume 28, sections 493–94.

GALLE, formerly POINT DE GALLE, city and seaport, S Sri Lanka, capital of Southern Province. Galle exports rubber, tea, rope, coconut oil, fiber, and coir yarn. Galle was of little importance until the 16th century, when much of Sri Lanka was occupied by Portugal. During the Portuguese period and the later era of Dutch occupancy, it was a busy commercial port. Following the improvement of the port of Colombo by Great Britain during the 19th century, the prosperity of Galle declined. Pop. (1984 est.) 95,000.

GALLEGOS FREIRE, Rómulo (1884–1969), Venezuelan novelist and statesman, born in Caracas. He was a teacher from 1912 until 1930, and during this period he published several novels dealing with Venezuelan life. Gallegos's best-known work, *Doña Bárbara* (1929; trans. 1931), depicts the unsuccessful struggle against the forces of tyranny in Venezuela. Because the novel was deemed critical of the dictator Juan Vincente Gómez, Gallegos exiled himself in 1931. Upon his return to Venezuela he was appointed minister of education, but his efforts at school reform failed, and he was forced to resign. In 1945 he participated in the military coup that brought Rómulo Betancourt (1908–81) to power as provisional president. Gallegos was himself elected president, but served only three months in 1948 before he was forced into exile following a military coup. He returned to Venezuela in 1958.

GALLEY, in maritime history, genre name applied to a variety of large, seagoing warships propelled by oars and, more frequently, by sail. In the 18th and 19th centuries the name was applied also to certain classes of sailing-rowing warships and merchant ships, and to some types of small boat as well. The warships of Phoenicia, Greece, and other ancient maritime nations were galleys fitted with rams, and were in use as early as 850 BC. The earliest galleys probably were long, narrow, open boats of shallow draft, with short decks at the bow and sometimes at the stem, and with a narrow gangway extending down the center of the hull over the thwarts of the rowers. The oars pivoted on the gunwales or through oar ports cut in the topsides of the hull. A row of oarsmen sat on each side, protected from enemy missiles, at least to shoulder height, by a light, open rail on which were hung their shields or, in some instances, hides or heavy woven material.

Greek vase paintings show that these single-level, or one-banked, vessels had as many as 20 oars on a side and were about 24 m (about 80 ft) long. The maximum number of oars on a side in a single-banked galley appears to have been 25; such a galley would have been somewhat more than 30 m (100 ft) in length.

Multibanked Galleys. In ancient times, people lacked the technology to build long hulls, and as a result they began to employ two banks of rowers on a side. This innovation led to a marked increase in freeboard. The earliest two-banked galleys, or biremes, apparently had two decks, with oarsmen on each. Later, to reduce freeboard, galleys were built with the upper bank seated inboard of and between the rowers of the lower bank. Thus, the seats of the upper bank did not have to be above the heads of the lower bank. The two-banked galley was rowed with one man to the oar. As early as the time of the Assyrian Empire (c. 1700–600 BC), two-banked galleys were built with a complete fighting deck above the upper bank of oarsmen. Single-banked galleys with such decks also are shown in early Greek vase paintings.

The desire to increase the speed and ramming power of the galley led to the introduction, sometime before 500 BC, of three-banked galleys. This type was employed by ancient Greece, Rome, and other Mediterranean maritime nations. Considerable controversy exists regarding the seating arrangment of the oarsmen in these galleys. Enough evidence seems to exist, however, to assume that the lowest bank of oarsmen sat close to the side of the hull and rowed through oar ports about 84 cm (about 33 in) above the waterline, using possibly shorter oars than the other banks. The second bank rowed over the gunwale or through gunwale oar ports and sat inboard of the lower bank and between pairs of oarsmen in the lower bank. The third-bank oarsmen sat above and perhaps a little outboard of the lowermost bank and between pairs of oarsmen in the second bank. The oars of the third bank apparently pivoted on an outrigger, or

rowing frame, constructed by projecting the deck beams outboard and capping them with heavy timber.

The Athenian three-banked galley, called usually trireme, had 54 oarsmen in the lowest, or thalamite, bank, 54 in the second, or zygite, bank, and 62 in the uppermost, or thranite, bank. Such a galley would have a length of about 39 m (about 128 ft) and a beam of perhaps 4.6 m (15 ft) at the waterline and would draw about 1.2 m (about 4 ft) of water.

The early galleys appear to have been fitted with a single mast and sail, placed a little forward of amidships; some of the later three-banked galleys had two or three masts and sails, which were struck before going into battle. When cruising, the two- and three-banked vessels commonly used only one bank, the oarsmen working short watches so that all did not become tired at the same time.

About 325 BC four- and five-banked galleys (quadriremes and quinqueremes) appeared. How the oarsmen and oars were arranged in these craft and in the later multibanked ships is not known with certainty, but it seems improbable that the oar-per-man arrangement of the three-banked ships was continued in the four- and five-banked ships.

The later multibanked ships, ranging from the hexeris (six banks) to the tessaraconter (40

Roman bireme man-of-war, from a marble relief (c. 30 BC) in the Vatican collection.

A Venetian galley of the 14th century.
Mariners Museum, Newport News, Va.

banks), appear to have been cumbersome and inefficient. In any event these craft were replaced by the Liburnian galley in the 3d century AD. The Liburnian galley was a relatively small vessel designed for speed and using two banks of oars on a side and a large sail. Long a favorite cruiser with the Romans, it was used by them in 31 BC at the Battle of Actium.

Middle Ages and Later. Among the types developed in the Middle Ages were the Byzantine dromond, a fast, two-banked sailing galley having 25 oars on a side; the so-called Italian galley, which had oars on one level and in which one, two, or three men sat on the same bench to row, each with his own oar. The bench was canted to the centerline of the hull and raked from the centerline aft. The Italian galley carried 120 oarsmen and from 40 to 50 soldiers and sailors. It had a single mast and a triangular, lateen sail, a length of about 39 m (about 128 ft) and a beam of about 5 m (about 6.4 ft), and drew 1.4 m (4.5 ft) of water, fully loaded. The hull had only about 61 cm (about 24 in) freeboard to the deck, which was heavily crowned and watertight, except at hatches near the centerline. At the bow, in the fore end of the rowing frame, was a deck structure in which heavy missile weapons such as catapults and ballistae were located. The crew

lived on deck, and the officers were quartered at the extreme stern in a raised cabin with a heavily crowned roof.

In the 13th century the so-called tarida, a galley nearly twice as wide as the Italian type, appeared. Equipped with two masts and carrying about 150 oarsmen, it was used as a transport. Merchant galleys, from 46 to 52 cm (150 to 170 ft) long and with a beam of 5.5 to 7 m (18 to 23 ft), were introduced also. These vessels usually had three masts. By the middle of the 16th century the ordinary galley had an overall length of about 50 m (about 165 ft), a waterline length of 40 m (131 ft), a beam of about 5.5 m (about 18 ft), and a draft of 1.4 m (4.5 ft) loaded. The galley had 150 rowers, and the total crew aboard aggregated from 220 to 230 men. The rowing arrangement remained unchanged, but the oars were longer and counterbalanced. The galleys of this period carried three to five heavy guns, pointed forward, and a number of pivoted, small, light guns.

Another 16th-century development was the galleass, a three-masted rowing-sailing ship, about 50 m (about 165 ft) long, with 45 to 49 oars, up to 350 rowers, and a total crew of about 700 men.

The Battle of Lepanto in 1571 was the last of the great galley battles; thereafter the naval im-

A Venetian galley at the time of the Battle of Lepanto in 1571.

Mariners Museum, Newport News, Va.

portance of this type of ship steadily declined. The rowing man-of-war played a subordinate role in subsequent battles, and by the last half of the 18th century the naval galley was no more than a small gunboat employed in inland waters and in coastal defense.

Galleys continued in use as merchant ships, however. Merchant galleys were built in New England at the end of the 17th century and in the Mediterranean and Baltic countries as late as the first quarter of the 19th century.   H.I.C.

For further information on this topic, see the Bibliography in volume 28, section 557.

GALLIARD, lively 16th-century court dance of Italian origin, often paired with a musically related pavane or passamezzo. The basic galliard pattern, danced in six beats, was four springing steps and a leap (hence its nickname, cincopace, from Fr. *cinqpas,* "five steps"). The pattern's many variations were danced athletically by men and demurely by women. The music was in $\frac{3}{4}$ time, sometimes with alternating $\frac{6}{8}$ measures.

GALLICANISM, in ecclesiastical history, a combination of theological doctrines and political positions supporting the relative independence of the French Roman Catholic church and the French government in their relations with the pope. It was the opposite of ultramontanism, which called for active intervention of the pope in French internal affairs.

Three relatively distinct, although closely related, strands of Gallicanism existed. Ecclesiastical Gallicanism argued that the decisions of ecumenical councils had supremacy over the pope, that the pope was not infallible, and that all bishops were established by divine right as the successors of the apostles. Royal Gallicanism stressed the French kings' absolute independence from Rome in all temporal affairs. Parlementary Gallicanism, a position of the French royal courts, or parlements, was more radical and aggressive, advocating the complete subordination of the French church to the state and, if necessary, the intervention of the government in the financial and disciplinary affairs of the clergy.

The roots of Gallicanism can be traced back at least to the early Middle Ages and to the numerous struggles between the French kings and the popes over political authority and the power to fill clerical positions and collect certain taxes. The first coherent expositions of Gallicanism as a doctrine date from the late 14th and early 15th centuries, when Gallicanism was closely tied to the conciliar movement (*see* CONCILIAR THEORY) and the efforts to end the Great Schism (*see* SCHISM, GREAT) in the church. Thereafter, Gallicanism was greatly strengthened by certain institutional developments. Through the Concordat of 1516, the pope gave the French king the right to appoint all bishops in his realm. The development of the General Assembly of the French clergy in the 16th century strengthened the cohesion and independence of the French episcopacy in relation to Rome. The doctrine achieved its fullest triumph with the Four Gallican Articles of 1682, issued by the General Assembly under the leadership of Bishop J. B. Bossuet and accepted by King Louis XIV. The Four Articles, which reaffirmed the basic tenets of royal and ecclesiastical Gallicanism, were immediately rejected by the pope and later officially renounced by Louis himself. They were taught, however, in French universities and seminaries until the French Revolution (1789).

Following the Revolution, certain Gallican attitudes lingered among the French episcopacy until the mid-19th century. The declaration of the First Vatican Council (1869–70) on papal infallibility and the general triumph of ultramontanism among the French clergy, however, brought an end to the movement.   T.N.T.

GALLI-CURCI, Amelita (1889–1963), Italian-born American soprano, one of the most renowned coloraturas of all time. Born in Milan, Italy, she trained as a pianist and was largely self-taught as a vocalist, using cylinder recordings of her voice to check her progress. She made her debut in 1909 in Rome. She sang with the Chicago Opera Association (1916–25) and with the Metropolitan Opera in New York City (1920–30). A thyroid condition forced her to retire in 1930. Her portrayals included title roles in *Lakmé* by the French composer Léo Délibes and *Lucia di Lammermoor* by the Italian composer Gaetano Donizetti. Her commercial recordings rivaled those of the Italian tenor Enrico Caruso in popularity.

GALLIENI, Joseph Simon (1849–1916), French soldier and colonial administrator, born in Saint-Béat, and educated at the military academy of Saint-Cyr. From 1877 until 1881 he participated in the explorations and military campaigns in the upper Niger River region that resulted in the extension of French influence in western Africa. In 1886, after three years in Martinique, he became governor of Upper Senegal. In 1896, when Madagascar became a French colony, Gallieni was military commander. He was then appointed governor general of the island, and retained that post until 1905. He established firm French control of Madagascar and instituted a program of economic development. On his return to France he was made general of a division and in 1906 was named military governor of Lyon. At the beginning of World War I, Gallieni was chosen to head the military government of Paris. He is credited with persuading Gen. Joseph Jacques Césaire Joffre to attack the Germans on the line of the Ourcq River in the first Battle of the Marne. During that battle Gallieni dispatched several thousand troops from Paris, using every available means of transportation, including taxicabs, to reinforce the army of Gen. Michel Joseph Maunoury (1847–1923). For this action, which resulted in the repulse of the German right flank under Gen. Alexander von Kluck (1846–1934), Gallieni was called the savior of Paris. In 1915 he was made minister of war in the cabinet of Prime Minister Aristide Briand, but ill health caused him to resign shortly before his death in 1916. The title of marshal was awarded posthumously to Gallieni in 1921.

GALLIENUS, Publius Licinius Egnatius (d. 268), emperor of Rome (253–268). He was made joint ruler on the accession of his father, Valerian, in August 253. In 258 Gallienus defeated the Alamanni, a group of German tribes who were making incursions into the Roman provinces along the Danube River. The Alamanni rose again, however, and forced their way into Italy, where Gallienus gained a second victory over them near Mediolanum (now Milan). Meanwhile, Valerian had been engaged in wars with Shapur I, the Sassanid king of Persia (r. 241–72), by whom he was taken prisoner in 260 and put to death. Gallienus then became sole emperor, but in name only, because self-appointed rulers arose in all outlying parts of the Roman Empire. To use his troops most effectively, he established a highly mobile cavalry force that was retained by his successors. During an attack on Mediolanum, held by a usurper, Gallienus was killed in a plot instigated by some of his officers. He was succeeded by Claudius II, his cavalry commander.

GALLINULE, common name for any of a number of birds of the rail family, Rallidae. Gallinules are similar in appearance to coots, but their toes have an undivided marginal membrane. This membrane and the great length of the toes enable the gallinules to swim powerfully and walk on floating vegetation. The members of the genus *Gallinula*, all of which are dull-colored, are known as moorhens (*see* MOORHEN); the genus includes the species formerly called Florida or common gallinule. The remaining gallinules are generally brightly colored in purples, blues, and greens, often with red bills. One relatively small species (33 cm/13 in), the purple gallinule, *Porphyrula martinica*, is found in warm areas throughout the Americas, north to the Carolinas. Similar in color but much larger (51 cm/20 in) is the purple swamphen, *Porphyrio porphyrio*, which is confusingly called "purple gallinule" in many British books. This species occurs in warm areas of the Old World, from the Mediterranean countries east to Samoa, and in the cooler climate of New Zealand and nearby islands. A close relative, often placed in its own genus, *Notornis*, is the even larger takahe, *P. mantelli* (63 cm/25 in), a ponderous, flightless species of New Zealand that was thought to be extinct until it was rediscovered in 1948.

For further information on this topic, see the Bibliography in volume 28, sections 445, 473.

GALLIPOLI. See GELIBOLU.

GALLIPOLI CAMPAIGN (April 25, 1915–Jan. 8, 1916), major land and sea operation of World War I, in which British, French, Australian, and New Zealand forces unsuccessfully attempted an invasion of Turkey. The action was confined to the Dardanelles Strait and the tip of the Gallipoli (Gelibolu) Peninsula near İstanbul. The purpose of the campaign, devised by British munitions minister David Lloyd George, first lord of the admiralty Winston Churchill, Gen. Herbert H. Kitchener, and Adm. Sackville H. Carden (1857–1930), was to open up a new theater of war as an alternative to the stalemate in France, to relieve Turkish pressure on Russian forces in the Caucasus, and, by gaining control of İstanbul and the straits, to provide a direct link with Russia via the Black Sea. What initially was to be a naval operation failed in February 1915 when several British and French ships were damaged by floating mines. A land invasion was then decided on, but it was not begun until late April. An amphibious landing at that time was met with heavy resistance by the Turks. Excessive caution and timorous leadership by the British commander, Sir Ian Hamilton, resulted in several lost initiatives. Little headway was made beyond the several beachheads. In early August, after three months of stalemate and stagnation on the beaches, a new major offensive was begun. Once again, the caution and indifferent leadership of the British command offset the effect of heavy reinforcements. The Turkish forces, on the other hand, were inspired by the leadership of Mustafa Kemal (Kemal Atatürk, later president of Turkey) and the skill of their German commander, Otto Liman von Sanders (1855–1929). After a few more months of stalemate, Hamilton was replaced by Sir Charles Monro (1860–1929), who was sent to evaluate the situation. Monro recommended evacuation, and the allied forces were withdrawn in December and January.

British casualties were 205,000 out of 410,000; the French sustained a rate of 47,000 out of 79,000; Turkish, 250,000 to 300,000 out of 500,000. The fiasco badly stained the reputations of Churchill, Hamilton, and Kitchener. Despite its overall failure, however, the Gallipoli campaign weakened the Turks enough to facilitate the British seizure of Palestine in 1917. The action also distracted the Germans from a plan they had in 1915 to begin another offensive in France.   N.D.B.

For further information on this topic, see the Bibliography in volume 28, section 911.

GALLIUM, metallic element, symbol Ga, in group 13 (or IIIa) of the periodic table (*see* PERIODIC LAW); at.no. 31, at.wt. 69.2. Gallium melts at 30° C (86° F), boils at 2403° C (4357° F), and has a sp.gr. of 5.9.

Gallium was discovered spectroscopically by the French chemist Paul Émile Lecoq de Boisbaudran (1838–1912) in 1875, and isolated in the metallic state by him in 1876. It is blue-gray in color as a solid and silvery as a liquid. It is one of the few metals that is liquid at or near room temperature. It can be supercooled; like water, it expands on freezing. The element is about 34th in order of abundance in the crust of the earth. It occurs in small quantities in some varieties of zinc blende, bauxite, pyrite, magnetite, and kaolin. Gallium resembles aluminum in forming trivalent salts and oxides; it also forms a few monovalent and divalent compounds. The low melting point and high boiling point of the metal are used to advantage in high-temperature thermometers. Certain gallium compounds are excellent semiconductors and have been extensively used in rectifiers, transistors, photoconductors, and laser and maser diodes.

GALLOWAY, area, SW Scotland, bordered on the S by the Irish Sea. The communities of Wigtown and Kirkcudbright are here. Galloway was once a province and included a larger territory. The name Galloway, although still in use locally and historically, no longer has any political significance. The area was known to the Romans as Novantia, and its present name is derived from the Gaelic *Gall-Gael* ("Foreign Gaels"). The term was applied to its inhabitants because they were topographically separated from their northern kinsmen and preserved their distinct identity until the 12th century, their language remaining unchanged until the 15th century.

After the Roman evacuation, in the 5th century AD, Galloway came under the power of the Angles, during which time its inhabitants were called the Picts of Galloway; later the area was conquered by the Norsemen. In the 11th century Galloway was taken by Malcolm III MacDuncan (1031?–93), king of Scotland, who gave his son, later King David I, the title earl of Galloway and united the territory to the kingdom of Scotland. The area is famous for the beauty of its mountains, lakes, and moorland and also for its fine pasturelands. A native breed of hornless sturdy black beef cattle bears the name Galloway.

GALLSTONE. *See* GALLBLADDER.

GALLUP, city, seat of McKinley Co., NW New Mexico, on the Puerco R., near the Arizona border; inc. 1891. It is the processing center of an area rich in uranium and coal; tourism is also important. Gallup is a trading hub for Navajo and Zuñi Indians, who live nearby. The University of New Mexico, Gallup Branch (1957), and the Museum of Indian Arts and Crafts are here. An annual intertribal Indian ceremonial is held in Red Rock State Park here. Gallup was settled in 1880 and became a railroad terminal in 1895. It is named for David L. Gallup (1842–1924), a railroad paymaster. Pop. (1980) 18,167; (1990) 19,154.

GALLUP, George Horace (1901–84), American public opinion analyst and statistician, born in Jefferson, Iowa, and educated at the University of Iowa. He was head of the journalism department at Drake University (1929–31), professor of journalism and advertising at Northwestern University (1931–32), and professor at the Pulitzer School of Journalism, Columbia University (1935–37). In 1935 he founded and became director of the American Institute for Public Opinion, and in 1936 he established the British Institute of Public Opinion. Gallup was a pioneer in the use of statistical methods for measuring the interest of readers in the features and advertisements of magazines and newspapers and for determining public opinion on general issues. He extended his research to include the reactions of radio audiences and founded the Audience Research Institute in 1939. He directed research for many órganizations, won numerous awards, and wrote several books. He is best known for the Gallup poll, public opinion surveys on politics.

GALLUS, Gaius Vibius Trebonianus (205?–53), emperor of Rome (251–53). He served under Emperor Decius in the campaign against the Goths in 251 and is said to have contributed by his treachery to the death of Decius. Gallus thereupon became emperor, and shortly afterward he purchased peace with the Goths by agreeing to let them retain the booty and captives they had acquired in their war with Rome and by pledging to pay them a fixed annual tribute. In 253 the Roman Empire was again invaded by the Goths, but they were defeated in the Roman province of Moesia (in present-day Yugoslavia) by the provincial governor Aemilianus (206?–53), whose troops then proclaimed him emperor. Gallus marched forth to suppress the insurrection but was killed by his own soldiers before his army and that of Aemilianus could meet.

GALOIS, Évariste (1811–1832), French mathematician, best known for his development of group theory (*see* GROUP). Galois was born in the Paris suburb of Bourg-la-Reine and was educated at home. He was twice rejected for admission to the École Polytechnique, the leading school of French mathematics, and three papers he submitted to the Academy of Sciences were lost or rejected as incomprehensible. He then turned to political activism and was arrested and imprisoned for his outspoken republican convictions. Shortly before his death at the age of 21 he hastily wrote down some of his algebraic theories. With the publication of his manuscripts in 1846 and 1870, Galois's reputation as a mathematical giant became widely recognized. Several of his constructs, now termed Galois group, Galois field, and Galois theory, remain fundamental concepts in modern algebra.

GALSWORTHY, John (1867–1933), English novelist and playwright, who was one of the most popular English novelists and dramatists of the early 20th century. He was born in Kingston Hills, Surrey, and educated at Harrow School and the University of Oxford. He was admitted to the bar in 1890 but soon abandoned law for writing. Galsworthy wrote his early works under the pen name John Sinjohn. His fiction is concerned principally with English upper middle-class life; his dramas frequently find their themes in this stratum of society, but also often deal, sympathetically, with the economically and socially oppressed and with questions of social justice. Most of his novels deal with the history, from Victorian times through the first quarter of the 20th century, of an upper middle-class English

The Forsyte Saga, by John Galsworthy, adapted for British television as a series, achieved great success in the U.S. when it was presented over the educational television network WNET. Here, the Forsyte cast gathers for a group portrait.
WNET-TV

family, the Forsytes. The principal member of the family is Soames Forsyte, who exemplifies the drive of his class for the accumulation of material wealth, a drive that often conflicts with human values. The Forsyte series includes *The Man of Property* (1906), the novelette "Indian Summer of a Forsyte" (pub. in the collection *Five Tales*, 1918), *In Chancery* (1920), *Awakening* (1920), and *To Let* (1921). These five titles were published as *The Forsyte Saga* (1922). The Forsyte story was continued by Galsworthy in *The White Monkey* (1924), *The Silver Spoon* (1926), and *Swan Song* (1928), which were published together under the title *A Modern Comedy* (1929). These were followed in turn by *Maid in Waiting* (1931), *Flowering Wilderness* (1932), and *Over the River* (1933), published together posthumously as *End of the Chapter* (1934). Among the plays by Galsworthy are *Strife* (1909), *Justice* (1910), *The Pigeon* (1912), *Old English* (1924), and *The Roof* (1929). Galsworthy was awarded the 1932 Nobel Prize in literature.

GALT, Sir Alexander Tilloch (1817–93), Canadian statesman, born in London, and privately educated. He immigrated to Canada in 1835 to join the British American Land Co. as a clerk; he served as commissioner of the company from 1844 to 1855. In 1849–50 he held his first post as a public servant, representing Sherbrooke, a town in the province of Canada East (now Québec), in the newly established joint Canadian legislature. Reelected in 1853, he served until 1872 as a leading spokesman for the English-speaking minority of the province. From 1858 to 1862 and from 1864 to 1865 he was also minister of finance for the two parts of Canada. He helped introduce the Cayley-Galt tariffs in 1859. In 1867, when the confederation he had long advocated was achieved, Galt was named minister of finance under Sir John Alexander MacDonald in the first government of the Dominion of Canada. He resigned, however, later the same year. Knighted in 1869, he served as first Canadian high commissioner to Great Britain from 1880 to 1883.

GALT, John (1779–1839), Scottish author, born in Irvine, Ayr Co. Early in the 1820s he wrote a series of colorful novels about Scottish life, including *The Ayrshire Legatees* (1820); *The Annals of the Parish* (1821); and *The Entail,* a horrifying study of greed and obsession. Between 1825 and 1829 he served in Canada as an official of the Canada Co., a land-development organization. During this period he founded the town of Guelph (now in Ontario). Shade's Mills (Ontario) was renamed Galt in his honor in 1827. After his return from Canada to live in England and Scotland, he wrote several works, including *The Life of Lord Byron*

Luigi Galvani   New York Public Library

(1830), a biography of his friend, and *Lawrie Todd* (1830), the first novel to deal with Scottish settlers in Canada.

GALTON, Sir Francis (1822–1911), British scientist, best known for his work in anthropology and heredity and considered the founder of the science of eugenics.

Galton was born near Birmingham, England, and educated at King's College, London, and Trinity College, University of Cambridge. He traveled in Africa in 1844 and 1850 and subsequently wrote *Narrative of an Explorer in Tropical South Africa* (1853) and *Art of Travel* (1855). His study of meteorology led him to write *Meteorographica* (1863), the first book on modern methods of mapping weather.

Galton, a cousin of Charles Darwin, became interested in heredity and the measurement of humans; he collected statistics on height, dimensions, strength, and other characteristics of large numbers of people. He devoted special attention to fingerprints and devised a method of identification by fingerprinting. He also demonstrated fundamental techniques in statistical measurement, notably in the calculation of the correlation between pairs of attributes. Galton was knighted in 1909. Among his other works are *Hereditary Genius* (1869), *Inquiries into Human Faculty* (1883), *Natural Inheritance* (1889), and *Finger Prints* (1892).

GALVANI, Luigi (1737–98), Italian physiologist, noted for his studies of the effects of electricity on animal nerves and muscles. Born in Bologna, he was a medical student and later professor of anatomy at the University of Bologna. He accidentally discovered that the leg of a frog twitched when touched with an electrically charged scalpel. Galvani's name is still associated with electricity in the words *galvanism* and *galvanization*.

GALVANIZED IRON, iron or steel coated with a layer of zinc for protection against corrosion. Zinc is applied with greater ease and at lower cost than other metallic coatings such as tin, chromium, nickel, or aluminum.

The most widely used method of galvanizing is the hot dip process. The iron is pickled (immersed in acid) to remove dust, dirt, and grease. It is then washed and dipped into the spelter, that is, molten zinc. In a process known as sherardizing, the article to be galvanized is covered with zinc dust and heated in a tightly closed drum for several hours at 300° to 420° C (572° to 788° F). Other methods of galvanizing iron consist of depositing the zinc electrolytically and applying molten zinc in the form of a fine spray.

GALVANOMETER. *See* ELECTRIC METERS.

GALVESTON, city, seat of Galveston Co., SE Texas, at the NE end of Galveston Island; inc. 1839. Galveston is linked with the mainland by causeways and a bridge. A major seaport located on Galveston Bay, it is the state's chief cotton port; sulfur, grain, and petroleum are also shipped. The city is a commercial fishing center and a popular vacation spot, with many Victorian buildings and long stretches of beach nearby. Industries include insurance, medicine, and the manufacture of refined petroleum, processed food, and textiles. The University of Texas Medical Branch at Galveston (1881), Texas A & M University at Galveston (1971), and a junior college are here.

Galveston Island State Park and an archaeological site are nearby.

Spanish explorers probably visited the area as early as 1523. In the late 1700s the bay (and later the city) was named for Bernardo de Gálvez (1746–86), governor of Louisiana, later viceroy of Mexico. The modern city dates from a settlement established here in 1817 by the pirate Jean Laffite. The town was platted in 1836 and served briefly that year as capital of the Republic of Texas. During the American Civil War, the city, which was a Confederate supply port, changed hands several times. After a hurricane in 1900, which took about 6000 lives, a 16-km- (10-mi-) long seawall was constructed. Other hurricanes in 1961 and 1983 caused much damage here. Pop. (1980) 61,902; (1990) 59,070.

GALWAY, maritime county, W Republic of Ireland, in Connaught Province, bounded on the W by the Atlantic Ocean; after county Cork, Galway is the largest Irish county. Most of the E part of county Galway is a plain with extensive bogs, but Connemara Peninsula in the W, extending S from county Mayo to Galway Bay, is rugged in terrain, with Benbaun Mt., in the Twelve Pins (Twelve Bens) group, reaching a height of 730 m (2395 ft) above sea level. The Galway coast has many inlets and is dotted with islands. The county has numerous lakes, the largest being Lough Corrib, 43 km (27 mi) long. The economy of county Galway is based largely upon the growing of wheat, oats, barley, and potatoes and the raising of sheep, pigs, and poultry. Fishing, gathering kelp, and quarrying limestone, gravel, marl, and black and red marble are also important. The principal towns of the county are the county borough Galway, Ballinasloe, Tuam, and

University College, Galway, in county Galway. **Irish Tourist Board**

Loughrea. Several ancient encampments, burial sites, and ruins of castles and monasteries are in the county. Area, 5939 sq km (2293 sq mi); pop. (1986) 178,552.

GALWAY, city and seaport, W Republic of Ireland, in Connaught Province, county borough of county Galway, on Galway Bay. The city of Galway, in addition to being an export center for wool and agricultural produce from its hinterland, has fisheries, distilleries, iron foundries, flour and corn mills, and marble-polishing works. It is the site of University College (1845), a constituent college of the National University of Ireland.

The older section of the city is built in an irregular fashion, and many of the older buildings are Spanish in architecture. The new town, with spacious streets, is built on rising ground, which slopes gradually toward the bay and the Lough Corrib. Among the churches in Galway is Saint Nicholas, a cruciform structure dating from 1320. Walls, fragments of which remain, were built around the town about 1270, and the commercial development began about that time. From the 13th to the 17th century, Galway had considerable trade with Spain. Pop. (1986) 47,104.

GALWAY, James (1939–), British flutist, born in Belfast, Northern Ireland. He studied at the Royal College of Music and Guildhall School in London, the Paris Conservatoire, and privately under virtuoso French flutists Jean Pierre Rampal and Marcel Moyse (1889–1984). Between 1961 and 1975 he played in the orchestras of Sadler's Wells Opera, Covent Garden Opera, the London Symphony, the Royal Philharmonic, and the Berlin Philharmonic. In 1975 he launched his career as a concert soloist and made his debut in the U.S. in 1978. He became widely known through television appearances, an international concert schedule, and recordings ranging from classical and popular music to jazz and folk music.

GAMA, Vasco da (1469?–1524), Portuguese explorer and navigator, who was the first European to reach India by the sea route.

Da Gama was born in Sines, Alemtejo (now Baixo Alentejo). In his youth he participated in the wars against Castile. Commissioned by Emanuel, king of Portugal, to reach India by sea, da Gama sailed from Lisbon with four ships on July 9, 1497. In November he rounded the Cape of Good Hope (first rounded in 1486 by the Portuguese navigator Bartolomeu Dias) and anchored at Malindi on the east coast of Africa. With the aid of a pilot secured through Indian merchants in that port, da Gama directed his course eastward and on May 20, 1498, reached Calicut (now Kozhikode) on the Malabar Coast

Vasco da Gama   Granger Collection

of India. Because of the hostility of Muslim merchants, he could not establish a Portuguese trading station there. After fighting his way out of the harbor of Calicut, he returned to Portugal in 1499. Da Gama was welcomed with praise, rewarded financially, and permitted to use the prefix Dom with his name. To follow up the discoveries of da Gama, the Portuguese navigator Pedro Álvares Cabral was immediately dispatched to India, and he established a Portuguese trading post in Calicut. When news reached Portugal that those stationed in Calicut by Cabral had been massacred, da Gama, who had been given the title of admiral of India, was sent to avenge that act. On the route to Calicut he established Portuguese colonies at Mozambique and Sofala (now part of Mozambique), in east Africa. After arriving in Calicut, da Gama subdued the inhabitants and forced the raja to make peace. Bearing a rich cargo of spice, he left India and sailed back to Portugal in 1503. For the next 20 years he saw no active sea duty. He received the title of count of Vidigueira in 1519, and in 1524 he was named viceroy and sent to India to correct the mounting corruption among the Portuguese authorities there.

Da Gama reached India in the fall of 1524, but he died in Cochin only three months after his arrival.

GAMALIEL, name of several Jewish figures. In the Old Testament, Gamaliel is mentioned in Numbers as a prince of the tribe of Manasseh. In Jewish history of the New Testament period, Gamaliel is the name of a number of rabbis who were descendants of the rabbi and teacher Hillel. Of these the most notable were the following.

Gamaliel the Elder (fl. AD 20–50), rabbi of the Pharisees, president of the Sanhedrin and the first rabbi to be honored with the title of *rabban* (Heb., "teacher" or "master"), afterward granted to all heads of the Sanhedrin who were descendants of Hillel. Gamaliel was a renowned teacher of the Law. The New Testament records Gamaliel's name in two instances: in Acts 5:34–40, he advises the Sanhedrin to treat the disciples of Jesus Christ with moderation; in Acts 22:3, St. Paul boasts that the great rabbi was his instructor in the Law.

Gamaliel of Jabneh, or Gamaliel the Younger (fl. late 1st cent. AD), scholar, grandson of Gamaliel the Elder. He was the head of the school of Jabneh, a town near Jaffa (now Tel Aviv-Jaffa, Israel), which became the center of Judaism and Jewish studies after the destruction of Jerusalem in AD 70. Gamaliel's authority over the Jews was recognized by the Romans, who designated him "patriarch." He dedicated himself to the preservation of Judaism and made notable contributions to its ritual; these included a revision of the 18 Benedictions recited thrice daily by orthodox Jews and the substitution of the present simple Pesach, or Passover, service for the paschal sacrifice that was forbidden after the destruction of the Temple.

GAMBA, VIOLA DA. See VIOL.

GAMBETTA, Léon (1838–82), French lawyer and statesman, who played a leading part in the formation of the Third Republic.

Gambetta was born on April 2, 1838, in Cahors, and educated in law in Paris. He began to practice in 1860 and through speeches and articles soon became known for his opposition to the regime of Emperor Napoleon III. In 1868, while defending a journalist who had been banned by the government, Gambetta attacked, in a speech that made him famous, the coup d'etat of 1851, by which Napoleon had established the Second Empire.

Gambetta was elected to the Chamber of Deputies in 1869. Although he first opposed the declaration of war against Prussia in 1870, he worked vigorously for the French cause once war had been declared. On Sept. 4, 1870, three days after the Battle of Sedan, in which Napoleon III was captured by the Germans, Gambetta led the Parisian republicans to proclaim the establishment of the Third Republic. He escaped from besieged Paris in a balloon, which was established headquarters at Tours, and attempted to reorganize the French army in the provinces. Assuming the direction of French affairs, he was, by popular consent, dictator of France for five months. Urging the French to fight on, he regarded the military surrender (at Metz) as an act of treason, and resigned from the provisional government.

Gambetta was one of the most radical members of the National Assembly. To disseminate his republican beliefs, he founded *La République Française,* which became one of the most influential newspapers in France and strongly opposed attempts to restore the monarchy. His fiery speeches were celebrated, and his popularity and political strength never wavered. When Jules Grévy was elected president of France in 1879, Gambetta became president of the Chamber of Deputies, and in 1881 he became premier of France. His ministry, however, lasted only two months because his policies, which aimed at the formation of a strong executive government, were unpopular with almost all political factions. Gambetta died near Paris on Dec. 31, 1882. He is considered one of France's most notable patriots, orators, and statesmen.

GAMBIA, river, W Africa, rising in the Futa Jallon Mts., in Guinea. It flows generally W through the nations of Senegal and The Gambia before emptying into the Atlantic Ocean by a wide estuary near Saint Mary's Island, the site of Banjul, the capital of The Gambia. A sandbar at the mouth does not obstruct navigation even during low tide. The river from source to outlet extends little more than 480 km (about 300 mi) in a straight line, but because of its sinuous course, the actual length is about 1125 km (about 700 mi). The flood period of the Gambia is from June to November, at which time the Barraconda Rapids, some 443 km (275 mi) from the mouth of the river, are traversable by small craft. For a long time, the Gambia R. was the only important artery of trade in The Gambia. It was discovered by the Portuguese about 1446 and was explored in 1455 by the Venetian navigator Alvise da Ca Da Mosto (1432?–1511?).

GAMBIA, THE, also Gambia, republic within the Commonwealth of Nations. It is situated on the W coast of Africa, enclosed on the N, E, and S by Senegal and fronting the Atlantic Ocean on the W. The Gambia has an area of 11,295 sq km (4361 sq mi).

LAND AND RESOURCES

The Gambia extends for about 320 km (about 200 mi) inland from the Atlantic Ocean on both sides of the lower Gambia R. It is only some 50 km (some 30 mi) wide at its widest point. The river is lined with mangrove swamps.

Climate. The Gambia has a subtropical climate with distinct hot and cool seasons. During the cool season, from December to April, the hot, dry, dusty winds of the harmattan blow from the Sahara. Temperatures during the year range from 7.2° to 43.3° C (45° to 110° F). The rainy season lasts from June to October. The average annual rainfall is about 1020 mm (about 40 in).

Natural Resources. The main natural resources of The Gambia are agricultural. The soil is mostly poor and sandy, except in the riverine swamps, but is ideally suited for the cultivation of peanuts, upon which the economy is dependent.

Plants and Animals. The mangrove, oil palm, and rubber vine grow in profusion, and cedar and mahogany trees abound. The fauna includes the leopard, wild boar, crocodile, hippopotamus, and several species of antelope. Such game birds as the guinea fowl and sand grouse are plentiful.

POPULATION

The great majority of the inhabitants of The Gambia are Muslim and live in farming villages. The Christian minority lives mainly in Banjul.

Population Characteristics. The population of The Gambia (1983 prelim.) was 695,886, making it one of the least populous African countries. The estimated population in 1989 was 835,000, yielding an overall density of about 74 persons per sq km (about 191 per sq mi). The population comprises the Mandingo, the largest ethnic group (representing about 40% of the country's inhabitants); the Fulani (about 19%), who predominate in the E part of the country; the Wolof (about 15%), who live mainly in Banjul and the W region; the Serahuli (about 10%), whose rulers introduced Islam into the region in the 12th century and who are primarily traders and nomads; the Jola (about 10%), who live in the W region; and the small Aku community, partly descended from liberated slaves.

Banjul, formerly called Bathurst, the capital, is the only seaport and large city. It had a population (1983) of 44,188.

Religion and Language. About 95% of the people of The Gambia are Muslim. Most of the rest are followers of traditional religions. A small minority are Christian. English is the official language. The principal African languages are Wolof and Mandinka.

Education. Primary education is free but not compulsory. In the mid-1980s The Gambia had 189 primary schools, 24 secondary schools, and 9 postsecondary schools. Their combined enrollment totaled about 82,200. The country has teacher-training, vocational, and nursing schools but no university.

Sir Dawda K. Jawara (seated behind small table) leads a discussion with the village authorities of Queenala during an election campaign. United Nations

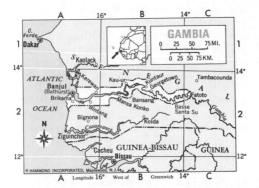

ECONOMY

The Gambia is dependent largely on the production of a single crop, peanuts. The estimated national budget in the late 1980s included revenue of $66 million and expenditure of $75 million, including $22 million in development outlays.

Agriculture and Fishing. About 75% of the working population of The Gambia is engaged in agriculture. Rice and millet, as well as cattle, sheep, goats, and poultry, are raised for local consumption. Peanuts are grown primarily for export; the annual crop amounted to 110,000 metric tons in the late 1980s, when the sale of peanuts and peanut products accounted for about one-third of total yearly exports by value. The government has introduced the raising of cotton, sisal, citrus fruits, and tobacco to diversify agricultural production. The coastal villages engage in fishing. In the late 1980s the annual fish catch was about 14,400 metric tons, mostly from marine waters.

Manufacturing, Currency, and Trade. Manufacturing in The Gambia is limited mainly to the processing of peanuts and other primary products and to the building of fishing boats. Other manufactures include beverages, clothing, footwear, and handicrafts. The unit of currency, adopted in 1971, is the dalasi (8.3 dalasi equal U.S.$1; 1990), consisting of 100 butut; it is issued by the Central Bank of The Gambia (1971). Other banks in The Gambia include the Standard Chartered Bank Gambia Ltd., The Gambia Commercial and Development Bank, and the Agricultural Development Bank. The cost of The Gambia's yearly imports is usually much more than its export earnings; in the late 1980s annual imports totaled $105 milllion and exports and reexports were valued at $74 million. The main trade partners were Great Britain, Germany, China, Italy, the U.S., Senegal, and Ghana. The Gambia's tourist industry is a growing source of foreign exchange.

Transportation and Communications. The Gambia R. is navigable for about 240 km (about 150 mi) from the Atlantic Ocean by small oceangoing vessels. There are about 2390 km (about 1485 mi) of roads; the construction of a major road S of the river has reduced the importance of the river as a major artery of transportation. The country has no railroads. An international airport is located at Yundum, near Banjul. Broadcasters include government-operated Radio Gambia and a commercial station, Radio Syd. About 110,000 radios and 3600 telephones were in use in the late 1980s.

GOVERNMENT

The Gambia is a republic governed under a constitution that became effective in 1970. The head of state and government of The Gambia is a president, who is popularly elected to a 5-year term. The president appoints a cabinet, headed by a vice-president. The unicameral Parliament, called the House of Representatives, consists of 36 popularly elected members, 5 chiefs chosen by leaders of the country's ethnic groups, 8 non-voting members nominated by the president, and the attorney general. The members all serve terms of up to five years.

The judicial system consists of a supreme court with unlimited jurisdiction, an appeal court, and subordinate magistrate and divisional courts. Civil actions between Muslim citizens are handled by special Muslim courts. Minor civil and criminal cases are tried in group tribunals.

HISTORY

Stone Age tools and crude pottery have been found near Banjul, indicating early occupation of the river mouth, and evidence of iron works dating from the 8th century AD also exists. Numerous ethnic groups inhabited the region before the first contact with Europeans, but no unified grouping existed. When the Portuguese arrived in 1455, they found some native Mandingo and Wolof states that paid tribute to the Mali Empire. The Portuguese did not establish a settlement but sold trading rights along the river to English merchants. Throughout the 17th century companies of European traders secured charters to the area, and a struggle developed between the British and the French for supremacy. The British obtained possession of Banjul Island from the local king in 1816 and founded the town of Bathurst (now Banjul). Five years later the British settlements in the region were placed under the administrative control of Sierra Leone. In 1888 The Gambia became a separate crown colony; the boundaries were delimited some years later.

After World War II Britain began to develop the area and to train Gambians for civil administration posts. Political parties soon formed in the 1950s, and the first elections based on universal suffrage were held in May 1960. The colony became independent on Feb. 18, 1965, with Sir Dawda K. Jawara, former minister of education, as prime minister. In a national referendum in 1970, the Gambians voted to form a republic. Jawara became its first president and was reelected in 1972 and 1977. A Libyan-backed coup attempt was thwarted, with Senegalese aid, in 1980. After another coup attempt in 1981, The Gambia joined with neighboring Senegal to form the confederation of Senegambia; President Abdou Diouf (1935–) of Senegal became president of the confederation, and Jawara was made vice-president. Jawara retained the presidency of The Gambia in the elections of 1982 and 1987. The confederation with Senegal collapsed in 1989, but a new friendship treaty was signed in 1991.

For further information on this topic, see the Bibliography in volume 28, section 1012.

GAMBIER ISLANDS, also Mangaréva Islands, group of small coral islands, Tuamotu Archipelago, French Polynesia (an overseas territory of France), in the S Pacific Ocean. Mangaréva, the group's largest island, is the site of the chief settlement, Rikitea. Other islands include Akamaru, Aukéna, and Taravai. Copra is the principal product. The islands were discovered by the British in 1797 and were annexed by France in 1881. Area, about 16 sq km (about 6 sq mi); pop. (1983) 582.

GAMBLING, wagering of money or other consideration of value on an uncertain event that is dependent either wholly on chance, as in roulette, or partly on chance and partly on skill, as in certain card games and in sporting contests. Gambling has been practiced by people throughout history. Anthropologists, who have found evidence of games of chance among the most primitive peoples, contend that the attitude of early humankind toward gambling derived from the general attitude toward the environment. To them the world was a mysterious place controlled by gods or supernatural beings whose favor or disfavor was manifested through chance situations and through the outcome of such events as hunts, wars, and games of chance; instruments of divination frequently included objects used in gambling.

As people gradually acquired knowledge of the nature of their environment and interpreted it in terms of cause and effect, their attitude toward gambling changed. Games of chance became pastimes, but the ancient belief that a lucky gambler was favored of the gods persisted and still survives in various forms. Among the upper classes of the peoples of antiquity, gambling was frequently associated with profligacy and licentiousness. During the Middle Ages, in times of trouble, the rabbis in European Jewish communities banned dice games and other games of chance. Gambling was also proscribed by some Oriental religions, such as Confucianism, by the Koran of Islam, and by the moral codes of many Protestant denominations.

Modern Forms. In modern times gambling occurs in practically all nations and takes a great variety of forms. Among the most widespread are betting on the outcome of horse and dog races; of bull, cock, and prize fights; of wrestling matches; and of such games as baseball, football, basketball, and hockey. Attempts on the part of professional gamblers to fix the outcome of such games have caused numerous scandals and provoked many representatives of organized sports to oppose professionally arranged betting on such events. Other common forms of gambling include roulette, card and dice games, and bingo. Games of this type, as well as slot machines, constitute a major industry in Nevada, where gambling was legalized in 1931, and in Atlantic City, N.J., which legalized casino gambling in 1978. Similar games are played at the most famous European gambling resort, the casino of Monte Carlo, which provides the principality of Monaco with much of its revenue. The lottery, a form of gambling that dates from ancient times, often is used as a money-raising technique by governments, religious groups, and charities.

Government Control. In general, the attitudes of governments toward gambling have been that the practice should be discouraged or regulated. To this end, the British Parliament in 1845 passed an act providing that "all contracts or agreements, by way of gaming or wagering, shall be null and void, and that no suit shall be brought in any court of law for recovering money alleged to have been won upon a wager." Similar legislation has been enacted in all the states of the U.S.; some states have considerably more restrictive laws against gambling and betting, particularly if professionally organized. Nevertheless, all but a few states now have legalized at least some forms of gambling, which has become a growing source of state revenue.

One form of public betting that is acceptable in many states is the pari-mutuel system, which originated in France. It consists of a pool of betting moneys. Those who correctly predict winners of the first three places share the total moneys minus a percentage for track management. Pari-mutuel betting is often employed for horse and dog races and for jai alai games. The pari-mutuel system serves as protection against dishonesty and facilitates collection of gambling taxes. In order to raise additional revenue, New York City on April 7, 1971, opened the first legalized off-track betting system (OTB) in the U.S., enabling the public to place horse racing bets at special locations throughout the city.

At the present time one of the more permissive countries in regard to gambling is Great Britain. Under laws enacted there in 1960 and 1963, betting offices for making wagers on races and games have been licensed; games of chance are allowed in private clubs and homes; and mechanical gambling devices such as slot machines are legal, provided that the odds are not weighted too heavily in favor of the concessionaire, who is permitted only expenses and a "fair" recompense.

GAMBLING, PATHOLOGICAL, behavior disorder in which an individual becomes progressively unable to resist the impulse to gamble. Listed in 1980 as "pathological gambling" in the American Psychiatric Association diagnostic manual, this disorder afflicts 2 to 3 percent of the U.S. adult population. Four out of five problem gamblers are men, and over 90 percent have gambled since their mid-teens. Compulsive gamblers are usually competitive, hardworking, bright individuals addicted to the activity of gambling. They show little interest in passive games of chance, such as lotteries. Gamblers Anonymous, an organization with a 12-step self-help program, has some 300 chapters in the U.S. to help reformed gamblers, who experience psychological withdrawal effects similar to those of drug addicts. Recovery often takes two years or more.

GAMBOGE, gum resin obtained from the bark of various Asian trees of the genus *Garcinia* or from American trees of the genus *Vismia*. Gamboge is orange-red in the resin form and becomes bright yellow when powdered. The best-quality gamboge, obtained from Singapore and from the Canton (Guangzhou), China, area, is a product of *G. hanburyi*, a tree native to southeast Asia; the word gamboge is derived from the name Cambodia. Gamboge is used as a yellow pigment by artists, as a resin in varnishes, and, in medicine, as a cathartic and diuretic.

GAMELAN. *See* INDONESIAN MUSIC.

GAME LAWS, laws regulating the hunting or trapping of wild game: mammals, birds, or fish. As construed in the courts of the U.S., game is generally held to mean all wildlife fit for food; under some statutes the term is also held to include animals valuable for their fur. Oysters and clams that have been planted in beds by commercial fishers generally are not considered game, but the private property of the fishers.

Early game laws in Europe (such as the medieval English Forest Laws) were enacted to make hunting the sole privilege of the nobility and to prevent poaching; in the 19th century such laws were generally modified to allow anyone with a license to hunt. Game laws in the U.S. are directed at protecting wildlife from indiscriminate slaughter and capture, restricting their taking and molestation to certain so-called open periods of the year, or prohibiting the hunting and killing of game entirely. Apart from the states' police power, the ownership of fish and game resides in the people of the states. Where no individual has any property rights to be affected, the legislature, as the representative of the people, may withhold or grant to individuals the right to hunt and kill game or may qualify or restrict that right. In other words, to hunt and kill game is a privilege either expressly granted or implied by sovereign authority rather than an individual right.

Each of the 50 states has its own game laws, which are administered by fish and game commissions or by other agencies. These laws differ widely in some respects. Under most statutes, the possession or sale of certain fish or game during certain so-called closed seasons is prohibited. Occasionally these statutes expressly apply only to game caught within the state. The contrary, however, has obtained in most states, where these statutes have been held to apply to out-of-season possession or sale of game whether or not it was caught within the state. Certain statutes place limitations on the age, sex, or size of game allowed to be hunted, and bag limits per hunter may be set for the day or for the hunting season. Many states require hunting and fishing licenses, for which a nominal fee is charged. Such licenses permit the taking of certain varieties during stipulated periods. Where waters lie between two states the right of fishery is generally regulated by an agreement between the two states.

When lands or waters are owned by a private individual, the exclusive right of hunting or fishing thereon belongs to the owner or tenant. The owner of land on both sides of a stream has the exclusive right to fish in the stream, but the rights of the owner of land on one side only extend to the center of the stream.

See also FISHING; HUNTING; WHALING.

GAMELIN, Maurice Gustave (1872–1958), French general, who commanded the Allied forces at the beginning of World War II. Born in Paris, and educated at the Saint-Cyr military school, Gamelin rose from the rank of major to brigadier general during World War I. Named chief of the general staff in 1931, he directed the extension of the Maginot line. In 1935 he became inspector general of the French army and vice-president of the Higher Council of War. During the initial period of inactivity in World War II, Gamelin was commander in chief of the French and British armies on the western front. When the Germans broke through in May 1940, he was removed from command. After France's defeat the pro-German Vichy government charged him with responsibility for the French entry into the war and the resulting disaster. Later interned in northern Italy by the Germans, he was released and repatriated in 1945.

GAME PRESERVE. *See* CONSERVATION; FISH AND WILDLIFE SERVICE, UNITED STATES.

GAMES, recreational activities generally, but not invariably, played according to prescribed formulas and patterns, and involving equipment such as cards, dice or other counters, or specially marked boards. As differentiated from sports, games are usually more passive in nature, often involving intellectual skill more than physical capability. Games may be classified by type, such as board games, including chess and checkers (qq.v.); card and dice games; guessing games, including charades (q.v.); word and letter games, for example, bingo (q.v.); and the games unique to children. Recently, computer and video games have become popular for children and adults.

See CHILDREN'S GAMES; DICE AND DICE GAMES; and individual articles on various card games.

For further information on this topic, see the Bibliography in volume 28, section 767.

GAMES, ANCIENT, athletic contests and other types of public spectacle that were a feature of the religious and social life of ancient Greece and Rome. In Greece the games served at first as an element in various religious observances: Some were held in honor of the gods, some as offerings of thanksgiving. Others, in later times, were held in honor of living persons. The Greek games, with their attendant processions, feasts, and music, played an important role in developing the appreciation of physical beauty that is typical of Greek art and literature. Until a relatively late stage in Greek history, the participants in the games were drawn from among the citizens rather than from among professional athletes. As the games took on an increasingly professional character, they rapidly declined in public esteem. The four major cycles of games were the Olympian Games, the Pythian Games, the Isthmian Games, and the Nemean Games.

The Roman games, like those of the Greeks, were partly religious in nature. To ensure the continued favor of the gods, the consuls of Rome were required at the beginning of each calendar

A black-figured Athenian amphora, dating from the 6th century BC, depicts a boxing match. The sport was an integral part of the Olympian Games of ancient Greece.
Metropolitan Museum of Art–Rogers Fund

year to hold games dedicated to the gods. Funds for these spectacles were at first supplied by the public treasury. Later, corrupt politicians used the games to win the favor of the populace and vied with one another in the lavishness and extravagance of the games, which were held on the flimsiest of pretexts and eventually lost their original religious meaning and purpose.

The Roman games differed radically from the Greek games in several respects. In Greece the people were often participants, whereas in Rome they were mere spectators, and only professional athletes, slaves, and prisoners customarily took part. Also, the Greek games depended for their entertainment value chiefly on competition among athletes, whereas the Roman games were often characterized by the staging of battles fought to the death and involved large numbers of human beings and also beasts.

GAMETE, sexual reproductive cell that fuses with another sexual cell in the process of fertilization. The cell resulting from the union of two gametes is called a zygote; the zygote usually undergoes a series of cell divisions until it develops into a complete organism.

Gametes, also called germ cells, vary widely in structure. The simplest sexual organisms are isogamous, that is, they produce a single kind of gamete. The identical gametes unite in pairs to produce zygotes. Although all isogametes are apparently alike in structure, they are thought to be different in physiological constitution, because gametes from the same individual do not successfully unite. The simplest isogametes, those of lower fungi such as molds, are small cells that grow on the ends of body filaments and become detached when mature. Other lower organisms, such as lower algae and protozoa, have gametes, which are formed by division of the protoplasm of single cells.

All higher plants are heterogamous, that is, they produce two kinds of gametes. The female gamete is called the egg; the male gamete is called the sperm. The organ of gamete production in plants is called a gametangium.

All animals and animallike lower organisms that reproduce sexually, except a few protozoans, are also heterogamous. The male gametes are called spermatozoa; female gametes, ova or eggs. The gamete-producing organs of animals are called gonads. The formation of gametes in the gonads of animals is called gametogenesis. By this process the number of chromosomes in the sex cells is reduced in number from diploid to haploid, which is half the number of chromosomes in the normal body cells of the species. The diploid number of human chromosomes, for example, is 46. When a human sex cell divides to form two gametes, each gamete receives only half, or 23, of the normal complement of chromosomes. This type of cell division is called meiosis. The normal total of chromosomes is restored in fertilization when two gametes fuse, each contributing half of the chromosomes required by the zygote.

GAME THEORY, mathematical analysis of any situation involving a conflict of interest, with the intent of indicating the optimal choices that, under given conditions, will lead to a desired outcome. Although game theory has roots in the study of such well-known amusements as checkers, ticktacktoe, and poker—hence the name—it also involves much more serious conflicts of interest arising in such fields as sociology, economics, and political and military science.

Aspects of game theory were first explored by the French mathematician Émile Borel (1871–1956), who wrote several papers on games of chance and theories of play. The acknowledged father of game theory, however, is the Hungarian-American mathematician John von Neumann, who in a series of papers in the 1920s and '30s established the mathematical framework for all subsequent theoretical developments. During World War II military strategists in such areas as logistics, submarine warfare, and air defense drew on ideas that were directly related to game theory. Game theory thereafter developed within the context of the social sciences. Despite such empirically related interests, however, it is essentially a product of mathematicians.

Basic Concepts. In game theory, the term *game* means a particular sort of conflict in which *n* number of individuals or groups (known as players) participate. A list of rules stipulates the conditions under which the game begins, the possible legal "moves" at each stage of play, the total number of moves constituting the entirety of the game, and the terms of the outcome at the end of play.

Move. In game theory, a move is the way in which the game progresses from one stage to another, beginning with an initial state of the game through the final move. Moves may alternate between players in a specified fashion or may occur simultaneously. Moves are made either by personal choice or by chance; in the latter case an object such as a die, instruction card, or number wheel determines a given move, the probabilities of which are calculable.

Payoff. Payoff, or *outcome,* is a game-theory term referring to what happens at the end of a game. In such games as chess or checkers, payoff may be as simple as declaring a winner or a loser. In poker or other gambling situations the payoff is usually money; its amount is predetermined by antes and bets amassed during the course of play, by percentages or by other fixed amounts calculated on the odds of winning, and so on.

Extensive and normal form. One of the most important distinctions made in characterizing different forms of games is that between extensive and normal. A game is said to be in extensive form if it is characterized by a set of rules that determines the possible moves at each step, indicating which player is to move, the probabilities at each point if a move is to be made by a chance determination, and the set of outcomes assigning a particular payoff or result to each possible conclusion of the game. The assumption is also made that each player has a set of preferences at each move in anticipation of possible outcomes that will maximize the player's own payoff or minimize losses. A game in extensive form contains not only a list of rules governing the activity of each player, but also the preference patterns of each player. Common parlor games such as checkers and ticktacktoe and games employing playing cards such as "go fish" and gin rummy are all examples.

Because of the enormous numbers of strategies involved in even the simplest extensive games, game theorists have developed so-called normalized forms of games for which computations can be carried out completely. A game is said to be in normal form if the list of all expected outcomes or payoffs to each player for every possible combination of strategies is given for any sequence of choices in the game. This kind of theoretical game could be played by any neutral observer and does not depend on player choice of strategy.

Perfect information. A game is said to have perfect information if all moves are known to each of the players involved. Checkers and chess are two examples of games with perfect information; poker and bridge are games in which players have only partial information at their disposal.

Strategy. A strategy is a list of the optimal choices for each player at every stage of a given game. A strategy, taking into account all possible moves, is a plan that cannot be upset, regardless of what may occur in the game.

Kinds of Games. Game theory distinguishes different varieties of games, depending on the number of players and the circumstances of play in the game itself.

One-person games. Games such as solitaire are one-person, or singular, games in which no real conflict of interest exists; the only interest involved is that of the single player. In solitaire only the chance structure of the shuffled deck and the deal of cards come into play. Single-person games, although they may be complex and interesting from a probabilistic view, are not rewarding from a game-theory perspective, for no adversary is making independent strategic choices with which another must contend.

Two-person games. Two-person, or dual, games include the largest category of familiar games such as chess, backgammon, and checkers or two-team games such as bridge. (More complex conflicts—*n*-person, or plural, games—include poker, Monopoly, Parcheesi, and any game in which multiple players or teams are involved.) Two-person games have been extensively analyzed by game theorists. A major difficulty exists, however, in extending the results of two-person theory to *n*-person games is predicting the interaction possible among various players. In most two-party games the choices and expected payoffs at the end of the game are generally well-known, but when three or more players are involved, many interesting but complicating opportunities arise for coalitions, cooperation, and collusion.

Zero-sum games. A game is said to be a zero-sum game if the total amount of payoffs at the end of the game is zero. Thus, in a zero-sum game the total amount won is exactly equal to the amount lost. In economic contexts, zero-sum games are equivalent to saying that no production or destruction of goods takes place within the "game economy" in question. Von Neumann and Oskar Morgenstern (1902-77) showed in 1944 that any *n*-person non–zero-sum game can be reduced to an $n + 1$ zero-sum game, and that such $n + 1$ person games can be generalized from the special case of the two-person zero-sum game. Consequently, such games constitute a major part of mathematical game theory. One of the most important theorems in this field establishes that the various aspects of maximal-minimal strategy apply to all two-person zero-sum games. Known as the minimax theorem, it was first proven by von Neumann in 1928; others later succeeded in proving the theorem with a variety of methods in more general terms.

Applications. Applications of game theory are wide-ranging and account for steadily growing interest in the subject. Von Neumann and Morgenstern indicated the immediate utility of their work on mathematical game theory by linking it with economic behavior. Models can be developed, in fact, for markets of various commodities with differing numbers of buyers and sellers, fluctuating values of supply and demand, and seasonal and cyclical variations, as well as significant structural differences in the economies concerned. Here game theory is especially relevant to the analysis of conflicts of interest in maximizing profits and promoting the widest distribution of goods and services. Equitable division of property and of inheritance is another area of legal and economic concern that can be studied with the techniques of game theory.

In the social sciences, *n*-person game theory has interesting uses in studying, for example, the distribution of power in legislative procedures. This problem can be interpreted as a three-person game at the congressional level involving vetoes of the president and votes of representatives and senators, analyzed in terms of successful or failed coalitions to pass a given bill. Problems of majority rule and individual decision making are also amenable to such study.

Sociologists have developed an entire branch of game theory devoted to the study of issues involving group decision making. Epidemiologists also make use of game theory, especially with respect to immunization procedures and methods of testing a vaccine or other medication. Military strategists turn to game theory to study conflicts of interest resolved through "battles" where the outcome or payoff of a given war game is either victory or defeat. Usually, such games are not zero-sum games, for what one player loses in lives and injuries is not won by the victor. Some uses of game theory in analyses of political and military events have been criticized as a dehumanizing and potentially dangerous oversimplification of necessarily complicating factors. Analysis of economic situations is also usually more complicated than zero-sum games because of the production of goods and services within the play of a given "game."   J.W.D.

For further information on this topic, see the Bibliography in volume 28, section 374.

GAMETOPHYTE.   See ALTERNATION OF GENERATIONS.

GAMMA GLOBULIN, mixture of proteins in plasma, the fluid portion of blood. It contains antibodies produced in the liver, spleen, bone marrow, and lymph glands to protect the body from invading viruses or bacteria. Each disease antigen (invading protein) stimulates production of a specific antibody (q.v.), which circulates in the blood for a period of time. Since the gamma globulin contains these antibodies, it is sometimes taken from patients who have recovered from chicken pox, hepatitis (qq.v.), and other infectious diseases and given to confer a rapid but short-term immunity on persons recently exposed to those diseases. Persons who suffer from an unusual deficiency of gamma globulin known as agam-

maglobulinemia are deficient in antibodies and may require periodic infusions of gamma globulin to maintain protection.

In 1969 scientists in England and at Rockefeller University (New York City) determined the chemical structure of gamma globulin, an important advance in the knowledge of immunity.

GAMMA RAY.   See RADIOACTIVITY; X RAY.

GAMMA-RAY ASTRONOMY, field of astronomy involving the observation of gamma rays from outer space. A gamma ray is a very-high-energy form of electromagnetic radiation, with a wavelength even shorter than that of X rays. Gamma rays are produced by changes in atomic nuclei and are also decay products of collisions between cosmic rays (q.v.) and interstellar matter. Their study aids in understanding the high-energy processes occurring in outer space, such as those associated with neutron stars and quasars.

Although highly energetic, most gamma rays are absorbed by the earth's atmosphere. Gamma-ray astronomy did not really begin until the space age provided satellite-borne detecting devices (*see* SATELLITE, ARTIFICIAL). In 1991 NASA launched the 17-ton Compton Gamma Ray Observatory into high earth orbit. Within only a few months of operation, its four telescopes had already detected over 100 gamma-ray "bursters," sources of energy so intense as to exceed by many times the total energy of an exploding supernova, but lasting from only a fraction of a second to 100 seconds. Adding to the list of known gamma-ray sources, such as the pulsar in the Crab nebula (*see* NEBULA) and the binary star system Cygnus X-3, the observatory identified a quasar, 3C279, as a powerful gamma-ray emitter.

GAMOW, George (1904–68), Russian-American theoretical physicist, born in Odessa, Ukraine, and educated at the University of Leningrad (now Saint Petersburg). His early work in nuclear physics was done at the universities of Leningrad, Göttingen, Copenhagen, and Cambridge. Gamow became professor of physics at Leningrad in 1931 but left the Soviet Union in 1933. The following year he moved to the U.S., and he became a naturalized citizen in 1940. He was professor of theoretical physics at George Washington University (1934–56) and professor of physics at the University of Colorado (1956–68). Gamow made important contributions in a wide variety of fields, including radioactivity and cosmogony, as well as astrophysics and nuclear physics. He was one of the leading exponents of the theory of the evolutionary universe. He wrote many books for the general public, including *The Birth and Death of the Sun* (1940) and *One, Two, Three . . . Infinity* (1947).

GANDER

GANDER, town, E Newfoundland Island, Newfoundland; inc. 1954. Gander developed after the site was chosen for the construction of an air base in 1935. During World War II, the airport served as an Atlantic base for British, Canadian, and U.S. aircraft. In 1945 the base became a civilian airport, which the Canadian government acquired in 1949 after Newfoundland became a province. The Air Control Center in Gander plays a major role in controlling flights over the North Atlantic. Pop. (1986) 10,207; (1991) 10,339.

GANDHI, Indira Priyadarshini, *née* NEHRU (1917–84), prime minister of India (1966–77; 1980–84), whose controversial political career ended with her assassination by Sikh conspirators.

Gandhi was born on Nov. 19, 1917, in Allahabad, the only child of Jawaharlal Nehru, later the first prime minister of India. A graduate of Visva-Bharati University, Bengal, she also studied at the University of Oxford, England. In 1938 she joined the National Congress party and became active in India's independence movement. In 1942 she married Feroze Gandhi (1913–60), a Parsi lawyer also active in the party. Shortly after, both were arrested by the British on charges of subversion and spent 13 months in prison.

When India won its independence in 1947 and Nehru took office as prime minister, Gandhi became his official hostess. (Her mother had died in 1936.) She also served as his confidante on national problems and accompanied him on foreign trips. In 1955 she was elected to the executive body of the Congress party, becoming a national political figure in her own right; in 1959 she became president of the party for one year. In 1962, during the Chinese-Indian border war, she coordinated civil defense activities.

Following the death of her father in May 1964, Gandhi became minister of information and broadcasting in Lal Bahadur Shastri's government. In this post she extended broadcasting time, liberalized censorship policies, and approved a television education project in family planning. When Shastri died suddenly in January 1966, Gandhi succeeded him as prime minister. The following year she was elected to a 5-year term by the parliament members of the dominant Congress party. She led her party to a landslide victory in the national elections of 1971.

In 1975 Gandhi was convicted of a minor infraction of the election laws during the 1971 campaign. Maintaining innocence, she charged that the conviction was part of an attempt to remove her from office and, instead of resigning, declared a national state of emergency on June 26. Although her conviction was soon overturned by the Indian Supreme Court, the emergency was continued.

Indira Gandhi UPI

Gandhi placed many aspects of life in India under her strict control, and thousands of dissenters were imprisoned. Many saw in these actions the influence of her younger son, Sanjay Gandhi (1946–80), a political neophyte on whom she relied more and more for assistance. Hoping to demonstrate popular support for her regime, which critics contended was undermining India's democratic system, Gandhi called a general election in March 1977; she lost her seat in parliament, and the Congress party was defeated. In the elections of January 1980, however, she made a spectacular comeback and was able to form a new majority government. When Sanjay died in a plane crash that June, she began grooming her older son, Rajiv Gandhi (1944–91), as her successor. On Oct. 31, 1984, after she had moved vigorously to suppress Sikh insurgents, she was shot to death by Sikh members of her security guard. Rajiv then served as prime minister until 1989. He was killed in a bombing at an election rally in Madras on May 21, 1991.

For further information on this person, see the section Biographies in the Bibliography in volume 28.

GANDHI, Mohandas Karamchand, called Mahatma Gandhi (1869–1948), Indian nationalist leader, who established his country's freedom through a nonviolent revolution.

Gandhi was born in Porbandar in the present state of Gujarat on Oct. 2, 1869, and educated in law at University College, London. In 1891, after having been admitted to the British bar, Gandhi returned to India and attempted to establish a law practice in Bombay, with little success. Two years later an Indian firm with interests in South Africa retained him as legal adviser in its office in Durban. Arriving in Durban, Gandhi found himself treated as a member of an inferior race. He was appalled at the widespread denial of civil liberties and political rights to Indian immigrants to South Africa. He threw himself into the struggle for elementary rights for Indians.

Passive Resistance. Gandhi remained in South Africa for 20 years, suffering imprisonment many times. In 1896, after being attacked and beaten by white South Africans, Gandhi began to teach a policy of passive resistance to, and noncooperation with, the South African authorities. Part of the inspiration for this policy came from the Russian writer Leo Tolstoy, whose influence on Gandhi was profound. Gandhi also acknowledged his debt to the teachings of Christ and to the 19th-century American writer Henry David Thoreau, especially to Thoreau's famous essay "Civil Disobedience." Gandhi considered the terms *passive resistance* and *civil disobedience* inadequate for his purposes, however, and coined another term, Satyagraha (Skt., "truth and firmness"). During the Boer War, Gandhi organized an ambulance corps for the British army and commanded a Red Cross unit. After the war he returned to his campaign for Indian rights. In 1910, he founded Tolstoy Farm, near Durban, a cooperative colony for Indians. In 1914 the government of the Union of South Africa made important concessions to Gandhi's demands, including recognition of Indian marriages and abolition of the poll tax for Indians. His work in South Africa complete, he returned to India.

Campaign for Home Rule. Gandhi became a leader in a complex struggle, the Indian campaign for home rule. Following World War I, in which he played an active part in recruiting campaigns, Gandhi, again advocating Satyagraha, launched his movement of passive resistance to Great Britain. When, in 1919, Parliament passed the Rowlatt Acts, giving the Indian colonial authorities emergency powers to deal with so-called revolutionary activities, Satyagraha spread through India, gaining millions of followers. A demonstration against the Rowlatt Acts resulted in a massacre of Indians at Amritsar by British soldiers; in 1920, when the British government failed to make amends, Gandhi proclaimed an organized campaign of noncooperation. Indians in public office resigned, government agencies such as courts of law were boycotted, and Indian children were withdrawn from government schools. Throughout India, streets were blocked by squatting Indians who refused to rise even when beaten by police. Gandhi was arrested, but the British were soon forced to release him.

Economic independence for India, involving the complete boycott of British goods, was made

Mahatma Gandhi, shown during a 1938 tour of jails in Calcutta, where, with a view to negotiating the release of political prisoners, he interviewed them. UPI

a corollary of Gandhi's swaraj (Skt., "self-ruling") movement. The economic aspects of the movement were significant, for the exploitation of Indian villagers by British industrialists had resulted in extreme poverty in the country and the virtual destruction of Indian home industries. As a remedy for such poverty, Gandhi advocated revival of cottage industries; he began to use a spinning wheel as a token of the return to the simple village life he preached, and of the renewal of native Indian industries.

Gandhi became the international symbol of a free India. He lived a spiritual and ascetic life of prayer, fasting, and meditation. His union with his wife became, as he himself stated, that of brother and sister. Refusing earthly possessions, he wore the loincloth and shawl of the lowliest Indian and subsisted on vegetables, fruit juices, and goat's milk. Indians revered him as a saint and began to call him *Mahatma* (Skt., "great-souled"), a title reserved for the greatest sages. Gandhi's advocacy of nonviolence, known as *ahimsa* (Skt., "noninjury"), was the expression of a way of life implicit in the Hindu religion. By the Indian practice of nonviolence, Gandhi held, Great Britain too would eventually consider violence useless and would leave India.

The Mahatma's political and spiritual hold on India was so great that the British authorities dared not interfere with him. In 1921 the Indian National Congress, the group that spearheaded the movement for nationhood, gave Gandhi complete executive authority, with the right of naming his own successor. The Indian population, however, could not fully comprehend the unworldly *ahimsa*. A series of armed revolts against Great Britain broke out, culminating in such violence that Gandhi confessed the failure of the civil-disobedience campaign he had called, and ended it. The British government again seized and imprisoned him in 1922.

After his release from prison in 1924, Gandhi withdrew from active politics and devoted himself to propagating communal unity. Unavoidably, however, he was again drawn into the vortex of the struggle for independence. In 1930 the Mahatma proclaimed a new campaign of civil disobedience, calling upon the Indian population to refuse to pay taxes, particularly the tax on salt. The campaign was a march to the sea, in which thousands of Indians followed Gandhi from Ahmadabad to the Arabian Sea, where they made salt by evaporating sea water. Once more the Indian leader was arrested, but he was released in 1931, halting the campaign after the British made concessions to his demands. In the same year Gandhi represented the Indian National Congress at a conference in London.

Attack upon the Caste System. In 1932, Gandhi began new civil-disobedience campaigns against the British. Arrested twice, the Mahatma fasted for long periods several times; these fasts were effective measures against the British, because revolution might well have broken out in India if he had died. In September 1932, while in jail, Gandhi undertook a "fast unto death" to improve the status of the Hindu Untouchables. The British, by permitting the Untouchables to be considered as a separate part of the Indian electorate, were, according to Gandhi, countenancing an injustice. Although he was himself a member of the Vaisya (merchant) caste, Gandhi was the great leader of the movement in India dedicated to eradicating the unjust social and economic aspects of the caste system.

In 1934 Gandhi formally resigned from politics, being replaced as leader of the Congress party by Jawaharlal Nehru. Gandhi traveled through India, teaching *ahimsa* and demanding eradication of "untouchability." The esteem in which he was held was the measure of his political power. So great was this power that the limited home rule granted by the British in 1935 could not be implemented until Gandhi approved it. A few years later, in 1939, he again returned to active political life because of the pending federation of Indian principalities with the rest of India. His first act was a fast, designed to force the ruler of the state of Rajkot to modify his autocratic rule. Public unrest caused by the fast was so great that the colonial government intervened; the demands were granted. The Mahatma again became the most important political figure in India.

Independence. When World War II broke out, the Congress party and Gandhi demanded a declaration of war aims and their application to India. As a reaction to the unsatisfactory response from the British, the party decided not to support Britain in the war unless the country were granted complete and immediate independence. The British refused, offering compromises that were rejected. When Japan entered the war, Gandhi still refused to agree to Indian participation. He was interned in 1942 but was released two years later because of failing health.

By 1944 the Indian struggle for independence was in its final stages, the British government having agreed to independence on condition that the two contending nationalist groups, the Muslim League and the Congress party, should resolve their differences. Gandhi stood steadfastly against the partition of India but ultimately had to agree, in the hope that internal peace would be achieved after the Muslim demand for

Fishermen pole their small boats from the banks of the Ganges River in Calcutta to the fishing grounds a few miles offshore in the Bay of Bengal.

United Nations

separation had been satisfied. India and Pakistan became separate states when the British granted India its independence in 1947. During the riots that followed the partition of India, Gandhi pleaded with Hindus and Muslims to live together peacefully. Riots engulfed Calcutta, one of the largest cities in India, and the Mahatma fasted until disturbances ceased. On Jan. 13, 1948, he undertook another successful fast in New Delhi to bring about peace, but on January 30, 12 days after the termination of that fast, as he was on his way to his evening prayer meeting, he was assassinated by a fanatic Hindu.

Gandhi's death was regarded as an international catastrophe. His place in humanity was measured not in terms of the 20th century but in terms of history. A period of mourning was set aside in the UN General Assembly, and condolences to India were expressed by all countries. Religious violence soon waned in India and Pakistan, and the teachings of Gandhi came to inspire nonviolent movements elsewhere, notably in the U.S. under the civil rights leader Martin Luther King, Jr.

For further information on this person, see the section Biographies in the Bibliography in volume 28.

GANGES (Hindi *Ganga*), major river of the Indian subcontinent, formed in the S ranges of the Himalaya, in N Uttar Pradesh State, India. Except for extensive streams of the E delta in Bangladesh, the river is in India. The Ganges Basin, one of the most fertile regions of the world and also one of the most densely populated, lies between the Himalaya and the Vindhya Range, and embraces an area of more than 1 million sq km (more than 386,100 sq mi).

187

The river, about 2510 km (about 1560 mi) long, rises in a snowfield situated among three Himalayan mountains all more than 6706 m (22,000 ft) high. It issues as the Bhagirathi R. from an ice cave, 3139 m (10,300 ft) above sea level, and falls 107 m per km (350 ft per mi). About 16 km (about 10 mi) from the source is Gangotri, the first temple on its banks and a traditional resort of pilgrims. At the village of Devaprayag, 214 km (133 mi) from the source, the Bhagirathi joins the Alaknanda to form the Ganges.

The Ganges, after descending 2827 m (9276 ft), or an average of about 11 m per km (about 60 ft per mi), flows W to the border of the great plain of Hindustan at Hardwar, 253 km (157 mi) from its source and 312 m (1024 ft) above sea level. From Hardwar it continues S and then SE to Allahabad after a winding course of 785 km (488 mi), made unnavigable by shoals and rapids.

At Allahabad, the Ganges is joined by the Jumna R. from the SW, and from that point the river flows E past Mirzapur, Varanasi, Ghazipur, Patna, Monghyr, and Bhagalpur, receiving on the S the Son R. and on the N the Gumti, Ghaghra, Gandak, and Kosi rivers. In the Rajmahal Hills, at the head of the Ganges delta, 906 km (563 mi) from Allahabad, the river turns S and begins a descent of 455 km (283 mi) to the Bay of Bengal. Near Pakaur, the Bhagirathi (assuming the former name of the river) and, 114 km (71 mi) lower down, the Jalangi R. branch off from the main stream, and after individual courses of 193 km (120 mi) each, unite to form the Hooghly R., the westernmost and principal channel of navigation, on which the city of Calcutta stands. The main branch of the Ganges, from which numerous minor tributaries flow, continues in Bangladesh, as the Padma R., to the town of Shivalaya (Sibalay), where it unites with the Jamuna, the main branch of the Brahmaputra, and finally runs through the Meghna estuary into the Bay of Bengal.

Between the Meghna estuary and the W channel of the Hooghly R. are the several mouths of the deltaic channels. The N portion of the delta is fertile and well cultivated. The S section consists mostly of swampland, known as the Sundarbans, because of the sundari tree that flourishes there. The marshes are infested by several species of crocodile. From year to year the Ganges exchanges old channels for new ones, particularly in the alluvial basin of its lower reaches.

The Ganges is regarded by Hindus as the most sacred river in the world. Many important religious ceremonies are held in cities on its banks, including Varanasi, Hardwar, and Allahabad.

For further information on this topic, see the Bibliography in volume 28, sections 426, 1082.

GANGRENE, mass death or necrosis of individual cells or tissues of a living organism. The immediate physiological cause of gangrene is blockage of arterial blood supply. Among the symptoms of gangrene are loss of sensation and function. The affected part, usually a limb, becomes cold, turns progressively darker in color, and finally undergoes decomposition. Gangrene may take two forms, dry gangrene or moist gangrene.

Dry, or chronic, gangrene occurs when arteries are blocked gradually and tissues are bloodless. It may be a result of arteriosclerosis (*see* ARTERY), or follow frostbite, injury, or the vascular collapse that often accompanies diabetes.

If the dead, bloodless tissue becomes infected by the anaerobic bacterium *Clostridium,* the condition is called moist, or acute, gangrene. It is also known as gas gangrene because of its putrid-smelling gaseous discharge. The victim's temperature rises sharply, and he or she suffers great pain, acute anemia, and prostration. Moist gangrene may follow contamination of a wound with dirt or other infected matter. It once occurred frequently with war wounds and still occurs among diabetics and after abortions performed under unsanitary conditions. Moist gangrene is fatal unless treated with antibiotics. In severe cases amputation is necessary.

GANNET, common name for three species of seabirds constituting the genus *Morus,* of the family Sulidae in the order Pelecaniformes, particularly the northern gannet, *M. bassanus.* Adults have a pure white body, black wingtips, a yellow-tinged head and neck, and webbed feet. Juveniles are dark brown, speckled with white. The wingspan is about 2 m (about 6 ft), and the body length about 89 cm (about 35 in). The gannet is a powerful flyer and catches fish by plunging into the water, often from 30 m (100 ft) above the surface. Its note is a deep, prolonged croak. Gannets breed in colonies on cliffs and rocks; the female lays one egg, which is usually pale greenish blue flaked with chalky white. The northern gannet is seen in the North Atlantic Ocean and is abundant in the Gulf of Saint Lawrence, Canada, and in the Firth of Forth, Scotland. In the winter, it has been seen off the east coast of the U.S. as far south as Florida.

GANNETT, Henry (1846–1914), American cartographer, born in Bath, Maine, and educated at Harvard University in the Lawrence Scientific School and the Hooper Mining School. He was (1872–79) a topographer for the Hayden Survey, directed by the American geologist Ferdinand Vandeveer Hayden (1829–87), preparing maps in Wyoming and Colorado. The U.S. Geological Survey retained him as chief geographer

GARBO

in 1882. Gannett was the geographer for the 10th (1880), 11th (1890), and 12th (1900) censuses of the U.S. and assistant director of the census of the Philippine Islands (1902) and Cuba (1907–8). He was one of the founders and later a president of the National Geographic Society. Among his works are *A Manual of Topographic Surveying* (1893), *The Building of a Nation* (1895), and *Gazetteer of Texas* (1902).

GANSU, also Kansu, province, N China. Long and narrow in outline, it is dominated by a complex system of semiarid loess-covered plateaus and basins. The high Nan Shan and Qilian (Ch'i-lien) mountain ranges extend along much of the S border. Terraced and irrigated agriculture produces wheat, millet, kaolin, and soybeans. Major resources include petroleum, iron ore, copper, and coal. Lanzhou (Lan-chou), the capital, is an important transportation junction and industrial center; other cities include Yumen and Tianshui (T'ien-shui).

Gansu first came under Chinese administration in the Ch'in dynasty (221–206 BC) and thereafter served as the main corridor between E China and Central Asia. Trade flowed through the region on the Old Silk Road. It became a Muslim stronghold by the 13th century and was the base of the violent Muslim Rebellion (1862–78). It was subsequently reduced in size. The province was hit by devastating earthquakes in 1920 and 1932. Traditionally one of the poorer Chinese provinces, it grew rapidly when reached by rail and industrialized in the 1950s. Area, 450,000 sq km (173,746 sq mi); pop. (1982) 19,570,000.

GANYMEDE, in Greek mythology, a handsome young Trojan prince whom the god Zeus, in the guise of an eagle, snatched from the midst of his companions and bore up to Mount Olympus. He was granted immortality and replaced Hebe, goddess of youth, as cupbearer to the gods. Ganymede was later identified with the constellation Aquarius, "the Water Bearer."

GANYMEDE, in astronomy. *See* JUPITER (planet).

GAR (A.S. *gār*, "spear"), name commonly given to certain fishes with long, narrow bodies and bony, sharp-toothed beaks. Technically the name is restricted to seven or eight species in two genera, *Lepisosteus* and *Atractosteus*, of the family Lepisosteidae. These primitive fish are primarily freshwater. They range from southern Québec through eastern North America to Cuba and Costa Rica. The largest, the tropical gar, reaches a length of 3.7 m (12 ft). The teeth are needlelike, the dorsal fin sits far back on the heavily scaled body, and the lung has blood vessels that enable the gar to breathe in stagnant water. The vertebrae have a ball-and-socket structure similar to that found in some reptiles. The fish spawn in the spring in large groups, and their roe is poisonous to many animals, including humans.

GARBAGE. *See* SOLID WASTE DISPOSAL.

GARBO, Greta, professional name of GRETA GUSTAFFSON (1905–90), Swedish-American actor, born in Stockholm, and educated at the Royal Dramatic Academy. Following her successful performance as the Countess Elizabeth Dohna in the Swedish film *Gösta Berling's Saga* (1923), Garbo was hired by MGM studios and settled in the

Greta Garbo and Charles Bickford in the motion picture Anna Christie *(1930), based on the play by Eugene O'Neill.*
Metro-Goldwyn-Mayer

U.S. Her first American film, *The Torrent* (1926), was a great success and was followed by *The Temptress* (1926) and *Flesh and the Devil* (1927), which established her position as one of the most popular film stars of the time. Garbo's first sound picture was the compelling *Anna Christie* (1930), based on the American dramatist Eugene O'Neill's play. Other film appearances include superb performances in *Susan Lennox—Her Fall and Rise* (with Clark Gable, 1931), *Grand Hotel* (1932), *Queen Christina* (1933), *Anna Karenina* (1935), *Camille* (1936, released 1937), and *Ninotchka* (1939). After completing *Two Faced Woman* (1941), she retired. In 1950 Garbo was chosen the best actress of the half century in a poll conducted by the theatrical newspaper *Variety*. She became a U.S. citizen in 1951 and received a special Academy Award in 1954.

GARBORG, Arne Evenson (1851-1924), Norwegian poet, novelist, and language reformer, born in Time, and educated at the University of Christiania (now the University of Oslo). In 1877 he founded the weekly publication *Fedraheim*, in which he advocated the adoption of a Norwegian literary language based on Old Norse and known as Landsmål; he also advocated a revival of Norwegian national folk dances, costumes, and customs. His works include *The New Norwegian Language and the National Movement* (1887), two cycles of lyric poems, and the religious novels *A Freethinker* (1878) and *Weary Souls* (1891).

GARCÍA ÍÑIGUEZ, Calixto (1836?-98), Cuban revolutionist, born in Holguín. In 1868 he became a leader of the Cuban insurrection against Spanish rule. He was commander in chief of the Cuban forces in 1873, when he was captured and taken to Spain. In 1895 he escaped to New York City. When the Spanish-American War broke out in 1898, García Íñiguez cooperated actively with the U.S. Army and distinguished himself in the battle for El Caney (July 1, 1898). His name became famous after the war through the inspirational essay "A Message to García" (1899) by the American writer Elbert Hubbard (1856-1915).

GARCÍA LORCA, Federico (1898-1936), Spanish writer, the most popular poet of the Spanish-speaking world and one of the most powerful dramatists in the modern theater.

García Lorca was born on June 5, 1898, in Fuente Vaqueros, and educated at the universities of Granada and Madrid. During his youth he wrote poetry and studied music. From 1919 to 1934 he lived principally in Madrid, where he organized theatrical performances and gave readings of his poems, which were first collected in *Libro de poemas* (Book of Poems, 1921).

García Lorca organized in 1922 the first festival of *cante jondo,* or deep song, an ancient type of Andalusian Gypsy song that influenced his own poetry considerably. His first successful play, the historical drama *Mariana Pineda,* appeared five years later. After the publication of *Primer romancero gitano* (First Book of Gypsy Ballads, 1928), on Andalusian Gypsy themes, García Lorca became renowned among both the intelligentsia and the common people of Spain.

García Lorca lived in New York City in 1929-30, writing the poems published posthumously in *Poet in New York and Other Poems* (1940; trans. 1940). In 1931, after returning to Spain, he organized a popular traveling theater for the Spanish government. His tragedy of rural life *Blood Wedding* (1933; trans. 1939), a true story of jealousy and death among the peasants of Andalusia written in vivid symbolic language, marked a new departure in the modern poetic theater. It was followed by the great tragedies *Yerma* (1935; trans. 1941) and *La casa de Bernarda Alba* (The House of Bernard Alba, 1936); and the tragic comedy *Doña Rosita la soltera* (Doña Rosita the Spinster, 1935). García Lorca was assassinated on Aug. 19-20, 1936, by Franco's Nationalists during the Spanish civil war.

García Lorca's other works include the comedy *The Shoemaker's Prodigious Wife* (1930; trans. 1941) and *Lament for the Death of a Bullfighter and Other Poems* (1935; trans. 1937).

Concerned principally with the themes of fate and death in the lives of country people and Gypsies, García Lorca's works portray elemental human passions and emphasize the interpenetration of dreams and reality in their lives. In addition the plays incorporate elements from traditional Spanish and Spanish Gypsy popular songs as well as from surrealist poetry. His spontaneous and refined language is marked by startling images and highly original metaphors.   E.F.

GARCÍA MÁRQUEZ, Gabriel (1928-), Colombian short-story writer and novelist, born in Aracataca, and initially trained in journalism. From 1959 to 1961 he worked for a Cuban news agency. Living in political exile, mainly in Mexico from the 1960s on, he began to turn to literature. His best known novels are *One Hundred Years of Solitude* (1967; trans. 1970), the epic story of a Colombian family, which shows the stylistic influence of the American novelist William Faulkner; and *The Autumn of the Patriarch* (1975; trans. 1976), about political power and corruption. *Chronicle of a Death Foretold* (1981; trans. 1983) is the story of murder in a Latin American town. His *Collected Stories* was published in English translation in 1984. García Márquez is admired for his weaving of realism with fantasy in narratives that take place in a fictional Colombian village. He was awarded the Nobel Prize for literature in 1982.

GARCÍA MORENO, Gabriel (1821–75), Ecuadorian statesman, born in Guayaquil, and educated in law at the University of Quito; he became rector of the university in 1857. In 1859 he led the rebellion that overthrew the government of President Francisco Robles (1811–93); he was a member of the provisional government until 1861, when he became president for a 4-year term. From then until his death García Moreno held the real power, although he was not nominally the president from 1865 to 1869. During his regime he established a program of road building and of educational reform. In 1862 he made the Catholic church the dominant force in Ecuador. In 1869 he ousted the nominal president and formally resumed the office again. At the beginning of his third term, he was assassinated.

GARCILASO DE LA VEGA (1539?–1616), Spanish historian and soldier, born in Cuzco, Peru, the son of Sebastián de la Vega y Vargas (1500–59), a conqueror of Peru; his mother was an Inca princess, niece of Huayana Capac, and he called himself "El Inca." He went to Spain in 1560 and became a captain in the army. He later settled in Córdoba. He is best known for his two-part history of the Incas of Peru and the Spanish conquest of Peru, *Royal Commentaries of Peru* (1609 and 1617; trans. 1869–71). He also wrote a romanticized account of the expedition of the Spanish explorer Hernando de Soto, *Florida of the Inca* (1605; trans. 1951).

GARDA, LAKE (anc. *Lacus Benacus*), lake, N Italy, in the provinces of Verona, Brescia, and Trento. Italy's largest lake, it is 51 km (32 mi) long and from 5 to 16 km (3 to 10 mi) wide and has a total area of 370 sq km (143 sq mi). The Sarca R. is its chief affluent, and the lake is drained by the Mincio R., which discharges into the Po R. Parts of the lake are exposed to sudden storms, but its W and S shores are sheltered and have a mild climate. The latter regions are noted for the cultivation of lemons, mulberries, olives, and figs. The lake abounds in fish. Many villas are situated on its shores. On the peninsula of Sirmione (anc. Sirmio), at the S end of the lake, are the ruins of a Roman villa and a castle of the Scaligers, an Italian family of the 16th century.

GARDEN, Mary (1874–1967), American operatic soprano, noted for her dramatic talent, born in Aberdeen, Scotland, and reared in the U.S. She made her debut at the Opéra-Comique in Paris in 1900 at the premiere of *Louise,* by the French composer Gustave Charpentier, when the singer of the title role became ill. In 1902 she created the role of Mélisande in *Pelléas et Mélisande,* by the French composer Claude Debussy. From 1910 to 1931 she sang with the Chicago Grand Opera Company, serving briefly (1921–22) as its director.

GARDENA, city, Los Angeles Co., SW California, in the Gardena Valley, near Los Angeles; inc. 1930. Motor-vehicle parts, aluminum products, and electronic equipment are manufactured here. The community, settled in the mid-19th century, was named by an early resident who considered the region a beautiful garden spot. Pop. (1980) 45,165; (1990) 49,847.

GARDEN CITY, city, Wayne Co., SE Michigan, a residential suburb of Detroit; inc. as a city 1933. The area was settled in 1832, but the community did not grow substantially until the early 1920s. It was then developed so that most houses had space for a garden, hence its name. Pop. (1980) 35,640; (1990) 31,846.

GARDEN OF EDEN. *See* EDEN.

GARDEN GROVE, city, Orange Co., SW California, near the Santa Ana R., a suburb of Long Beach; settled 1870, inc. as a city 1956. Although chiefly residential, it has some light industry. In a former fruit- and vegetable-growing area, the city still hosts an annual strawberry festival. Its name, suggested by an early resident, was first given (1874) when a school district was formed here. Pop. (1980) 123,351; (1990) 143,050.

GARDENIA, genus of shrubs and small trees of the family Rubiaceae (*see* MADDER), named for Alexander Garden (1730–91), an American physician and naturalist. The genus contains about 200 species native to tropical and subtropical countries. Gardenias are popular greenhouse plants because of their beautiful and fragrant flowers. A few species are hardy enough to survive outdoors in warm temperate summers. Propagation is by cuttings.

Flowers of gardenias are usually white and funnel shaped or salverform (tubular with a

Cape jasmine, Gardenia jasminoides   W. Atlee Burpee Co.

spreading limb), with the tube much longer than the calyx. The fruit is a large berry, which in several species contains α-crocetin, a crystalline compound used for yellow silk dyes.

The Cape jasmine, *G. jasminoides,* is one of the most popular species of gardenia in the U.S. Native to China, it is an evergreen shrub up to 1.5 m (5 ft) high, with heavily scented waxy, white flowers. Two common greenhouse plants of the U.S., *G. thunbergia* and *G. rothmannia,* are shrubs or small trees; in *G. thunbergia,* the flowers are white, with long tubes; *G. rothmannia* bears pale yellow flowers with purple markings and has short tubes. Their hardwood is used in South America for agricultural implements. A dwarf species from Japan, *G. radicans floreplana,* is about 46 cm (about 18 in) high, has double flowers, and is cultivated as a houseplant.

For further information on this topic, see the Bibliography in volume 28, sections 453, 592–93.

GARDENING, cultivation of plants in enclosed areas for ornamental purposes. It is contrasted with agriculture and horticulture (qq.v.), both of which are concerned with plants grown on a large scale for economic or other gain to the cultivator. Scientific research in plants is normally a matter for the botanist. *See* BOTANICAL GARDEN; BOTANY; PLANT BREEDING.

Gardening is often a matter of recreation for the home gardener, who usually follows the patterns and methods established by commercial and professional gardeners but adapted to smaller operations. The gardener also may purchase some plants, seeds, and tools from a commercial nursery, which provides various services to householders and small-scale gardeners. The history of gardening and the traditional forms of present-day gardens are discussed in LANDSCAPE ARCHITECTURE.

The type of garden planted by the average

A formal bed of hydrangeas and tulips at Hampton Court, the huge 16th-century palace near London. The palace gardens cover 18 ha (44 acres) and include two orangeries and a maze.
Susan McCartney–Photo Researchers, Inc.

homeowner generally depends on a number of cultivation variables, as well as on individual tastes and preferences. Among such variables are soil type and fertility, wind and sun exposure, air pollution (if in or near large urban centers), position of existing trees and shrubs, visual effect desired, amount of land available, size and design of buildings, need for walks and pathways, desire for privacy, and ease of maintenance. Local regional climate determines the plants available and useful to the home gardener (*see* PLANT DISTRIBUTION). The U.S. Department of Agriculture has divided the continental U.S., the subject of this article, into zones that are based on the average minimum temperature for that zone in any given year. *See* SOIL; SOIL MANAGEMENT; UNITED STATES OF AMERICA: *The Land.*

Trees and Shrubs. Trees and shrubs, which are relatively permanent materials in the garden design, should be planted before more temporary plantings. Evergreens (such as pine, fir, spruce, juniper, and hemlock), rhododendrons, and some forms of holly are suitable as background material for a garden that will be green year-round. Many plants that are deciduous in the northern U.S. remain green throughout the year in warmer areas (*see* DECIDUOUS PLANTS). Another desirable feature in trees is spectacular autumn foliage; some excellent species are dogwood, mountain ash, the maples, redbud, poplar, white ash, and American beech. Copper beeches are popular for their naturally dark red leaves. Other trees such as dogwood, magnolia, mimosa, and tulip tree offer lovely spring blossoms. Good trees for milder areas include willow oak, tulip tree, and loblolly pine. In the Deep South, camphor trees, jacaranda, citrus, and eucalyptus are good choices. A large majority of tropical and subtropical species will not survive drastic temperature fluctuations, and thus they are not suitable for cold-weather environments, except when kept in a greenhouse (q.v.) during the winter, or sometimes in the home. Crab apple, honey locust, hawthorn, ginkgo, and plane trees adapt well to areas of high air pollution. Seaside plants must be able to withstand considerable wind and salt spray. Deciduous trees are generally best planted in the fall after they have shed their leaves. *See also* EVERGREEN; TREE.

Shrub species for gardens include euonymus, bayberry, honeysuckle, forsythia, ilex, rhododendron, azalea, cotoneaster, mountain andromeda, and lilac. In the Deep South, Natal plum, gardenia, santolina, floribunda rose, and myrtle are suitable and will be evergreen. Many other shrubs, including privet, holly, barberry, aborvitae, and nandina, are trimmed and clipped into hedges or are used as border and foundation plantings. A foundation planting is made up of plants, often evergreen, set in the ground close to a building and useful in hiding its unattractive features. An important plant in any garden is the rose (q.v.).

Lawns. Different lawn grasses have been developed for best results according to climate (*see* GRASSES). Preferred in cooler areas are the Kentucky bluegrasses, fine fescues, and bent grasses, the last being particularly well suited for formal gardens. In the South, Saint Augustine grass or buffalo grass (good for shady areas), centipede grass, and Bermuda grass are best. Ground covers can substitute for lawns. They require little maintenance, control soil erosion, and are excellent underplantings for trees and shrubs. Low-growing plants such as ivy (q.v.), pachysandra, periwinkle, dwarf juniper, and lily of the valley are typical.

Beds and Borders. Long, narrow strips in the garden planted with a large variety of plants are referred to as borders. They may include hardy perennials, annuals, and shrubs. Keynotes in a border are harmony of color and a succession of blooms throughout the growing season. Plants grouped together for a mass effect form a flower or shrub bed. Low-growing species are used to edge a flower bed, driveway, path, or lawn. Shrubs and perennials form the backbone of a border or bed, annuals being used to fill the spaces in between and to contribute a continuous colorful display of flowers. Perennials are those plants that will live on indefinitely, although some may die down to the ground in cold weather. Types often found in the garden include impatiens, alyssum, delphinium, day lily, feverfew, candytuft, moss pink, and violet. Biennials are plants that require two years to complete their life cycle. They bloom in the second year after the seeds are sown in the garden. They are useful in the flower garden because they often bloom early in summer, when few perennials are in flower. Favorite biennials include Canterbury bells, some forget-me-not varieties, and hollyhock. Many perennials, including such plants as foxglove, and sweet William, are treated as biennials.

Annuals, which complete their life cycle in one season, are used most often as filler plants to harmonize with other plantings. They offer dramatic colors not often found in perennials and are usually good as cut flowers. Most require bright sun. In cooler climates, some tender perennials are grown as annuals. Zinnia, ageratum, petunia, dianthus, phlox, and baby's breath are all grown as annuals.

Rock garden in the 100-ha (250-acre) New York Botanical Garden. The institution has conservatories, laboratories, an extensive library, and a herbarium with 4 million specimens.

Narcissus, crocus, hyacinth, lily, tulip, gladiolus, and dahlia are all treated as bulb plants (*see* BULB). They have a longer dormancy period than most plant species, flowering very briefly. Many bulbs need annual chilling and will not grow in gardens in milder climates that do not experience frost. According to species, bulb plants flower from early spring through autumn. In the garden, they are generally planted in beds or borders or among low ground covers. Narcissus may be planted in drifts on uncultivated ground.

Special Gardens. Gardens may be of many different types of designs, as a rock garden, a herb garden, a wild-flower garden, or a water garden. They may also manifest different styles or gardening techniques, as in a bonsai garden or an espalier garden.

A rock garden duplicates the natural environmental conditions in which rock and mountain plants thrive. It is somewhat easier to cultivate than an ordinary garden because the contained plants are hardier and more resistant to drought and cold and require far less fertilizer than plants that succeed in other types of gardens. Slightly sloping ground that is well drained naturally or artificially is the best location. Rock gardens are often terraced to prevent the washing away of topsoil by rain. The most suitable plants for rock gardens are flowering, hardy perennials. Among the cultivated alpine plants that meet these requirements are the aconite (monkshood), anemone, rockfoil or saxifrage, cinquefoil, and sedum (creeping stonecrop). In addition, rock gardens are often planted with dwarf trees and shrubs.

Herb gardens have, by common practice, come to include a large number of shrubs as well. Most of the plants cultivated are perennial, and all are used primarily today in culinary recipes, sachets, and perfumes. Some of the more familiar herbs are parsley, thyme, lavender, basil, salvia, marjoram, dill, mint, sage, and chive. Some are used cut fresh from the garden; others are best dried and stored.

Wild-flower gardens generally require a rich, acid soil. They may include native marsh or bog plants as well as typical forest-floor wild flowers. A setting as close as possible to the natural environment of the species is important in the garden design. Native orchids, cranberry, gentians, bloodroot, partridgeberry, ferns, and trillium are commonly used wild flowers. Water gardens, styled around natural or artificial ponds, are typically planted with hardy water lilies and marsh marigold, among others.

The Japanese style in gardening emphasizes year-round continuity by using a maximum of evergreen plants. Color is restricted to spring-flowering azaleas and the fall berries of other shrubs. Stone lanterns—stones selected for texture, shape, and size—and walking paths are sometimes included. Streams and waterfalls may be natural or artificial, with raked sand or rocky beds to create the illusion of a landscape in miniature. A gardening technique typical of the Japanese is the bonsai, a method originally developed in China, involving the deliberate, artificial dwarfing of plants by special methods of cultivation. The tree or shrub is planted in a shallow container or an urn and is starved of plant food. The space for root growth is limited, and the roots are pruned. As the plant grows, the shoots also are pruned, and the branches are twisted or bent with wire so that the full-grown bonsai, often less than 61 cm (less than 24 in) tall, will have the appearance of an aged, gnarled tree or shrub. Favorite plants for bonsai gardens include pine and fir trees and such hardwood flowering shrubs as azaleas and Japanese quinces, as well as shrubs known for their foliage, including hollies and cut-leaf maples.

Another gardening technique, known as espalier, was originally developed in France. Espalier gardening involves the planting of a tree or woody shrub close to a wall or trellis—thus the popular name wall trees. The plant is trained flat by tying its branches to the support. The result is a two-dimensional effect. Pruning is important in determining the shape of the flattened plant against the trellis. The design or pattern of growth may be candelabra shaped, U shaped, T shaped, or palmlike. Espalier gardening has special decorative effect where space is limited.

See also entries on individual plants mentioned.

For further information on this topic, see the Bibliography in volume 28, sections 451–52, 592–93, 675.

GARDEN REACH, municipality, E India, in West Bengal State, on the Hooghly R., adjacent to Calcutta. The community, named for a section of the river, was once chiefly residential but now has industries, including tanning and jute and cotton ginning and milling. An extensive dry-dock basin and a power station are situated here. During the recapture of Calcutta by the British in 1756–57, Robert Clive seized the fort in the W end of Garden Reach. Pop. (1981) 191,107.

GARDINER, Stephen (1488?–1555), English cleric and statesman, who fought to preserve the basic tenets of the Roman Catholic faith within the Anglican church.

Born in Bury Saint Edmunds, Gardiner was educated at the University of Cambridge, from which he received the degree of doctor of civil law in 1520 and that of doctor of canon law the next year. He was subsequently named archdeacon of Taunton. In 1525 Gardiner was employed as secretary to Cardinal Thomas Wolsey, lord chancellor to King Henry VIII. From 1528 to 1533 Gardiner was engaged in negotiations with Pope Clement VII to obtain for King Henry a divorce from Catherine of Aragón. For his efforts in 1531 he received the bishopric of Winchester.

In 1533 Gardiner was counsel for Henry VIII in the court that declared the king's marriage dissolved. Two years later he joined with the other bishops in approving the act of 1534 that made Henry supreme head of the English church, and he wrote a treatise of vindication entitled *De Vera Obedientia* (On True Obedience, 1535). He was a reformer only insofar as repudiating the pope was concerned, for in matters of doctrine and practice he advocated retention of the Roman Catholic faith. The promulgation in 1539 of the Six Articles embodying Catholic principles was accomplished largely through his effort. He opposed the extreme Protestant party and was imprisoned shortly after the accession of Henry's son, King Edward VI. Released for a brief period, Gardiner was again arrested in 1548 and placed in the Tower of London. In 1551 he was deprived of his bishopric. On the accession of Queen Mary I he was released and his see restored to him.

Appointed lord chancellor, Gardiner retained that post until his death. He participated in the persecution of Protestants but was unsuccessful in his attempts to save the lives of Thomas Cranmer, archbishop of Canterbury, and of John Dudley, duke of Northumberland. Gardiner also served (1540–47, 1553–55) as chancellor of the University of Cambridge.

GARDINERS ISLAND, also Gardiner's Island, island of SE New York, forming a part of the town of East Hampton, in Gardiners Bay, near the E end of Long Island. The island has an area of 1335 ha (3300 acres). It was purchased from the Indians in 1639 by Lion Gardiner (1599–1663), an English colonist, who, in settling there, is said to have established the first English settlement in what is now the state of New York. The island has remained in possession of the Gardiner family, but its status was under discussion in the early 1980s. Legend holds that the pirate William Kidd buried some of his treasure on the island in 1699.

GARDNER, Erle Stanley (1889–1970), American detective novelist, born in Malden, Mass. His numerous novels are notable for their fast action and revelations of legal ingenuity, the latter due in part to Gardner's work as an attorney. The style is vigorous and realistic. The character of lawyer-detective Perry Mason appeared in more than 80 novels, with titles such as *The Case of the Velvet Claws* (1933) and *The Case of the Duplicate Daughter* (1960).

GARFIELD, industrial city, Bergen Co., NE New Jersey, at the confluence of the Passaic and Saddle rivers; settled 1679 by the Dutch, inc. as a city 1917. Major products include textiles, rubber goods, chemicals, paper products, and machinery. Once known as Cadmus' Melon Patch and later as East Passaic, the community was renamed in 1881 for President James A. Garfield. Pop. (1980) 26,803; (1990) 26,727.

GARFIELD, James Abram (1831–81), 20th president of the U.S. (1881), who during his brief term asserted presidential prerogatives against the demands of congressional leaders.

Garfield was born in a log cabin in Cuyahoga Co., Ohio, on Nov. 19, 1831. Raised in poverty by his widowed mother, and doing every kind of rough frontier work, he managed to secure a college education and to develop oratorical skills that quickly led him from lay preaching for the Disciples of Christ into politics. He was married in 1858 to Lucretia Rudolph (1832–1918) and was elected to the Ohio legislature the year after. When the American Civil War came, he raised a regiment and soon displayed considerable talent as an administrator and military leader.

Military and Congressional Career. In January 1862, when Union victories were rare, Garfield's troops defeated a Confederate army at Middle Creek, making Garfield a hero and resulting in his promotion to brigadier general of volunteers. Military glory and his antislavery record won him a seat in Congress in 1863. Garfield went to

James Abram Garfield   Clarence Hornung

196

Washington with brilliant prospects marred only by his lack of wealth and his tendency, already manifest, to participate in rather dubious business undertakings that traded on his military fame and political position.

Garfield was a talented parliamentarian, a hard worker, and a skilled negotiator in Congress. His work on the House Appropriations Committee made a real contribution to improving the management of the U.S. government. When James G. Blaine advanced to the Senate in 1876, Garfield succeeded him as leader of the House Republicans; as such he was a brilliant debater and a consistent but sensible partisan. In 1880, when Republican factions deadlocked at the national convention, he was an obvious compromise choice for the party's presidential nomination.

Garfield as President. Factional battling within the Republican party marked the 1880 campaign, which was further marred by the airing of two financial scandals that loosely implicated Garfield—one involving the paving of Washington, D.C., streets and the other the building of the transcontinental railroads. Then, as throughout his career, Garfield deflected his accusers, but he could never fully deter them. With the Republican factions finally cooperating and a New Yorker, Chester Arthur, as his vice-presidential candidate, Garfield became president with a scant margin of 10,000 votes.

Garfield's brief administration was consumed largely by a war with Sen. Roscoe Conkling of New York over patronage. Garfield had appointed James Blaine, Conkling's greatest enemy, as secretary of state and then named a Blaine supporter to the politically critical position of collector of the Port of New York. Conkling, upholding the tradition of "senatorial courtesy," questioned the president's right to make New York appointments over the objection of the state's senator. After a bitter battle in which it became clear that the Senate would confirm Garfield's nominee, Conkling and Thomas Platt (1833–1910)—New York's junior senator—resigned their seats, seeking vindication through reelection by the New York legislature. Conkling's plan backfired: The legislature sent two new senators to Washington, ending Conkling's career and giving Garfield a triumph.

On July 2, 1881, Charles Jules Guiteau (c. 1840–82), a disappointed office seeker, shot Garfield; he lingered on until September 19, when he finally succumbed. Garfield's death at the hands of a frustrated office seeker created a powerful impetus for civil reform. His administration, which initiated prosecutions for mail-contract frauds in the previous administration, in addition to fighting the battles with Conkling, had importance principally in asserting the power of the president against Congress and in attacking corruption in government.   R.D.Ma.

For further information on this person, see the section Biographies in the Bibliography in volume 28.

GARFIELD HEIGHTS, city, Cuyahoga Co., NE Ohio, near Cleveland; settled 1786, inc. 1932. It is chiefly residential, with some industry; manufactures include metal products and chemicals. The city probably is named for President James A. Garfield. Pop. (1980) 34,938; (1990) 31,739.

GARIBALDI, Giuseppe (1807–82), Italian nationalist revolutionary and leader in the struggle for Italian unification and independence.

Garibaldi was born on July 4, 1807, in Nice, France, and was largely self-educated. He spent his youth as a sailor on Mediterranean merchant ships. In 1833 he joined Young Italy, the movement organized by the Italian revolutionary Giuseppe Mazzini to achieve the freedom of the Italian people and their unification into a self-governing republic. Garibaldi was condemned to death in 1834, but he escaped to South America, where he lived for 12 years. There he displayed unusual qualities of military leadership while participating in the revolt of the state of Rio Grande do Sul against Brazil, as well as later in a civil war in Uruguay.

Return to Italy. When the revolutionary tide that swept over Europe in 1848 engulfed Italy, Garibaldi returned and again took part in the movement for Italian freedom and unification, thereafter known as the Risorgimento (literally, "revival"). He organized a corps of about 3000 volunteers, which, in the service of the Piedmontese ruler Charles Albert (1798–1849), king of Sardinia, unsuccessfully fought the Austrians in Lombardy. In 1849 he led his volunteers to Rome to support the Roman Republic established by Mazzini and others. Garibaldi successfully defended the city against attacks by superior French forces for 30 days but was finally compelled to make terms with the French. Although he was allowed to depart from Rome at the head of about 5000 of his followers, the line of retreat lay through territory controlled by the Austrians; the larger part of his force was killed, captured, or dispersed, and Garibaldi had to flee Italy to save his life.

Garibaldi went to the U.S. in 1848, settled in Staten Island, N.Y., working as a candlemaker, and became a citizen. In 1854 he returned to Italy and bought a modest home on the island of Caprera northeast of Sardinia. At that time Garibaldi had separated politically from Mazzini,

Giuseppe Garibaldi   Italian State Tourist Office

an undeviating republican; Garibaldi believed that the road to freedom and unity for Italy lay in alliance with the liberal ruler Victor Emmanuel II, king of Sardinia, and his premier, Conte Camillo Benso di Cavour. Thousands of other Italian patriots and revolutionaries were influenced by Garibaldi's position, a fact that did much to enhance the fortunes of the Sardinian monarch and influence the course of Italian history.

Struggle for Unification. Garibaldi was deeply involved in the complicated military and political struggles that took place in the following years. In 1859 he led a successful expedition against the Austrian forces in the Alps; in 1860 he led a force of 1000 men from Genoa to Sicily, then ruled by the king of Naples. Distinctively clad in bright red shirts, Garibaldi's men became known as the Red Shirts and as The Thousand. Between May and August 1860, Garibaldi conquered Sicily and set up a provisional insular government. He then crossed to the Italian mainland; took Naples; defeated the Neapolitans in a decisive engagement on the banks of the Volturno River on Oct. 26, 1860; and besieged the fortress of Gaeta, which fell in February 1861.

Later that year, the kingdom of Italy was established with Victor Emmanuel as king; Rome, a papal possession garrisoned by French troops, was not included in the new kingdom, nor were areas in the north of the peninsula held by the

Austrians. Garibaldi, declining all honors and positions in the new kingdom, retired to his island home on Caprera. In the following year, however, he organized the Society for the Emancipation of Italy and visited Sicily, where he raised a force of volunteers with the object of capturing Rome and including it in a unified Italian state. He was opposed by Victor Emmanuel, who defeated him at the Battle of Aspromonte, Aug. 29, 1862. Garibaldi was wounded and captured in that battle but was soon pardoned and released.

In 1866, despite the opposition of the Italian government, Garibaldi again raised a volunteer force with the aim of annexing the Papal States to the kingdom of Italy. After a number of initial engagements, he was defeated by combined papal and French forces at the Battle of Mentana on Nov. 3, 1867. He was taken prisoner but was held only a short time.

For about two years thereafter Garibaldi lived the life of a farmer on Caprera. In 1870 he offered his services to the French government and fought with his two sons in the Franco-Prussian War. Rome was annexed to Italy in October 1870, and Garibaldi was elected a member of the Italian parliament in 1874. In his last years he sympathized with the developing socialist movement in Italy and other countries. Garibaldi died on Caprera on June 2, 1882. His autobiography was published in 1887.

For further information on this person, see the section Biographies in the Bibliography in volume 28.

GARLAND, city, Dallas, Collin, and Rockwall counties, NE Texas, a residential and industrial suburb of Dallas; settled 1850s, inc. 1891. Products include defense-related electronics, processed food, machine parts, chemicals, and paint; steel and other metals are fabricated here. Amber University (1971) is located in Garland. The community originated in 1887 when the settlements of Embree and Duck Creek were amalgamated and named for U.S. Attorney General Augustus H. Garland (1832–99). Pop. (1980) 138,857; (1990) 180,650.

GARLAND, (Hannibal) Hamlin (1860–1940), American writer, born in West Salem, Wis. For years he worked on farms in his native state and in Iowa and South Dakota. His experiences during this period furnished the central theme for many short stories; bitter denunciations of American farm life, they were collected and published under the titles *Main-Travelled Roads* (1890) and *Other Main-Travelled Roads* (1910).

Garland's other works include *Crumbling Idols* (1894), a volume of essays on literature and art; two important studies of frontier life, *A Son of the Middle Border* (1917) and *A Daughter of the Middle Border* (1921), the latter of which won the Pulitzer Prize for biography in 1922; *Afternoon Neighbors* (1934), a book of memoirs; and *The Mystery of the Buried Crosses* (1939), concerned with psychic research.

GARLAND, Judy, professional name of FRANCES GUMM (1922–69), American motion picture actor and singer. Born in Grand Rapids, Minn., Garland

.Judy Garland is congratulated by enthusiastic members of the audience after a Carnegie Hall concert in 1961. **UPI**

made her singing debut at the age of 30 months in her father's theater. Later she and her sisters formed a vaudeville act called the Gumm Sisters, and from 1927 to 1935 the sisters toured the U.S. Her film career, which began in 1935, included appearances in such motion pictures as *The Wizard of Oz* (1939), for which she received a special award from the Academy of Motion Picture Arts and Sciences; *Ziegfeld Girl* (1941); *The Clock* (1944); *Meet Me in St. Louis* (1944); and *The Pirate* (1948). After 1950 she appeared primarily in nightclubs, concerts, and on television; her first engagement at the Palace Theater in New York City (1951–52) broke vaudeville box-office records. Her later films were *A Star Is Born* (1955), *Judgment at Nuremberg* (1961), *I Could Go on Singing* (1963), and *A Child Is Waiting* (1963).

GARLIC, common name for several strongly scented herbs belonging to the genus *Allium,* of the family Liliaceae (*see* LILY), and for the bulbs of these plants, used as a flavoring. Garlic, like the related onion (q.v.), has small, six-part, whitish flowers borne on umbels. The fruit is a capsule containing black, kidney-shaped seeds. Common garlic, *A. sativum,* is native to the Old World, cultivated since ancient times. The bulb, which has a strong characteristic odor and taste, is covered with a papery skin and may be broken into constituent bulblets, called cloves. Garlic is used as a flavoring in cooking and pickling, sometimes in the form of whole or grated cloves and sometimes in the form of a cooked extract, as in sauces and dressings. In medicine garlic is used as a digestive stimulant, diuretic, and antispasmodic. Other possible mild medicinal uses are under investigation. The British wild garlic, *A. oleraceum;* the American wild garlic, *A. candense;* and the field garlic of both Europe and the Americas, *A. vineale,* are also used for seasoning. The false garlic, *Nothoscordum bivalve,* or crow poison, is a North American species with pale yellow or pale green flowers closely related to garlic but lacking the characteristic garlic odor. It is poisonous to livestock.

GARMISCH-PARTENKIRCHEN, town, S central Germany, in Bavaria. It is an internationally famous winter sports center situated in the Bavarian Alps at the foot of the Zugspitze, Germany's highest peak. The town, formed in 1935 by the merger of Garmisch and Partenkirchen, was the site of the 1936 Olympic Winter Games. Pop. (1989 est.) 25,900.

GARNEAU, François Xavier (1809–66), Canadian historian, born in Québec, and educated at Québec Seminary. In 1830 he became a notary. He subsequently traveled in France and England. On his return to Canada in 1833 he was appointed translator for the legislative assembly of Lower Canada (now Québec Province). From 1844 until 1864 he served as secretary to the city of Québec. Garneau is considered the first national historian of French Canada. His writings include *Histoire du Canada* (History of Canada, 3 vol., 1845–48) and *Voyage en Angleterre et en France* (Travels in England and France, 1855).

GARNER, John Nance (1868–1967), 32d vice-president of the U.S. (1933–41), born near Detroit, Red River Co., Tex., and educated in law in Clarksville. He was admitted to the bar in 1890 and served (1898–1902) two terms in the Texas state legislature. He was then elected to the U.S. House of Representatives, where he served from 1903 to 1933, becoming Speaker of the House in his last term. In 1932 and 1936 he was elected to the vice-presidency on the Democratic ticket headed by Franklin D. Roosevelt. He broke with Roosevelt when the latter sought a third term, and he retired from politics in 1941.

For further information on this person, see the section Biographies in the Bibliography in volume 28.

GARNET, general name of a group of related minerals, often used as gemstones and abrasives. Garnets crystallize in the isometric system, usually as rhombic dodecahedrons, tetragonal trisoctahedrons, or combinations of the two (*see* CRYSTAL). The different varieties of garnet exhibit almost all colors except blue. Brown, red, green, yellow, black, and colorless stones are common. Darker stones are usually opaque, and light ones may be transparent or translucent. The hardness (q.v.) of garnet varies from 6 to 7.5, and the specific gravities of specimens may be anywhere between 3.6 and 4.3. Garnets have a vitreous or resinous luster, and some varieties exhibit considerable brilliance. Chemically, garnets are compound silicates, and the varieties are usually differentiated by their chemical composition. The composition of individual gems varies widely, and the formulas given below are only approximate.

Grossularite, $Ca_3Al_2(SiO_4)_3$, is a light-colored or colorless garnet, usually found in shades of green, red, yellow, or brown. Yellow gems of this variety are often called hyacinths, and yellow and cinnamon-brown specimens are marketed under the names of hessonite, essonite, or cinnamon stone.

Pyrope, $Mg_3Al_2(SiO_4)_3$, is the variety of garnet most often used for gem purposes and is prized for its ruby red color. Pure pyrope has no color, but all specimens contain impurities that produce a number of shades from red to black.

Spessartite, $Mn_3Al_2(SiO_4)_3$, is not a popular

The grand staircase of the Paris Opéra (1861–75), masterpiece of the French architect Charles Garnier.

gemstone because of its color, which is usually brownish, although it occasionally has a reddish cast. It is found in the Alps, in Sri Lanka, and in Nevada and Virginia.

Almandite, $Fe_3Al_2(SiO_4)_3$, was formerly much used in jewelry and is known by the popular name of carbuncle. It occurs in a range of hues from deep red to black, but usually only stones that are both red and transparent are regarded as gems. Some specimens have a violet cast, and some exhibit asterism, showing a four-rayed star in reflected light. Almandite is a widely distributed mineral, found in India, Australia, South America, and North America.

Uvarovite, $Ca_3Cr_2(SiO_4)_3$, is an emerald green variety of garnet found largely in tiny crystals too small for gem use. Comparatively rare, it occurs chiefly in the northern Ural Mountains in Russia.

Andradite, $Ca_3Fe_2(SiO_4)_3$, is a type of garnet that varies widely in composition and color. An opaque, black variety, called melanite, is sometimes used for jewelry by people who are in mourning. A transparent yellow variety that re-

sembles topaz, and is sometimes misleadingly called topazolite, is found in Italy.

For further information on this topic, see the Bibliography in volume 28, sections 433, 690.

GARNIER, (Jean Louis) Charles (1825–98), French Beaux-Arts architect, best known for his Paris Opera House. His eclectic Second Empire style drew on Renaissance, baroque, and neoclassical prototypes. The Paris Opéra (1861–75), arguably one of the masterpieces of 19th-century architecture, is an elaborate combination of styles but nonetheless has an underlying harmony. In both grandeur and ornateness—it was decorated inside and out with sculpture, fresco, and colored marble—it overshadows his later private residences and public buildings. In 1990, after the Paris Opera company moved to the newly built Opéra de la Bastille, the Garnier Opera House continued to be used as the home of the Paris Opera Ballet.

GARNIERITE, amorphous, brittle mineral composed of hydrous nickel and magnesium silicate, with the formula $(Ni,Mg) SiO_3 \cdot n H_2O$; it ranges in color from pale green to nearly white, with an earthy luster. It has a hardness (q.v.) of only 1 to 3 and a sp.gr. ranging from 2.3 to 2.8, and it occurs as earthy masses. Garnierite is one of the most important ores of nickel (q.v.) and is extensively mined in New Caledonia and in Oregon and North Carolina in the U.S. Genthite, an apple-green variety of garnierite, is found in the states of Oregon, Georgia, and Pennsylvania; in Spain; and in Ontario Province, Canada.

GARNISHMENT, in law, statutory proceeding by which chattels, rights, or credits that belong to the defendant in an action, but which are in the possession of a third person, are seized and applied to the claim of the plaintiff. Garnishment is, in effect, a warning or notice given to the third person not to pay money or turn over property to the defendant. It has been called an equitable attachment of the claims or assets of a defendant when those claims or assets are in the hands of a third person. It is not a common-law process and is regulated by statute in the states of the U.S. An example of garnishment is the order of a court to an employer of a judgment debtor to pay over to a creditor, at fixed intervals, a fixed amount of the wages of an employee in satisfaction of the claim of the creditor.

GARONNE (Lat. *Garumna*), principal river of SW France, rising in Spain in the Maladeta range of the Pyrenees Mts. The total length of the Garonne is about 645 km (about 400 mi), and it drains an area of about 85,470 sq km (about 33,000 sq mi). About 48 km (about 30 mi) from the source the river enters France in Haute-Garonne Department and flows generally NE to Toulouse, where it receives the waters of several streams, including the Neste, Salat, and Ariège. Beyond Toulouse the river becomes navigable, turns to the NW, and receives the waters of its principal tributaries, the Tarn and Lot rivers. At the Bec d'Ambès, near Bordeaux, the Garonne joins the Dordogne R. to form the Gironde estuary. Oceangoing ships navigate the river as far as the port of Bordeaux. A lateral canal parallel to the Garonne was built (1838–56) to provide a direct waterway between Bordeaux and the Canal du Midi at Toulouse. More than 50 locks control the flow of the canal, which has a fall of about 128 m (about 420 ft). The peninsula between the Garonne and Dordogne is a famous wine-producing region. The Garonne frequently overflows its banks, causing much damage; destructive flooding occurred in 1770, 1856, and 1930.

GARRETT, João Baptista da Silva Leitão, Visconde de Almeida. *See* ALMEIDA GARRETT, JOÃO BAPTISTA DA SILVA LEITÃO, VISCONDE DE.

GARRICK, David (1717–79), British actor, theatrical manager, and playwright, regarded as one of the greatest actors of the British theater.

Garrick was born on Feb. 19, 1717, in Hereford, a descendant of a French Huguenot family that had settled in England. He was educated at the Lichfield Grammar School and at a school run by the British lexicographer Samuel Johnson near Lichfield. Garrick and his master became friends, and when Johnson closed the school in 1737 and went to London to seek his fortune, Garrick accompanied him. Subsequently Garrick studied law; later he became a wine merchant; eventually he turned from business to the stage. He made his debut as a professional actor at Ipswich in 1741 in *Oroonoko or the Royal Slave,* a play by the British dramatist Thomas Southerne (1660–1746). His success led to his appearance in London the same year in the title role of Shakespeare's *Richard III,* in which he scored a sensational triumph. During the following six months Garrick appeared in 18 different roles and rapidly established himself as one of the best actors of the time. Between 1742 and 1747 he acted at the three principal British theaters, the Drury Lane Theatre and Covent Garden Theatre in London, and the Smock Alley Theatre in Dublin. He usually played opposite the celebrated British actor Margaret Woffington (c. 1718–60). In 1747 he became co-manager and owner of the Drury Lane.

As a theatrical manager Garrick worked to make the plays of Shakespeare popular in 18th-century England, producing 24 of them. He was also instrumental in reforming a number of stage traditions, particularly in ending the practice of permitting privileged persons to sit on the stage during a performance. In 1749 he married the Viennese dancer Eva Maria Veigel (1724–1822). By 1766 Garrick rarely appeared on the stage, but he retained the managership of the Drury Lane. In 1769 he produced the plays that were part of a celebration held at Stratford-on-Avon to commemorate the 200th anniversary of Shakespeare's birth (although 1564 is commonly accepted as the year of Shakespeare's birth). In addition, Garrick was chiefly responsible for the celebration itself, which marked the beginning of a revival of popular interest in Shakespearean drama. In 1776 he sold his interest in the Drury Lane and gave a series of farewell performances in his favorite roles; his last stage appearance was in June of that year, in *The Wonder!* by the British playwright Susannah Centlivre (1667?–1723).

Garrick was equally skilled in tragedy, comedy, and farce. His acting was noted for its naturalness, vivacity, and power of characterization. His

The masthead of the Liberator, *official newspaper of the abolitionist movement, founded in 1831 by William Lloyd Garrison and edited by him for 34 years.*
Bettmann Archive

wide repertory included 17 Shakespearean roles, among them Hamlet, King Lear, Macbeth, and Benedick in *Much Ado About Nothing;* and roles in plays by a wide variety of other dramatists, including *Zaire,* by the French author Voltaire, *Every Man in His Humour* by the English dramatist Ben Jonson, and *The Provoked Wife* by the English dramatist Sir John Vanbrugh. Among plays written by Garrick himself are *The Lying Valet* (1740) and *Miss in Her Teens* (1747). In 1831 the Garrick Club, named in his honor, was founded in London; its members today include many leading actors and writers.

GARRISON, William Lloyd (1805–79), American abolitionist, who founded the influential antislavery newspaper *Liberator.*

Garrison was born Dec. 10, 1805, in Newburyport, Mass. Indentured at the age of 14 to the owner of the *Newburyport Herald,* he became an expert printer. The struggles of oppressed peoples for freedom engaged his sympathies in his youth. In articles written anonymously or under the pseudonym Aristides, in the *Herald* and other newspapers, he attempted to arouse Northerners from their apathy on the question of slavery in the U.S.

In 1829 Garrison entered into partnership with the American antislavery agitator Benjamin Lundy (1789–1839) to publish a monthly periodical, *The Genius of Universal Emancipation,* in Baltimore, Md. Lundy believed in gradual emancipation, and Garrison at first shared his views; but he soon became convinced that immediate and complete emancipation was necessary. Because Baltimore was then a center of the domestic slave trade in the U.S., Garrison's eloquent denunciations of the trade aroused great animosity. A slave trader sued him for libel; he was fined, and, lacking funds to pay the fine, was jailed. After his release from prison Garrison dissolved his partnership with Lundy and returned to New England. In partnership with another American abolitionist, Isaac Knapp (1804–43), Garrison launched the *Liberator* in Boston in 1831; the newspaper became one of the most influential journals in the U.S.

Garrison was also a pacifist and involved in other reform movements. He was deeply convinced that slavery had to be abolished by moral force. He appealed through the *Liberator* and through his speeches, especially those to the clergy, for a practical application of Christianity in demanding freedom for the slaves. His campaign aroused great opposition. The state of Georgia offered (1831) a reward of $5000 for his arrest and conviction under Georgia law, and he received hundreds of abusive letters, many of which threatened him with assassination. Undaunted, he helped to organize the New England Anti-Slavery Society in 1832; the next year, after a trip to England, where he enlisted the aid of abolitionist sympathizers, he played a leading role in establishing the national American Anti-Slavery Society, of which he was president from 1843 until 1865.

As Garrison's demands on the Northern clergy went unheeded and his attacks on them increased, opposition to his policy developed within abolitionist ranks. A further cause of dissension was Garrison's advocacy of equal rights for women generally and especially within the abolitionist movement. The cleavage was still further increased when Garrison later became convinced that the slavery clauses of the U.S. Constitution were immoral and that, consequently, it was equally immoral to take an oath in support of the Constitution. In 1840 he publicly burned a copy of the federal Constitution and denounced it as "a covenant with Death and an agreement with Hell"; he chose as his motto "No union with slaveholders" and, still true to his pacifist beliefs, advocated peaceful separation of the free states from the slave states.

With the outbreak of the American Civil War, he predicted the victory of the North and the end of slavery, and he ceased to advocate disunion. Promulgation (1863) of the Emancipation Proclamation by Abraham Lincoln removed the last difference between Garrison and Lincoln, and Lincoln paid public tribute to Garrison's long and uncompromising struggle to abolish slavery. In 1865, after the de facto abolition of slavery, Garrison discontinued the *Liberator* and advocated dissolution of the antislavery societies.

He then became prominent in campaigns by reformers to promote free trade and abolish customhouses on a world scale; to achieve suffrage for American women and justice for American Indians; and to establish Prohibition and eliminate the consumption of tobacco in the U.S. He died in New York City on May 24, 1879.   O.Ha.

GARTER SNAKE, common name for several harmless, semiaquatic snakes of the genus *Thamnophis*, subfamily Colubrinae. The garter snakes are the most common snakes (*see* SNAKE) in the U.S. where 12 species are widely distributed. They also are found in Canada and most of Mexico. Garter snakes have coarse, ridged scales and three longitudinal stripes on a dark brown or black body, one on either side and one along the back. The snakes are viviparous, averaging 20 young in one litter. They feed only on cold-blooded animals such as earthworms, frogs, toads, salamanders, and fish. When in danger, wild garter snakes secrete a foul-smelling fluid from glands at the base of the tail.

The best-known garter snakes in the U.S. are the common garter snake, *T. sirtalis*, and the ribbon snake, *T. sauritus*. Northern varieties of the common garter snake prefer a dry habitat and are found in woods or in rocky crevices. Southern varieties are found in swamps or along streams and dive into water when alarmed. The common garter snake has its lateral stripes on the second and third rows of scales, counting upward from the abdominal plates. A large specimen is 1 m (3 ft) long and 2.5 cm (1 in) in diameter. A western variety of garter snake has a brick-red tinge to its sides, and a common eastern variety is strongly spotted but stripeless.

The ribbon snake differs from other members of *Thamnophis* in several respects: Its coloration is more intense, and the lateral stripes are on the third and fourth rows of scales. The ribbon snakes are slender, less than 1.2 cm (0.5 in) in diameter. They eat small fish and are consequently always found near water. They rarely produce more than 12 young in a litter.

For further information on this topic, see the Bibliography in volume 28, sections 470–71.

GARVEY, Marcus (1887–1940), American advocate of black nationalism, born in Saint Ann's Bay, Jamaica. He left school at the age of 14 to serve as a printer's apprentice. In 1916, having lived in Costa Rica, Panama, and England, he moved to the U.S. and settled in New York City. There, he incorporated his Universal Negro Improvement Association (UNIA), founded two years earlier in Jamaica, and started a weekly newspaper, the *Negro World*. A persuasive orator and author, Garvey urged American blacks to be proud of their race and preached their return to Africa, their ancestral homeland. To this end he founded (1919) the Black Star Line to provide steamship transportation and the Negro Factories Corp. to provide economic independence. At that time he claimed 2 million members for the UNIA. He suffered a series of economic disasters, however, and in 1922 he was arrested for mail fraud. Garvey served as his own defense attorney at his trial, was convicted, and went to prison in 1925. His sentence was commuted two years later, but he was immediately deported to Jamaica, where he died in relative obscurity. Social

Garter snake, Thamnophis sirtalis

historians generally agree that in spite of Garvey's failures his "back to Africa" movement had a lasting effect on black life in America.

For further information on this person, see the section Biographies in the Bibliography in volume 28.

GARY, city, Lake Co., NW Indiana, a port of entry on Lake Michigan; inc. 1909. Once one of the largest steel-producing centers in the world, the city still contains steel refineries; however, Gary now has many retail enterprises and diversified manufacturing, including the production of motor-vehicle parts, cement, plastic products, and clothing. Gary is the seat of Indiana University Northwest (1922) and is adjacent to Indiana Dunes National Lakeshore, which includes huge dunes along Lake Michigan.

The community was established after the United States Steel Corp. bought the site in 1905. The site was chosen because of its location on a navigable waterway midway between great iron ore reserves to the N and coal deposits to the S and E. The settlement was named in honor of Elbert Gary, the chairman of the board of directors of U.S. Steel. On Oct. 7, 1919, during a widespread strike among workers in the steel industry, the city was occupied by federal troops, which remained until the strike ended on Jan. 7, 1920. In 1967 Gary became one of the first major U.S. cities to elect a black mayor when it chose Richard G. Hatcher (1933–). Large-scale urban renewal projects started in the 1970s have yet to take hold. The 1990 population, about 83% black, continues to decline, with many residents moving to the suburbs. Pop. (1980) 151,953; (1990) 116,646.

GARY, Elbert Henry (1846–1927), American corporation official, born in Wheaton, Ill., and educated at Union College of Law (now part of the University of Chicago). In 1898 he became president of the Federal Steel Co., which he helped to found. Gary was one of the organizers of the United States Steel Corp. and served as chairman of the board of directors from 1903 to 1927. Although Gary was responsible for a number of reforms in the working conditions of employees in United States Steel plants, he consistently opposed efforts to institute the closed shop and to shorten the 12-hour working day. He defeated striking employees in the general steel strike of 1919 but was forced by public opinion to institute the 8-hour day in 1923.

GARY, Romain, real name ROMAIN KACEW (1914–80), French novelist and diplomat, born in Vilna (now Vilnius), Lithuania. He achieved literary success in 1945 with *L'education européenne* (trans. 1960), an account of the lives of Polish Resistance fighters during World War II. Gary entered the French diplomatic corps following the war and until his death combined writing with government service. *The Roots of Heaven* (1956; trans. 1958) demonstrates his concern for African wildlife. *Promise at Dawn* (1960; trans. 1962) is an autobiographical tribute to his mother. Other novels by Gary include *The Talent Scout* (1960; trans. 1961), the tragicomedy *The Dance of Genghis Cohn* (1965; trans. 1968), and *Your Ticket Is No Longer Valid* (1975; trans. 1977). Gary committed suicide in December 1980.

GASCOIGNE, George (1525?–77), English poet, born probably in Cardington, Bedfordshire, and educated at the University of Cambridge. He studied law and from 1557 to 1559 represented Bedford in Parliament. His play *The Supposes,* the first English comedy in blank verse, was produced in 1566. It was based on *Gli suppositi* (The Suppositions, 1509), by the Italian poet Ludovico Ariosto. An authorized edition of his work, *The Posies of George Gascoigne* (1575), contains short poems and *Jocasta,* a blank-verse adaptation of *Phoenissae,* by the Greek dramatist Euripides. *Jocasta* is regarded by some scholars as the earliest English translation of a Greek tragedy. This volume also includes what appears to be the earliest English critical essay on prosody, "Certain Notes of Instruction Concerning the Making of Verse." Gascoigne is remembered as an innovator who adapted foreign literary forms to English. His best-known works, however, are his lyric poems, including "The Arraignment of a Lover" and "A Strange Passion of a Lover."

GASCONY (Fr. *Gascogne*), ancient duchy and part of a former province (Guyenne-et-Gascogne) in southwestern France, with its capital at Auch. Gascony was bounded on the west by the Bay of Biscay and on the south by the Pyrenees Mountains, and extended north and east to the old provinces of Guyenne and Languedoc. The duchy included the modern departments of Landes, Gers, Basses-Pyrénées, and Hautes-Pyrénées, and part of the departments of Haute-Garonne, Lot-et-Garonne, Tarn-et-Garonne, and Ariège.

The name Gascony is derived from Vasconia, the Latin name for the region after it was invaded by the Vascones (or Basques), who late in the 6th century crossed the Pyrenees from Spain to the former Roman district of Novempopulana, or Aquitania Tertia, in Gaul. In the 7th century Gascony became tributary to the Merovingian kings but retained much of its independence as a duchy; in 813 the title of duke of Gascony became hereditary. The history of the duchy during the 9th and 10th centuries is obscure. In the 11th century Gascony came under the sovereignty of the dukes of Aquitaine (q.v.), or Guyenne, but a century later the kings of England gained control, which they held until 1453, when the duchy was annexed by France.

GASES, collective term for one of the three visibly different states of ordinary matter, liquid and solid being the other two. Solids have well-defined shapes and are difficult to compress. Liquids are free-flowing and bounded by self-formed surfaces. Gases expand freely to fill their containers and are much lower in density than liquids and solids.

The Ideal Gas Law. The atomic theory of matter defines states, or phases, in terms of order. Molecules have a certain freedom of motion in space. These microscopic degrees of freedom are associated with the concept of macroscopic order. Molecules in a solid are arranged in a regular lattice, their freedom restricted to small vibrations about lattice sites. In contrast, there is no macroscopic spatial order in a gas. Molecules move at random, bounded only by the walls of their container.

Empirical laws have been developed that correlate macroscopic variables. For common gases, the macroscopic variables include pressure (P), volume (V), and temperature (T). Boyle's law states that in a gas held at a constant temperature the volume is inversely proportional to the pressure. Charles's law, or Gay-Lussac's law, states that if a gas is held at a constant pressure the volume is directly proportional to the absolute temperature (q.v.). Combining these laws gives the ideal gas law: $PV/T = R$ (per mole), also known as the equation of state of an ideal gas. The constant R on the right-hand side of the equation is a universal constant, the discovery of which is a cornerstone of modern science.

The Kinetic Theory of Gases. With the advent of the atomic theory of matter, the above-mentioned empirical laws acquired a microscopic basis. The volume of a gas reflects simply the position distribution of its constituent molecules. More exactly, the macroscopic variable V represents the available amount of space in which a molecule can move. The pressure of a gas, which can be measured with gauges placed on the container walls, registers the average change of momentum experienced by molecules as they collide with, and subsequently rebound from, the walls. The temperature of a gas is proportional to the average kinetic energy of the molecules, or to the square of the average velocity of the molecules. The reduction of these macroscopic measures to such mechanical variables as position, velocity, momentum, and kinetic energy of the molecules, which can be correlated through Newton's laws of mechanics (q.v.),

should yield all the empirical gas laws. This turns out to be generally true.

The physics that relates the properties of gases to classical mechanics is called the kinetic theory of gases. Besides providing a basis for the ideal gas equation of state, the kinetic theory can also be used to predict many other properties of gases, including the statistical distribution of molecular velocities and transport properties such as thermal conductivity, the coefficient of diffusion, and viscosity.

Van der Waals equation. The ideal gas equation of state is only approximately correct. Real gases do not behave exactly as predicted. In some cases the deviation can be extremely large. For example, ideal gases could never become liquids or solids, no matter how much they were cooled or compressed. Thus, modifications of the ideal gas law, $PV = RT$, were proposed. Particularly useful and well known is the van der Waals equation of state: $(P + a/V^2)(V - b) = RT$, where a and b are adjustable parameters determined from experimental measurements carried out on actual gases. They are material parameters rather than universal constants, in the sense that their values vary from gas to gas.

The van der Waals equation also has a microscopic interpretation. Molecules interact with one another. The interaction is strongly repulsive in close proximity, becomes mildly attractive at intermediate range, and vanishes at long distance. The ideal gas law must be corrected when attractive and repulsive forces are considered. For example, the mutual repulsion between molecules has the effect of excluding certain territory around each molecule from intrusion by its neighbors. Thus, a fraction of space becomes unavailable to each molecule as it executes random motion. In the equation of state, a volume of exclusion (b) should be subtracted from the volume of the container (V); thus, $(V - b)$.

Phase transitions. At low temperatures (reduced molecular motion) and at high pressures or reduced volumes (reduced intermolecular spacing), the molecules in a gas come under the influence of one another's attractive force. Under certain critical conditions, the entire system enters a high-density bound state and acquires a bounding surface. This signifies the onset of the liquid state. The process is known as a phase transition. The van der Waals equation permits such a phase transition. It also describes a two-phase coexistence region that terminates on a critical point (q.v.), above which no physical distinction can be found between the gas and the liquid phases. These phenomena are consistent with experimental observations. For actual use one has to go to equations that are more sophisticated than the van der Waals equation.

Improved understanding of the properties of gases over the past century has led to large-scale exploitation of the principles of physics, chemistry, and engineering for industrial and consumer applications.

See ATOM AND ATOMIC THEORY; MATTER, STATES OF; THERMODYNAMICS.

For further information on this topic, see the Bibliography in volume 28, sections 389, 402, 406.

GASES, FUEL, any combustible gaseous mixture used as fuel to provide energy (q.v.) for domestic or industrial use (*see* COMBUSTION; FUEL).

Fuel gases consist principally of hydrocarbons, that is, of molecular compounds of carbon and hydrogen. The properties of the various gases depend on the number and arrangement of the carbon and hydrogen atoms within their molecules. All these gases are odorless in the pure state, and carbon monoxide (q.v.) is toxic. It is therefore common practice to add sulfur compounds to manufactured gas; such sulfur compounds, which are sometimes normally present in the gas, have an unpleasant smell and serve to give warning of a leak in the supply lines or gas appliance. In addition to their combustible components most gases have varying amounts of noncombustible nitrogen and water as their end products.

The devices used to burn gas for either heat or illumination consist of a burner nozzle and some means of mixing air with the gas before it reaches the nozzle, as, for example, in the Bunsen burner (q.v.) invented by the German chemist Robert Wilhelm Bunsen. *See* LAMP.

Fuel gases still in use are coal gas, made by the destructive distillation of coal (*see* COAL; COKE); producer gas and blast-furnace gas, made by the interaction of steam, air, and carbon; natural gas, drawn from gas deposits in the earth; and bottled gases, made from the lighter hydrocarbons.

Coal Gas. The most important coal-gasification processes aim chiefly at production of so-called pipeline quality gas, which is reasonably interchangeable with natural gas. Gas from coal, besides having pumping and heating specifications, must meet strict limits on content of carbon monoxide, sulfur, inert gases, and water. To meet these standards, most coal-gasification processes culminate with gas cleanup and methanation operations. Various hydrogasification processes, in which hydrogen reacts directly with coal to form methane, are used today; these processes bypass the indirect step of producing synthesis gas, hydrogen and carbon monoxide, before an upgrading yields methane. Other coal-gas processes include the carbon dioxide acceptor process, employing the lime-bearing material dolomite, and the molten salt process. These processes work indirectly to produce synthesis gas first. Other gases manufactured formerly from coal and coke, such as illumination gas and coke-oven gas, are of little or no importance today.

Producer and Blast-Furnace Gases. Producer gas is a form of water gas, a term applied to steam-process gases. It is made by burning low-grade fuel (such as lignite or bituminous coal) in a

Industry makes extensive use of natural gas for fuel. Here it provides a flame to heat a mix in an asphalt plant.
Trans-Canada Pipe Lines Ltd.

closed vessel, called a producer, while passing a continuous stream of steam and air through the producer. Because of the air present in the producer, the resulting gas is approximately 50 percent incombustible nitrogen and is low in fuel value, having only about 28 percent the heating value of coke-oven gas.

Blast-furnace gas, which results from the interaction of limestone, iron ore, and carbon in blast furnaces, has some heating value because of its carbon monoxide content but contains about 60 percent nitrogen. Enormous quantities are produced during the operation of furnaces. Most of this gas is consumed in heating the air blast and driving the compressors for the blast. The heating value of blast-furnace gas is about 16 percent of that of coke-oven gas. For a discussion of oil gas, made by the pyrolysis of petroleum hydrocarbons, see CRACKING.

Natural Gas. A certain amount of natural gas almost always occurs in connection with oil deposits and is brought to the surface together with the oil when a well is drilled. Such gas is called casing-head gas. Certain wells, however, yield only natural gas.

Natural gas contains valuable organic elements that are important raw materials of the natural-gasoline and chemical industries. Before natural gas is used as fuel, heavy hydrocarbons such as butane, propane (qq.v.), and natural gasoline are extracted as liquids. The remaining gas constitutes so-called dry gas, which is piped to domestic and industrial consumers for use as fuels; dry gas, devoid of butane and propane, also occurs in nature. Composed of the lighter hydrocarbons methane and ethane, dry gas is used also in the manufacture of plastics, drugs, and dyes.

Bottled Gas. Several of the lighter hydrocarbons, such as propane, butane, pentane, and mixtures of these gases are liquefied and employed as fuels. These so-called bottled gases, which are usually stored in steel cylinders, make possible the use of appliances such as cooking stoves and heaters in localities where a centralized gas supply is not available. Such bottled gases are produced from natural gas and petroleum.

See also ENERGY SUPPLY, WORLD; FUELS, SYNTHETIC; PETROLEUM.

For further information on this topic, see the Bibliography in volume 28, section 540.

GASKELL, Elizabeth Cleghorn, *née* STEVENSON (1810–65), English novelist, born in London. Her first novel was *Mary Barton, a Tale of Manchester Life* (pub. anonymously in 1848), an attack on the behavior of factory employers during the 1840s, a time of depression and hardship for the British working class. The book won her the friendship of Charles Dickens, who requested a contribution to his new magazine, *Household Words;* between 1851 and 1853 she contributed the papers later published under the title of *Cranford* (1853). This book, concerning elegant gentility among women in a country town, has become an English classic.

Gaskell's other works include a biography (1857) of her friend the novelist Charlotte Brontë and the novels and stories *The Moorland Cottage* (1850); *Ruth* (1853); *North and South* (1855), another compassionate study of conditions in Manchester; and the posthumously published *Wives and Daughters* (1866).

GASOHOL, a blend of nine parts unleaded gasoline and one part alcohol (ethanol or methanol), used extensively in some countries to reduce the cost of gasoline as automobile fuel. Raw materials for methanol production are coal and organic wastes, especially waste-wood products, while ethanol may be distilled from grain, sugar crops, or almost any starchy plant (*see* ALCOHOL). Although in most of the world in the early 1980s it remained more expensive than gasoline, gasohol is derived from renewable sources.

Alcohol was used interchangeably with gasoline in the first internal-combustion engines in the 1870s, and gasoline-alcohol blends have been used periodically in Europe when petroleum (q.v.) was in short supply. Two gasoline-alcohol blends, alcoline and agrol, were sold in the U.S. in the 1930s but were unable to compete successfully with low-cost gasoline. The oil shortages of the 1970s prompted a revival of interest in alcohol blends, an interest further increased in 1985 by the proposed banning of leaded gasolines by the end of the 1980s. Gasohol can be used without modifying the carburetor, ignition timing, or fuel lines of an automobile and provides a slightly higher octane than unleaded regular gasoline (q.v.).

For further information on this topic, see the Bibliography in volume 28, section 540.

GASOLINE, mixture of the lighter liquid hydrocarbons (q.v.) used chiefly as a fuel for internal-combustion engines. It is produced by the fractional distillation of petroleum (q.v.); by condensation or adsorption from natural gas; by thermal or catalytic decomposition of petroleum or its fractions; by the hydrogenation of producer gas or coal; or by the polymerization of hydrocarbons of lower molecular weight. See INTERNAL-COMBUSTION ENGINE.

Gasoline produced by the direct distillation of crude petroleum is known as straight-run gasoline. It is usually distilled continuously in a bubble tower (*see* DISTILLATION), which separates the gasoline from the other fractions of the oil having higher boiling points, such as kerosene, fuel oil, lubricating oil, and grease. The range of temperatures in which gasoline boils and is distilled off is roughly between 38° and 205° C (100° and 400° F). The yield of gasoline from this process varies from about 1 percent to about 50 percent, depending on the petroleum. Straight-run gasoline now makes up only a small part of U.S. gasoline production because of the superior merits of the various cracking (q.v.) processes.

In many parts of the country natural gas contains a percentage of natural gasoline that may be recovered by condensation or adsorption. The most common process for the extraction of natural gasoline includes passing the gas as it comes from the well through a series of towers containing a light oil called straw oil. The oil absorbs the gasoline, which is then distilled off. Other processes involve adsorption of the gasoline on activated alumina, activated carbon, or silica gel.

High-grade gasoline can be produced by a process known as hydrofining, that is, the hydrogenation of refined petroleum oils under high pressure in the presence of a catalyst such as molybdenum oxide. Hydrofining not only converts oils of low value into gasoline of higher value but also at the same time purifies the gasoline chemically by removing undesirable elements such as sulfur. Producer gas, coal, and coal-tar distillates can also be hydrogenated to form gasoline. See HYDROGENATION.

For use in high-compression engines, it is desirable to produce gasoline that will burn evenly and completely in order to prevent knocking, the sound and damage caused by premature ignition of a part of the fuel and air charge in the combustion chamber of an internal-combustion engine. The antiknock characteristics of a gasoline are directly related to its efficiency and are indicated by its octane number. This is a rating that describes performance of a fuel in comparison with that of a standard fuel containing given percentages of isooctane and heptane. If the performance of the rated fuel is the same as that of a standard fuel with a certain percentage of isooctane, the octane number given the rated fuel is the same as the percentage of isooctane in the standard fuel. The higher this number, the less likely a fuel is to cause knocking. Cracked gasoline has better antiknock characteristics than straight-run gasoline, and any gasoline can be further improved by the addition of such substances as tetraethyl or tetramethyl lead. In recent years, however, the emission of lead from gasolines combined with such additives has been proved dangerous to living beings; among other effects, it raises blood pressure. Thus research on new ways to reduce the knocking characteristics of gasolines has continued.

Low-lead gasolines were introduced in the early 1970s as a result of increased public concern about air pollution (q.v.). Automobiles equipped with catalytic converters to reduce the engine's emission of pollutants cannot use even low-lead gasoline because lead "poisons" the catalyst. In 1985 the U.S. Environmental Protection Agency ruled that the allowable lead content in gasoline had to be reduced by 91 percent by 1986, from 1.1 to 0.1 grams per gallon. The EPA also proposed the complete banning of leaded gasoline by 1988, but this did not happen. (European countries were moving more slowly in this direction and had not yet set a date for the elimination of lead.) As a result, producers of ethyl and methyl alcohols and other octane-raising chemicals are competing for the probable increased market for gasohol (q.v.) in the future.   S.Z.L.

For further information on this topic, see the Bibliography in volume 28, sections 536, 540.

GASPÉ, city, Gaspé-Est Co., SE Québec Province, Canada, on the Gaspé Peninsula, at the mouth of the York R.; inc. 1958. Principal industries including fishing, fish processing, and tourism. Forillon National Park is nearby. The site of Gaspé was visited in 1534 by the French explorer Jacques Cartier, who claimed the area for France. The fishing community that later developed here was sacked by British troops under Gen. James Wolfe in 1758. Pop. (1981) 17,261; (1986) 17,350.

GASPÉ, Philippe Joseph Aubert de (1786–1871), French-Canadian novelist, born in Québec. He wrote what is considered the first noteworthy French-Canadian novel, *Les anciens canadiens* (1863; The Canadians of Old). This historical romance is set in the 1760s and describes life in Québec, from folklore to contemporary social mores, but focuses on the growing suspicion of the British, who had then begun to rule Canada.

GASPÉ PENINSULA or **GASPÉSIE**, broad peninsula, SE Québec Province, Canada. It is bordered by the Saint Lawrence R. on the N, by the Gulf of Saint Lawrence on the E, by Chaleur Bay on the S, and by the Matapédia R. on the W. The peninsula is dominated by forested ranges of the Appalachian mountain system, such as the Chic-Chocs (or Shickshock) Mts., in the N interior, which include one of the Gaspé's loftiest points, Mt. Jacques-Cartier (1268 m/4160 ft). The peninsula has numerous rivers and lakes and large areas of wilderness, which afford excellent opportunities for hunting and fishing. Noted for its rugged beauty, the Gaspé coast is dotted with many pic-

The Gaspé village of Percé and the Three Sisters rock formation.　　　J. Ehlers–Bruce Coleman, Inc.

turesque villages and towns, including Matane, Gaspé, and Percé. Île Bonaventure and Percé Rock, small islands off Percé, on the E coast, are favorite tourist spots. The principal industries of the Gaspé communities are fishing, lumbering and wood processing, and dairying. Copper ore is mined near Murdochville, one of the few settlements of the interior. The peninsula has several large parks, notably Forillon National Park, on the E coast, and Gaspésie Provincial Park, in the Chic-Chocs.

GASPERI, Alcide De. *See* DE GASPERI, ALCIDE.

GASSENDI, Pierre (1592–1655), French philosopher and savant, born in Champtercier, near Digne, and educated at Digne and at the universities of Aix and Avignon. In 1617 he was appointed professor of philosophy at the University of Aix. During the next years he taught, traveled to Flanders and Holland, and worked on studies in science and philosophy. In 1634 he was appointed provost of the cathedral at Digne, and in 1645 he became professor of mathematics at the Collège Royal in Paris. He retired in 1648. As a philosopher he first became known through his attacks on the theories of Aristotle; he also participated in a controversy with the French philosopher René Descartes over the nature of matter. In 1647 his *De vita et Moribus Epicuri* (On the Life and Character of Epicurus) was published, followed two years later by two more works on the ancient Greek philosopher Epicurus. Gassendi's theories are considered to have prepared the way for modern empirical methods, anticipating

those of the English philosopher John Locke and the French philosopher Étienne Bonnot de Condillac; he was chiefly responsible for reviving interest in the philosophy of Epicureanism in modern times. His scientific work was mainly in the fields of astronomy and cartography.

GASTONIA, city, seat of Gaston Co., SW North Carolina, on the Catawba R., on the Piedmont Plateau; settled late 1700s, inc. 1877. It is an industrial hub located near Charlotte; manufactures include textiles, machinery, metal products, and plastics. The Schiele Museum of Natural History and Planetarium is here, and Belmont Abbey College (1876) is nearby. The city is named for William Gaston (1778–1844), a state legislator and judge. Pop. (1980) 47,333; (1990) 54,732.

GASTRITIS, acute or chronic inflammation of the mucosal lining of the stomach. The ailment was first described in 1833 by the American military surgeon William Beaumont, who was able to study the mucosa of a man who had suffered a gunshot wound in the abdomen. The wound healed with an opening in the stomach wall, through which Beaumont was able to observe the patient's digestive process. In gastritis the inflammation may be marked by the erosion of surface cells of the mucosa, formation of granular nodules, and hemorrhage. In chronic gastritis, there is a growth of fibrous tissue on the lining. Weight loss and delayed emptying of the contents of the stomach may accompany the disease. Gastritis may be caused by excessive consumption of alcohol, abnormal secretion of hydrochloric acid in the gastric juices, and various infections ranging from syphilis and tuberculosis to fungus. Psychological stress may also be involved in the development of gastritis.

GASTROPOD, any mollusk (q.v.) of the class Gastropoda, which includes snails and slugs. The Gastropoda (Gr. *gaster,* "stomach"; *pous,* "foot") are generally characterized by a single shell and an asymmetric body. They form the second largest class in the animal kingdom, outnumbered only by insects. The most recent estimate of the number of known species is 37,500, a revision downward from an earlier estimate of about 80,000.

Gastropods vary considerably in structure and way of life. The smallest species are barely visible, whereas the largest, a sea slug, weighs up to 13 kg (29 lb). Evolutionarily the animals are successful, being common in most marine and freshwater habitats and the only mollusks to flourish on land. The three gastropod subclasses are the Prosobranchia, the Opisthobranchia, and the Pulmonata, described below.

Body Structure. The ancestors of gastropods had bilateral symmetry; that is, they had right and left sides. The animals evolved, however, so as to become asymmetric. This happened through two processes, the first of which was torsion, a twisting of the body. Originally the gills and anus of a gastropod were at the hind end of the body. The left half of the body began to increase in relative size, however, and the upper part of the body (including the shell) rotated like a turret so that the gills and anus were now above the head. The change may have taken place to protect the head or make it easier for the body to balance the shell.

The second process leading to asymmetry was the development of a coiled shell, which usually spirals to one side. Not all shells followed this pattern; sometimes the shell is cap-shaped, with little or no coiling involved. The latter kind of snail, called a limpet, can cling to rocks or shells with its broad foot. When the shell is deep, however, it is usually coiled, and the snail can then crawl about freely. If it needs protection, it can withdraw into the shell and close the opening with a doorlike structure, called an operculum, on the foot. A further development is seen in slugs, which have lost or reduced the shell. Young slugs usually have well-developed shells, but these are either shed or kept as a small remnant in the adult. Both snails and slugs crawl slowly, mainly using waves of muscular contraction of the single foot; some, however, can swim.

In ancestral gastropods a space called a mantle cavity, with two gills and various body openings, existed above the head. In land snails and some other species the gills have become lost or reduced, and the mantle cavity has been transformed into a lung. In most gastropods the head usually bears eyes and tentacles. The animals can see and smell fairly well, although their behavior is not complicated. The mouth is usually

A freshwater snail of the family Planorbidae. Planorbids are pulmonates, that is, they breathe with a primitive lung rather than with gills.

William H. Amos–Bruce Coleman, Inc.

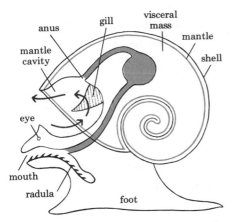

anus
gill
visceral mass
mantle cavity
mantle
shell
eye
mouth
radula
foot

Structure of a typical gastropod, the snail, shows how the body has become twisted up within the shell, leaving mouth, anus, and gills at forward end.

From Helena Curtis: *Biology*, Third Edition, Worth Publishers, Inc., New York, 1979

equipped with a rasplike tongue called a radula; this is also found in other mollusks. Generally used in scraping up food, the radula may be considerably modified. In cone shells the teeth on the tongue become dartlike, and some species can inflict a dangerous wound. In oyster drills, the radula can bore through a shell.

The gut of a gastropod is a coiled tube with various glands and sometimes a gizzard. The nervous, circulatory, and reproductive systems are well developed.

Life Cycle. Lower gastropods have separate sexes and reproduce by spawning eggs into the water, where they are fertilized with sperm and develop. The young larvae swim about, settle, and mature. In advanced gastropods fertilization takes place internally, and coverings are produced that protect the eggs and young, which are sometimes also guarded by the female. At times the whole development process is internal.

In the more modified subclasses Opisthobranchia and Pulmonata, the animals are almost always hermaphroditic (containing both male and female reproductive organs). This allows them to mate with any mature animal of the same species. In some Pulmonata an ability to self-fertilize is common, and a few snails can reproduce without fertilization of the eggs.

Ecology and Importance. The abundant and diverse gastropods are an important part of the food web, whether as herbivores, carnivores, or omnivores. Some are parasites, and many specialize by feeding on unusual, hard to eat, or poorly digestible materials. They are also important as a source of food for other animals. Among the gastropods eaten by humans are the abalone, other

marine snails such as the conch and the periwinkle, and land snails of various types. The abalone is taken commercially and as sport.

A few gastropods are harmful. Some snails and slugs damage crops and garden plants, and others are pests in oyster beds. In some parts of the world, freshwater snails harbor blood flukes, worms that cause a serious disease in humans.

Classification. The first gastropods appeared in the early Cambrian period, about 600 million years ago. The most primitive living gastropods are of the subclass Prosobranchia and are mostly marine with a few freshwater and terrestrial species. The three suborders are Archaeogastropoda (archaic forms such as abalone and limpets), Mesogastropoda, and Neogastropoda (advanced forms such as oyster drills and cone shells).

The subclass Opisthobranchia is almost wholly marine. The shell tends to be reduced, and the gill migrates toward the rear of the body. Eight orders exist, including the less modified tectibranches (bubble shells, sea hares, and allies), the shell-less nudibranches, and two groups of pteropods that swim in the plankton.

In the subclass Pulmonata the mantle cavity has become a lung, and the operculum is lost. The group has a few marine forms. Most terrestrial snails and slugs belong to the order Stylommatophora, and most freshwater snails belong to Basommatophora.

See also ABALONE; BUBBLE SHELL; CONCH; CONE; COWRIE; DRILL; LIMPET; PERIWINKLE; SLUG; SNAIL.

M.T.G.

For further information on this topic, see the Bibliography in volume 28, section 465.

GAS TURBINE, engine that employs gas flow as the working medium by which heat energy is transformed into mechanical energy. Gas is produced in the engine by the combustion of certain fuels. Stationary nozzles discharge jets of this gas against the blades of a turbine wheel, causing it to spin. The impulse force of the gas striking the turbine wheel is transmitted to a shaft as mechanical torque, and thus the shaft is made to turn.

A simple gas-turbine plant usually includes a compressor that pumps compressed air into a combustion chamber. Fuel (q.v.) in gaseous, fine-powder, or liquid-spray form is also injected into the chamber, and combustion (q.v.) takes place there. Then the combustion products pass from the chamber through a series of nozzles to the turbine wheel. The spinning wheel in turn drives the compressor and also powers a dynamo or similar device.

Such a simple gas-turbine plant has relatively low mechanical efficiency, about 10 to 15 per-

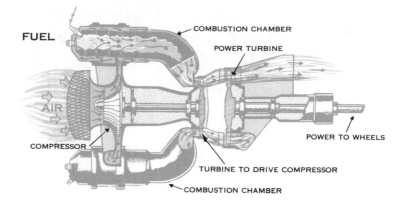

FUEL

COMBUSTION CHAMBER

POWER TURBINE

AIR

A gas turbine engine.

COMPRESSOR

POWER TO WHEELS

TURBINE TO DRIVE COMPRESSOR

COMBUSTION CHAMBER

cent. A conventional gasoline engine has an efficiency of about 20 to 25 percent. The efficiency of a gas turbine is limited by the necessity to operate a compressor. It is also limited by the inability of most materials to function well at the temperatures at which turbines must operate. With auxiliary apparatus, however, the efficiency may be raised to between 20 and 30 percent.

Such efficiency-increasing auxiliary equipment includes intercoolers, regenerators, and reheaters. With an intercooler, the compressor is divided into two or more stages, and the compressed air is cooled by a heat-exchanging device between the stages. This cooling reduces the amount of work that must be done to achieve the second stage of compression. Thus it permits more of the output of the turbine to be used for productive work. The regenerator is a heat exchanger that uses the heat of the exhaust gas to preheat the compressed air before it reaches the combustion chamber. As a result, less fuel is required to produce a given gas temperature. The reheater uses a second combustion chamber, in which fuel is burned to reheat the exhaust gases from a high-pressure turbine so that they can drive a low-pressure turbine.

Gas turbines have been applied to the propulsion of ships and railroad locomotives. A modified form of gas turbine, the turbojet, is used for airplane propulsion. Gas-turbine engines are gaining importance as power sources for generating electricity. They are also being adapted for use in trucks and automobiles, operating on any of several liquid fuels, including kerosene and inexpensive diesel oil. The chief disadvantage of the gas turbine in cars is that the engine provides no braking force when the driver takes his or her foot off the accelerator.

See also AIRPLANE; AUTOMOBILE; JET PROPULSION; TURBINE.

For further information on this topic, see the Bibliography in volume 28, section 536.

GAS WARFARE. *See* CHEMICAL AND BIOLOGICAL WARFARE.

GATES, Horatio (1728?–1806), American revolutionary soldier, whose career was marked by heroism at the start and near disgrace at the end.

Born in Maldon, England, Gates entered the British army and served as a lieutenant in Nova Scotia in 1749. In 1755 he fought as a captain under Gen. Edward Braddock during the French and Indian War (1754–63). In 1761 he returned to England, where except for one voyage to New York, he remained until 1772. In that year, having retired from the army, he moved to an estate in Berkeley Co., Va. (now West Virginia). He supported the colonial cause at the outbreak of the American Revolution in 1775 and was appointed adjutant general in the regular army with the rank of brigadier general.

In 1776–77 Gates was in command at Fort Ticonderoga on Lake Champlain with the rank of major general. In August 1777, through the influence of the New England delegates in Congress, he succeeded in supplanting Gen. Philip John Schuyler as commander of the Northern Department. The army under his command successfully defeated the British under Gen. John Burgoyne at the battles of Stillwater and Saratoga, N.Y., forcing the British to surrender on Oct. 17, 1777. Gates received the credit for this success, which had actually been achieved through the efforts of Schuyler and Benedict Arnold. Gates was appointed to the Board of War and spent much of the winter of 1777–78 in the York, Pa., headquarters of the Congress. There he took part in the Conway Cabal, an unsuccessful attempt to wrest the command from Gen. George Washington.

Gates retired to his farm in the winter of 1780 but was recalled by Congress and given command of the Army of the South. Owing partly to his poor leadership, his forces were disastrously defeated near Camden, S.C., on Aug 16, 1780, by the British general Charles Cornwallis. Gates was replaced by Gen. Nathanael Greene. The charges that were to have been preferred against Gates were dropped, and he spent the final months of the war serving under Washington. After the war he returned to his Virginia estate; in 1790 he freed his slaves and moved to a farm in what is now New York City.

GATES OF THE ARCTIC NATIONAL PARK, N Alaska, proclaimed a national monument 1978, redesignated a national park 1980. Lying N of the Arctic Circle, this park encompasses a vast tundra wilderness. The landscape includes broad valleys and the rugged peaks of the Brooks Range. The park provides a habitat for diverse wildlife, including arctic caribou, grizzly bear, moose, Dall sheep, wolf, and various birds of prey. Area, 30,448.2 sq km (11,756.1 sq mi).

GATESHEAD, borough, in the metropolitan county of Tyne and Wear, NE England, on the Tyne R., opposite Newcastle upon Tyne. Gateshead is an industrial center located in a large coal-mining region; coal and iron ore are the chief commodities handled by its port. Manufactures include iron and steel goods and processed foods. Probably settled in Saxon times, Gateshead received its first charter in 1164. The industrial development and growth of the community date from the 19th century. Pop. (1981) 211,658.

GATINEAU, city, Hull Co., SW Québec Province, on the Ottawa R.; inc. 1946. Gatineau is the site of one of Canada's largest pulp and paper mills, established in 1927. Building materials and alcohol are also produced here. Gatineau Provincial Park is adjacent to the city. Pop. (1986) 77,708; (1991) 92,284.

GATINEAU, river, S Québec Province. It rises in a chain of lakes NE of Réservoir Baskatong and flows for 386 km (240 mi) S to join the Ottawa R. at Hull. Long a major route for floating logs to processing plants, the river is now a main source of hydro-electricity. The lower Gatineau is a resort area. The river is named for Nicholas Gatineau, a fur trader who died in the early 1680s.

GAUCHO, a cowboy or herdsman of the pampas, or prairies, of Argentina and Uruguay, who lived on the grass plains of southern South America from the mid-18th to the mid-19th century. Gauchos were essentially nomadic mestizos (people of mixed Indian and Spanish descent). Bold and skillful riders, they earned an adventurous livelihood on cattle ranges or by illegal horse and cattle trading at the Brazilian frontier. The weapons used by the gaucho in capturing wild horses and cattle, often for their hides, were the lasso and the bola, a cord-and-weight type of sling thrown to entangle the legs of quarry. Leather making was an additional source of income for

the gauchos, and many of them were also wandering minstrels. Politically, they played an important role as Indian fighters and revolutionaries in the history of Argentina.

The characteristic apparel of the gaucho included a flat, brimmed hat; baggy trousers over boots; a wide belt of silver or coins; a woolen poncho; and a colorful scarf.

In the latter part of the 19th century, the modernization of the cattle-raising business, the arrival in South America of European farmers, and the portioning of the pampas marked the passing of the gaucho's hardy, independent way of life. Like the cowboy of North America, however, he lives on as a heroic figure in the folklore, music, and literature of South America.

GAUDÍ Y CORNET, Antoni (1852–1926), Spanish architect, one of the most creative practitioners of his art in modern times. His style is often described as a blend of neo-Gothic and Art Nouveau, but it also has surrealist and cubist elements.

Born June 25, 1852, in Reus, Catalonia, Gaudí was the son of a coppersmith. He attended the School of Architecture in Barcelona (1874–78), where he spent his life. As a student he was already involved in several building projects. His

The unusual and still unfinished Expiatory Church of the Sagrada Familia, in Barcelona, Spain, was designed by Antoni Gaudí. **Magnum**

earliest major assignment was the Casa Vicens (1878–80), a private home in Barcelona. This and other work brought him the patronage of an industrialist, Eusebio Güell, for whom he carried out many important commissions, including the Palacio Güell (1885–89), distinguished by parabolic arches and rich ironwork, and the bizarre Park Güell (1900–14), with its stone trees, reptilian fountains, and mosaics of broken ceramic pieces set in concrete.

In 1883 Gaudí was appointed official architect of the huge Church of the Sagrada Familia, which, although still unfinished at his death, is acknowledged as his masterpiece. Its lofty semi-cubist towers, with mosaic-covered finials, dominate the Barcelona skyline, and its imaginative forms, colors, and textures are unmatched in European architecture.

Among Gaudí's other celebrated works are two apartment buildings, the Casa Batlló (1907) and the Casa Milá (1905–07). These large stone and iron structures minimize traditional straight lines and flat surfaces by the use of rounded, irregularly spaced openings and a roof and balconies that have a wavelike appearance.

Gaudí was deeply involved in Catalan nationalism, of which he was a leader. He died June 10, 1926, in Barcelona.

GAUGAMELA, BATTLE OF, sometimes called the Battle of Arbela, engagement between the armies of Alexander the Great and the Persian monarch Darius III, fought on Oct. 1, 331 BC. The Persian defeat in the battle signaled the decline of their empire and the opening of the East to the Macedonians.

Marching north from Egypt early in 331 BC, Alexander invaded the Persian Empire for the second time. Darius assembled an army of about 250,000 men on the plain of Gaugamela, some 97 km (about 60 mi) from Arbela (now Irbil, Iraq). The Persians formed a front line of chariots, supported by archers and cavalry. The infantry was massed behind the chariots, and light cavalry guarded the flanks. Alexander, with 40,000 infantry and 7000 cavalry, moved his forces near the Persian position in late September. On October 1, Alexander began the battle by attacking the Persian left flank. Little progress was made until the Persian cavalry became fully engaged on the left flank, leaving the infantry exposed. Alexander then led a charge of his best cavalry into the enemy's center, broke it, and attacked the Persian flanks and rear. Darius fled, and the Persian army began to retreat in disorder. The Persians were chased for about 80 km (50 mi) by Alexander's men, who killed large numbers of the fleeing Persians. The Persians lost 40,000 to 90,000 men in the battle; the Macedonians lost fewer than 500.

GAUGUIN, (Eugène Henri) Paul (1848–1903), French postimpressionist painter, whose lush color, flat two-dimensional forms, and primitivistic subject matter helped form the basis of modern art.

Gauguin was born in Paris on June 7, 1848, into a liberal middle-class family. After an adventurous early life, including a 4-year stay in Peru with his family and a stint in the French navy, he became a successful Parisian stockbroker, settling into a comfortable bourgeois existence with his wife and five children. In 1874, after meeting the artist Camille Pissarro and viewing the first impressionist exhibition, he became a collector and amateur painter. He exhibited with the impressionists (1879–86), and in 1883 he gave up his secure existence to devote himself to painting; his wife and children, without adequate subsistence, were forced to return to her family. From 1886 to 1891 Gauguin lived mainly in rural Brittany, where he was the center of a small group of experimental painters known as the school of Pont-Aven. Under the influence of the painter Émile Bernard (1868–1941), Gauguin turned away from impressionism and adapted a less naturalistic style, which he called synthetism. He found his inspiration in primitive art, in medieval stained glass, and in Japanese prints; he was introduced to Japanese prints by the Dutch artist Vincent van Gogh when he spent two months in Arles, in the south of France, in 1888. Gauguin's new style was characterized by the use of large flat areas of nonnaturalistic color, as in *Yellow Christ* (1889, Albright-Knox Gallery, Buffalo, N.Y.).

In 1891, ruined and in debt, Gauguin sailed for the South Seas to escape European civilization and "everything that is artificial and conventional." Except for one visit to France (1893–95), he remained in the Tropics for the rest of his life, first in Tahiti and later in the Marquesas Islands. The essential characteristics of his style changed little in the South Seas, retaining its archaic qualities of expressive color, denial of perspective, and thick, flat forms. Under the influence of the tropical setting and Polynesian culture, however, Gauguin's subject matter became more distinctive and his scale larger. His subjects ranged from scenes of ordinary life, such as *Two Women on the Beach* (1891, Musée de l'Impressionisme, Paris), to brooding scenes of superstitious dread, such as *The Spirit of the Dead Is Watching* (1892, A. Conger Goodyear Collection, New York City). His masterpiece was the monumental allegory *Where Do We Come From? What Are We?*

Hail Mary *(1891), oil on canvas, by Paul Gauguin. This monumental picture, the first major work Gauguin painted during his stay in Tahiti, he titled* Ia Orana Maria *in the native language. The words are the greeting of the angel Gabriel to the Virgin Mary during the annunciation. The salutation, the angel, and the halos on the heads of Mary and Jesus are all that the artist borrowed from conventional European portrayals. Every other element has been transposed into its Tahitian equivalent.*
Metropolitan Museum of Art–Bequest of Samuel A. Lewisohn, 1951.

Where Are We Going? (1897, Museum of Fine Arts, Boston), which he painted shortly before attempting suicide. A modest stipend from a Parisian art dealer sustained him until his death at Atuana in Marquesas on May 9, 1903.

Gauguin's bold experiments in coloring led directly to the 20th-century Fauvist style (*see* FAUVISM) in modern art, and his strong modeling influenced the Norwegian artist Edvard Munch and the later expressionist school.

GAUL (Lat. *Gallia*), ancient Roman designation of that portion of western Europe which is substantially identical with France, although extending beyond the boundaries of the modern country. It was bounded on the west by the Atlantic Ocean, on the south by the Pyrenees Mountains and the Mediterranean Sea, on the north by the English Channel, and on the east by the Alps and the Rhine River. The inhabitants, called the Gauls (Lat. *Galli*), were among the most prominent of Celtic peoples and played an important role in the ethnic distribution of the early peoples of Europe. The first historic mention of Gaul occurs about 600 BC, when Phocaean Greeks founded the colony of Massilia (Marseilles) on the southern coast. Greeks of a later period called the country Galatia, which in Roman times became Gallia.

Tribes in the Three Parts of Gaul. Julius Caesar, in his *Commentaries,* recounted his conquest of Gaul, that part called Gallia Transalpina. He spoke of the country as being divided into three parts ("*in partes tres divisa est*"), inhabited by the Belgae, the Aquitani, and the Galli (or, "as they are known in their own tongue," Celtae). The Belgae dwelt in the north, with the Sequana (Seine) and Matrona (Marne) rivers as their southern boundary; the Aquitani lived in the south, between the Garumna (Garonne) River and the Pyrenees; and the Celtae inhabited the region between the Belgae and the Aquitani. According to Caesar, the three nations differed in language, customs, and laws. His account is fundamentally correct, although he did not mention all the tribes of Gaul; nor did he recognize that the Aquitani were ethnically distinct from the Belgae and Celtae, between whom many affinities existed, notably that of language. The Belgae and the Celtae were tall, of fair complexion, gregarious, and given to fighting in large numbers. The Aquitani, in contrast, were dark, reserved, and fond of fighting in small bands.

Caesar mentioned a number of tribes belonging to the three nations distinguished by him. The Celtae included the Helvetii, the Sequani, and the Aedui, along the Rhône and Sâone rivers; the Arverni among the mountains (Cévennes); the Carnutes and Senones along the Loire River; and the Armorican, or maritime, tribes, such as the Veneti, between the Loire and Seine rivers. The Belgae included the Bellovaci, Nervii, Suessiones, Aduatuci, Remi, and Menapii. The Tarbelli were a tribe of the Aquitani. The memory of several of these tribes is preserved in the names of French cities, such as Soissons (Suessiones) and Reims (Remi).

Two Main Divisions. To the Romans, Gaul consisted of two main divisions: Gallia Cisalpina (in present-day northern Italy) and Gallia Transalpina. Gallia Cisalpina, or "Gaul this side of the Alps" as viewed from Rome, was also called Gallia Citerior, or Hither Gaul, to distinguish it from Gallia Ulterior, or Farther Gaul, better known as Gallia Transalpina, or "Gaul across the Alps." Rome gradually extended its way over all Gallia Cisalpina, establishing colonies in the various Gaulish towns. In 49 BC, Julius Caesar conferred Roman citizenship on the inhabitants of these towns. Many illustrious Romans were born in the territory of Gallia Cisalpina, including the poets Vergil and Gaius Valerius Catullus, the historian Livy, and the statesmen and writers Pliny the Elder and Pliny the Younger.

In time, the Romans crossed the Alps, pushing their conquests as far as the Pyrenees. The territory between the Alps and the Pyrenees became a Roman province known as Gallia Provincia, and the city of Narbo (Narbonne) on the southern coast was made the capital. The wars of Julius Caesar, which concluded in 50 BC with the subjugation of all Gallia Transalpina, resulted in the formation of a new province, Aquitania (see AQUITAINE). In 27 BC the Roman emperor Augustus divided Gaul into four administrative regions: Gallia Narbonensis, extending from the Alps to the Cévennes; Aquitania, bounded on the north by the Liger (Loire) River, and incorporating 14 more tribes than the original Aquitania established by Caesar; Gallia Lugdunensis, comprising

the area bounded by the Loire, Seine, and Sâone rivers, and taking its name from the town of Lugdunum (Lyon); and Gallia Belgica, between the Seine and Rhine rivers, with the North Sea as the northern boundary. This administrative organization endured until the 4th century AD, when Emperor Diocletian reorganized the empire. Gaul was once again divided into two sections, each with several provinces. Long before, as early as the 1st century AD, Emperor Claudius had contributed much to the Romanization of Gaul. During the period of the Roman Empire, the Gauls enjoyed close relations with the Romans, and the fortunes of Gaul in both war and peace were virtually indivisible from those of Rome.

In the 5th century AD, with the downfall of the Western Roman Empire, Gaul was overrun by successive incursions of the Goths, Franks, and Huns, who gradually destroyed the Roman power. The last Roman outposts in Gaul capitulated to the Frankish king Clovis I in 486, and the foundations of a new empire were laid in the Merovingian dynasty, inaugurating the beginning of medieval Europe.

GAULLE, Charles de. See DE GAULLE, CHARLES ANDRÉ JOSEPH MARIE.

GAUNT, JOHN OF. See JOHN OF GAUNT.

GAUR, also seladang, largest wild ox, *Bos gaurus*, found in the forests of India, Burma, and the Malay Peninsula. The adult is dark brown to black; the legs from above the knees to the hooves are white. The thick, curved horns are covered with white hair at the junction with the broad forehead and are black-tipped. The adult male is almost 2 m (6 ft) high at the shoulder and reaches a length of 3 m (9.5 ft) from nose to tail. The gaur feeds on grass and shoots of bamboo and other trees. Sometimes hunted for food, it has never been successfully domesticated.

GAUSS, Carl Friedrich (1777–1855), German mathematician, noted for his wide-ranging contributions to physics, particularly the study of electromagnetism.

Born in Braunschweig on April 30, 1777, Gauss studied ancient languages in college, but at the age of 17 he became interested in mathematics and attempted a solution of the classical problem of constructing a regular heptagon, or seven-sided figure, with ruler and compass. He not only succeeded in proving this construction impossible, but went on to give methods of constructing figures with 17, 257, and 65,537 sides. In so doing he proved that the construction, with compass and ruler, of a regular polygon with an odd number of sides was possible only when the number of sides was a prime number of the series 3, 5, 17, 257, and 65,537 or was a multiple of two or more

Carl Friedrich Gauss   Yerkes Observatory

of these numbers. With this discovery he gave up his intention to study languages and turned to mathematics. He studied at the University of Göttingen from 1795 to 1798; for his doctoral thesis he submitted a proof that every algebraic equation has at least one root, or solution. This theorem, which had challenged mathematicians for centuries, is still called "the fundamental theorem of algebra" (*see* ALGEBRA; EQUATIONS, THEORY OF). His volume on the theory of numbers, *Disquisitiones Arithmeticae* (Inquiries into Arithmetic, 1801), is a classic work in the field of mathematics.

Gauss next turned his attention to astronomy. A faint planetoid, Ceres, had been discovered in 1801; and because astronomers thought it was a planet, they observed it with great interest until losing sight of it. From the early observations Gauss calculated its exact position, so that it was easily rediscovered. He also worked out a new method for calculating the orbits of heavenly bodies. In 1807 Gauss was appointed professor of mathematics and director of the observatory at Göttingen, holding both positions until his death there on Feb. 23, 1855.

Although Gauss made valuable contributions to both theoretical and pratical astronomy, his principal work was in mathematics and mathematical physics. In theory of numbers, he developed the important prime-number theorem (*see* e). He was the first to develop a non-Euclidian geometry (*see* GEOMETRY), but Gauss failed to publish these important findings because he wished to avoid publicity. In probability theory, he developed the important method of least squares and the fundamental laws of probability distribution, (*see* PROBABILITY; STATISTICS). The normal probability graph is still called the Gaussian curve. He made geodetic surveys, and applied mathematics to geodesy (*see* GEOPHYSICS). With the German physicist Wilhelm Eduard Weber, Gauss did extensive research on magnetism. His applications of mathematics to both magnetism and electricity are among his most important works; the unit of intensity of magnetic fields is today called the gauss. He also carried out research in optics, particularly in systems of lenses. Scarcely a branch of mathematics or mathematical physics was untouched by Gauss.

GAUTAMA BUDDHA. *See* BUDDHA.

GAUTIER, Théophile (1811–72), French poet, critic, and novelist, who was a prominent figure for 40 years in the artistic and literary life of Paris.

Gautier was born on Aug. 31, 1811, in Tarbes, and educated in Paris. In the 1830s he supported the romantic movement, then superseding the classical movement in French literature and the drama. As a poet, however, Gautier opposed the principles of romanticism, avoiding in his work the expression of strong emotions and emphasizing instead technique and finish of style. These qualities are characteristics of his early *Poésies* (1830) and *Albertus* (1832); they are particularly strong in his masterpiece *Émaux et camées* (Enamels and Cameos, 1852; enlarged ed., 1872). The impersonality and technical expertness of his poetry foreshadowed the Parnassian school of French poetry, which succeeded the romantic school. Gautier became a leader of the Parnassians, who held that poetry should be concerned with artistic effect rather than with life ("art for art's sake"); he particularly influenced the work of one of the most important of the group, Charles Baudelaire.

As a novelist, Gautier is known chiefly for his *Mademoiselle de Maupin* (1835), an expression of the hedonistic philosophy of life. He was also a noted writer of exotic short stories, among which are *"La morte amoureuse"* (The Love-Death, 1836) and *"Une nuit de Cleopatre"* (One of Cleopatra's Nights). In addition, he was among the best and most influential critics of his time. Among his critical writings are *Histoire de l'art dramatique depuis vingt-cinq ans* (History of Dramatic Art During the Last Twenty-five Years, 6 vol., 1858–59), and *Rapport sur le progrès des lettres depuis vingt-cinq ans* (Report on the Progress of Literature During the Last Twenty-five Years, 1868).

Gautier died on Oct. 23, 1872, in the Paris suburb of Neuilly.

GAVARNI, real name G<small>UILLAUME</small> S<small>ULPICE</small> C<small>HEVA-</small>LIER (1804–66), French caricaturist and illustrator, born in Paris and largely self-taught as an artist. He began his career as an engraver and after 1830 was a fashion illustrator. Subsequently he became a caricaturist, specializing in satiric studies of Parisian life, which he contributed to a number of Parisian periodicals, including the magazine *Charivari.* Among his better-known works are the series *Les fourberies de femme en matière de sentiment* (Treachery of Women in Matters of Sentiment) and *Les lorettes* (The Prostitutes). Gavarni lived in London from 1847 to 1851; deeply moved by the economic misery of the poorer classes there, he thenceforth used his satiric approach to life to stress social problems. Gavarni was also a watercolorist and a noted illustrator of books. In all, Gavarni executed about 8000 drawings, lithographs, and watercolors.

GAVIAL, common name for either of two Asian crocodiles (*see* C<small>ROCODILE</small>) distinguished by an extremely long, slender snout, terminating in a lumpy, erectile nob of flesh in which the nostrils are set. The forward portions of the two bones of the lower jaw are fused. The feet are webbed. Gavials are fish eaters, and they are too timid to be dangerous to humans.

The Indian gavial, *Gavialis gangeticus,* has been known to reach a length of 9 m (30 ft). The Malayan gavial, *Tomistoma schlegeli,* is about half the size of the Indian. *Rhamphosuchus crassidens,* an extinct Indian crocodile similar to the gavial, was 15 m (50 ft) long.

GÄVLE, city and seaport, E Sweden, in Gävleborg Co., on an occasionally icebound inlet of the Gulf of Bothnia. The port serves an extensive mining and lumbering area and is noted for the export of timber, wood pulp, and iron and steel. The principal imports of Gävle are coal, coke, oil, and grain. The leading industries in the city are brewing, shipbuilding, tobacco and wood processing, and the manufacture of chemicals and textiles. Gävle was chartered in the 1440s. It was rebuilt after being badly damaged by fire in 1869. Pop. (1985 est.) 87,784.

GAVOTTE, French dance for a circle of couples, to music in moderately fast $\frac{4}{4}$ time. It originated among the peasants, known as Gavots, of the Pays de Gap region of the former province of Dauphiné. It was introduced at the French court in the 16th century and remained in vogue until the French Revolution began in 1789. Stylized gavotte music was often used as one of the movements of the instrumental suite.

GAWAIN. *See* A<small>RTHURIAN</small> L<small>EGEND</small>.

GAY, John (1685–1732), English dramatist and poet, who was one of the outstanding writers of the neoclassical period in English literature. He was born in Barnstaple. His early poetry includes *The Shepherd's Week* (1714) and *Trivia, or the Art of Walking the Streets of London* (1716), the latter a studiedly artificial counterpart of Vergil's *Georgics.*

Gay is famous for his *Fables* (two series, 1727 and, posthumously, 1738), tales in verse considered the best of their kind in English. His fame as a playwright rests primarily on *The Beggar's Opera* (1728), a social satire that two centuries later inspired *The Threepenny Opera* (1928; trans. 1933) by the German dramatist Bertolt Brecht and the German-born American composer Kurt Weill. *The Beggar's Opera,* in various adaptations, is still popular. A sequel, entitled *Polly* (1729), was banned from the stage but was published and widely read. Gay composed the lyrics to many songs, including "'Twas When the Seas Were Roaring," and he wrote many ballads, the most familiar of which is "Sweet William's Farewell to Black-eyed Susan."

GAYA, city, NE India, in Bihar State, on the Phalgu R. (an affluent of the Ganges). A number of sacred shrines are located in and near Gaya, notably the Vishnupad Hindu temple built in 1787, and Buddh Gaya to the S, the site of the Great Enlightenment of Buddha. The temples are regularly visited by hundreds of thousands of pilgrims each year. The city, which became a municipality in 1865, is the site of Magadh University (1962) and of an archaeological museum. The principal products manufactured in the city include metal articles, mats, bamboo baskets, cotton rope, and jute twine. Pop. (1981 prelim.) 246,778.

GAYAL, massive, semidomesticated ox, *Bos frontalis,* found in India. The gayal is similar to the gaur (q.v.), from which it may have been bred, but is smaller and has longer horns, placed lower on the forehead and farther apart. Gayals are raised in Assam for meat and milk; they roam freely in the jungle during the day and return to the village at night. Gayals interbreed with other bovine species, and excellent beef cattle have been obtained by crossing gayal bulls with English cows.

GAY-LUSSAC, Joseph Louis (1778–1850), French chemist and physicist, known for his studies on the physical properties of gases. He was born in Saint Léonard and educated at the École Polytechnique and the École des Ponts et Chaussées in Paris. After holding several professorships he became professor of physics at the Sorbonne from 1808 to 1832.

In 1804 he made balloon ascensions to study magnetic forces and to observe the composition and temperature of the air at different altitudes. In 1809 he formulated a law of gases that is still associated with his name. Gay-Lussac's law of combining volumes states that the volumes of the gases involved in a chemical reaction (both reactants and products) are in the ratio of small whole numbers. In connection with these studies he investigated, with German naturalist Baron Alexander von Humboldt, the composition of water and found it forms when two parts of hydrogen and one of oxygen unite.

In 1809 Gay-Lussac worked on the preparation of potassium and boron and investigated the properties of chlorine and hydrocyanic acid. In the field of industrial chemistry, he developed improvements in various manufacturing and assaying processes. In 1831 he was elected to the Chamber of Deputies and in 1839 to the Senate.

GAY-LUSSAC'S LAW. *See* GASES.

GAZA (Arab. *Ghazze*), city and seaport of Israeli-occupied Palestine, near the Mediterranean Sea and Egypt. The city is on the road and railroad running from Egypt N to Lydda, Israel. Gaza has bazaars and markets and several small industries producing black pottery and coarse fabric for cloaks.

Gaza was an important city in the 15th century BC, when the Egyptian king Thutmose III made it a base for his army in a war with Syria. In biblical times Gaza was one of the five royal cities of the ancient Philistines and the place where Samson met his death (see Judg. 16:21–30). In the 8th century BC it was conquered by the Assyrians; from the 3d to the 1st century BC, Egyptian, Syrian, and Hebrew armies fought for its possession. For a time during Roman occupation it was called Minoa. In the 7th century AD it became a sacred Muslim city, but the Crusaders found it

almost deserted in the 12th century. Gaza fell to the French general Napoleon Bonaparte during his Egyptian campaign. In 1917, during World War I, the city was taken from Turkey by British forces under Gen. Edmund Henry Hynman Allenby.

By the terms of the UN plan of 1947 providing for the partition of Palestine into a Jewish state and an Arab state, Gaza was to have been included in the Arab area. In 1948, during the war between newly established Israel and the Arab League, Arab forces retained Gaza and the surrounding area (about 324 sq km/125 sq mi), later called the Gaza Strip. The strip, which extends along the Mediterranean Sea for a distance of about 40 km (about 25 mi) to the Sinai Peninsula, came under the control of Egypt by the terms of the Arab-Israeli armistice agreement of 1949. In the course of the war some 200,000 Arab refugees from Israel settled in the strip, doubling the former population.

In the spring of 1956 several military clashes between Egypt and Israel took place in the Gaza Strip. Israel accused Egypt of using the area as a base for commando raids into Israeli territory. In October 1956, shortly before the invasion of the Suez Canal Zone of Egypt by French and British forces, Israeli troops seized the Gaza Strip and advanced into the Sinai Peninsula. The following March a UN emergency force replaced the Israeli troops, and Egypt regained control of the civil administration of the strip. Israeli forces seized the area again during the Arab-Israeli war of June 1967. The 1979 peace treaty between Egypt and Israel called for eventual self-rule for the Arabs in the Gaza Strip (also called Gaza District). Beginning in December 1987, Gaza was the site of violent demonstrations by Palestinians demand-

Gayal, Bos frontalis

ing self-rule. Pop. of Gaza Strip (1987 est.) 561,000.

GAZELLE, common name for any of several small antelopes (*see* ANTELOPE) of the subfamily Antilopinae, characterized by a sandy color, with a streak of white or red on the side of the face. The knees are often tufted with hair. Horns are generally present in both the male and female, are curved forward, and usually are ringed from base to tip. In four Asian species, typified by the Persian gazelle, *Gazella subgutturosa,* the female is hornless. The gazelle is noted for its grace and gentleness. It is found in Africa and Asia, on deserts or open plains.

One of the best known of the true gazelles is the dama of the Sudan, *G. dama,* first described by the French naturalist G. L. L de Buffon. A subspecies, *G. dama mhorr,* is one of the largest gazelles, reaching 91 cm (36 in) in height. The most strikingly marked animal of this group is Grant's gazelle, *G. granti,* which is fawn colored, with the abdomen and rump pure white. The face from horns to nose is marked with a reddish band, on each side of which are streaks of white. The horns, which are first curved forward and then back, reach a length of 76 cm (30 in) in the male and 43 cm (17 in) in the female. The most common gazelle in northern Africa is the dorcas gazelle.

Of the animals closely related to the true gazelles, the springbok of southern Africa is best known. Another related antelope, the dibatag of eastern Africa, *Ammodorcas clarkei,* has short horns up to 30 cm (12 in) high, present only in the male. It has a long neck and an extremely long tail that it holds forward over its back when walking or running. The dibatag is usually found in small groups of two or three; groups of more than five are extremely rare. The gerenuk, *Litocranius walleri,* found in eastern Africa, has an excessively elongated neck and a more solid skull than the true gazelles. The horns, present only in the male, reach an average length of 30 cm (12 in) and are more strongly curved forward at the points than those of the true gazelles.

For further information on this topic, see the Bibliography in volume 28, sections 475, 478.

GAZETTEER, geographical dictionary in which political and physical features of the earth, such as countries, cities, rivers, and mountains, are listed alphabetically, and some information, usually descriptive and statistical, is given about them. The term originally meant anyone who wrote a gazette, or newspaper; it acquired its geographical connotation in the 18th century because of the popularity of *The Gazetteer's or Newsman's Interpreter* (1703), a geographical

dictionary by the English historian Lawrence Echard (1670?–1703).

The oldest known work of this type was the *Ethnika* (probably early 6th cent.) of the Byzantine geographer Stephanus Byzantinus, parts of which are extant. One of the first modern gazetteers was *La guide des chemins pour aller et venir par tous les pays et contrées du royaume de France* (Road Guide to All Districts and Regions of the Kingdom of France, 1552), prepared by the French printer and writer Charles Estienne (1504–64). Many gazetteers, for the most part full of serious errors, were compiled during the 17th and 18th centuries. The 19th century was a great period of development in gazetteers, because of greater knowledge of geography and the need for geographical information in international commerce.

GAZIANTEP, formerly AINTAB (anc. *Doliche*), city, S Turkey, capital of Gaziantep Province, at an elevation of about 1067 m (about 3500 ft) above sea level, in a wide and treeless valley, near the border with Syria. The principal products of Gaziantep are striped silk and cotton dress material, tent cloth made from black goat's hair, morocco leather, soap processed from olive oil, and a sweet confectionery paste made from grapes. The dyeing of yarn is also important. Pistachio nuts, cereal grains, tobacco, and raw cotton are transported from the surrounding agricultural region to the city for export. The ancient city of Doliche, probably of Hittite origin, is thought to date from before 1000 BC. A mound a short distance to the NW of Gaziantep marks the center of worship of a Baal that was called Zeus Dolichenus by the Greeks. Pop. (1985) 466,302.

GDAŃSK (Ger. *Danzig*), city and seaport, N Poland, the administrative center of Gdańsk Province, on the Gulf of Danzig. The city was formerly the administrative center of the free city of Danzig. The harbor, equipped with extensive facilities for the accommodation of oceangoing vessels, lies in the lee of Hel Peninsula. Two dredged arms of the Vistula R. extend through the city, which has numerous bridges. Except for the industrial areas and the Langgarten, the modern section of Gdańsk, the city has a medieval appearance and many narrow, winding streets and gabled houses with open-air balconies of carved stone. Among the noteworthy buildings is the Church of Saint Mary (1343–1505), which contains the celebrated painting *The Last Judgment* by the Flemish painter Hans Memling. Other notable structures include the town hall, a Gothic-style edifice; the exchange, formerly the merchants guild, built in 1379; and the Church of Saint Catherine. The Langgarten, which replaced

(1895–96) fortifications removed from the N and W sides of the city, has spacious public gardens, wide streets, and many examples of modern architecture. Cultural and educational institutions in Gdańsk include Gdańsk Polytechnical University (1945), the University of Gdańsk (1970); music, art, and trade schools; a municipal library; and a number of theaters.

Commercially, Gdańsk is one of the most important cities in Poland: It has not only port facilities and inland-water connections with the valley of the Vistula but also direct rail connections with Warsaw and other major points in the country and on the Continent. The port, serviced by foreign and domestic steamship lines, shares with Gdynia the bulk of Polish import trade and handles a considerable portion of the exports. The industrial equipment of Gdańsk, severely damaged during World War II, has been repaired or replaced. The city ranks among the foremost manufacturing centers of Poland; manufactures include ships, railway cars, furniture, sugar, fertilizer, nuts and bolts, military weapons, bricks, amber products, cigarettes, and numerous other commodities.

The historical origins of the city are obscure, but it is known that the town existed as early as 970. During the first three centuries of the recorded history of the town, Gdańsk was successively attacked by the Danes, Swedes, and Pomeranians. The Teutonic Knights conquered it in 1308. In 1358 Gdańsk joined the Hanseatic League, and in the following centuries, particularly the 16th and 17th, it became one of the leading commercial cities of Europe. In the course of the Swedish-Polish wars of the 17th and 18th centuries the city lost its commercial supremacy. In 1793, with the partition of Poland, the city became a possession of Prussia. In 1807, after Napoleon won a victory over Prussia, it was established as a free city, controlled by the French and the Saxons. It was returned to Prussia in 1815 by the Congress of Vienna. By the terms of the Treaty of Versailles (1919), following World War I, the city was established as the administrative center of the free city of Danzig, a territory 1953 sq km (754 sq mi) in area, under the control of the League of Nations. In 1939, at the outbreak of World War II, the German government incorporated Danzig into the Third Reich. At the Potsdam Conference in 1945, Danzig was awarded to Poland. The city was the scene of wide labor unrest in 1970, in the early '80s, and again in Spring '88. The Polish labor federation Solidarity was organized here in 1980. Pop. (1986 est.) 468,600.

GDYNIA, city, seaport, and naval base, N Poland, in Gdańsk Province, on the Gulf of Danzig (an inlet of the Baltic Sea), near the city of Gdańsk. Following World War I, most of the shipping of Poland passed through what was then Danzig, a free city under the protection of the League of Nations. In 1924, for reasons of national prestige as well as military security, Poland began construction of a new Polish port at Gdynia, at the time a fishing village with a population of about 1500. By 1934 Gdynia had become one of the most important ports in E Europe, with harbor facilities capable of handling the largest oceangoing vessels. Shortly after the German invasion of Poland in September 1939, Gdynia, then with a population of about 120,000, was occupied by the Germans and renamed Gotenhafen. It remained under German control until March 1945, when the Germans were overcome by Soviet and Polish forces. Pop. (1985 est.) 246,500.

GE. See GAEA.

GEAR, toothed wheel or cylinder used to transmit rotary or reciprocating motion from one part of a machine to another. Two or more gears, transmitting motion from one shaft to another, constitute a gear train. At one time various mechanisms were collectively called gearing. Now, however, the word *gearing* is used only to describe systems of wheels or cylinders with meshing teeth. Gearing is chiefly used to transmit rotating motion, but can, with suitably designed gears and flat-toothed sectors, be employed to transform reciprocating motion into rotating motion, and vice versa.

Simple Gears. The simplest gear is the spur gear, a wheel with teeth cut across its edge parallel to the axis. Spur gears transmit rotating motion between two shafts or other parts with parallel axes. In simple spur gearing, the driven shaft revolves in the opposite direction to the driving shaft. If rotation in the same direction is desired, an idler gear is placed between the driving gear and the driven gear. The idler revolves in the opposite direction to the driving gear and therefore turns the driven gear in the same direction as the driving gear. In any form of gearing the speed of the driven shaft depends on the number of teeth in each gear. A gear with 10 teeth driving a gear with 20 teeth will revolve twice as fast as the gear it is driving, and a 20-tooth gear driving a 10-tooth gear will revolve at half the speed. By using a train of several gears, the ratio of driving to driven speed may be varied within wide limits.

Internal, or annular, gears are variations of the spur gear in which the teeth are cut on the inside of a ring or flanged wheel rather than on the outside. Internal gears usually drive or are driven by a pinion, a small gear with few teeth. A rack, a flat, toothed bar that moves in a straight line, op-

Gearing: (1) spur; (2) hypoid; (3) herringbone, or double helical; (4) helical.

erates like a gear wheel with an infinite radius and can be used to transform the rotation of a pinion to reciprocating motion, or vice versa.

Bevel gears are employed to transmit rotation between shafts that do not have parallel axes. These gears have cone-shaped bodies and straight teeth. When the angle between the rotating shafts is 90°, the bevel gears used are called miter gears.

Helical Gears. These have teeth that are not parallel to the axis of the shaft but are spiraled around the shaft in the form of a helix. Such gears are suitable for heavy loads because the gear teeth come together at an acute angle rather than at 90° as in spur gearing. Simple helical gearing has the disadvantage of producing a thrust that tends to move the gears along their respective shafts. This thrust can be avoided by using double helical, or herringbone, gears, which have V-shaped teeth composed of half a right-handed helical tooth and half a left-handed helical tooth. Hypoid gears are helical bevel gears employed when the axes of the two shafts are perpendicular but do not intersect. One of the most common uses of hypoid gearing is to connect the drive shaft and the rear axle in automobiles. Helical gearing used to transmit rotation between shafts that are not parallel is often incorrectly called spiral gearing.

Another variation of helical gearing is provided by the worm gear, also called the screw gear. A worm gear is a long, thin cylinder that has one or more continuous helical teeth that mesh with a helical gear. Worm gears differ from helical gears in that the teeth of the worm slide across the teeth of the driven gear instead of exerting a direct rolling pressure. Worm gears are used chiefly to transmit rotation, with a large reduction in speed, from one shaft to another at a 90° angle.

See also AUTOMOBILE.

For further information on this topic, see the Bibliography in volume 28, section 392.

GEBANG PALM, common name for a fan-leafed tree, *Corypha elata,* of the family Arecaceae (*see* PALM), native to the Malay Peninsula. The trunk grows 18 to 24 m (60 to 80 ft) tall and about 60 cm (about 24 in) in diameter, and bears large, fan-shaped leaves composed of leaflets as much as 152 cm (60 in) long. The central pith of the stem yields sago, a starch used as a food. Young leaves of gebang palm are plaited into baskets and bags; fibers of the petioles are made into mats, ropes, baskets, and nets; mature leaves are used for thatching.

GEBER *or* **JABIR,** full name ABU MUSA JABIR IBN HAYYAN (c. 721–c. 815), Arabian alchemist. He is supposed to have lived in Kufah and Baghdad (both now in Iraq), and more than 500 treatises have been ascribed to him. Contemporary scholars, however, believe that most of these works date from the 9th to the 12th century. In addition, several works printed in Latin and ascribed to Geber, which is the Latin transcription of his Arabic name, probably date from the 14th century. These works give detailed descriptions of chemical processes, including experiments on the properties of metals. They develop the theory—of great importance to medieval and Renaissance scholars—that all metals are composed of mercury and sulfur and that it is possible to transmute base metals into gold.

GECKO, common name for any of the numerous small, heavy-bodied lizards of the families Gekkonidae and Uroplatidae, the latter represented only by three species found on the island of Madagascar. The gecko is often seen at night, in tropical regions, running upside down on the ceilings of houses. On each toe is a disk that enables geckos to cling to smooth surfaces. The disk is composed of closely set, concave areas that create suction. Geckos vary in length from 10 to 30 cm (4 to 12 in). They have broad, flattened heads and thick, stumpy tails. The skin is coated with minute, granular scales. In most species the two large eyes are each covered by an immovable, transparent membrane. The tongue is thick and sticky and is used to capture insects. The animal makes a loud, clicking noise that sounds

The gecko, with a suction disk on each toe, is able to cling to smooth surfaces, even upside down.
Gordon S. Smith–National Audubon Society

like "gecko"; it is the only lizard that produces any sound other than hissing. It is oviparous and lays white, hard-shelled eggs. The gecko is not venomous, although in some regions it is feared and called "poison lizard."

For further information on this topic, see the Bibliography in volume 28, section 470.

GEDDES, Norman Bel (1893–1958), American theatrical and industrial designer, born in Adrian, Mich. His talents as a designer were first employed in the theater, in which he staged more than 200 plays, including Max Reinhardt's famous production of *The Miracle* (1923). His many industrial designs included automobiles, hotels, furniture, and railroad trains. His Futurama exhibit for the New York World's Fair of 1939–40 included a revolutionary plan for a nationwide traffic system, which he elaborated in his book *Magic Motorways* (1940). His autobiography, *Miracle in the Evening,* was published posthumously in 1960.

GEDDES, Sir Patrick (1854–1932), British biologist and sociologist, known for his theories of civic planning.

Geddes was born in Bollater, Scotland, on Oct. 2, 1854, and educated at Perth Academy. His biological work centered on studies in the evolution of sex. Early in his career Geddes became interested in problems of human environment, which led him to an extensive study of sociology and particularly of city planning. He established in Edinburgh the first British school of sociology and helped found (1903) the Sociological Society of London. Geddes's theories stemmed from his belief that human beings can best develop in a favorable and integrated environment. He studied a number of cities and drew up plans for the improvement of Edinburgh and numerous cities in India. Few of his plans were brought to com-

pletion, but his influence was extensive and is reflected in the achievements of many city planners. He died on April 17, 1932, in Montpellier, France. Geddes's works include *City Development* (1904) and *Cities in Evolution* (1915).

GEELONG, city and seaport, SE Australia, in Victoria State, on Corio Bay (an inlet of Port Philip Bay), near Melbourne. It contains an excellent landlocked harbor with railroad and dock facilities for the shipping of wool and wheat. The chief industries in the city are tanning, oil refining, the manufacture of flour, salt, and woolen textiles, and the assembling of automobiles and farm machinery. Geelong, incorporated in 1849, grew rapidly after the discovery (1851) of gold in Victoria. The city is the site of Deakin University (1974). Pop. (1986 est., greater city) 148,300.

GEᶜEZ, the scriptural and liturgical language of The Ethiopian Orthodox church. Also called classical Ethiopic, Geᶜez belongs to the South Peripheral branch of the Semitic languages (q.v.). It was in use by at least the 3d or 4th century AD and became extinct as a spoken language by the 14th century. It still survives as a literary language, however, and Geᶜez literature flourished from the 13th to 17th century. The modern language Tigrinya, spoken in northern Ethiopia, is descended from spoken Geᶜez. Early writing in Geᶜez, examples of which survive from the 3d or 4th century, were written in a consonant-only alphabet of South Semitic origin. In later inscriptions of the 4th century and after, a system of vowel notation was introduced, with vowel sounds indicated by lengthening or shortening strokes or adding a stroke, hook, or circle. Today this alphabet is also used to write the modern languages of Ethiopia.

The earliest Geᶜez inscriptions were written with lines running alternately from right to left and left to right (boustrophedon writing, from the Greek for "oxplow"). Later, under Greek influence and in contrast to other Semitic scripts, writing from left to right prevailed.

GEHENNA (Gr. *Geenna;* Heb. *Ge Hinnom*), Valley of Hinnom, near Jerusalem, where Solomon, king of Israel, built "an high place," or place of worship, for the gods Chemosh and Moloch, according to 1 Kings 11:7. Because some of the Israelites are supposed to have sacrificed their children to Moloch there (see 2 Kings 23:10), the valley came to be regarded as a place of abomination. In a later period it was made a refuse dump, and perpetual fires were maintained there to prevent pestilence. Thus, in the New Testament, Gehenna became synonymous with hell.

GEHRIG, Lou, full name HENRY LOUIS GEHRIG (1903–41), American professional baseball play-

Lou Gehrig   UPI

er, born in New York City and educated at Columbia University. From 1924 until 1939, when he was stricken with the spinal disease amyotrophic lateral sclerosis (q.v.) and forced to abandon his career, he played first base for the New York Yankees of the American League. Called the Iron Horse, he established a record for the number of consecutive games played by a professional baseball player, taking part in 2130 games in succession. His lifetime batting average was .340. Gehrig was elected to the Baseball Hall of Fame in 1939, and in 1940 he was appointed a commissioner on the New York State Parole Board. The story of his life was made into a motion picture entitled *Pride of the Yankees* (1942).   B.K.K.

GEIGER, Abraham (1810–74), German rabbi and theologian, born in Frankfurt am Main, and educated at the universities of Heidelberg and Bonn. He became rabbi at Wiesbaden in 1832. Three years later he assisted in the founding of the Jewish theological review *Zeitschrift für Jüdische Theologie.* In Breslau (now Wrocław, Poland), where he served as rabbi from 1840 until 1863, Geiger became the leader of the Reform movement in Judaism. From 1863 until 1870 he was rabbi in Frankfurt. He was called to Berlin in 1870 to become chief rabbi of the Jewish congregation of that city and to head the newly

established Jewish seminary there. His principal works include *Lehr- und Lesebuch zur Sprache der Mischna* (A Grammar and Reader of the Language of the Mishnah, 1845); *Studien* (1850), studies from the works of the medieval Jewish philosopher Maimonides; and *Das Judentum und seine Geschichte* (Judaism and Its History, 1865–71).

GEIGER COUNTER. *See* PARTICLE DETECTORS.

GEIJER, Erik Gustaf (1783–1847), Swedish historian and poet, born in Rausater, Varmland Co. After a period as a teacher at the University of Uppsala, Geijer helped to found the Gothic Society, dedicated to the celebration of Swedish tradition, and wrote many poems and essays. He set many of his poems to music and composed hymns. Among Geijer's historical works are *Svea rikes häfder* (Records of Sweden, 1825), the first volume of a projected complete history of his country, considered authoritative for the period it covers; and *Svenska folkets historia* (A History of the Swedish People, 3 vol., 1832–36), a description of Swedish history until 1654.

GEISHA, class of professional dancing and singing women of Japan; the word is of Chinese origin and denotes an individual of artistic accomplishments. It is sometimes erroneously used by Europeans to designate a prostitute. Traditionally, and until recent times, the geisha began her training at the age of seven and, when sufficiently proficient, was bound by her parents in a contract with an employer for a term of years. She could seldom escape from this contract except by marriage. Following World War II, however, the selling of a daughter became illegal, and the practice disappeared.

GEJIU, also Ko-chiu or Kokiu, city, SW China, in Yunnan Province. Located in a rugged region near the border with Vietnam, the city has been a major mining center for silver and tin since about the 13th century, and it is now the country's most important producer of tin ore; lead and iron ore also are mined. In the city are large plants for smelting and processing tin. Pop. (1987 est.) 201,100.

GEL, colloidal suspension of solid particles in a liquid, with the particles forming a loose but definite network that gives the suspension some degree of elastic firmness (*see* COLLOID). Jellies are typical gels, made by using pectin (q.v.). Agar (q.v.) is another common gel-forming substance, used industrially and as a growth medium in laboratories. Silica gels are widely used in industry and research. *See* GELATIN.

GELA, formerly TERRANOVA DI SICILIA, city, S Italy, on the S coast of Sicily. The city is a resort and fishing port, as well as an industrial center, with petroleum refineries. The ancient city, of which ruins remain, was founded by colonists from Rhodes and Crete in about 688 BC. The city flourished until 405 BC, when it was sacked by the Carthaginians. Its destruction was completed in 282 BC by a band of mercenaries from Messina. The modern city was founded in 1233 by Frederick II of the Holy Roman Empire. It was known as Terranova di Sicilia until it was renamed Gela in 1927. During World War II the city was taken by Allied landing forces in 1943. Pop. (1990 est.) 79,600.

GELASIUS I, Saint (d. 496), pope (492–96), born in Rome. He was one of the first popes to assert both the parity of the papacy with the temporal power and papal jurisdiction over the general councils of the church. By ordering that both bread and wine be used in the Communion service, he drove out of the church the heretical Manichaeans, who had vowed never to drink wine. Gelasius was among the foremost writers of his time. Many of his letters have been preserved, and by tradition he is credited with writing part of the so-called Leonine Sacramentary, a 6th-century compilation. He can hardly have had any part, however, in the 7th-century Sacramentary that commonly bears his name, *Sacramentarium Gelasianum* (Gelasian Sacramentary), which contains a section of the liturgy.

GELATIN, protein substance obtained by boiling animal bones and connective tissue containing collagen in water or dilute acid. It is colorless, transparent, brittle, odorless, and tasteless in a purified form. Gelatin dissolves in hot water and forms a gel or jelly upon cooling. It is insoluble in organic solvents, such as ether, chloroform, and benzene. When placed in cold water, gelatin

Geishas dancing in Kyoto, Japan. A geisha (the word literally means "art person" in Japanese) is a professional woman skilled in the art of conversation and, often, in dancing, singing, and performing on musical instruments. She is employed to provide diverting company for men, especially at business parties.
Ronny Jacques–Photo Researchers, Inc.

225

takes up five to ten times its own weight and swells to an elastic, transparent mass.

Gelatin in its purest form is used as a constituent of foods, being highly nutritious and easily digested and absorbed. It cannot, however, completely replace other proteins because it lacks some essential amino acids. Gelatin is used in making jams and jellies, ice cream and marshmallows and as a setting for other foods in aspics. It is employed in photography in the preparation of film, plates, and paper; in bacteriology as a culture medium; and in medicine as a coating for capsules, pills, and some surgical dressings. It is also used in dyeing and in photomechanical printing processes.

Glue is an impure form of gelatin. A purified form of gelatin obtained from the air bladders of certain fishes, including sturgeon, cod, catfish, and carp, is called isinglass.

GELÉE, Claude. *See* CLAUDE LORRAIN.

GELIBOLU (Eng. *Gallipoli*), city and seaport, NW Turkey, in Çanakkale Province, on a narrow peninsula extending into the Dardanelles. Situated in European Turkey, it has two harbors and is strongly fortified. Lignite, copper, and petroleum are mined in the area surrounding the city. Roman and Byzantine ruins are in the immediate vicinity. The city has long been strategic in the defense of İstanbul (formerly Constantinople) and was the scene of a major military campaign in World War I, the Gallipoli and Dardanelles campaign. Pop. (1985) 16,715.

GELL-MANN, Murray (1929–), U.S. physicist, noted for his classification of subatomic particles and his proposal of the existence of quarks. Born in New York City, Gell-Mann attended Yale University and received a Ph.D. degree from the Massachusetts Institute of Technology in 1951. He taught at the University of Chicago from 1952 to 1955, when he joined the faculty of the California Institute of Technology. Gell-Mann was awarded the 1969 Nobel Prize in physics for work begun in Chicago in 1953. His research in particle physics concerned the interactions between protons and neutrons. On the basis of a proposed property called "strangeness," conserved by particles involved in strong and electromagnetic interactions (*see* CONSERVATION LAWS), Gell-Mann grouped related particles into multiplets, or families. In 1963 he and, independently, his colleague George Zweig (1937–) advanced the quark theory; they hypothesized that quarks—particles carrying fractional electric charges—are the smallest particles of matter. Research in particle physics has made use of and thus far supported these theories. *See* ATOM AND ATOMIC THEORY; ELEMENTARY PARTICLES; QUARK.

GELON, also called Gelo (540?–478 BC), tyrant of Gela and Syracuse, Sicily, born in Gela. He was an officer in the army of Hippocrates (r. 498–491 BC), whom he succeeded as tyrant of Gela in 491 BC. About six years later, Gelon made himself master of Syracuse also and established the seat of his government there; under his rule Syracuse became preeminent among Greek cities in Sicily. When King Xerxes I of Persia invaded the Greek archipelago about 481 BC, Gelon refused to join in the fight against him. The next year an army from Carthage invaded Sicily, and Gelon won a decisive victory against it at Himera on the north coast. That victory blocked the northward progress of Carthage for 70 years and consolidated Gelon's popularity as leader of the Greek states in Sicily. He was considered a wise and just ruler; after his death the Syracusans gave him divine honors.

GELSENKIRCHEN, city, W central Germany, in North Rhine-Westphalia, a port on the Rhine-Herne Canal, in the Ruhr industrial district, near Dortmund. Manufactures include iron and steel, refined petroleum, chemicals, and soap; coal is mined nearby. The city, which developed as a major industrial center after 1850, was severely damaged during World War II. Pop. (1987 est.) 283,600.

GEMARA (Aram. "completion" or "perfection"), in Judaism, either of the commentaries contained in the two versions of the Talmud, the Babylonian and the Palestinian. The Gemara pertaining to the Babylonian Talmud is written in East Aramaic, and that pertaining to the Palestinian Talmud is written in West Aramaic. The Gemara includes discussions, explanations, and amplifications of the Mishnah, the traditional doctrine of Judaism developed by rabbinical decisions during the first few centuries of the Christian era. Of the two commentaries, the Gemara of the Babylonian Talmud is the more extensive and elaborated.

GEMINI (Lat. "twins"), northern constellation of stars in the ecliptic. Gemini is the third sign of the zodiac. Its most prominent features are two bright stars, Castor and Pollux; it also includes a star cluster visible to the naked eye on clear, moonless nights. The astronomers of ancient Egypt symbolized this constellation by a pair of young goats; the Arabians by peacocks; and the Greeks by twin children.

GEMINIANI, Francesco (1687–1762), one of the leading Italian virtuoso violinist-composers of his time. Born in Lucca, he studied under the Italian violinist-composer Arcangelo Corelli and in 1714 settled in England, establishing a career as a brilliant performer. Of his compositions the best

The gemsbok of South Africa, Oryx gazella
South African Tourist Corp.

known are his concerti grossi, opus 2 and 3. Through his teaching he transmitted the technique and style of Corelli to later generations. *The Art of Playing on the Violin,* an invaluable 18th-century treatise on violin playing, was for many years misattributed to Geminiani.

GEMSBOK, common name for *Oryx gazella,* the largest and best known of the four species of oryx, or straight-horned antelope (q.v.). Herds of ten or more gemsbok are still seen in southwestern Africa, their sandy-gray flanks nearly invisible against the desert and brushland habitat. Both sexes have sharply pointed horns that extend up to about 1.2 m (about 3.7 ft). The gemsbok stands more than 122 cm (more than 4 ft) high and has a horselike posture and gallop. The horns are lowered parallel to the ground and the animals lunge with great accuracy when holding off lions and other predators. They are also swift runners that can outpace a horse or a pack of African hunting dogs. Gemsbok can survive dry seasons, eating melons and plant bulbs. Their long horns and striking facial markings have made them prized hunting trophies.

For further information on this topic, see the Bibliography in volume 28, sections 475, 478.

GEMSTONES, minerals that are treasured for their beauty and durability. A large number of minerals have been used as gems. Their value generally depends on four elements: the beauty of the stone itself; its rarity; its hardness (q.v.) and toughness; and the skill with which it has been cut and polished. Stones such as diamonds, rubies, and emeralds represent one of the greatest concentrations of money value. During times of war or economic disturbance many people convert their wealth into precious stones, which are transportable and more easily sold.

Optical Properties. The beauty of gems depends to a large extent on their optical properties. The most important optical properties are the degree of refraction (*see* OPTICS) and color. Other properties include fire, the display of prismatic colors; dichroism, the ability of some gemstones to present two different colors when viewed in different directions; and transparency. Diamond is highly prized because of its fire and brilliancy, ruby and emerald because of the intensity and beauty of their colors, and star sapphire and star ruby because of the star effect, known as asterism, as well as for their color.

In certain gemstones, notably opals, brilliant areas of color can be seen within the stone; these areas change in hue and size as the stone is moved. This phenomenon, known as play of color, differs from fire and is caused by interference and reflection of the light by tiny irregularities and cracks inside the stone. Opals also exhibit milky or smoky reflections from within the gem. Gems that are fibrous in structure show

227

Front row: Round-cut diamond, oval cabochon turquoise, oval opal. Middle row: Oval cabochon jade, heart-shaped sapphire, cushion-shaped ruby, emerald-cut emerald. Back row: Cushion-shaped amethyst, octagon topaz, pear-shaped quartz.

Alice Su–H. Stern Jewelers

irregular interior reflections similar to those seen on watered or moiré silk. This optical property, which is called chatoyancy, is exhibited by several gems, notably the tigereye and cat's-eye.

The appearance of a gem as seen by reflected light is another optical property of gemstones and is called luster. The luster of gems is characterized by the terms metallic, adamantine (like the luster of the diamond), vitreous (like the luster of glass), resinous, greasy, silky, pearly, or dull. Luster is particularly important in the identification of gemstones in their uncut sate.

Identification of Gems. A gem cannot always be identified by sight alone. It is therefore necessary to rely on measurement of the optical properties that can be determined without harming the stone in any way.

The gemologist uses an instrument called a refractometer to measure the characteristic property of the stone, known as refractive index, which is its relative ability to refract light. In addition, an instrument called the polariscope is employed to determine whether a gem is doubly or singly refracting (*see* CRYSTAL). Emeralds, rubies, sapphires, amethysts, and synthetic rubies and sapphires are all doubly refracting, whereas diamonds, spinels, synthetic spinels, garnets, and

glass are singly refracting. A special dark-field illuminator with a binocular microscope is employed for examining the interior of a gemstone to determine whether it is of natural or artificial origin, and to search for inclusions characteristic of a given gemstone.

These tests usually are sufficient to identify the rather limited number of materials used as gemstones; occasionally, however, other instruments are required, including a dichroscope, which measures the property called dichroism, or a spectroscope to determine the characteristic absorption spectra (*see* SPECTROSCOPY; SPECTRUM). Hardness, the test ordinarily associated with gem testing, is never used on cut stones by the gemologist.

Another physical test that can be given to an unknown stone is the determination of its specific gravity (*see* DENSITY). For exact determinations various weighing devices are used, but rough approximations of the specific gravity of lighter stones can be made by means of a series of liquids of known specific gravity. If the stone will float in a liquid having a specific gravity of 4 and sink in a liquid with a specific gravity of 3, the specific gravity of the stone must lie between these limits and be approximately 3.5.

Gem Materials. The accompanying table lists precious and semiprecious gem minerals with the names commonly applied to them. See separate articles on many of the gems mentioned.

LIST OF GEM MATERIALS

Gem Material	Gem Names	Gem Material	Gem Names
Diamond	Diamond	Spinel	Ruby spinel
			Blue spinel
Corundum	Ruby		Flame spinel
	Sapphire		
		Chrysoberyl	Alexandrite
Beryl	Emerald		Cat's-eye
	Aquamarine		Yellow
	Golden beryl		chrysoberyl
Topaz	Topaz	Zircon	Jacinth or
			hyacinth
Garnet	Almandite		Jargon
	Pyrope		
	Demantoid	Opal	Black opal
	Hessonite		White opal
			Fire opal
Tourmaline	Red tourmaline		
	Green	Quartz	Amethyst
	tourmaline		Citrine
			Tigereye
Peridot	Peridot		Cat's-eye
	Chrysolite		Jasper
Chalcedony	Bloodstone		
	Heliotrope	Turquoise	Turquoise
	Chalcedony		
	Agate	Nephrite	Jade
	Onyx		
		Jadeite	Jade

Artificial Gems. The term *artificial gem* is used to describe either an imitation of a natural gemstone or a synthetic gem that is chemically identical to naturally occurring gems.

Imitation gem. Such a gem may be made of flint glass, often silvered on the back to increase the brilliance. Since World War II, colored plastics have replaced glass, especially in costume jewelry. Plastics are cheaper, more easily molded, and lighter in weight.

During the 19th century, artificial pearls were made by blowing hollow beads of glass and pouring into them a mixture of liquid ammonia and the white matter from the scales of fish such as the bleak, roach, or dace. A much better type of artificial pearl, the indestructible bead, was introduced shortly after 1900. The bead is made of solid glass with only a narrow hole for the thread. Pearl essence, consisting of the crushed scales of certain herring, is applied to the outside of the glass and covered with a transparent, colorless lacquer.

The most successful imitation of a diamond is strontium titanate, made by a flame-fusion technique. Its index of refraction is almost identical

Important gem types. Top: Quartz (agate). Center: Garnet (spessartite with tourmaline). Right: Almandite.
Smithsonian Institution

to that of a diamond, and it has a higher dispersion. Thus, it has the brilliance and greater fire than the diamond. It scratches easily, however. A harder material simulating the diamond is rutile, or titanium oxide.

Synthetic gems. The term is limited by the U.S. Federal Trade Commission to manufactured materials that duplicate a natural gemstone chemically, physically, and optically. Synthetic gems can be distinguished under a microscope because they are more perfect than natural gemstones and contain no irregularities.

Synthetic diamonds were first made by the General Electric Co. in the U.S. in 1955. In their process, carbonaceous compounds are subjected to pressures of 56 metric tons per sq cm (360 metric tons per sq in) at temperatures of 2760° C (5000° F). The diamonds thus produced are suitable only for industrial use.

In the late 1960s a method was developed for "growing" diamonds by heating a diamond particle to a high temperature and subjecting it to methane gas. The gas decomposes into carbon atoms, which adhere to the diamond crystal. The crystal structure of the enlarged diamond is identical to that of a natural diamond. Diamonds of about 1 carat (200 mg or 0.007 oz) have been produced by this method, but their cost is still considerably higher than that of naturally occurring diamonds.

Sapphires are made in an apparatus resembling an oxyhydrogen torch. The flame is directed into a fireclay support inside an insulated chamber. The oxygen gas carries finely powdered pure aluminum oxide into the flame, and the powder fuses into droplets, forming a cylindrical boule, or matrix, on the support. The size of the resulting sapphire is controlled by varying the gas flow, temperature, and amount of powder. Boules weighing up to 200 carats (40 g or 1.41 oz) can be produced by this technique. Perfect rubies and sapphires up to 50 carats (10 g or 0.353 oz) have been cut from such a boule.

Rubies are made by the same process by adding 5 to 6 percent chromium oxide to the aluminum oxide. Colors other than red are produced by adding different metallic oxides. Stars can be added to synthetic rubies or sapphires by adding an excess of titanium oxide to the aluminum oxide powder and heating to temperatures greater than 1000° C (greater than 1832° F). In gems made with this technique, synthetic stars appear sharper than naturally occurring stars.

Emeralds, some of which are of gem quality, are synthesized by still-secret methods. They can be distinguished from natural emeralds by their red glow under ultraviolet light.

Gem Cutting. The shaping and polishing of gem materials to enhance their beauty and, in some cases, to remove imperfections is performed by expert workers known as lapidaries. Their trade, although highly skilled, is not as exacting as that of the diamond cutter.

Materials and equipment. Gems are shaped entirely by being ground on abrasive wheels or revolving abrasive disks. For minerals that are no harder than quartz, natural sandstone wheels are sometimes used, but for the harder stones, such as rubies and sapphires, synthetic grinding wheels of cemented Carborundum (silicon carbide) must be employed.

The first step in the cutting of a gem is to saw it roughly to shape. Thin abrasive disks or metal disks charged with powdered diamond or other abrasives are employed in this process. Wheels (called laps) made of Carborundum or of abrasive-charged cast iron are used to shape the stone. The stone to be shaped is cemented to the end of a wooden stick called a dop and is held against the revolving wheel or lap with the aid of a supporting block placed adjacent to the wheel. This supporting block contains a number of holes in which the end of the dop can be rested. By changing the dop from one hole to another the lapidary is able to control the angle of the facet, or face, being ground. When the stone has been ground to the required shape, it is brought to a high polish on wooden or cloth wheels charged with a fine abrasive such as rouge or tripoli powder.

The cabochon cut. Left: Single cabochon with flat bottom. Right: Hollow cabochon.

Gem Cuts. The oldest and simplest of the many standardized shapes or cuts given to gemstones is the cabochon cut, in which the stone is smoothly rounded. The cabochon cut is essential if a star or cat's-eye is to be visible, and is the most satisfactory cut for opal, moonstone, and colorful opaque gems. Cabochon-cut stones usually are rounded on the back; this is sometimes advantageous in improving appearance, but often is done in order to give the stone extra weight.

Various forms of faceted cuts, in which the gem is given a number of symmetrical plane surfaces, or facets, are universally employed in the cutting of diamonds and are used extensively for

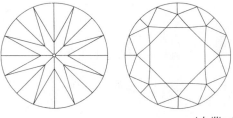

A brilliant.

other stones as well. The most common cut is the brilliant. In this cut the top of the stone is ground to a flat so-called table from which the sides of the stone slope outward to the broadest portion of the stone, which is known as the girdle. Below the girdle, the sides slope inward at a slightly broader angle to a tiny flat surface, the culet, parallel to the table at the bottom of the stone. The ordinary brilliant-cut stone has 32 facets besides the table in the top portion of the stone (called the crown or bezel) above the girdle, and 24 facets besides the culet on the bottom portion of the stone (called the pavilion or base) below the girdle. In rare cases the number of facets is increased by some multiple of 8. Scientific studies have worked out proportions of the size and inclination of the facets that give the maximum brilliance to a given gem.

In addition to the round brilliant, stones are cut in a variety of square, triangular, diamond-shaped, and trapezoidal faceted cuts. The use of such cuts is largely determined by the original shape of the stone. Large rubies, sapphires, and emeralds are often cut square or rectangular with a large table facet surrounded by a relatively small number of supplementary facets. The emerald cut, which is frequently also used for diamonds, resembles the brilliant, but has a large square or rectangular facet at the top and a total of 58 facets in all, although more or less facets may be used, again added or subtracted in multiples of 8. *See also* JEWELRY.

Gem Engraving. Designs are cut in precious or semiprecious stones either as cameos, in which the design is raised in relief above the surface, or as intaglios, in which the design is incised into the surface (*see* CAMEO). Intaglios were formerly often used as seals for making impressions on wax or damp clay.

The technique of gem engraving requires, on all hard stones, the use of a rotating metal tool. The stone is fastened to a wooden handle and moved against the tool, which does not itself perform the cutting of the design but merely rubs abrasive powder on the stone. The ancients probably used emery powder for this purpose,

but since Roman times the abrasive has been a mixture of diamond dust with oil.

Ancient engraving. Intaglio cutting probably started during the 4th millennium BC, in Mesopotamia, during the Elamite and Sumerian civilizations (*see* SUMERIAN ART AND ARCHITECTURE). The first seals, made of stone, were usually cylindrical and were suspended on a cord. The art reached its peak about 2800 BC, in elaborate cuttings on cylindrical rock crystal; these commonly dealt with the adventures of the mythical king Gilgamesh. By the 1st millennium BC the art had spread throughout Asia Minor and Egypt. Although the cylindrical form was still common, domed and conical seals with flat surfaces for the intaglios became popular. The Egyptians initially adopted the cylinder but later produced seals of various shapes, including that of the scarab beetle, often cut in one of the colored quartzes, such as amethyst, carnelian, or jasper. Unlike the people of Asia Minor, they engraved symbols rather than pictorial scenes (*see* EGYPTIAN ART AND ARCHITECTURE). Although the Egyptians made use of the quartzes for their engravings, the most

An impression on clay made by an intaglio-cut cylindrical Babylonian seal, dating from about 2000 BC.
Metropolitan Museum of Art–Gift of David Dows

popular material for the making of seals was glazed earthenware. The earliest Cretan gems were carved in soft steatite, but by about 1700 BC harder stones such as chalcedony were employed. The engraving of seals for the bezels of rings was first practiced about 1100 BC.

The carvings on the gems of Greece and Rome provide a complete miniature history of the art of every period during which they were made (*see* GREEK ART AND ARCHITECTURE). The Greek gems of the 6th century BC were cut in agate, carnelian, and chalcedony; by the 4th century BC the last had become the most popular material, although lapis lazuli, agate, jasper, and rock crystal were also employed. Gems of the Hellenistic period,

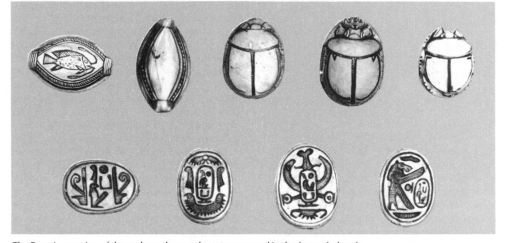

The Egyptian version of the seal was the scarab, a stone carved in the form of a beetle or engraved with various symbolic designs.   Metropolitan Museum of Art

dating from about 330 BC, were cut in a large variety of stones, including garnet, beryl, topaz, sard, agate, and amethyst. The use of glass as a substitute for more precious stones was introduced about this time. The cameo, usually made of one of the layered quartzes (such as sardonyx) or in colored glass, made its first appearance in Hellenic Greece and was brought to a high artistic level by the Roman craftsmen. The cameo was commonly employed in articles of personal adornment, such as brooches or clasps. The intaglio gems of Rome were usually used as the bezels of rings.

Revival in Europe. By the 2d century AD gem engraving had declined in Asia Minor, the best examples being talismans produced by the adherents of the Gnostic heresy. They are frequently connected with the symbolism attached to the worship of Mithras. In Europe a limited number of gems were engraved, usually for bishops' rings, until the 7th century, but the art then declined until the end of the 14th century, when Florentine and German engravings made their appearance. In Italy the art received impetus from the ardor with which the Medici family collected gems. Although the artists of the Renaissance based their designs on those of the Greek and Roman artists, they employed a freedom of interpretation that made their work individual. On the other hand, the revival of gem engraving that took place in the 18th and 19th centuries produced works that so closely resembled the classical originals that it is difficult to tell them apart.   GEMOLOGICAL INSTITUTE OF AMERICA

For further information on this topic, see the Bibliography in volume 28, sections 433, 690.

GENE, unit of inheritance, a piece of the genetic material that determines the inheritance of a particular characteristic, or group of characteristics. Genes are carried by chromosomes in the cell nucleus and are arranged in a line along each chromosome (q.v.). Every gene occupies a place, or locus, on the chromosome. Consequently, the word *locus* has become loosely interchangeable with the word *gene.*

The genetic material is deoxyribonucleic acid, or DNA (*see* NUCLEIC ACIDS), a molecule that forms the "backbone" of the chromosome. Because the DNA in each chromosome is a single, long, thin, continuous molecule (*see* GENETICS), the genes must be parts of that molecule; and because DNA is a chain of minute subunits known as nucleotide bases, each gene includes many bases. Four different kinds of bases exist in the chain—adenine, guanine, cytosine, and thymine—and their sequence in a gene determines its properties.

Genes exert their effects through the molecules they produce. The immediate products of a gene are molecules of ribonucleic acid (RNA); these are copies of the DNA, except that RNA has the base uracil instead of thymine. The RNA molecules from some genes play a direct part in the metabolism of the organism, but most are used to make protein (q.v.). Proteins are chains of subunits known as amino acids (q.v.), and the sequence of bases in the RNA determines the sequence of amino acids in the protein by means of the genetic code (*see* GENETICS: *Gene Action: DNA and the Code of Life: The Genetic Code*). The sequence of amino acids in a protein dictates whether it will become part of the structure of the organism, or whether it will become an enzyme (q.v.) for promoting a particular chemical reaction. Thus, changes in the DNA (*see* MUTATION) can produce changes that affect the structure or the chemistry of an organism.

The nucleotide bases in DNA that code the structure of RNAs and proteins are not the only components of genes; groups of bases adjacent to the coding sequences affect the quantities and dispositions of gene products. In higher organisms (animals and plants, rather than bacteria and viruses), the noncoding sequences outnumber the coding ones by a factor of ten or more, and the functions of these noncoding regions are largely unknown. This means that geneticists cannot yet set precise limits to the sizes of animal and plant genes. B.C.C.

For further information on this topic, see the Bibliography in volume 28, sections 443–44, 449.

GENEALOGY, history of the descent of a family, often rendered in a tabular list (family tree) in the order of succession, with the earliest known ancestor placed at the head and later generations placed in lines of direct and collateral descent. Genealogical tables are familiar from the Bible, especially the so-called Tree of Jesse (see Matt. 1:1–17). Genealogy also covers the study and research of pedigrees.

Practical Use. The most practical use of genealogy is in the proving of wills, when knowledge of descent is necessary, especially if a dispute occurs, to ensure that property goes to the right person. Genealogy has also been used when legitimacy is in question. One of the best and most practical modern uses of genealogy is in the medical field; physicians have, with considerable success, examined genealogical records for the origin of unusual diseases in present-day families.

Methods. The traditional method of those wishing to find their ancestors is to question parents and grandparents, for they are likely to possess written records and family Bibles, and their memories are often clear and accurate. From this start the researcher may visit libraries and courthouses and seek documentary evidence from municipal and village records and from church registers, which record weddings, christenings, and funerals. In the case of Americans, a family may be traced back to the time of its arrival in the new country. Research in the country of a family's origin is usually the most difficult because records may no longer exist and work may have to be conducted in a foreign language. British research is relatively easy because records were immaculately kept and few have been lost. Fortunately for U.S. researchers, American Mormons have the best worldwide modern records,

for their missionaries spent many years copying pertinent documents in many foreign countries.

In the U.S., and to some extent in Europe and Great Britain, genealogy has developed into a major hobby. The great surge in U.S. interest started in the 1930s, increased somewhat after World War II, but reached a crescendo in the 1970s, especially after the publication of *Roots* (1976) by Alex Haley (1921–92), which showed that despite few extant records, it is possible with hard work and good luck to construct one's family history. Genealogical research is an important adjunct to the study of history. P.W.F.

GENE BANK, term applied to a facility where plant genes are stored, usually in the form of seeds but also as whole plants, pollen, and cell cultures. Gene banks provide a broad range of plant genes from which breeders can develop new plant varieties with desired characteristics such as higher yield and better resistance to disease and weather. To this end, breeders should have as large a variety of plant genes as possible. The need for such gene banks increases as agricultural lands impinge further upon undeveloped areas, with subsequent loss of species and strains of wild plants.

The U.S. maintains its own gene banks. In addition, in 1974 a consortium of government and private organizations set up the International Board for Plant Genetic Resources (IBPGR), which maintains more than 40 gene banks worldwide, about half of them in developing countries. Since its creation a debate has continued between developed countries, which are poor in plant diversity but lead in devising new, patentable plant forms, and developing countries, which supply most of the genetic resources for such work and feel that the new plants should be more freely available to all. The latter countries have sought to gain greater international control over the IBPGR through the UN's Food and Agriculture Organization, which houses the IBPGR itself.

GENERAL, in the U.S. Army and Air Force and in the ground and air forces of most countries, the title used to address any officer above the rank of colonel, including, in ascending order, brigadier general, major general, lieutenant general, and general. The term is also used as a suffix to denote military or civilian officers of wider range of authority than their subordinates, as in the modern terms postmaster general and inspector general. The term was first used in its present sense toward the close of the 16th century in England when the general was the commander in chief of the army, the lieutenant general was second in command and commander of the cavalry, and the major general was chief of staff and commander of foot troops. In the 17th century the first lords of the admiralty were called generals at sea. Later the rank of field marshal was made superior to that of general in the armies of Europe.

The title of general, although unofficially given to George Washington during the American Revolution, was first officially created in the U.S. by Congress in 1799. Washington, Ulysses S. Grant, William T. Sherman, Philip H. Sheridan, and John J. Pershing were the only men to hold this rank permanently until World War II, when many generals were appointed. The U.S. Army and Air Force chiefs of staff hold this title by statutory designation, as do several others holding high-ranking positions. The insignia in the U.S. is four silver stars on each shoulder strap and collar lapel. In December 1944, the rank of general of the army was created, with an insignia of five silver stars, in order to make U.S. commanders equal to European field marshals. This rank was held by Omar N. Bradley, Dwight D. Eisenhower, Douglas MacArthur, and George C. Marshall, as well as Henry H. Arnold (1886–1950) of the Air Force. Previously, general of the army had been an honorary rank, conferred only on Pershing after World War I.

GENERAL ACCOUNTING OFFICE (GAO), independent agency of the U.S. government, created in 1921 to audit federal expenditures. The agency is directed by the comptroller general of the U.S., who is appointed by the president with the consent of the Senate. The GAO seeks to advise and assist Congress in the legislative administration of public funds by providing independent examination of spending operations and programs, and generally to improve efficiency and economy in the government. Its responsibilities extend beyond the national level whenever federal funds are involved.

Under its audit authority, the GAO has access to the records of most federal departments, excluding certain independent agencies. Other responsibilities include settlement of federal contracts and examination of transportation rates or claims involving the U.S. government.

GENERAL AGREEMENT ON TARIFFS AND TRADE (GATT), treaty signed at the Geneva Trade Conference in 1947 by representatives of 23 non-Communist nations, including the U.S. The major achievement of this agreement was the formation of an international forum dedicated to the expansion of multilateral trade and the conciliation and settlement of international trade disputes. Since it became effective in January 1948, the treaty has been accepted by an increasing number of nations. By 1988, 96 nations, representing

a predominant share of world trade, adhered to GATT as full contracting parties; others participate under various arrangements, including de facto treaty acceptance. Although trade negotiations are ongoing in nature, since 1947 GATT members have sponsored eight specially organized rounds of negotiations. The seventh conference, the Tokyo Round, was completed in 1979. The eighth round of trade negotiations, the Uruguay Round, began in late 1986 and was expected to last four years.

Trade Policies. GATT members continue to study and propose policies to minimize new and existing trade barriers, including reducing import tariffs and quotas and abolishing preferential trade agreements between member countries. Tariff concessions are negotiated on the principle of reciprocity. Once a concession is made on an item, it applies to all contracting parties so that the item is bound against higher tariffs. A country can request an escape clause in order to withdraw its original concession in case a tariff reduction causes serious injury to its domestic industry.

A basic foundation of GATT is the principle of nondiscriminatory trade relations between member nations. Countries under GATT's jurisdiction agree to a policy of most-favored-nation status among members. These nations agree to treat all other GATT members equally. All tariffs, whether or not determined by a concession, are included under this policy. GATT members have advocated the abolition of all nontariff barriers to trade. The first attempt to reduce such barriers was made during the Kennedy Round talks (1962–67). Negotiations have continued in recent years, and much emphasis was placed on further reducing these barriers during the Tokyo Round.

Revisions to GATT. The first major revisions to the treaty were ratified in 1955. Member nations agreed on stronger provisions regarding the treatment of subsidies designed to reduce imports or increase exports. During the 1960s, GATT was revised to reflect the increased interest by developed countries in the trade problems of developing nations. On the basis of these reforms, developing countries are no longer bound by reciprocity to tariff concessions made by other contracting parties.

See also COMMERCIAL TREATIES; FOREIGN TRADE; TARIFF.   C.M.A.

GENERAL ASSEMBLY, one of the six principal organs of the UN. It is made up of all the UN member nations, with each having one vote. According to the UN Charter, the General Assembly may discuss any question or matter brought before it and may make recommendations to any member nations and also to the Security

View of the Assembly Hall during a regular meeting of the General Assembly. **United Nations**

Council; the assembly may not, however, make recommendations on matters that the council has under consideration, except at the request of the council. The most important and frequently misunderstood aspect of the General Assembly is that, according to the charter, its resolutions are not legally binding; the force of its recommendations rests on their representation of world public opinion.

The assembly meets in one regular session each year, opening on the third Tuesday of September and ordinarily concluded by Christmas. It may also meet in special sessions at the request of a majority of the members. On the basis of the "Uniting for Peace" resolution of November 1950, the assembly may also meet in emergency session on 24-hour notice, at the request of a majority of the members of the Security Council, in matters in which a council decision has been blocked by a Great Power veto.

The assembly passes resolutions by simple majority, except on important questions, such as recommendations on peace and security; election of members to any of the other five UN organs; admission, suspension, and expulsion of members; and budgetary matters. Decisions in these matters require a two-thirds majority. The assembly elects a president and 21 vice-presidents for each session. The agenda, which rarely contains less than 100 items, is distributed among seven main committees. Two of these committees deal with political and security questions while the remaining committees deal with economic and financial; social, humanitarian, and cultural; trusteeship; administrative and budgetary; and legal questions.

The organization of the work of each session is the task of the General (Steering) Committee, which consists of the president, the 21 vice-presidents, and the chairpersons of the seven main committees (who are elected by those bodies). A nine-member Credentials Committee passes on the validity of accreditations. The assembly is assisted by two standing committees and may set up ad hoc bodies.

The General Assembly has exclusive authority to set the UN budget, paid for by all members according to an agreed-upon quota. The U.S. makes the largest contribution, amounting to 25 percent of the budget.

For the role of the General Assembly in international politics, *see* UNITED NATIONS.   L.H.

For further information on this topic, see the Bibliography in volume 28, section 190.

GENERAL FEDERATION OF WOMEN'S CLUBS, international organization founded in New York City in 1890, with the aim of uniting women's clubs and similar organizations throughout the world for mutual benefit. Member organizations must not require partisan political tests for their own membership, must not be secret societies, and must uphold state and national laws. The official publication is *The Clubwoman*. The main office is in Washington, D.C.

GENERAL SERVICES ADMINISTRATION (GSA), independent agency of the U.S. government responsible for the management of property and records belonging to the federal government. The GSA is charged specifically with the construction and operation of buildings; procurement and distribution of supplies; disposal of surplus property; management of government traffic and communications; stockpiling of strategic and critical materials; and management of the government's automatic data processing resources program. Among the publications issued by the GSA are the *Federal Register,* a report on the actions of all government agencies published five times a week, and the *United States Government Manual,* which explains the organization and functions of federal government agencies.

The GSA, established by the Federal Property and Administrative Services Act of 1949, assumed many functions formerly executed by other government agencies. It is directed by an administrator, who is appointed by the president. Currently it consists of various operating services, including the Public Buildings Service, the Federal Supply Service, the Federal Property Resources Service, and the Information Resources Management Service. In 1984 the GSA's National Archives and Records Service became an independent agency. *See* NATIONAL ARCHIVES AND RECORDS ADMINISTRATION.

GENERATION, interval of time between the birth of parents and the birth of their offspring. This is usually taken to be approximately 30 years. All children of one set of parents are members of the same generation although they may be years apart in age.

In anthropology, the term *generation* refers to one degree in the line of descent from a particular ancestor. Where records have been kept, anthropologists can trace the descent of various branches of a tribe through many generations.

In sociology, members of a society who were born at about the same time are considered of the same generation. Thus, social scientists attempt to explain the behavior patterns of a particular generation by studying the customs and events of that time. Often, striking differences are found between the generations; for example, during the Vietnam War young adults in the U.S. and other countries tended to be highly vocal antiwar activists. The older generation, many of whom had served in the armed forces during World War II, were frequently more conservative in their reactions to the war, at least during the first few years. Such differences in attitudes and beliefs often cause misunderstandings and antagonistic feelings between generations.

GENERATOR, ELECTRIC. *See* ELECTRIC MOTORS AND GENERATORS.

GENESEE, river rising on the Allegheny Plateau in N Pennsylvania, flowing N through W New York State to empty into Lake Ontario, near Rochester. It is about 257 km (about 160 mi) long and is noted for its falls, especially the falls SW of Rochester, which are 34 m (110 ft) high. The falls of the river at Rochester are used to generate hydroelectric power.

GENESIS, book of the Old Testament. The English title is derived from the words *Genesis kosmou* (Gr., "origin of the cosmos"), the title of the book in the Septuagint. The Jews, who know each of the five books comprising the Pentateuch (q.v.) by either the opening word or the first significant word, entitle it *Bereshith* (or *Bereshit*), "In the beginning."

Genesis, the first book of the Bible, tells of the beginning of the world from the time when "God created the heaven and the earth" (1:1) until the death of Joseph, the 11th son of the Hebrew patriarch Jacob. The book falls into two unequal parts. The first part (chap. 1–11) is concerned with the primeval history of humankind and contains stories about the first man and the first woman, their original sin, the first man to die and the first murderer, the flood that God sent to destroy all things save the immediate family of one "just man" (6:9) and the creatures committed to him for preservation, and the confounding of the speech and scattering abroad of later people. The first part of Genesis also contains the first covenant (q.v.) made by God with humanity in the person of Noah (see 9:9–17). The second part (chap. 12–50) is mainly an account of the lives of the Hebrew patriarchs Abraham, Isaac, and Jacob, that is, a history of the origins of the Hebrew nation (*see* HEBREWS; JEWS).

Purpose. The basic aim of Genesis is to relate all of creation (q.v.) and history to God, and, specifically, to explain the role of Israel in the world. Thus, for example, the genealogies in the first part of the book (see 5, 10, 11:10–32) connect Adam with Abraham and recount the number of years between the two; and the covenants made by God with Noah and with Abraham (see 17:2–21) express new and permanently intended binding relationships between God and humankind and God and the Hebrew nation.

Sources. Scholars have shown convincingly that the Book of Genesis was compiled from several sources. For a general discussion of the process of compilation, *see* BIBLE: *The Old Testament.*

Interpretation. Genesis is regarded by many as a literal rendition of creation, the view of most Christians and Jews until the latter half of the

19th century. Some see the book as myth or legend expressive merely of tribal beliefs, superstitions, and mores. Intensive scholarship and related scientific investigation have revealed that numerous events, places, and persons described and named in Genesis most probably did occur and exist. Those that could not literally or historically occur or exist as described and named had, and still have for some people, a figurative origin and existence. Therefore, although it may seem irrelevant to dwell, for example, on Adam and Eve and on their sin in Eden, the story of humanity's fall from grace remains for many contemporary inheritors of Western culture a viable, commonly understood expression of a recurring, inwardly felt, and otherwise inexplicable experience. See BIBLICAL SCHOLARSHIP.

GENET, any of several species of small carnivores constituting the genus *Genetta* and related to the civet (q.v.). Genets inhabit forests and dense grasslands throughout Africa; one species, *G. genetta,* is also found in southwestern Europe and western Asia. The color is pale yellow or gray, with rows of brown or black spots and a stripe down the back and tail. Some species have banded tails. The animal's length varies from 43 to 58 cm (17 to 23 in), and the tail may be as long as the body. Genets hunt at night, singly or in pairs, and prey on small mammals and birds. They live up to ten years.

GENÊT, Edmond Charles Édouard (1763–1834), French diplomat, born in Versailles. At the age of 18 he succeeded his father as secretary interpreter at the ministry of foreign affairs. He was attached to the French embassy at Saint Petersburg (now Leningrad) from 1787 to 1792, when the Russian government, objecting to his liberal opinions, expelled him. Late in 1792 he was appointed French minister to the U.S. Citizen Genêt, as he was called, took up his duties in April 1793 and began an active campaign to involve the U.S. in the French Revolution. He raised troops for projected military operations against the Spanish possessions in America and used American ports for the equipping of privateers that attacked British shipping. When George Washington insisted on maintaining American neutrality, Genêt threatened to appeal directly to the American people for aid. Washington thereupon demanded his recall, and in 1794 the French government sent a new minister with orders to arrest Genêt and return him for trial. Believing that Genêt's life would be endangered if he returned to France, where the Girondist party had lost power, Washington refused his extradition. Genêt then settled on a farm on Long Island, N.Y., and later in Rensselaer County, N.Y., as a naturalized American citizen.

GENET, Jean (1910–86), French novelist and dramatist, whose writings, dwelling upon bizarre and grotesque aspects of human existence express profound rebellion against society and its conventions.

Born Dec. 19, 1910, in Paris, Genet was the illegitimate child of a prostitute. He was caught stealing at the age of ten and by early adolescence had begun to serve a series of sentences for theft and homosexual prostitution that spanned nearly 30 years. In 1947, following his tenth conviction for theft, he was sentenced to life imprisonment. While he was in prison Genet had been writing and publishing, and his growing literary reputation induced a group of leading French authors to petition for his pardon, which was granted in 1948 by the president of France.

Genet's first novel, an autobiographical work about homosexuality and life in the underworld, was *Our Lady of the Flowers* (1944; trans. 1964). His later novels include *The Thief's Journal* (1949; trans. 1961), *The Miracle of the Rose* (1951; trans. 1967), and *Funeral Rites* (1953; trans. 1969). Lyric imagery and use of underworld argot are characteristic of his prose.

In 1947 Genet turned to drama, the medium in which he made his greatest impact. His first play, *The Maids* (1947; trans. 1954), one of his most successful, marked his entry into the movement known as the theater of the absurd. In the play two maids take turns at playing the role of their mistress, seeking their identities amid ever-shifting reality and illusion. In the plays *Deathwatch* (1949; trans. 1954), *The Balcony* (1957; trans. 1958), *The Blacks* (1959; trans. 1960), and *The Screens* (1961; trans. 1962), Genet often used role playing and the inversion of good and evil as techniques for commenting on the falseness of social and political values.

All Genet's works expose his deep sense of sympathy with the outcasts of society as they are confronted by omnipresent crime, sex, and death. His plays are filled with ritual, cruelty, and his conviction of the absurdity of moral concepts. Although his writings were at first considered pornographic, Genet was soon recognized as an existentialist grappling with problems of identity and alienation, and he came to be regarded as one of the most influential 20th-century writers. In 1983 he was awarded the Grand Prix National des Lettres.

GENETIC DISEASES. See BIRTH DEFECTS.

GENETIC ENGINEERING, altering the inherited characteristics of an organism in a predetermined way, by introducing into it a piece of the genetic material of another organism. Such a transfer of genetic material—that is, of deoxyribonucleic acid, or DNA (*see* GENETICS; NUCLEIC ACIDS)—is made possible through the use of so-called restriction enzymes. These enzymes (*see* ENZYME), produced by various species of bacteria, are each capable of recognizing a particular sequence of the chain of chemical units, called nucleotide bases, that make up the DNA molecule, and of breaking the chain where the sequence occurs. Fragments of DNA produced by the same restriction enzyme tend to join together, and these linkages can be made permanent. Thus, if the DNA strands of two organisms are treated with the same restriction enzyme, they subsequently can be combined to form a hybrid DNA molecule. If this molecule can be incorporated into a cell, an organism can be produced that has characteristics of both parent organisms.

Genetic engineering thus far has been mainly carried out with bacteria and viruses. The reason is that the process works in a very small proportion of the organisms treated. With bacteria and viruses, large numbers of organisms can be screened to pick out the few successful transfers. This can be done, for example, by incorporating into the DNA that is to be transferred a gene (q.v.) that confers resistance to some chemical, and then subjecting the recipient organisms to the chemical. Only those with a successful transfer will then survive.

One of the problems of introducing genes from higher organisms into bacteria is the presence within the donor genes of intervening, noncoding sequences called introns (*see* GENETICS: *Gene Action: DNA and the Code of Life: Introns*). Bacteria do not seem to have the enzymes for removing introns. Therefore, they tend to produce an imperfect product or no product at all. This problem can be circumvented, however, by using messenger ribonucleic acid from the cytoplasm of the higher organism's cells as a template for the production of DNA, with no intervening sequences, which can then be introduced into the bacterium.

Benefits. The process of genetic engineering is potentially very important. For example, the gene for insulin (q.v.), normally found only in higher animals, can now be introduced into a bacterial cell. The bacteria can then be grown in large quantities, giving an abundant source of insulin at a relatively low cost. Another example is the gene for interferon (q.v.)—a rare substance of great potential value in the treatment of viral infections (and possibly of cancer). The same technique is being applied to the production of complex organic molecules such as enzymes.

Genetic engineering also offers the hope of cures for many inherited diseases, once the problem of low efficiencies of effective transfer of genetic material is overcome. One promising strategy might be to introduce into a person afflicted with a genetic deficiency some of his or her own cells that have been transformed to normality in laboratory culture, thus making the material more readily acceptable to the person's body. By the mid-1980s the U.S. was preparing to undertake the first such attacks on genetic diseases (*see* BIRTH DEFECTS).

Another development has been the refinement of the technique called cloning, which produces large numbers of genetically identical individuals by transplanting whole cell nuclei (*see* CLONE). With other techniques scientists can isolate sections of DNA representing single genes, determine their nucleotide sequences, and reproduce them in the laboratory. Ways have been developed for making DNA with a predetermined nucleotide sequence, using purely chemical methods. This offers the possibility of creating entirely new genes with commercially or medically desirable properties. The great commercial potential of genetic engineering, however, is also leading to a growing number of lawsuits over patent rights on techniques.

Hazards. While the potential benefits of genetic engineering (or recombinant DNA technology, as it is also called) are considerable, so may be the potential dangers. For example, the introduction of cancer-causing genes into a common infectious organism, such as the influenza virus, could be hazardous. Consequently, in most nations experiments with recombinant DNA are closely regulated, and those involving infectious agents can be conducted only under the strictest conditions of containment.

In the U.S., the National Institutes of Health (NIH) set up the Recombinant DNA Advisory Committee (RAC) in the 1970s to assess the hazards of such research. In 1978 the NIH approved field experiments using altered bacteria, on a case-by-case basis. Although research efforts not funded by the federal government are not required to submit environmental-impact statements to the RAC, most of them have been doing so on a voluntary basis. The problems entailed in such work, however, were exemplified in the mid-1980s when the Environmental Protection Agency withdrew a field-test permit and the Department of Agriculture a genetically modified swine vaccine because of insufficient care being taken in clearance procedures.

See also MUTATION.   B.C.C.

For further information on this topic, see the Bibliography in volume 28, sections 38, 449.

GENETICS, scientific study of how physical, bio-chemical, and behavioral traits are transmitted from parents to their offspring. The word itself was coined in 1906 by the British biologist William Bateson. Geneticists are able to determine the mechanisms of inheritance because the off-spring of sexually reproducing organisms do not exactly resemble their parents, and because some of the differences and similarities between parents and offspring recur from generation to generation in repeated patterns. The investigation of these patterns has led to some of the most exciting discoveries in modern biology.

Emergence of Genetics. The science of genetics began in 1900, when several plant breeders independently discovered the work of the Austrian monk Gregor Mendel, which, although published in 1866, had been virtually ignored. Working with garden peas, Mendel described the patterns of inheritance in terms of seven pairs of contrasting traits that appeared in different pea-plant varieties. He observed that the traits were inherited as separate units, each of which was inherited independently of the others (see MENDEL'S LAWS). He suggested that each parent has pairs of units but contributes only one unit from each pair to its offspring. The units that Mendel described were later given the name *genes* (see GENE).

Physical Basis of Heredity. Soon after Mendel's work was rediscovered, scientists realized that the patterns of inheritance he had described paralleled the action of chromosomes (see CHROMOSOME) in dividing cells, and they proposed that the Mendelian units of inheritance, the genes, are carried by the chromosomes. This led to intensive studies of cell division.

Every cell comes from the division of a preexisting cell. All the cells that make up a human being, for example, are derived from the successive divisions of a single cell, the zygote (see FERTILIZATION), which is formed by the union of an egg and a sperm. The great majority of the cells produced by the division of the zygote are, in the composition of their hereditary material, identical to one another and to the zygote itself (assuming that no mutations occur; see below). Each cell of a higher organism is composed of a jellylike layer of material, the cytoplasm, which contains many small structures. This cytoplasmic material surrounds a prominent body called the nucleus. Every nucleus contains a number of minute, threadlike chromosomes. Some relatively simple organisms, such as blue-green algae and bacteria, have no distinct nucleus but have cytoplasm, which contains one or more chromosomes.

Chromosomes vary in size and shape and usually occur in pairs. The members of each pair, called homologues, closely resemble each other. Most cells in the human body contain 23 pairs of chromosomes, whereas most cells of the fruit fly *Drosophila* contain four pairs, and the bacterium *Escherichia coli* has a single chromosome in the form of a ring. Every chromosome in a cell is now known to contain many genes, and each gene is located at a particular site, or locus, on the chromosome.

The process of cell division by which most of the cells of an organism come to have identical sets of genes is called mitosis (see REPRODUCTION). In mitotic division each chromosome divides into two equal parts, and the two parts travel to opposite ends of the cell. After the cell divides, each of the two resulting cells has the same number of chromosomes and genes as the original cell (see CELL: *Division, Reproduction, and Differentiation*). Every cell formed in this process thus has the same array of genetic material. Simple one-celled organisms and some multicellular forms reproduce by mitosis; it is also the process by which complex organisms achieve growth and replace worn-out tissue.

Higher organisms that reproduce sexually are formed from the union of special sex cells known as gametes (see GAMETE). Gametes are produced by a special type of cell division called meiosis, which differs from mitosis in one important way: In meiosis a single chromosome from each pair of chromosomes is transmitted from the original cell to each of the new cells. Thus, gametes contain only half the number of chromosomes that are found in the other body cells. When two gametes unite in fertilization, the resulting cell, called the zygote, contains the full, double set of chromosomes. Half of these chromosomes normally come from one parent and half from the other.

The Transmission of Genes. The union of gametes brings together two sets of genes, one set from each parent. Each gene—that is, each specific site on a chromosome that affects a particular trait—is therefore represented by two copies, one coming from the mother and one from the father (for exceptions to this rule, see Sex and Sex Linkage, below). Each copy is located at the same position on each of the paired chromosome of the zygote. When the two copies are identical, the individual is said to be homozygous for that particular gene. When they are different—that is, when each parent has contributed a different form, or allele, of the same gene—the individual is said to be heterozygous for that gene. Both alleles are carried in the genetic material of the individual, but if one is dominant, only that one will be manifested. In later generations, however, as was shown by Mendel, the recessive trait may show itself again (in individuals homozygous for its allele).

For example, the ability of a person to form pigment in the skin, hair, and eyes depends on the presence of a particular allele (*A*), whereas the lack of this ability, known as albinism, is caused by another allele (*a*) of the same gene. (For convenience, alleles are usually designated by a single letter; the dominant allele is represented by a capital letter and the recessive allele by a small letter.) The effects of *A* are dominant; of *a*, recessive. Therefore, heterozygous persons (*Aa*), as well as persons homozygous (*AA*) for the pigment-producing allele, have normal pigmentation. Persons homozygous for the allele that results in a lack of pigment (*aa*) are albinos. If a couple who both are heterozygous (*Aa*) have a large number of children, approximately one-fourth of them will be homozygous *AA*, one-half heterozygous *Aa*, and one-fourth homozygous *aa*. Three-fourths of the children will be normal and one-fourth albino. Both alleles will be carried in the genetic material of heterozygous offspring, who will produce gametes bearing one or the other allele. A distinction is made between the appearance, or outward characteristics, of an organism and the genes and alleles it carries. The observable traits constitute the organism's phenotype, and the genetic makeup is known as its genotype.

Not always is one allele dominant and the other recessive; instead, the inheritance of two alleles sometimes results in intermediate characteristics. The herb called four-o'clock, for example, may have flowers that are red, white, or pink. Plants with red flowers have two copies of the allele *R* for red flower color and hence are homozygous *RR*. Plants with white flowers have two copies of the allele *r* for white flower color and are homozygous *rr*. Plants with one copy of each allele, heterozygous *Rr*, are pink—a blend of the colors produced by the two alleles.

The action of genes is seldom a simple matter of a single gene controlling a single trait. Many genes are known to affect more than one trait. On the other hand, many characteristics require the simultaneous action of a number of genes. For example, the action of at least two dominant genes is required to produce purple pigment in the purple-flowered sweet pea. Sweet peas that are homozygous for either or both of the recessive alleles involved in the color traits produce white flowers. Thus, the effects of a gene can depend on which other genes are present.

Quantitative Inheritance. Traits that are expressed as variations in quantity or extent, such as weight, height, or degree of pigmentation, usually depend on many genes as well as on environmental influences. Often the effects of different genes appear to be additive—that is, each gene seems to produce a small increment or decrement independent of the other genes. The height of a plant, for example, might be determined by a series of four genes: *A, B, C,* and *D*. Suppose that the plant has an average height of 25 cm (10 in) when its genotype is *aabbccdd,* and that each replacement by a pair of dominant alleles increases the average height by approximately 10 cm (about 4 in). In that case a plant that is *AABBccdd* will be 46 cm (18 in) tall, and one that is *AABBCCDD* will be 66 cm (26 in) tall. In reality, the results are rarely as regular as this. Different genes may make different contributions to the total measurement, and some genes may interact so that the contribution of one depends on the presence of another. The inheritance of quantitative characteristics that depend on several genes is called polygenic, or multifactorial, inheritance.

Gene Linkage and Gene Mapping. Mendel's principle that genes controlling different traits are inherited independently of one another turns out to be true only when the genes occur on different chromosomes. The American geneticist Thomas Hunt Morgan and his coworkers, in an extensive series of experiments using fruit flies (which breed rapidly), showed that genes are arranged on the chromosomes in a linear fashion; and that when genes occur on the same chromosome, they are inherited as a single unit for as long as the chromosome itself remains intact. Genes inherited in this way are said to be linked.

Morgan and his group also found, however, that such linkage is rarely complete. Combinations of alleles characteristic of each parent can become reassorted among some of their offspring. During meiosis, a pair of homologous chromosomes may exchange material in a process called recombination, or crossing-over. (The effect of crossing-over can be seen under a microscope as an X-shaped joint between the two chromosomes.) Crossovers occur more or less at random along the length of the chromosomes, so the frequency of recombination between two genes depends on their distance from each other on the chromosome. If the genes are relatively far apart, recombinant gametes will be common; if they are relatively close, recombinant gametes will be rare. In the offspring produced by the gametes, the crossovers show up as new combinations of visible traits. The more crossovers that occur, the greater the percentage of offspring that show the new combinations. Consequently, by arranging suitable breeding experiments, scientists can plot, or map, the relative positions of the genes along the chromosome.

In recent years geneticists have used organisms such as bacteria, molds, and viruses, which rapidly produce extremely large numbers of offspring, to detect recombinations that occur only rarely. Thus, they are able to make maps of genes that are quite close together. The method introduced at Morgan's laboratory has now become so exact that differences occurring within a single gene can be mapped. These maps have shown that not only do the genes occur in linear fashion along the chromosome, but they themselves are linear structures. The detection of rare recombinants can reveal the existence of structures even smaller than those observed through the most powerful microscopes.

Studies of fungi, and more recently of fruit flies, have shown that recombination of alleles can sometimes take place without reciprocal exchanges between chromosomes. Apparently, when two different versions of the same gene occur together (in a heterozygote), one of them may be "corrected" to match the other. Such corrections may take place in either direction (for example, the allele A may be changed to a, or vice versa). This process has been called gene conversion. Occasionally, several adjacent genes may undergo conversion together, and the likelihood of two genes being coconverted is related to their distance apart. This provides another way of mapping the relative positions of genes on the chromosome.

Sex and Sex Linkage. Another contribution to genetic studies made by Morgan was his observation in 1910 of sexual differences in the inheritance of traits, a pattern known as sex-linked inheritance.

Sex is usually determined by the action of a single pair of chromosomes. Abnormalities of the endocrine system (q.v.) or other disturbances may alter the expression of secondary sexual characteristics, but they almost never completely reverse the sex. A human female, for example, has 23 pairs of chromosomes, and the members of each pair are much alike. A human male, however, has 22 similar pairs and one pair consisting of two chromosomes that are dissimilar in size and structure. The 22 pairs of chromosomes that are alike in both males and females are called autosomes. The remaining chromosomes, in both sexes, are called the sex chromosomes. The two identical sex chromosomes in the female are called X chromosomes. One of the sex chromo-

somes in the male is also an X chromosome, but the other, shorter one is called the Y chromosome. When gametes are formed, each egg produced by the female contains one X chromosome, but the sperm produced by the male can contain either an X or a Y chromosome. The union of an egg, which always bears an X chromosome, with a sperm also bearing an X chromosome produces a zygote with two X's: a female offspring. The union of an egg with a sperm that bears a Y chromosome produces a male offspring. Modifications of this mechanism occur in various plants and animals.

The human Y chromosome is approximately one-third as long as the X, and apart from its role in determining maleness, it appears to be genetically inactive. Thus, most genes on the X have no counterpart on the Y. These genes, said to be sex-linked, have a characteristic pattern of inheritance. The disease called hemophilia (q.v.), for example, is usually caused by a sex-linked recessive gene (h). A female with HH or Hh is normal; a female with hh has hemophilia. A male is never heterozygous for the gene because he inherits only the gene that is on the X chromosome. A male with H is normal; with h he has hemophilia. When a normal man (H) and a woman who is heterozygous (Hh) have offspring, the female children are normal, but half of them carry the h gene—that is, none of them is hh, but half of them bear the genotype Hh. The male children inherit only the H or the h; therefore, half the male children have hemophilia. Thus, in normal circumstances a female carrier passes on the disease to half her sons, and she also passes on the recessive h gene to half her daughters, who in turn become carriers of hemophilia. Many other conditions—including red-green color blindness, hereditary nearsightedness, night blindness, and ichthyosis (a skin disease)—have been identified as sex-linked traits in humans.

Gene Action: DNA and the Code of Life. For more than 50 years after the science of genetics was established and the patterns of inheritance through genes were clarified, the largest questions remained unanswered: How are the chromosomes and their genes copied so exactly from cell to cell, and how do they direct the structure and behavior of living things? Two American geneticists, George Wells Beadle and Edward Lawrie Tatum, provided one of the first important clues in the early 1940s. Working with the fungi Neurospora and Penicillium, they found that genes direct the formation of enzymes through the units of which they are composed. Each unit (a polypeptide) is produced by a specific gene. This work launched studies into the chemical na-

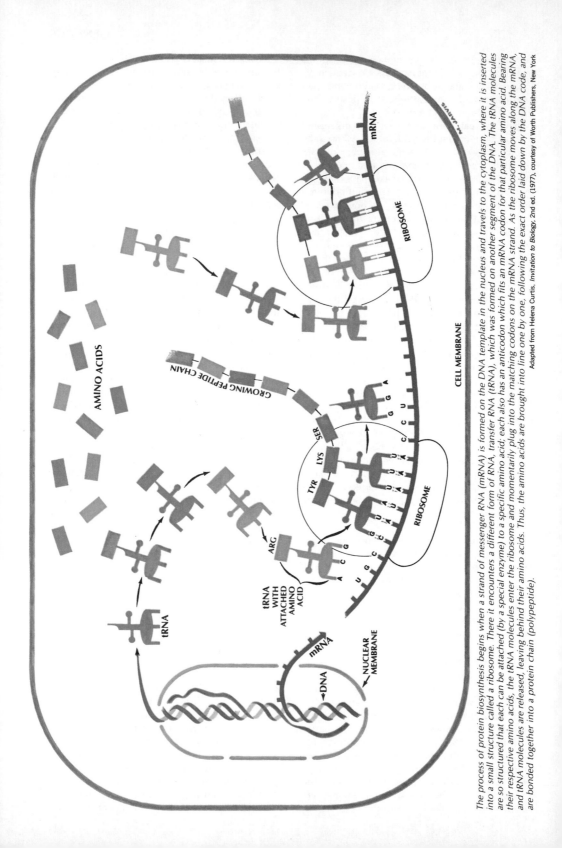

The process of protein biosynthesis begins when a strand of messenger RNA (mRNA) is formed on the DNA template in the nucleus and travels to the cytoplasm, where it is inserted into a small structure called a ribosome. There it encounters a different form of RNA, transfer RNA (tRNA), which was formed on another segment of the DNA. The tRNA molecules are so structured that each can be attached (by a special enzyme) to a specific amino acid; each also has an anticodon which fits an mRNA codon for that particular amino acid. Bearing their respective amino acids, the tRNA molecules enter the ribosome and momentarily plug into the matching codons on the mRNA. As the ribosome moves along the mRNA, and tRNA molecules are released, leaving behind their amino acids. Thus, the amino acids are brought into line one by one, following the exact order laid down by the DNA code, and are bonded together into a protein chain (polypeptide).

Adapted from Helena Curtis, Invitation to Biology, 2nd ed. (1977), courtesy of Worth Publishers, New York

FIRST LETTER	SECOND LETTER				THIRD LETTER
	U	**C**	**A**	**G**	
U	phenylalanine	serine	tyrosine	cysteine	U
	phenylalanine	serine	tyrosine	systeine	C
	leucine	serine	(end chain)	(end chain)	A
	leucine	serine	(end chain)	tryptophan	G
C	leucine	proline	histidine	arginine	U
	leucine	proline	histidine	arginine	C
	leucine	proline	glutamine	arginine	A
	leucine	proline	glutamine	arginine	G
A	isoleucine	threonine	asparagine	serine	U
	isoleucine	threonine	asparagine	serine	C
	isoleucine	threonine	lysine	arginine	A
	methionine	threonine	lysine	arginine	G
G	valine	alanine	aspartic acid	glycine	U
	valine	alanine	aspartic acid	glycine	C
	valine	alanine	glutamic acid	glycine	A
	valine	alanine	glutamic acid	glycine	G

The genetic code. Letters represent uracil, cytosine, adenine, and guanine, the four nucleotide bases of messenger RNA. When combined in three-letter "words," or codons, they specify a single amino acid or an instruction, such as "end the chain." Thus, reading the code for the amino acids in the first box, the first, second, and third codon letters are UUU (for uracil-uracil-uracil), and the amino acid they specify is phenylalanine. The codon UUC also specifies this amino acid. Leucine is specified by either UUA or UUG. The code is the same in all living matter, from bacteria to humans.

ture of the gene and helped to establish the field of molecular genetics.

That chromosomes were almost entirely composed of two kinds of chemical substances, protein and nucleic acids (qq.v.), had long been known. Partly because of the close relationship established between genes and enzymes, which are proteins, protein at first seemed the fundamental substance that determined heredity. In 1944, however, the Canadian bacteriologist Oswald Theodore Avery proved that deoxyribonucleic acid (DNA) performed this role. He extracted DNA from one strain of bacteria and introduced it into another strain. The second strain not only acquired characteristics of the first but passed them on to subsequent generations. By this time DNA was known to be made up of substances called nucleotides. Each nucleotide consists of a phosphate, a sugar known as deoxyribose, and any one of four nitrogen-containing bases. The four nitrogen bases are adenine (A), thymine (T), guanine (G), and cytosine (C).

In 1953, putting together the accumulated chemical knowledge, geneticists James Dewey Watson of the U.S. and Francis Harry Compton Crick of Great Britain worked out the structure of DNA. This knowledge immediately provided the means of understanding how hereditary information is copied. Watson and Crick found that the DNA molecule is composed of two long strands in the form of a double helix, somewhat resembling a long, spiral ladder. The strands, or sides of the ladder, are made up of alternating phosphate and sugar molecules. The nitrogen bases, joining in pairs, act as the rungs. Each base is attached to a sugar molecule and is linked by a hydrogen bond to a complementary base on the opposite strand. Adenine always binds to thymine, and guanine always binds to cytosine. To make a new, identical copy of the DNA molecule, the two strands need only unwind and separate at the bases (which are weakly bound); with more nucleotides available in the cell, new complementary bases can link with each separated strand, and two double helixes result. If the sequence of bases were AGATC on one existing strand, the new strand would contain the complementary, or "mirror image," sequence TCTAG. Since the "backbone" of every chromosome is a single long, double-stranded molecule of DNA, the production of two identical double helixes will result in the production of two identical chromosomes.

The DNA backbone is actually a great deal

longer than the chromosome but is tightly coiled up within it. This packing is now known to be based on minute particles of protein known as nucleosomes, just visible under the most powerful electron microscope. The DNA is wound around each nucleosome in succession to form a beaded structure. The structure is then further folded so that the beads associate in regular coils. Thus, the DNA has a "coiled-coil" configuration, like the filament of an electric light bulb.

After the discoveries of Watson and Crick, the question that remained was how the DNA directs the formation of proteins, compounds central to all the processes of life. Proteins are not only the major components of most cell structures, they also control virtually all the chemical reactions that occur in living matter. The ability of a protein to act as part of a structure, or as an enzyme affecting the rate of a particular chemical reaction, depends on its molecular shape. This shape, in turn, depends on its composition. Every protein is made up of one or more components called polypeptides, and each polypeptide is a chain of subunits called amino acids (q.v.). Twenty different amino acids are commonly found in polypeptides. The number, type, and order of amino acids in a chain ultimately determine the structure and function of the protein of which the chain is a part.

The genetic code. Since proteins were shown to be products of genes, and each gene was shown to be composed of sections of DNA strands, scientists reasoned that a genetic code must exist by which the order of the four nucleotide bases in the DNA could direct the sequence of amino acids in the formation of polypeptides. In other words, a process must exist by which the nucleotide bases transmit information that dictates protein synthesis. This process would explain how the genes control the forms and functions of cells, tissues, and organisms. Because only four different kinds of nucleotides occur in DNA, but 20 different kinds of amino acids occur in proteins, the genetic code could not be based on one nucleotide specifying one amino acid. Combinations of two nucleotides could only specify 16 amino acids ($4^2 = 16$), so the code must be made up of combinations of three or more successive nucleotides. The order of the triplets—or, as they came to be called, codons—could define the order of the amino acids in the polypeptide.

Ten years after Watson and Crick reported the DNA structure, the genetic code was worked out and proved biologically. Its solution depended on a great deal of research involving another group of nucleic acids, the ribonucleic acids (RNA). The specification of a polypeptide by the

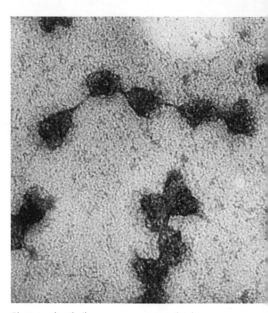

Photograph of ribosomes on a strand of messenger RNA. As the ribosomes move along the strand, translation of the genetic code takes place. Dr. Alexander Rich

DNA was found to take place indirectly, through an intermediate molecule known as messenger RNA (mRNA). Part of the DNA somehow uncoils from its chromosome packing, and the two strands become separated for a portion of their length. One of them serves as a template upon which the mRNA is formed (with the aid of an enzyme called RNA polymerase). The process is very similar to the formation of a complementary strand of DNA during the division of the double helix, except that RNA contains uracil (U) instead of thymine as one of its four nucleotide bases, and the uracil (which is similar to thymine) joins with the adenine in the formation of complementary pairs. Thus, a sequence adenine-guanine-adenine-thymine-cytostine (AGATC) in the coding strand of the DNA produces a sequence uracil-cytosine-uracil-adenine-guanine (UCUAG) in the mRNA.

Transcription. The production of a strand of messenger RNA by a particular sequence of DNA is called transcription. While the transcription is still taking place, the mRNA begins to detach from the DNA. Eventually one end of the new mRNA molecule, which is now a long, thin strand, becomes inserted into a small structure called a ribosome, in a manner much like the insertion of a thread into a bead. As the ribosome bead moves along the mRNA thread, the end of the thread may be inserted into a second ribosome, and so on. Using a very high-powered microscope and special staining techniques, scientists can photograph mRNA molecules with their associated ribosome beads.

Ribosomes are made up of protein and RNA. A group of ribosomes linked by mRNA is called a polyribosome or polysome. As each ribosome passes along the mRNA molecule, it "reads" the code, that is, the sequence of nucleotide bases on the mRNA. The reading, called translation, takes place by means of a third type of RNA molecule called transfer RNA (tRNA), which is produced on another segment of the DNA. On one side of the tRNA molecule is a triplet of nucleotides. On the other side is a region to which one specific amino acid can become attached (with the aid of a specific enzyme). The triplet on each tRNA is complementary to one particular sequence of three nucleotides—the codon—on the mRNA strand. Because of this complementarity, the triplet is able to "recognize" and adhere to the codon. For example, the sequence uracil-cytosine-uracil (UCU) on the strand of mRNA attracts the triplet adenine-guanine-adenine (AGA) of the tRNA. The tRNA triplet is known as the anticodon.

As tRNA molecules move up to the strand of mRNA in the ribosome beads, each bears an amino acid. The sequence of codons on the mRNA therefore determines the order in which the amino acids are brought by the tRNA to the ribosome. In association with the ribosome, the amino acids are then chemically bonded together into a chain, forming a polypeptide. The new chain of polypeptide is released from the ribosome and folds up into a characteristic shape that is determined by the sequence of amino acids. The shape of a polypeptide and its electrical properties, which are also determined by the amino acid sequence, dictate whether it remains single or becomes joined to other polypeptides, as well as what chemical function it subsequently fulfills within the organism.

In bacteria, viruses, and blue-green algae, the chromosome lies free in the cytoplasm, and the process of translation may start even before the process of transcription (mRNA formation) is completed. In higher organisms, however, the chromosomes are isolated in the nucleus and the ribosomes are contained only in the cytoplasm. Thus, translation of mRNA into protein can occur only after the mRNA has become detached from the DNA and has moved out of the nucleus.

Introns. A recent and unexpected discovery is that in higher organisms the genes are interrupted. Within the length of a sequence of nucleotides that codes a particular polypeptide may be one or more interruptions by noncoding sequences; within some genes as many as 50 of these intervening sequences, or introns, may be found. During transcription the introns are copied into RNA along with the coding sequences, producing an extra-large RNA molecule. The sequences corresponding to the introns are then exactly chopped out of the RNA, by special enzymes in the nucleus, to form the mRNA that is exported to the cytoplasm.

The functions (if any) of introns are not understood, although the suggestion has been made that the processing of RNA by chopping out the intervening sequences may be involved in regulating the quantity of polypeptide produced by the gene. Introns have also been found in genes that code for special RNAs, such as those that are components of the ribosomes. The discovery of introns was made possible by new methods of determining the exact sequence of nucleotides in molecules of DNA and RNA. These methods were developed by the British molecular biologist Frederick Sanger; for this work he received a second Nobel Prize in chemistry in 1980.

Repeated sequences. Direct studies of DNA have also shown that, in higher organisms, some sequences of nucleotides are repeated many times throughout the genetic material. Some of these repeated sequences represent multiple copies of genes that code polypeptides, or of genes that code special RNAs (almost always, there are many copies of genes that produce the RNA components of ribosomes). Other repeated sequences do not seem to code polypeptides or RNAs, and their function is unknown. Among them are sequences that seem able to jump from place to place in a chromosome, or from one chromosome to another. These "transposons," or transposable elements, may cause mutations (see below) in the genes adjacent to their points of arrival or departure.

Gene Regulation. Knowing how protein is made allows scientists to understand how genes can produce specific effects on the structures and functions of organisms. This does not explain, however, how organisms can change in response to changing environmental circumstances, or how a single zygote can give rise to all the different tissues and organs that make up a human being. Most of the cells in these tissues and organs contain identical sets of genes but nevertheless make different proteins; clearly, in the cells of any one tissue or organ some genes are acting but others are not. Different tissues have different arrays of genes in the active state. Thus, part of the explanation for the development of a complex organism must lie in the ways by which genes are specifically activated.

GENETICS

The processes of gene activation in higher organisms are still obscure, but through the work of the French geneticists François Jacob (1920–) and Jacques Lucien Monod, a good deal is known about these processes in bacteria. Near each bacterial gene is a segment of DNA known as the promoter. This is the site at which RNA polymerase, the enzyme responsible for the production of mRNA, sticks to the DNA and starts transcription. Between the promoter and the gene there is often a further segment of DNA called the operator, where another protein—the repressor—can stick. When the repressor is attached to the operator, it stops the RNA polymerase from moving along the chromosome and producing mRNA; consequently, the gene is inactive. The presence of a chemical substance in the cell, however, may cause the repressor to become detached and the gene to become active. Other substances may affect the degree of gene activity by altering the ability of the RNA polymerase to bind to the promoter. The repressor protein is produced by a gene called the regulator.

In bacteria several genes may be controlled simultaneously by one promoter and one or more operators. The entire system is then called an operon. Apparently, operons do not occur in complex organisms, but quite possibly each gene has its own individual system of promoters and operators, and introns and repeated sequences may also play a role.

Cytoplasmic Inheritance. Some constituents of the cell (q.v.) besides the nucleus contain DNA. They include the cytoplasmic bodies known as mitochondria (the energy producers of the cell) and the chloroplasts of plants, where photosynthesis (q.v.) takes place. These bodies are self-reproducing. The DNA is replicated in a manner similar to that in the nucleus, and sometimes its code is transcribed and translated into proteins. In 1981 the entire sequence of nucleotides in the DNA of a mitochondrion was determined; apparently, mitochondria use a code only slightly different from that used by the nucleus.

The traits determined by cytoplasmic DNA are more often inherited through the mother than through the father, because sperm and pollen usually contain less cytoplasmic material than do eggs. Some cases of apparent maternal inheritance are actually due to the transmission of viruses from mother to offspring through the egg cytoplasm.

Mutations. Although the replication of DNA is very precise, it is not uniformly perfect. Very rarely, mistakes do occur, and the new piece of DNA contains one or more changed nucleotides. A mistake of this kind, which is called a mutation (q.v.), may happen in any part of the DNA. If it occurs in the sequence of nucleotides that codes for a particular polypeptide, it may change an amino acid in the polypeptide chain. This change may seriously alter the properties of the resulting protein. For example, the polypeptides distinguishing normal hemoglobin and sickle-cell hemoglobin differ by only a single amino acid. When a mutation occurs during the formation of

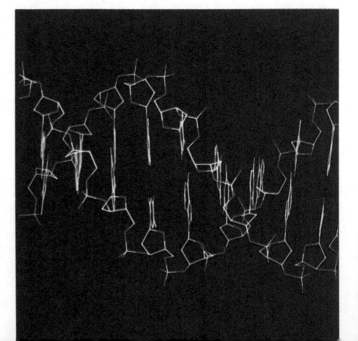

A computer-generated depiction of a small segment of a DNA molecule. The main units of the molecule form a double spiral, with cross-links.   Merck & Co., Inc.

gametes, it will be passed on to the following generation.

Gene mutation. Mutations were first reported in 1901 by the Dutch botanist Hugo De Vries, one of Mendel's rediscoverers. In 1929 the American biologist Hermann Joseph Muller found that the rate of mutation can be increased greatly by X rays. Later, other forms of radiation, as well as high temperatures and various chemicals, were also found to be capable of inducing mutations. The rate can also be increased by the presence of particular alleles of certain genes, known as mutator genes, some of which seem to cause defects in the mechanisms maintaining the fidelity of DNA replication. Others may be transposable elements (see above).

Most gene mutations are harmful to the organisms that carry them; the function of a complex system such as a protein is more easily destroyed than improved by a random change. Thus, the number of individuals carrying a particular mutant gene at any time is usually the consequence of two opposing forces: the tendency to increase because of the propagation of new mutant individuals in a population, and the tendency to decrease because mutant individuals survive or reproduce less well than their peers. Recent human activities have tended to make the increase larger by exposure to medical X rays, radioactive materials, and mutation-causing chemicals.

Mutations are usually recessive, and their harmful effects are not expressed unless two of them are brought together into the homozygous condition. This is most likely to occur as a result of inbreeding, the mating of closely related organisms that may have inherited the same recessive mutant gene from a common ancestor. For this reason, inherited diseases are more common among children whose parents are cousins than they are in the human population as a whole.

Chromosome mutations. The substitution of one nucleotide for another is not the only possible kind of mutation. Sometimes a nucleotide may be entirely lost or one may be gained. In addition, more dramatic and obvious changes may occur, or the chromosomes themselves may alter in form or number. A section of chromosome may become detached, turn over, and then reattach to the chromosome at the same site. This is called an inversion. If the detached section unites with a different chromosome, or a different part of the original chromosome, it is called a translocation. Sometimes a piece of chromosome will be lost from one member of a pair of homologous chromosomes and gained by the other member. One of the pair is then said to have a deficiency and the other a duplication. Deficiencies are usually lethal in the homozygous condition, and duplications are often so. Inversions and translocations are more frequently viable, although they may be associated with mutations in genes near the points where the chromosomes have been broken. Most of these chromosomal rearrangements are probably the consequences of errors in the process of crossing over.

Another kind of mutation occurs when a pair of homologous chromosomes fails to separate at meiosis. This can produce gametes—and hence zygotes—with extra chromosomes and others with one or more chromosomes missing. Individuals with an extra chromosome are known as trisomics, and those with a missing chromosome as monosomics. Both conditions tend to result in severe disabilities. People with Down's syndrome (q.v.), for example, are trisomics, with three copies of the 21st chromosome.

Sometimes an entire set of chromosomes may fail to separate at meiosis; thus, a gamete with twice the normal number of chromosomes is produced. If such a gamete fuses with one containing the normal number of chromosomes, the offspring will have three homologous sets rather than the normal two. If two gametes with twice the normal number fuse, the offspring will have four homologous sets. Organisms with additional sets of chromosomes are known as polyploids. Polyploidy is the only known process by which new species may arise in a single generation. Viable and fertile polyploids are found almost exclusively in hermaphroditic organisms, such as most flowering plants and some invertebrate animals. Plant polyploids are usually larger and sturdier in form than their normal diploid ancestors. Polyploid fetuses sometimes occur in humans, but they die at an early stage of fetal development and are aborted.

Genes in Populations. Population genetics, which investigates how genes spread through populations of organisms, was given a firm basis by the work of the English mathematician Godfrey H. Hardy (1877–1947) and the German obstetrician Wilhelm Weinberg (1862–1937). In 1908 they independently formulated what is now known as the Hardy-Weinberg law. This states that if two alleles of one autosomal gene (A and a) exist in a population, if their frequencies of occurrence (expressed in decimals) are p and q, respectively ($p + q = 1$), and if mating between individuals occurs at random with respect to the gene, then after one generation the frequencies of the three genotypes AA, Aa, and aa will be p^2, $2pq$, and q^2, respectively. These frequencies, in the absence of disturbances, will then remain constant from generation to generation. Any change of frequency, which signals an evolutionary change, must therefore be due to disturbances. These disturbances may include mutation, natural selection, migration, and breeding within small populations that may lose particular alleles by chance, or random genetic drift (*see* EVOLUTION).

Evidence indicates that most populations are a great deal more variable genetically than was supposed. Studies of the polypeptide products of genes have suggested that, on the average, about one-third of them have genetic variants at frequencies higher than could be expected from the balance between their generation by mutation and the selective disadvantage of the mutants. This has led to increased interest in the ways by which alternate alleles may be actively maintained in a state of balance so that neither replaces the other. One such balancing mechanism is heterozygous advantage, when the heterozygote survives better than either of the homozygotes. Another balancing mechanism, called frequency-dependent selection, depends on the relative advantage of rare varieties, for example, in populations subject to predators. Predators tend to concentrate on the variety that is common and to disregard rarer types. Thus, a variety can be at an advantage when it is rare but may begin to lose the advantage as natural selection for the protective trait makes it more common. Predators then begin to kill off the once-favored variety until at last an equilibrium is reached between the alleles in the population. Parasites may act in a similar fashion, becoming specialized to attack whichever is the commonest variety of host and thereby maintaining genetic variability in host populations.

Human Heredity. Most physical characteristics of humans are influenced by multiple genetic variables as well as by the environment. Some characteristics, such as height, have a relatively large genetic component. Others, such as body weight, have a relatively large environmental component. Still other characteristics, such as the blood groups (*see* BLOOD TYPE) and the antigens involved in the rejection of transplanted organs, appear to involve entirely genetic components; no environmental condition is known to change them. The transplantation antigens have recently been much studied because of their medical interest. The most important ones are produced by a group of linked genes known as the HLA complex. This group of genes not only determines whether transplanted organs will be accepted or rejected, it is also involved in the body's resistance to various diseases (including allergies, diabetes, and arthritis).

Susceptibility to various other diseases has an important genetic element. These diseases include schizophrenia, tuberculosis, malaria, several forms of cancer, migraine headaches, and high blood pressure. Many rare diseases are caused by recessive genes and a few by dominant genes.

The mapping of human genes to identify their position on particular chromosomes has proved difficult because the chromosomes are so numerous and because the time required to observe changes over generations is so lengthy. Recently, however, two useful techniques have been developed. The first, called chromosome banding, involves procedures that make each chromosome individually recognizable under the microscope. The second enables human cells grown in the laboratory to be fused with cells of another species, such as a mouse. Such hybrid cells have a tendency to lose chromosomes. When a chromosome is lost, the simultaneous loss of a polypeptide can sometimes be detected, thereby locating the gene for that polypeptide on a particular chromosome. With the use of these two methods, more than 200 human genes have been located.

See also GENE; GENETIC ENGINEERING; HEREDITY; HYBRID; MUTATION; NATURAL SELECTION; PLANT BREEDING. For additional information on individual scientists, see biographies of those whose names are not followed by dates.   B.C.C.

For further information on this topic, see the Bibliography in volume 28, sections 443–44, 449.

GENEVA, city, Ontario and Seneca counties, W New York, at the N end of Seneca Lake (one of the Finger Lakes); inc. as a city 1898. It is a farm-trade center; local industries manufacture processed food, printed materials, machinery, electronic equipment, and metal products. Geneva is the site of Hobart-William Smith Colleges (1822) and Rose Hill, a Greek Revival mansion built in 1839. The community, settled in the late 1780s, is named for Geneva, Switzerland. It grew after Seneca Lake was linked to the Hudson R. by the Erie Canal. Pop. (1980) 15,133; (1990) 14,143.

GENEVA (Fr. *Genève*; Ger. *Genf*), city, W Switzerland, capital of Geneva Canton, at the W extremity of Lake Geneva, where the Rhône R. issues from the lake. The Rhône divides Geneva into two almost equal parts. On the S, or left, bank stands the older part of the city, containing the financial and business districts, and two old residential districts, Eaux Vives and Carouge, the latter a working-class neighborhood. Narrow, crooked streets penetrate the old quarter everywhere except along the river bank, which contains broad avenues and modern quays. The

A scenic view along the Rhône River at Geneva. The river divides the city into two almost equal parts.

Rhône is spanned by several bridges, one of which traverses a small island, Rousseau's Island. The N, or right, bank is principally residential, containing the Quartier Saint-Gervais, in which are located large hotels; and the Les Délices district, containing the house of the same name in which the French writer and philosopher Voltaire lived from 1755 to 1758. The entire city is encompassed by boulevards laid out on the site of the ancient city walls.

Geneva contains many parks and squares, notably the Jardin Anglais and the Place Neuve on the left bank, and the Place des Alpes on the right bank. The principal buildings in the old section include the Romanesque Cathedral of Saint Peter, built in the 10th and 11th centuries; the Florentine-style city hall, erected in the 16th century; the Temple de l'Auditoire, where the Scottish religious reformer John Knox preached and the French theologian John Calvin taught; the 18th-century house where the French philosopher Jean Jacques Rousseau was born; the Rath Museum, containing an immense art collection; and the Museum of Natural History. Educational institutions in the city include the University of Geneva (founded as the Collège de Genève by Calvin in 1559) and various industrial and technical schools, of which the École d'Horlogerie (School of Watchmaking) is particularly prominent. Watchmaking and the manufacture of jewelry have contributed to making Geneva an important manufacturing center. Other industries include enameling, the production of music boxes and scientific instruments, and diamond cutting. Geneva is also an important banking and financial center.

Center of Diplomacy. Geneva became a world center in 1920 with the founding of the League of Nations, which established its headquarters in the city. Several important conferences took place in Geneva between the two world wars, notably the Naval Disarmament Conference in 1927 and the World Disarmament Conference of 1932. The departure of the League of Nations in 1939 dealt a serious economic blow to Geneva, from which it slowly recovered during World War II. In 1947 Geneva was designated the European center for the UN, and in 1948 the International Labor Organization and the World Health Organization, followed by other international agencies, set up headquarters here. Geneva has remained a site for international diplomatic confrontations, notably the Asia Conference of 1954, concerning the disposition of Indochina, and the Geneva Summit Conference of 1955, at which the reunification of Germany was discussed. Beginning in 1962, several nations conducted disarmament negotiations in Geneva.

History. Before the Roman conquest of Gaul, Geneva was the northernmost city of the Allobroges, who became part of the Roman Empire in 121 BC. It became an episcopal seat in the 4th century, was conquered by the Burgundians in the 5th century, and eventually came under Frankish rule. In the first half of the 11th century Geneva was incorporated into the Holy Roman Empire. The ruling power of the city was conferred upon a prince-bishop, and the counts of Geneva were made feudal vassals. The Genevans, however, were unwilling to accept the bishop's authority and, desiring municipal independence, applied for help in the early 14th century to Amadeus VI, count of Savoy. From that time on, Geneva became the object of struggle between the citizens themselves, the counts of Savoy, the counts of Geneva, and the bishops of Geneva. The Reformation finally brought the city its independence; in 1536, the Genevans declared themselves Protestant and proclaimed their city a republic. John Calvin was invited to take up residence in Geneva. The city began to acquire a great influence over Protestant Europe and became the center of education for Protestant youth from many countries. During the French Revolution, aristocratic and democratic factions contended for control of Geneva. In 1798, however, France, then under the Directory, annexed Geneva and its surrounding territory. After the overthrow of Napoleon, Geneva recovered its independence, and in 1815, was admitted to the Swiss Confederation. The Congress of Vienna in 1815 increased its territory and guaranteed its neutrality. From 1841 to 1878, the history of the city was one of political strife, but democratic elements eventually triumphed. The referendum was introduced in 1879, and in 1891 the initiative and recall were introduced. In 1907, by a referendum, the state and church were separated, and the theocracy, which had generally controlled Geneva, became a minor political factor. Pop. (1986 est.) 159,895.

For further information on this topic, see the Bibliography in volume 28, section 996.

GENEVA, LAKE, also Lac Léman *or* Lake Leman (Ger. *Genfersee*), largest lake in central Europe, about 583 sq km (about 225 sq mi) in area, straddling the border between Switzerland and France. The largest part of the lake, about 363 sq km (about 140 sq mi), is in W Switzerland. The two most populous lakeside cities, Geneva and Lausanne, are in Switzerland; on the French side are the notable spas Thonon-les-Bains and Évian-les-Bains. Shaped like a crescent, the lake lies about 380 m (about 1250 ft) above sea level. It is 72 km (45 mi) long, varies from about 2.4 to 13 km (about 1.5 to 8 mi) in width, and has a maximum depth of about 310 m (about 1015 ft). The Rhône R. enters the lake at its E end and issues from it at the W extremity; the deposits of the Rhône at its point of issue have contracted the lake area considerably, towns and villages once on the shore now being miles inland. About 20 small streams flow into the lake, which is surrounded by the Alps on the S and E and the Jura Mts. on the N and W. Lake Geneva is frequently subject to the phenomena known as seiches, which occasion a rise and fall of about 0.6 to 1.5 m (about 2 to 5 ft) in depth in the course of half an hour; these phenomena are said to be caused by variances in atmospheric pressure on different parts of the surface of the water.

GENEVA, UNIVERSITY OF, institution of higher learning, in Geneva. The university is under the jurisdiction of the department of instruction of the canton and is also financed by the state. Founded in 1559 by the French theologian and reformer John Calvin as Schola Genevensis, the Academy of Geneva (also known as Calvin's Academy) became noted for the teaching of Protestant, and particularly Calvinistic, doctrines. Incorporated as a university in 1873, it comprises faculties of science, letters, economics and social science, law, medicine, Protestant theology, and psychology and educational sciences. It grants the licentiate and doctoral degrees, which are roughly equivalent to the U.S. degrees of master and doctor.

GENEVA CONVENTIONS. *See* RED CROSS.

GENEVIÈVE, Saint (c. 422–c. 500), patron saint of Paris, born in nearby Nanterre, France. She decided on a life of religious devotion at an early age. In 451 she was in Paris and is said to have predicted the invasion of the Huns led by Attila and to have saved the city by her prayers. By tradition she is credited with the conversion to Christianity of Clovis I, king of the Franks, and, through him, his entire nation. On her death, St. Geneviève was buried at Mont-les-Paris, in the Church of Saints Peter and Paul, which came to be known as the Church of Saint Geneviève. Louis XV, king of France, erected a new church in her memory in 1764; in 1793, during the French Revolution, the government changed this church into the Panthéon, where busts of famous Frenchmen are enshrined. Her traditional feast day is January 3.

GENGHIS KHAN, original name Temujin (1167?–1227), Mongol conqueror, whose nomad armies created a vast empire under his control, from China to Russia. He was born near Lake Baykal in Russia, the son of Yesukai (d. 1180?), a Mongol chief and ruler of a large region between the Amur River and the Great Wall of China. At the age of 13, Temujin succeeded his father as tribal chief. His early reign was marked by successive revolts of his subject tribes and an intense struggle to retain his leadership, but the Mongol ruler soon demonstrated his military genius and conquered not only his intractable subjects but his hostile neighbors as well. By 1206 Temujin was master of almost all of Mongolia. In that year, a convocation of the subjugated tribes proclaimed him Genghis Khan (Chin. *chêng-sze,* "precious warrior"; Turk. *khān,* "lord"), leader of the united Mongol and Tatar tribes; the city of Karakorum was designated his capital.

The khan then began his conquest of China. By 1208 he had established a foothold inside the Great Wall, and in 1213 he led his armies south and west into the area dominated by the Juchen Chin (or Kin) dynasty (1122–1234), not stopping until he reached the Shantung Peninsula. In 1215 his armies captured Yenking (now Peking), the last Chin stronghold in northern China, and in 1218 the Korean Peninsula fell to the Mongols.

In 1219, in retaliation for the murder of some

Genghis Khan

Mongol traders, Genghis Khan turned his armies westward, invading Khoresm, a vast Turkish empire that included modern Iraq, Iran, and part of Western Turkestan. Looting and massacring, the Mongols swept through Turkestan and sacked the cities of Bukhara and Samarkand. In what are now northern India and Pakistan, the invaders conquered the cities of Peshawar and Lahore and the surrounding countryside. In 1222 the Mongols marched into Russia and plundered the region between the Volga and Dnepr rivers and from the Persian Gulf almost to the Arctic Ocean.

The greatness of the khan as a military leader was borne out not only by his conquests but by the excellent organization, discipline, and maneuverability of his armies. Moreover, the Mongol ruler was an admirable statesman; his empire was so well organized that, so it was claimed, travelers could go from one end of his domain to the other without fear or danger. At his death, on Aug. 18, 1227, the Mongol Empire (q.v.) was divided among his three sons and gradually dissipated. Four of his grandsons, however, became great Mongol leaders in their own right. Genghis Khan's invasions were of great historical importance long after his death, for the Turks, who fled before him, were driven to their own invasion of Europe.

GENIE. *See* JINNI.

GENITAL ORGANS. *See* REPRODUCTIVE SYSTEM.

GENIUS, in Roman mythology, a protecting, or guardian, spirit. It was believed that every individual, family, and city had its own genius. The genius received special worship as a household god because it was thought to bestow success and intellectual powers on its devotees. For this reason, the word came to designate a person with unusual intellectual powers. The genius of a woman was sometimes referred to as a juno. In art, the genius of a person was frequently depicted as a winged youth; the genius of a place, as a serpent.

GENOA (Ital. *Genova;* anc. *Genua*), city, NW Italy, capital of Genoa Province, in Liguria Region, a seaport on the Gulf of Genoa (an arm of the Ligurian Sea). The city lies beside a fine natural harbor at the foot of a pass in the W Apennines. It rivals Marseille, France, as the leading European port of the Mediterranean Sea and is the commercial center of the heavily industrialized sections of Piedmont and Lombardy, the rich agricultural regions of N Italy and of central Europe. The harbor facilities, which were heavily damaged during World War II, have been expanded and modernized. Shipbuilding is the leading industry of Genoa. Other important industries are the manufacture of iron and steel products, motors and automotive parts, refrigeration equipment, munitions, chemicals, soap, and the processing of agricultural products. Processing plants include sugar and edible-oil refineries, canneries, tanneries, breweries, and distilleries.

The old quarter of the city covers a narrow strip of coastal plain E and N of the old port, which was enlarged in modern times by the addition of an outer harbor protected by breakwaters. Industrial and residential sections were developed E and W along the shore and on the hills back of the old port. In the heart of the old quarter is the Romanesque-Gothic Church of San Donato, dating from the 12th and 13th centuries, and, on the harbor front, is the Palazzo San Giorgio, which was built in the 14th century by order of the first Genoese doge, Simone Boccanegra (1300?–63), and which later became the seat of the powerful Bank of Saint George.

Work on the Cathedral of San Lorenzo in Genoa was begun, according to some accounts, with the first rich booty from the Crusades. The cathedral, consecrated in 1118, contains a wealth of art treasures. The massive 16th-century Palazzo Ducale, former residence of the doges, now houses the law courts. On the Piazza San Matteo are the houses of the Doria family and the Church of San Matteo, founded by the family in 1125 and containing the tomb of the Genoese admiral and statesman Andrea Doria. Toward the NW, near the Stazione Marittima, at which ocean liners dock, stands the 13th-century Church of the Annunziata, noteworthy for its interior containing many fine works of art. The birthplace of Christopher Columbus is also among the historic places of Genoa. The city is the seat of the University of Genoa (1471).

History. Genoa's history goes far back into ancient times. A city cemetery, dating from the 4th century BC, testifies to the occupation of the site by the Greeks, but the fine harbor probably was in use much earlier. Destroyed by the Carthaginians in 209 BC, the town was rebuilt by the Romans, who used it as a base during their wars with the Ligurians (*see* LIGURIA). Under the Romans, the city enjoyed municipal rights and exported skins, wood, and honey.

Little is known of Genoese history from the fall of the Roman Empire (476) until the 11th century, by which time the city had become a maritime republic governed by consuls. Genoa then contributed ships to the campaign against Saracen corsairs in Italian waters. The Genoese, in alliance with Pisa, eventually drove the Saracens from settlements on the islands of Corsica

The harbor of Genoa, probably an important Mediterranean port as early as the time of the ancient Greeks.
Italian State Tourist Office

and Sardinia, which thereafter became prizes in a long naval war between the two city-states. In the 12th century the Genoese extended their mastery over the adjacent coast and nearby mountain valleys and laid the foundations of future naval greatness and prosperity. Genoese ships transported Crusaders to the Middle East and returned laden with booty. Genoese merchants, profiting from the newly awakened European demand for goods from the Middle East, were to be found in all the principal centers of trade. Genoese forts and trading posts spread through the eastern Mediterranean and the Aegean seas and eventually into the Black Sea. Their trade, facilitated by friendly relations with the Byzantine Empire, brought Genoa and Venice into increasing rivalry, which broke into open warfare in the mid-13th century, just as Genoese power reached its height. At the Battle of Meloria (1284), Genoa crushed Pisa, the power of which thereafter declined; the Venetians were defeated at Curzola in 1299. The oligarchy of prosperous merchants and bankers that had ruled the Genoese Republic after 1257 subsequently dealt on equal terms with the courts of popes and kings. Genoese expansion, in fact, had been largely the work of citizens whose primary concern was the advancement of their private interests. As a result, the city was torn between factions contending for control of the government. The rival groups did not hesitate to call in outside powers to aid them. Even the dogeship, the institution of first magistrate, established in 1339, was unable to master the ensuing disorders. Although the struggle sapped Genoese strength, and despite continued bitter rivalry with Venice, the Genoese largely held their own for several decades. In 1380, however, their fleet fell into Venetian hands at Chioggia, a blow from which their naval power never recovered. Venice drew far ahead, and Genoese overseas possessions were lost one by one, although the last, Corsica, was held until 1768, when it was ceded to France. Internal strife finally ended under the rigid dogeship that Andrea Doria had established with the help of the Holy Roman emperor in 1528, and Genoa prospered as a shipbuilding port and banking center.

Although powerful neighbors, France and Piedmont, dominated the city, Genoese independence was respected until 1797, when Napoleon Bonaparte abolished the dogeship and incorporated Genoa into the newly organized Ligurian Republic, which in turn was absorbed by the French Empire in 1805. The city was annexed by the kingdom of Sardinia in 1815. In the last quarter of the 19th century the port of Genoa was widened and modernized, and the city at-

tracted a variety of industries that process imported raw materials and goods for export. During World War II repeated bombings heavily damaged the industrial sections and harbor of the city. Pop. (1988 est.) 722,000.

For further information on this topic, see the Bibliography in volume 28, section 961.

GENOCIDE, in international law, the crime of destroying, or committing conspiracy to destroy, a national, ethnic, racial, or religious group. It was thus defined in the Convention on Prevention and Punishment of the Crime of Genocide, which was adopted by the UN General Assembly on Dec. 9, 1948.

The crime of genocide has been committed or attempted many times in recorded history. The best-known example in this century was the systematic effort carried on by Nazi Germany during the 1930s and '40s to destroy the Jewish population of Europe. By the end of World War II some 6 million Jews had been killed in Nazi concentration camps.

At the 1945 war crimes trials (q.v.), the Nuremberg Tribunal established the principle of individual accountability of those who were responsible for carrying out Nazi extermination policies. The following year, the UN General Assembly drafted the convention to outlaw the practice of genocide.

The preamble to the convention declares that in all periods of history "genocide has inflicted great losses on humanity," and that it is the aim of the contracting parties to eliminate genocide through international cooperation. The first article of the convention declares genocide a crime whether committed in time of peace or war. The second and third articles define genocide in detail. The fourth article establishes the principle that punishment for genocide shall apply to guilty "constitutionally responsible rulers," public officials, and private individuals. The fifth article imposes on the signatory nations the obligation of enacting legislation to give effect to the provisions of the convention and to provide suitable penalties for persons found guilty.

Other articles exclude genocide from the category of political crimes and explicitly deny to persons accused of genocide immunity from extradition; they also provide that persons accused of genocide shall be tried "by a competent tribunal of the state in which the act was committed," or by such international tribunal as may have the necessary jurisdiction.

GENRE PAINTING, type of painting concerned with the realistic depiction of scenes from everyday life. Originally the term was applied to all paintings that were factual representations of na-

Woman and Child in a Courtyard *(c. 1660), painting by Pieter de Hooch.*
National Gallery of Art, Washington–Widener Collection

ture (animals, fruit, and landscapes), as well as scenes of ordinary life, rather than to works of imagination, such as religious and historical paintings. Genre paintings deal with ordinary life, including family life, sports, street scenes, picnics, festivals, and tavern scenes. They are usually characterized by human interest and by the care and finish with which they are executed.

Early Genre Painting. Genre painting originated in ancient times. Many of the scenes painted on the walls of Egyptian tombs represent the daily life of the people of ancient Egypt. Excavations in the ancient cities of Pompeii and Herculaneum (qq.v.) have revealed many genre paintings, both conventional and erotic. In the late Middle Ages genre painting reappeared, represented chiefly in the religious calendars that formed part of the illuminations, or illustrations, of manuscript books; the calendars show people going about the occupations appropriate to each season of the year (see ILLUMINATED MANUSCRIPTS).

In Italy during the early Renaissance, many of the religious and historical pictures of such painters as the 15th-century Florentines Ghirlandaio and Benozzo Gozzoli and the later Vene-

tians Giorgione and the Bassano family are considered genre paintings because of their contemporaneous backgrounds and costumes as well as their use of people of the times as models. In 17th-century Italy, Mannerist painters such as Caravaggio executed genre paintings of extreme realism and dramatic power.

In the 15th century the Flemish painter Petrus Christus (c. 1420–73) in some of his religious paintings represented scenes from ordinary life, and in the following two centuries genre painting rose to its highest level in history with the work of the Flemish artists Pieter Brueghel the Elder, David Teniers, and Adriaen Brouwer.

Dutch Genre Painting. The greatest national school of genre painting was that of the Netherlands in the 17th century. Probably never before or after was the ordinary life of a nation depicted so fully as was the Dutch life of this period. Not only the great masters but also the less outstanding Dutch painters excelled in it. The most important of the Dutch genre painters were the so-called little masters, including Gerard Ter Borch, Jan Steen, Gabriel Metsu, Pieter de Hooch, Gerard Dou, and Adriaen van Ostade. The three leading 17th-century Dutch masters, Rembrandt, Frans Hals, and Jan Vermeer, also created genre paintings of unrivaled beauty.

Later Genre Painting. French genre painting showed a vital development in the work of Antoine Watteau, Nicolas Lancret, Jean Baptiste Chardin, and Jean Honoré Fragonard. One of the most noted English genre painters was the great satirist William Hogarth.

In the 19th century, genre painting was widely practiced in both Europe and the U.S. Among the outstanding European painters in this style were the French painters Jean Léon Gérôme (1824–1904) and Jean Meissonier (1815–91), the English painter William Powell Frith (1819–1909), and the American painter William Sidney Mount, known as the "Jan Steen of Long Island." Among the many 19th- and 20th-century American painters whose work included genre painting were Robert Henri, John Sloan, George Wesley Bellows, George B. Luks, Charles E. Burchfield, Reginald Marsh, Grant Wood, and Thomas Hart Benton. For additional information on individual artists, see biographies of those whose names are not followed by dates.

GENS, in anthropology, a term referring to the descent of a group of people from common ancestors through the paternal line. Usually this group is somewhat larger than an extended family, but it shares a common or family name. The term *gens* was first introduced into anthropological usage in the late 18th century to replace *clan* (q.v.). Today, however, it is not used extensively.

GENS (Lat., "race," "tribe," or "male line of descent"; from *genere,* "to beget"), term occasionally used by the ancient Romans to designate a community, the members of which were not necessarily connected by any known ties of blood, although it is likely that such a connection was taken for granted.

Gens had a more specific meaning, however, in the constitutional law of ancient Rome. According to one ancient authority, Publius Mucius Scaevola (fl. 2d cent. BC), those persons alone belonged to the same gens who bore the same gentile name, were born freemen, had no slaves among their progenitors, and had suffered no degradation in social status. The gens, which usually owned a burial place for its members, embraced all who could trace their descent through the male line to a common ancestor, whom they all worshiped. The middle of the three names customarily borne by a Roman was that of his gens. In early times, membership in a gens was a condition of Roman citizenship, and the gens was a political unit, a subdivision of a curia, which in turn was part of a tribe. According to tradition, the ancient Romans were divided into 3 tribes and 30 curiae by Romulus, founder of Rome. Originally, only members of the patrician class bore the gentile name, but in time it was extended to the plebeians. Gens and clan are sometimes used synonymously.

GENSERIC. *See* GAISERIC.

GENTIAN, common name for a family of flowering plants, the Gentianaceae, containing about 74 genera and 1200 species, and for its representative genus, *Gentiana.* The family is mainly a temperate group. *G. acaulis,* a perennial herb with dark blue flowers, is native to the Alps and Pyrenees and cultivated as an ornamental. Some members of the family, for example, the genera *Voyria* and *Bartonia,* are saprophytes (plants that absorb dead organic matter for their food).

The family belongs to the order Gentianales. Members of the order usually have simple (undivided) leaves that are opposite each other on the stem and flowers with four or five petals united

The gentian family contains many blue-flowered species. Shown here is the bottle gentian, also known as the closed, or blind, gentian, Gentiana andrewsii.
Grant Heilman Photography

into a floral tube, or corolla. The ovary is usually superior—that is, borne above and free from other floral parts—and is composed of two fused carpels (ovule- or egg-bearing floral parts). Most families in the order have food-conducting tissue (phloem) located in the usual position external to the water-conducting tissue (xylem) but also internal to it; this unusual feature helps to distinguish the order.

The order contains four other families. The two largest are the milkweed (q.v.) family, Asclepiadaceae, and the dogbane (q.v.) family, Apocynaceae, each having about 2000 species. Flowers in the milkweed family characteristically bear pollen in waxy sacs produced by anthers fused around the gynoecium (female flower organ). Included in the Asclepiadaceae are the commonly cultivated milkweeds and butterfly weeds as well as many cultivated succulents. Among the members of the dogbane family are some that yield important drugs and rubber. Ornamentals include periwinkle (q.v.), *Vinca;* oleander (q.v.), *Nerium;* and frangipani, *Plumeria.* The only other large family in the order is the Loganiaceae, with about 500 species, including many poisonous plants (*see* STRYCHNOS) and the Carolina, or yellow, jasmine. The remaining family, the Saccifoliaceae, contains a single species, *Saccifolium bandeirae,* a small shrub native to Guyana.

Plants of the order Gentianales are members of the class Magnoliopsida (*see* DICOTS) in the division Magnoliophyta (*see* ANGIOSPERM). M.R.C.

For further information on this topic, see the Bibliography in volume 28, sections 451–52, 592–93.

GENTILE, Giovanni (1875–1944), Italian philosopher, political leader, and educator, born in Castelvetrano, Sicily. Educated at Pisa, he taught there and at Palermo and Rome. Gentile was a dedicated supporter of the Fascist movement, serving as Benito Mussolini's minister of education (1922–24) and also as a member of the Fascist Grand Council. He was killed in Florence by Italian Communists on April 15, 1944.

Gentile was directing editor (1925–37) of the *Enciclopedia italiana,* and his major individual works include *The Theory of the Mind as Pure Act* (1916; trans. 1922), *Sistema di logica come teoria del conoscere* (System of Logic as Theory of Knowing, 1917), and *The Philosophy of Art* (1931; trans. 1972). Gentile's theory of active idealism stressed the importance of the act of thinking in the articulation of an individual's experience. P.Fu.

GENTILE DA FABRIANO (c. 1370–1427), Italian painter in the International Gothic style. Origi-

nally named Gentile di Niccolò di Giovanni di Massio, he was born in Fabriano, Ancona Province. Much of his work has been lost, but what remains shows the influence of the French and Flemish version of the International Gothic style then current in Lombardy. His work is characterized by sparkling color and graceful figures with animated and smiling faces. Gentile was active in a number of Italian cities. In Venice in 1411 he executed frescoes for the Ducal Palace and greatly influenced Pisanello and the early Venetian school. In Florence in 1423 he painted his masterpiece, *Adoration of the Magi* (Uffizi), and in Rome in 1427 he painted frescoes illustrating the life of Saint John the Baptist (Saint John Lateran) and the Holy Family (Santa Maria Maggiore). Other important paintings are *Madonna in Glory* (Brera, Milan), *Presentation in the Temple* (Louvre, Paris), and *Madonna with Saints* (Berlin Museum).

GENTILESCHI, surname of two Italian baroque painters, who were father and daughter.

Orazio Gentileschi (1562?–1639), originally named Orazio Lomi, born in Pisa. Gentileschi worked in Rome, where he executed murals for a number of palaces; in Genoa; and after 1626 in England, where King Charles I and George Villiers, duke of Buckingham, were his patrons. Among Gentileschi's paintings, noted for their vivid color but considered weak in design, are *David After the Death of Goliath* (Palazzo Doria, Genoa), *Saints Cecilia and Valerian* (Palazzo Borghese, Rome), *Joseph and Potiphar's Wife* (Hampton Court, England), and *Flight into Egypt* (Louvre, Paris).

Artemisia Gentileschi (c. 1593–1651), born in Rome. She studied with her father and with the celebrated painter of the school of Bologna, Guido Reni. About 1638 she visited England, where she won renown as a portrait painter. Gentileschi was one of the few artists of her time to experiment with paintings of night scenes, of which her *Lot and His Daughters* (Galleria Borghese, Rome) is a prime example. Among her other paintings, noted for their skillful use of chiaroscuro (light and dark contrasts), are a self-portrait (Hampton Court), *Mary Magdalen* (Pitti Gallery, Florence), and *Christ Among the Doctors* (New York Historical Society, New York City).

GENTOFTE, municipality, E Denmark, on Sjaelland Island, in Copenhagen Co. Part of metropolitan Copenhagen, it is chiefly residential and contains some light manufacturing industries. Pop. (1990 est.) 65,300.

GENUS, in biology, category of classification of living things; specifically, a group of species (*see*

The Adoration of the Magi, *by Gentile de Fabriano.*

SPECIES AND SPECIATION) closely related in structure and evolutionary origin. The position of a genus, in classification of the kingdoms of living forms, is below family (q.v.) or subfamily, and above species.

A genus name always differs from the name used for any other genus of living forms. An organism is named by assigning it a binomial, consisting of a genus name followed by a species name. In the scientific name of the tiger lily, *Lilium tigrinum,* for example, *Lilium* is the genus name and *tigrinum* is the species name. In zoological nomenclature, the genus and species names may be identical; the gorilla, for example, is *Gorilla gorilla.* In botanical nomenclature, the genus name may never be assigned as a species name. The scientific name applied to a family is always a modification of the name of one of the genera; the genus involved is termed the type genus. *See* CLASSIFICATION; TAXONOMY.

GEOCHEMISTRY, the application of chemical principles and techniques to geologic studies, to understand how chemical elements are distributed in the crust, mantle, and core of the earth. Over a period of several billion years, chemical differentiation of the earth's crust has created vast rafts of silica-rich rocks, the continents, which float on iron- and magnesium-rich rocks of the ocean basins. *See also* SILICON.

In its emphasis on the chemical composition of earth materials, geochemistry overlaps with several other branches of earth science, notably mineralogy, petrology, and the study of ore deposits. Pioneering work in the field was done early in the 20th century by Scandinavian petrologists such as V. M. Goldschmidt (1888–1947) and P. Eskola (1883–1964), who established the principles governing chemical changes that rocks undergo during metamorphism (*see* METAMORPHIC ROCK). In 1921, using new techniques such as X-ray diffraction, Goldschmidt devised the modern geochemical classification of the elements. Published in the interval from 1925 to 1940, as the 8-volume *Geochemical Laws of the Distribution of Elements,* his work laid the basis for the science of crystal chemistry. Over the past 30 years, geochemistry has taken on an increasingly practical aspect in response to heightened public awareness of environmental problems.

Environmental Geochemistry. Among the various branches of earth science, environmental geochemistry is unique in focusing directly on public health issues related to the environment. Trace elements, normally present in minute amounts in rocks, soil, and water, are a major influence on health. Some are essential to growth and metabolism (*see* NUTRITION, HUMAN); others are toxic; and some are beneficial in minute quantities but toxic if concentrated (*see* LOCOWEED).

The type of bedrock beneath the soil in an area helps determine the kinds of trace elements in the water and vegetation of the area. Geochemical analyses of soil, water, and plants indicate how trace elements are distributed. These findings may have serious health implications, revealing, for example, correlations between trace-element distribution and incidence of cardiovascular disease. *See also* SOIL: *Soil Chemistry*; WATER POLLUTION.

Geochemical studies also provide data with which to assess the health hazards of toxic elements and carcinogenic minerals. Selenium is especially harmful to wildlife in heavily irrigated areas, and indoor radon (q.v.) has become a major health concern because it increases the risk of lung cancer. Data on the health effects of the various asbestos (q.v.) minerals suggest enough variation in carcinogenicity to warrant greater discrimination in state and federal regulations governing the use and disposal of these minerals.

Exploration Geochemistry. Rudimentary forms of geochemical prospecting for ore deposits, as described by the German Scientist Georgius Agricola in his *De Re Metallica* (1556), have been practiced since the 8th and 9th century AD. Modern methods of exploration geochemistry begin with systematic collection of samples of soil, rock, vegetation, and water. Data obtained by analysis of the samples is now interpreted using computer programs written specifically for this purpose. In current world markets, with the price of most nonferrous metals at an all-time low, exploration for metallic mineral deposits is confined largely to precious metals, and the chief targets of geochemical prospecting are gold and platinum-group metals.

For further information on this topic, see the Bibliography in volume 28, section 419.

GEODE, in geology, a more or less spherical structure, several centimeters wide, found in limestones and shales. A geode first formed as a cavity with walls composed of the cryptocrystalline quartz called chalcedony (q.v.). As water passed through the cavity, the dissolved minerals slowly lined the hollow, so that geodes are often partly filled with colorful layers of quartz, sometimes with sulfide minerals as the innermost layer. *See also* AGATE.

GEODESIC DOME. *See* DOME.

GEODETIC SURVEYING. *See* SURVEYING.

GEOFFREY OF MONMOUTH (c. 1100–54), English historian and ecclesiastic. He was the author of *Historia Regum Britanniae* (History of the Kings of Britain), a work purporting to delineate the lives of British kings from Brutus the Trojan, the mythical progenitor of the British people, to Caedwalla, king of North Wales (r. about 625–34). Although the work is known to have existed as early as 1139, copies now extant are believed to date from 1147. The history is based on the writings of the early British chroniclers Gildas and Nennius and on popular legends, but includes much fictitious material, including the first extensive collection of tales dealing with King Arthur, which afterward formed the basis for the Arthurian legend. Geoffrey earned the patronage of Robert, earl of Gloucester (fl. 1100–47), and was named archdeacon of Llandaff about 1140 and bishop of Saint Asaph in 1152.

GEOGRAPHICAL SOCIETIES, organizations with the express aim of encouraging, and in some cases planning and financially supporting, geographic research and expeditions. They preceded university departments of geography, and functioned as centers in which journeys and explorations were planned, talks were given, and periodicals were published. Geographical societies have been established in many countries in all parts of the world. They may be of private or government sponsorship; most publish periodicals or journals, and some also publish maps. The earliest societies include Paris (1821), Berlin (1827), Mexico (1833), Frankfurt (1836), Brazil (1838), the Imperial Russian Geographical Society (1845), and the Finnish Geographical Society (1888). The Royal Geographical Society (1830) in Great Britain and the American Geographical and Statistical Society (1851) in the U.S. are among those that publish notable scholarly journals. The National Geographic Society (1888) has achieved a wide popularity with its publications, films, and maps. Other significant U.S. societies are the Association of American Geographers (1904) and the American Society for Professional Geographers (1943). Of lesser standing, but still significant in the development of geography in the U.S. were the Appalachian Mountain Club (1876), the Geographic Society of the Pacific (1881; since 1890, the Geographical Society of California), the Geographical Society of Philadelphia (1891), the Sierra Club (1892), the Mazamas (1894), the Geographical Society of Chicago (1889), the Alaska Geographical Society (1898), the Harvard Travellers Club (1902), and the American Alpine Club (1902). The most prominent international geographical organization, the International Geographical

Union (1922), sponsors commissions and working groups and arranges quadrennial international geographical congresses.   G.J.M.

GEOGRAPHIC DISTRIBUTION OF ANIMALS. *See* ANIMAL DISTRIBUTION.

GEOGRAPHIC EXPLORATION. *See* EXPLORATION, GEOGRAPHIC.

GEOGRAPHY, science that deals with the spatial distribution of all phenomena on the earth's surface. The word *geography* was adopted in the 3d century BC by the Greek scholar Eratosthenes and means "earth description." Geographic study encompasses the environment of the surface of the earth and the relationship of humans to this environment, which includes both physical and cultural geographic features. Physical geographic features include the climate, land and water, and plant and animal life. Cultural geographic features include artificial entities, such as nations, settlements, lines of communication, transportation, buildings, and other modifications of the physical geographic environment. Geographers make use of the disciplines of economics, history, systematic botany, geology, and mathematics in their studies.

BRANCHES OF GEOGRAPHY

The science may be divided into two fundamental branches: systematic and regional geography. Systematic geography is concerned with individual physical and cultural phenomena. Regional geography is concerned with various areas of the surface of the earth for the purpose of determining the peculiar combinations of physical and cultural features that characterize each region and distinguish one region from another. Because the division is based only on a difference in approach to geographic studies, the two branches are interdependent and ordinarily are combined in practical applications. Each branch is further subdivided into several fields to permit specialization in particular aspects of the comprehensive study.

Systematic Geography. This branch encompasses the major classifications of physical geography and cultural geography. Each classification comprises the specialized fields dealing with the spatial aspects of specific phenomena, rather than with the phenomena, per se, that constitute the focus of disciplines other than geography.

Physical geography. Physical geography includes the following fields: geomorphology, allied to geology (q.v.) and dealing with the form and structure of the surface of the earth; climatology, allied to meteorology (q.v.) and concerned with climatic conditions; biogeography, allied to biology (q.v.) and dealing with plant and animal life; soils geography, allied to podology (*see* SOIL;

SOIL MANAGEMENT) and concerned with the distribution of soil; hydrography, allied to hydrology and dealing with the distribution of seas, lakes, rivers, and streams in relation to the utilization of their waters; oceanography, which deals with the waves, tides, and currents of oceans and the ocean floor (*see* OCEAN AND OCEANOGRAPHY); and cartography, allied to mathematics and geodesy and dealing with graphic representation and measurement of the surface of the earth.

Cultural geography. This classification, sometimes called human geography, embraces virtually all phases of human social life in relation to the physical earth. Economic geography deals with the industrial use of the geographic environment. Natural resources, such as mineral and oil deposits, forests, grazing lands, and farmlands, are studied with reference to their situation, productivity, and potential. Manufacturing industries rely on geographic studies for information concerning raw materials, labor, supply, and ease of distribution. Marketing studies concerned with plant locations and sales potential are based on geographic considerations. The establishment of transportation facilities, trade routes, and resort areas frequently depends on the results of geographic studies.

Cultural geography also includes political geography, which is allied to political science (q.v.). This field deals with human social activities that are related to the locations and boundaries of cities, nations, and groups of nations.

Military geography constitutes a continuing study for the purpose of providing military leaders with an intimate knowledge of all areas in which they may be required to operate. Among the many other fields of cultural geography are ethnography, allied to ethnology (q.v.), historical geography, urban geography, demography, and linguistic geography.

Regional Geography. This branch of geography is concerned with the differences and similarities among the various regions of the earth. Regional geography seeks explanations for this variety among places by studying in each area the peculiar combination of spatially related features that distinguishes it from bordering areas.

Studies in regional geography may be restricted to the intensive development of a small area (the study of which is called microgeography) or may include large areas, such as Asia, Latin America, or the Mediterranean region. The broad areas, called macrodivisions, are based on the similarity of certain cultural criteria within each region.

In each of the large cultural regions, numerous

smaller areas with further distinguishing characteristics may be identified. For example, a particular area may be differentiated from its surrounding areas by language, by the predominant type of agriculture, by the terrain, by the market orientation, or by the combination of two or more such characteristics.

TOOLS AND METHODS OF GEOGRAPHY

Before the 19th century geographic writing could be characterized as descriptive, that is, it was largely the simple recording of observations and data. As more accurate methods of obtaining and analyzing data were developed, geographic writings became more explanatory, and after the mid-20th century, more theoretical.

It remains the geographer's goal, however, to describe the human habitat on the surface of the earth. To do this it is necessary to record the results of both systematic and regional studies. Geographers have compiled many charts, graphs, and textbooks that record detailed observations of individual geographic features of the earth as a whole and of local regions. When used for comparative purposes, this type of material is easiest to understand if it is supported by graphic representations such as maps. *See* MAP.

Data Collection. Data may be collected in the field or from secondary sources, such as censuses, statistical surveys, maps, and photographs. Advances made since World War II in the design of aerial cameras and high-resolution lenses, in aerial photogrammetric techniques, including the use of special infrared and other films, and in techniques for obtaining three-dimensional views of the landscape from the air have made possible more detailed studies of the earth and its resources. Geographers have also made use of radar, artificial satellites, bathysphere descents, and deep drilling into the earth's crust to obtain information about the environmental features of the earth. With the great increase in available data produced by these advances, geographers have begun to use the computer both to list and to analyze data.

Mapping. The map is the most important tool of geography and may be used to record either simple data or the results of a geographic study. In addition to providing a wealth of factual information, the map permits a visual comparison between areas because it may be designed to indicate, by means of symbols, not only the existence but also the form of all geographic features of a given area.

A standard pattern of cultural map symbols has been developed for identifying such cultural features as homes, factories, and churches; dams, bridges, and tunnels; railways, highways, and travel routes; and mines, farms, and grazing lands.

Quantitative Methods. Techniques that employ mathematical or statistical processes to analyze data are known as quantitative methods. The use of quantitative methods enables geographers to treat a larger amount of data and a larger number of variables in a more objective manner. Frequently, geographers collect data and then advance a theoretical explanation for an observed phenomenon. They then test this theory using quantitative methods. Sometimes the theories are expressed as mathematical statements, called models. Nevertheless, in geography, where the human variable is almost always present, theories are not expected to be universally precise, but rather to explain an observed tendency.

HISTORY OF GEOGRAPHY

Hundreds of individuals have contributed to the development of geography, and the fruits of their work have accumulated for several thousand years. Numerous travelers, surveyors, explorers, and scientific observers have added to this growing store of information. Only during the last two centuries, however, has it been possible to collect and record really accurate geographic information. The major conceptual framework that guides present-day geographers is of even more recent derivation, having originated in the 19th century.

Ptolemy of Alexandria　　　　Bettmann Archive

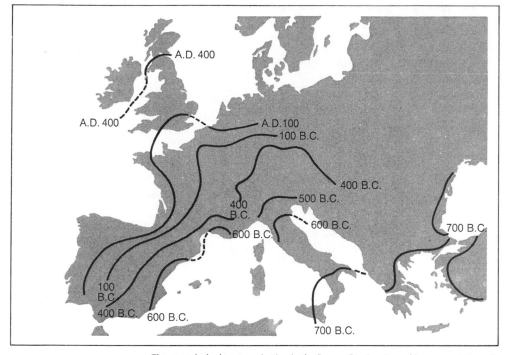

The spread of urban organization in the Roman Empire. A graphic representation of a spatial diffusion, this map could be used as a research tool by cultural, historical, or urban geographers. Reprinted from *Annals of the Association of American Geographers* by permission of the Association.

Early Geographers. The earliest geographers were concerned with exploring unknown areas and with describing the observable features of individual places. In antiquity such ancient peoples as the Chinese, Egyptians, and Phoenicians made long journeys and recorded their observations of strange lands. One of the first known maps was made on a clay tablet in Babylonia as early as 2300 BC. By 1400 BC the shores of the Mediterranean Sea had been explored and charted, and during the next thousand years Britain was visited, and most of the African coastline was navigated.

The ancient Greeks, however, gave the Western world its first important knowledge relating to the form, size, and general nature of the earth.

Aristotle in the 4th century BC was the first to demonstrate that the earth was actually round. He based his hypothesis on the arguments that all matter tends to fall together toward a common center, that the earth throws a circular shadow on the moon during an eclipse, and that in traveling from north to south new constellations become visible and familiar ones disappear. The Greek geographer Eratosthenes calculated with amazing accuracy the circumference of the earth.

The Greeks' travels, conquests, and colonizing activities in the Mediterranean region resulted in the accumulation of considerable geographic information and stimulated geographic writing.

The early Roman geographers produced a number of massive works on geography, notably a 17-volume encyclopedia by the Greek geographer and historian Strabo that served as a valuable source of information for military commanders and public administrators of the Roman Empire.

In the 2d century AD the Alexandrian astronomer Ptolemy synthesized accumulated Greek and Roman geographic learning. In his famous *Geographike syntaxis* he divided the equatorial circle into 360 degrees and constructed an imaginary north-south, east-west network over the surface of the earth to serve as a reference grid for locating the relative positions of known landmasses, such as islands and continents. Although he elected to use less accurate measurements of the circumference of the earth than those of Eratosthenes, Ptolemy nevertheless contributed useful descriptions and maps of the known world. His maps clearly indicated his understanding of the problems involved in representing a spherical earth on a plane surface.

261

GEOGRAPHY

Medieval Geography. During the Middle Ages little travel and exploration and practically no advancement in geography took place. Among Europeans only the Vikings were active in exploration. The Arabs, however, interpreted and tested the works of the earlier Greek and Roman geographers and explored southwestern Asia and Africa. As early as the 8th century Muslim scholars were translating the works of the Greek geographers into Arabic; only after these Arabic texts had been translated into Latin did Greek geographic learning become known in the Christian world. Among the major figures of Arab geography were al-Idrisi, who was known for his detailed maps, and Ibn Batuta and Ibn Khaldun, both of whom wrote about their extensive travels. The Mongols and Chinese also learned much about Asia, but their findings on the whole remained unknown to the Western world.

The trips of the Venetian Marco Polo in the 13th century, the Crusades of the 12th and 13th centuries, and the Portuguese and Spanish voyages of exploration of the 15th and 16th centuries opened up new horizons and stimulated geographic writings. Among the most notable of the accounts of voyages and discoveries that were published in the 16th century were those by the Venetian Giambattista Ramusio (1485–

1557), by Richard Hakluyt in England, and by Theodore de Bry (1528–98) in what is now Belgium. No longer could the concept of a spherical earth be considered heretical, as ecclesiastical authorities previously had contended, for exploration proved beyond a doubt the global nature of the earth.

Geography from the 17th to the 19th Century. Important in the history of geographic method is *Geographia generalis* (1650) by the German geographer Bernhardus Varenius. Varenius suggested that geography be divided into three separate branches, the first dealing with the form and dimensions of the earth; the second with tides, climates, seasons, and other variables depending upon the relative position of the earth in the cosmos; and the third dealing with comparative studies of particular regions on the globe. His work remained a standard authority for more than a century.

The first comprehensive geographic work printed in English was published in 1625 by the English geographer Nathaniel Carpenter (1589–1628?), who emphasized the spatial interrelationships of the physical features on the earth's surface. His approach subsequently became an important geographic point of view.

Many other European contributors increased

Marco Polo's father and uncle starting on their first journey to China (from a 14th-cent. manuscript).
Bettmann Archive

Gerhardus Mercator and Jodocus Hondius, whose maps reflected the notable increase in geographic knowledge attained by the 16th century. Bettmann Archive

geographic knowledge during the following two centuries. In the 18th century the German philosopher Immanuel Kant played a decisive role in placing geography within the framework of science. Kant divided knowledge gained from observation into two categories. One category, comprising phenomena perceived in accordance with a logical system, resulted in such classifications as the orders, genera, and species of plants and animals, regardless of when or where they occur. The other category included phenomena perceived in terms of time and space, with classification and description according to time viewed as history, and classification and description according to space viewed as geography. Kant subdivided geography into six branches, one of which, physical geography, was considered basic to the five other branches. The other branches recognized by Kant were mathematical, moral, political, commercial, and theological geography.

Alexander von Humboldt and Carl Ritter, both

of Germany, made major contributions to geographic theory in the early 19th century. An extensive traveler and a brilliant field observer, Humboldt applied his knowledge of physical processes to the systematic classification and comparative description of phenomena observed in the field and devised methods for measuring the phenomena he observed. Humboldt produced a number of superb geographic studies based on his travels in America. His work *Kosmos* (1844), which describes the physical geography of the earth, is considered one of the great geographic works of all time.

The views of Ritter differed in part from those of Humboldt. Whereas Humboldt utilized the systematic approach of treating physical features as separate phenomena, Ritter contributed greatly to the regional approach to geography. He laid stress on the comparative study of particular areas and on the associated features that characterized those areas. His 19-volume work *Die Erdkunde im Verhaltnis zur Natur und Ge-*

LAND-USE ZONES

BASED ON MODEL OF J. H. von THÜNEN

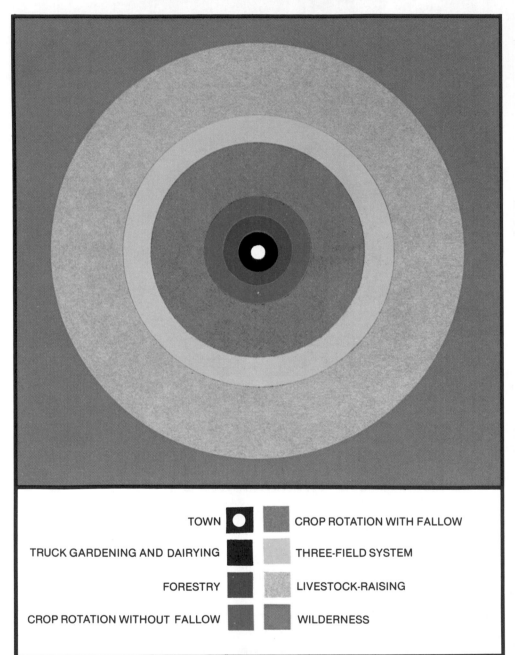

TOWN		CROP ROTATION WITH FALLOW
TRUCK GARDENING AND DAIRYING		THREE-FIELD SYSTEM
FORESTRY		LIVESTOCK-RAISING
CROP ROTATION WITHOUT FALLOW		WILDERNESS

In his work The Isolated State *(1826), Johann H. von Thünen sought to explain the location of agricultural activities. To do this he made a number of simplifying assumptions: The area under question is a level plain, isolated from outside influences, with uniform soils and climate and with a market (town) at its center. This model illustrates his findings. The land closest to the town is most valuable because transport costs are lowest; therefore, high-value commodities are produced here. Commodities that have a low value yield per unit area are grown on less costly land farther from the town. The proximity of the forest zone illustrates the former importance of wood as a fuel.*

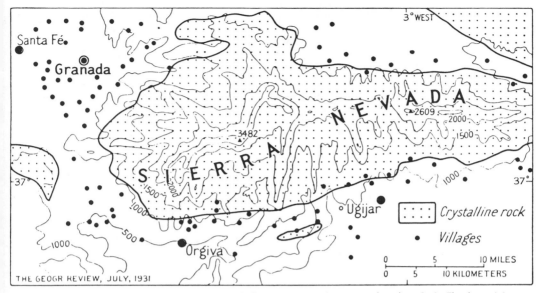

The distribution of villages in a mountainous area of southern Spain. The determining variable here is the hard crystalline rock, which impedes the availability of groundwater. If this were not plotted on the map, it might be assumed that the location of villages was limited merely by altitude. Reprinted from *The Geographical Review* by permission of the American Geographical Society.

schichte des Menschen (Geography and Its Relation to Nature and the History of Man, 1822–59) is a masterly treatment of Asia and parts of Africa. Ritter was a keen field observer, well trained in natural sciences and history. He called his work comparative geography, considering it analogous to comparative anatomy, and proceeded from observation to observation to arrive at laws and principles. Although his approach was largely regional rather than systematic, Ritter acknowledged that without systematic studies regional studies would be impossible.

Another German geographer, Friedrich Ratzel, also made significant contributions to geographic thinking. He is best known for his work *Anthropogeographie* (1882), which attempted to show that the distribution of people on the earth had been determined by natural forces. Describing geography as the science of distribution, he favored the study of restricted areas, which he claimed would provide the basis for generalizations about larger areas or about the world as a whole. The German geographers Ferdinand von Richthofen and Alfred Hettner (1859–1942) welded the ideas of Humboldt, Ritter, and Ratzel into a coherent system. *Die Geographie: Ihre Geschichte, ihr Wesen, und ihre Methoden* (Geography: Its History, Its Nature, and Its Methods, 1927), by Hettner, is a valuable work on the history of geographic methodology.

Outstanding among French geographers of the late 19th century was Paul Vidal de la Blache, who opposed the idea that the physical environment strictly determines human activities. He viewed human beings as determining agents operating in a physical environment, which could be molded to their needs in accordance with their development. He favored studies of small areas, stressing spatial differentiations as a result of both physical and cultural processes.

Greatly facilitating the emergence of geographic learning in the 19th century was the establishment of geographic societies, many of which sponsored geographic study and exploration and published periodicals devoted to geographic study. Among the earliest of these societies were those at Paris (1821), Berlin (1827), and London (Royal Geographical Society, 1830). Of particular significance to geography in the U.S. was the founding of the American Geographic Society in 1852 and the National Geographic Society in 1888. International geographic conferences were initiated in 1871 at Antwerp.

The 20th Century. During the first half of the 20th century, numerous geographic writers—British, American, French, and German—continued to carry on the tradition of their German and French predecessors. Studies of small areas all over the world, based on field observations, extended the frontiers of geographic knowledge, but the traditions and methodology inherited from the late 19th century remained essentially unaltered. Beginning in the 1950s, however, geographers made increasing use of quantitative methods. The change in methodology in the 1950s and '60s was so rapid that it is sometimes called the quantitative revolution. The goals of the geographer have remained basically the same, although the tendency now is to find practical applications for geographic studies.

Location theory, which is concerned with the analysis of variables that influence the location of an entity (such as a town or a factory), has been in the vanguard in its use of quantitative methods. The seminal work of location theory, done by the German agriculturalist Johann Heinrich von Thünen (1783–1850), is strikingly modern in its methodology. Thünen devised a method of analysis to explain the relationship of several variables that influence the location of agricultural activities. He also constructed a model of this arrangement under ideal conditions. In the 1930s the German geographer Walter Christaller proposed a central place theory to explain the location of urban centers in quantitative terms. The value of the work of these men was not fully realized until the 1950s.

By the 1960s the unity of the discipline had given way to diversity, and a certain amount of friction developed between geographers who used the quantitative approach and those who used a more descriptive approach. In the 1970s the descriptive approach was used with new vigor, and proponents revived interest in the field when they turned to studies such as the human perception of geographic phenomena, regional studies, and medical geography. The quantitative and descriptive approaches have not only continued to coexist, but have been mutually influential. See also GEOPHYSICS.

For additional information on individual geographers, see biographies of those whose names are not followed by dates.   J.H.T. & G.J.M.

For further information on this topic, see the Bibliography in volume 28, sections 861–63, 866.

GEOLOGICAL SURVEY, UNITED STATES (USGS), research agency of the U.S. Department of the Interior, established in 1879. It is responsible for interpreting and mapping the geology, hydrology, and topography of the U.S. and its territories and for investigating and appraising mineral, energy, and water resources. The agency investigates such natural hazards as volcanoes, earthquakes, and landslides. It performs scientific research and publishes the results of its studies.

GEOLOGY (Gr. *gē*, "earth"; *-logia*, "knowledge of"), field of science concerned with the origin of the planet earth, its history, its shape, the materials forming it, and the processes that are act-

ing and have acted on it. It is one of several related subjects commonly grouped as the earth sciences, or geoscience, and geologists are earth scientists concerned primarily with rocks and derivative materials that make up the outer part of the earth. To understand these materials, geologists make use of knowledge from other fields, such as physics, chemistry, and biology; thus, geological fields such as geochemistry, geophysics (qq.v.), geochronology (see DATING METHODS), and paleontology (q.v.), now important disciplines in their own right, incorporate other sciences, enabling geologists to understand better the working of earth processes through time.

Although each earth science has a particular focus, they all frequently overlap with geology. Thus, the study of the earth's waters in relation to geological processes involves knowledge of hydrology (see WATER) and oceanography (see OCEAN AND OCEANOGRAPHY), and the measurement and mapping of the earth's surface forms involve knowledge of cartography (see MAP) and geodetics (see SURVEYING). Clues to the origin of the earth are also sought by the study of extraterrestrial bodies, especially the moon, Mars, and Venus. Originally limited to earth-based telescopic observation, such studies were given a powerful impetus by the space exploration that began in the 1960s (see SPACE EXPLORATION: *Space Programs—Unmanned*).

As a major science, geology not only involves the study of landforms and other surface features of the earth but also is concerned with the structure and inner parts of the planet. Such knowledge is of basic scientific interest, but it is also placed at the service of humanity. Thus, the focus of applied geology is on the search for useful minerals within the earth, the identification of geologically stable environments for human constructions, and the foreknowledge of natural hazards associated with the geodynamic forces described below.

HISTORY OF GEOLOGICAL THOUGHT

Ancient peoples considered many geological features and processes as the work of gods and goddesses, and they regarded the natural environment with fear and wonder as dangerous and mysterious. Thus, the ancient Sumerians, Babylonians, and other peoples, although they made remarkable discoveries in mathematics and astronomy, went astray in geological inquiries by simply personifying geological processes. Irish legends, for example, suggest that giants were responsible for certain natural phenomena such as a weathered formation of basaltic columns, now known as the Giant's Causeway. Such mythology was also popular among the civilizations of the New World; for example, furrows on the flanks of what came to be known as Devil's Tower in Wyoming were thought by American Indians to be the claw marks of a giant bear.

Ancient to Medieval Times. Similarly, in ancient Greece and Rome, many of the gods were identified with geological processes. For example, volcanic eruptions in Sicily were ascribed to the local Roman volcano god, Vulcan. The Greek philosopher Thales of Miletus, in the 6th century BC, has been credited with making the first clean break with this traditional mythologizing. He regarded geological processes as natural and orderly events that could be studied in the light of reason, rather than as supernatural interventions. The Greek philosopher Democritus advanced this naturalistic philosophy with the theory that all matter is composed of atoms. Building on his atomic theory, he offered rational explanations of all manner of geologic processes: earthquakes, volcanic eruptions, the hydrologic cycle, erosion, and sedimentation. His teachings, as expounded by the Roman poet Lucretius in his poem *On the Nature of Things,* are readily available in English translation. Aristotle, the most influential natural philosopher of ancient times, recognized in the 4th century BC that fossil seashells embedded in sedimentary rock strata were similar to shells found along the beach. From this observation he surmised that the relative positions of land and sea must have fluctuated in the past, and he also realized that such changes would require great lengths of time. Theophrastus, Aristotle's pupil, contributed to geological thought by writing the first book on mineralogy. Called *Concerning Stones,* it formed the basis of most mineralogies throughout the Middle Ages and even later.

The Renaissance. The Renaissance was truly a new beginning for the earth sciences; people began to observe geological processes much as the ancient Greeks had done. Were Leonardo da Vinci not better known as a painter and engineer, he might still be recognized as a pioneer of natural science. He realized, for example, that landscapes are sculptured by erosive processes

A famous geological phenomenon is the Garden of the Gods near Colorado Springs, Colo., a group of huge, grotesquely shaped sedimentary rock formations of red and white sandstone.   Stewart's Commercial Photographs

and that fossil shells in Apennine limestones were the remains of marine organisms that had lived on the floor of a former sea that must have extended over Italy.

Following Leonardo, the French natural philosopher Bernard Palissy (c. 1510–90) wrote on the nature and scientific study of soils, groundwater, and fossils. The classic works on minerals written in this period, however, were by Georgius Agricola, a German mining expert who published *De Re Metallica* (1556) and *De Natura Fossilium* (1546). Agricola recorded the most recent developments in geology, mineralogy, mining, and metallurgy at that time, and his works were widely translated.

17th Century. Niels Stensen (1638–86), a Dane—better known by the Latinized version of his name, Nicolaus Steno—stands prominent among 17th-century geoscientists. In 1669 he showed that the interfacial angles of quartz crystals were constant, regardless of the shape and size of the crystals, and that by extension, the structure of other crystal species should also be constant. Thus, by drawing attention to the significance of crystal form, Steno laid the foundation for the science of crystallography. Steno's observations on the nature of rock strata led him to formulate the law of superposition, one of the basic principles of stratigraphy (see below).

18th and 19th Centuries. Geological thought during the 18th century was characterized by debates between contrasting schools. Plutonists, who proposed that the earth's rocks were all originally solidified from a molten mass and later altered by other processes, were opposed by Neptunists, whose leading exponent was the German geologist Abraham Gottlob Werner. Werner hypothesized that the earth's crust is a series of layers derived from mechanical and chemical sedimentary deposits laid down by a vast ocean, in a regular sequence, like the layers of an onion. By contrast, the Scottish geologist James Hutton and the Plutonists, as his followers were called, distinguished sedimentary rocks from intrusive rocks of volcanic origin.

In 1785, Hutton introduced the concept of uniformitarianism, according to which the history of the earth can be interpreted solely on the basis of everyday geologic processes familiar to modern observers. He reasoned that most such processes, operating as slowly as they do today, would have taken millions of years to produce the modern landscape. This theory set him at odds with theologic opinions of the day, which held that the earth was barely 4000 years old. Hutton's antagonists, led by the French naturalist Georges Cuvier, believed that abrupt, violent changes—natural catastrophes such as floods and earthquakes—were responsible for the earth's geologic features. For this reason, they were known as catastrophists.

The debate that raged between these two schools began to tip in favor of the uniformitarians with the publication of Charles Lyell's *Principles of Geology* (1830–33). Born in 1797, the year Hutton died, Lyell became a major influence on modern geologic theory, courageously attacking theological prejudices concerning the age of the earth and rejecting attempts to interpret geology in the light of scripture.

In the American colonies, the noted surveyor, draftsman, and mapmaker Lewis Evans (1700–56) had already made remarkable contributions to American geological knowledge before Lyell's influential work. For Evans, river erosion and fluvial deposition were self-evident processes that had been at work in the past. Through the work of Evans, in addition, the concept of isostasy—that the density of the earth's crust decreases as its thickness increases—also appeared for the first time in American geological writings.

Besides Lyell's work, the primary 19th-century developments in geology were the following: new reactions to traditional geological concepts, the fostering of glacial theory, the beginnings of American geomorphology, theories of mountain building, the advent of marine exploration, and the development of the so-called structuralist school (see below). Geological explorations, mainly in the American West, were major scientific events.

Glacial theory. The glacial theory drew on the work of Lyell and many others. First propounded about 1840 and later universally accepted, the theory states that glacial drift had been deposited by glaciers and ice sheets moving slowly from higher to lower latitudes during the Pleistocene epoch (*see* QUATERNARY PERIOD). The Swiss naturalist Horace Bénédict de Saussure (1740–99) had been among the first to credit glaciers in the Alps with the power to move large boulders. The Swiss-American naturalist Louis Agassiz correctly interpreted the environmental impact of this erosive and transporting agent and, with his colleagues, accumulated diverse forms of evidence that supported concepts of glacial advance and retreat for continental and mountain glaciers.

Stratigraphy. Advances in stratigraphy were made by the English geologist William Smith, who traced out the strata of England and represented them on a geological map that remains substantially unchanged today. Smith first traced strata over relatively short distances; he then correlated stratigraphic units of the same age but of different rock content. After the development of evolutionary theory by Charles Darwin later in the 19th century, this knowledge led to the principle of faunal succession. According to this principle the life in each period of earth history is unique for that specific period, fossil remains provide a basis for recognizing contemporaneous deposits around the world, and fossils can be used to assemble scattered fragments of the record into a chronological sequence known as the geologic time scale (see below).

Cycles of geologic activity. Many 19th-century geologists came to understand the earth as a thermally and dynamically active planet, internally as well as externally. Those known as structuralists or neocatastrophists believed that catastrophic or structural upheavals accounted for the formation of the earth's topographic features. Thus, the English geologist William Buckland (1784–1856) and his followers postulated frequent changes of sea level and upheaval of landmasses to explain geological successions and breaks, or unconformities, in stratigraphic sequences. Hutton, by contrast, regarded earth history in terms of overlapping, successive cycles of geological activity. He referred to long belts of folded rocks, which were taken to be the result of a variety of such cycles, as orogenic belts, and he referred to mountain formation through the processes of folding and uplift as orogenesis. Other geologists later supported these orogenic concepts, and they distinguished four major orogenic periods: the

Huronian (end of the Precambrian era); the Caledonian (lower Paleozoic era); the Hercynian, or Variscan (end of the Paleozoic era); and the Alpine (end of the Cretaceous period).

Surveys. Exploration of the western U.S. in the 19th century provided a whole new body of geological data that had an immediate effect on geomorphological theory. Early survey parties to the American West, under the auspices of the government, were headed by such figures as Clarence King (1842–1901), Ferdinand Vandeveer Hayden (1829–87), and John Wesley Powell, among others. Grove Karl Gilbert (1843–1918), the most outstanding of Powell's associates, recognized a form of topography caused by faults in the earth's crust, and he deduced a system of laws governing landform development.

20th Century. Technological advances made in the 20th century provided new, sophisticated tools for geologists, enabling them to measure and monitor earth processes with a precision previously unattainable. In terms of basic theory, the field of geology underwent a major revolution with the introduction and development of the plate tectonics (q.v.) hypothesis, that the earth's crust is divided into a number of plates that move about, collide, and separate over geologic time. The great crustal plates of the earth are now understood to begin at midocean and other ridges, or spreading centers, and to move toward submarine trenches, or subduction zones, where the crustal material again de-

A simplified map of the earth's crustal plates.   USGS

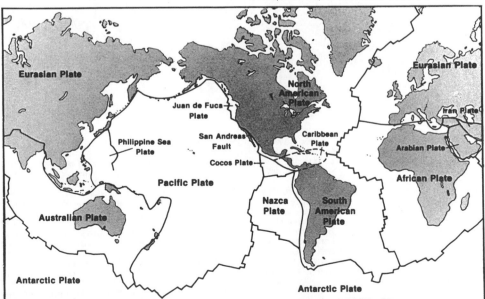

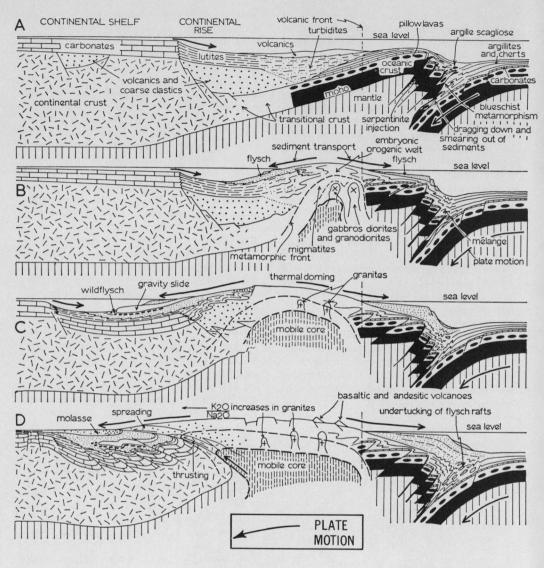

Schematic diagrams illustrating a model for the evolution of a mountain belt such as the Andes in South America, developed by the underthrusting of a continent by an oceanic plate. (A) Oceanward-driven wedges of oceanic crust, mantle, and flysch, or largely sandstone deposits, thicken toward the trench where the oceanic plate is descending. As the plate reaches depths exceeding 100 km (about 62 mi) beneath the continental rise, submarine volcanic deposits are erupted behind the volcanic front. (B) As the heat flux generated by the rise of basaltic and calc-alkaline magmas, or molten rock materials, increases, an embryonic orogenic welt, or mountain-forming ridge, rises above an expanding dome consisting of a core of rising gabbroic and granodioritic magmas. As the welt rises above sea level, sedimentary and volcanic deposits of the lower continental rise are transported both toward the continent and away toward the trench. (C) The sedimentary and volcanic pile is affected by high-temperature deformation and metamorphism as the mobile core expands, and the deformation wave, accompanied by flysch, arrives at the continental margin. At about this time, the continental shelf subsides, to form a trough in which massive rock slides from the welt, caused by gravity, accumulate. (D) The gravity rock slides are in turn buried under sheets of metamorphosed rock thrust toward the continent by the expanding mobile dome, and away from the continent toward the trench, burying also the sedimentary and flysch deposits. An additional lateral thrust is provided by the spreading of the orogenic welt, resulting in a broad symmetry of thrust direction and sediment distribution. The external troughs also begin to accumulate sediments known as molasse.

John F. Dewey & John M. Bird–Journal of Geophysical Research

The Devils Tower National Monument in Crook Co., Wyo., resembles a volcanic neck, but the polygonal joints in the igneous mass are more consistent with a cooling laccolith, an igneous intrusion between sedimentary beds. The undisturbed sedimentary strata can be seen at the base.
U.S. Geological Survey

scends. The places on the earth where major earthquakes occur tend to outline the boundaries between these crustal plates, suggesting that seismic activity can be interpreted as the result of the horizontal movements of the crustal plates.

This hypothesis is related to the concept of continental drift, first proposed in modern form by the German geophysicist Alfred Wegener in 1912. The hypothesis gained support later in the century as deep-sea exploration (q.v.) provided evidence for seafloor spreading—the outflow of new crustal material along midocean ridges. The concept of plate tectonics has since been related to the origin and growth of continents, the generation of continental as well as oceanic crust, and the nature of the earth's underlying layers and their evolution through time. Thus, 20th-century geologists have developed a theory that unifies many of the major processes that have shaped the earth and its landforms.

THE GEOLOGIC TIME SCALE

Records of the earth's geological history are obtained from four major types of rock, each pro-

duced by a different kind of crustal activity: (1) Erosion (q.v.) and sedimentation produce successive layers of sedimentary rocks (*see* SEDIMENTARY ROCK); (2) molten rock, pushed upward from deep-lying magma chambers, cools and forms surface rocks or the upper part of the earth's crust, providing records of volcanic activity; (3) geological structures developed from pre-existing rocks form records of past deformations; and (4) records of plutonism, or magmatic activity deep within the earth, are supplied by studying the deep-lying metamorphic and granitic rocks. A time chart of the earth's geological events is developed by dating these past geological episodes by using various radiometric and relativistic methods.

The divisions of the resulting geologic time scale are based primarily on changes in fossil forms found from one stratum to the next. The first five-sixths of the estimated 4 to 6 billion years of the earth's history, however, is recorded in rocks that contain almost no fossils; an adequate fossil record for stratigrapahic correlation

271

exists only for the past 600 million years, beginning at the time when Lower Cambrian deposits were laid. Scientists therefore conveniently separate the earth's vast span of existence into two major time divisions: the Cryptozoic (hidden life), or Precambrian; and the Phanerozoic (obvious life), or Cambrian, and the more recent time divisions.

Fundamental differences in the fossil assemblages of early, middle, and late Phanerozoic rocks gave rise to the designation of three great eras: the Paleozoic (ancient life), the Mesozoic (middle life), and the Cenozoic (recent life). The principal divisions of time in each of these eras constitute geological periods, during which rocks of corresponding systems were laid down worldwide. The periods generally are named for the regions where rocks of the period in question are well exposed; for example, the Permian period is named for the European province of Perm in Russia. Some periods are named instead

for typical deposits, such as the Carboniferous period for its coal beds; or for ancient peoples, such as the Ordovician and Silurian periods, named after the Ordovices and Silures of ancient Britain and Wales. The Cenozoic's Tertiary and Quaternary periods are further divided into epochs and ages, from the Paleocene to the Holocene, or most recent time. Besides these time periods, geologists also use time-rock divisions called systems; such systems are similarly divided into series and, sometimes, still smaller units called stages.

The discovery of radioactivity enabled 20th-century geologists to devise new dating methods and thereby assign absolute ages, in millions of years, to the divisions of the time scale. The following is an overview of these divisions and the life forms on which they are based. The scantier fossil record of Precambrian times, as stated, does not permit similar clear divisions. For a description of the earth's formation and

GEOLOGIC TIME SCALE

ERA	PERIOD		APPROXIMATE TIME BOUNDARIES*	LIFE FORMS ORIGINATING
		EPOCH		
CENOZOIC	QUATERNARY	RECENT	10,000	MAN
		PLEISTOCENE	2,500,000	
	TERTIARY	PLIOCENE	12,000,000	GRAZING AND CARNIVOROUS MAMMALS
		MIOCENE	26,000,000	
		OLIGOCENE	38,000,000	
		EOCENE	54,000,000	
		PALEOCENE	65,000,000	
MESOZOIC	CRETACEOUS		136,000,000	PRIMATES- FLOWERING PLANTS
	JURASSIC		195,000,000	BIRDS
	TRIASSIC		225,000,000	DINOSAURS-MAMMALS
PALEOZOIC	PERMIAN		280,000,000	
	CARBON-{ PENNSYLVANIAN		320,000,000	REPTILES
	IFEROUS{ MISSISSIPPIAN		345,000,000	FERN FORESTS
	DEVONIAN		395,000,000	AMPHIBIANS-INSECTS
	SILURIAN		430,000,000	VASCULAR LAND PLANTS
	ORDOVICIAN		500,000,000	FISH-CHORDATES
	CAMBRIAN		570,000,000	SHELLFISH-TRILOBITES
PRECAMBRIAN			(700,000,000) (1,500,000,000) (3,500,000,000) 4,650,000,000+ [FORMATION OF THE EARTH]	ALGAE EUCARYOTIC CELLS PROCARYOTIC CELLS

*Beginning date for each period or epoch

An 1898 photograph of the Badlands in Washington Co., now part of Shannon Co., S.D., illustrates the gullies, ridges, flat-topped hills, and strangely shaped columns that are characteristic of differential erosion and weathering of horizontal strata of varied resistance. Badlands are created by weathering and stream erosion.
U.S. Geological Survey

earlier history, along with a discussion of the origin of life on earth, *see* EARTH; EVOLUTION; LIFE.

Cambrian Period (570–500 million years ago). An explosion of life populated the seas, but land areas remained barren. Animal life was wholly invertebrate, and the most common animals were arthropods called trilobites (now extinct), with species numbering in the thousands. Multiple collisions between the earth's crustal plates gave rise to the first supercontinent, known as Gondwanaland.

Ordovician Period (500–430 million years ago). The predecessor of today's Atlantic Ocean began to shrink as the continents of that time drifted closer together. Trilobites were still abundant; important groups making their first appearance included the corals, crinoids, bryozoans, and pelecypods. Armored, jawless fishes—the oldest known vertebrates—made their appearance as well; their fossils are found in ancient estuary beds in North America.

Silurian Period (430–395 million years ago). Life ventured onto land in the form of simple plants called psilophytes, with a vascular system for circulating water, and scorpionlike animals akin to now extinct marine arthropods called eurypterids. Trilobites decreased in number and variety, but the seas teemed with reef corals, cephalopods, and jawed fishes.

Devonian Period (395–345 million years ago). This period is also known as the age of fishes, because of their abundant fossils in Devonian rocks. Fishes had also become adapted to fresh water as well as to salt water. They included a diversity of both jawless and jawed armored fishes, early sharks, and bony fishes, from the last of which amphibians evolved. (One subdivision of the sharks of that time is still extant.) On land areas, giant ferns were widespread.

Carboniferous Period (345–280 million years ago). Trilobites were almost extinct, but corals, crinoids, and brachiopods were abundant, as were all groups of the mollusks. Warm, humid climates fostered lush forests in swamplands, where the major coal beds of today were formed. Dominant plants included treelike lycopods (*see*

273

LYCOPSID), horsetails, ferns, and extinct plants called pteridosperms, or seed ferns. Amphibians spread and gave rise to reptiles, the first vertebrates to live entirely on land; and winged insects such as the dragonfly appeared.

Permian Period (280–225 million years ago). The earth's land areas became welded into a single landmass that geologists call Pangaea, and in the North American region the Appalachians were formed. Cycadlike plants and true conifers appeared in the northern hemisphere, replacing the coal forests. Environmental changes resulting from the redistribution of land and sea triggered the greatest mass extinction of all time. Trilobites and many fishes and corals died out as the Paleozoic era came to an end.

Triassic Period (225–195 million years ago). The beginning of the Mesozoic era was marked by the reappearance of Gondwanaland, as Pangaea split apart into northern (Laurasia) and southern (Gondwanaland) supercontinents. Forms of life changed considerably in the Mesozoic, known as the age of reptiles. New pteridosperm families appeared, and conifers and cycads became major floral groups, along with ginkgos and other genera. Such reptiles as dinosaurs and turtles appeared, as did mammals.

Jurassic Period (195–136 million years ago). As Gondwanaland rifted apart, the North Atlantic Ocean widened and the South Atlantic was born. Giant dinosaurs ruled on land, while marine reptiles such as ichthyosaurs and plesiosaurs increased in number. Primitive birds appeared, and modern reef-building corals grew in coastal shallows. Crablike and lobsterlike animals evolved among the arthropods.

Cretaceous Period (136–65 million years ago). The Rocky Mountains began to rise in North America. Dinosaurs flourished and evolved into highly specialized forms, but they abruptly disappeared at the end of the period, along with many other kinds of life. (Theories to account for these mass extinctions are currently of great scientific interest.) The floral changes that took place in the Cretaceous were the most marked of all alterations in the organic world known to have occurred in the history of the earth. Gymnosperms were widespread, but in the later part of the period angiosperms (flowering plants) appeared.

Tertiary Period (65–2.5 million years ago). In the Tertiary, North America's land link to Europe was broken, but its ties to South America were forged toward the end of the period. During Cenozoic times, life forms both on land and in the sea became more like those of today. Grasses became more prominent, leading to marked changes in the dentition of plant-eating animals. With most of the dominant reptile forms having vanished at the end of the Cretaceous, the Cenozoic became the age of mammals. Thus, in the Eocene epoch, new mammal groups developed such as small, horselike animals; rhinoceroses; tapirs; ruminants; whales; and the ancestors of elephants. Members of the cat and dog families appeared in the Oligocene epoch, as did species of monkeys. In Miocene times, marsupials were numerous, and anthropoid (humanlike) apes first appeared. Placental mammals reached their zenith, in numbers and variety of species, in the Pliocene, extending into the Quaternary period.

Quaternary Period (2.5 million years ago to present). Intermittent continental ice sheets covered much of the northern hemisphere. Fossil remains show that many primitive prehuman types existed in south-central Africa, China, and Java by lower and middle Pleistocene times; but modern humans (*Homo sapiens*) did not appear until the later Pleistocene. Late in the period, humans crossed over into the New World by means of the Bering land bridge. The ice sheets finally retreated, and the modern age began.

FIELDS OF GEOLOGICAL STUDY

The discipline of geology deals with the history of the earth, including the history of life, and covers all physical processes at work on the surface and in the crust of the earth. Broadly, geology thereby includes studies of interactions between the earth's rocks, soils, waters, atmosphere, and life forms. In practice, geologists specialize in a branch of either physical or historical geology. Physical geology, including fields such as geophysics, petrology, and mineralogy, focuses on the processes and forces that shape the exterior of the earth and operate within the interior, while historical geology is primarily concerned with the evolution of the earth's surface and its life forms through time, and involves investigations into paleontology, stratigraphy, paleogeography, and geochronology.

Geophysics. The aim of geophysics is to deduce the physical properties of the earth, along with its internal composition, from various physical phenomena. For example, geophysicists study the geomagnetic field, paleomagnetism in rocks and soils, heat-flow phenomena within the earth, the force of gravity, and the propagation of seismic waves (*see* SEISMOLOGY). As a subfield, applied geophysics investigates relatively small-scale and shallow structural features within the earth's crust, such as salt domes, synclines, and faults, for human-related purposes. Exploration geophysics also combines physics with geological information to solve practical problems related to searching for oil and gas, locating water-bearing strata, detecting new metal-ore deposits, and various forms of civil engineering.

Geochemistry. Geochemistry is concerned with the chemistry of the earth as a whole, but the subject is further divided into such areas as sedimentary geochemistry, organic geochemistry, the new field of environmental geochemistry, and several others. Of great interest for the geochemist are the origin and evolution of the earth's elements and the major classes of rocks and minerals. The geochemist specifically studies the distribution and amounts of the chemical elements in minerals, rocks, soils, life forms, water, and the atmosphere. Knowledge of the circulation of the elements in nature—for example, the carbon, nitrogen, phosphorus, and sulfur geochemical cycles—is of practical significance, as is the study of the distribution and abundance of isotopes and of their stability in nature. Exploration geochemistry, or geochemical prospecting, is the practical application of theoretical geochemical principles to mineral exploration.

Petrology. Petrology deals with the origin, occurrence, structure, and history of rocks, particularly igneous and metamorphic rocks. (The study of the petrology of sediments and sedimentary rocks is known more particularly as sedimentary petrology.) Petrography, a related discipline, is concerned with the description and characteristics of crystalline rocks as determined by microscopic examination under polarized light (*see* MICROSCOPE). Petrologists study changes that occur spontaneously in rock masses when magmas solidify, when solid rocks melt partially or wholly, or when sediments undergo chemical or physical transformation. Workers in this field are specifically concerned with the crystallization of minerals and solidification of glass from molten materials at high temperatures (igneous processes), the recrystallization of minerals at high temperatures without the intervention of a molten phase (metamorphic processes), the exchange of ions between minerals of solid rocks and migrating fluid phases (metasomatic and diagenetic processes), and sedimentary processes including weathering, transport, and deposition.

Mineralogy. The science of mineralogy (q.v.) deals with minerals in the earth's crust and also those found outside the earth, such as lunar samples or meteorites. (Crystallography, a branch of mineralogy, involves the study of the external form and internal structure of natural and artifi-

Stalactites (top) and stalagmites (bottom), such as those found in the Carlsbad Caverns in New Mexico, are formed by precipitation of dissolved carbonates from water dripping in the cave. Santa Fe Railway

cial crystals.) Mineralogists study the formation, occurrence, chemical and physical properties, composition, and classification of minerals. Determinative mineralogy is the science (and art) of identifying a mineral from its physical and chemical properties. Economic mineralogy focuses on the geological processes responsible for the formation of ore minerals, especially those with industrial or strategic importance.

Structural Geology. Originally concerned with analyzing the deformation of sedimentary strata, structural geologists now study the distortions of rocks in general. Commonly investigated structural forms or shapes lead to a comparison of observed features and, eventually, to the classification of related types. Comparative structural geology, concerned with large external features, contrasts with theoretical and experimental approaches, which employ the microscopic study of mineral grains in deformed rocks. Oil and coal geologists must employ structural geology in their daily work, especially in petroleum exploration, where the detection of structural traps that can hold petroleum is an important source of information to the geologists.

Sedimentology. Also referred to as sedimentary geology, this study of sedimentary deposits and their origins deals with ancient and recent marine and terrestrial deposits and their faunas, floras, minerals, textures, and evolution in time and space. Sedimentologists study numerous intricate features of soft and hard rocks in their natural sequences, with the goal of restructuring the earth's earlier environments in their stratigraphic and tectonic frameworks. The study of sedimentary rocks includes data and methods borrowed from other branches of geology, such as stratigraphy, marine geology, geochemistry, mineralogy, and environmental geology.

Paleontology. Paleontology, the study of prehistoric life, deals with fossil animals (paleozoology) and fossil plants (paleobotany) in relation to existing plants and animals. Investigation of microscopic fossils (micropaleontology) involves techniques different from that of larger specimens. Fossils, the remains of or indications of life in the geologic past, as preserved by natural means in the earth's crust, are the chief data of paleontology. Paleontography is the formal, systematic description of fossils (plants and animals), and invertebrate paleontology is frequently regarded as a separate subdiscipline from vertebrate paleontology.

Geomorphology. Meaning "form and development of the earth," geomorphology (q.v.) involves the attempt to furnish a working model for the outer part of the earth. Geomorphologists explain earth-surface morphologies in terms of established principles related to glacial action, fluvial processes, wind transport and deposition, and weathering. Major subfields focus on tectonic influences on landforms (morphotectonics), the influence of climate on morphogenetic processes and associated landform assemblages (climatic geomorphology), and the measurement and statistical analysis of landform data (quantitative geomorphology).

Economic Geology. This major branch of geology is geared to the analysis, exploration, and exploitation of geological materials of use to humans, such as fuels, metals and nonmetallic minerals, water, and geothermal energy. Kindred fields include the science of locating economic or strategic minerals (exploration geology), processing ores (see METALLURGY), and the practical application of geological theories to mining (mining geology).

Engineering (Environmental) Geology. Engineering geologists apply geologic principles in investigating the natural materials—soil, rock, surface water, and groundwater—that impinge on the design, construction, and operation of civil engineering projects. Representative of such projects are dams, bridges, highways, pipelines, housing developments, and waste-management systems. A recent offshoot, environmental geology, involves collection and analysis of geologic data for the purpose of resolving problems created by human use of the natural environment. Chief among such problems are the risks to life and property that result from building homes and other structures in areas subject to geologic hazards, particularly earthquakes (see EARTHQUAKE), landslides (see LANDSLIDE), coastal erosion, and flooding. The scope of environmental geology is exceptionally broad, comprising as it does physical sciences such as geochemistry and hydrology, as well as biological and social sciences. See also ENGINEERING: *Geological and Mining Engineering.*

GEOLOGICAL PROCESSES

Geological processes may conveniently be divided into those that originate within the earth (endogenic processes) and those that originate externally (exogenic processes).

Endogenic Processes. The rifting of the great lithospheric plates, the continual drifting of continental crust, and the expansion of oceanic crust from midoceanic spreading centers all set deep-seated dynamic forces into action. Diastrophism is a general term for all crustal movements produced by endogenic earth forces that produce ocean basins, continents, plateaus, and mountains. The so-called geotectonic cycle relates these larger

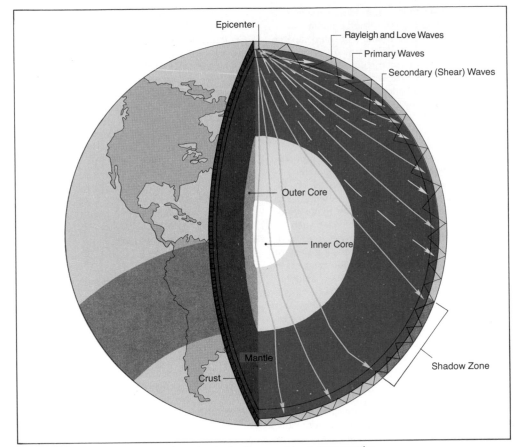

Cross section of the earth showing the paths of seismic waves. Primary waves are the fastest; they pass through solids, liquids, and gases; secondary waves travel only through solids, and therefore do not penetrate the molten outer core. Rayleigh and Love waves are surface waves. The epicenter is that point on the surface of the earth that is immediately above the origin of the earthquake, and the shadow zone is an area that receives no direct waves.

structural features to gross crustal movements and to the kinds of rocks that form various stages of their development.

Orogenesis, or mountain building, tends to be a localized process that distorts preexisting strata. Epeirogeny affects large parts of the continents and oceans, primarily through upward or downward movements, and produces plateaus and basins. Slow, gradual displacement of crustal units particularly affects cratons, or stable regions of the crust. Rock fractures and displacements that range in scale from a few centimeters to several kilometers are called faults. Faulting is commonly associated with plate boundaries that glide past one another—for example, the San Andreas Fault—and with sites where continents are rifted apart, such as the Eastern Rift Valley, in East Africa. Geysers and hot springs, like volcanoes, are often found in tectonically unstable areas.

Volcanoes are produced by outpouring of lavas from deep within the earth. The Columbia plateau of the western U.S. is overlaid by volcanic basalts that are more than 3000 m (10,000 ft) thick and cover 52,000 sq km (20,000 sq mi). Such plateau basalts are derived from fissure volcanoes. Other kinds of volcanoes include shield volcanoes, which are broad and convex in profile, such as those forming the Hawaiian Islands, and strato volcanoes, such as Mount Fuji or Mount Saint Helens, which are composed of interleaved layers of different materials.

Earthquakes are caused by the abrupt release of slowly accumulated strain by faulting or volcanic activity, or both. Sudden motion at the earth's surface is a manifestation of endogenic processes that can wreak havoc through seismic

GEOMETRIC PROGRESSION

sea waves (tsunamis), landslides, surface collapse or subsidence, and related phenomena.

Exogenic Processes. Any natural medium capable of picking up and moving earth material is referred to as a geomorphic agent. Running water, groundwater, glaciers, wind, and movements within bodies of standing water (such as tides, waves, and currents) are all primary geomorphic agents. Because they originate outside the earth's crust, these geological processes are designated as epigene or exogenic.

Weathering is a collective name for a group of processes responsible for the disintegration and decomposition of rock in place. Physical, chemical, or biological weathering is a prerequisite to erosion. Mass wasting (the gravitative transfer of material downslope) involves creep and such actions as earthflow, debris avalanches, and landslides. Hydraulic action is the sweeping away of loose material by running water; the companion process performed by wind is known as deflation. The action of ice moving over a land surface is sometimes called scouring; plucking and gouging are erosional processes restricted to glaciers. Aggradation, or the accumulation of sediments, contributes to the general leveling of the earth's surface as a result of deposition, which occurs when the medium transporting the sediments loses power.

ORGANIZATIONS

Numerous geological organizations provide their members with a wide range of services. Primarily they act as forums for the dissemination of knowledge, by means of professional journals, letters, and other communications. In addition they provide codes of professional conduct, short courses of practical instruction, job placement services, and certify specialists. Representative American organizations include the Geological Society of America, the American Geological Institute, the American Geophysical Union, the American Institute of Mining, Metallurgy, and Petroleum Engineers, the American Petroleum Institute, the American Association of Petroleum Geologists, and the Association of Exploration Geophysics. Other organizations include the Association of Geoscientists for International Development, the Geological Association of Canada, the Geological Society of London, the Geological Society of Australia, the Geoscience Information Society, the International Union of Geological Sciences, the Society of Economic Geologists, and the Society of Economic Paleontologists and Mineralogists.   C.W.F.

For additional information on individual scientists, see biographies of those whose names are not followed by dates.

For further information on this topic, see the Bibliography in volume 28, sections 417–29.

GEOMETRIC PROGRESSION, in mathematics, sequence of numbers in which the ratio of any term, after the first, to the preceding term is a fixed number, called the common ratio. For example, the sequence of numbers 2, 4, 8, 16, 32, 64, 128 is a geometric progression in which the common ratio is 2, and 1, $\frac{1}{3}$, $\frac{1}{9}$, $\frac{1}{27}$, $\frac{1}{81}$, $\frac{1}{243}$, . . . $\frac{1}{3}j$, . . . is a geometric progression in which the common ratio is $\frac{1}{3}$. The first is a finite geometric progression with seven terms; the second is an infinite geometric progression. In general, a geometric progression may be described by denoting the first term in the progression by a, the common ratio by r, and, in a finite progression, the number of terms by n. A finite geometric progression may then be written formally as

$$a, ar, ar^2, ar^3, ar^4, \ldots, ar^{n-1}$$

and an infinite geometric progression as

$$a, ar, ar^2, \ldots, ar^i, \ldots$$

In general, if the nth term of a geometric progression is denoted by a_n, it follows from the definition that

$$a_n = ar^{n-1}$$

If the symbol S_n denotes the sum of the first n terms of a geometric progression, it can be proved that

$$S_n = \frac{a(1 - r^n)}{1 - r}$$

The terms in a geometric progression between a_i, and a_j, $i < j$, are called geometric means. The geometric mean between two positive numbers x and y is the same as the mean proportional $\sqrt{xy}$ between the two numbers. In particular, a_n is the geometric mean or mean proportional between a_{n-1} and a_{n+1}.

The formal sum of the terms of an infinite geometric progression, written as

$$a_1 + a_2 + a_3 + a_4 + a_5 + \ldots + a_{n-1} + a_n \ldots$$

is called a geometric series (*see* SEQUENCE AND SERIES). In analysis it can be proved that a geometric series converges if the absolute value of the common ratio is less than 1; otherwise, the series diverges. If the series does converge, the limit, S, can be shown to be

$$S = \lim_{n \to \infty} S_n = \frac{a}{1 - r}$$

The symbol $\lim_{n \to \infty} S_n$ is read "the limit of S_n as n increases without bound."

Geometric series and geometric progressions have many applications in the physical, biological, and social sciences, as well as in investments and banking. Many problems in compound interest and annuities are easily solved using these concepts. *See also* ARITHMETIC PROGRESSION.

J.Si.; REV. BY J.Le.B.

For further information on this topic, see the Bibliography in volume 28, sections 369, 372.

GEOMETRY (Gr. *geō*, "earth"; *metrein*, "to measure"), branch of mathematics that deals with the properties of space. In its most elementary form geometry is concerned with such metrical problems as determining the areas and diameters of two-dimensional figures and the surface areas and volumes of solids. Other fields of geometry include analytic geometry, descriptive geometry, analysis situs or topology, the geometry of spaces having four or more dimensions, fractal geometry, and non-Euclidean geometry.

Demonstrative Geometry. The derivation of the term geometry is an accurate description of the works of the early geometers, who were concerned with such problems as measuring the size of fields and laying out accurate right angles for the corners of buildings. This type of empirical geometry, which flourished in ancient Egypt, Sumer, and Babylonia, was refined and systematized by the Greeks. In the 6th century BC the Greek mathematician Pythagoras laid the cornerstone of scientific geometry by showing that the various arbitrary and unconnected laws of empirical geometry could be proved to follow as logical conclusions from a limited number of axioms, or postulates. These postulates were taken by Pythagoras and his successors to be self-evident truths, but in modern mathematical thinking they are considered to be a group of convenient but arbitrary assumptions.

Typical of the postulates that were developed and accepted by Greek mathematicians is this statement: "A straight line is the shortest distance between two points." From these axioms, a number of theorems about the properties of points, lines, angles, curves, and planes can be logically deduced. Typical of these theorems are these statements: "The sum of the interior angles of any triangle is equal to the sum of two right angles," and "The square of the hypotenuse of a right-angled triangle is equal to the sum of the squares of the other two sides" (known as the Pythagorean theorem). The demonstrative geometry of the Greeks, which dealt chiefly with polygons and circles and corresponding three-dimensional figures, was drawn up in a rigid set of *Elements* by the Greek mathematician Euclid. Euclid's text, in spite of its imperfections, has served as a basic textbook in geometry almost to the present day.

The Greeks introduced construction problems, which require a certain line or figure to be constructed by the use of straightedge and compass alone. Simple examples are the construction of a line that will be twice as long as another line or of a line that will divide a given angle into two equal angles. Three famous construction problems dating from the time of the ancient Greeks resisted the efforts of many generations of mathematicians to solve them: duplicating the cube (constructing a cube double the volume of a given cube); squaring the circle (constructing a square equal in area to a given circle); and trisecting the angle (dividing a given angle into three equal parts). None of these constructions is possible with straightedge and compass alone, but the impossibility of squaring the circle was not finally proved until 1882.

The Greeks, particularly Apollonius of Perga, made a study of the family of curves known as conic sections (see below) and discovered many of their fundamental properties. The conic sections are important in many fields of physical science; for example, the orbits of the planets around the sun and the orbits of electrons in an atom are basically conic sections.

Archimedes, one of the greatest of Greek scientists, made a number of important contributions to geometry. He devised ways to measure the areas of a number of curved figures and the surface areas and volumes of solids bounded by curved surfaces, such as paraboloids and cylinders. He also worked out a method for approximating the value of π (the ratio between the diameter and circumference of a circle) and stated that numerically it lay between $3\frac{10}{71}$ and $3\frac{10}{70}$. *See* PI.

Geometry, like most other sciences, advanced little from the end of the Greek era to the end of the Middle Ages. The next great stride in the science was taken by the French philosopher and mathematician René Descartes, whose epoch-making treatise *A Discourse on Method* was published in 1637. This work forged a link between geometry and algebra by showing how to apply the methods of one discipline to the other. This is the basis of analytic geometry, a subject that underlies much modern work in geometry.

Another important development of the 17th century was the investigation of the properties of geometrical figures that do not vary when the figures are projected from one plane to another. A simple example of a theorem in projective geometry is illustrated in Fig. 1. If points *A, B, C* and *a, b, c* are placed anywhere on a conic section,

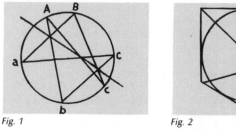

Fig. 1

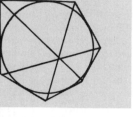

Fig. 2

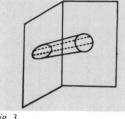

Fig. 3

such as a circle, and the points interconnected *A* to *b* and *c*, *B* to *c* and *a*, and *C* to *b* and *a*, the three points at which the corresponding lines intersect will lie in a straight line. Similarly, if any six tangents are drawn to a conic section, as in Fig. 2, and lines are drawn connecting the opposite intersections of these tangents, the connecting lines will meet at a single point. This theorem is said to be projective, since it is equally true for all the conic sections, and the sections themselves may be transformed into one another by suitable projections, as in Fig. 3, which shows the projection of a circle as an ellipse in another plane.

Analytic Geometry. In analytic geometry straight lines, curves, and geometric figures are represented by numerical and algebraic expressions (*see* ALGEBRA); using a set of axes and coordinates. Any point in a plane may be located with respect to a pair of perpendicular axes by specifying the distance of the point from each of these axes. In Fig. 4, point *a* is 1 unit from the vertical *y*-axis and 4 units from the horizontal *x*-axis. The coordinates of point *a* are 1 and 4, and the point is located by the statements $x = 1$, $y = 4$. Positive *x* numbers are located at the right side of the *y*-

axis and negative numbers to the left; positive *y* numbers are above the *x*-axis and negative *y* numbers below. Thus, point *b* in Fig. 4 has the coordinates $x = 5$, $y = 0$. Points in three-dimensional space can be similarly located with respect to three axes, of which the third, usually called the *z*-axis, is perpendicular to the other two at their point of intersection, which is called the origin.

In general, a straight line can always be represented by a linear equation in two variables, *x* and *y*, in the form $ax + by + c = 0$. In the same way, equations can be derived for the circle, ellipse, and other conic sections and regular curves. The problems treated in analytic geometry are of two classic kinds. The first is: Given a geometric description of a set of points, determine the algebraic equation that is satisfied by these points. For example, the collection of points that lie on the straight line passing through the points *a* and *b* satisfies the linear equation $x + y = 5$. In general, $ax + by = c$. The second kind of problem is: Given an algebraic statement, describe the locus of the points that satisfy the statement in geometric terms. For example, a circle of radius 3 and with its center at the origin is the locus of points that satisfy the equation $x^2 + y^2 = 9$. From such equations as these it is possible to solve algebraically such geometrical construction problems as bisecting a given line or angle, constructing a perpendicular to a given line at a given point, or drawing a circle that will pass through three given points not on the same straight line.

Analytic geometry has been of great value in the development of mathematics because it has unified the concepts of analysis (number relationships) and geometry (space relationships). The study of non-Euclidean geometry and the geometries of spaces that have more than three dimensions would not have been possible without the analytic approach. Similarly, the techniques of analytic geometry, which made possible the representation of numbers and of algebraic expressions in geometric terms, have cast new light on calculus (q.v.), the theory of

Fig. 4

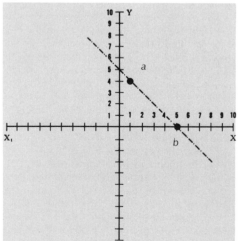

functions, and other problems in higher mathematics.

Descriptive Geometry. The science of making accurate, two-dimensional drawings, or representations, of three-dimensional geometrical forms and of solving graphically problems relating to the size and position in space of such forms is called descriptive geometry. Descriptive geometry is the basis of much of engineering and architectural drafting (*see* DRAFTING).

The usual technique of representing lines, surfaces, or solids in plane drawings is by means of orthographic projection. In this type of projection, the object to be represented is referred to one or more imaginary planes that are at right angles to one another. A point in space is represented by the point in the reference plane touched by a ray perpendicular to the plane and passing through that point. A line in space is represented by a line in the projection plane that joins the projections of the two end points of the line. *See* PERSPECTIVE.

Conic Sections. Conic sections are curves formed by the intersection of a plane with the surface of a right circular cone (q.v.) extended infinitely far on both sides of the vertex. The surface of the cone on either side of the vertex is called a nappe of the cone. Consider a cone, letting α be the angle between the axis of the cone and the generatrix of the cone. If the cone is cut by a plane that makes an angle with the axis that is greater than a, the intersection is a closed curve called an ellipse (q.v.); see Fig. 5. If the plane is perpendicular to the axis, the intersection is a circle (q.v.), which is considered a special case of

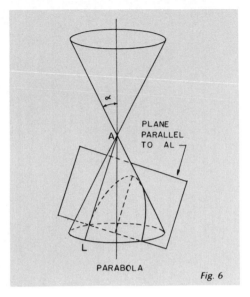

PLANE PARALLEL TO AL

PARABOLA

Fig. 6

the ellipse. If the plane intersects the axis at an angle equal to α, so that the plane is parallel to the surface of the cone, the intersection is an open curve of infinite extent called a parabola (q.v.); see Fig. 6. If the cone is intersected by a plane that is either parallel to the axis or makes an angle with it smaller than α, and if the plane does not contain the vertex of the cone, the intersection is called a hyperbola (q.v.); see Fig. 7. In this case the cone is necessarily intersected in both nappes, and it follows that the hyperbola has two branches, each of which is infinite in extent.

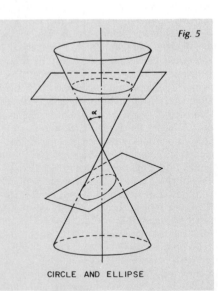

Fig. 5

CIRCLE AND ELLIPSE

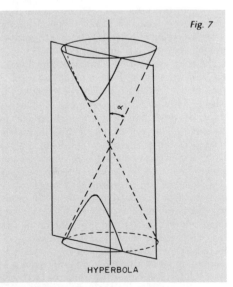

Fig. 7

HYPERBOLA

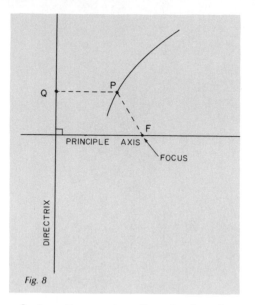

Fig. 8

Conic sections are two-dimensional or plane curves, and therefore a desirable definition of conics avoids the notion of a cone, which is three-dimensional. A conic may be defined as the set of points of which the distances from some fixed point are in a constant ratio to the distances of the points from a fixed line that does not pass through the fixed point. The fixed point is called the focus, and the line is called the directrix. The constant ratio is called the eccentricity of the conic and is usually denoted by the letter e. If P is a point and Q is the foot of a line from P perpendicular to the directrix (see Fig. 8), the point P is on the conic if and only if $[FP] = e[QP]$, in which $[FP]$ and $[QP]$ are the distances between the respective points. When $e = 1$, the conic is a parabola; when $e > 1$, it is a hyperbola; and when $e < 1$, it is an ellipse.

The conic sections have numerous mathematical properties that give them important applications in mathematical physics. For example, the orbit (q.v.) of any astronomical object such as a planet or comet around any other object such as the sun is always one of the conic sections. Artificial satellites have elliptical orbits around the earth. Reflection of light (or of sound or any other form of ray) by mirrors molded to the curve of a conic section has particular characteristics: Rays emanating in any direction from the center of a circle are reflected back to the center; rays emanating in any direction from one of the two foci (geometrical centers) of an ellipse are reflected to the other focus; the rays emanating from the focus of a parabola are reflected out in parallel lines; rays emanating from one focus of a hyperbola are reflected in such a direction that they appear to emanate from the other focus.

Non-Three-Dimensional Geometry. The development of projective and analytical geometry led mathematicians to the possibility of studying the geometry of spaces with more than three dimensions. Understanding such spaces does not require extraordinary feats of visualization or other mental gymnastics. Any point in the physical universe can be located by reference to three given axes; the physical universe is said, therefore, to be three-dimensional. The same space, however, becomes four-dimensional if it is regarded as made up not of points but of an infinity of spheres, because then four references must be given to determine or locate each individual sphere: the three coordinates of its center point and the length of its radius. Similarly a "three-dimensional" space that can be drawn on a flat piece of paper can be imagined, the space consisting of all the circles that can be drawn on a plane surface. In this case the three dimensions consist of the coordinates of the center of a circle and its radius. The use of geometrical concepts involving more than three dimensions has had a number of important applications in the physical sciences, particularly in the development of the theory of relativity (q.v.).

Analytical methods may also be used to investigate regular geometrical figures in four or more dimensions and to compare them with similar figures in three or fewer dimensions. Such geometry is called structural geometry. A simple example of this approach to geometry is the definition of the simplest geometrical figure that can be drawn in spaces of zero, one, two, three, four, or more dimensions. In the first four of these spaces, the figures are the familiar point, line, triangle, and tetrahedron. In a space of four dimensions the simplest figure can be shown to be composed of five points as vertices, ten line segments as edges, ten triangles as faces, and five tetrahedra. A tetrahedron similarly analyzed is composed of four vertices, six line segments, and four triangles; see Fig. 9. Geometry in four or more dimensions (n-dimensional geometry, in mathematical terms) was developed by the 19th-century British mathematician Arthur Cayley. Another dimensional concept, that of fractional dimensions, also arose in the 19th century. In the 1970s, the concept was separately developed as fractal geometry (see FRACTAL).

Non-Euclidean Geometry. One of the postulates of Euclid's geometry of the plane states that through a point outside a given line it is possible to draw only one line parallel to the given line, that is, one that will never meet the given line no

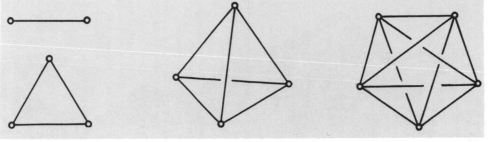

Fig. 9

matter how far the lines are extended in either direction. For many centuries mathematicians believed that this postulate could be proved on the basis of the remaining postulates, but all efforts to discover such a proof were fruitless. Then in the first part of the 19th century the German mathematician Carl Friedrich Gauss, the Russian mathematician Nikolay Ivanovich Lobachevsky, and the Hungarian mathematician János Bolyai independently demonstrated the possibility of constructing a consistent system of geometry in which Euclid's postulate of the unique parallel was replaced by a postulate stating that through any point not on a given straight line an infinite number of parallels to the given line could be drawn. Later, about 1860, the German mathematician Georg Friedrich Bernhard Riemann showed that a geometry in which no parallel lines occurred was equally possible.

The details of these two types of non-Euclidean geometry are complex, but both systems can be demonstrated by means of simple models. The Bolyai-Lobachevsky geometry, often called hyperbolic non-Euclidean geometry, describes the geometry of a plane consisting only of the points on the inside of a circle in which all possible straight lines are chords of the circle. As can be

seen from Fig. 10, an infinite number of parallels to line L can be drawn through the point P. Similarly Riemannian, or elliptic non-Euclidean geometry, is the geometry of the surface of a sphere in which all straight lines are great circles. Fig. 11 makes apparent the impossibility of drawing any pair of parallel lines on this surface.

For comparatively small distances, such as those commonly experienced, Euclidean geometry and the non-Euclidean geometries are essentially equivalent. However, in dealing with astronomical space and such problems of modern physics as relativity and the theory of wave propagation, non-Euclidean geometries give a more precise description of the observed phenomena than does Euclidean geometry. For example, the theory of relativity developed primarily by Albert Einstein is based on a Riemannian geometry of curved space.　　　　　　　J.Si.; REV. BY J.Le.B.

For further information on this topic, see the Bibliography in volume 28, section 372.

GEOMORPHOLOGY, scientific study of landforms and landscapes. The term usually applies to the origins and dynamic morphology (changing structure and form) of the earth's land surfaces, but it can also include the morphology of the seafloor and the analysis of extraterrestrial

Fig. 10

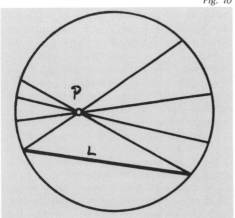

Fig. 11

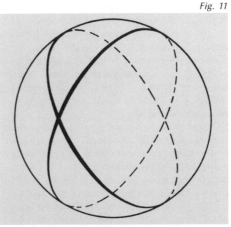

Crustal movement has caused the originally horizontal strata south of Heavens Peak in Glacier National Park, Montana, to become warped or bent through a process known as folding.   U.S. Geological Survey

terrains. Sometimes included in the field of physical geography, geomorphology is really the geological aspect of the visible landscape. The science has developed in two distinctive ways that must be integrated in order for the whole picture of landscapes to emerge.

Historical Geomorphology. One approach to the science of landforms is by means of historical, cyclic geomorphology. The concepts involved were worked out at the turn of the 20th century by the American geologist William Morris Davis, who stated that every landform could be analyzed in terms of structure, process, and stage. The first two are also treated by process geomorphology, discussed below; but the third, by introducing the element of time, is subject to a far greater degree of interpretation. Davis argued that every landform underwent development through a predictable, cyclic sequence: youth, maturity, and old age.

Historical geomorphology relies on various chronological analyses, notably those provided by stratigraphic studies of the last 2 million years, known as the Quaternary period (q.v.). The relative chronology usually may be worked out by observation of stratigraphic relationships, and the time intervals involved may then be established more precisely by dating methods (q.v.)

such as historical records, radiocarbon analysis, tree-ring counting (dendrochronology), and paleomagnetic studies. By applying such methods to stratigraphic data, a quantitative chronology of events is constructed that furnishes a basis for calculating long-term rates of change.

Process Geomorphology. This second branch of geomorphology analyzes contemporary dynamic processes at work in landscapes. The mechanisms involved—weathering and erosion (qq.v.)—combine processes that are in some respects destructive and in others constructive. The bedrock and soil provide the passive material, whereas the climatic regime and crustal dynamics together provide the principal active variables.

Underlying Dynamics. In geomorphological processes, gravity is an all-pervading, essentially invariable energy factor; a second variable, energy flow is provided by solar radiation. The latter is expressed either as a direct thermal variable or, indirectly, through the hydrologic cycle, which involves evaporation of water from the ocean, atmospheric transport of water, precipitation as rain or snow, and a return to the ocean by various processes. A third energy factor is heat flow from the earth's interior. Although of a magnitude considerably less than solar energy, this heat flow ultimately is responsible for creating major geological structures such as faults, but rates of change tend to be quite low (usually less than 1 mm per year). Nonetheless, in particular zones—for example, along crustal-plate boundaries (see PLATE TECTONICS) such as the San Andreas fault—stress may build up until released catastrophically in violent displacements of up to 12 m (40 ft). Locally, heat flow from the interior is concentrated in eruptions of magma (molten rock), producing various volcanic landforms.

Weathering and Erosion. Weathering is often a combination of three processes: the mechanical process, as in the growth of ice or salt crystals or in thermal heating and cooling; the chemical process, as in acid-water solutions that tend to dissolve minerals such as calcite and feldspar; and the biological process, as in the effect of plant roots, which generate both mechanical and chemical energy. Erosion is the dislodging, removal, and transport of material, either in solution or in particle form. The energy to accomplish this may be provided in the form of raindrops, running water, wind, waves, or simply gravity (as in a landslide).

An eroding landmass tends to rise to compensate for the removal of the load, but it eventually stabilizes as land relief decreases and stream gradients decline. The resulting surface, almost flat, is called a peneplain. It may be interrupted, here and there, by isolated hills called monadnocks consisting of rocks especially resistant to erosion. The theoretical base level of such a surface—the ultimate grade of streams—is mean sea level. For a peneplain to form and not be destroyed by renewed erosion, sea level must remain stable for millions of years. However, since the end of the Quaternary Ice Age (see ICE AGES), 10,000 years ago, sea level has risen a hundred feet or more.

Human-induced soil erosion is a feature of the present day and of the last few millennia, because clearing land of native vegetation or excessive grazing by domesticated animals exposes the soil to massive erosion. In this way some 3 billion metric tons of particulate material are washed from the surface of the U.S. alone each year. In undisturbed natural settings, on the other hand—notably in low-relief continental interiors—erosion rates are very slow (except in semiarid areas where thunderstorms produce flash floods). In structurally active belts such as in youthful mountains, which as a rule coincide with plate boundaries that recently collided or rifted, erosion rates may be enormous.

Of all the different processes acting on the earth's surface, rain and rivers are the most vigorous erosive agents. By contrast, although wave action on a rocky coast is often impressive, the rate of retreat of the shoreline is generally very slow. Sand dunes in the Sahara are also impressive, but the sand is only a relatively thin veneer; and the moraines left by giant continental glaciers are likewise only superficial scrapings of ancient soils. In general, without human interference, the landscape is stable. R.W.Fa.

For further information on this topic, see the Bibliography in volume 28, sections 417, 422.

GEOPHYSICS, branch of science that applies physical principles to the study of the earth. Geophysicists examine physical phenomena and their relationships within the earth; such phenomena include the earth's magnetic field, heat flow, the propagation of seismic (earthquake) waves, and the force of gravity. The scope of geophysics also broadly includes outer-space phenomena that influence the earth, even in subtle ways; the effects of the sun on the earth's magnetic field; and manifestations of cosmic radiation and the solar wind.

AREAS OF STUDY

Subdivision of the wide-ranging subject matter of geophysics into various branches involves categorizing specific endeavors. Strictly speaking, however, the discipline embraces all fields devoted to researching the earth's interior, atmosphere, hydrosphere (waters), and ionosphere (ionized upper atmosphere). Related fields are included in the following descriptions.

Solid Earth Physics. Embracing all fields devoted to the earth's interior, solid earth physics involves studying the behavior of earth materials from the crust down to the core (see EARTH), particularly as they relate to the earth's size and shape, gravity, magnetism, and seismicity. The specialized field of geodesy is concerned with determining the earth's size and shape and locating precise points on its surface. Involved in this study are the determination of the earth's gravitational field and observation of variations in the earth's rotation, the location of the poles, and tides. Two new techniques for making geodetic measurements, Very Long Baseline Interferometry (VLBI) and Satellite Laser Ranging (SLR), have been used to determine, within a fraction of a centimeter, the rates at which the continents are moving toward or away from each other. See PLATE TECTONICS.

Terrestrial Magnetism. Geomagnetism refers to the study of magnetic phenomena exhibited by the earth and its atmosphere. Generation of the magnetic field seems to be related to the motion of fluid, electrically conducting material within the earth, so that the planet acts as a self-exciting

The San Andreas fault, photographed in connection with earthquake research in Parkfield, Calif.

James Balog, 1986–Black Star

dynamo. The conducting material and the geomagnetic field may mutually control each other. Study of this problem is known as magnetohydrodynamics or hydromagnetics. The study of how the magnetic field has changed throughout the earth's history, called paleomagnetism, provided the first strong evidence for the theory of plate tectonics. See EARTH: *Terrestrial Magnetism.*

Gravity and Tides. Gravity (see GRAVITATION) is the attractive force exerted by the mass of the earth. The gradient of the gravitational potential—that is, the force of gravity—is perpendicular to the surface of the earth, which means that the force acts in the vertical direction. Gravimeters are highly sensitive balances used to make relative gravity measurements. Differences in relative gravity due to variations in the earth's density below the measurement site are referred to as Bouguer anomalies.

The rotation of the earth in the gravity fields of the moon and sun imposes periodicities in the gravitational potential at any point on the earth's surface. Tides are the most obvious effect; in addition to marine tides, solid earth tides occur as slight crustal deformations (see TIDE).

Seismology. Comprehensive understanding of global seismic activity became possible with the recognition that major earthquakes are triggered by movement of the earth's tectonic plates. In addition, much of what we are able to surmise about the earth's mantle and core has been gained by studying the passage of earthquake waves through the center of the earth. In this decade, geophysicists have also made great strides in understanding the structure of the crust and upper mantle, a zone known as the lithosphere (*See* EARTH: *Composition*). Major accomplishments in lithospheric research have been made possible through the use of an echosounding technique originally developed for finding oil and gas: seismic reflection profiling. *See* SEISMOLOGY.

Hydrology. This is the principal science dealing with continental water on and under the earth's surface and in the atmosphere. The constant circulation of water from land and sea through the biosphere (q.v.) and atmosphere by evaporation, evapotranspiration (loss of water from the soil by evaporation and transpiration by plants), and precipitation and runoff constitutes the so-called hydrologic cycle. *See* WATER.

Volcanology. Volcanologic studies are concerned with the surface eruption of gas-charged magmas (molten rock materials) from within the earth and with the structures, deposits, and landforms associated with such activity (*see* VOLCANO).

Although no single set of volcanic activities reliably indicates future volcanic events, certain processes provide geophysicists with clues to possible forthcoming eruptions. Such phenomena include changes in the strength and orientation of the earth's magnetic field; swarms of microearthquakes; increased heat flow in the earth, sometimes detected by thermocouples (*see* THERMOELECTRICITY) or from infrared aerial photos; variations in local electrical currents within the earth; increased exhalations of gases from fumaroles and vents; and the tumescence (bulging upward) of magma domes.

Terrestrial Electricity. Static or alternating electric currents that flow through the ground are induced by natural or artificial electric or magnetic fields. Electrical resistivity deep within the earth is explored by so-called magnetotelluric probing. Geophysicists have determined from effects of induced currents or geomagnetic variations that, in general, conductivity increases with depth in the mantle. *See* EARTH: *Terrestrial Electricity.*

Atmospheric Phenomena. Physics of the lower atmosphere, where air is dense enough to be subject to the laws of fluid dynamics (*see* FLUID MECHANICS), is the province of meteorology (q.v.). In recent years, the techniques of remote sensing (q.v.) have begun to play a major role in monitoring storms and other transient atmospheric phenomena, such as lightning (q.v.).

Phenomena of the upper atomsphere are the subject of aeronomy and magnetospheric physics (*see* IONOSPHERE). The earth's magnetic field reacts with the solar wind (*see* SUN) to form a sort of sheath, called the magnetosphere, that acts as a gigantic natural dynamo, more than 100,000 km (more than 60,000 mi) across. When high-energy particles streaming from the sun penetrate this sheath and enter the Van Allen belts, the phenomena known as aurora (q.v.) are created (*see* RADIATION BELTS).

GEOPHYSICAL SURVEYS

Geophysical exploration, commonly called applied geophysics or geophysical prospecting, is conducted to locate economically significant accumulations of oil, natural gas, and other minerals, including groundwater. Geophysical investigations are also employed with engineering objectives in mind, such as predicting the

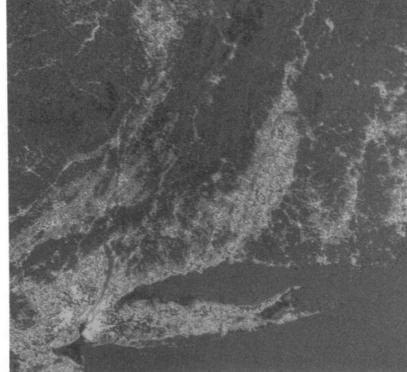

Geophysical surveys by satellites show broad patterns of surface conditions on the earth. Here, the New York City area is seen in computer-created false colors, from white and red for warmer areas to deep blue and violet for cooler ones. NASA

Workers on the Glomar Challenger, a U.S. research ship, manipulate core casings used to retrieve samples of the earth's crust from the seafloor.
Deep Sea Drilling Project Photo, Scripps Institution of Oceanography

behavior of earth materials in relation to foundations for roads, railways, buildings, tunnels, and nuclear power plants. Surveys are generally identified by the property being measured—namely, electrical, gravity, magnetic, seismic, thermal, or radioactive properties.

Used primarily in the search for oil, gas, and base metals, electrical and electromagnetic surveys map variations in the conductivity or capacitance of rocks (*see* ELECTRICITY). Measured by special tools lowered into holes drilled for oil and gas, conductivity variations provide geophysicists with clues from which they can judge the hydrocarbon-bearing potential of rock strata. Direct and alternating electrical currents are measured in ground surveys, but the lower radio frequencies are used both in ground and in airborne electromagnetic surveys.

Gravity surveys measure density variations in local rock masses. Used mainly in petroleum exploration, these surveys are based on use of a device called a gravimeter. Gravity surveys are made on land, at sea, and down boreholes.

In ground magnetic surveys, variations in the earth's magnetic field are measured at stations placed closely together; aeromagnetic surveys

may also be conducted, especially in petroleum exploration. Devices called magnetometers, towed by aircraft or behind a seismic research ship, help to detect magnetic anomalies or to distinguish geologic features that might appear similar from seismic data alone.

Measurement of seismic-wave travel time is one of the most common geophysical methods used in surveys. Seismic exploration is divided into refraction and reflection surveys, depending on whether the predominant portion of the seismic waves' travel is horizontal or vertical. Refraction seismic surveys are used in engineering geophysics and petroleum exploration, and to locate groundwater or buried stream channels containing placer mineral deposits. Seismic reflection surveys, on the other hand, detect boundaries between different kinds of rocks; this detection assists in the mapping of geologic structures. Seismic energy is detected on land by using devices called geophones, which react to on-site ground motions; and in water by using piezometric devices, which measure hydrostatic pressure changes.

Geothermal surveys concentrate on temperature variations and the generation, conduction, and loss of heat within the earth. Geothermometry is also important to volcanologic studies as well as to locating geothermal energy resources. *See* GEOTHERMICS.

Radioactivity surveys, conducted on the ground and from the air, measure natural radiation from the earth. Geiger and scintillation counters (*see* PARTICLE DETECTORS) are used in searching for ores of uranium as well as in searching for rare earth metals, potash deposits, and other radioactive materials.

ORGANIZATIONS AND PROGRAMS

Major national and international geophysical bodies that publish mainly in English include the American Geophysical Union (AGU), American Meteorological Society (AMS), International Union of Geodesy and Geophysics (IUGG), International Council of Scientific Unions (ICSU), Royal Astronomical Society, Seismological Society of America, Society of Exploration Geophysicists, and World Meteorological Organization (WMO). Such organizations take part in extensive research and exploration efforts, as well as gathering and publishing the results of research.

Programs of geophysics are designed to collect, exchange, analyze, and synthesize data from many sites over extended periods of time. The International Geophysical Year (IGY, 1957–58), for example, was an international program that concentrated on exploration of the solar and terrestrial atmospheres. It was followed in 1964–65 by the International Years of the Quiet Sun (IQSY) to compare times of maximum and minimum solar activity and their effects on terrestrial phenomena. Solid earth geophysical programs of the same decade included the World Magnetic Survey Board of IUGG and the Upper Mantle Program coordinated by ICSU. The International Hydrological Decade (IHD, 1965–74) was launched by the United Nations Educational, Scientific, and Cultural Organization (UNESCO) to deal with a variety of water-related topics of practical significance to humanity. The International Indian Ocean Expedition (IIOE, 1961–66) was one of several oceanographic geophysical programs. Geological programs for drilling far into the earth's crust, such as the Deep Sea Drilling Program completed in 1983 and the succeeding Ocean Drilling Program (qq.v.), are also of importance to geophysicists (*see* OCEAN AND OCEANOGRAPHY); the world's deepest well—already more than 12,000 m (40,000 ft) deep—is being drilled in the Kola Peninsula, in northern Russia. Geodetic data provided by satellites of the U.S. Navstar Global Positioning System are helping to measure seismic and plate-tectonic movements. The World Weather Watch (WWW), an ongoing atmospheric science program managed by ICSU and WMO, is a global data collecting, processing, and dissemination system serving all nations. The Global Atmospheric Research Program (GARP) is a research endeavor geared to quantitative weather prediction.   C.W.F.

For further information on this topic, see the Bibliography in volume 28, section 419.

GEOPOLITICS, term used to designate the determining influence of the environment (elements such as geographical features, social and cultural forces, and economic resources) on the politics of a nation. The Swedish political scientist Rudolf Kjellén (1864–1922), who developed a system of political science based on the interaction of sociological, political, and physical forces, coined the word geopolitics in his work *Staten som Livsform* (The State as an Organism, 1916).

A sovereign state occupies a particular territory with unique physical features that partly determine viable forms of economic, social, political, and military organization. In addition, the geographical location of a state must be considered in relation to those of other states, each with its own unique geopolitical qualities. In the 20th century, for example, Belgium and Poland have been "fighting places," one located between Germany and France, the other between Germany and Russia.

Geopolitics, as developed by the German general Karl Haushofer, became important in Germany during the period of National Socialism; it provided a pseudoscientific rationale to justify that nation's territorial expansion. One facet of German geopolitics was the theory called *Lebensraum* ("living space"). According to this theory, the "living space" is defined as all the territory that a country is alleged to need in order to achieve self-sufficiency.

Many scholars have looked to geopolitics for a deeper understanding of the fundamental structure of power relations between states. For a better conception of the political rivalry between the U.S. and USSR, for example, geopolitical theorists looked for the roots of foreign policy imperatives in the domestic conditions of those two countries. As early as 1904, the British geographer Sir Halford MacKinder noted a geopolitical antagonism between the Eurasian land power (that is, Russia) and the leading sea power (then Great Britain, subsequently the U.S.). Various geopolitical explanations were offered for the U.S.-Soviet struggle for influence in Africa, Eurasia, and Latin America from the late 1940s through the early '90s, when the USSR broke up.   C.S.G.

For further information on this topic, see the Bibliography in volume 28, section 171.

Saint George and the Dragon *(1504–5), a painting by Raphael.*
National Gallery of Art, Washington–Mellon Collection

GEORGE, Saint (d. about 303), Christian martyr and patron saint of England, born in Cappadocia (eastern Asia Minor). His life is obscured by legend, but his martyrdom at Lydda, Palestine, is generally considered a matter of historical fact, testified to by two early Syrian church inscriptions and by a canon of Pope Gelasius I, dated 494, in which St. George is mentioned as one whose name was held in reverence. The most popular of the legends that have grown up around him relates his encounter with the dragon. A pagan town in Libya was victimized by a dragon (representing the devil), which the inhabitants first attempted to placate by offerings of sheep, and then by the sacrifice of various members of their community. The daughter of the king (representing the church) was chosen by lot and was taken out to await the coming of the monster, but George arrived, killed the dragon, and converted the community to Christianity. In 1222 the Council of Oxford ordered that his feast, on April 23, be celebrated as a national festival, and in the 14th century he became the patron saint of England and of the Order of the Garter.

GEORGE I (1660–1727), king of Great Britain (1714–27) and elector of Hannover (1698–1727), first of the Hannoverian line of British rulers.

George was born in Osnabrück, Hannover (now in Lower Saxony state, Germany), on May 28, 1660, the son of Ernest Augustus, elector of Hannover (1629–98), and Sophia (1630–1714), granddaughter of King James I of England. George succeeded Queen Anne by the terms of the Act of Settlement (*see* SETTLEMENT, ACT OF). Thoroughly German in tastes and habits, he never learned the English language, and he made periodic lengthy visits to Hannover, which always remained his primary concern, despite his dutiful efforts to attend to his new kingdom's needs. He remained, however, unpopular in Britain, a fact that contributed to Jacobite plots to replace him with James II's son, James Edward Stuart, known as the Old Pretender. George appointed only Whigs as his ministers and advisers, reasoning that the Tories were favorable to the Stuart cause. He took a keen interest in foreign affairs, and it was his judgment that made possible the formation in 1717 of the third Triple Alliance with the Netherlands and France. For domestic policies he relied on his ministers, James Stanhope, 1st earl Stanhope (1673–1721), Charles Townshend, 2d viscount Townshend of Raynham, and Robert Walpole. Their sound administrative skills strengthened the position of the house of Hannover in Great Britain. He was succeeded by his son, George II. George died in Osnabrück on June 11, 1727.

GEORGE II (1683–1760), king of Great Britain and Ireland (1727–60), and elector of Hannover (1727–60), the son of King George I.

George was born at Herrenhausen Palace in Hannover (now in Lower Saxony state, Germany) on Nov. 10, 1683, and he grew up a German prince. In 1705 he married Caroline of Ansbach, an intelligent woman who wielded great influence over her husband and thereby on government. Like his father, George II was more interested in Hannover than in Great Britain, and during his many absences from London Caroline frequently acted as regent. During the war of the Austrian Succession (1740–48), the king subordinated the interests of Great Britain to those of his German principality. This policy was unpopular in Great Britain, but the king won admiration for his courage at the Battle of Dettingen in Bavaria (1743), the last engagement in which a British monarch participated in person. George II contributed to the material progress of Great Britain, mainly because he was shrewd enough to listen to his wife and heed the advice of his ministers. He retained Sir Robert Walpole as chief minister only upon Caroline's insistence, and he later relied on Henry Pelham (1696–1754), and, toward the end of his reign, William Pitt the Elder, although he had originally disliked him. George's reign was marked by the suppression of the last major Jacobite rebellion (see JACOBITES) and by the successful prosecution—at Pitt's initiative—of the Seven Years' War. He was succeeded by his grandson George III. George died at Kensington Palace, London, on Oct. 25, 1760.

GEORGE III (1738–1820), king of Great Britain and Ireland (1760–1820), who presided over the loss of Britain's American colonies; he was also elector of Hannover (1760–1815) and, by decision of the Congress of Vienna, king of Hannover (1815–20).

George was born in London on June 4, 1738, the oldest son of Frederick Louis, prince of Wales (1707–51), and the grandson of King George II. The first of the Hannoverian house to be born and educated as an Englishman, he was primarily interested in his royal prerogatives as king of Great Britain—in contradistinction to his two predecessors, to whom Hannover was the main concern. George's aim was to rule as well as reign, and he was a skillful and astute intriguer; by 1763 he had managed to regain many of the powers that strong Whig ministries had appropriated during the reigns of the first two Georges. His problem was that he lacked the self-confidence and the mature statesmanship to form and achieve any long-term policy. After the dismissal of several ministers who did not satisfy him, the king found a firm supporter in Frederick North, 2d earl of Guilford, prime minister from 1770 to 1782. Lord North executed the royal policies that provoked the American Revolution. The unsuccessful conclusion of that protracted conflict forced North to resign, and during the government crisis that followed—when three cabinets came and went in less than two years—the king himself was almost induced to abdicate. He then took a political gamble by placing the government in the hands of the 24-year-old William Pitt, thereby restoring stability for the rest of the century. In line with his belief in royal authority, George favored the wars with France (1793–1815) that grew out of the French Revolution.

In 1809 the king became blind. As early as 1765 he had suffered an apparent dementia, and in 1788 his derangement recurred to such a degree that a regency bill was passed, but the king recovered the following year. It is now thought likely that he had inherited porphyria, a defect of the metabolism that may in time lead to delirium. In 1811 he succumbed hopelessly, and his son, later George IV, acted as regent for the rest of his reign. George III died at Windsor Palace on Jan. 29, 1820.

GEORGE IV (1762–1830), king of Great Britain and Ireland (1820–30), and king of Hannover (1820–30).

George was born in London on Aug. 12, 1762, the eldest son of King George III. As prince of Wales, he became notorious for his profligacy and extravagance. Despite his father's strongly anti-Catholic views, he secretly married a Roman Catholic, Mrs. Maria Anne Fitzherbert (1756–1837), in 1785; less than two years later, to obtain money for his debts, he allowed Parliament to

GEORGE V

declare the marriage illegal, which in fact it was by the terms of acts governing royal marriages and succession. In 1795, again to liquidate his debts, he agreed to a marriage with his cousin, Caroline of Brunswick, but he became estranged from her in 1796 after the birth of their daughter, Princess Charlotte (1796–1817). His misconduct alienated the British people, and when he tried to divorce Caroline, charging her with adultery, she was so enthusiastically supported by the London crowds that her trial had to be abandoned. His cleverness and gracious manners, however, gave him the name of "first gentleman of Europe." George became prince regent in 1811, when his father became mentally unable to discharge his duties, and succeeded to the throne in 1820. The outstanding act of his reign was the Catholic Emancipation Act, which the king opposed. George IV died at Windsor Palace on June 26, 1830, and was succeeded by his brother William IV.

GEORGE V (1865–1936), king of Great Britain and Northern Ireland, and emperor of India (1910–36), of the house of Saxe-Coburg-Gotha (later changed to Windsor).

George was born in London on June 3, 1865, the second son of Edward VII. He was known as the Sailor Prince; he entered the Royal Navy in 1877 and, after an active naval career and successive promotions, rose to the rank of vice admiral in 1903. The death of his elder brother, Albert Victor, duke of Clarence and Avondale (1864–92), made George second in line to the succession. He married his brother's fiancée, Princess Victoria Mary of Teck, later Mary, queen consort of England, and was created duke of York in 1892. After his father succeeded Queen Victoria on the throne in 1901, George became prince of Wales. Six children were born to George and Mary: Edward Albert, later Edward VIII; Albert Frederick George, later George VI; Victoria Alexandra Alice Mary (1897–1965); Henry William Frederick Albert, duke of Gloucester (1900–74); George Edward Alexander Edmund, duke of Kent (1902–42); and John Charles Francis (1905–19).

The outstanding event of the reign of George V was World War I. Following England's declaration of war on Germany, the king renounced all the German titles belonging to him and his family and changed the name of the royal house to Windsor. He died at Sandringham House, Norfolk, on Jan. 20, 1936.

GEORGE VI (1895–1952), king of Great Britain and Northern Ireland (1936–52), and emperor of India (1936–47), of the house of Windsor. George was born in Sandringham, Norfolk, on Dec. 14, 1895, the second son of King George V,

and he was educated at Trinity College, University of Cambridge, and the Royal Naval College on the Isle of Wight. In 1923 he married Lady Elizabeth Bowes-Lyon (1900–   ), and they had two daughters: Elizabeth Alexandra Mary, later Queen Elizabeth II, and Margaret Rose. George succeeded to the throne after the abdication of his older brother, Edward VIII. Following his coronation in 1937, King George, accompanied by the queen consort, began a series of state goodwill visits, traveling to France in 1937 and to Canada and the U.S. in 1939. These visits were interrupted by World War II, during which the king visited many fronts in Europe, but were resumed in 1947, when the royal family spent several months in South Africa. In the last three years of his life, illness prevented any further trips. The reign of George VI was marked by the relinquishment of the title of emperor of India, following the partition of India in 1947 into Pakistan and India. He died at Sandringham on Feb. 6, 1952, and was succeeded by Elizabeth II.

GEORGE I (1845–1913), king of Greece (1863–1913), the first Greek monarch of the house of Glücksburg. The second son of King Christian IX of Denmark, he was known as Prince William and was nominated for the Greek throne by the British government after the revolution that deposed his predecessor, King Otto, in 1862. The Danish prince was elected to the throne by the Greek National Assembly and was crowned as George I, king of the Hellenes, after being approved by the Great Powers. In 1867 he married Olga, niece of Alexander II of Russia. George followed a consistent expansionist policy; the Ionian Islands, part of Epirus, and most of Thessaly were joined to Greece during his reign. After winning a victory over Turkey in the First Balkan War, he was assassinated in Salonika in 1913. He was succeeded by his son, Constantine I.

GEORGE II (1890–1947), king of Greece (1922–23, 1935–41, 1946–47), eldest son of King Constantine I, of the house of Glücksburg, born at Tatoi, the royal estate near Athens. In 1921 he married Princess Elizabeth of Romania (1894–1956). He succeeded to the throne after the abdication of his father, but was himself deposed a year later, in 1923. Returned to the throne by a plebiscite in 1935, George was, however, given little authority, the actual power being in the hands of the military dictator Ioánnes Metaxas. The German invasion of Greece in 1941 caused him to take refuge first in Egypt and then in London, where he established a government in exile. Following another plebiscite, George returned to Greece in 1946. The following year he died and was succeeded by his brother Paul I.

Water-skiers on Lake George.

GEORGE, David Lloyd. *See* LLOYD GEORGE, DA-VID, 1ST EARL OF DWYFOR.

GEORGE, Henry (1839–97), American economist and social philosopher, born in Philadelphia. In 1855 he sailed as a cabin boy to Australia and India, where he was appalled by the extremes of wealth and poverty. Later he settled in San Francisco and became a printer and free-lance writer, eventually editing newspapers there and in Oakland, Calif. In 1871 George wrote the pamphlet *Our Land and Land Policy,* in which he argued that the boom in the West, resulting from the development of the railroads, was actually making most people poor and only a few rich. The reason, George asserted, was that landownership is concentrated in the hands of the few; these few reap the benefit of the rise of the value of land, although the rise is not a result of their own efforts but instead is due to the increase in population and the development of the economy. George recommended shifting the tax burden from buildings to land, his solution being the single tax.

His book *Progress and Poverty* (1879), in which he developed this idea, brought him fame as an opponent of poverty and injustice in modern capitalism. Thereafter George wrote and lectured on his ideas, touring the U.S., Great Britain, and Ireland. In 1886, with labor and liberal support, George ran second in a three-man race for mayor of New York City. In 1897, as an independent Democrat, he was again a candidate for mayor of New York City, but he died during the campaign. His writings include *Social Problems* (1884), *Protection or Free Trade* (1886), and *The Science of Political Economy* (1897).

GEORGE, LAKE, lake of NE New York State, lying in the foothills of the Adirondack Mts., covering an area of 114 sq km (44 sq mi). Its waters are discharged into Lake Champlain, to the N, through a narrow channel. The swift descent from Lake George to Lake Champlain is marked by rapids and falls. Lake George is fed by mountain streams and underground springs. More than 200 wooded islands dot the lake. The waters abound in fish, and the surrounding mountains provide excellent facilities for hunting and winter sports. The principal communities on the lake are the villages of Lake George, Bolton Landing, and Hague, which are popular vacation resorts.

The first European to see Lake George was Father Jogues, a French Jesuit missionary, taken captive by the Mohawk Indians in 1642. Father Jogues later named the lake Lac Saint Sacrament. In 1755, the British soldier and colonial official Sir William Johnson renamed it Lake George in honor of George II. During the French and Indian War and during the American Revolution, Lake George, on a transportation route between New York and Canada, was the scene of many battles. The most famous was the Battle of Lake George, fought on Sept. 8, 1755, in which a force of French and Indians was defeated by a British colonial force under Gen. William Johnson. The battle is commemorated by a monument in Lake George Battleground Park at Lake George village.

GEORGE, Stefan (1868–1933), German lyric poet, born in Rüdesheim, and educated in philosophy and art history at the universities of Darmstadt, Berlin, Munich, and Paris. In Paris he became an enthusiastic follower of the symbolist movement, and in England was influenced by the Pre-

Raphaelites. After extensive travel in Europe, George returned to Germany and established a circle of literary disciples (the George-Kreis), of which he remained the autocratic guiding spirit. A number of famous German poets were members of this "art for art's sake" group; in revolt against contemporary realism and devoted to reviving German poetry, they wished to purify the literary language and restore to it aural sensuality and the spirit of Greek classicism.

A complete edition of his poetry—much of which was originally privately printed and distributed—was published in 18 volumes between 1927 and 1934. Little of this large body of difficult, complex, and highly personal verse has been translated into English. Selections, however, were published in *The Works of Stefan George* (1949; 2d ed., 1974), translated by Olga Marx (b. 1894) and Ernst Morwitz (1887–1971).

Although the Nazis, in recognition of George's contributions to German poetry and national ideals, wished to honor him, the poet refused their offers and went into exile in Switzerland in 1933.

GEORGE JUNIOR REPUBLIC, private self-governing, self-supporting, and coeducational boarding school. It was founded as a self-contained community in Freeville, N.Y., in 1895 by the philanthropist William Reuben George (1866–1936). It originally consisted of 144 boys and girls between the ages of 12 and 21, all of whom were from New York City. The community was established in the belief that boys and girls were capable of self-support and self-government and that the lack of such responsibilities contributed to juvenile delinquency.

Under the founder's direction the community was organized as a village under the laws of New York State. It prospered and grew in size and became the model for similar ventures in other states, a number of which later made up the National Association of Junior Republics. Members of George Junior Republic attend high school, work at paying jobs, learn practical skills, and share in the management of the community.

GEORGETOWN, capital, largest city, and chief port of Guyana, on the Atlantic Ocean, at the mouth of the Demerara R. The city lies 1.5 m (5 ft) below high-tide level and is protected from floods by a sea wall (completed 1882). Many older buildings are raised on brick stilts above the flood level. Sugar refining is a major industry. Exports include sugar, rice, bauxite, and diamonds. The University of Guyana (1963) and a large tropical botanical garden are here. The multiracial population includes large numbers of East Indians and Amerindians.

Georgetown was founded by the British in 1781 and named for King George III. It passed for a while to the French, who largely rebuilt it, and in 1784 to the Dutch, who called it Stabroek. Regaining control in 1812, the British government restored the name Georgetown and made the city the colonial capital of British Guiana. In 1966 it became the capital of independent Guyana. Pop. (1985 est., greater city) 200,000.

The George Washington Bridge   Port of New York Authority

GEORGE TOWN, formerly PINANG or PENANG, city, NW Malaysia, on the island of Pinang, capital of Pinang State, in the Strait of Malacca. One of the country's major seaports, it is a distribution point for rubber and agricultural products. Settled in 1786 by agents of the British East India Co., the community prospered as a port of call for ships trading between India and China. The Pagoda of 10,000 Buddhas and an art museum are here, and the University of Science (1969) is nearby, at Minden. Pop. (1980 prelim.) 250,578.

GEORGETOWN UNIVERSITY, institution of higher learning, in Washington, D.C., and the oldest Roman Catholic and Jesuit university in the U.S. First planned in 1785, the institution was founded as Georgetown Academy by John Carroll in 1789; students entered in 1791, and in 1805 Georgetown was placed under the direction of the Society of Jesus in Maryland. A congressional act in 1815 empowered the institution to grant academic degrees. At present, Georgetown consists of a college of arts and sciences and schools of business administration, foreign service, languages and linguistics, law, medicine, nursing, graduate studies, and summer and continuing education.

GEORGE WASHINGTON BRIDGE, two-level suspension toll bridge for vehicular traffic, northeast U.S., spanning the Hudson R. between New York City and Fort Lee, N.J. It was designed by the Swiss-American engineer Othmar Ammann (1879–1971). Construction began in 1927, and the bridge was opened on Oct. 25, 1931. The length between anchorages is 1451 m (4760 ft) and the length of the center span is 1067 m (3500 ft). At the center the bridge is 65 m (212 ft) above the river. The bridge has a width of 36 m (119 ft), of which 27 m (90 ft) is used for roadway. The upper level carries eight lanes of motor-vehicle traffic and two footways, and the lower roadway, completed in 1962, has six lanes for motor-vehicle traffic. The upper roadway is suspended from four steel cables, each 91 cm (36 in) in diameter and composed of 26,474 wires. The total weight of cable wire is 25,673 metric tons. The cables are carried by saddles on top of two 184-m- (604-ft-) high steel towers. The bridge is operated by the Port Authority of New York and New Jersey.

GEORGE WASHINGTON UNIVERSITY, privately controlled institution of higher learning, in Washington, D.C., founded in 1821. The university was known as Columbian College until 1873, when the college and professional schools were incorporated as Columbian University. In 1904 the name was changed to George Washington University. The university includes eight degree-granting schools and colleges: Columbian College (undergraduate liberal arts); a graduate school of arts and sciences; and professional schools in law, medicine, engineering and applied science, education, business and public management, and international affairs. The university's Division of Continuing Education offers courses at off-campus locations.

GEORGIA, one of the South Atlantic states of the U.S., bounded on the N by Tennessee and North Carolina, on the E by South Carolina and the Atlantic Ocean, on the S by Florida, and on the W by Alabama. The Savannah R. forms part of the E border and the Chattahoochee R. part of the W border.

Georgia entered the Union on Jan. 2, 1788, as the fourth state. During the American Civil War it was a member of the Confederate States of America. Once principally a farming state, known for its considerable cotton output, Georgia in the early 1990s had an economy centered on manufacturing and service industries. Atlanta, the state capital, serves as a major economic center for the South. Georgia is named for George II of England and is known as the Empire State of the South.

LAND AND RESOURCES

Georgia, with an area of 153,953 sq km (59,441 sq mi), is the 24th largest U.S. state and the biggest in land area E of the Mississippi R.; 4% of its land area is owned by the federal government. The state is roughly rectangular in shape, and its extreme dimensions are about 515 km (about 320 mi) from N to S and about 410 km (about 255 mi) from E to W. Elevations range from sea level, along the Atlantic Ocean, to 1458 m (4784 ft), atop Brasstown Bald, near the N boundary. The mean elevation of the state is 183 m (600 ft). The coastline along the Atlantic is 161 km (100 mi) long.

Physical Geography. Encompassing parts of six geographical regions, Georgia has a varied landscape. The S half of the state is made up of sections of the Atlantic Coastal Plain and the East Gulf Coastal Plain. The two regions had similar origins and are much alike. Each is underlain mainly by soft, unconsolidated sedimentary beds of sand and clay. A substantial part of the East Gulf Coastal Plain is underlain by limestone, which is studded with water-filled holes (sinkholes). The Atlantic Coastal Plain has richer topsoil. The two regions gradually increase in elevation toward the interior. The Atlantic coast is broken by many inlets and contains much marsh and swamp; offshore are the Sea Islands (a chain that continues N into South Carolina and S into Florida). Straddling the S border of the two coastal plains is the Okefenokee Swamp, which is also partly in Florida.

Most of the N half of Georgia is made up of a part of the Piedmont Plateau, an area of rolling hills underlain by hard crystalline rocks such as granite. The fall line (q.v.) is at the S edge of this region. Rivers flowing from the Piedmont Plateau onto the coastal plains descend in falls and rapids at the fall line. Elevations in the Piedmont section increase to the N, from about 150 m (about 500 ft) at the fall line to about 365 m (about 1200 ft) at its N edge.

Three regions of the Appalachian Mts. make up N Georgia. The most elevated of the regions is the Blue Ridge, in the NE, an area of rounded, forested mountains separated by narrow valleys. The Blue Ridge is underlain by extremely hard crystalline rocks such as gneiss. To the W of the Blue Ridge is the Valley and Ridge Region, where wide, flat, fertile valleys extending NE to SW are separated by narrow, steep-sided ridges. The NW corner of Georgia, made up of a section of the Cumberland Plateau, contains narrow, relatively infertile valleys bordered by ridges.

Rivers and Lakes. One group of Georgia rivers flows to the Atlantic Ocean. The Savannah and Altamaha are the main rivers in this group. The Altamaha collects the waters of two important central Georgia rivers, the Ocmulgee and Oconee. A second group of Georgia rivers flows toward the Gulf of Mexico. The Chattahoochee and the Flint are the principal rivers of this group.

Georgia has no large natural lakes, but dams on rivers have formed a number of large bodies of water. These include Lake Seminole, Walter F. George Lake, and Lake Sidney Lanier, on the Chattahoochee R.; Lake Sinclair, on the Oconee R.; Hartwell and Strom Thurmond lakes, on the Savannah R.; and Allatoona Lake, on the Etowah R. Parts of some lakes are in neighboring states.

Climate. The two Coastal Plain regions of Georgia and the Piedmont Plateau area have a humid subtropical climate. The S location, relatively low elevation, and nearness to the comparatively warm waters of the Atlantic and Gulf of Mexico produce a climate with long, hot summers, short, mild winters, and rainfall at all times of year. The climate is classified as humid continental in the Blue Ridge, Valley and Ridge, and Cumberland Plateau regions of the N. Summer temperatures in these areas are cooler than in S Georgia, and winters are colder, although not severe. Some winter snowfall occurs in the N regions. Because moist marine air is forced to rise when it meets the mountains, the Blue Ridge receives the most precipitation in the state. In Georgia as a whole, the rainier times of the year are in winter and summer; the average yearly precipitation is about 1270 mm (about 50 in). The recorded tem-

Cane Creek Falls near Dahlonega, in northern Georgia.
Georgia Dept. of Commerce

perature in the state has ranged from –27.2° C (–17° F), in 1940 near Rome in the NW, to 44.4° C (112° F), in 1952 at Louisville in the E.

Plants and Animals. About 60 percent of Georgia's land area is covered with forest. In the Coastal Plain regions the woodland, part of the Southeastern Pine Forest of the U.S., is dominated by slash and longleaf pine. Hardwood trees, notably the large live oak, are intermixed with the pine. Swamp trees, such as cypress and tupelo, and marsh grasses grow in some low-lying areas. The forest in the Piedmont region is mainly a mixture of oak and pine. In N Georgia the forest covering the mountains is composed principally of oak, hickory, maple, and other hardwood trees. The state's forest, particularly in the N, also contains many beautiful flowering trees and shrubs such as redbud, dogwood, and azalea.

Wild animals in Georgia include many deer, raccoon, opossum, fox, and squirrel, plus small numbers of black bear in the mountains and the SE forest. Ducks, geese, and quail are numerous, as are songbirds such as the mockingbird and wood thrush. Georgia's freshwater rivers and lakes contain many bass, bream, trout, perch, crappie, and catfish, and crabs, oysters, shrimp, and shad are to be found in the state's coastal marine waters.

Mineral Resources. Georgia contains sizable deposits of several important minerals. The inner Coastal Plain regions have deposits of kaolin, a high-grade white clay. Beautiful marble is found on the Piedmont Plateau N of Atlanta, and Stone Mt., E of Atlanta, is one of the largest known single masses of exposed granite in the world. Other minerals found in the state include coal, sand and gravel, talc, soapstone, barite, manganese, and bentonite. Much of the state's soil has a reddish tint because of its high clay content.

POPULATION

According to the 1990 census, Georgia had 6,478,216 inhabitants, an increase of 18.6% over 1980. The average population density in 1990 was 42 people per sq km (109 per sq mi). Whites made up 71% of the population and blacks 27%; other groups included 15,275 persons of Korean origin, 13,926 persons of Asian Indian background, 12,926 American Indians, and 12,657 persons of Chinese ancestry. About 109,000 persons were of Hispanic origin. Baptists made up 50.8% of the state population, followed by Methodists (11.5%) and Roman Catholics (6.3%). In 1990 approximately 63% of all Georgians lived in areas defined as urban, and the rest in rural areas. The state's biggest cities were Atlanta, the capital; Columbus; Savannah; Macon; and Albany.

EDUCATION AND CULTURAL ACTIVITY

Georgia has an extensive educational system, many cultural institutions, and a variety of historical places.

Education. In the colonial era, Georgia's children were educated in one-room rural schools and in a few church-supported academies. Publicly financed elementary schools were organized in 1872, and the state supported high schools beginning in 1912. In the late 1980s, Georgia's public educational facilities included 1732 public elementary and secondary schools, which each year enrolled about 828,400 elementary pupils and 298,100 secondary students. In addition, some 82,800 students attended private schools.

In the same period, Georgia had 95 institutions of higher education, with a combined annual enrollment of about 239,200 students. These institutions included the University of Georgia, at Athens, and Emory University, Georgia Institute of Technology, and Georgia State University (1913), all at Atlanta.

Cultural Institutions. Georgia has an extensive public library system. The state's largest libraries

The domed Georgia state capitol (center), built in 1889, stands near the modern skyscrapers of Peachtree Center in downtown Atlanta.   © 1990 Bill Losh–FPG International

are located in Atlanta, Columbus, Macon, and Savannah. Outstanding collections on Georgia's history are available at historical societies in Atlanta and Savannah. The Carter Presidential Center in Atlanta houses Jimmy Carter's presidential papers.

Notable museums are the Telfair Academy of Arts and Sciences, in Savannah; the Atlanta Museum and the High Museum of Art, in Atlanta; the Georgia Museum of Art, in Athens; the National Infantry Museum, at Fort Benning; and the Museum of Coastal History, on Saint Simons Island. Atlanta and Savannah support symphony orchestras, and Atlanta and Augusta have opera companies.

Historical Sites. Many historical sites and monuments are located in Georgia. The remains of old Indian mounds and villages are in Ocmulgee National Monument, near Macon, and Fort Frederica National Monument, on Saint Simons Island, includes a fort constructed in the 18th century by the British. Civil War battle sites are in Chickamauga and Chattanooga National Military Park, in the NW corner of the state; and in Kennesaw Mountain National Battlefield Park, near Marietta. Andersonville National Historic Site encompasses a Civil War prisoner-of-war camp, and Fort Pulaski National Monument, on Tybee Island, includes a fort attacked by Union forces in 1862. President Franklin D. Roosevelt's "Little White House" is in Warm Springs.

Sports and Recreation. Georgia's best-known sports event is the Masters, a golf tournament held at Augusta every April. Atlanta is the site of the annual Peach Bowl postseason college football game. The city also is the home of major league baseball, basketball, and football teams. Popular outdoor-recreation activities in Georgia

The Colonial Dames House in Savannah, built in the classical revival style, reflects the serenity and graciousness of the Old South still to be encountered here.

INDEX TO MAP OF GEORGIA

Cities and Towns

☉ County seat

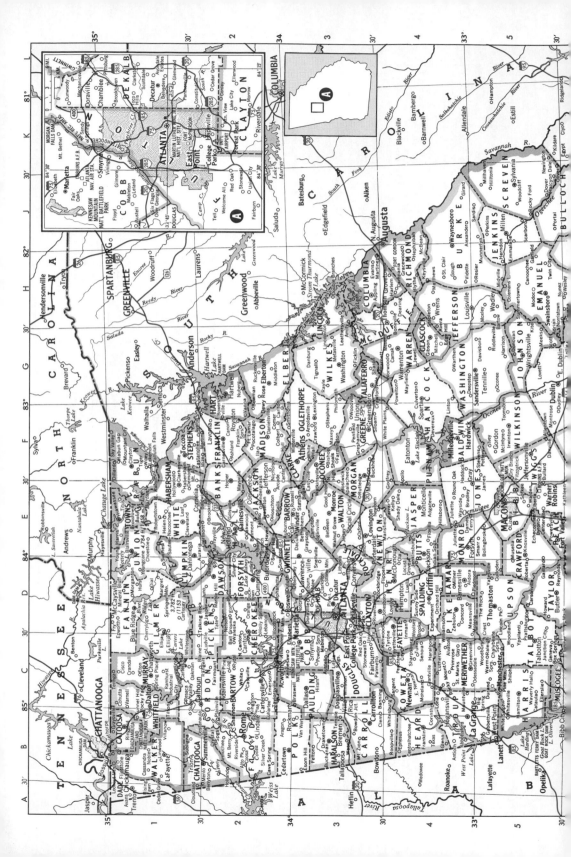

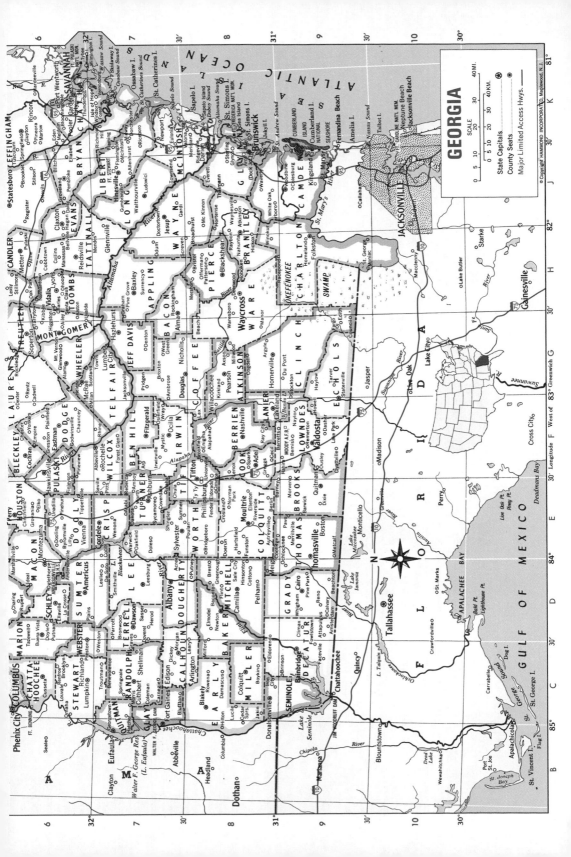

GEORGIA

SCALE

0 10 20 30 40 MI.

0 5 10 20 30 40 KM.

⊛ State Capitals

⊚ County Seats

── Major Limited Access Hwys.

© Copyright HAMMOND INCORPORATED, Maplewood, N.J.

include swimming, fishing, hunting, hiking, and golfing. Cumberland Island National Seashore includes unspoiled beaches, dunes, and marshes.

Communications. Georgia is served by a broad range of communications media. In the early 1990s the state had 196 AM and 184 FM radio-broadcasting stations and 46 television stations. The state's first radio station, WSB, began operation in Atlanta in 1922. Atlanta is the headquarters of the Turner Broadcasting System, a major cable-television company that in 1980 established the Cable News Network.

Georgia was served by 36 daily newspapers with a combined daily circulation of about 1.2 million copies in the early 1990s. Among the leading dailies were the *Constitution* and the *Journal,* published in Atlanta; the *Columbus Ledger-Enquirer;* the *Macon Telegraph;* and the *Savannah Morning News.* The oldest newspaper was the *Chronicle,* first published in Augusta in 1785.

GOVERNMENT AND POLITICS

Georgia is governed under a constitution that was adopted in 1982; previous constitutions had been adopted in 1777, 1789, 1798, 1861, 1865, 1868, 1877, 1945, and 1976. State constitutional amendments may be proposed by a two-thirds vote of the legislature or by a constitutional convention; to take effect, an amendment must be ratified by a majority of the persons voting on the issue in a general election.

Executive. Georgia's chief executive is a governor, who is popularly elected to a 4-year term and is prohibited from serving more than two successive terms. The same regulations apply to the lieutenant governor, who succeeds the governor should the latter resign, die, or be removed from office. Other officials popularly elected to 4-year terms are the secretary of state, attorney general, commissioner of agriculture, commissioner of labor, commissioner of insurance (who

Midway Church, in Midway, Liberty Co., originally built in 1752, was destroyed by fire during the American Revolution and rebuilt in 1792.

Georgia Dept. of Industry and Trade

also serves as comptroller general), and superintendent of schools.

Legislature. The bicameral Georgia legislature is the General Assembly, and it consists of a house of representatives, which has 180 members, and a senate, which has 56 members. All state representatives and state senators are popularly elected to 2-year terms.

Judiciary. Georgia's highest tribunal is the supreme court, made up of seven justices popularly elected to 6-year terms. The chief justice is elected by the court for the duration of the justice's term of office. The second highest court is the court of appeals, consisting of nine judges popularly elected to 6-year terms. The principal trial courts are the superior courts, which have 148 judges.

Local Government. County government is important in Georgia. In the early 1990s the state had 159 counties, almost all of which were administered by boards of commissioners. Most cities and towns were governed by popularly elected mayors and councils.

National Representation. Georgia is represented in the U.S. Congress by 2 senators and 11 representatives. The state has 13 electoral votes in presidential elections.

Politics. The Democratic party has dominated state and local politics in Georgia. Democrats have held the governorship continuously in the state since 1872, and they retain control of both houses of the state legislature by large majorities. The Democratic party also dominated national politics in the state from 1872 through 1960. In 1964, however, Georgia for the first time cast its electoral votes for a Republican presidential candidate. George C. Wallace, running as the nominee of the American Independent party, carried the state in 1968. Jimmy Carter, a one-term governor (1971–75), became in 1976 the first native Georgian to win election to the U.S. presidency.

ECONOMY

Georgia was primarily an agricultural state until the mid-20th century. In the early 1990s, manufacturing was a leading economic sector, and Atlanta was a major commercial, financial, transportation, and manufacturing center for the southeastern U.S. Several large federal military facilities, such as Fort Benning, near Columbus, were major contributors to the state's economy.

Agriculture. The Georgia economy has an important agricultural sector. Sales of livestock and livestock products account for nearly 60% of the yearly farm income and sales of crops for the rest. The output is produced on about 46,000

Okefenokee Swamp in southeast Georgia, extending into northern Florida. This 72-km (45-mi) long area consists of lakes and islands covered with vines and cypress forests. Much of it is a wildlife refuge.

Georgia Dept. of Industry and Trade, Tourist Division

Tobacco, a leading crop of Georgia, is harvested in the southern part of the state. Carolyn Carter

farms, averaging 106 ha (263 acres) in size. Leading agricultural products include broiler chickens, chicken eggs, peanuts, corn, soybeans, and cattle. Georgia usually ranks with Arkansas and Alabama as the top three U.S. producers of broiler chickens; most broilers are raised in the NE part of the state. Georgia typically leads all states in peanut and pecan production and ranks fifth in the volume of tobacco output; these three crops are grown mainly in the S half of the state. Other major crops include cotton, hay, beans, and peas. In addition, Georgia produces large quantities of peaches, especially in Peach Co., near Macon. Many hogs are raised in the state.

Forestry. A substantial amount of timber is cut each year from Georgia's extensive commercial timberland. Approximately two-thirds of the annual harvest is softwood, much of which is used to make paper. Naval stores such as turpentine, pitch, and rosin are produced from the pine trees of the SW part of the state.

Fishing. The relatively small commercial fishing industry of Georgia operates mainly in the coastal waters of the Atlantic Ocean. The yearly marine catch is about 7300 metric tons and has a total value of approximately $20 million. Edible shellfish make up the bulk of the catch in terms of both volume and value, and shrimp is the leading variety landed. Crabs, oysters, and clams also are caught.

Mining. The principal minerals recovered in Georgia are clays, stone, and sand and gravel. Georgia is the leading state in the production of clay, and kaolin—a clay used in producing china, paint, paper, and other goods—is the most important single mineral product. It is mined chiefly along the fall line, from Columbus to Augusta. Fuller's earth is another major type of clay produced in the state. Granite and marble are quarried in great quantities in N Georgia. Other important mineral products include barite, feldspar, and mica.

Manufacturing. Georgia contains more than 9000 manufacturing establishments, which together are responsible for the employment of more than 500,000 workers. Manufacturing accounts for

305

GEORGIA

DATE OF STATEHOOD: January 2, 1788; 4th state

CAPITAL:	Atlanta
MOTTO:	Wisdom, justice and moderation
NICKNAME:	Empire State of the South
STATE SONG:	"Georgia on My Mind" (words by Stuart Gorrell; music by Hoagy Carmichael)
STATE TREE:	Live oak
STATE FLOWER:	Cherokee rose
STATE BIRD:	Brown thrasher
POPULATION (1990):	6,478,216; 11th among the states
AREA:	153,953 sq km (59,441 sq mi); 24th largest state; includes 3943 sq km (1522 sq mi) of inland water
COASTLINE:	161 km (100 mi)
HIGHEST POINT:	Brasstown Bald, 1458 m (4784 ft)
LOWEST POINT:	Sea level at the Atlantic coast
ELECTORAL VOTES:	13
U.S. CONGRESS:	2 senators; 11 representatives

POPULATION OF GEORGIA SINCE 1790

Year of Census	Population	Classified As Urban
1790	83,000	0%
1820	341,000	2%
1850	906,000	4%
1880	1,542,000	9%
1900	2,216,000	16%
1920	2,896,000	25%
1940	3,124,000	34%
1960	3,943,000	55%
1980	5,463,000	62%
1990	6,478,216	63%

POPULATION OF TEN LARGEST CITIES

	1990 Census	1980 Census
Atlanta	394,017	423,022
Columbus	179,278	169,441
Savannah	137,560	141,390
Macon	106,612	116,896
Albany	78,122	74,550
Roswell	47,923	23,337
Athens	45,734	42,549
Augusta	44,639	47,532
Marietta	44,129	30,829
Warner Robins	43,726	39,893

CLIMATE

	ATLANTA	SAVANNAH
Average January temperature range	0.6° to 10.6° C (33° to 51° F)	3.9° to 16.1° C (39° to 61° F)
Average July temperature range	20.6° to 30.6° C (69° to 87° F)	21.7° to 32.8° C (71° to 91° F)
Average annual temperature	16.1° C (61° F)	18.9° C (66° F)
Average annual precipitation	1219 mm (48 in)	1295 mm (51 in)
Average annual snowfall	38 mm (1.5 in)	8 mm (0.3 in)
Mean number of days per year with appreciable precipitation	113	113
Average daily relative humidity	70%	71%
Mean number of clear days per year	108	104

CUMBERLAND PLATEAU
BLUE RIDGE
VALLEY & RIDGE REGION
Chattahoochee R.
PIEDMONT PLATEAU
Savannah R.
ATLANTIC COASTAL PLAIN
Chattahoochee R.
EAST GULF COASTAL PLAIN
Flint R.

NATURAL REGIONS OF GEORGIA

ECONOMY

State budget .... general revenue $11.2 billion
                         general expenditure $11.4 billion
                         accumulated debt $3.1 billion
State and local taxes, per capita $1801
Personal income, per capita.................... $13,631
Population below poverty level 14.7%
Assets, insured commercial banks (392) .... $64.3 billion
Labor force (civilian nonfarm) 2,945,000
    Employed in wholesale and retail trade   25%
    Employed in services   21%
    Employed in manufacturing   18%
    Employed in government   17%

	Quantity Produced	Value
FARM PRODUCTS		**$3.9 billion**
Crops		**$1.6 billion**
Peanuts	611,000 metric tons	$459 million
Tobacco	46,000 metric tons	$172 million
Corn	1.2 million metric tons	$105 million
Hay	1.0 million metric tons	$72 million
Soybeans	267,000 metric tons	$57 million
Peaches	59,000 metric tons	$39 million
Livestock and Livestock Products		**$2.3 billion**
Chickens		
(broilers)	1.7 million metric tons	$1.2 billion
Eggs	4.3 billion	$289 million
Cattle	173,000 metric tons	$276 million
Hogs	200,000 metric tons	$233 million
Milk	649,000 metric tons	$227 million
MINERALS		**$1.4 billion**
Clays	9.8 million metric tons	$1.0 billion
Stone	46.1 million metric tons	$275 million
Sand, gravel	6 million metric tons	$26 million
FISHING	7300 metric tons	**$20 million**

	Annual Payroll
FORESTRY	**$14 million**
MANUFACTURING	**$13.2 billion**
Apparel and textile mill products	$2.8 billion
Transportation equipment	$1.4 billion
Food and kindred products	$1.1 billion
Paper and allied products	$938 million
Printing and publishing	$733 million
Industrial machinery and equipment	$730 million
Electronic equipment	$726 million
Chemicals and allied products	$572 million
Lumber and wood products	$518 million
Fabricated metal products	$499 million
Stone, clay, and glass products	$431 million
Primary metals	$389 million
Rubber and plastics products	$357 million
OTHER	**$49.2 billion**
Government	$12.5 billion
Services	$12.2 billion
Retail trade	$6.0 billion
Wholesale trade	$5.3 billion
Transportation, communications, and public utilities	$5.3 billion
Finance, insurance, and real estate	$4.2 billion
Construction	$2.9 billion

PRINCIPAL PRODUCTS OF GEORGIA

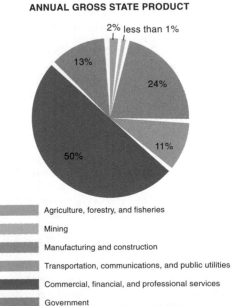

ANNUAL GROSS STATE PRODUCT

2% less than 1%

13%

24%

11%

50%

- Agriculture, forestry, and fisheries
- Mining
- Manufacturing and construction
- Transportation, communications, and public utilities
- Commercial, financial, and professional services
- Government

Sources: U.S. government publications

A lumberjack atop a mountain of pulpwood. Georgia is a leader in lumber production.   Georgia Dept. of Commerce

mountains of the N part of the state, the Atlanta area, and the Atlantic coast. Near Atlanta is Stone Mountain State Park, which features the equestrian figures of the Confederate leaders Robert E. Lee, Stonewall Jackson, and Jefferson Davis carved on the N face of the granite mountain. Points of interest in the coastal area include Savannah, one of the oldest cities in the U.S., and Cumberland, Saint Simons, and Jekyll islands. Among the notable attractions of the W part of the state are Warm Springs, which was frequented by Franklin D. Roosevelt, and Plains, the hometown of Jimmy Carter.

Transportation. Georgia has an extensive system of modern transportation facilities. Among them are about 176,380 km (about 109,600 mi) of federal, state, and local roads, including 1931 km (1200 mi) of the Interstate Highway System. The first railroad in Georgia was opened in 1837; in the early 1990s the state was served by some 6470 km (some 4020 mi) of operated Class I railroad

Georgia has rapidly industrialized in recent years. Substantial amounts of steel are produced at modern mills in and near Atlanta.   Georgia Dept. of Commerce

about 19% of the annual gross state product. The leading types of manufactures, based on annual payroll, are apparel and textiles, transportation equipment, processed foods, and paper and kindred products. The principal textiles produced are woven cotton fiber, floor covering, and yarn and thread. NW Georgia contains the largest concentration of tufted-carpet producers in the U.S. and accounts for more than 50% of the nation's output. Many other textile mills, as well as clothing factories, are in the Piedmont Plateau region of the state, especially in small towns.

The state produces a great variety of foodstuffs, notably processed peanuts and fruit, dressed broilers, and frozen shrimp. The manufacture of transportation equipment, mainly motor vehicles and aircraft, is concentrated in the Atlanta metropolitan area. The state has many paper mills, and cellophane and rayon are made from the cellulose of pine trees. Much pine lumber and hardwood flooring also are produced, and an important furniture industry is centered at Toccoa. Other fabricated goods made in Georgia include industrial machinery, electronic equipment, chemicals, metal products, and bricks and tiles.

Tourism. In the early 1990s, more than 32 million travelers visited Georgia each year, and the state annually earned over $10 billion from tourism. The major tourist attractions of Georgia include the

track. The Atlanta area is a major rail hub as well as the site of William B. Hartsfield International Airport, one of the busiest in the U.S. Georgia has 275 airports and 89 heliports. Its principal seaports are Savannah and Brunswick; along the coast is a section of the Atlantic Intracoastal Waterway. Parts of the Chattahoochee, Flint, and Savannah rivers are used to transport freight.

Energy. In the early 1990s, Georgia had an installed electricity generating capacity of about 20.7 million kw, and its annual electricity production was about 97.6 billion kw. Approximately 70% of the electricity was generated from fossil fuels, about 25% by nuclear power plants, and about 5% by hydroelectric installations (mainly on the Chattahoochee, Etowah, and Savannah rivers). J.D.Lo.

HISTORY

The major Indian groups in Georgia at the time of European settlement were the Lower Creeks and the Cherokees, both of which had established cultures. The earliest known European settlement in Georgia was the Spanish mission of Santa Catalina, established in 1566 on Saint Catherines Island. The mission was overrun in 1680 by the British and their Indian allies.

The Colonial and Revolutionary Periods. In 1732, the British philanthropists James Oglethorpe and John Percival (1683–1748) secured a royal charter to establish a colony in the area, providing for a board of trustees to govern it. The early settlers included many English debtors, but also Scots, Germans, Swiss, and some German Jews. Oglethorpe arrived with the first group and founded Savannah in 1733. The British desired a buffer between South Carolina and the Spanish in Florida and the French in Louisiana. Georgia served this purpose well. It did not begin to prosper economically, however, until the charter expired in 1753, and economic growth became pronounced after the appointment of James Wright (1716–85) as royal governor in 1760. Relations between the colonists and the Indians were generally friendly, and slavery was prohibited until 1749.

Although loyalty to the British crown was strong in Georgia, the colony joined the American Revolution and sent representatives to the Second Continental Congress. The British seized Savannah in 1778, but guerrilla fighters prevented them from gaining control of the interior, and they evacuated the state in 1782.

Disputes with the Federal Government. After the Revolution, Georgia supported a strong central government and was one of three states to ratify the Constitution unanimously. This popular support, however, did not prevent conflict with the new national government. Georgia claimed virtually all of what is now Mississippi and much of

Alabama, and granted this territory to private land companies. These grants (the Yazoo Land Frauds) were declared invalid in 1800 by the U.S. Congress. Georgia agreed in 1802 to cede these lands to the U.S. and received a federal commitment to remove the Indians to the West. After a series of constitutional squabbles involving the state, the president of the U.S., and the U.S. Supreme Court, by 1838 the Creeks and Cherokees were largely removed from Georgia, thus opening up vast new cotton lands that were quickly settled by whites.

Antebellum Politics and the American Civil War. Two factions dominated Georgia politics in the early 19th century, one representing the coastal communities and the slaveholders and the other including the up-country people and the non-slaveholders. Nonslaveholders frequently failed to support the coastal planters in their struggles with the North over slavery. Nevertheless, when the final showdown came in 1861, a majority voted to secede from the Union. Federal forces quickly blockaded the state and captured many offshore islands. Georgia provided large numbers of troops for the Confederate army, but Gov. Joseph E. Brown (1821–94) also resisted the authority of the Confederate government in Montgomery on the basis of states' rights. In 1864 Georgia was invaded by Union forces under Gen. William Tecumseh Sherman, which took Atlanta on September 2 and then proceeded on the famous "March to the Sea," ending in Savannah in December.

The Post–Civil War Period. Georgia adopted a new constitution and ratified the 13th amendment abolishing slavery in 1865, but was nevertheless placed under federal military control by terms of the Reconstruction Acts of 1867. Because of continuing resistance by state officials to the political conditions established by the federal government, however, Georgia was not restored to the Union until July 1870.

State politics were staunchly Democratic after Reconstruction. The Bourbons (conservative Democrats) dominated from 1872 until 1890, combining support for business interests with low taxes and limited public services. In Atlanta, the journalist and lecturer Henry W. Grady (1851–89) led the "New South" movement, which advocated industrial development and urbanization for the region. Poor agricultural conditions created widespread support for the Populists, who challenged the Bourbons for political power in the 1890s but quickly faded thereafter.

White Supremacy. In 1908 new voter registration requirements virtually disenfranchised blacks, and the county unit system of Democratic primary voting (1917) placed political power firmly in the hands of rural white voters. Eugene Talmadge (1884–1946), elected governor in 1933, opposed most New Deal measures, especially those promoting social and racial equality. The election of Ellis Arnall (1907–   ) as governor in 1942 ushered in a period of reform, which included abolition of the poll tax and adoption of a new constitution in 1945. Talmadge was again elected governor in 1946, but he died before he could take office. The General Assembly declared his son, Herman E. Talmadge (1913–   ), governor, but this action was nullified by the state supreme court. Talmadge eventually won election, however, in 1948.

Georgia was very much a part of southern resistance to the civil rights movement. In response to the 1954 Supreme Court decision declaring public school racial segregation unconstitutional, an amendment was adopted permitting state support of private education as an alternative to public schools. The state legislature passed a law in 1955 to implement this tactic if federal courts ordered any public school to integrate. After 1959, however, closing schools to avoid integration became a local option.

Racial Compromise and Economic Growth. In 1961 the University of Georgia and the Atlanta public school system were integrated. White and black leaders in Atlanta worked to avoid violence and meet black demands, while the Southern Christian Leadership Conference, a major civil rights organization led by Martin Luther King, Jr., made its headquarters in the city.

Georgia's population increased rapidly in the 1960s and '70s. Atlanta, the state capital, became the leading financial and transportation hub of the Southeast, with one of the country's busiest commercial airports and by 1990, a metropolitan area population of approximately 2.8 million. Light industry, tourism, and military and defense installations far outdistanced agriculture in contributions to the state's economy.   B.A.Br.

For further information on this topic, see the Bibliography in volume 28, sections 1183, 1187.

GEORGIA, REPUBLIC OF, formerly GEORGIAN SOVIET SOCIALIST REPUBLIC, independent republic, SE Europe, in W Caucasia. It is bordered on the N by Russia; on the E by Azerbaijan; on the S by Azerbaijan, Armenia, and Turkey; and on the W by the Black Sea. Georgia includes the Abkhaz, Adzhar, and South Ossetian autonomous regions. Tbilisi is the capital and largest city; other important cities include Kutaisi, Sukhumi, and Batumi. Area, about 69,700 sq km (about 26,900 sq mi); pop. (1989) 5,443,000.

For a map of this area, *see* UNION OF SOVIET SOCIALIST REPUBLICS.

Georgia has a mostly mountainous terrain, more than one-third of which is heavily wooded. The main ridge of the Caucasus Mts. forms the N boundary, the Lesser Caucasus occupying the S and central parts of the republic. Georgia is drained principally by the Rioni R., which flows through a broad valley to the Black Sea; and the

Two Georgians in cossack uniforms leap high in the air in the mock combat of a sword dance. Georgians are noted for their folk dances.   Leo DeWys Inc.

Kura R., which flows E from Turkey, its rapid waters being a primary source of hydroelectric power. The climate has wide regional variations, from humid subtropical in the W coastal lowlands to drier and colder in the E mountains.

Agriculture is an important feature of the Georgian economy, although arable land is scarce. Reclamation of swampy coastal lowlands around the mouth of the Rioni R. has added much fertile land; this region produces tea and citrus fruit. Other crops are grapes, tobacco, and silk. Livestock raising is also important. Georgia has acquired increasing importance as an industrial region because of the abundance of electric power, mineral deposits (manganese, iron ore, molybdenum, and gold), and fuel (coal and petroleum). Marble, alabaster, and diatomite shale are also mined. Industries produce iron and steel, cement, motor vehicles, and textiles. The Georgian Black Sea coast is an important resort area. The population of the republic is about two-thirds Georgian, with Armenians, Russians, Azerbaijanians, Ossetians, and Abkhazians the largest ethnic minorities.

From about the 6th century BC, Georgia was colonized by Ionian Greeks; the W region was known as Colchis and the E region as Iberia. In about the 4th century BC Georgia was united into a single kingdom, with Mtskheta as its capital. Christianity was introduced in the 4th century AD. Until the 7th century, control over Georgia was contested by the Persian and Byzantine empires. The region was conquered by the Arabs in the 7th century and by the Seljuk Turks in the 11th century. King David II expelled the Turks in the early 12th century, reuniting Georgia as a kingdom. The kingdom was crushed by Mongol invaders in the 13th century. Thereafter Georgia was under the control of Iran and the Ottoman Empire until the 18th century. A Georgian kingdom was proclaimed in the mid-18th century, but Russia obtained control of the state's foreign affairs in 1783. In 1801 the last Georgian king abdicated, and Georgia became a part of the Russian Empire.

In 1918, following the Russian Revolution, Georgia became an independent state. In 1921 Soviet troops invaded, and the region was incorporated in the USSR. In 1922 Georgia was joined with Armenia and Azerbaijan to form the Transcaucasian SFSR. When the Transcaucasian SFSR was dissolved in 1936, Georgia was made a constituent republic of the Soviet Union. Georgia declared independence from the USSR in April 1991 and held presidential elections in May, but political conditions within the republic remained unstable throughout the year. When the USSR dissolved in December, Georgia was the only one of the 12 remaining Soviet republics that did not join the Commonwealth of Independent States (q.v.).

GEORGIA, STRAIT OF, channel, NW Washington and SW British Columbia, about 240 km (about 150 mi) long and up to 48 km (30 mi) wide. It separates part of Vancouver Island from the mainland. Linked to the Pacific Ocean by waterways to the SW and NW, it forms a section of the Inside Passage between Washington and Alaska. It has many islands and receives the Fraser R. near the city of Vancouver.

GEORGIA, UNIVERSITY OF, state-supported institution of higher learning, in Athens, Ga., founded in 1785. The school was opened in 1801 and functioned until the outbreak of the American Civil War, when the faculty and most of the students joined the Confederate army. The institution reopened in 1866, and in 1872 it received the proceeds of the sales of lands received by the state under the Land Grant Act of 1862. The university consists of the College of Arts and Sciences, conferring the baccalaureate and higher degrees; colleges of agriculture, business, education, and veterinary medicine; the Henry W. Grady College of Journalism and Mass Communication; the D. B. Warnell School of Forest Resources; a graduate school; and schools of family and consumer sciences, law, pharmacy, and social work.

GEORGIA INSTITUTE OF TECHNOLOGY, state-supported institution of higher learning in Atlanta, Ga. Founded in 1885 and commonly known as Georgia Tech, the institute forms part of the state university system and comprises the colleges of architecture, computing, engineering, and sciences and the Ivan Allen College of Management, Policy, and International Affairs. Undergraduate and graduate degrees are granted in various engineering disciplines, including aerospace, ceramic, chemical, civil, computer, electrical, environmental, health physics, health systems, industrial, materials, mechanical, metallurgical, nuclear, polymer, and textile, as well as engineering science and mechanics, operations research, and statistics. Degrees are also offered in other branches of the natural and social sciences.

GEORGIAN BAY, large NE arm of Lake Huron, SE Ontario, about 200 km (about 124 mi) long and 80 km (50 mi) wide. It is partially separated from Lake Huron by the Manitoulin Islands and by the Bruce Peninsula. Numerous rivers, which drain the lake regions of S Ontario, empty into the bay. It is linked with Lake Ontario by the Trent Canal system. Georgian Bay has a very irregular shoreline and includes numerous islands, notably the Thirty Thousand Islands along its E shore. Many of the islands, including those of Georgian Bay Islands National Park, are frequented by vacationers. The bay was discovered in 1612 by the French explorer Étienne Brûlé and was later named for George IV of Great Britain.

GEORGIAN BAY ISLANDS NATIONAL PARK, SE Ontario, established 1929. The park comprises 59 scenic islands, all but one located on the E side of Georgian Bay, an inlet of Lake Huron. Flowerpot Island, in W Georgian Bay, contains oddly shaped rock pillars. Facilities for outdoor recreation are available in the park, especially on Beausoleil Island. Area, 25 sq km (10 sq mi).

GEORGIAN LANGUAGE. See CAUCASIAN LANGUAGES.

GEORGIAN LITERATURE, literature of the inhabitants of the Republic of Georgia. It is written in the Georgian language. The earliest work to survive, *The Martyrdom of the Saint Shushanik* (474–84), and the thousands of palimpsests of the 5th, 6th, and 7th centuries indicate that at least the Gospels, the Epistles of Saint Paul, and about 150 Psalms had been translated into Georgian during that period. Several Georgian translations of the complete Bible from the 8th and 9th centuries also survive.

The Golden Age of Georgian literature came under Queen Thamar (c. 1160–1212), during whose rule (1184–1212) Georgia reached its political as well as its cultural peak. The best-known work is the secular *The Man in the Tiger's Skin,* by the late 12th-century poet Shotha Rusthaveli (fl. 1190), the national epic of Georgia. Beginning in this period, Persian stories and myths became a strong literary influence. They were much evident in the writings of the royal poet King Theimuraz I (1589–1663) and denounced by a later royal poet, King Archil (1647–1713). Persian influence remained strong until the rise of Georgian nationalism in the 18th century.

Among the important 18th-century writers were King Vakhtang (1675–1737) and Sulkhan Saba Orbeliani (1655?–1725?), author of a collection of moral tales and of a Georgian dictionary as well as of poems and a journal of his extensive travels in Western Europe. Other writers include the poets David Guramishvili (1705–92) and Bessarion (Besiki) Gabashvili.

During the 19th century, Western European influence became strong. Among the poets were Alexander Chavchavadse (1786–1846) and Grigol Orbeliani (1804–83). Their poetry was noted for its patriotic themes and extravagant praise of wine and women. Nikoloz Baratashvili (1814–46) also showed European influence.

In the late 19th century the most influential Georgian man of letters was the patriotic Ilia Chavchavadse (1837–1907). From 1921 to 1991

The doorway of Ely House in Dublin exemplifies the Georgian style in English 18th-century domestic architecture. Irish Tourist Board

Georgia was part of the Soviet Union. Much literature continued to be produced in the Georgian language, but it belonged to the cultural tradition of the USSR.

GEORGIAN SOVIET SOCIALIST REPUBLIC. See GEORGIA, REPUBLIC OF.

GEORGIAN STYLE, neoclassical style of architecture and interior design, popular in Great Britain during the reigns of the first four Georges, or from about 1715 to 1820. The Georgian style developed from the Roman Palladian style (*see* PALLADIO, ANDREA) used by the 17th-century English architect Inigo Jones, and was largely employed in domestic architecture and in planned sections of towns, such as the Adelphi section of London designed by the 18th-century Scottish-English architect Robert Adam, the Circus and the Royal Crescent built by the English architects John Wood the Elder and John Wood the Younger (1728–81) in the resort town of Bath, and the whole of New Town in Edinburgh. Among the finest examples of the style used for a public building in the second half of the 18th century is Somerset House, London, designed by the English architect Sir William Chambers. The Customs House, the Four Courts, and other Georgian buildings that give Dublin its 18th-century character were designed by the English architect James Gandon (1743–1823). The style was superseded in England by the Greek and Gothic revivals of the 19th century. In colonial North America, the influence of the Georgian style is evident in very few buildings before the American Revolution. By 1785, however, in the newly formed U.S., the Georgian style had become extremely popular in a native version called the Federal style. This evolved into a monumental neoclassical style exemplified by Thomas Jefferson's elegant designs (1817–26) for the University of Virginia at Charlottesville. This version of the Georgian style remained popular for public buildings in the U.S. well into the 20th century. See also AMERICAN ART AND ARCHITECTURE; NEOCLASSICAL ART AND ARCHITECTURE.

For further information on this topic, see the Bibliography in volume 28, sections 663, 676.

GEOSYNCLINE, in geology, a major structural feature of the earth's crust. A geosyncline begins as a belt of especially active sedimentation and eventually becomes troughlike. This trough may remain intact for millions of years, but as a rule, the sediments deposited in it become severely folded and uplifted to form a mountain chain.

The concept of a geosyncline was first developed in the 1850s when the American geologist James Hall (1811–98), working on a geological survey of New York State, noticed that sedimentary formations of the Devonian period (q.v.) became progressively thinner toward the northwest, where they wedged out on the Canadian Shield; whereas, to the southeast, formations of

that age became gradually thicker. Also, whereas the formations on the edge of the shield were almost flat, those in the southeast were increasingly folded. Similar troughlike features were found to have been the antecedents of most mountain belts. The American mineralogist James Dwight Dana coined the name geosyncline for these features, from the common geological term syncline (a structural trough) and the prefix geo- (earth), to imply their global importance.

Two kinds of geosynclines were later identified: miogeosynclines, developed along continental shelves, and eugeosynclines, developed seaward along continental rises. Miogeosynclines are found where rivers bring enough sediment to the sea for huge, subsiding deltas to form, as at the mouths of the Nile and the Mississippi. Eugeosynclines coincide with the deep ocean trenches that form where one plate of the earth's crust plunges (is subducted) beneath another (see PLATE TECTONICS). Sediments and volcanic rocks in these trenches have been crumpled and thrust up from the ocean floor to form mountains such as the Coast Ranges of western North America. R.W.Fa.

GEOTHERMAL ENERGY. See GEOTHERMICS; ENERGY SUPPLY, WORLD.

GEOTHERMICS, science pertaining to the earth's interior heat. Its main practical application is in finding natural concentrations of hot water, the source of geothermal energy, for use in electric power generation and direct heat applications such as

Geothermal generating plant, one of 15 installations in Sonoma Co., Calif., that transform the internal heat of the earth into electric energy. Joseph H. Wherry

space heating and industrial drying processes. Heat is produced within the crust and upper mantle of the earth (q.v.) primarily by decay of radioactive elements. This geothermal energy is transferred to the earth's surface by diffusion and by convection movement of magma (molten rock) and deep-lying circulating water. Surface hydrothermal manifestations include hot springs, geysers, and fumaroles. Hot springs have been used since ancient times for therapy and for recreational purposes. Early Norse settlers in Iceland brought water from neaby hot springs into their shelters by means of wooden conduits.

Steam produced from the naturally hot fluid that exists in geothermal systems is an alternative to pressurized steam produced in power plants by burning fossil fuels, by utilizing nuclear energy, or by other means. Modern drilling in geothermal systems reaches concentrations of water and steam, heated by much deeper magma, at depths up to 3000 m (10,000 ft). Steam is purified at the wellhead before being transported in large, insulated pipes to turbines.

Geothermal energy was developed for electrical power in 1904 in Tuscany, Italy, where power production continues today. Geothermal fluids are also used to heat groups of buildings in Budapest, Hungary; a Paris suburb; all of Reykjavík and other Icelandic cities; most of Klamath Falls, Oreg.; and (since 1890) part of Boise, Idaho.

The world's largest geothermal power complex is in the U.S. at The Geysers of northern California. As of 1991, The Geysers had a generating capacity of approximately 1400 megawatts (MW), enough to satisfy most of the electrical demand of the San Francisco metropolitan area 170 km (105 mi) to the south. Geothermal power plants are operating at other sites in California, Nevada, Utah, and Hawaii, for a total U.S. capacity of approximately 2800 MW in 1990. The U.S. has an estimated total potential of 23,000 MW a year for 30 years, based on all known hydrothermal systems hotter than 150° C (300° F). A possible technique for future development of geothermal energy has been tested in New Mexico by drilling into hot, dry rock beneath a quiescent volcanic system and injecting surface water that returns as superheated steam. Worldwide, installed geothermal capacity in 18 countries was approximately 5800 MW in 1990, and as much as 9000 MW is planned by 1995. J.H.W.

For further information on this topic, see the Bibliography in volume 28, sections 417, 534.

GERA, city, central Germany, in Thuringia, on the White Elster R. It is an industrial center and rail junction. Chief manufactures include iron castings, machinery, musical instruments, furniture, textiles, carpets, dyestuffs, and leather goods. Among the

Dwarf bedding geraniums in a variety of colors.
Ferry-Morse Seed Company

city's historical buildings is Osterstein Palace (17th-18th cent.). Established in the 10th century and chartered in 1224, Gera was sacked by Swedish forces in 1639, during the Thirty Years' War, and was largely destroyed by fire in 1686 and 1780. Pop. (1987 est.) 132,900.

GERANIUM, common name for the plant family Geraniaceae, and for its representative genus, *Geranium.* The family contains 14 genera and about 730 species of mostly temperate herbs or shrubs. The genus *Geranium*—commonly called cranesbill because the fruit bears a long "beak" formed from the persistent style—contains about 250 species, many of which are cultivated. The garden geranium is actually a related genus, *Pelargonium.* The two genera have several structural differences, the most significant being the presence of a nectar-producing spur on the calyx (the outer floral envelope) of *Pelargonium.* The two are easily distinguished vegetatively, however, *Pelargonium* being thick-stemmed, succulent, and usually strongly scented, and *Geranium* being low, spreading, and unscented.

The family Geraniaceae belongs to the order Geraniales, which contains four other families and a total of about 2600 species. The family Oxalidaceae (*see* OXALIS) contains about 900 species of mostly subtropical and tropical herbs. The family Balsaminaceae (*see* BALSAM) contains about 850 species, all but one of which are in the genus

Impatiens. The two remaining families are the Limnanthaceae, with 2 genera and only 8 species of temperate North American herbs, and the Tropaeolaceae, with 3 genera and about 88 species of Central and South American herbs. The nasturtium (q.v.) is a member of the Tropaeolaceae.

The flowers of the order are hypogynous, that is, the various parts arise from below the ovary (female part of the flower); usually the flowers have twice as many stamens (male flower parts) as petals or sepals (outer floral whorl); and the style (elongated part of the pistil) often persists after the flower has withered and the fruit has begun to develop.

Plants of the order Geraniales are members of the class Magnoliopsida (*see* DICOTS) in the division Magnoliophyta (*see* ANGIOSPERM). M.R.C.

For further information on this topic, see the Bibliography in volume 28, sections 451–52, 592–93.

GERBIL, common name for any of several small, burrowing rodents forming the subfamily Gerbillinae, of the family Cricetidae, which also includes the hamster. Gerbils are about 13 cm (about 5 in) long, excluding the equally long tufted tail. They have soft, sand-colored fur, a mouselike face, and long hind legs that enable them to leap about like rodents such as jerboas and kangaroo rats (*see* JERBOA; KANGAROO RAT). Sometimes called sand rats or desert rats, they are found in the dry, sandy areas and grasslands of western Asia and Africa. Colonies usually live together in a long tunnel, plugging the entrance with earth to retain moisture. Most species are active at night and feed on seeds, grasses, and roots. They require little water.

Gerbils may live up to four years; litters of two to nine young are born as often as once a month during the first two years. About 12 genera and more than 70 species are known. The Mongolian gerbil, *Meriones unguiculatus,* became a popular pet after it was introduced as a laboratory animal. It is clean, active, and friendly.

For further information on this topic, see the Bibliography in volume 28, sections 461, 475, 595.

GERIATRICS, specialized branch of medicine that deals with the diseases of older persons and their therapy. The study of the aging process itself is called gerontology (q.v.). Increased interest in geriatrics is due largely to the greater number of older persons in society, which is in turn a result of social and medical changes that have extended the life expectancy in the U.S. from an average of 47 years in 1900 to 75.9 years in 1990. The elderly population is expected to increase rapidly over the next 30 years, with the number of persons over 85 growing most rapidly.

In 1975 the U.S. Congress established the National Institute on Aging (NIA) to sponsor research on aging and on therapy for the problems of older persons. In 1978 the Institute of Medicine of the National Academy of Sciences issued a report recommending greater integration of knowledge on aging and geriatrics into the curriculum of medical schools. Some physicians have advocated establishing special geriatric care units in hospitals and outpatient health clinics. Nevertheless, Robert Butler (1927–), the first director of the NIA, identified one of the limits to advancing the study of geriatric medicine when he observed that traditional medical education trains physicians to think in terms of cure. This concept is not usually applicable in geriatrics, as many medical conditions of elderly persons can only be ameliorated, not cured.

One problem of the elderly is intellectual impairment. A 1980 task force of the NIA stated that 10 percent of persons over the age of 65 years have some serious mental impairment. They disputed, however, the notion of the inevitability of the process and stated that normal aging does not include gross intellectual impairment, confusion, depression, hallucinations, or delusions. The task force estimated that intellectual impairment can be reversed in close to 20 percent of these cases. Treatable causes of mental deterioration include alterations in functioning of the thyroid gland (q.v.), sleep disorders, depression resulting from bereavement, infectious and metabolic diseases, and the side effects of therapeutic drugs. This last cause is especially important, because the average person over the age of 65 takes 13 different medicines in a year. Because some of these drugs may interact and cause toxic effects, and because the human metabolism clears drugs from the body less rapidly as people get older, an increased probability exists of interference with mental function. The NIA task force stressed that physicians treating older persons must be alert to these effects.

Mental changes in the elderly may also be due to irreversible conditions, such as the degenerative brain disease called Alzheimer's disease (q.v.). No cure exists and the course of the illness is variable, usually leading to death within five to ten years. Mental impairment can also result from multiple small strokes (*see* STROKE).

Older persons are also more susceptible to diseases found in people of all ages, as witnessed by their increased risk of death from influenza infection or exposure to cold. Heat, too, is more dangerous to the elderly. In the heat wave of 1980 the mortality rate among persons over the age of 65 was found to be more than ten times greater than that among other age groups.

In addition, progressive diseases tend to become more severe in old age. These include heart disease (*see* HEART), arthritis, diabetes mellitus, glaucoma (qq.v.), and cataracts (*see* CATARACT). The weakening of the immune system (q.v.) may lead to an increased incidence of cancer in older persons.

See also AGING.

For further information on this topic, see the Bibliography in volume 28, sections 296, 450.

GÉRICAULT, (Jean Louis André) Théodore (1791–1824), French painter, perhaps the most influential artist of his time, and a seminal figure of the 19th-century romantic movement in art.

Géricault, born into a wealthy Rouen family on Sept. 26, 1791, studied with the French painters Carle Vernet (1758–1836) and Pierre Guérin (1774–1833) and also traveled to Italy to study. He was greatly influenced by the work of Michelangelo and other Italian Renaissance painters, as well as that of the Flemish master Peter Paul Rubens. Early in his career, Géricault's paintings began to exhibit qualities that set him apart from such neoclassical French painters as Jacques Louis David. Géricault soon became the acknowledged leader of the French romantics. His *Charging Chasseur* (1812, Louvre, Paris) and *Wounded Cuirassier* (1814, Louvre) display violent action, full of bold design and color, and evoke powerful emotion. These characteristics appeared in heightened form in his immense and overpowering canvas *Raft of the Medusa* (1818–19, Louvre), showing the dying survivors of a contemporary shipwreck. The painting's disturbing combination of idealized figures and realistically depicted agony, as well as its gigantic size, aroused a storm of controversy between neoclassical and romantic artists. In 1820 Géricault traveled to England, where he painted his *Race for the Derby at Epsom* (Louvre). At the time of his death in Paris on Jan. 26, 1824, Géricault was engaged in painting a series of portraits of insane people that demonstrate the preoccupation of the romantic artists with unusual and neurotic subjects. Among his other works are a number of bronze statuettes, a superb series of lithographs, and hundreds of drawings and color sketches.

GERM, general term employed loosely to designate any minute pathogenic agent. The term is applied to disease-producing microorganisms, such as bacteria, protozoa, and fungi (qq.v.), and to pathogenic agents of uncertain classification, such as Rickettsia (q.v.) and viruses (*see* VIRUS).

The term germ became widely used after the development of the germ theory of disease in the 19th century. Scientists and science writers after the beginning of the 20th century have tended to use the specific technical names of particular microorganisms.

GERMAIN, George Sackville, 1st Viscount Sackville (1716–85), British soldier and statesman, son of Lionel Cranfield Sackville, 1st duke of Dorset (1688–1765), educated at Trinity College, Dublin. He became an officer in the British army and served with distinction in the War of the Austrian Succession (1740–48). As a major general during the Seven Years' War (1756–63), he commanded an unsuccessful attack on Saint-Malo, France (1758). In the following year, at the Battle of Minden, he refused the orders of his commander to lead a cavalry charge that would have ensured a decisive allied victory. He was court-martialed in 1760 and was dismissed from the military service. Known after 1770 as Lord George Germain, he served as colonial secretary under Lord North from 1775 to 1782. In this capacity he was directly responsible for the conduct of British policy during the American Revolution and was blamed for the failure of the Saratoga campaign (1777).

GERMANIC LANGUAGES, subfamily of the Indo-European languages (q.v.). Germanic languages are spoken by more than 480 million people in northern and western Europe, North America, South Africa, and Australia. In their structure and evolution they fall into three branches:

1. East Germanic (extinct): the Gothic language (q.v.) and some other extinct languages. Substantial information survives only for Gothic.

2. North Germanic or Scandinavian: western group—the Icelandic language, the Norwegian language (qq.v.), and Faroese (intermediate between Icelandic and western Norwegian dialects); eastern group—the Danish language and the Swedish language (qq.v.).

3. West Germanic: Anglo-Frisian group—the English language and the Frisian language (qq.v.; *see also* AMERICAN ENGLISH); Netherlandic-German group—Netherlandic, or Dutch-Flemish (*see* DUTCH LANGUAGE; FLEMISH LANGUAGE) and the Low German (Plattdeutsch) dialects, Afrikaans (q.v.), the German language (q.v.) or High German, and the Yiddish language (q.v.).

In terms of unwritten regional dialects, the Scandinavian languages form a single speech area of high mutual intelligibility (except for Icelandic, which was long isolated and retains many archaisms), within which Danish has diverged the most. The Netherlandic-German dialects form another speech area. In both areas, speech varies gradually from one village to the next, although over wide distances greater differences accumulate. Also, in both areas more than one literary norm arose, corresponding to political and historical divisions. These norms are what are usually meant by terms such as Swedish language. *See* GRIMM'S LAW; RUNES; VERNER'S LAW.

GERMANIC MYTHOLOGY. *See* SCANDINAVIAN MYTHOLOGY.

GERMANIC PEOPLES, group of tribes united by language and custom that conquered most of western and central Europe in the 5th century AD. By the 2d century BC the Germanic groups had already occupied northern Germany and southern Scandinavia. Two of the most important early historical accounts of the ancient Germans are contained in the works of two Roman authors: Julius Caesar's *Commentaries* (51 BC) and Tacitus's *Germania* (AD 98). By comparing the two it is possible to trace the evolution of Germanic society in the intervening period. In Caesar's time, land tenure did not involve private property; instead, fields were divided annually among clans. By the time of Tacitus, however, land was distributed annually to individuals according to social class. The basic sociopolitical unit was the *pagus* (clan). In Caesar's period, some *pagi* had military leaders as chiefs, but only during wartime. By Tacitus's time, however, several *pagi,* at least, had full-time, elected chiefs. These leaders did not have absolute power but were limited by a council of nobles and an assembly of fighting men. Military chiefs had groups (*comitatus*) of men who swore allegiance to them both in peace and war.

The first clash between Romans and Germanic peoples was in the 2d century BC, when the Cimbri and Teutons invaded Gaul and were defeated in present-day Provence. By this period, however, much of Germany was occupied by such Germanic tribes as the Suevi, Cherusci, and others. When the Romans in turn attempted to conquer the area east of the Rhine early in the first century AD, they were defeated by the Cherusci chief Hermann (Arminius). By the mid-2d century AD Germanic pressures on the Roman frontiers intensified. The emperor Marcus Aurelius waged successful warfare against the Marcomanni, Quadi, and Iazyges. By this period, German mercenaries were beginning to be used by the Roman armies. During the 3d century AD more migrations caused a crisis within the empire, as Goths, Alamanni, and Franks penetrated German borders. The movement was stopped temporarily during the reigns of the emperors Diocletian and Constantine the Great, but it re-

Gothic tribes in Germany during the early Middle Ages lived in round reed or twig huts and dressed in clothing made of animal skins.

From *The World We Live in and How It Came to Be,* by Gertrude Hartman, 1931, Macmillan Co.

sumed under pressure from the non-Germanic Huns, who came out of Central Asia in the 4th century. In the 5th century the Germans occupied the whole Western Roman Empire; over the next few hundred years, they adopted Christianity and laid the foundations of medieval Europe. Germanic languages are still spoken today in Germany, Austria, Switzerland, Scandinavia, the Netherlands, Belgium, South Africa, and the English-speaking countries.   M.S.C.

For further information on this topic, see the Bibliography in volume 28, section 889.

GERMANICUS CAESAR (15 BC–AD 19), Roman general, son of the general Nero Claudius Drusus, and nephew and adopted son of Emperor Tiberius. Germanicus took part in campaigns against the Pannonian, Dalmatian, and Germanic tribes in eastern and northern Europe. In AD 12 he was consul, and the following year Emperor Augustus appointed him to command the eight Roman legions on the Rhine. In AD 14, on the death of Augustus, the legions mutinied, but Germanicus quelled the insurrection, after which he led the soldiers into battle. He routed the Marsi, a German tribe, and the next year met the German leader Arminius (Hermann), chief of the Cherusci, who in AD 9 had destroyed three Roman legions and driven their general, Publius Quintilius Varus (fl. 13 BC–AD 9), to suicide. The engagement was indecisive, but in AD 16 Germanicus, at great risk to his own troops, won two victories over Arminius and claimed Germany for Rome.

Emperor Tiberius recalled Germanicus to Rome in AD 17 because he felt the Germans could most successfully be dealt with through diplomacy. The young general was received with great enthusiasm and honored with a triumph, the traditional celebration for victorious generals. Tiberius then dispatched him to settle a dispute that had arisen in the eastern provinces of Armenia and Parthia. On this mission, Germanicus was stricken with a fatal illness at Antioch. His friends charged that he had been poisoned on orders from Tiberius, who was supposed to have been jealous of his popularity. Germanicus, widely mourned in the provinces and in Rome, was survived by his wife Agrippina and six children. These included Caligula, later emperor, and a daughter, Agrippina the Younger, who became the mother of Emperor Nero.

GERMANIUM, metalloid element, symbol Ge, in group 14 (or IVa) of the periodic table (*see* PERIODIC LAW); at.no. 32, at.wt. 72.59. Germanium melts at about 937° C (about 1719° F), boils at about 2830° C (about 5126° F), and has a sp.gr. of 5.3.

The Russian chemist Dmitry Mendeleyev predicted its existence and chemical properties in 1871; because of its position under silicon in the periodic table, he called it ekasilicon. The element was actually discovered in the silver-sulfide ore argyrodite by the German chemist Clemens Alexander Winkler (1838–1904) in 1866. The metal is hard, brittle, grayish-white, and crystalline in structure. Germanium is in the same chemical family as carbon, silicon, tin, and lead and resembles these elements in forming organic derivatives, such as tetraethyl germanium and tetraphenyl germanium. Germanium forms hydrides—germanomethane, or germane, GeH_4; germanoethane, Ge_2H_6; and germanopropane, Ge_3H_8—analogous to those formed by carbon in the methane series (*see* CHEMISTRY, ORGANIC). The most important compounds of germanium are the oxide GeO_2 (germanic acid) and the halides. Germanium is separated from other metals by distillation of the tetrachloride.

Germanium ranks 54th in order of abundance of the elements in the earth's crust. It occurs in small quantities in the ores of silver, copper, and zinc, and in the mineral germanite, which contains 8 percent germanium. Germanium and its compounds are used in a variety of ways. Suitably prepared germanium crystals have the property of rectifying, or passing electrical currents in one direction only, and so were used extensively during and after World War II as detectors for ultra-high-frequency radio and radar signals. Germanium crystals also have other specialized electronic uses. Germanium was the first metal employed in the transistor (q.v.), the electronic device that requires far less current than the vacuum tube. Germanium oxide is used in the manufacture of optical glass and as a drug in the treatment of pernicious anemia.

GERMAN LANGUAGE, language of the German people and other peoples akin to or at one time politically united with the Germans. German belongs to the Netherlandic-German group within the western branch of the Germanic languages (q.v.), a subfamily of the Indo-European languages (q.v.). It comprises two main groups of dialects, High German (including standard literary German) and Low German. Together, they form a continuum from Switzerland north to the sea; a local dialect can be understood by speakers of nearby dialects but not necessarily by speakers of far-away dialects.

Chief Characteristics. The development of German was affected by several systematic shifts of certain consonants. The so-called Germanic consonant shift distinguished the ancient Proto-Germanic tongue from other Indo-European speech. In this shift, which is described by Grimm's law (q.v.), an Indo-European *p, t, k* changed to a Germanic *f, th, h,* respectively; Indo-European *b, d, g* to Germanic *p, t, k;* and similarly Indo-European *bh, dh, gh,* to Germanic *b, d, g.* After the western Germanic dialects had developed their own distinctive traits, the High German sound shift occurred. Datable to AD 500–700, it set the High German dialects off from other West Germanic speech. During that period the Germanic *p,* when used initially, or after consonants, or when doubled, became *pf* (High German *Pflantze,* Low German *Plante,* "plant"); when used medially or finally after vowels it became *ff* or *f* (High German *hoffen,* Low German *hopen,* "to hope"). Under the same conditions the Germanic *t* became *z* (pronounced *ts,* as in *Pflantze*) or *ss* (High German *essen,* Low German *eten,* "to eat"). After vowels, *k* became *ch* (High German *machen,* Low German *maken,* "to make"); in all other cases *k* remained unchanged except in the extreme south of Germany, where it first became *kch,* and later *ch.* A later change, found also in Low German, is that of the Germanic *th* to *d* (High German *das,* Low German *dat,* "that").

Another characteristic of German, as well as of all the Germanic languages, is that the principal accent falls regularly upon the first syllable of a word; in verbal combinations, however, the root syllable, not the prefix, is stressed.

The phonological characteristics of the German language include the use of the glottal stop before every initial stressed vowel in simple words or independent parts of a word; the pronunciation of *u, o, ü,* and *ö* with full lip-rounding; the tenseness of long vowels and the laxness of short vowels; the articulation of *r* lingually and gutturally; the voicing of the single *s* before and between vowels, and the devoicing of the final *b, d, g* to *p, t, k,* respectively; the use of the affricates *pf* and *ts;* and the pronunciation of *w* as *v* and of *v* as *f.* Vowels are nasalized only in words borrowed from French.

German is an inflected language, with three genders, four cases, and a strong and weak declension of qualifying adjectives. Because of the declensional and conjugational endings, some parts of speech are more precisely identified than in languages that show less inflection. Word order is strictly regulated; for example, subject and predicate are inverted when preceded by an adverb, prepositional phrase, or dependent clause; the verb is placed in the final position in a subordinate clause introduced by a relative pronoun or conjunction. In the formation of new words, German makes extensive use of compounds of two or more independent words and of prefixes

and suffixes (*Oberbaumeister; Handelsluftfahrt; Geteilheit; teilbar*). The poetic and philosophical vocabulary and scientific and technical terminology of German are particularly rich.

High German. The usually cited dividing line, south of which High German is spoken, runs eastward from Aachen, south of Düsseldorf, Kassel, Magdeburg, and Berlin, to Frankfurt-an-der-Oder. High German is in turn divided into two categories: Upper German, in Switzerland, Austria, Liechtenstein, and southern Germany, and Middle German, across Luxembourg and the middle of Germany.

Upper German consists of (1) Alamannic (designated as Swabian in its northeastern sector), spoken in the southern regions of Baden-Württemberg and of Alsace, the southwestern corner of Bavaria, and the German-language areas of Switzerland, including the major cities of Basel, Zürich, and Bern; (2) Bavarian-Austrian, used in the southeastern section of Germany east of the Lech River and south of Nuremberg, including Munich, and in Austria, including the cities of Innsbruck, Vienna, and Graz; (3) the branches of the Franconian dialect, classified as South Franconian, found between Karlsruhe and Heilbronn, and East Franconian, used in the vicinity of Nuremberg, Würzburg, Bamberg, and Fulda; and (4) Langobardic, spoken at one time in the parts of Lombardy (Italy) occupied by the Germanic tribe of the Langobards, and surviving today only in certain geographical names of that area. The Langobardic dialect is of great historical interest because it is the earliest (mid-7th cent. AD) recorded German dialect, whereas the majority of German dialects can be traced back only to the 8th, 9th, or 10th centuries.

Middle German consists of (1) Rhine Franconian, spoken in most of the Palatinate and Hesse, which contain the cities of Mainz, Heidelberg, Frankfurt am Main, and Marburg; (2) Mosel-Franconian, used on both sides of the Mosel River and centering in the city of Trier; (3) Ripuarian, used between Aachen and Cologne; (4) Thuringian, heard in the environs of Weimar, Jena, and Erfurt; (5) Upper Saxon, spoken in Saxony, including the cities of Dresden and Leipzig; and (6) Silesian, used in Lower and Upper Silesia, northwest and southeast of Wrocław (formerly called Breslau, now in Poland).

Low German. The second principal division of German, Plattdeutsch or Low German, includes Low Franconian, which is very closely related to Netherlandic (Dutch-Flemish) and is spoken only in the west, in a narrow fringe along the border between the Netherlands and Germany; and Low Saxon, which is used in the northern lowlands as far east and northeast as the Elbe River, including the cities of Münster, Kassal, Bremen, Hannover, Hamburg, and Magdeburg. As a result of the colonization of the Baltic regions by the Teutonic Knights, Low German spread throughout the lands east of the Elbe to Brandenburg, Mecklenburg, and Pomerania, as well as parts of Prussia.

History. Until the middle of the 14th century Latin was the official written language of the Holy Roman Empire, which comprised most of the German-speaking regions of present-day Europe. During the reign (1314–47) of Louis IV, Holy Roman emperor, German was adopted as the language of official court documents. Between 1480 and 1500 it was introduced for official use in many municipalities and courts of Saxony and Meissen and was adopted also by the universities of Leipzig and Wittenberg. By 1500 German had become generally accepted as the official language of all parts of Saxony and Thuringia and was the written language of the educated classes. In addition the publication of books in German increased in the East Middle German towns of Wittenberg, Erfurt, and Leipzig, as well as in such western and southwestern cities as Mainz, Strassburg, Basel, Nuremberg, and Augsburg. These developments helped reduce regional differences and standardize the literary language.

Standard written German emerged during the first quarter of the 16th century in the eastern midland area of Erfurt, Meissen, Dresden, and Leipzig, where the inhabitants, originally from regions farther west and southwest, spoke a dialect based on the Middle and Upper German dialects of High German. Largely by means of Luther's translation of the Bible into German and his German pamphlets, hymns, and catechisms, the High German standard spread from the eastern midland throughout the rest of Germany. Thus, the term High German came to mean, on the one hand, all German dialects except those belonging to the Low German branch of the language, and, on the other hand, the literary language of Germany. By 1600 this literary language was firmly established, although its present form did not become recognizable until about the middle of the 18th century.

The various sections of Germany and of other European nations where German was spoken adhered to different standards of spelling until the 20th century. In 1901 a conference, in which representatives of northern and southern Germany, Austria, and Switzerland took part, devised a uniform system of orthography that later came into acceptance. This system is outlined in *Rechtschreibung der Deutschen Sprache* (Orthography of the German Language, published in many editions), by the German philologist Konrad Duden (1829–1911).

No generally accepted standard of German pronunciation exists. As the result of the work of a commission established in 1898, composed of university professors and representatives of the German theater, certain norms of pronunciation were, however, accepted. These rules have been codified in *Deutsche Buhnenaussprache* (German Stage Pronunciation), first published in 1898 and again in 1957 as *Deutsche Hochsprache* (Standard German). The speech even of highly educated Germans is affected by the pronunciation peculiar to their native dialects. Various German-speaking groups, such as the Swabians, Saxons, Austrians, and Swiss, can be distinguished readily by their characteristic types of pronunciation.

Usage. German is spoken by many millions of people throughout the world. Approximately 71 million German-speaking persons live in Germany, and several million under foreign administration. In addition, German is spoken by almost 7 million people in Austria, about 300,000 in Luxembourg, 3,400,000 in the northern section of Switzerland, and about 1,500,000 in Alsace-Lorraine. Reliable statistics are not available concerning the number of German-speaking persons who inhabit those regions of eastern Europe from which Germans were expelled at the end of World War II.

Outside Europe, the largest number of people using German as their mother tongue live in the U.S. An important group of German-speaking people in the U.S. are the so-called Pennsylvania Dutch, who left the Palatinate region of Germany during the late 17th and the 18th centuries and settled in the southeastern part of Pennsylvania. They speak the Rhine-Franconian dialect with relatively few admixtures of English. Other countries with a fairly large number of German-speaking citizens are Canada (approximately 330,000), Brazil (550,000), and Argentina (250,000).   O.S.

For further information on this topic, see the Bibliography in volume 28, section 842.

GERMAN LITERATURE, literature written in the German language (q.v.) from the 8th century to the present, and including the works of German, Austrian, and Swiss authors. It may be divided into periods corresponding generally to successive phases in the development of the German language and to the growth and unification of Germany as a nation. *See also* AUSTRIAN LITERATURE; SWITZERLAND: *Literature.*

Old High German Period (800–1100). The oldest known literary work in German is the epic *Hildebrandslied* (Lay of Hildebrand), which survives in a fragment dating from about AD 800. This work describes, in mixed Low and High German alliterative verse, the confrontation and the beginning of a battle between the legendary hero Hildebrand and his son. Other legends deal with such heroic personalities as Theodoric, king of the Ostrogoths; Attila, king of the Huns; and Siegfried, identified by some authorities as the German chief Arminius, who defeated the Romans in the Teutoburger Wald, a forest in Lower Saxony in AD 9.

This pagan tradition was disowned by the Roman Catholic church, which remained the dominant force in German literature from the 4th to the 12th century. As early as 381 Ulfilas, bishop of the Goths, translated the Bible into the vernacular, and an anonymous priest wrote *Muspilli* (900; trans. 1885), an alliterative poem in Bavarian dialect depicting the destruction of the world by fire on Judgment Day. Another important work, written in the old Low German dialect, is the epic *Heliand* (9th cent.; trans. 1830), in which Christ is represented as a German prince with feudal retainers as his disciples.

Under the Frankish ruler Charles Martel and his successors, many abbeys were founded, among them the famous Sankt Gallen (now in Switzerland) and Fulda in Germany. In these abbeys the monks preserved ancient literature as well as the history of their own time. During this period, however, the major literary works were written in Latin, with German being used primarily in translations from the older language. An example of an epic written in Latin is the *Walthariuslied* (c. 930; *Lay of Walter*, 1858) by Ekkehard I the Elder (c. 910–73) of Sankt Gallen, which tells of the escape of the hero Walter and his bride from the court of Attila. In addition to such epics, written for the royal courts, a popular oral literature developed during the 9th and 10th centuries. It consisted largely of tales and ballads, which were not written down until about the 14th century.

Middle High German Period (1100–1370). Although prose writing and drama were found primarily in the form of didactic religious works throughout the Middle High German period, poetry developed as a mode of secular expression, and epic, lyric, and satiric forms appeared, giving voice to the virtues of chivalry and courtly love. The *Spielleute*, or wandering minstrels, entertained their listeners with stories of adventure sometimes based on the experiences of warriors returning from the Crusades. Among the epic poems of the period, *König Rother* (King Rother, c. 1150) had the greatest success. Another important style was the court epic, which reached its highest form in the works of Hartmann von Aue (c. 1170–c. 1235), Gottfried von Strassburg, Wolfram von Eschenbach, and Heinrich von Veldeke (fl. 1160–1200). Although the works of such French writers as Chrétien de Troyes and others served as models for the German epics, the German writers expressed their own ideals, found their own form and style, and very often added depth to the stories. A variation of the court epic was the epic in which an animal was the central figure. *Reinecke Fuchs* (c. 1180; *Reynard the Fox*, 1840) by Heinrich der Glîchezaere (fl. 1170–89) is the best example. The greatest of the German epics is the *Nibelungenlied* (q.v.), set down in the early 13th century by an unknown author.

Lyric poetry during the Middle High German period developed in the form of the *Minnesang*, or courtly lyric, composed by the lyric poets known as minnesingers (q.v.). The great master of this type of poetry is Walther von der Vogelweide. His works, which include love songs, religious lyrics, and epigrams, express personal and political idealism and assert his independence of papal authority.

In the second half of the 13th century the nature of the epic began to change as characters from the middle class and the peasantry were introduced. The peasantry, once an object of derision, became increasingly important in literature, figuring prominently in such works as *Meier Helmbrecht*, a 13th-century tale of peasant life.

The Reformation (1500–1700). The rise of the middle class in the 14th and 15th centuries and the struggles of the peasants against the nobility culminated in the great 16th-century religious revolution known as the Reformation. This movement was reflected in literature, especially by Martin Luther, whose translation of the Bible established New High German as the literary language of Germany. In secular literature the aristocratic *Minnesang* was discarded in favor of the *Meistergesang* ("master song"), written by guilds of artisans known as Meistersinger (q.v.). Also popular were the simple lyric poems later collectively titled *Volkslied* ("folk songs"; *see* FOLK MUSIC). The *Schwank*, a farcical form of comic anecdote, gave popular expression to the stories of such sly rogues as Till Eulenspiegel. In the famous *Das Narrenschiff* (1494; *The Ship of Fools*, 1509) the humanist poet Sebastian Brant satirized more than 100 contemporary forms of foolishness and immorality. Another successful author was Johann Fischart (1546–90), a satiric poet and

.hie krieget mit fange K walth' vod vogelweide · h wolfran von Gfchalbach. h"Rennander alte der tugenthafte schuber hemrich vo Ofternnge vij klmgefor von vngerlant.

A poetical and musical congress in 1207 at the Wartburg, a castle overlooking Eisenach, with the famous minnesingers Walther von der Vogelweide and Wolfram von Eschenbach among the participants (from the 14th-cent. manuscript Treatise on the Minnesingers*).* Bibliothèque Nationale, Paris

polemical writer for the Protestant cause, who based his material on the adventures of Gargantua and Pantagruel, characters created by the French satirist François Rabelais. This period marked the first appearance in literature of the legendary scholar Johann Faust in the anonymous prose fiction *Historia von Dr. Johann Fausten,* published in 1587.

Late in the 15th century German drama, hitherto restricted to passion plays and other religious spectacles, began to take on secular form in the *Fastnachtsspiele* ("Shrovetide plays"), allegorical comic dramas performed during the carnival season. Worldly elements gradually penetrated even the religious Christmas and Easter plays. Among the important dramatists of the Reformation period were Burkard Waldis (c. 1495-1557), who also wrote satiric fables, Nikodemus Frischlin (1547-90), and Hans Sachs, a poet and dramatist who was noted for his *Fastnachtsspiele.*

An attempt to bring French influences into German literature was made during the early 17th century by the critic Martin Opitz (1597-

1639). In his principal work, *Das Buch von der deutschen Poeterey* (Book of German Poetry, 1624), Opitz demanded that German writers imitate contemporary French models in style, meter, and pattern. Although some of the literary academies carried his rules to extremes of complicated formality, several poets, influenced by Opitz, achieved an increased individuality of expression. Among them were Simon Dach (1605-59); Paul Flemming (1609-40); Johann Scheffler (1624-77), commonly called Angelus Silesius; and Baron Friedrich von Logau (1604-55). Protestant poetry of the 17th century reached its height in the hymns of Paul Gerhardt (1607-76).

The development of German literature was halted for more than a generation by the Thirty Years' War. The effects of the conflict can be seen in the work of the novelist Hans Jakob Christoph von Grimmelshausen. His tale of a disillusioned farmer's son, *Der abenteuerliche Simplicissimus* (1669; *The Adventurous Simplicissimus,* 1912), is the first great novel in the German language. Such comedies as *Peter Squenz* (1663) by the satirist Andreas Gryphius also describe the disillusionment and disenchantment that inevitably followed the war.

18th Century. By the beginning of the 18th century German cultural life had become increasingly receptive to new literary models and ideas. Such novels as *Robinson Crusoe* by the English novelist Daniel Defoe were widely read in Germany, leading to the decline of the heroic narrative and to greater realism in German fiction. A notable critic of the period was Johann Christoph Gottsched (1700–66), whose *Versuch einer critischen Dichtkunst vor die Deutschen* (Attempt at a Critical Theory of Poetry for the Germans, 1730) established standards derived from the logic and precision of French literature. Gottsched also attempted to reform the drama, both as a literary arbiter and as a translator of French, Greek, and Latin plays. His literary influence, however, was challenged by a group of young writers who wished to liberate German literature from the restrictive influence of foreign models. Stimulated by the nationalism of Frederick the Great, but influenced also by his extensive cultural interests, these writers led one of the greatest periods in German literature. Among the successive phases of this era were the preclassical period (1748–88), the Sturm und Drang ("storm and stress") movement (beginning c. 1770), and the classical (1788–98) and romantic (1798–1832) periods.

Johann Christoph Friedrich von Schiller, in a portrait painted by Gerhard von Kügelgen three years after Schiller's death on the basis of existing drawings of the poet.   German Information Center

Preclassical period. Christian Fürchtegott Gellert (1715–69), an early writer of the preclassical period, enjoyed great popularity with his didactic fables, poems, novels, and comedies. Of greater importance, however, was the poet and dramatist Friedrich Gottlieb Klopstock. In his religious epic *Messias* (4 vol., 1751–73; *The Messiah*, 1810) and in his collection of odes he introduced strong personal emotion into German poetry. Even more important, Klopstock's conception of the holy mission of the poet profoundly influenced subsequent writers. Christoph Martin Wieland, author of the epic *Oberon* (1780; trans. 1798), also affected the course of German literature by translating Shakespeare's plays into German. Wieland's *Agathon* (1766–77; *The History of Agathon*, 1773) is considered the earliest psychological novel in German literature.

The dramas of Gotthold Ephraim Lessing, notable for their characters and passion, formed the foundation of modern German drama. He gave the German stage its first tragedy of everyday life in *Miss Sara Sampson* (1755; trans. 1789), and in his dramatic poem *Nathan der Weise* (1779; *Nathan the Wise*, 1781) he made an ardent appeal for religious tolerance. *Minna von Barnhelm* (1767; *The Disbanded Officer*, 1786) is a skillful comedy. In his influential critical treatise *Laokoon* (1766; trans. 1930), Lessing brought the spirit of the Enlightenment to Germany (*see* ENLIGHTENMENT, AGE OF).

Sturm und Drang. The philosopher Johann Gottfried von Herder was the dominant figure of this new movement, which took its name from the play *Sturm und Drang* (1776) by Friedrich Maximilian von Klinger (1752–1831), one of a group of young writers who were delighted by Herder's rejection of traditional authorities. The members of this group abandoned rationalism and the concern with form and structure that had characterized classical and French drama. Influenced by Herder's study of primitive peoples and folk culture, they emphasized the use of national or folk elements, and sought inspiration in the *Volkslied* and other aspects of German culture. Their longing for emancipation was symbolized in poems and dramas centering on heroic individualists possessed by uncontrolled emotions and engaged in immense conflicts.

Many elements of Sturm und Drang can be found in the early dramas of two of the greatest German authors, Johann Wolfgang von Goethe and Friedrich von Schiller. Goethe's early play *Götz von Berlichingen* (1773; trans. 1799), greatly influenced by Shakespeare's dramas, concerns a 16th-century knight, opposed to aristocracy and the church, who leads a revolt of the peasants.

Introspective melancholy, another feature of Sturm und Drang, is clearly shown in Goethe's novel *Die Leiden des jungen Werthers* (1774; *The Sorrows of Young Werther,* 1779). The sentimental hero, disappointed in love, kills himself; hundreds of young male readers are said to have followed Werther's example. Goethe's most important work of this period is the so-called *Urfaust,* the oldest preserved version of his long poetic drama *Faust* (2 vol., 1808–32; trans. 1834), completed in the last years of the poet's life. Schiller, in his *Die Räuber* (1781; *The Robbers,* 1800) and *Kabale und Liebe* (1783; *Intrigue and Love,* 1849), emphasized the political aspects of Sturm und Drang, attacking political tyranny and social corruption.

Classical period. The development of Goethe and Schiller, after the period of their early dramas, represents one of the major achievements of the classical period in German literature—an era notable for its emotional restraint, temperance of thought, and lucidity of expression. Both writers were influenced by the extensive philosophical activity of the period, which culminated in the idealism of the philosopher Immanuel Kant and his disciple Johann Gottlieb Fichte. During the classical period, moreover, Goethe and Schiller became close friends despite differences in their philosophical attitudes. Schiller believed in absolute ethical ideals, which provide the motive force of his greatest dramatic works: the *Wallenstein* trilogy (1798–99; trans. 1839), *Maria Stuart* (1800; trans. 1833), *Die Jungfrau von Orleans* (1801; *The Maid of Orleans,* 1835), and *Wilhelm Tell* (1804; *William Tell,*

Immanuel Kant (from a 19th-cent. engraving).

Johann Wolfgang von Goethe (from a 19th-cent. engraving).

1825). Goethe derived his philosophy from his experiences as lyric poet, balladeer, dramatist, novelist, essayist, scientist, and political figure. He lived according to the ideal expressed in his *Faust:* never to be satisfied with what one is, but to strive incessantly to learn, to improve, to accomplish. His writings clearly show his development from youthful rebellion to the search for emotional restraint, objectivity, beauty, and the ideal human personality. The two parts of *Faust,* moreover, have often been considered representative of the prevailing tendencies of German literature; the first part contains many elements of the literary movement known as romanticism, and the second represents the classicism most admired by Goethe.

These elements may also be found in the work of the poet Friedrich Hölderlin, whose admiration for the harmony of the classical world was vitiated, as Goethe and his contemporaries saw it, by his visionary religious attitude. Hölderlin himself explored the conflict between absolute ideals and the problems of existence in his epistolary novel *Hyperion* (2 vol., 1797–99; trans. 1927) and in his poetry. Another highly individualistic writer of the late classical period, the dramatist and short-story writer Heinrich von Kleist, portrayed heroic characters in conflict with their destiny. His comedies *Der zerbrochene Krug* (1806, pub. about 1811; *The Bro-*

ken Pitcher, 1961) and *Amphytrion* (1807; trans. 1962) depict human conflict in an almost tragic manner. The tales of the humorist Johann Friedrich Richter (usually known by the pseudonym Jean Paul), with their fantasy and their sense of the grotesque, bring him close to the romantic movement, which dominated German literature at the beginning of the 19th century.

Romantic period. The increasing romantic tendency of German literature, as expressed, for example, in some of the later writings of Goethe, became dominant in 1798, with the first issue of the journal *Athenaeum,* edited by three friends, the writer Ludwig Tieck and the critics August Wilhelm von Schlegel and Friedrich von Schlegel. Romanticism (q.v.) in the literature of Germany, as in that of other countries, resulted from a fusion of political, philosophical, and artistic elements. The Napoleonic Wars awakened a new sense of national identity in German writers, while increasing their admiration for such heroic individuals as Napoleon and Ludwig van Beethoven. The nationalistic elements of romanticism were furthered in Germany by the philosopher and theologian Friedrich Ernst Daniel Schleiermacher, who stressed the virtues of national independence and influenced such poets as Ernst Moritz Arndt and Karl Theodor Körner (1791–1813). The work of the philosopher Friedrich Wilhelm Joseph von Schelling gave the movement a philosophical base for its mysticism and belief in the ultimate oneness of the natural and spiritual world. Folktales and mythology, another concern of German romanticism, received attention in the collections made by two scholars, the Grimm brothers, Jacob Ludwig Karl and Wilhelm Karl. A notable collection of German folk songs was formed by the poet and dramatist Clemens Maria Brentano and his brother-in-law Achim von Arnim, *Des Knaben Wunderhorn* (3 vol., 1805–8; *The Boy's Magic Horn,* 1841).

Romantic themes characterize the work of the poet Baron Friedrich von Hardenberg, known as Novalis, author of the mysterious and deeply religious *Hymnen an die Nacht* (1800; *Hymns to the Night,* 1889) and of the novel *Heinrich von Ofterdingen* (1802; trans. 1842). Ludwig Tieck, poet, dramatist, and novelist, lacked the depth and religious feeling of Novalis, but he was extremely facile, gifted in the expression of poetic, fantastic, and satiric elements. Joseph von Eichendorff praised the beauty of nature in his poems and the virtues of idleness in his prose work *Aus dem Leben eines Taugenichts* (1826; *The Love Frolics of a Young Scamp,* 1864). The genuine tenderness of folk songs can be found in the poems of Adelbert von Chamisso, but many have tragic elements, as does his prose work, *Peter Schlemihls wundersame Geschichte* (1814; *Peter Schlemihl's Remarkable Story,* 1927). The great balladeer of this generation was Ludwig Uhland. One of the masters of poetry and prose was Eduard Friedrich Mörike; the calm composure in his writing contrasted with the melancholy of Nikolaus Lenau's poetry. Most of the romantic poets were also gifted storytellers, but the most original prose writer of this period was E. T. A. Hoffmann, the master of tales dealing with the supernatural.

Revolution and Reaction (1832–71). During the 1830s a new generation of writers turned from the fantasies of romanticism to participate in political events. Forming a movement known as Junges Deutschland (Young Germany), they supported the attempts of liberal elements in various parts of Germany to modify the absolute rule of the surviving feudal princes. The major philosopher of this period was G. W. F. Hegel, whose rationalistic idealism greatly influenced the lyric poet and critic Heinrich Heine. The latter, a dominant figure among the new writers, began his career with ironic poems on romantic themes. He became famous with the publication of his *Buch der Lieder* (1827; *Book of Songs,* 1846). After the failure of the revolution of 1830, he fled to Paris, where he wrote his major poetry and produced many critical articles on contemporary art and politics. A perceptive observer, Heine anticipated many of the techniques of modern journalism. Another political exile, Ludwig Börne (1786–1837), attempted to invigorate German political

Heinrich Heine   German Information Center

activity in his *Briefe aus Paris* (Letters from Paris, 1830–33).

19th-century drama. Political ideas dominated the German drama of the 19th century. In addition to Kleist, Christian Dietrich Grabbe (1801–36) and other writers produced significant plays. Most important, however, was the revolutionary dramatist Georg Büchner, a pioneer in psychological realism whose works continue to be widely performed. His *Dantons Tod* (1835; *Danton's Death*, 1927) explores the sense of futility and apathy that affected the French revolutionary leader Georges Jacques Danton at the close of his life. In *Wozzeck* (1836; trans. 1927)—well known in the modern operatic version by the Austrian composer Alban Berg—Büchner depicts the tragic disintegration of a poor soldier victimized by an unjust and cruel society. The topic, style, and deep psychological insight of this play mark it as the beginning of modern German drama.

Psychological realism and political perception also characterize the historical tragedies of Friedrich Hebbel and the poetic dramas of the Austrian playwright Franz Grillparzer. Ferdinand Raimund (1790–1836) wrote comedies that took place in a world of fairy tales and magic happenings but reflected his deep melancholy. Entertaining satires were composed by Johann Nepomuk Nestroy (1801–62); and Ludwig Anzengruber (1839–89) wrote plays of peasant life, anticipating, in his concern with social problems, the literary movement known as naturalism.

The German theater of the 19th century was profoundly influenced by the composer Richard Wagner. A participant in the unsuccessful revolution of 1848, Wagner produced numerous prose writings describing the importance of the drama in the development of civilization and calling for a union of the arts in the form known as music drama. As a poet, he wrote the texts of his music dramas, celebrating the great traditions of German literature in such works as *Die Meistersinger von Nürnberg* (1867) and *Parsifal* (1882). Wagner in turn was influenced by the philosophy of Arthur Schopenhauer, whose darkly pessimistic thought may be considered typical of the defeatist temper that followed the political repression of 1848. Schopenhauer, in his principal work *Die Welt als Wille und Vorstellung* (1819; *The World as Will and Idea,* 1883), conceived of a fundamental active principle, the will, that operates as a driving force in all forms of existence and that, in human beings, causes inevitable dissatisfaction and suffering unless balanced by a sense of saintly resignation. This conception of a primal governing force in human behavior was to have a significant influence on subsequent German literature and philosophy.

19th-century prose. The popular storytellers of the mid-19th century included the poet Baroness Annette Elisabeth von Droste-Hülshoff, known for her novella *Die Judenbache* (1842; *The Jew's Beech,* 1958). Detailed descriptions of nature characterize the novels of Adalbert Stifter (1805–68); *Der Nachsommer* (Indian Summer, 1857) and *Witiko* (3 vol., 1865–67) are his best-known works. The Swiss novelist Gottfried Keller, in his autobiographical novel *Der grüne Heinrich* (4 vol., 1854–55; *Green Henry,* 1960), continued the tradition of the Bildungsroman that began with a work by Goethe, *Wilhelm Meisters Lehrjahre* (4 vol., 1795–96; *Wilhelm Meister's Apprenticeship,* 1824). Rural life, and the problems of the individual in an expanding society, are portrayed by the novelists Albert Bitzius (1797–1854), who used the pseudonym Jeremias Gotthelf, and Wilhelm Raabe (1831–1910). Conrad Ferdinand Meyer (1825–98), a poet and novelist, chose characters from the Middle Ages for many of his ballads and stories. The unity of human beings and nature forms a recurrent theme in the poetry and novellas of Theodor Storm (1817–88). *Immensee* (1852; trans. 1863), one of his best-known stories, is a lyrical, nostalgic tale of childhood. His later, darker style is shown in *Der Schimmelreiter* (1888; *Rider of the White Horse,* 1915), which shows the effect of the sea on the lives of shore dwellers. Theodor Fontane, a writer of ballads and novels, is noted for his perceptive criticisms of German society at the end of the 19th century.

The prevailing idealism of German philosophy was rejected in favor of materialism by Paul Johann Anselm von Feuerbach, whose work influenced the German revolutionists Karl Marx and Friedrich Engels. Among the many scholars who furthered the development of the science of history during this period were Leopold von Ranke, considered a founder of the objective writing of history, Theodor Mommsen, an expert in Roman studies, and Jakob Burckhardt, noted for *Kultur der Renaissance in Italien* (1860; *The Civilization of the Renaissance in Italy,* 1878). The development of Germany as a nation was studied by Wilhelm Häring (1798–1871), who used the pseudonym Willibald Alexis, and by the ardent nationalist Heinrich von Treitschke.

German Nationalism (1871–1945). After the unification of the German states in 1871, the revolutionary tendencies of German literature began increasingly to conflict with the militarism and economic materialism of the German middle class. Representing, in the main, the latter, the

Prussian statesman and first chancellor of the German Empire, Prince Otto von Bismarck, expressed the prevailing view of contemporary society in his memoirs entitled *Gedanken und Erinnerungen* (1898; *Bismarck: His Reflections and Reminiscences,* 1898). A powerful criticism of existing social values, however, was advanced by the poet and philosopher Friedrich Wilhelm Nietzsche. In such works as *Jenseits von Gut und Böse* (1886; *Beyond Good and Evil,* 1907) and *Wille zur Macht* (1901; *The Will to Power,* 1967), Nietzsche rejected both the traditional religious values of bourgeois morality and the prevailing idealism of German philosophy. His poetic vision of a new type of human being as the dominant figure of a radically transformed society is presented in the prose poem *Also sprach Zarathustra* (1883; *Thus Spoke Zarathustra,* 1896). This new type, the *Übermensch* ("superman"), would embody the best qualities of the creative individual, who is the highest expression of the "will to power," the force that produces all human endeavor.

Friedrich Wilhelm Nietzsche   Bettmann Archive

Nietzsche's concern with the inner forces of the human personality profoundly influenced the course of early 20th-century thought. In psychology, Sigmund Freud and the Swiss psychologist and psychiatrist Carl Gustav Jung were greatly indebted to Nietzsche for their theories of the human psyche. From Nietzsche's idea of the cyclical recurrence of events, the philosopher of history Oswald Spengler formulated his principles of historical determinism. These developments in psychology and historical studies,

when combined with Nietzsche's conception of the artist as a radical critic of society, influenced the major literary movements of the late 19th and early 20th centuries: naturalism, expressionism (qq.v.), and the epic theater.

Naturalism. The naturalistic movement in literature occurred after the rise of realism (q.v.). Realism calls for an art reflecting both the good and the evil forces that affect human life. Naturalism, on the other hand, is a form of artistic determinism and depicts a bleak world in which people are trapped and doomed to defeat and disaster by uncontrollable forces. Symbols often used by naturalistic writers include sickness; insanity; senility; hypocrisy in religion, family relationships, and government; and the entrapping forces of economics, heredity, race, class, and environment. The artistic principles of the naturalist movement were described by the critic and writer Arno Holz (1863–1929) in his treatise *Die Kunst* (Art, 1891). Holz was also the coauthor, with Johannes Schlaf (1862–1941), of three dramatic naturalistic stories under the collective title *Papa Hamlet* (1889). Certain elements of naturalism, especially those dealing with the erotic aspects of life, appear in the dramas of the Austrian physician and playwright Arthur Schnitzler. The principal representative of the naturalist movement, however, was the dramatist Gerhart Hauptmann. In his play *Vor Sonnenaufgang* (1899; *Before Dawn,* 1909), he depicted human beings as victims of heredity and environment, doomed to hopeless struggles against forces beyond their control. This theme, and the manner of its presentation, anticipated many similar treatments in modern literature. A later Hauptmann play, *Die Weber* (1892; *The Weavers,* 1899), introduced the social group as hero of the drama. Hauptmann's later writings represent a transition from naturalism to the literary movement known as impressionism, in which precise realism is replaced by a depiction of the impressions that objects make on the individual vision of the artist.

Among other principal movements in the German literature of the early 20th century were neoclassicism (*see* CLASSIC, CLASSICAL, AND CLASSICISM), neoromanticism, symbolism (*see* SYMBOLIST MOVEMENT), surrealism, Dada (qq.v.), and, most important, expressionism, in which the emphasis on psychological problems became especially pronounced.

Expressionism. Originating in painting, expressionism began to influence German literature about 1910. A reaction to naturalism and impressionism, which were concerned primarily with the realistic representation of existence, the new movement had as its object the expression, or portrayal, of the inner feelings, experiences, and reactions of the artist or writer. The expressionist writer embodied Nietzsche's concept of the artist as a critic of traditional values. Like the painter, moreover, the poet or novelist was expected to portray the powerful forces within the human personality. Exaggerated emotional language and the depiction of abstract types rather than realistic characters became means to this end. The German playwright Frank Wedekind, an early expressionist with a sense of grotesque humor, fought against social convention and demanded a new sexual morality. Such forces as adolescent rebellion and amoral sexuality are portrayed in his plays *Frühlings Erwachen* (1891; *The Awakening of Spring,* 1909) and *Die Büchse der Pandora* (1904; *Pandora's Box,* 1918). The latter was the basis both for a film (1928) and for *Lulu,* an opera by the Austrian composer Alban Berg.

The conflict of generations became for several expressionist writers a symbol of the criticism of traditional values, as in *Der Sohn* (The Son, 1914) by Walter Hasenclever (1890–1940). Antiwar attitudes found expression after World War I in plays by Ernst Toller, Fritz von Unruh, and others. Georg Kaiser, in his immense dramatic production, was a specialist in epigrammatic dialogue, which suited the abstract, symbolic nature of his characters. Carl Zuckmayer (1896–1977), perhaps the most popular dramatist of his generation, is especially noted for his vivid characterizations. Among his best-known works are the drama *Der Hauptmann von Köpenick* (1931; *The Captain of Koepenick,* 1932) and the script for *Der blaue Engel* (The Blue Angel, 1930), a film by Josef von Sternberg (1894–1969).

The expressionist movement produced several poets of remarkable originality. Their central topic was the crisis of individual and collective values, as in the poems of Georg Trakl (1887–1914), filled with longing and loneliness; or of Georg Heym (1887–1912), who expressed despair over the misery and solitude of urban life. Franz Werfel, an Austrian writer, the greatest poet of expressionism, wrote of his longing for harmony between people and nature.

Epic theater. The most original and stimulating dramatist of the modern period was Bertolt Brecht. He began as an expressionist but soon developed his own style by introducing his epic theater, using ballads, documentary techniques, and other innovations as commentary on the dramatic action. Like Wagner, he believed in the mission of the stage as the center of political and moral teachings. In his many plays, among them *Mutter Courage und ihre Kinder* (1941; *Mother*

Courage and Her Children, 1963), *Der kaukasische Kreidekreis* (1944–45; *The Caucasian Chalk Circle,* 1948), and *Der gute Mensch von Sezuan* (1943; *The Good Woman of Setzuan,* 1948), he wrote dramatic parables to educate his audience. Brecht's influence was worldwide, and many younger writers adopted the dramatic techniques he developed. Among Brecht's disciples, Peter Weiss (1916–82), best known for his passionate documentary drama *Marat/Sade* (1964; trans. 1965), Rolf Hochhuth (1931–), and Heinar Kipphardt (1922–82) have been successful with the so-called documentary theater in which historical events are presented onstage. The Swiss dramatist Friedrich Dürrenmatt has enlivened the theater with a number of eclectic, cynical, and melodramatic plays. Max Rudolf Frisch holds stronger beliefs and deeper moral convictions than Dürrenmatt, but has been less successful in attracting an international audience.

The 20th-century novel. The strong narrative trend that can be felt in some of Hauptmann's plays became prominent in his novel *Der Narr in Christo Emanuel Quint* (1910; *The Fool in Christ, Emanuel Quint,* 1911), the story of a religiously enraptured young carpenter whose martyrdom is frustrated by the profane world. Schnitzler's prose forfeited action in favor of interior monologue. In *Leutnant Gustl* (1901; *None but the Brave,* 1926) and *Fräulein Else* (1924; trans. 1925) he created a new technique of dealing with the subconscious. *Der Mann ohne Eigenschaften* (3 vol., 1930–42; *The Man Without Qualities,* 1953–60) by the Austrian writer Robert Musil (1880–1942) is an intellectual and psychological mirror of a dying cultural epoch in Europe. Hermann Broch (1886–1951), in his trilogy *Die Schlafwandler* (1931–32; *The Sleepwalkers,* 1932), also described the disintegration and decay of the old bourgeois society. Monumental pictures of historical events and personalities can be found in the writings of Ricarda Huch (1864–1947). In prose Franz Werfel's best-known works are the novels *Die vierzig Tage des Musa Dagh* (1933; *The Forty Days of Musa Dagh,* 1934) and *Das Lied von Bernadette* (1941; *The Song of Bernadette,* 1942). Alfred Döblin (1878–1957) in his most expressionistic novel *Alexanderplatz, Berlin* (1930; trans. 1931) found an original montagelike style for presenting the situation of Berlin workers.

The most eminent modern German novelists are Thomas Mann, Hermann Hesse, and Franz Kafka. Mann, in his first novel, *Buddenbrooks* (1901; trans. 1904), stated a recurrent theme of his work: the conflict between the smug, prosperous representatives of healthy bourgeois life and the perceptive, often sickly artist. The con-

Thomas Mann   Alfred A. Knopf

scrutable world haunted by loss of faith and direction. Kafka's apparently simple narrative style gave a new depth to the expressionist principle, suggesting the mystery of human experience through suggestive symbols.

Modern poetry. The modern era of German poetry begins with Nietzsche, who wrote lyric poetry of the impressionist and expressionist schools. His influence can be traced in the lyrics and prose of Gottfried Benn (1886–1956), whose almost nihilistic disillusion and despair underlay his search for positive values. A strong resentment of social injustice characterizes the poems of Richard Dehmel (1863–1920). Hugo von Hofmannsthal developed his poetic gifts in lyric poems and in librettos for operas by the German composer Richard Strauss. The leading exponent of the symbolist movement in German poetry was Stefan George, who, like Nietzsche, attempted to revive the role of the poet as a critic of materialism and corruption. A similar mission was proposed by perhaps the best known of modern German poets, Rainer Maria Rilke. In his *Die Sonette an Orpheus* (1923; *Sonnets to Orpheus,* 1936), Rilke sought to convey the poet's mysterious perceptions of beauty.

Conflict and Revival Since 1946. The conflict between the radical artist, as conceived by Nietzsche, and an increasingly materialistic, militaristic society reached its extreme phase during the 1930s. The rise of National Socialism and the totalitarian government of Adolf Hitler virtually destroyed German culture. The National Socialists

flicts and difficulties of the creative personality are the topic of many of Mann's masterly novels and short stories. In *Der Zauberberg* (1924; *The Magic Mountain,* 1927) he offered what is in effect an allegory of Western intellectual life on the eve of World War I. A bitter opponent of National Socialism, Mann left Germany in 1933, and several of the four volumes of *Joseph und seine Brüder* (1933–44; *Joseph and His Brothers,* 1933–44) were finished in exile. His despair over the fate of Germany and his concern with the creative artist are eloquently portrayed in *Doctor Faustus* (1947; trans. 1948), a study of German cultural life during the rise of National Socialism. Heinrich Mann, the brother of the great novelist, was also an opponent of fascism and is known for such political satires as *Der Untertan* (1918; *The Patrioteer,* 1921).

The writings of Hesse express a sense of spiritual loneliness, often tempered by the wisdom and the mysticism of Oriental philosophy. Hesse described the alienation and duality of nature of modern people in his *Demian* (1919; trans. 1923) and *Steppenwolf* (1927; trans. 1929). Perhaps his greatest work, *Das Glasperlenspiel* (1943; trans. as *Magister Ludi,* 1949; trans. as *The Glass Bead Game,* 1969), advocates a new ethical and intellectual aristocracy. Hesse, once little read except in Germany, enjoyed a considerable revival during the 1960s, especially among U.S. students.

No modern writer in German has exercised a more extraordinary influence on contemporary fiction than the Austrian writer Kafka. His novels *Der Prozess* (1925; *The Trial,* 1937), *Das Schloss* (1926; *The Castle,* 1930), and *Amerika* (1927; trans. 1938) and his many short stories offer a fascinating account of a disjointed and in-

Hermann Hesse   German Information Center

imposed a trivial realism and a nationalistic fanat-
icism on literature. Many writers were compelled
to leave Germany, either as victims of persecution or because they were unwilling to live under
an oppressive dictatorship. During this period
the only significant German literature was produced by writers in exile from their native land—
among them, for example, Thomas Mann and
the German-Swedish poet Nelly Leonie Sachs,
cowinner of the 1966 Nobel Prize in literature,
who lived in exile in Sweden from 1940, continuing to write in German. "O the Chimneys," her
most famous poem, is a moving testament to the
tragedy of the Jews under Nazism.

After the collapse of the Hitler regime, a considerable revival of German literature occurred.
Many new writers continued work in the 20th-
century novel and in modern poetry. The radio
play became a promising new art form; many
such dramas, devoted to analyses of modern life,
have been contributed by writers otherwise
known as poets, short-story writers, and novelists—including Marie Luise Kaschnitz (1901-74),
Günther Eich (1907-72), Wolfgang Weyrauch
(1907-80), Ilse Aichinger (1921-), and Siegfried
Lenz (1926-).

Outstanding among the new generation of
German novelists who gained success after
World War II are Heinrich Böll, winner of the
1972 Nobel Prize in literature, Uwe Johnson,
Günter Grass, and Lenz, members of Gruppe 47,
a group of dynamic young writers committed to
free expression and dissatisfied with complacent
attitudes toward the war. Böll's *Billard um Halb-
zehn* (1959; *Billiards at Half-Past Nine,* 1962)
probes German history in a story of one family
over the last half century. Like his *Gruppenbild
mit Dame* (1971; *Portrait with Lady,* 1972), it be-

Heinrich Theodor Böll

Günter Grass and his family.　　　　Foto–Studio–Rama

came popular in English translation. A semiautobiographical trilogy by Johnson, *Jahrestage*
(1970-73; *Anniversaries,* 1975), treats moral and
political issues in the U.S. of the 1960s and
Germany in the 1930s. Grass's sprawling novels,
often dealing with the conflict between modern
society and its critics, include *Die Blechtrommel*
(1959; *The Tin Drum,* 1963), a freewheeling satire
on Nazi Germany, made into a film in 1979; *Der
Butt* (1976; *The Flounder,* 1978); and *Kopfge-
burten; oder, Die Deutschen sterben aus* (1980;
Headbirths; or, The Germans Are Dying Out,
1982).

For additional information on individual authors, see biographies of those whose names are
not followed by dates.　　　　　　　　　　F.G.G.

*For further information on this topic, see the
Bibliography in volume 28,* sections 842, 933.

GERMAN MEASLES, also rubella, contagious disease of short duration, caused by virus infection.
The disease is characterized by a rose-colored
rash and frequently by other mild symptoms,
such as a slight fever, sore throat, and swelling of
the lymph glands behind the ears. The rash,
which lasts from one to four days, first appears
on the face and spreads rapidly to the chest,
limbs, and abdomen. German measles is most
common among teenagers and young adults and
rarely occurs in infants or in adults over the age
of 40. It has an incubation period of 14 to 21 days,
more commonly 17 or 18 days. An attack of the
disease usually confers lifelong immunity.

Although far less severe than measles (q.v.),
German measles can have severe consequences
for women in the first three months of pregnancy. The newborn child may be afflicted with
various congenital abnormalities, including heart
defects, mental retardation, deafness, and cataracts (*see* FETUS). The incidence of these malfor-

mations is so high that many physicians recommend therapeutic abortion, if miscarriage has not already resulted from the disease. An attack of rubella after the fourth month of pregnancy rarely causes birth defects. Pregnant women who are exposed to German measles are given gamma globulin (*see* BLOOD: *Plasma*) in an effort to prevent contraction of the disease. Women of childbearing age are advised to be immunized with attenuated live virus vaccines several months before anticipated pregnancy.

The rubella virus was isolated and identified in 1961, and by the early 1970s the vaccine was readily available. Administered in primary and secondary schools and community health departments, the vaccine has dramatically reduced the incidence of German measles among U.S. school-age children.

For further information on this topic, see the Bibliography in volume 28, sections 448, 487.

GERMAN POINTER, either of two dog breeds, the German shorthaired pointer, or kurzhaar, and the German wirehaired pointer, or drahthaar. Both breeds closely resemble one another except for the wiry coat of the drahthaar, with its soft, thick undercoat. The dogs were bred in the late 19th century for sports use as scent hounds on both land and water. The dogs are also good retrievers. Male adults stand about 62.5 cm (25 in) at the shoulder and weigh about 32 kg (70 lb). The coat is light to dark brown, with whitish to liver-colored patches. The ears droop, and the tail is docked to about two-fifths of the original length to avoid entanglements in brush. The German shorthaired pointer was recognized by the American Kennel Club in 1930, and the German wirehaired pointer was recognized in 1959.

GERMAN SHEPHERD DOG, breed of working dog that originated in northern Europe several centuries ago. The dogs were originally used to

German shepherd dogs.   Walter Chandoha

protect flocks of sheep and are still used for this purpose. More recently they have been trained to aid police forces in capturing criminals and to guide the blind—hence the designations "police dog" and "Seeing Eye dog." German shepherds are also used as guard dogs by the military. The dog is more than medium size, standing 61 to 66 cm (24 to 26 in) high at the shoulder. It has a long, muscular body and gives an impression of power and ruggedness. The dog has a long head; a wedge-shaped muzzle; dark-brown eyes of medium size placed somewhat obliquely; medium-sized ears, set high; short, compact feet with hard pads and dark nails; and a bushy tail. The dog has a double coat, consisting of an outer coat with straight hairs of medium length and a thick woolly undercoat. The color may be any of many varieties between light gray and jet black; the main colors are brindle, black and tan, tan, brown and black. The German shepherd dog is noted for loyalty, intelligence, and courage.

GERMAN SOUTHWEST AFRICA. *See* NAMIBIA.

GERMANTOWN, BATTLE OF, engagement of the American Revolution, fought on Oct. 4, 1777, between Americans under the command of Gen. George Washington and British and Hessian troops under Sir William Howe. The British had occupied Philadelphia after the defeat of the Americans at the Battle of the Brandywine (Sept. 11, 1776), and their army was encamped at Germantown, Pa. Washington decided to launch a surprise attack against the encampment, and at dawn on October 4, in the midst of a heavy fog, the American troops advanced into Germantown by two roads, with Gen. Nathanael Greene leading the detachment on the left and Gen. John Sullivan that on the right. Gen. Anthony Wayne and Washington accompanied Sullivan, who was successful at first, forcing the enemy back and capturing a battery. A British force took refuge in the Chew mansion, a large stone house on the line of the American advance, and an American force was detained in an attempt to dislodge them. Meanwhile, a detachment of the Americans under the command of Greene, whose advance had been less successful, had been drawn too far toward the right wing; in the resulting confusion, they mistook the firing in the vicinity of the Chew house for an enemy attack and opened fire on their own troops. This incident threw the American troops into a panic and forced a retreat. The British lost about 550 men in killed and wounded; the Americans, 673. Although the attack itself had failed, Washington's ability to take the offensive so soon after his defeat at Brandywine, coupled with the subsequent American victory over the British general John

Burgoyne at Saratoga, N.Y., on October 17, encouraged the American people and led France to form an alliance with the Americans.

GERMANY, a country of central Europe inhabited chiefly by German-speaking peoples. For most of the more than 1000 years of German history, Germany was a geographical term for an area occupied by many states. A unified nation for only 74 years (1871–1945), it was divided after World War II into the Federal Republic of Germany (FRG), or West Germany, and the German Democratic Republic (GDR), or East Germany. On Oct. 3, 1990, Germany was once again united, as the land that had been East Germany became part of the FRG.

As a geographical area, Germany consists of three regions—the northern plain, the central uplands, and a mountainous area in the south. It is crossed by the Rhine, Weser, Elbe, and Oder rivers flowing north and by the Danube flowing east. Lacking geographical boundaries except for the North Sea and the Baltic Sea, it was in the path of migrations and invasions from the east and west, and the fluidity of the population helped delay German unification.

Also working against national unity was the ethnic variety of the "Germans." Germans of Roman descent shared the west and southwest with those of Celtic ancestry, who also lived in the south. Those of Germanic, or Teutonic, origin occupied the north, center, south, and east, while Baltic peoples inhabited the northeast and Slavs the east and southeast. Generally, the north and east were Protestant, and the south and west were Roman Catholic.

These differences encouraged devotion to particular homelands, on the one hand, and antipathy toward neighboring groups, on the other. Germans sometimes engaged in divisive civil wars but at other times merged their differences in supranational empires. Individualistic, and yet submissive to authority, they were slow to develop effective representative government.

This article surveys the history of Germany before 1949. For details of geography, economy, government, history, and cultural life after 1949, see GERMANY, EAST; GERMANY, WEST. See also EUROPE (map pages); GERMAN LANGUAGE; and GERMAN LITERATURE. For information on the Federal Republic of Germany in 1990 and imediately after, see the history section of WEST GERMANY.

ORIGINS OF THE GERMANS

Archaeological evidence shows that what is now Germany was inhabited from earliest times.

Stone Age Peoples. During the Old Stone Age, the German forests were thinly populated by wandering bands of hunters and gatherers. They belonged to the earliest forms of *Homo sapiens,* such as Heidelberg man, who lived about 400,000 years ago. Somewhat later more advanced forms of *Homo sapiens* appeared, as exemplified by skeletal finds near Steinheim, some 300,000 years old, and near Ehringsdorf, from about 100,000 years ago. Another human type was Neanderthal man, found near Düsseldorf, who lived about 100,000 years ago. The most recent type, which appeared by 40,000 BC, was Cro-Magnon man, a member of *Homo sapiens sapiens,* essentially of the same group as modern Europeans.

During the New Stone Age, the indigenous hunters encountered farming peoples from the more advanced southwest Asia, who were migrating up the Danube Valley into central Germany about 4500. They mixed and settled in villages to raise crops and breed stock. Villagers of this Danubian culture lived with their animals in gabled wooden houses, made pottery, and traded with Mediterranean peoples for fine stone and flint axes and shells. As their hand-hoed fields wore out, they moved on, often returning years later.

Bronze Age Peoples. The Bronze Age began in central Germany, Bohemia, and Austria about 2500 with the working of copper and tin deposits by prospectors from the eastern Mediterranean. About 2300, new waves of migrating peoples arrived, probably from southern Russia. These battle-ax–wielding Indo-Europeans were the ancestors of the Germanic tribes that settled in northern and central Germany, the Baltic and Slavic peoples in the east, and the Celtic peoples in the south and west. The central and southern groups mixed with the so-called Bell-Beaker people, who moved east from Spain and Portugal about 2000. The Bell-Beaker folk, probably Indo-Europeans, were skilled metalworkers. They developed a thriving Bronze Age culture in Germany and traded amber from the Baltic coast for bronze, pottery, and beads from the Mediterranean.

From 1800 to 400, Celtic peoples in southern Germany and Austria developed a sequence of advanced metalworking cultures—Urnfield, Hallstatt, and La Tène—each of which spread throughout Europe. They introduced the use of iron for tools and weapons. The La Tène Celts did fine metalwork and used ox-drawn plows and wheeled vehicles. The Germanic tribes absorbed much Celtic culture and eventually displaced the Celts themselves.

Germans and Romans. From the 2d century BC to the 5th century AD the Germanic and Celtic tribes, constantly pressed by migrations from the north and east, were in contact with the Romans. Roman accounts by Julius Caesar and Tacitus describe these encounters.

The Cimbri and Teutons, about to invade Italy, were defeated by the Roman general Gaius Marius in 101 and 102 BC. The Suevi and other tribes in Gaul (modern France), west of the Rhine, were subdued by Julius Caesar around 50 BC. The Romans tried unsuccessfully to extend their rule to the Elbe, and the emperors held the border at the Rhine and the Danube. Between the two rivers they erected a limes, a line of fortifications to keep out raiding tribes.

In the 2d century AD the Romans prevented confederations of Franks, Alamanni, and Burgundians outside the empire from crossing the Rhine. But in the 4th and 5th centuries, the pressure proved too much for the weakened Romans. The Huns, sweeping in from Asia, set off waves of migration, during which the Ostrogoths, Visigoths, Vandals, Franks, Lombards, and other Germanic tribes overran the empire.

BEGINNINGS OF A GERMAN STATE

In the late 5th century the Frankish chieftain Clovis defeated the Romans, and he established a kingdom that included most of Gaul and southwestern Germany. He converted his subjects, believers in the Arian heresy, to orthodox Christianity.

Carolingian Germany. Clovis's work was carried on in the 8th century by Charlemagne, who fought the Slavs south of the Danube, annexed southern Germany, and ferociously subdued and converted the pagan Saxons in the northwest. As champion of Christianity and supporter of the papacy against the restive people of Rome, Charlemagne was crowned emperor of the Romans by Pope Leo III in Rome in 800. This milestone event revived the Roman imperial tradition in the west, but it also set a precedent for the dependence of the emperors on papal approval.

The Carolingian Empire was based on the social structure of the late Roman Empire. The official language of the court and the church was Latin, but Franks in Gaul adopted the Latinate vernacular that became French, and Franks and other Germanic tribes in the east spoke various languages that became German. The only relic of Old High German is the *Hildebrandslied* (Lay of Hildebrand), a fragmentary 8th-century poem, based on early pagan heroic tales, about the tragic duel between a father and son.

Carolingian rulers encouraged missionary work among the Germans. St. Willibrord founded the monastery of Echternach, and St. Boniface founded Reichenau and Fulda and reformed the Frankish church. Non-Frankish Germans, however, retained much pagan belief beneath their newly acquired faith. The *Heliand,* a 9th-century epic, depicts Christ as a Saxon warrior king.

Charlemagne *(1512–13), by Albrecht Dürer. Charlemagne's 9th-century revival of Roman imperialism inspired the Holy Roman emperors.*

Scala–Editorial Photocolor Archives

East Francia. The Carolingian Empire, unwieldy and prey to tribal dissension, did not long survive Charlemagne's death in 814. By the Treaty of Verdun (843), the empire was divided among his three grandsons. One received West Francia (modern France). Another got the imperial title and an area running from the North Sea through Lotharingia (Lorraine) and Burgundy to Italy. The third, Louis the German, received East Francia (modern Germany). The Treaty of Mersen (870) divided the middle kingdom, with Lotharingia going to East Francia and the rest to West Francia. In 881 Charles the Fat of East Francia, heir of Louis the German, received the imperial title. Six years later he was deposed by Arnulf, the last Carolingian emperor.

The Tribal Duchies. By the 10th century East Francia was being buffeted by new waves of pa-

GERMAN RULERS AND REGIMES

Holy Roman Emperors

(elected German kings, who also ruled the Holy Roman Empire, later regarded as the First Reich; for list, see HOLY ROMAN EMPIRE)   800–1806

Electors of Brandenburg and Dukes of Prussia

George William	1619–40
Frederick William the Great Elector	1640–88
Frederick III	1688–1713

(became Frederick I, king of Prussia, 1701; the Hohenzollern dynasty continued to rule as kings of Prussia until 1918)

Kings of Prussia

Frederick I	1701–13
Frederick William I	1713–40
Frederick II, the Great	1740–86
Frederick William II	1786–97
Frederick William III	1797–1840
Frederick William IV	1840–61
William I	1861–88

(became also German Emperor William I, 1871)

German Emperors

(of the Deutsches Reich, or Second Reich)

William I	1871–88
Frederick III	1888
William II	1888–1918

Presidents

(of the Deutsches Reich, known as the Weimar Republic)

Friedrich Ebert	1919–25
Paul von Hindenburg	1925–33

Führer

(of the Deutsches Reich, or Third Reich)

Adolf Hitler	1933–45

gan Danes, Magyars, and Moravians from the north and east and was virtually torn apart by rival tribes. The Carolingians had granted tribal military leaders (dukes) and appointed officials (counts and margraves) lands as temporary fiefs for their services to the state, and many of the high clergy had also received fiefs. As royal authority declined, these feudal lords, or princes, provided local government and defense. The secular lords gradually made their fiefs hereditary. The greatest of them were the rulers of five stem (tribal) duchies—Franconia, Swabia, Bavaria, Saxony, and Lorraine. Lesser warriors joined princely retinues out of tribal loyalty and in exchange for smaller grants of land and other gifts. Common people lost the right to bear arms. They worked the fields of warriors and churchmen in return for protection and a share of the crops. Thus, the Carolingian governmental system blended with the German tradition of free tribesmen to form a society in which a military nobility was supported by an agricultural peasantry of freemen and serfs.

By ancient German tradition, the kings were elected. Because no noble family wanted to be subject to another family or to a strong king, weak kings were often chosen, and none could safely assume the loyalty of his nobles. These conditions delayed for centuries the consolidation of a strong German state.

EARLY MIDDLE AGES

Medieval German kings had three major concerns. One was checking the rebellious princes—usually with the help of churchmen. The second was controlling Italy and being crowned emperor of the West by the pope, a policy considered an essential part of the Carolingian heritage. The third was expansion to the north and east.

The Saxon Kings. When the last Carolingian died without an heir, the Franks and Saxons elected Conrad, duke of Franconia, their king; he proved incompetent. After his death in 918 they chose the Saxon duke Henry I, the Fowler, a sober, practical soldier, who made peace with a rival king chosen by the Bavarians, defeated Magyars and Slavs, and regained Lorraine.

Otto I, the Great. At Henry's death in 936, the princes elected his son Otto I, who combined extraordinary forcefulness, dignity, and military prowess with great diplomatic skill and genuine religious faith. Determined to create a strong centralized monarchy, Otto gave the duchies to his relatives and then broke them up into nonhereditary fiefs granted to bishops and abbots. By nominating these churchmen and subjecting them to the royal court, he ensured their loyalty. This Ottonian system of government through alliance with the German state church was carried much further by his successors.

Otto also had to defend his realm from outside pressures. In the west he strengthened his hold on Lorraine and gained influence over Burgundy (Arles). In the north and east he defeated the Danes and Slavs, and he permanently broke the power of the Magyars (Hungarians) at the Battle of the Lechfeld in 955. Otto established the archbishopric of Magdeburg (968) and other sees as centers of civilization in the conquered lands. Germans settled these regions.

Wanting to emulate Charlemagne as the divinely sanctioned emperor of Christendom, Otto began the disastrous policy of German entanglement in Italy. The temptation was the greater because Italy was a rich land and a scene of feudal disorder and Saracen invasions. When Adelaide (931–99), widowed queen of the Lombards, asked Otto for help against her captor, Berengar (c. 900–66), king of Italy, Otto invaded Italy in 951, married her, and took her dead husband's title.

The papacy at this time was struggling to hold its land against encroaching nobles from the north and Byzantine Greeks and Saracens from the south. When Pope John XII appealed to Otto for aid against Berengar, Otto invaded Italy a second time, defeated Berengar, and was crowned emperor by the pope in 962. By a treaty called the Ottonian Privilege, Otto guaranteed the pope's claim to papal lands, and all future papal candidates had to swear fealty to the emperor.

Later Saxon kings. Otto's successors in the 10th and 11th centuries continued his German and Italian policies as best they could. Otto II established the Eastern March (Austria) under the Babenbergs as a military outpost but was defeated by the Saracens in his efforts to secure southern Italy. The pious Otto III supported the Benedictine reform movement originating in Cluny, Burgundy, which encouraged a more austere, disciplined life. The childless Henry II, gentle and devout, also encouraged the Cluniac movement and sent out missionaries from his court in the new bishopric of Bamberg.

Salian Kings. For 100 years (1024–1125) German kings were chosen from the Salian line, which was related to the Saxons. The Salians brought the empire to its height.

High tide of empire. Conrad II, a clever and ruthless ruler, reasserted royal authority over princely opposition by making the fiefs of lesser nobles hereditary and by appointing as officials and soldiers ministerials, lower-class men responsible directly to him. He seized Burgundy, strengthened his hold on northern Italy, and became overlord of Poland.

Conrad's son Henry III, the Black, was the first undisputed king of Germany. A pious visionary, he introduced to a Germany torn by civil strife the Cluny-inspired Truce of God, a respite from war lasting from Wednesday night to Monday morning, and tried in vain to extend it to a permanent peace. He ended the payment by new bishops of tribute to the Crown (simony), although he still invested churchmen, who remained his vassals. During his reign he deposed three rival popes and created four new ones, notably the reform-minded Leo IX.

Henry IV. While still a child, Henry IV succeeded his father, Henry III, in 1056. During his mother's regency, long-restive princes annexed much royal land; cities, popes, and Normans controlled Italy; and the Lateran synod of 1059 declared that only cardinals could canonically elect the pope. Wily, opportunistic, and headstrong in an era of violence and treachery, as ruler Henry sought to recover lost imperial power. His efforts to retrieve crown lands aroused the Saxons, who resented the Salian kings. He crushed a Saxon rebellion in 1075 and proceeded to confiscate land, thus intensifying their enmity.

Henry's control of the clergy embroiled him with the militant reform pope Gregory VII, who wanted to free the church from secular bondage. When Gregory forbade lay investiture of churchmen, Henry had him deposed by the Synod of Worms in 1076. The pope promptly excommunicated Henry and released his subjects from their oath of loyalty to him. To keep his crown, Henry cleverly sought the pope at Canossa in the Apennines in January 1077, where, after three days of humble penitence, he was forgiven. The princes, however, elected a rival king, Rudolf of Swabia. The result was nearly 20 years of civil war. In 1080 Gregory excommunicated Henry again and recognized Rudolf. Deposing Gregory, Henry marched on Rome, installed the antipope Clement III (c. 1025–1100), and was crowned emperor in 1084. Henry returned to Germany to continue the civil war against a new rival king (Rudolf had died in 1080). Finally, betrayed and imprisoned by his son Henry, the emperor was forced to abdicate.

Compromise. The treacherous, brutal, and greedy Henry V vainly continued his father's struggle for supremacy. Suffering military defeats, he lost control of Poland, Hungary, and Bohemia. Despite the support of churchmen, ministerials, and the towns, he could not suppress the princes, who forced the weary emperor and Pope Callistus II to compromise on investiture. They accepted the Concordat of Worms (1122), which stipulated that clerical elections in Germany were to take place in the imperial presence without simony and that the emperor was to invest the candidate with the symbols of his temporal office before a bishop invested him with the spiritual ones. The pope, however, had the better of the bargain, and the rivalry between empire and papacy took on new dimensions.

Early Medieval Society. German kings had no fixed capital, but traveled unceasingly about their realm. They had no income beyond that from their family lands and gifts from churchmen. Feudalism was the rule. The great lords, theoretically vassals of the king, in fact usurped royal rights to build castles and administer justice. The vast majority of common people lived on country manors belonging to nobles or churchmen. The few cities, such as Trier and Cologne, were chiefly Roman foundations or imperial fortifications. There, merchants, artisans, and uprooted peasants settled as free citizens under the authority of a prince. The cities also sheltered Jews, who were not allowed to hold land.

The clergy, which included many nobles, spread the faith, provided education, and carried on the functions of government. Monasteries such as Reichenau, Regensburg, Fulda, Echternach, and Saint Gall became centers of scholarship. Monks wrote Latin works (such as the *Walthariuslied*, based on a German legend) and translated biblical and other Christian texts into Old High German. Their illuminated manuscripts with flat, dignified images imitated the art of classical antiquity and Byzantium. Churches, notably Saint Michael at Hildesheim and the cathedrals of Mainz, Speyer, and Worms, were massive, stone-vaulted basilicas with towers and small, round-arched windows. Their walls were adorned with painted murals and expressive sculpture in wood and bronze.

HIGH MIDDLE AGES

In the 12th and 13th centuries Germany and Italy were rent by rivalry between two princely families. The Hohenstaufen, or Waiblingen, of Swabia, known as Ghibellines in Italy, held the German and imperial crowns. The Welfs of Bavaria and Saxony, known as Guelphs in Italy, were allied with the papacy.

Henry V died childless in 1125. The princes, avoiding the principle of heredity, passed over his nephews, Frederick (1090–1147) and Conrad Hohenstaufen, to choose Lothair, duke of Saxony. As emperor, Lothair II revived German efforts to convert and dominate the east. To assert his authority in Italy, he made two expeditions supporting the pope, who crowned him in 1133. In Germany he fought a civil war with the Hohenstaufen princes, who refused to accept him as emperor.

The Hohenstaufen Kings. At Lothair's death the princes avoided his powerful Welf son-in-law and heir, Henry the Proud (1108–39), lord of Bavaria and Saxony. Instead, they chose Conrad Hohenstaufen. Civil war erupted again, this time between the weak but charming Conrad III and the Welf dukes Henry the Proud and his son Henry the Lion. It continued while Conrad led the ill-fated Second Crusade and was paralleled by the Guelph-Ghibelline conflict in Italy. The struggle in Germany was temporarily resolved at Conrad's death by the election of his nephew Frederick, a Hohenstaufen born of a Welf mother.

Frederick I, Barbarossa.

Frederick I, Barbarossa. Handsome and intelligent, warlike, just, and charming, Frederick Barbarossa was the ideal medieval Christian king. Regarding himself as the successor of Augustus, Charlemagne, and Otto the Great, he took the title Holy Roman emperor and spent most of his reign shuttling between Germany and Italy trying to restore imperial glory in both.

In the north he joined Germany and Burgundy by marrying Beatrice (d. 1184), heiress to Burgundy. He declared an imperial peace; to ensure

it, he placated the Welfs by recognizing Henry the Lion as duke of Saxony and Bavaria, and for balance he made Austria a duchy. But when Henry refused to contribute troops to a critical Italian campaign, Frederick and jealous princes exiled him as a traitor. Henry's duchies were split up, Bavaria going to the Wittelsbach family.

In the south, Frederick made six expeditions to Italy to assert full imperial authority over the Lombard city-states and the popes. On his first trip he was crowned (1155) emperor. On his second, he had the Diet of Roncaglia (1158) declare his rights, and he installed podestas (imperial representatives) in the cities. Some cities had Ghibelline sympathies, but most objected to being ruled and taxed by uncouth, greedy foreigners. The popes needed imperial support against a Roman rising, but they believed that their spiritual office gave them sovereignty over the emperors. Also, they wanted to maintain independent control of the Papal States. Consequently, some cities revolted against imperial authority and formed the Lombard League in alliance with Pope Alexander III. Frederick reacted by creating an antipope. On his next two trips, Ghibelline cities joined Guelph cities in a revived league and threw out the podestas. Alexander, who had excommunicated Frederick, fled to his Norman allies in Sicily, and Frederick captured (1166) Rome.

During his fifth invasion of Italy, lacking the support of Henry the Lion, Frederick was defeated by the league at the Battle of Legnano (1176). As a result, the Peace of Constance (1183) recognized the autonomy of the cities, which remained only nominally subject to the emperor.

Bracelet, Mosan enamel on gilt copper, one of a pair, was probably part of the regalia of Holy Roman Emperor Frederick Barbarossa. Sotheby Parke Bernet, Inc.

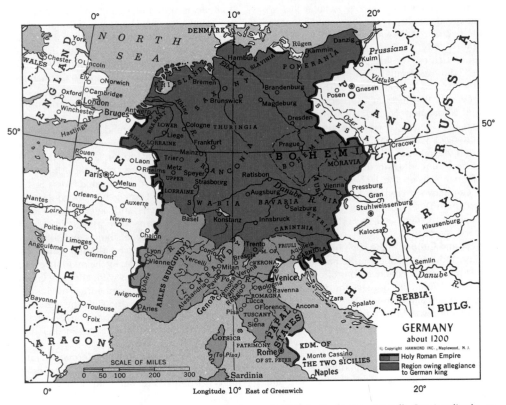

GERMANY
about 1200
© Copyright HAMMOND INC., Maplewood, N. J.
■ Holy Roman Empire
■ Region owing allegiance
to German king

SCALE OF MILES
0 50 100   200   300

Longitude 10° East of Greenwich

Stubbornly, Frederick made a last trip in which he gained new support among the quarrelsome cities. He died leading the Third Crusade.

Henry VI. More ambitious even than his father, Henry VI wanted to dominate the known world. To secure peace in Germany, he put down a rebellion by the returned exile Henry the Lion and then restored him to power. He forced the northern Italian cities to submit to him and seized Sicily from a usurping Norman king. Intending to create an empire in the Mediterranean, he exacted tribute from North Africa and the weak Byzantine emperor. Henry died suddenly in 1197 while planning a crusade to the Holy Land.

The empire immediately fell apart. Henry's infant son, Frederick II, inherited Sicily, but northern Italy reasserted its independence. The Germans refused to accept a child or make the Crown hereditary in the Hohenstaufen line. Once more civil war raged as two elected kings—the Hohenstaufen Philip of Swabia and the Welf Otto of Brunswick, son of Henry the Lion—struggled for the Crown. When Otto invaded Italy, Pope Innocent III secured the election of Frederick II on the promise that Frederick would give up Sicily so as not to surround the pope.

Frederick II, Stupor Mundi. Outstandingly accomplished in many fields, the new king was called Stupor Mundi ("wonder of the world"). He was gracious and amiable but also crafty and ruthless. Determined to keep Sicily as his base of operations, he revised his coronation promise, giving Germany rather than Sicily to his young son Henry. In Sicily he suppressed the barons, reformed the laws, founded the University of Naples, and kept a brilliant court, where he shone as scientist, artist, and poet. He was also an excellent soldier, diplomat, and administrator.

To gain German support for his campaigns in northern Italy, Frederick allowed the princes to usurp royal powers. The confirmation of their rights by the Privilege of Worms (1231) made them virtually kings in their own territories. Henry, when he came of age, objected to this policy and revolted but was quickly deposed and imprisoned by his father.

An aggressive emperor such as Frederick was regarded as dangerous by the popes. Angered by his claims to Lombardy, Pope Gregory IX excommunicated him for his delay in leading a promised crusade. Frederick finally went to Jerusalem in 1228, was crowned king, and gained the chief Christian sites in the Holy Land. His success did not mollify Gregory, however, who in his absence invaded Sicily. Frederick rushed home and made peace. But he was soon battling (1237) in northern Italy against the second Lombard League of cities. The league was allied with the pope, who excommunicated him again. Frederick then seized the Papal States. The new pope, Innocent IV, fled to Lyon and declared him deposed. Undaunted, Frederick was making headway against the league when he suddenly died.

Frederick's young son Conrad IV inherited Sicily and the imperial title, but Italy and Germany were never united again. The popes, allied with the French, ousted the Hohenstaufens from Sicily. Germany suffered the turmoil of the Great Interregnum (1254–73), during which foreigners claimed the Crown and the princes won a 6-century ascendancy.

Society and Culture in the High Middle Ages. By the late 13th century the empire had lost Poland and Hungary and effective control of Burgundy and Italy. Within its borders the principalities were virtually autonomous. The ancient right of royal election was limited to seven princes, who purposely chose weak men unlikely to thwart their own dynastic ambitions.

The church continued to be a dominant force in society. Cistercian monks and Premonstratensian canons settled new lands in the east, and

Dominican and Franciscan friars preached and taught in the towns. The Teutonic Knights moved their headquarters to Marienburg in eastern Germany, where they led a crusade against the pagan Prussians. The knights opened the Baltic coast to the German church and to German merchants.

The struggle between emperors and princes benefited the towns, who paid taxes to the emperors in exchange for freedom from feudal obligations. Trade greatly increased. Cologne and Frankfurt gave access to the fairs of Champagne. Mainz lay on the route across the Alps to Italy. Lübeck and Hamburg dominated North Sea and Baltic trade, and Leipzig was in contact with Russia. Rhine towns and, later, north German towns began to form trade associations, called Hansas. The rich burghers built city walls, cathedrals, and elaborate town halls and guildhalls as expressions of civic pride. By the mid-13th century, French Gothic influences were affecting German architecture. The lofty cathedrals of Bamberg, Strasbourg, Naumburg, and Cologne were richly decorated with sculpture, and they were filled with light from the stained glass in their large, pointed-arched windows.

French culture also affected German literature. Wandering nobles and knights, called minnesingers, wrote and recited courtly love poems in

At Ehrenfels castle (13th cent.), on the Rhine River near Rudesheim, Germany, the medieval archbishops of Mainz collected river tolls.

the tradition of Provençal troubadours and French trouvères. Foremost among them were Reinmar von Hagenau (c. 1160-1210) and Walther von der Vogelweide. Other poets, called *Spielleute*, composed epics. Gottfried von Strassburg and Wolfram von Eschenbach dealt with Christian themes from the French Arthurian cycle. Nonetheless, the two most important epics—the *Niebelungenlied* and the *Gudrunlied*—were based on pagan Germanic traditions.

LATE MIDDLE AGES AND EARLY RENAISSANCE

By the late Middle Ages, the great stem duchies had been broken up and new principalities created. Three princely families—Habsburg, Wittelsbach, and Luxemburg—struggled for dynastic rights to the imperial crown.

Princely Rivalry. In 1273 the electors ended the Great Interregnum by choosing Rudolf of Habsburg, a minor Swabian prince unable to repossess the lands they had usurped. Rudolf I concentrated on aggrandizing his family. Aided by the Wittelsbachs and others, he defeated the rebellious Ottokar II of Bohemia (1230-78) and took the lands Ottokar had usurped—Austria, Styria, Carinthia, and Carniola—for his two sons, thus making the Habsburgs one of the great powers in the empire.

On Rudolf's death the electors chose Adolf of Nassau (c. 1250-98) but deposed him when he asserted his authority. They next chose Rudolf's son, Albert of Austria, but when he displayed appetite for additional territory, he was murdered. Still seeking a weak emperor, the electors voted for Henry, count of Luxemburg. Anxious to restore imperial claims to Italy, Henry VII crossed the Alps in 1310 and temporarily subdued Lombardy; he was crowned by the Roman people, because the popes had left Rome and were then living in Avignon, France—the so-called Babylonian Captivity. He died trying to conquer Naples from the French.

Civil war then raged until the Wittelsbach candidate for the throne, Louis the Bavarian, defeated his Habsburg rival at the Battle of Mühldorf in 1322. Louis IV obtained a secular coronation in Italy, but Pope John XXII, objecting to his interference in Italian politics, declared his title invalid and excommunicated him. Louis then called for a church council and installed an antipope in Rome. At Rhense in 1338 the electors made the momentous declaration that henceforth the king of the Germans would be the majority electoral choice, thus avoiding civil war, and that he would automatically be emperor without being crowned by the pope. This was reflected in the title, official in the 15th century, Holy Roman Empire of the German Nation.

The Luxemburg Line. The popes, of course, objected. Clement VI opened negotiations with Charles, king of Bohemia, grandson of Henry VII. In 1347 he was chosen by five of the seven electors, who had previously deposed Louis. Charles IV diplomatically ignored the question of papal assent. In the Golden Bull (1356) he specified the seven electors as the archbishops of Mainz, Trier, and Cologne, the count palatine of the Rhine, the duke of Saxony (an old title for a new state in the east), the margrave of Brandenburg, and the king of Bohemia. Because the bull made their lands indivisible, granted them monopolies on mining and tolls, and secured them "gifts" from candidates, they were the strongest of all the princes.

Having ensured the power of the princes, the astute Charles entrenched his own dynasty in Bohemia. He bought Brandenburg and took Silesia from Poland to build a great state to the east. To obtain cash, he encouraged the silver, glass, and paper industries of Bohemia. He adorned Prague, his capital, with new buildings in the late Gothic style, founded a noted university, and kept a brilliant court.

Charles's son, Sigismund, forced Pope John XXIII to call the Council of Constance (1414-18), which ended the Great Schism in the papacy. But as the king of Bohemia he was chiefly concerned with his own dynastic lands. Bohemia was convulsed by the Hussite movement, which combined traditional Czech national feeling with desire for much-needed church reform. Sigismund invited the reformer John Huss (Jan Hus) to state his views, under imperial protection, at the Council of Constance, but failed to prevent the council from subsequently burning him as a heretic. This led to the Hussite Wars by which the moderate Calixtine Hussites won some concessions from the church and Sigismund in exchange for their reconciliation.

The Habsburg Line. When Sigismund died without an heir, the electors unanimously chose his Habsburg son-in-law Albert of Austria, who became emperor as Albert II. From then on, the imperial crown became in practice, although not in theory, hereditary in the Habsburg family. Albert II died in the midst of civil war in Bohemia and an Ottoman invasion of Hungary. His cousin and successor, Frederick III, lost Hungary and Bohemia and sold Luxemburg to France, while he struggled with the German princes and the Turks on his borders. In 1486 the princes forced him to cede his authority to his son, but he retained the title of Holy Roman Emperor until 1493.

Maximilian I, knight and art patron, enthusiastically laid many plans, which never materialized.

His chief success was in arranging marriages to benefit his family. By his own marriage to Mary of Burgundy (1457–82) he acquired a rich territory that included the thriving Flemish towns. French-speaking Burgundy was the initial cause of the Habsburg-Valois feud that lasted for the next three centuries. By marrying his son, Philip the Handsome, to the heiress of Spain, Maximilian acquired Spain and its possessions in Italy and the New World. By betrothing his grandson Ferdinand to the heiress of Hungary and Bohemia, he added those states to the inheritance.

15th-Century Society. In Germany as in the rest of Europe, the 15th century was a time of transition from the land economy of the Middle Ages to the money economy of modern times. The process created painful tensions among all classes of society.

The nobility. The German nobility ranged from the great electors and other princes of the 240 states of the empire to the minor knights who held fiefs directly from the emperor. They had supreme jurisdiction in their own lands, checked only by diets representing nobles, clergy, and burghers, which alone could levy the taxes needed to pay for new arms and mercenary soldiers. As prices rose and income from land did not, all the nobility felt pressed for funds. Some squeezed more goods and services out of their peasants. Others resorted to raiding their peers

or the cities, and still others sold their military services as mercenaries.

The cities. As centers of commerce, the cities became increasingly important in a money economy. In the south, Nuremberg and Augsburg, home of the Fugger bank, thrived on mines and trade with Italy. In the north, Lübeck, Hamburg, and other cities of the Hanseatic League carried on brisk trade with Britain and Scandinavia. Within the cities the old merchant guilds and new craft guilds, both virtually hereditary, struggled for power. Common laborers had no say. As their trade grew, cities' demand for freedom from attack and from local tolls levied on roads and rivers often led to war with the nobles.

The peasants. Perhaps one-third of the peasants, like the rest of the population, had been carried off by the Black Death that swept Europe in the mid-14th century. Of the survivors, some had lost their land through frequent subdivision among heirs. Many of these streamed to the cities, while others charged landlords more for their labor. Most small peasants, however, lost whatever rights and freedoms they had traditionally possessed, as lords strove to keep them on the land and make them as profitable as possible. The peasants, especially in southern Germany, finally resorted to violent protest.

The church. Cries for church reform had been raised at least as early as the 11th-century Clu-

Woodcut from the Mazarin Bible (c. 1455), printed by Johann Gutenberg, the inventor of movable type. Printing contributed to the rapid spread of ideas in modern times. Tower News Service–Editorial Photocolor Archives

niac movement. During the late Middle Ages and early Renaissance they became more insistent. On the political level, the church lost prestige as a result of the unedifying Babylonian Captivity and the ensuing Great Schism in the papacy.

On the economic level, the increasingly widespread need for cash led to criticism of the church's wealth. People objected that the church owned much land and bore heavily on its tenants but paid no taxes. Economic and political concerns came together in growing German resentment at sending money to maintain the pope in Rome.

The church was also attacked on the intellectual level by the humanist study of classical antiquity, which spread north from Italy. Nicholas of Cusa proposed a heliocentric theory of astronomy that undermined the accepted biblical view of creation. Literary humanists such as Conradus Celtes (1459–1508), Willibald Pirkheimer (1470–1530), Johann Reuchlin, and Erasmus of Rotterdam urged linguistic purity in the study of biblical and other texts and satirized abuses in the church. The invention of printing from movable type by Johann Gutenberg made it possible to produce Bibles, other books, and pamphlets in great quantity at low cost. As a result, the new learning could circulate widely, preparing the intellectual ground for the Reformation.

AGE OF RELIGIOUS STRIFE

The spiritual concerns of Martin Luther combined with secular ambitions of the German princes to produce the Protestant Reformation. The movement for church reform created religious liberty at the cost of Western Christian unity. Religious strife intensified European political wars for 100 years.

The Protestant Reformation. Charles V succeeded his grandfather Maximilian as Holy Roman emperor in 1519. He devoted his life to preserving a medieval empire united in faith, a fruitless effort in the pluralistic society created by religious reformers and secular forces.

Luther. A key figure of the new age was Martin Luther, an Augustinian friar who was disturbed by abuses within the church. He was particularly aroused by the unscrupulous campaign to sell indulgences, or remissions of punishment for sin. In 1517 Luther published a list of 95 theses attacking indulgences, and these stirred up much controversy.

In 1520 Luther published three pamphlets stating his beliefs in the liberty of the Christian conscience informed only by the Bible, the priesthood of all believers, and a state-supported church. Because these doctrines struck at the root of church authority, Pope Leo X issued a bull

Martin Luther, *by Lucas Cranach. Luther led the Protestant Reformation, which encouraged German national feeling.*   Josse–Editorial Photocolor Archives

condemning Luther's works. Luther burned the bull and was then excommunicated. Charles V summoned him to defend himself at the Diet of Worms (1521) and, when Luther refused to recant, outlawed him. On his way home, however, Luther was rescued by Frederick the Wise (1463–1525), elector of Saxony; installed in the Wartburg castle, he began to translate the Bible into German.

Lutheran ideas, partly a continuation of Hussite traditions, were sympathetically received by many. Matters of conscience, however, were often carried to extremes or mixed with socioeconomic grievances. The fanatical Karlstadt urged iconoclastic attacks on church painting, statuary, and stained glass. The mercenary knight Franz von Sickingen (1481–1523) led impecunious south German knights against ecclesiastical lords in the hope of gaining church lands. Peasant groups, wanting a return to old ways, looted and burned castles and monasteries in the Peasants' War (1524–26).

These revolutionaries looked to Luther for guidance in reordering the church and German society, but Luther did not want to mix religious with secular concerns. Emerging from the Wartburg to restore order, he checked Karlstadt and urged the princes to crush every rising, which they did. The peasants then lost all traditional

341

rights, sense of initiative, and status, while the princes set up state churches supported by confiscated Catholic lands. In these new churches the service was in German, and the clergy were permitted to marry.

Conflict and compromise. At this early stage, a break with Rome did not seem inevitable. Many Lutherans would have remained in the church if nonbiblical practices had been eliminated. Charles V, busy with foreign wars, wanted to make peace at home, but Luther was not conciliatory. Furthermore, Protestants, as the reformers came to be called, were themselves divided. In addition to Lutherans there were Reformed Christians, inspired by the Swiss theologian Huldreich Zwingli, who wanted to set up theocratic states based on the Bible, and radical Anabaptists, mostly poor people who wanted to form churches independent of the state.

At the Diet of Augsburg (1530) Lutherans and Reformed Christians presented separate confessions of faith, indicating that they could not compromise with the Catholics or each other. The Anabaptists were not represented at all. Both the princes and the pope blocked Charles's desire for a council to mediate the dispute. Despairing of peaceful means, Charles led his troops against the Protestant princes and cities of the Schmalkaldic League (1531), routing them at the Battle of Mühlberg in 1547. By this time, however, many nobles, who had acquired secularized Catholic lands, were staunch Protestants, and they forced on Charles the compromise Peace of Augsburg (1555). It recognized Lutheranism, but not the Reformed (Calvinist) faith, whose theocratic doctrines seemed revolutionary to the princes. Most significant, it gave the princes the right to choose the religion for their territory.

Luther died in 1546, his work done. Charles, who had failed at a hopeless task, abdicated in 1556. His vast empire was divided, with the Spanish and Burgundian lands going to his son Philip II and the imperial title and the German lands going to his brother Ferdinand.

The Catholic Reformation. While the emperors Ferdinand I and his son Maximilian II (1527–76) were occupied with the threat of Turkish invasion, Protestantism in Germany grew apace. Its progress was checked, however, by the Counter Reformation (q.v.). The long-delayed Council of Trent (1545–63), dominated by the Jesuits, abolished the sale of indulgences but also reformulated doctrine and worship so as to preclude reconciliation with Protestantism. The Jesuits established centers in German cities, where they won many Germans back to Catholicism. The

rulers of Bavaria, Austria, Salzburg, Bamberg, and Würzburg restored Catholicism by force, creating a Catholic bloc in southern Germany.

Tension mounted between Protestants and Catholics. Protestant princes under Frederick IV (1574–1610), count palatine, a Reformed Protestant, formed (1608) the Protestant Union. Maximilian I (1573–1651), duke of Bavaria, led (1609) the Catholic princes into the Catholic League. Emperor Rudolf II, a scholarly recluse in Prague, unable to govern, was forced to relinquish his authority to his brother Matthias (1557–1619), who proved no more effective.

Matthias was succeeded by his nephew, who ruled as Ferdinand II. The real power in Europe, however, was Philip II of Spain, with his well-armed troops highly paid in New World gold. Catholic France was determined not to be overwhelmed by Habsburgs on either side. Protestant England and the Netherlands were also opposed to a strong Habsburg dynasty. Denmark and Sweden were lured by the desire to dominate the Baltic. Taking advantage of the quarreling German states, all these countries intervened to make Germany the scene of a devastating, four-phase European War.

The Thirty Years' War. The trouble began in Protestant Bohemia, which refused to accept the Catholic Ferdinand as king or future emperor. In 1618 the Czechs set up their own government, supported by the Evangelical Union. After the death of Matthias in 1619, they chose the Protestant elector Frederick V (1596–1632), count palatine, as their king. Ferdinand, however, crushed the Bohemian forces at the Battle of Weisserberg (1620); Frederick, called the Winter King, was exiled; and Catholicism was restored by force. The Bohemian nobles were killed, deprived of their lands, or fined. As a result of the war the population declined by two-thirds.

Protestant princes objected to Spanish troops in Germany. They supported Christian IV of Denmark, who, financed by the Dutch and English, invaded Germany in 1625. So began the second phase of the Thirty Years' War, which ended with Christian's defeat. The victorious Ferdinand issued the Edict of Restitution (1629), which ordered the return of all Catholic church property seized by Protestants since 1552.

The third phase of the war began when Gustav II Adolph of Sweden, who had long wanted to extend Swedish control of the Baltic, invaded Pomerania as the champion of the Protestant princes. The Swedish army won a brilliant victory at Breitenfeld (1631) and took Mainz and Prague, but the war dragged on for years, the two opposing armies devastating the countryside and accomplishing little. In 1635 a truce was declared, and the Edict of Restitution was revoked.

The Swedish, however, were still land-hungry, and the French, led by Cardinal Richelieu, were determined to subdue the Habsburgs. Accordingly, in the fourth phase of the war, the French paid subsidies to the Swedish army to keep it fighting, and French troops crossed the Rhine. After another 13 years of struggle, Emperor Ferdinand III and the princes were ready for peace.

The Peace of Westphalia. The long war resulted in a draw, finalized by the Peace of Westphalia in 1648. The religious status quo of 1624 was accepted, meaning that the Habsburg lands and the south and west were Catholic, the Reformed faith was recognized, and Protestants could retain acquired lands.

Politically, the Holy Roman Empire, or First Reich, continued in name, but it had lost all claim to universality or effective centralized government. Economically and socially, Germany had lost about half of its people to war, famine, and plague and much of its livestock, capital, and trade. Bands of refugees and mercenaries roamed the countryside, seizing what they could.

Cultural Life in the Renaissance and Reformation. Renaissance classicism and the Protestant Reformation deeply affected the arts of the 16th century and transformed education.

The visual arts. In painting and sculpture the late Gothic style, characterized by religious devotion and love of fine detail, lingered on. Great effort was expended on stained-glass windows and altarpieces by such masters as the painters Matthias Grünewald and Stephen Lochner and the sculptors Veit Stoss, Peter Vischer the Elder, Adam Kraft, and Tilman Riemenschneider. The Renaissance style, marked by classical motifs and interest in the natural world, was introduced from Italy by Albrecht Dürer, who brought German painting to heights previously unknown. Lucas Cranach and Hans Holbein the Younger expressed the humanist emphasis on the individual in portraits. Dürer and Martin Schongauer combined Gothic and Renaissance elements in the new arts of woodcut and copper engraving, used for printed book illustration.

Architecture was late Gothic until the Reformation, when church building virtually stopped. Protestants frowned on church art, but they spent lavishly on the steep-roofed, half-timbered, decoratively painted houses of the burghers and on imposing palaces and guildhalls in the Renaissance style.

Literature and scholarship. Medieval tradition continued in popular German literature in the form of folk songs, anecdotes about folk heroes, and religious and secular folk plays. Folk and classical themes provided source material for the Meistersinger, lyric poets who wrote according to the strict forms of the earlier minnesingers. Foremost among them was Hans Sachs, a cobbler of Nuremberg.

The most important development in literature was Luther's translation of the Bible into a vigorous vernacular that helped give the German people a unified literary language. Luther and others wrote German hymns for Protestant congregations, a liturgical innovation that laid the foundation for German church music and influenced worship throughout the Protestant world. Melanchthon, a professor at the University of Wittenberg, lucidly presented Protestant doctrines in Latin to the non-German world. He and other humanists introduced classical scholarship to universities in Cologne, Leipzig, Vienna, and other cities, and he helped found new universities in Königsberg, Jena, and Marburg.

Education. Medieval German education had been limited chiefly to schools and universities run by religious orders to train churchmen and a few government officials. Even the new humanist learning was at first intended for a small, scholarly elite. But Luther, consistent with his belief in the priesthood of all believers and individual study of the Bible, thought that state schools should be open to children of every class. In the Protestant states, primary schools were set up to teach German and religion. Latin was the principal subject in the secondary schools (*Gymnasiens*) founded by Melanchthon, which presented for the first time a graded course of study. Saxony and other Protestant states gradually opened *Gymnasiens*, which influenced German education into the 20th century. In the Catholic states similar but highly centralized schools were established. All these schools were attended chiefly by boys whose families could afford the fees.

RISE OF AUSTRIA AND PRUSSIA

In the late 17th and 18th centuries, the empire was overshadowed by France and England. Its creaking framework was supported by lesser German princes, who wanted its protection, and undermined by greater princes, who wanted freedom to develop on their own. The Wettins of Saxony, expanding eastward, became kings of Poland. The Welfs of Brunswick-Lüneburg became electors of Hannover and gained great influence when Elector George inherited England in 1714. The Wittelsbachs of Bavaria intrigued for a crown in the Spanish Netherlands. Dominating the other princes were the Habsburgs of Austria, who also held Bohemia and Hungary, and the

343

Hohenzollerns of Brandenburg, who became kings of Prussia.

Foreign Wars. Scarcely had they recovered from the Thirty Years' War when the princes and the emperor plunged into a variety of new dynastic struggles.

French wars. In the west the princes were involved in four wars by which Louis XIV strove to extend French territory to the Rhine. In the War of the Devolution (1667–68), Great Elector Frederick William of Brandenburg accepted a pension from Louis in return for political support. In the Dutch War (1672–78), however, Frederick William turned against Louis and lost his conquests in Pomerania. But he later benefited Brandenburg by offering refuge to Huguenots (French Calvinists), whom Louis had exiled by revoking the Edict of Nantes in 1685. Some 20,000 Huguenots migrated east, bringing with them weaving skills and French culture.

Louis's invasion of the Palatinate led to the War of the League of Augsburg (1688–97), which won him Strasbourg and Alsace.

The War of the Spanish Succession (1701–14) was fought over the right of Louis XIV's grandson, Philip V, to inherit the Spanish throne. Bavaria sided with France, because Louis promised the elector the crown of the Spanish Netherlands. Brandenburg supported the successive emperors Leopold I and Joseph I in return for imperial recognition of Prussia as a kingdom. The other European states also allied with the empire to block unification of France and Spain. Large, well-trained, well-equipped armies fought in Bavaria and western Germany, wreaking havoc and ruin. When both sides were exhausted, they accepted the Peace of Utrecht.

Northern wars. Encroached on from the west, the German princes turned to the north and east, where they came into conflict with Sweden in the Baltic. In the First Northern War (1655–60) the emperor and the elector of Brandenburg supported Poland and Denmark against Charles X Gustav of Sweden. The outcome did not effect much change.

In the Great Northern War (1700–21), which paralleled the War of the Spanish Succession, Saxony, Poland, Brandenburg-Prussia, Hannover, Denmark, and Russia joined forces against Sweden. At the end of it, the treaties of Stockholm and Nystadt restored Poland to Augustus, transferred Stettin and West Pomerania from Sweden to Brandenburg-Prussia, and gave Sweden's eastern Baltic lands to Russia.

Turkish wars. The Germans had also to reckon with the Ottoman Turks, who, after a period of quiescence, were vigorously expanding in southeastern Europe. When the Turks invaded Hungary in 1663, imperial troops managed to defeat them and win a 20-year truce. More eager to check the Catholic Habsburgs than the Muslim Turks, Louis XIV and the Hungarians encouraged Turkish aggression. When the truce was up, the Ottomans besieged Vienna in 1683. In this emergency imperial troops, combined with those of John III Sobieski of Poland, rescued the city. The Turks were driven beyond the Danube, and Hungary was compelled to recognize the Habsburg right to inherit the Hungarian crown. The Turkish wars continued, however, until the brilliant general Prince Eugene of Savoy led imperial troops to victory at Senta (1697). By the Treaty of Karlowitz (1699) the Habsburgs regained most of Hungary. The depopulated country was resettled with German veterans, and imperial authority centralized in Vienna was imposed.

Austro-Prussian Rivalry. By 1740 the other German states had fallen behind, leaving Austria and Prussia as rivals for dominance in central Europe.

Growth of Prussia. The Hohenzollerns, who had been granted Brandenburg in the 15th century, had acquired a number of additional, geographically unconnected territories in the west. Outside the empire to the east was the most important area, Prussia, which they had inherited as a Polish duchy in 1618 and converted into an independent kingdom in 1701. Gradually, all the Hohenzollern lands came to be known as the kingdom of Prussia.

Frederick William I of Prussia was a sturdy, hardheaded soldier determined to unite his disparate possessions into a modern military state. Crushing local customs and interests, he created an honest, efficient bureaucracy, which filled the treasury and ran the country for the benefit of a large standing army. He tried to convert his intellectual and artistic son Frederick into an image of himself.

Frederick II, the Great, an unhappy genius, was equally at home on the battlefield and enjoying French literature and music in his Sans Souci (Carefree) Palace near Berlin. He spent most of his life, however, aggrandizing Prussia at the expense of Austria and Poland and refining and reorganizing the Prussian government and economy the better to serve the army.

War of the Austrian Succession. Emperor Charles VI, anxious to keep Habsburg lands unified, issued the Pragmatic Sanction in 1713, declaring that his only child, Maria Theresa, should succeed him. When he died in 1740, the electors of Bavaria and Saxony rejected the Pragmatic Sanction on the grounds that they had prior claims through their wives. Frederick II offered his support to Maria Theresa in exchange for the rich province of Silesia. Convinced of the justice of her cause, she indignantly refused. Frederick promptly invaded Silesia, precipitating the War of the Austrian Succession (1740–48). The Bavarians, Saxons, and French invaded Austria and Bohemia, while Great Britain, the Netherlands, and Russia came to the aid of Austria.

Alarmed by Frederick's military victories, Maria Theresa made peace with him in 1742, ceding him Silesia. Austria and its allies succeeded, however, in driving the French from Bohemia and conquering Bavaria to replace the lost Silesia. By the Treaty of Aix-la-Chapelle, Maria Theresa's husband, Francis, duke of Lorraine, was recognized as emperor, although it was she who actually ruled. In return, Maria Theresa gave up Bavaria and allowed Prussia to keep Silesia.

Seven Years' War. The emergence of Prussia as a major power led to a radical shift of alliances and to new hostilities. Maria Theresa, bent on reconquering Silesia, made an alliance with Elizabeth of Russia. George II of Britain, fearing possible French attack on Hannover, made a treaty of neutrality with Frederick. The old Habsburg-Valois rivalry was forgotten as the Austrian minister, Prince Kaunitz, maneuvered Louis XV, fearful of Prussia, into an alliance with Maria Theresa. Frederick, anticipating encirclement, struck first by invading Saxony and Bohemia, beginning the Seven Years' War (1756–63).

Violence spread as the Austrians invaded Silesia, the Russians marched into Prussia, and the French attacked Hannover. Despite good leadership, Frederick soon found himself hard pressed by many enemies. He was conveniently rescued by the death of Elizabeth of Russia and the succession of Peter III, who admired Frederick and at once made peace. The exhausted French also wanted peace. The Treaty of Hubertusburg restored the status quo, with Frederick keeping Silesia.

Bitterly disappointed, Maria Theresa devoted herself to internal affairs. She gradually reorganized the government and established uniform taxes, a customs union, and state-supported elementary schools. She encouraged nobles and commoners to take government and army posts. Wise, warmhearted, and tactful, she was loved by all her subjects. She did not always agree, however, with her idealistic son, Joseph. Joseph II was an enlightened monarch who impatiently tried to create an efficient, modern Germanic bureaucracy without regard for the strong prejudices within its empire.

Eastward expansion. Prussia was anxious to annex Polish territory separating Brandenburg and Prussia. Austria, still regretting Silesia, looked to the east for compensation. Both countries feared the new Russian presence. A weak Poland seemed ample excuse for intervention, and in 1772 Austria, Prussia, and Russia agreed to the first partition of Poland.

When the Bavarian throne became vacant, Joseph tried to annex Bavaria. Frederick objected and formed the League of Princes against the emperor. Blocked by Frederick in the short War of the Bavarian Succession (1778–79), Joseph turned east again. A Turkish war (1788–91) proved fruitless, and he was left out of the second partition of Poland (1793). Not to be overlooked, he insisted that Austria share in the third partition (1795), in which Poland entirely disappeared.

The Baroque Age and the Enlightenment. The end of religious strife and of the Turkish threat gave Germans new confidence. In the 18th century, German culture, nourished by French, English, and Italian developments, reached a brilliant flowering.

The princely courts. The princes, resisting imperial control and overriding local diets, made themselves absolute monarchs on the model of Louis XIV. They centralized their governments and established mercantile economies. Engaging the foremost artists, they made their capitals artistic and intellectual centers, resplendent with

Frederick the Great, *by J. Schroder. After defeat by Austria at Kolin (1757) in the Seven Years' War, Frederick ponders the fate of Prussia.*   Bettmann Archive

palaces, churches, museums, theaters, gardens, and universities.

Social and cultural life centered in the courts, which were the chief source of status. Courtiers scorned burghers and peasants as uncouth citizens, useful only to pay taxes to support court life. Princes maintained their courts also by accepting foreign subsidies and selling peasant boys as mercenary soldiers. To escape war and taxes, many Germans migrated to North America. **Art and music.** In the Catholic south, great numbers of churches and monasteries were built or rebuilt. They borrowed the dramatic baroque style that had developed out of the Italian and French Renaissance, transforming it into a graceful, playfully exuberant, rococo style that was uniquely German. Outstanding are the church at Vierzehnheiligen by Balthasar Neumann; the Karlskirche, Vienna, by J. B. Fischer von Erlach; and the churches of the brothers C. D. Asam (1686–1739) and E. Q. Asam (1692–1750). The baroque-rococo style was also used for palaces, such as Schönbrunn, outside Vienna, and the Zwinger in Dresden.

In the baroque period, instrumental music, mostly for chamber groups or keyboard, took the form of complex, highly structured polyphonic suites, preludes, and fugues by such masters as Heinrich Schütz and J. S. Bach. In the preclassical and classical periods, after 1720, orchestral music became more dominant and the compositions themselves longer and more abstract, with the development of sonata form and symphonic structure. Experimentation with orchestral forces and textures by C. P. E. Bach and others culminated in the great achievements of F. J. Haydn, W. A. Mozart, and Ludwig van Beethoven. Instrumental and vocal music were combined in the religious chorales and oratorios of J. S. Bach and G. F. Handel and in the Italian-inspired operas of Handel and G. P. Telemann. Opera truly came of age in the hands of C. W. Gluck and was carried to greater refinement by the versatile Mozart.

Literature and thought. In reaction against the religious concerns of the tumultuous 16th and early 17th centuries was the growth of rationalism and the scientific spirit, which produced the European Enlightenment. Absorbing the works of British and French thinkers, German professors discarded the theology of a world in which sinful men and women needed divine grace. They adopted the optimistic, secular philosophy of a world ordered by natural law in which all humans, innately rational and good, could, through education, aim at perfection.

The first major German philosopher, G. W. von Leibniz, posited a universe ruled by a natural,

preestablished harmony. The idealist philosopher Immanuel Kant analyzed the power of reason and asserted a rational basis for ethics. The playwright G. E. Lessing returned to the structure of classical drama and introduced to German theater the English principle of toleration and an interest in ordinary middle-class life.

Rationalism was soon opposed by a current stressing intuition and feeling. In religion it took the form of an evangelical revival, known as Pietism. Many middle- and lower-class Germans became followers of the Lutheran pastors P. J. Spener and A. H. Francke (1663–1727), who urged individual Bible study and personal experience of spiritual regeneration expressed in ethical conduct. The University of Halle (1694) became a center of Pietist education, charity, and training of missionaries. Pietism had a lasting influence on Lutheranism and on many German thinkers.

In literature the antirationalist tendency led to the late 18th-century Sturm und Drang (literally, storm and stress) movement. Writers in this revolutionary spirit viewed nature as a constantly changing force and valued humans for their individual passions rather than universal reason. Contributing to this spirit was the insistence of J. G. von Herder on the influence of history on literature, especially the importance of medieval folk songs and tales. Inspired by the French Revolution, antirationalism broadened into early romanticism, primarily concerned with the will and feelings of the unique, creative individual. The philosopher J. G. Fichte saw the universe as based on the moral will of God. August von Schlegel translated Shakespeare's plays, which emphasize history and individual character. Novalis wrote mystical Christian lyric poetry.

These contrasting and yet complementary streams came together in the work of three German literary masters: Friedrich von Schiller, who wrote classical dramas in historical settings, infused with moral conviction and the struggle for freedom; Friedrich Hölderlin, who wrote lyrical poems of profound spiritual anguish modeled on classical Greek forms; and Johann Wolfgang von Goethe, the sage of Weimar, a giant of European literature. Goethe's early autobiographical novel, *The Sorrows of Young Werther* (1774; trans. 1779), was in the romantic spirit. The more disciplined dramas *Egmont* (1788) and *Torquato Tasso* (1790), inspired by his Italian travels, were in the classical vein. He harmoniously combined both romantic and classical outlooks in the dramatic masterpiece *Faust* (1832).

AGE OF NATIONALISM

Enlightenment theories of representative government, combined with romantic stress on freedom and the distinctive history of a people, inspired Germans and other ethnic groups with a desire for national unification and liberal reform. The conquests of Napoleon subsequently aroused their sense of national identity.

Napoleonic Wars. For 18 years the German states variously engaged in five wars of defense against the well-trained, unified armies of revolutionary and Napoleonic France. In the first two wars the French took the left bank of the Rhine. In the third, Napoleon conquered Vienna and Berlin. In 1806 he reorganized the western German states, to compensate for their left-bank losses, into the Confederation of the Rhine. Austria and Prussia were excluded and lost much territory. In 1809 Austria led a fourth war against France, while Napoleon was occupied in Spain, but in the process it lost more land.

In 1812, Napoleon's disastrous retreat from Moscow, pursued by the Russians, encouraged the allies to make another effort. Frederick William III of Prussia, joined by Austria and Russia, led a War of Liberation, in which Napoleon was defeated at Leipzig (1813). After much bloodshed the allies took Paris in 1814.

At the Congress of Vienna (1814–15) the allies redrew the map of Europe. Austria, which gave up the Austrian Netherlands and its Swabian lands in the west, was compensated in the south and east by Salzburg, the Tirol, Lombardy and Venetia in Italy, and Illyria and Dalmatia on the Adriatic Sea. Prussia lost most of its Polish territory but gained much of Saxony and Swedish Pomerania as well as land in the Rhineland and Westphalia, including the undeveloped iron and coal resources of the Ruhr and Saar.

The German Confederation. The Congress of Vienna replaced the Holy Roman Empire of more than 240 states with the German Confederation of 39 states represented by a powerless diet. Opinions differed on what the character of the new confederation should be. Many Germans wanted to fashion a liberal government on British and French models according to a constitution guaranteeing popular representation, trial by jury, and free speech. They also hoped for national unification. Such ideas were especially popular among journalists, lawyers, and professors and with impatient university students, who formed secret societies for rapid action. These aims also appealed to the various restive peoples within the Austrian Empire.

Liberalism and nationalism were bitterly opposed by the rulers of Prussia and Austria and by the recently crowned kings of Bavaria, Hannover, Württemberg, and Saxony, who dreaded any encroachment on their individual sovereignty. Accordingly, Austria, Prussia, Russia, and Britain formed the Quadruple Alliance to suppress—by

Congress of Vienna *(1815), engraving after a painting by J. B. Isabey. After the Napoleonic Wars, the congress created the German Confederation.*   Bettmann Archive

force if necessary—any threat to the Vienna settlement. The German rulers supported the repressive system instituted by the Austrian foreign minister Prince Klemens von Metternich. Frederick William III blocked reforms planned by his ministers. Prussia outmaneuvered Austria by instituting a customs union of most German states except Austria.

The July Revolution in Paris in 1830 set off liberal risings in many German states. Metternich had the confederation forbid public meetings and ban petitions. Nevertheless, in 1848 another wave of revolutions, beginning in Paris, washed over Europe. Nationalist groups revolted in Hungary, Bohemia, Moravia, Galicia, and Lombardy. Metternich resigned and Emperor Ferdinand I abdicated in favor of his young grandson Francis Joseph. Uprisings also took place in Bavaria, Prussia, and southwest Germany. The frightened rulers agreed to send delegates to an assembly in Frankfurt.

The rebellions were soon crushed, however. In Austria a liberal constitutional assembly was dissolved, and a constitution providing highly centralized, although representative, government was imposed. Hungary, which had declared itself a republic, was forcibly subdued. In Prussia Frederick William IV imposed an authoritarian constitution.

Meanwhile, the Frankfurt Assembly wrote a liberal constitution for a united Germany under a hereditary emperor. Austria refused to allow its German lands to be included, so the assembly regretfully decided that "Germany" should consist of the German states without Austria. For lack of an alternative, they offered the crown to Frederick William, who loftily refused it. The assembly dispersed in failure; unity was to be achieved with Prussian military might.

The German Empire. After the failure of the Frankfurt Assembly, both Prussia and Austria put forth conflicting plans for union. On the brink, Prussia backed down, but only temporarily. William I was determined that neither Austria nor a newly aggressive France should thwart Prussian ambitions. He and his chief minister, Otto von Bismarck, decided that Prussia must become unassailable. Bismarck, a Prussian Junker (aristocrat) of forceful intellect, overbearing manner, and deep loyalty to the Crown, used unification as a means to that end.

Unification. Bismarck planned a realpolitik (politics of reality) that astutely combined diplomacy with "blood-and-iron" militarism in order to eliminate Austrian influence and bring about unification on Prussian terms. As a preliminary he bought the neutrality of Russia, Italy, and France with friendly treaties. His first step was to invite Austria in 1864 to join an invasion of Schleswig-Holstein. These two duchies were ruled by Den-

THE UNIFICATION OF GERMANY 1815-1871

© Copyright HAMMOND INC., Maplewood, N.J.

SCALE OF MILES
0   50   100   150   200

----- Southern boundary of the North German Confederation, 1867
▬▬▬ Boundary of the German Empire, 1871
▓ Prussia in 1815
▓ Prussian annexations to 1871

Longitude 10° East of Greenwich

mark. The Austrians and Prussians quickly defeated the Danes but soon fell out over control of the conquered duchies.

On that excuse Bismarck took a second step by launching the Seven Weeks' War against Austria. Skillfully coordinating three armies, Gen. Helmuth von Moltke made short work of the Austrians at Königgrätz in 1866. Bismarck, however, did not want to alienate Austria irrevocably; he made an easy peace. Austria gave up Venetia to Italian nationalists. Prussia annexed Schleswig-Holstein, Hannover, and other states and organized the North German Confederation (1867) without Austria.

To overcome south German fears of an enlarged Prussia, Bismarck took a third step, the Franco-Prussian War. In 1870 the aggressive French emperor Napoleon III unwisely pressed William I to promise that a Hohenzollern would never take the vacant Spanish throne. Bismarck distorted William's account of the incident to make it seem as if the French had been insulted and then published the account. The outraged French declared war. Stirred by national loyalty, the south German states joined forces behind Prussia, whose seasoned armies conquered the disorganized French at Sedan and, after a long siege, took Paris in 1871. With these events Bismarck convinced the south German states that Prussian hegemony was inevitable. At Versailles in 1871 he persuaded a reluctant William to take a new title as head of the German Empire, the Second Reich.

The age of Bismarck. Having sufficiently aggrandized Prussia, the Iron Chancellor, as Bismarck was called, worked for peace. He constructed a series of alliances designed to protect Germany from aggression. At the Congress of Berlin (1878) Bismarck mediated a settlement in the Balkans, where various Slavic groups kept rising against the decaying Ottoman Empire. To distract German nationalists from expanding into that explosive area, he consented to Germany's acquiring colonies in Africa and the Pacific. Germany found its colonies valuable chiefly for prestige, however.

At home, Bismarck encouraged the Industrial Revolution, which developed rapidly after 1850 as Germans applied advanced industrial technology to the iron and coal resources of the Ruhr and Saar. The population rose by a third, and factories boomed, transforming rural farmers into urban producers of steel for machinery, railways, and ships. This enlarged city population demanded a share in the government.

The empire, however, did not function democratically. The 25 nominally sovereign states (plus

Prince Otto von Bismarck created the German Empire in 1871 and served as its chancellor until 1890 (from a painting by R. C. Woodville). Bettmann Archive

Alsace-Lorraine) of the North German Confederation were ruled by a Bundesrat of princes dominated by Prussia and a powerless Reichstag of elected deputies, while the chancellor was responsible only to the emperor. Bismarck's scorn for the ordinary citizen and his distrust of the Roman Catholic Center party and the workers' Social Democratic party further discouraged parliamentary government.

Mindful of old papal-imperial rivalry, Bismarck believed that the Catholic church, which had declared the infallibility of the pope in 1870, threatened the supremacy of the German state. He therefore initiated the Kulturkampf ("culture struggle") during which he exiled or suppressed many religious orders and dismissed or imprisoned disobedient priests. Church-state strife cooled in 1879, chiefly because Bismarck needed the Center party's support against the Liberals to obtain high tariffs that would protect German agriculture and industry from cheap imports.

Bismarck next turned his wrath on the Socialist party, forerunner of the Social Democratic party. Blaming on them two attempts by non-Socialists to assassinate William, he had a new Reichstag elected, which supported tariffs and outlawed the Socialists. To forestall workers' demands and to ensure healthy army recruits, he provided state insurance for sickness, accidents, and old age. When the outlawed Socialists won many seats in the election of 1890, Bismarck prepared to abolish the constitution. Suddenly, however, he was dismissed by the new emperor, William II, who wanted to rule in his own right.

19th-Century Art and Thought. With little scope for political action, many middle-class Germans turned to cultural pursuits, through which they influenced the Western world.

The arts. German painting, reacting from the neoclassicism of Anton Raphael Mengs (1728–79), became romantic, as exemplified by the vast, allegorical landscapes of C. D. Friedrich and P. O. Runge (1777–1810). Later painting was realistic. Architecture was romantic Gothic or imposing neoclassical.

Music also became romantic. Much of it was inspired by literature, for example, the art songs, or lieder, of F. P. Schubert, Johannes Brahms, and Hugo Wolf and the operas of Richard Wagner. Instrumental music with literary or pictorial allusions, called program music, took the form of symphonic poems by Franz Liszt. Pure music, in contrast to program music, by such masters as Brahms, Robert Schumann, and Felix Mendelssohn continued classical forms. Late romantic music tended toward the dramatic and thickly textured, as in the complex symphonies of Gustav Mahler and the emotionally intense tone poems of Richard Strauss.

Romantic literature, inspired by the lyrics of Goethe, Schiller, and Heinrich Heine, included the work of such poets and storytellers as Ludwig Tieck, Clemens Brentano, Joseph von Eichendorff, E. T. A. Hoffmann, and J. L. Uhland. These romantics often used German folk materials such as the songs and tales collected by Jacob and Wilhelm Grimm. The conflict between the individual and society, first treated by Goethe, was expressed in the novels of Adalbert Stifter (1805–68) and Gottfried Keller, a Swiss, and in the dramas of Franz Grillparzer and Friedrich Hebbel. Their interest in psychology was part of the more realistic approach to the world that gradually superseded romanticism. Realistic criticism of society was evident in the ironic lyrics of Heine and took the extreme form of social determinism in the naturalist poems of Arno Holz (1863–1929) and the plays of Hermann Sudermann and Gerhart Hauptmann.

Education and thought. The French capture of Berlin in 1806 shocked the Prussians into an effort to recover in cultural dignity what they had lost in political fact. Under Wilhelm von Humboldt, the educational system was reorganized to stress the individuality of the student and the moral duty of the state to educate its citizens. Elementary schools emphasized experience instead of memorization. *Gymnasien* combined classical, Christian, and patriotic values to prepare middle-class as well as aristocratic students for the university. The University of Berlin became an outstanding center of humanistic, historical, and, especially, scientific studies.

German nationalism found justification in the work of the foremost thinkers of the day, J. G. Fichte and Friedrich Schleiermacher. The romantic Friedrich von Schelling presented all history as developing toward an absolute harmony of mind and matter. He influenced the absolute idealist G. W. F. Hegel, who synthesized nature and mind in the progress of the Absolute World Spirit to its embodiment in the Prussian state.

Opposing nationalism, the revolutionary philosophy of Karl Marx cast the Hegelian dialectic in materialistic terms, declaring that all ideas arise from economic systems. Marx urged workers throughout the world to unite in violently overthrowing existing governments and creating a new classless society.

Much more pessimistic was the view of Arthur Schopenhauer, who saw the world as a scene of painful, unavoidable conflict among individual wills. Drawing on Schopenhauer, Freidrich Nietzsche valued the creative "will to power" of the heroic individual, which sets him apart from the inferior masses. Extreme nationalists, mixing the Nietzschean superman with a romantic glorification of the German people, developed a hazy but heady concept of German racial superiority that contributed to two world wars.

WORLD WAR AND DEFEAT

The nationalism that created Germany in the 19th century led it into two disastrous wars and consequent division in the 20th century.

World War I. No European power wanted World War I, but they all feared Germany—newly unified, outstripping them in population and industry, and aggressively self-assertive—as a dangerous rival. Specifically, France wanted to recover Alsace-Lorraine; Britain, a seafaring country, felt threatened by German colonial expansion and William II's insistence on a large navy; Austria and Russia feared pressure within their tottering empires. Germany itself had nightmares of a war on two fronts. All these powers sought protection in huge, peacetime, standing armies and in an intricate system of international alliances.

Bismarck's delicate balance of powers proved too difficult for William II to maintain. Refusing (1887) to renew the Reinsurance Treaty with Russia, he continued the Triple Alliance (1882) of Germany, Austria, and Italy. Rebuffed, Russia made (1894) an alliance with France. Britain, long neutral, settled its colonial differences with

William II, emperor of Germany, helped maneuver his country into World War I. Bettmann Archive

France in the Entente Cordiale (1904) and its Middle East dispute with Russia in 1907, resulting in the Triple Entente. Thus, Europe was divided into two armed camps.

Steps toward war. Crises in Morocco and the Balkans intensified antagonisms. William twice interfered in Morocco (1905, 1911), which France claimed, to protect German interests in Africa. Austria's annexation (1908) of the Turkish provinces of Bosnia and Hercegovina spoiled Serbia's hopes of gaining them. The assassination, with Serbian knowledge, of the liberal Austrian archduke Francis Ferdinand in Sarajevo in June 1914 proved to be the spark that set off the war. Germany rashly assured Austria of full support, resulting in an Austrian ultimatum that Serbia could not accept. Because military advantage depended on rapid mobilization, the powers then moved with headlong speed. Austria declared war on Serbia. Russia, to defend Serbia, mobilized against Austria and Germany. Germany gave Russia 12 hours to demobilize, called up its own troops, and, receiving no answer, declared war on Russia. Assuming that France would aid Russia, Germany also declared war on France.

The Germans hoped that a quick conquest of France would secure the western front and release forces for the east. Avoiding the fortified French frontier, German armies swept through neutral Belgium, hoping to take Paris by surprise. This violation of international law brought Britain to the aid of France and destroyed all sympathy for the Central Powers.

Course of war. German forces nearly reached Paris. The British and French miraculously turned back the overstretched German lines at the Battle of the Marne, however, and the two sides dug trenches for a ferocious war of attrition that would last for four years. Meanwhile, the Russians attacked on the east, plunging Germany into the dreaded two-front war.

The Germans several times defeated the ill-equipped Russians, but they could make no headway in the west. The Allies blockaded Germany to cut off food and raw materials. Desperate to break the blockade, the Germans declared unrestricted submarine warfare. After several U.S. ships were sunk, the U.S. entered the war in 1917. The next year Russia, in the throes of two revolutions, sued for peace, which was concluded at Brest-Litovsk in 1918. Thus freed in the east, in 1918 the Germans launched a final, all-out offensive in the west, but the united Allies slowly turned the tide.

Recognizing the situation as hopeless, the German high command urged William to let a new civil goverment sue for peace. Moreover, U.S. President Woodrow Wilson insisted on dealing with civilians. William grudgingly appointed Prince Max of Baden (1867–1929) chancellor, and while he negotiated with Wilson, fighting continued, sailors mutinied, socialists struck, workers and the military formed Communist councils, and revolution broke out in Bavaria. Prince Max announced the abdication of William II and resigned. A leader of the Social Democrats proclaimed Germany a republic.

Versailles treaty. Having surrendered and changed its government, Germany expected a negotiated peace rather than the harsh terms imposed by the Treaty of Versailles in 1919. But the Allies were determined to receive reparation for their losses and to see that their enemy was never again in a position to endanger them. Accordingly, Germany lost Alsace-Lorraine to France and West Prussia to Poland, creating a Polish Corridor between Germany and East Prussia. It also lost its colonies and had to give up most of its coal, trains, and merchant ships, as well as its navy. Germany had to limit its army and submit to Allied occupation of the Rhineland for 15 years. Worst of all, the Germans had to accept full responsibility for causing the war and, consequently, pay its total cost. These last provisions particularly rankled; Germans did not consider themselves more guilty than anyone else and could not possibly pay all that was demanded.

The Versailles treaty, understandable from the Allies' immediate point of view, did not ensure lasting peace. Germany was neither crushed completely nor encouraged to return to the European community. Instead, by accepting the treaty, Germany gained a bad name among its citizens, crippling its chances of success.

The Weimar Republic. In Weimar in 1919, a national assembly, dominated by Social Democrats, wrote a democratic constitution for the new German Reich. But the prospects of the Weimar Republic, as it was familiarly known, were dim. For most Germans it bore the stigma of military defeat and the Versailles treaty, which they regarded as only temporary. In addition, as parliamentary government, it was opposed on principle by both conservative militarists and revolutionary socialists. Both sides, using private armies, frequently tried to overthrow the government, as in the military Kapp *Putsch* (1920) and the uprising of the Communist Spartacists (1919) under Karl Liebknecht and Rosa Luxemburg.

The economic situation made matters worse. Because Germany could not meet reparations re-

In the inflationary year 1925, Germans found it cheaper to start fires with millions of almost worthless paper marks than to buy kindling wood. UPI

quirements, France invaded the Ruhr in 1923 to take over the coal mines. The government encouraged the workers to resist passively, printing vast amounts of money to pay them. The resulting inflation wiped out savings, pensions, insurance, and other forms of fixed income, creating a social revolution that destroyed the most stable elements in Germany.

Aided by the Dawes Plan (1924), which set reasonable annual amounts of reparations and provided for foreign loans, the brilliant minister Gustav Stresemann reorganized the monetary system and encouraged industry. For five years Germany enjoyed relative peace and prosperity; in 1926 it joined the League of Nations. The worldwide depression of 1929, however, plunged the country once more into disaster. Millions of unemployed, disillusioned by capitalist democracy, turned to communism or to the National Socialist (Nazi) German Workers' party led by Adolf Hitler.

Hitler and the Third Reich. A former army corporal, Hitler hated aristocrats, capitalists, Communists, liberals, Jews, and other so-called non-Aryans. He had already tried to topple the government in the beer hall *Putsch* in Munich in 1923. After six months in prison, he continued to build up the Nazi party. A gifted public speaker, he rapidly won supporters by denouncing the Weimar government as weak and treacherous. He proposed giving the jobs of Jews, whom he painted as villainous, to deserving Germans, and he promised to recover Germany's strength and honor. In return, he demanded complete loyalty and obedience of people to himself as their *Führer* ("leader"). To reinforce his message, brown-shirted storm troopers attacked Communists, Jews, and other party targets.

In the depths of the depression of 1932, the Nazis were the largest party in the Reichstag. In 1933 the National party, made up chiefly of aristocrats and industrialists, had Hitler appointed chancellor in the hope that they could use him to control the Communists. To secure supreme power for himself, Hitler called new elections. Blaming a fire in the Reichstag house, set by the Nazis, on the Communists, he banned the Communist party. In the new Reichstag the Nazis, Nationals, and Catholic Center passed the revolutionary Enabling Act allowing the government to dictate all aspects of German life.

Armed with this power, Hitler set out to make the Third Reich, as he called the new totalitarian Germany. The groundwork had been laid in World War I, when the military ran the government. From that foundation, Hitler proceeded with frightening efficiency. Consolidating legisla-

Public appearances by Hitler and displays of soldiers and the swastika, symbol of the Nazis, encouraged German patriotism in World War II. Bettmann Archive

tive, executive, judicial, and military authority in himself, he remained chancellor, became head of state after the death of Paul von Hindenburg, headed a new court system, and commanded the armed forces.

All political parties except the Nazis were banned. People with one or more Jewish grandparents were deprived of citizenship, barred from civil service and professions, and heavily fined. Churches had to cooperate with the government. Strikes were forbidden, and the unemployed were enrolled in labor camps or the army as Germany strove to be economically self-sufficient. An elite, professional army, enlarged by conscription, was established to carry out Hitler's plan for conquest. Publishing and teaching became means of propaganda. Children were also indoctrinated through the Hitler Youth movement. Gigantic rallies with blown-up posters, marching ranks, and frenzied speeches whipped up enthusiasm. Backing up the propaganda were the Gestapo (secret police), the SS (elite guard), and an elaborate system of concentration camps.

Some Germans did not take Hitler seriously, but others accepted his emphasis on race and violence. Outspoken dissenters left the country or took the consequences.

World War II. Many of Europe's problems were left unresolved by World War I. Germany's willingness to seek a solution by force, while other countries wanted to avoid violence at all costs, led to World War II.

Steps toward war. Hitler planned to threaten and bluff the European powers into allowing him gradually to revise Germany's boundaries. His goal, to unite all Germans and give them "living space" (*Lebensraum*), did not seem unreasonable to some statesmen, who realized that the Versailles treaty had been unjust. At the time, no single demand of Hitler's seemed worth risking war to protest. Germany left the League of Nations in 1933 and, virtually unopposed, began (1935) to rearm; it then reoccupied (1936) the Rhineland. Germany signed an anti-Communist pact with Japan and made an alliance with Fascist Italy, creating the Rome-Berlin Axis. In 1938 it declared an Anschluss (union) with Austria. At Munich that year, Britain, France, and Italy timorously acceded to Hitler's demand for the German-populated Sudetenland of Czechoslovakia, on his promise that Germany would then be satisfied.

In March 1939, breaking his word, Hitler occupied the remainder of Czechoslovakia. In August, dramatically reversing his anti-Communist policy, he made a nonaggression pact with the Soviet Union containing a secret clause on the partition of Poland. His repeated demands for Danzig in the Polish Corridor led to a Polish-British pact and Polish mobilization. On September 1, Germany invaded Poland. Britain and France promptly declared war on Germany. World War II had begun.

Course of war. In a few weeks of blitzkrieg (literally, lightning war), mechanized German divisions overwhelmed the ill-equipped Poles, taking western Poland. The Soviets, not to be outdone, seized the eastern part. Encouraged by success, in 1940 Germany swallowed Denmark, Norway, and the Low Countries and invaded France, which rapidly collapsed. British and French forces were hastily evacuated from Dunkirk to England. Hitler then blockaded Britain with submarines and bombed the country with his new air force. He made a ten-year military pact with the other Axis powers—Italy and Japan. In 1941, to aid faltering Italian forces, he sent troops to North Africa, Greece, and Yugoslavia. To block Soviet ambitions in agricultural eastern Europe, which industrial Germany needed, he suddenly invaded the Soviet Union. As the Soviets retreated eastward, German armies engulfed the rich Ukraine.

At this point, Hitler was master of continental Europe. In 1942, however, Britain was still resisting, and the U.S., which had entered the war after an attack by Japan, was sending supplies to Britain and the Soviet Union. Hitler then ordered total mobilization of men and resources. Throughout Europe, conquered peoples, especially Slavs and Jews, were executed or enslaved in German war factories, while their countries were drained of food and raw materials.

In 1943 the tide began to turn. Supply lines in the Soviet Union were overextended, and the Germans were gradually driven west. Axis forces in North Africa were defeated, and Italy was invaded. Germany itself, from 1942 on, was being systematically bombed. Although defeat was inevitable, a deranged Hitler refused to surrender. The war dragged on as British and U.S. forces invaded Normandy in 1944 and swept inexorably east while the Soviets marched west. Hitler committed suicide just before Soviet tanks rolled into Berlin in April 1945.

Occupation. Germany's unconditional surrender ended the Third Reich. The Allies reduced Germany to its prewar western boundaries and assigned a large portion on the east to Poland. Setting up four occupation zones, they tried war criminals and dismantled factories. But as their policies diverged, Germany was split into two parts. Britain, the U.S., and, eventually, France wanted to rebuild Germany into a major Western European power capable of countering the expansionist tendencies of the Soviet Union. In 1948 they merged their zones into one region, supplied with U.S. aid, and encouraged the Germans to form a democratic government. The Soviet Union, on the other hand, imposed a Communist German government, under Soviet domination, on East Germany. In 1949 this practical polarization of Germany was legalized by the creation of two German states.

20th-Century Art and Thought. The era of relative peace and prosperity that preceded World War I gave rise to artistic and intellectual reaction against traditional forms and conceptions. The avant-garde increasingly separated itself from the general public as it experimented with new ideas and techniques. Continuing to flourish in the Weimar period, it was suppressed by the Nazis. Many artists and thinkers emigrated to avoid a state-imposed return to sterotyped tradition. After World War II, German culture slowly recovered.

Art and music. About 1900, German and Austrian architects and designers employed the graceful floral curves of Jugendstil (Art Nouveau), especially in the Vienna *Sezession* movement. Closely

Dresden lost many cultural landmarks as well as factories in heavy bombing attacks by British and U.S. forces during World War II. UPI

GERMANY
1871–1918

GERMANY
after World War I

GERMANY
after World War II

Copyright by HAMMOND INC., Maplewood, N.J.

allied was a new interest in materials and structure, seen in the work of Peter Behrens, J. M. Olbrich (1867–1908), and Walter Gropius. Adaptation of aesthetics to the machine age inspired buildings in the starkly functional International Style developed at the Bauhaus school of design founded by Gropius in Weimar in 1919. Its principles spread through Europe and the New World.

German expressionist paintings emphasized the artists' feelings instead of objectively describing the outside world. Such painters as E. L. Kirchner, Emil Nolde, Franz Marc, Wassily Kandinsky (a Russian), and Paul Klee (a Swiss) used strident colors and distorted forms. In the 1920s

Otto Dix and Max Beckmann painted bitter social commentaries. Surrealist interests influenced Klee and Max Ernst. Kandinsky created the first nonrepresentational works.

In music, Richard Strauss and Carl Orff wrote innovative program works. At the same time Arnold Schoenberg and his pupils Anton von Webern and Alban Berg devised a revolutionary twelve-tone music that abandoned traditional melodies and harmonies for emphasis on rhythm and dissonance. The level of music education and performance remained high.

Literature and thought. Writers such as Franz Werfel, the poets Stefan George, Hugo von Hofmannsthal, and Rainer Maria Rilke, and the psychological novelists Thomas Mann, Hermann Hesse, and Franz Kafka turned from realistic description of the world to an expressionistic exploration of the mind and spirit. Often they used myth, symbol, and exaggerated language to convey inner truths, frustrations, ironies, ambiguities, and subconscious forces. Social criticism was the primary purpose of the playwrights Arthur Schnitzler, Frank Wedekind, and Carl Sternheim (1878–1942). Bertolt Brecht's narrative epic theater in Berlin in the 1920s attacked capitalist society. Expressionism influenced German film directors such as Robert Wiene (1881–1938), G. W. Pabst (1885–1967), and Fritz Lang, who produced work of great originality. After World War II such novelists as Uwe Johnson, Heinrich Böll, and Günter Grass continued to analyze German society.

A great influence on expressionism in the arts was the new science of psychoanalysis developed about 1900 by Sigmund Freud. Psychoanalysis seemed to undermine confidence in the progress of a rational human race in an orderly universe by focusing on the uncharted, amoral depths of the subconscious. Belief in rational, liberal Christianity was specifically attacked by the Swiss neoorthodox theologians Karl Barth and Emil Brunner. Existentialism, as developed by the philosophers Martin Heidegger and Karl Jaspers and the theologian Paul Tillich, sought to integrate religion, art, and science.

For further information on this topic, see the Bibliography in volume 28, sections 652–53, 657–61, 724, 842, 901, 906, 933–42.

GERMANY, EAST, officially German Democratic Republic (GDR; Ger. *Deutsche Demokratische Republik*), former republic of central Europe, bordered on the N by the Baltic Sea, on the E by Poland, on the S by Czechoslovakia and West Germany, and on the W by West Germany. The GDR had an area of 108,178 sq km (41,768 sq mi). East Germany was established on Oct. 7, 1949, as one of two successor states—West

Germany being the other—to the nation of Germany, defeated and occupied by the Allies in World War II. The GDR ceased to exist when it merged with West Germany on Oct. 3, 1990.

THE LAND

The area that was East Germany consists of two major geographical regions, a lowland plain covering the N two-thirds of the country and an area of uplands in the S. The lowlands, a part of the North German Plain, can be divided into three parts. In the N is an area, gently sloping toward the Baltic Sea, that was largely molded by glacial action. It is characterized by heavy clay soil, ridges of moraine, and numerous hollows (many now filled by lakes). The large island of Rügen lies off the coast, in the Baltic. The middle part of the lowlands, around Berlin, is a generally infertile area, covered largely by heath and pine forests. The S lowlands are covered with rich soil. The region of uplands is composed of mountain ranges that contain several large basins and valleys. The principal ranges are the Harz Mts. and the Thüringer Wald, in the SW, and the Erzgebirge, or Ore Mts., in the S. The Erzgebirge include the loftiest point of eastern Germany, the Fichtelberg (1213 m/3980 ft high).

Eastern Germany has few large rivers. The most important river is the Elbe, which winds through the region from the border with Czechoslovakia, in the SE, to the former boundary with West Germany, in the NW, and then continues to the North Sea. Tributaries of the Elbe in eastern Germany include the Saale, Mulde, and Havel rivers; the last named widens into several lakes near Berlin. The Oder, along with the smaller Neisse R., forms most of eastern Germany's border with Poland. The largest lake is the Müritzsee (117 sq km/45 sq mi), located in the N.

Climate. Eastern Germany has a temperate climate, with generally cooler temperatures prevailing in the uplands of the S. The mean annual temperature for the country is 8.5° C (47.3° F). The average temperature in January is −1° C (30° F), and the mean temperature in July is 18° C (64° F). Yearly precipitation averages 584 mm (23 in). The lowlands receive less moisture than the uplands, the W slopes of which get up to 1524 mm (60 in) of precipitation yearly.

Natural Resources. Eastern Germany has few large-scale deposits of economically important natural resources. The most abundant is lignite, found chiefly near Leipzig and Cottbus. It is used for heating and in industry, and various products, including gasoline, are made from it. Rock salt

Bautzen, in east central Germany, is a city of about 50,000, and is the site of the May 1813 defeat of Prussian and Russian armies by Napoleon's French forces. At the end of the block is St. Peter's Church (13th–14th cent.). © 1990, Ulrike Welsch

The Elbe, one of Europe's important commercial waterways. This view is from a promontory in Saxon Switzerland, a mountainous region of eastern Germany near Dresden; the Czech border is nearby.   Wolfgang Krammisch–Bruce Coleman, Inc.

and potash are also found in sizable quantities. Eastern Germany has relatively small amounts of natural gas, crude petroleum, and silver and of copper, iron, lead, nickel, tin, and zinc ores. Deposits of kaolin have long been used by the celebrated porcelain industry of Meissen.

Plants and Animals. A little more than one-quarter of eastern Germany is forested. Most of the woodland is in the uplands of the S, but forests are also located near Berlin and in the lake districts of the N. Coniferous trees, especially spruce and other pines, predominate, but numerous deciduous species, such as beech, birch, and oak, also flourish. The region has many species of flowering plants.

Eastern Germany has a small variety of indigenous wildlife. Many deer live in the forests, which also shelter some bears, wild boars, wolves, foxes, and wildcats. Few reptiles are found. Sprat and other herring, flounder, and cod inhabit the coastal waters of the Baltic Sea; carp and trout are found in freshwater streams.

Soils. The soil of the N lowlands of eastern Germany contains much clay, and, with fertilizer, it can produce ample crops. The central lowlands consist mainly of sandy soil not suited to agriculture. Much of the S lowlands is made up of fertile loess. Scattered valleys and basins in the uplands of the S have productive farmland.

Electric Power. More than 88% of the electricity produced in eastern Germany is generated by thermal plants using lignite and imported coal. About 10% of the region's electricity is produced by nuclear-power facilities and less than 2% by hydroelectric installations. In the late 1980s about 114 billion kwh of electricity were generated yearly.

POPULATION

The population of eastern Germany consists principally of two groupings of the Caucasoid race. People of the predominant type, known as the Alpine, are concentrated in the central and S parts of eastern Germany, and persons of the Teutonic grouping live mainly in the N.

Population Characteristics. According to the 1981 official census, the GDR had 16,732,500 inhabitants, including East Berlin. The UN estimated the population at 16,644,000 in 1985; the average population density was about 154 persons per sq km (about 398 per sq mi). Eastern Germany is highly urbanized, with three-quarters of the people living in communities of 2000 or more.

Political Divisions. The GDR was divided into 15 districts (*Bezirke*): Cottbus, Dresden, East Berlin, Erfurt, Frankfurt, Gera, Halle, Karl-Marx-Stadt, Leipzig, Magdeburg, Neubrandenburg, Potsdam, Rostock, Schwerin, and Suhl. After the merger

357

with the Federal Republic of Germany, the eastern region was organized as five states: Mecklenburg-Pomerania, Brandenburg, Saxony-Anhalt, Thuringia, and Saxony.

Principal Cities. The GDR claimed East Berlin (pop., 1987 est., 1,246,900) as its capital. This claim, however, was not recognized by the three Western occupying powers, which maintained that East Berlin had a special status apart from East Germany. Large cities in the GDR included Leipzig (549,200), a manufacturing and commercial center; Dresden (519,500), an industrial city; Karl-Marx-Stadt (313,300), a manufacturing center known for its textiles; Magdeburg (289,600), an inland port with a large iron and steel industry; Rostock (250,700), a major seaport near the Baltic; Halle (235,700), a railroad hub and manufacturing center; and Erfurt (218,000), an industrial and transportation center.

Religion. Nearly half the people of East Germany were estimated to belong to a Protestant church affiliated with the Federation of Evangelical Churches in the GDR. A few small independent Protestant churches also existed, and about 7% of the population was Roman Catholic. The Jewish community numbered less than 1000.

Language. German, the official language of the GDR, is spoken by virtually all the inhabitants of eastern Germany. Sorbs, a significant linguistic minority of about 100,000, live in the Lusatia region (which includes the cities of Cottbus and Bautzen) and speak a Slavic language.

Education. Schooling in the GDR was compulsory for children between the ages of 6 and 16. Education was free, and many students were given study grants. Virtually all adults in eastern Germany are literate.

After World War II the basic educational system in the GDR was reorganized by the Soviet occupation authorities. The traditional structure, consisting of separate primary, intermediate, and specialized secondary schools, was abandoned. In its place general schools with integrated curricula were established. Attendance for ten years at such comprehensive schools (*Polytechnische Oberschule,* or polytechnical high schools) was required. Each comprehensive school was divided into a lower school (grades one to three), a middle school (grades four to six), and an upper school (grades seven to ten). The program in the upper school included training in industry and agriculture. A small number of comprehensive schools offered gifted children intensive instruction in the arts, mathematics, natural sciences, sports, or other specialized areas. On completion of the basic 10-year course, a number of possibilities for advanced education were available.

Students wishing to attend a university continued their studies for two years at an extended polytechnical high school, there preparing for the examinations for the *Abitur* (diploma), necessary for university entrance. Industrial and commercial skills were taught in *Berufsschulen,* vocational schools that provided 2- and 3-year programs and included apprenticeships. A *Berufsschule* graduate wanting to go on to more specialized training, such as that required to become an engineer, administrator, or other professional, attended a *Fachschule,* or technical school. A *Berufsschule* graduate who wished to enter a university could prepare for the *Abitur* during a 3-year course at a workers' and peasants' faculty.

In the late 1980s some 2,047,300 East German students were enrolled at the primary and secondary levels. Vocational and technical schools had a combined enrollment of about 366,300 students.

In the late 1980s the GDR had 53 centers of higher learning. These included seven universities, at East Berlin, Dresden, Greifswald, Halle, Jena, Leipzig, and Rostock. More than 132,000 persons were enrolled annually in institutions of higher education in the late 1980s.

CULTURAL LIFE

Cultural life in East Germany, as in West Germany, had a long tradition of multiple centers and of state support. Unlike the West, government aid in a controlled socialist society was accompanied by a high degree of political influence on artistic and intellectual life. The state encouraged the entire population to participate actively in the cultural life of the nation. It subsidized about 600 museums, 44 important libraries, more than 100 theaters, and about 80 major orchestras. The "work, live, and learn in a socialist way" movement promoted collective cultural experiences in factories and offices. The state and trade unions ran local cultural centers. The state fostered thousands of amateur clubs for music, dance, theater, fine arts, and film.

Museums and Libraries. The museum and library collections and the historic buildings of East Germany, like those of West Germany, suffered heavily during World War II. The Nazis, moreover, destroyed or sold works they disapproved of. Many art treasures removed to the West for safety were not returned, nor were many works seized by Soviet occupation forces. The GDR made an effort to replenish collections. It rebuilt the great cathedrals of Magdeburg, Erfurt, Freiberg, and Naumburg, as well as many castles and town halls, most of which became museums. Efforts were made to combine urban renewal with preservation of historic structures in such towns as Stralsund, Rostock, Leipzig, and Neubrandenburg.

A leading art museum in eastern Germany is the State Art Collection in Dresden, formerly owned by the rulers of Saxony. It includes a world-famous gallery of old masters and fine collection of porcelain, both in the Zwinger, and decorative arts in the Green Vault. The Ancient, Far Eastern, and Islamic collections of the kings of Prussia are part of the State Museums of what was formerly East Berlin. Schwerin and Lindenau also have noteworthy art collections. Outstanding science museums include the Technical Museum in Dresden and the Natural History Museum of Humboldt University in Berlin. In that city the GDR established the postwar Museum of German History. Other historical museums are the Sans Souci Palace in Potsdam and the Wartburg Castle near Eisenach.

The largest libraries in the GDR were the German State Library (part of the former Prussian State Library; 6.8 million volumes), in Berlin, which was especially strong in science, and the German Library in Leipzig (8.3 million volumes). High school, university, local public, and trade union libraries were also maintained.

Theater and Music. All theaters in the GDR were owned by the state. The largest concentration were in East Berlin, which had the German State Opera, the Comic Opera, the Folk Theater, the German Theater, and the Berliner Ensemble (founded by the German dramatist Bertolt Brecht). Important opera houses included those in Leipzig and Dresden, and also of note were the Folk Theater in Rostock and numerous open-air and children's theaters. East Germany's foremost orchestras included the Staatskapelle of Berlin (18th cent.) and the Staatskapelle of Dresden (16th cent.), both attached to those cities' operas, as well as the Dresden Philharmonic, the Leipzig Gewandhaus Orchestra, and the postwar Berlin Symphony. The GDR had many chamber groups. Among famous choral societies were the Thomaner Choir in Leipzig and the Dresden Kreuzchor (both 13th cent.). Leipzig played host to a Bach festival and the Documentary Film Week, Halle to a Handel festival, and Berlin to a festival of music and drama. A workers' festival of performing and fine arts was held in a different city every two years.

ECONOMY

Before World War II the economy of the region was primarily agricultural, although important industries were located in some of the cities. The region suffered heavily during the war, and the rebuilding process after 1945 was handicapped by the large war reparations exacted by the Soviet Union.

Sustained postwar recovery began with the initiation in 1949–50 of a rehabilitation program, which was succeeded by a five-year plan cover-

Leipzig, eastern Germany's second largest city, has a centuries-old tradition of culture and learning. Shown here is the Thomaskirche (Church of St. Thomas), where Johann Sebastian Bach was the organist.   J. Messerschmidt–Bruce Coleman, Inc.

Sans Souci Palace (1745–47) in Potsdam, seen from the garden. It was built in the rococo style by Frederick the Great of Prussia, who read French literature and played the flute here.
J. Messerschmidt–Bruce Coleman, Inc.

ing 1951–55. A special effort was made to increase the production of the many industrial items supplied by western Germany before 1945. By the late 1950s the industrial capacity of the GDR had been restored to its prewar level. In the 1960s and early '70s the country's industrial plant was increased dramatically, so that by the end of the 1970s the GDR ranked among the world's leading economic powers. Among the nations of Eastern Europe it was outdistanced only by the USSR.

The country's economy was dominated by the state. Virtually all manufacturing industries, commercial and financial enterprises, and transportation facilities were nationalized. According to official statistics, industrial production increased by 113% between 1970 and 1985, agricultural output rose by 37%, and exports increased more than fivefold. By the late 1980s, the gross national product of the GDR was approximately $207.2 billion, or about $12,500 per capita.

What these generally favorable economic statistics masked was a rise in foreign debt and a deterioration of work standards, infrastructure, and environmental quality. By 1990, when the GDR ceased to exist, agencies in the Federal Republic of Germany estimated that it would cost at least $200 billion to revamp the east's telecommunication and transportation systems, privatize its industries, pay off its foreign debt, subsidize the withdrawal of Soviet troops, finance the establishment of a unified German currency, and ease the economic hardships the former citizens of the GDR were expected to experience in making the transition to a market economy.

Agriculture. Until the end of World War II most of the farmland in eastern Germany was divided among large estates. In the immediate postwar years these holdings were broken up, and the land was redistributed in small parcels to peasants. This arrangement was judged inefficient by the GDR government, and beginning in 1952 peasants were urged to combine their resources by establishing collective farms. The socialization of agriculture moved forward quickly, and in the early 1980s about 84% of the farmland was held by collective farms. An additional 8% was controlled by state farms run directly by the government. About 47% of eastern Germany's land area is arable.

Although the relative importance of agriculture in the GDR's economy decreased drastically in comparison with industry, the country's farms markedly increased their output, largely through greater use of machinery and fertilizer. The best farmland is located in the S lowlands. The GDR's principal crops (with approximate annual output in the late 1980s) were potatoes (11.5 million metric tons), sugarbeets (4.6 million), barley (3.8 million), wheat (3.7 million), rye (4.6 million), and oats (508,000). The GDR's livestock in the late 1980s included 51 million chickens, 12.5 million hogs, 5.7 million cattle, and 2.7 million sheep.

Forestry and Fishing. Both forestry and fishing played relatively small roles in the East German economy. The cut of roundwood in the late 1980s was about 10.6 million cu m (about 374 million cu ft), more than 80% of which came from co-niferous trees. In the same year, about 193,600 metric tons of fish were caught. Approximately 90% of the catch came from marine fisheries.

Mining. In the late 1980s the GDR was by far the world's leading producer of lignite but produced insignificant quantities of other minerals. The leading minerals (with approximate annual output) were brown coal, including lignite (303 million metric tons), potash (potassium oxide content, 3.5 million), copper (10,000), crude petroleum (301,000 barrels), and natural gas (2.4 billion cu m/85 billion cu ft).

Manufacturing. From the 1950s East Germany placed much emphasis on increasing its manu-facturing plant. Heavy industry received particular attention. By the 1980s the GDR was a major industrial power, producing a vast range of goods, and the annual value of its manufactures was exceeded only by the USSR among the nations of Eastern Europe. Most of the leading industries were in the Berlin area and in the cities of the S.

East Germany had a large iron and steel indus-try, with huge mills at Eisenhüttenstadt and near Berlin. Yearly production of crude steel in GDR in the late 1980s was about 8.2 million metric tons. The country also produced great amounts of chemicals, such as sulfuric acid, caustic soda, and ammonia. Many chemical plants were in the region of Dessau, Halle, and Leipzig. A large petrochemical complex at Schwedt, in the NE, processed petroleum piped in from the Soviet Union. Machinery was produced in numerous cities, especially in the SW, and East Berlin had large factories making electronic equipment. Op-tical and precision instruments were manufac-tured in Jena and Görlitz. Rostock and Wismar were the chief centers of the shipbuilding indus-try. Textiles were produced in several cities, no-tably Cottbus, Karl-Marx-Stadt, and Leipzig, and motor vehicles were assembled in Dresden, Ei-senach, and Zwickau.

About 8000 companies were functioning in the GDR in 1990. Of these, fewer than one-fourth were expected to survive in the more competitive economy of a unified Germany.

Currency and Trade. The basic unit of currency in the GDR was the East German mark, or ost-mark, subdivided into 100 pfennigs. In July 1990, the currencies of East and West Germany were merged. Most East Germans were allowed to re-deem up to 4000 ostmarks for West German marks, or deutsche marks (DM), at par, and to exchange additional ostmarks for West German currency at a two-for-one ratio.

In the late 1980s, East Germany remained a major trading nation. About 60% of its foreign commerce was with the Soviet Union and other nations of Eastern Europe; approximately 7% was with West Germany. Annual imports cost about $31 billion, and exports earned approximately $30.8 billion. Because the GDR had few natural resources, it needed to import large quantities of such basic industrial raw materials as crude pe-troleum, coal, and iron ore; it also made heavy foreign purchases of grain and other foodstuffs. Principal exports were machinery, transport equipment, chemicals, and textiles.

Transportation. East Germany's transportation fa-cilities were concentrated in the industrial regions of the. S. The GDR had about 47,380 km (about 29,440 mi) of major roads, including some 1675 km (about 1040 mi) of limited-access ex-pressways (*Autobahnen*). In the late 1980s about 3.6 million passenger cars and nearly 435,000 commercial motor vehicles were in use. At the same time, East Germany's railroad operated 14,008 km (8704 mi) of track, about 22% of which was electrified. Oceangoing freight was handled at Wismar, Rostock, Stralsund, and other Baltic ports. Large amounts of goods were also carried on inland waterways. These include the Elbe R. and some of its tributaries, the Oder R., and several canals. The Elbe and Oder rivers are linked by a canal system. Dresden, Riesa, Magde-burg, and East Berlin were the main inland ports. The GDR's national airline, Interflug, provided domestic and international service. The principal airports were at Schönefeld (outside Berlin), Leipzig, Dresden, and Erfurt.

Communications. The mass media in East Ger-many were controlled by the government. Radio DDR provided the main domestic radio service; it offered two basic programs, with regional var-iations. A government-owned network supplied television service, and most viewers in the GDR could also receive West German programming.

The GDR had 39 daily newspapers, with a combined daily circulation of more than 9 mil-lion. The leading newspapers were produced by the dominant Socialist Unity party of Ger-many.

In the late 1980s, some 3.9 million telephones were in use. The GDR also had about 12,000 post offices and agencies.

Labor. Total employment in East Germany in the late 1980s was about 8.6 million persons. Women made up about 50% of the labor force. Manu-facturing, mining, and construction enterprises and public utilities employed more than 70% of all workers, and agriculture and commerce to-gether engaged about 20%. Almost all the work-ers belonged to a union affiliated with the Con-federation of Free German Trade Unions.

GOVERNMENT

From 1968 through 1989 the GDR was governed under a constitution that defined the country as a sovereign socialist state in which all political power was exercised by the working people. In practice, power resided with the Socialist Unity party of Germany (Sozialistische Einheitspartei Deutschlands, or SED), a Marxist-Leninist (Communist) organization. The 1968 constitution guaranteed the SED a leading role in national affairs, and its general secretary, as head of the party's political bureau, was usually the most powerful person in the country.

Central Government. Under the 1968 constitution, East Germany's unicameral parliament, the People's Chamber (Volkskammer), consisting of 500 deputies, met only for short sessions. To carry out its functions at other times, the People's Chamber elected a Council of State.

In the face of rising popular discontent, the SED and opposition groups agreed in December 1989 to hold free elections for a new People's Chamber of 400 members; this transitional body, chosen in March 1990, was charged with working out the constitutional arrangements under which the GDR would merge with the Federal Republic of Germany. On Oct. 3, 1990, the GDR ceased to exist, and the Basic Law of the FRG was extended to cover eastern Germany.

Health and Welfare. Medical service was nationalized in East Germany and was provided under the auspices of the Ministry of Health. Particular emphasis was placed on the prevention of disease. All employed persons were required to carry health insurance, which was offered by the trade union confederation and by the state. In the late 1980s East Germany had some 167,600 hospital beds and about 40,500 physicians.

Local Government. Each of the 15 districts (*Bezirke*) of East Germany had an elected assembly (*Bezirkstag*), which chose a council, headed by a chairperson, as its executive body. The districts were subdivided into counties, with such units as cities, boroughs, and villages. Elections were held in October 1990 for the governments of the re-created five states in eastern Germany.

Political Parties. After the Communist government of East Germany collapsed in 1989, the SED, which had long dominated the GDR's political life, reconstituted itself as the Party of Democratic Socialism and contested the elections held in March 1990. The party came in third following the Alliance for Germany, a conservative coalition backed by West Germany's Christian Democrats, and the Social Democratic party, which had close ties with the Social Democrats in West Germany.

Judiciary. The East German judicial system was headed by the supreme court, which sat in East Berlin. It supervised and heard appeals from district and county courts. Each of these tribunals consisted of three elected magistrates. Members of the supreme court were chosen by the People's Chamber, and district and county assemblies selected magistrates for courts within their jurisdictions. Social courts and disputes commissions handled minor proceedings.

Defense. The National People's Army was established in 1956. It consisted in the late 1980s of an army (with 120,000 members), a navy (16,000), and an air force (37,100). Paramilitary forces included some 49,000 border troops and a Workers' Militia with a potential strength of 500,000. When Germany reunified in 1990, these independent East German military organizations were dissolved, and the GDR's links to the Warsaw Pact were severed. The united Federal Republic of Germany became a full member of NATO, but no NATO troops were stationed in the eastern part of the country. The USSR pledged to withdraw its forces from eastern Germany by 1994.

HISTORY

The German Democratic Republic, established under Soviet auspices in 1949 in reaction to the Allied-sponsored founding of the Federal Republic of Germany, insisted on being internationally recognized as an independent Communist state. Despite Soviet demands for heavy reparations, it developed a potent economy and long held a key position in the Soviet bloc.

The Ulbricht Years. Walter Ulbricht, an old-line German Communist party stalwart, presided over the destiny of East Germany for more than a quarter of a century. Head of the Socialist Unity (Communist) party (1946–71), Ulbricht dominated the government as first deputy premier and as chairman of the Council of State (1960–73) as well.

Determined to transform the war-ravaged fragments of his country into a major Communist power, Ulbricht designed a foreign policy to foster friendly relations with other Communist states. In 1950 East Germany made a treaty with Poland, accepting the Oder-Neisse border, and joined the other Communist nations in the Council for Mutual Economic Assistance. In 1954 its position markedly improved when the Soviet Union ended its demands for reparations and granted the Democratic Republic diplomatic recognition. The next year East Germany helped found the Warsaw Pact, the Soviet answer to the North Atlantic Treaty Organization, and in 1956 it formed an army. Ulbricht made a treaty with the USSR in 1964, promising to help maintain communism in Eastern Europe, and negotiated

The Brandenburg Gate, famous memorial arch in Berlin . Built in 1788–91 by Frederick William II, it was damaged in World War II but has been repaired.

Vance Henry–Taurus Photos

an unfavorable trade agreement in 1965 in return for Soviet political support. In 1968 Ulbricht sent German troops to aid the Soviets in crushing an uprising in Czechoslovakia.

Relations with West Germany. East Germany's relations with capitalist West Germany were strained by the claim of the West German chancellor Konrad Adenauer that all Germans were one nation, and his consequent insistence on dealing with the Socialist Unity party rather than with the East German government. Matters were further complicated by the division of Berlin. To stop the flow of dissatisfied East Germans to the West, a situation seriously draining East Germany's trained work force, Ulbricht set up a three-mile police-guarded corridor along the western frontier, leaving only Berlin as a practical escape route. He finally blocked it in 1961 by building the heavily fortified Berlin Wall. In 1968 he imposed new restrictions on already limited travel from West Germany to West Berlin.

Strict party control. In domestic affairs, Ulbricht's first concern was to rebuild an economy that inherited only one-fourth of prewar Germany's resources but was required by the Soviet Union to pay three-fourths of overall German reparations to aid Soviet war recovery. He did so by imposing an iron discipline comparable to that of Joseph Stalin in the Soviet Union. The Socialist Unity party completely controlled the government, which had already taken over all large industry and agriculture and gradually acquired all small holdings as well. Emphasis was on heavy industrial production to satisfy Soviet requirements. In 1953 increased production quotas and food shortages caused worker revolts, which were put down by Soviet troops.

As a result of the Berlin Wall and the New Economic System of 1963, a policy characterized by some decentralization and by computerized planning, economic recovery in the area occurred rapidly. As workers' incomes and benefits improved and many of them were given advanced technological education, they became somewhat more reconciled to the Communist government. A more fully socialist constitution was accepted in 1968.

New Leadership. After 1971, when Ulbricht was succeeded by Erich Honecker (1912–) as party leader, no single figure dominated the East German government. Relations with West Germany improved as the West German chancellor Willy Brandt and Willi Stoph (1914–), the East German premier, agreed to ease West German travel to West Berlin (1972) and instituted formal diplomatic relations (1973). New trade, aid, and travel agreements were signed with West Germany in 1984, and in 1987 Honecker became the first East German head of state to pay an official visit to West Germany.

The End of the GDR. Communist rule unraveled in 1989 after Hungary, suspending a 20-year-old accord with the GDR, allowed thousands of East German citizens to cross the border from Hungary into Austria and thence to West Germany, where they received asylum. As the political crisis mounted, Honecker was forced out in October, and Egon Krenz (1937–) became president and party leader. In November the Berlin Wall was opened, other barriers to emigration were dropped, and tens of thousands of East Germans began streaming into West Berlin. Meanwhile, revelations of corruption among high officials during the Honecker era left the Socialist Unity party in complete turmoil. Krenz lost his state and party posts, and the Communist government agreed to allow free elections for a new People's Chamber, which took office in March 1990. By July the economy of the GDR had merged with that of West Germany, and on Oct. 3, 1990, the GDR ceased to exist and eastern Germany became part of the Federal Republic of Germany.   G.K.

For further information on this topic, see the Bibliography in volume 28, sections 935, 942.

GERMANY, WEST, former republic of central Europe, bordered on the N by the North Sea, Denmark, and the Baltic Sea; on the E by East Germany and Czechoslovakia; on the S by Austria and Switzerland; and on the W by France, Luxembourg, Belgium, and the Netherlands. The country had an area of 248,577 sq km (95,976 sq mi).

West Germany was established on May 23, 1949, as one of two successor states—East Germany being the other—to the nation of Germany, which was defeated and occupied by the Allies in World War II. In 1990 the East German government ceased to exist, and the former German Democratic Republic (GDR) became part of the Federal Republic of Germany (FRG; *Bundesrepublik Deutschland*), the name by which West Germany had officially been known.

This article deals with the state of West Germany (1949–90), the western region of unified Germany, and with the FRG, or unified Germany after 1990.

LAND AND RESOURCES

Western Germany consists of three major geographical regions of roughly equal size—a lowland plain in the N, an area of uplands in the center, and a mountainous region in the S. The lowlands, part of the North German Plain, have a varied topography that includes several river valleys and a large heath (the Lüneburger Heide). Along the coastline are areas of sand dunes and marshland. Off the coast are several islands, including the North Frisian Islands and the East Frisian Islands and Helgoland, in the North Sea, and Fehmarn, in the Baltic Sea. The central uplands region, the approximate boundaries of which are the latitude of Hannover, in the N, and the Main R., in the S, encompasses a complex terrain of low mountains, river valleys, and well-defined basins. The mountains include the Eifel and Hunsrück, in the W, the Taunus and Spessart, in the center, and the Fichtelgebirge, in the E. Much of southwestern Germany is dominated by two branches of the Jura Mts. One branch, the Black Forest, or Schwarzwald, is in the SW, and the other, made up of the Swabian Jura and the Franconian Jura, sweeps from the SW to the Frankenwald, Oberpfälzer Wald, and other mountains in the SE. In the extreme S are the Bavarian Alps, which contain Germany's loftiest peak, the Zugspitze (2962 m/9718 ft).

Western Germany has several major rivers. The most important is the Rhine, in the W, which forms part of the borders with Switzerland and France before flowing into the Netherlands. Among the tributaries of the Rhine in western Germany are the Lahn, Lippe, Main, Mosel, Neckar, and Ruhr rivers. Other important rivers include the Ems, Weser, and Elbe, which empty into the North Sea through large estuaries, and the Danube, which traverses much of the S before entering Austria. Western Germany has few large lakes. The largest is the Lake of Constance (Bodensee), which is partly in Austria and Switzerland.

Climate. Western Germany has a temperate climate, with an average annual temperature of 9° C (48° F). The mean January temperature varies from −6° to 1° C (21° to 34° F), according to location, and the average July temperature ranges between 16° and 20° C (61° and 68° F). The lowlands of the N have a somewhat warmer climate than the central and S regions. Precipitation is heaviest in the S, which yearly gets about 198 cm (about 78 in) of moisture, much of it in the form of snow. The central uplands receive a maximum of approximately 150 cm (59 in) of precipitation per year, and the lowlands in the N get up to about 71 cm (about 28 in) of moisture annually.

Natural Resources. Western Germany has large-scale deposits of several minerals. The most important is bituminous coal, which is found mainly in the Ruhr region and in the Saarland. Also important are substantial deposits of lignite, especially around Aachen, and of iron ore, found principally near Brunswick and in the region of the Lahn R. Potash is abundant in the SW, around Freiburg, and petroleum and natural-gas deposits occur in the N, near the mouths of the Ems and Weser rivers and E of Kiel. Western Germany

The Bavarian village of Hindelang nestles in the Allgäu Alps, near the Austrian Tirol. Set in a rich dairy land, Hindelang is a year-round resort center.
Toni Schneiders–Lindau–Bruce Coleman, Inc.

also has large deposits of rock salt, plus relatively small quantities of mercury, silver, sulfur, and lead, uranium, and zinc ores.

Plants and Animals. About 30% of western Germany is made up of woodland, most of which is in the S half of the region. Approximately two-thirds of the woodland is composed of pines and other conifers, and the rest is made up of deciduous species such as beech, birch, oak, and walnut. Vineyards cover many of the hillsides along the Rhine, Mosel, and Main rivers, and SW. Western Germany is noted for its orchards. A great variety of mosses and flowering plants also exists.

Western Germany has few wild animals. The more common mammals include deer, wild boars, hares, weasels, and badgers. Among the few reptiles is one poisonous snake, the adder. Finches, geese, and other migratory birds cross the country in great numbers. Herring, cod, and ocean perch are found in the coastal waters of the North Sea, and carp, catfish, and trout inhabit the country's rivers and streams.

Soils. Although most of western Germany has relatively infertile soil, several areas have rich earth. Areas of poorer soil, such as the lowlands of the N and the woodlands of the S, have earth containing much sand or clay. The region's best soil is composed of wind-deposited loess. Such earth is found in a wide belt (known as the Börde) along the S margins of the lowlands; in the W, between the Rhine R. and the Dutch border; in the SW; and in the S, near Ulm and Munich.

Electric Power. About 64% of the electricity produced in western Germany is generated in thermal plants using coal or lignite. Most of the remaining electricity is produced by nuclear-power plants, and western Germany also has several hydroelectric facilities (located mainly in the S). The annual output of electricity in the late 1980s was 415.8 billion kwh, placing West Germany among the world's top producers.

POPULATION

The people of western Germany consist mostly of two groupings of the Caucasoid race. The predominant Alpine type is concentrated in the central and S regions; persons of the Teutonic grouping live principally in the N.

Population Characteristics. In 1989, West Germany had an estimated population of 61,131,000, including West Berlin. The mean population density was about 246 persons per sq km (about 637 per sq mi). The region is highly urbanized, with nearly 90% of the people living in communities of at least 2000 persons.

365

Political Divisions. West Germany was divided into ten states (*Länder*): Baden-Württemberg, Bavaria, Bremen, Hamburg, Hesse, Lower Saxony, North Rhine-Westphalia, Rhineland-Palatinate, Saarland, and Schleswig-Holstein. West Berlin, which was legally a separate entity, was closely associated with the country. With the unification of Germany in 1990, West Berlin and East Berlin were reunited and five eastern states joined the FRG.

Principal Cities. The capital of West Germany was Bonn (pop., 1987 est., 291,400), an old university city on the Rhine R. The country's largest cities were Hamburg (1,571,300), a major seaport; Munich (1,274,700), a commercial and cultural center; Cologne (914,300), an industrial city with a famous cathedral; Essen (615,400), a steel-making center in the Ruhr; Frankfurt, or Frankfurt am Main (592,400), a commercial and manufacturing city; Dortmund (568,200), an industrial center with nearby coal mines; Stuttgart (565,200), a manufacturing and commercial city; Düsseldorf (560,600), a fashionable industrial and financial city; Bremen (522,000), a commercial center and seaport; Duisburg (514,600), a busy inland port; and Hannover (505,700), a manufacturing city and transportation hub. Closely associated with the country was West Berlin (1,879,200). Berlin became the capital of the united FRG; the seat of government was scheduled to shift from Bonn to Berlin over a 12-year period beginning in 1991.

Religion. About 47% of the people of western Germany are Protestants, the great majority of whom belong to a congregation affiliated with the Evangelical Church in Germany, a federation established after World War II. Most of the Protestants live in the N. Almost 45% of the people are Roman Catholics, concentrated in the Rhineland and Bavaria. About 30,000 Jews live in western Germany.

Language. German was the official language of West Germany and is spoken by almost all German citizens. Several regional dialects exist, some of which differ substantially from standard High German.

Education. Schooling in western Germany is compulsory and free for persons between the ages of 6 and 18. Although education is controlled by the individual state governments, national coordinating groups ensure that school systems and requirements are roughly the same throughout the region. Almost all adults in western Germany are literate.

All western German children begin their education with four years at a *Grundschule* (basic school). On completion of the *Grundschule* at about the age of ten, students are given extensive tests, the results of which largely determine their

A power plant in Boxberg, in a heavily industrialized region of SW Germany.
© 1990 Ulrike Welsch

INDEX TO MAP OF GERMANY

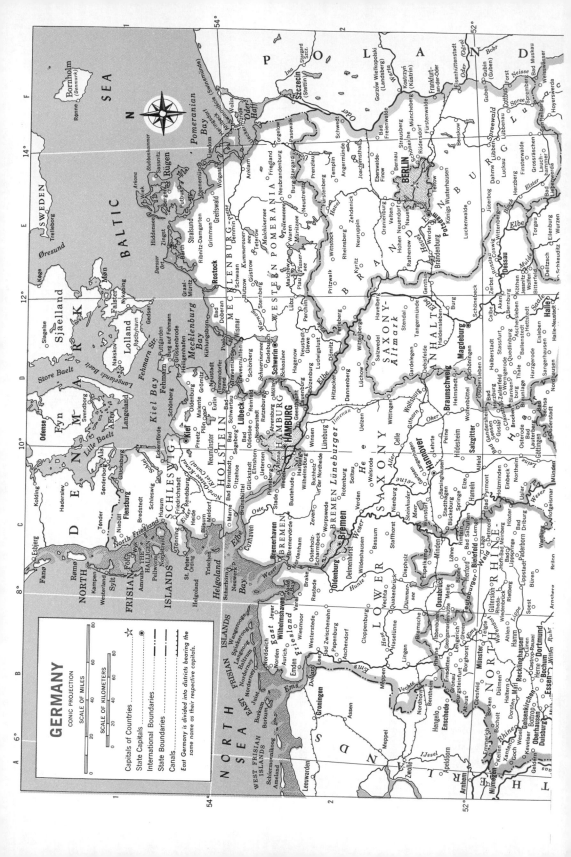

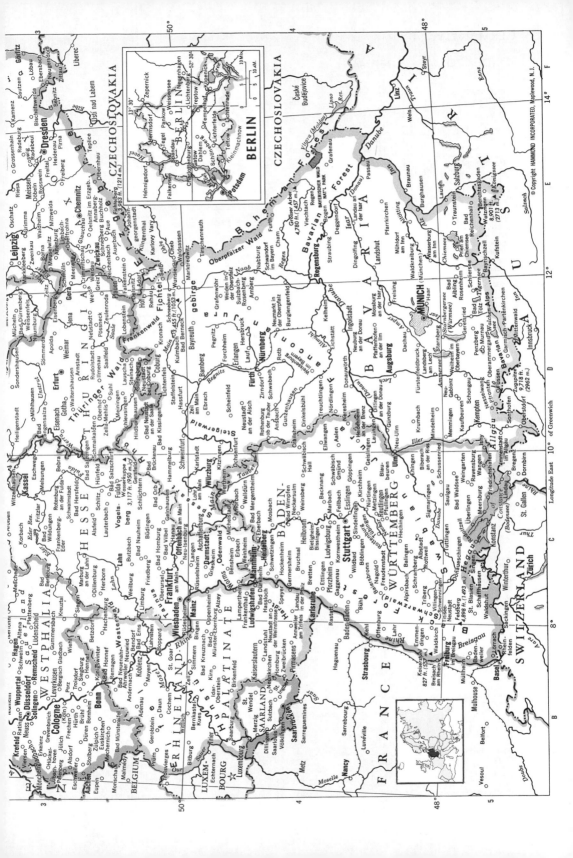

INDEX TO MAP OF GERMANY

subsequent types of schooling. Almost half of the students go on to a *Hauptschule* (senior school) for five years. They then undertake a 3-year vocational training program, which includes on-the-job experience plus classroom instruction at a *Berufsschule* (vocational school). Approximately one-fifth of the children who finish the *Grundschule* attend a *Realschule,* where they take a 6-year course emphasizing commercial and business subjects. After the *Realschule* these students may enter a 2-year vocational college (*Fachoberschule*). About one in four students enters a *Gymnasium* (academic high school) after the *Grundschule.* The *Gymnasium* offers a rigorous 9-year program that culminates with examinations for the *Abitur* (diploma), which is necessary for university entrance. Under reforms introduced in the 1970s, the rigid distinctions between the three types of schooling were loosened, and some students were permitted to change from one kind of school to another during the course of their education. Such midcourse changes were easiest at the small but growing number of comprehensive schools, which offered all three programs—vocational, commercial, and academic.

In the late 1980s *Grundschulen* in West Germany annually enrolled a total of about 3.7 million pupils who were instructed by some 212,100 teachers. *Berufsschulen* had about 2.5 million students and some 89,000 instructors; *Realschulen* had about 915,300 pupils and some 57,700 teachers; *Fachoberschulen* had about 312,500 students and some 22,900 instructors; *Gymnasien* had about 1.6 million pupils and some 120,200 teachers; and comprehensive schools had 244,300 students and some 19,300 instructors.

Western Germany has several types of specialized schools. Mentally or physically handicapped children are usually taught at separate institutions, and in the later 1970s about 385,000 handicapped pupils annually received instruction from a total of 30,500 teachers. Schools of continuing education for adults, such as the many *Volkshochschulen* (people's universities), offer a variety of courses and have some programs leading to diplomas.

Germany has long been known for the quality of its institutions of higher learning, and one of its universities, the Ruprecht-Karls-Universität in Heidelberg (1386), is among the oldest in Europe. Other leading universities in western Germany are at Berlin, Bonn, Erlangen, Frankfurt, Freiburg, Göttingen, Hamburg, Marburg an der Lahn, Munich, and Tübingen. In the late 1980s, 93 institutions with university status existed; they had a combined annual enrollment of about 1,060,000 students. Western Germany also has numerous teacher-training institutions, schools of fine arts, music, and filmmaking, and schools of theology.

CULTURAL LIFE

Unlike English and French cultural life, which is centered in the capital cities, London and Paris, German cultural life has traditionally flourished in many cities. For centuries they were the capitals of the many independent German states, whose rulers encouraged art, music, theater, and

Heidelberg, on the Neckar River. Renowned for its charming setting and its old castle (now largely in ruins), it is the quintessential university town, bustling with student life.
Edith Reichmann—Monkmeyer Press

scholarship as expressions of their power. Berlin was the cultural as well as the political capital of a united nation from 1871 to 1945 and became that again in 1990.

Western Germany has some 600 museums, 370 important libraries, 60 opera houses, 200 other theaters, and 80 major orchestras. These institutions receive large subsidies from their respective cities or states, continuing the tradition of princely support for the arts. Government aid enables many people to find employment in the arts and brings the arts within geographic and economic reach of a large part of the region's population, but it does not imply government control.

Museums and Libraries. World War II damaged or destroyed a great many museums, libraries, and historical buildings; but many treasures were safely stored away and thus preserved. A revival of interest in German history prior to the 20th century has encouraged rebuilding and new building, revitalizing old cities such as Munich and Bonn.

The outstanding art collections of the kings of Prussia are found in Berlin. The city's western sector has the State Museum of Prussian Cultural Treasures, which houses Egyptian art and old-master paintings in the Dahlem complex, and 19th- and 20th-century paintings in the National Gallery. The collections of the Bavarian rulers form the Bavarian State Art Galleries in Munich: old masters in the world-famous Alte Pinakothek and modern works in the Neue Pinakothek. The Bavarian National Museum, also in Munich, includes collections of sculpture, decorative art, and folk art. The Roman-Germanic Museum in Cologne displays Roman antiquities. Other art treasures are privately held by the church and by aristocratic families. Outstanding scientific collections are housed in the Senckenberg Museum of Natural History in Frankfurt and in the State Scientific Collections of Natural History and the German Museum, one of the foremost technological museums of the world, in Munich. The City Museums of Frankfurt contain fine art and folk art as well as an assortment of archaeological and historical material.

Important research libraries include the Bavarian State Library in Munich, the State Library of Prussian Cultural Treasures in Berlin, and the German Library in Frankfurt. Records of the Nazi period are in the federal archives in Koblenz. Excellent university libraries and many city and church lending libraries are found throughout the country.

Theater and Music. The theaters and concert halls of western Germany and the western sector of Berlin attract large audiences from all levels of society. Opera houses of the first rank are those of Berlin, Cologne, Hamburg, Munich, and Stuttgart. Stuttgart also maintains a fine ballet company. Repertory, open-air, and cabaret theaters thrive in Berlin, Hamburg, Recklinghausen, Hannover, and other cities. The Berlin and Munich Philharmonic orchestras and the Bamberg Symphony are world famous, as are the radio orchestras of Munich, Cologne, and Hamburg. International visitors flock to special festivals and fairs such as the Wagner festival at Bayreuth, the Bach festival at Ansbach, the "documenta" of visual arts at Kassel, film week in Berlin, and the Frankfurt Book Fair. Folk culture is preserved in folk museums, pageants, and festivals.

ECONOMY

Many industrial areas of western Germany were seriously damaged during World War II, and production of pig iron, steel, and other basic manufactures was at an extremely low level immediately following the war. In 1948 an ambitious program aimed at economic recovery was launched. The program was successful, largely because of aid received from the U.S. through the European Recovery Program. During the 1950s and '60s West Germany enjoyed a period of rapid industrial expansion and prosperity, which was known as the *Wirtschaftswunder* ("economic miracle"). By the late 1960s the country had become the leading industrial power of Western Europe and the world's second leading trading nation. The prosperity continued through the 1970s, although some strains, such as rising unemployment and an increasing rate of inflation, were evident by the end of the decade.

In the mid-1980s West Germany emerged as the world's leading export nation and the second leading importer. Its yearly gross national product (GNP), the market value of the country's total output of goods and services, was estimated at about $623.2 billion (including West Berlin) in constant dollars in 1985, compared to $289.5 billion in 1960. Industrial production increased by 22% between 1970 and 1985, while agricultural output rose by 18%; during the same period, consumer prices had the smallest rise of any non-Communist industrialized country. About 40% of the annual gross domestic product in the late 1980s originated in manufacturing, construction, and mining; roughly 58% was produced by the commercial sector, transportation, communications, and other services; and about 1.5% was produced by agriculture. The annual federal budget for the late 1980s included revenue of about $135 billion and expenditure of approximately $152 billion.

The economies of West Germany and East Ger-

Munich marketplace. Munich, which has long been both the business and the cultural metropolis of southern Germany, was founded as a marketplace (and mint) more than 800 years ago by a duke of Saxony.
German Information Service

many merged in July 1990. After the dissolution of the German Democratic Republic in October, the united Federal Republic of Germany faced the need to make massive investments to improve industrial, communication, and transportation facilities in the east; to ease the transition of eastern Germany from a centralized system to a market economy; and to harmonize the economy of the east with policies established by the European Community, of which West Germany was a founding member.

Agriculture. In the late 1980s agriculture played a small role in the West German economy, and the country imported much of its food. Farms were relatively small—about 75% of the units were made up of an area of 20 ha (49 acres) or less—and only some 1.3 million workers were engaged in agriculture.

About 30% of western Germany's land area is arable. The best farmland is located along the S fringes of the lowlands. The region's principal crops (with approximate annual output in the late 1980s) are sugar beets (19.6 million metric tons), potatoes (7.4 million), barley (9.6 million), wheat (12 million), oats (2 million), and rye (1.6 million). Western Germany also produces large quantities of grapes, some of which are used to make internationally famous wines. In the late 1980s the livestock population included some 72 million chickens, 23.7 million hogs, 14.9 million cattle, and 1.4 million sheep.

Forestry and Fishing. Western Germany has substantial forestry and fishing industries. The annual cut of roundwood in the late 1980s was about 28.7 million cu m (about 1 billion cu ft), approximately two-thirds of which came from coniferous trees.

The region's leading fishing ports are Bremen, Bremerhaven, and Cuxhaven, on the North Sea, and Kiel, on the Baltic Sea. In the late 1980s the annual catch totaled some 142,200 metric tons, almost all of which was marine fish, especially herring.

Mining. The mining industry plays a comparatively small role in the economy of western Germany. Several minerals are produced in sizable quantities, however. The leading minerals (with annual output in the late 1980s) include lignite (108.8 million metric tons), coal (76.3 million), crude petroleum (27.8 million), iron ore (metal content; 68,900), and natural gas (15.9 billion cu m/561 billion cu ft).

Manufacturing. The economy of western Germany is dominated by the manufacturing sector, which produces a great variety of articles. The leading types of fabricated goods are processed food, machinery, chemicals, electronic devices, and transportation equipment. Annual production in the late 1980s included some 35.9 million metric tons of crude steel and about 4 million passenger cars and minibuses.

Large-scale manufacturing enterprises are concentrated in several areas of western Germany. The most important industrial area encompasses the state of North Rhine-Westphalia, which includes the steel-producing Ruhr region plus other large manufacturing centers, such as Aachen, Cologne, and Düsseldorf, where chemicals, metal goods, machinery, and motor vehicles are manufactured. Another major industrial region is located around the confluence of the Rhine and Main rivers. Encompassing the cities of Frankfurt, Wiesbaden, Mainz, and Offenbach, it has large factories producing metals, electronic equipment, chemicals, pharmaceuticals, and motor vehicles. To the S, along the Rhine, is an important industrial area centered on the cities of Mannheim, Ludwigshafen, and Karlsruhe, where chemicals, machinery, and construction materials are manufactured. Stuttgart is the hub of a manufacturing region in which motor vehicles, electronic equipment, office machinery, textiles, and optical instruments are produced. Products of the Munich area include aircraft, motor vehicles, clothing, and beer. Several important industrial regions are located in northwestern Germany. These include the Hannover-Brunswick area, where steel, chemicals, and motor vehicles are produced. Another major manufacturing region includes such coastal port cities as Hamburg, Bremen, Kiel, and Wilhelmshaven. Among the products of this region are refined petroleum, processed food, beer, ships, office machinery, and printed materials. The western part of Berlin is also a major producer of electronic equipment.

Currency and Banking. The basic unit of currency in Germany is the deutsche mark, or DM (2.7775 marks equal U.S.$1; 1990). The mark is divided into 100 pfennigs.

The bank of issue is the Deutsche Bundesbank, headquartered in Frankfurt. The largest of Germany's many private commercial banks include the Deutsche Bank A.G., the Dresdner Bank A.G., and the Commerzbank A.G. Many savings banks and credit institutions exist.

Foreign Trade. Germany is a great trading nation. From the early 1950s through the 1980s West Germany generally received much more each year from foreign sales than it spent on purchases abroad. In the late 1980s annual exports of goods earned about $324.5 billion, and imports cost approximately $247.8 billion. The country's main exports were machinery, motor vehicles, chemicals, iron and steel, and textiles and clothing. Its principal imports included crude and refined petroleum, machinery, food, chemicals, clothing, and motor vehicles. West Germany's leading trade partners were France, the Netherlands, Italy, the U.S., Great Britain, Belgium and Luxembourg, and Japan.

Transportation. Western Germany has a highly developed transportation system that in the late 1980s included about 492,500 km (about 306,000 mi) of roads, with about 8435 km (about 5240 mi) of limited-access expressways (*Autobahnen*). In the late 1980s some 28.9 million passenger cars and 1.4 million commercial vehicles were in use. Western Germany has an excellent railroad system, the Deutsche Bundesbahn, which is run by the government. In the late 1980s it operated about 27,500 km (about 17,100 mi) of track, of which approximately 11,430 km (about 7100 mi) were electrified. The region's principal seaports are Hamburg, Wilhelmshaven, Bremen, Nordenham, and Emden, all located near the North Sea, and Lübeck, which serves Baltic shipping. The large merchant fleet included more than 1200 oceangoing vessels in the late 1980s. Much freight is shipped on the 4330 km (2691 mi) of inland waterways in western Germany. The most important of these is the Rhine R., but several canals are also heavily used; these include the Mittelland Canal, which traverses the N central part of the region, and the Nord-Ostsee Canal, or Kiel Canal, which links the North Sea and the Baltic. The leading inland port is Duisburg. The busiest of several international airports is near Frankfurt. Germany's principal airline, Deutsche Lufthansa A.G., operated by the government, offers extensive domestic and international service.

Communications. Western Germany is well supplied with modern communications media. Two national television networks broadcast, the ARD and the ZDF. In addition, regional telecasters offer a third program devoted mainly to educational and cultural offerings. Private cable television was begun in 1985. Western Germany also has ten regional radio broadcasters plus two international services, the Deutschlandfunk and the Deutsche Welle. In the late 1980s about 26.9 million radios and 23.7 million television receivers were licensed.

In the late 1980s western Germany had more than 350 daily newspapers with a combined daily circulation of about 25.3 million. Among the more influential newspapers are *Bild Zeitung, Frankfurter Allgemeine Zeitung, Frankfurter Rundschau, Süddeutsche Zeitung, Die Welt,* and *Westdeutsche Allgemeine Zeitung.* The region also has several widely read weekly publications. These include *Für Sie,* for women; *Der Spiegel,* an influential newsmagazine; *Stern,* an illustrated general-interest periodical; and *Die Zeit,* a sophisticated journal of politics and the arts.

Western Germany has efficient postal and telephone services, both of which are operated by the government. In the late 1980s about 41.7 million telephones were in use.

Labor. The work force in western Germany in the late 1980s comprised about 30.6 million persons.

About 27% of the labor force was employed in manufacturing and mining. The trade unions had some 9.3 million members, 7.8 million of whom belonged to a union affiliated with the Deutscher Gewerkschaftsbund (German Federation of Trade Unions). Relatively few strikes occur. Some enterprises, notably in the coal and steel industry, operate under a system of codetermination, in which workers and management have roughly equal say in establishing the major policies of their firm. From the late 1940s to the early '70s West Germany had virtually no unemployment. In the mid-1980s, however, about 9% of the labor force was unemployed.

GOVERNMENT

West Germany was governed under a Basic Law (*Grundgesetz*) promulgated on May 23, 1949, and later amended several times. The Basic Law, which described the country as a "democratic federal state based on social justice," resembled the constitution of the Weimar Republic (1919–33), but allowed a greater range of authority to the governments of the states. With the expansion of the Federal Republic of Germany to include the former German Democratic Republic on Oct. 3, 1990, West Germany's Basic Law was extended to what was formerly East Germany.

Central Government. Under the Basic Law the head of state of Germany is the federal president, who is elected to a 5-year term by a convention made up of members of the Bundestag (lower house of parliament) plus an equal number of persons chosen by the state legislatures. The president designates the chancellor, the country's chief executive official, who must then be approved by an absolute majority of the Bundestag. The president also names the cabinet ministers, in accordance with the proposals of the chancellor. The chancellor is responsible to the Bundestag, which may vote the chancellor out of office by a simple majority. The Basic Law provides, however, that the Bundestag must be able simultaneously to elect a successor, so that the country is never without a chancellor.

Legislature. The German parliament consists of two houses—the Bundestag, or lower house, and the Bundesrat, or federal council—both of which were expanded in 1990 to include representatives of eastern Germany. Members of the Bundestag are popularly elected to terms of up to four years by citizens aged 18 or over. One-half of the members are directly elected in single-member districts, and the rest are chosen under a system of proportional representation. The Bundestag may be dissolved by the federal president. The Bundesrat is made up of delegates chosen by the state governments, in a number varying from 3 to 5 according to state population.

In general, legislation is passed by a simple majority vote of the Bundestag. Laws dealing with matters of specific interest to the states, however, must also be approved by the Bundesrat. The Bundesrat may veto legislation passed by the Bundestag. A veto can be overridden if the Bundestag reapproves the legislation; for some types of laws it must override by the same proportionate majority by which the measure was vetoed in the Bundesrat. A two-thirds majority vote of both houses is necessary to amend the Basic Law; certain fundamental parts of the Basic Law may not be changed.

Political Parties. After general elections for a unified Bundestag in 1990, the leading German political parties, in order of representation, were the Christian Democratic Union (CDU), Social Democratic party of Germany (SPD), Free Democratic Party (FDP), Christian Social Union (CSU), Party of Democratic Socialism (PDS), and Green party.

The CDU is a conservative party emphasizing the rights of individuals. It has no organization in Bavaria, where its close ally, the somewhat more conservative CSU, is active. Both parties were established in 1945. The SPD, founded in 1875, had a Marxist orientation until 1959. In the 1980s and '90s it advocated a free-enterprise economy with sufficient public intervention to protect the general welfare.

The swing party in the lower house has often been the FDP (1948), a liberal group supported mainly by the middle class. The FDP joined with the CDU-CSU to form coalition governments during 1949–53 and 1961–66, and from 1969 to 1982 it formed coalition governments with the SPD. It again joined with the CDU-CSU in 1982 and took part in the governments formed after the elections of 1983, 1987, and 1990. Represented in the Bundestag for the first time in 1983 was the Green party, a leftist group concerned with environmental and peace issues. The PDS is the remnant of East Germany's Communist party.

Health and Welfare. Western Germany has a comprehensive social-insurance system, which includes sickness, accident, old-age, disability, and unemployment coverage. The insurance program is funded by compulsory contributions by employees and employers plus federal subsidies. In the late 1980s there were about 673,700 hospital beds and 171,500 physicians.

Local Government. The governments of the ten states (*Länder*) of western Germany have broad powers, including rights to levy taxes, formulate educational and cultural policies, and maintain police. Each state has a popularly elected assembly, which chooses a minister-president or (in Hamburg and Bremen) a first mayor to serve as chief executive. The states are subdivided into counties, municipalities, and communes.

Judiciary. The highest tribunal under the Basic Law is the Bundesverfassungsgericht (Federal Constitutional Court), which sits in Karlsruhe. It is the final interpreter of the Basic Law in all disputes. Six other important national courts are maintained—the Federal Court of Justice, the Federal Administrative Court, the Federal Financial Court, the Federal Labor Court, the Federal Court on Social Affairs, and the Federal Patent Court. Each state has a series of courts headed by an *Oberlandesgericht* (high state court). The death penalty is forbidden by the Basic Law.

Defense. The West German armed forces, or Bundeswehr, established in 1955, were fully integrated into the forces of the North Atlantic Treaty Organization. In the late 1980s the West German army had 340,700 members, the air force (Luftwaffe) had 106,000 members, and the navy had 36,000 members. The international agreements that allowed the unification of Germany in 1990 linked the gradual withdrawal of Soviet forces from eastern Germany with a pledge by NATO not to station forces in the east.

HISTORY

Since the Federal Republic of Germany was established in 1949, it has worked for close ties with the West, a strong capitalist economy, political stability within a democratic framework, and the unification of Germany. All these objectives had been accomplished by the end of 1990.

The Adenauer Years. For nearly 15 years (1949–63) the government of West Germany was dominated by the middle-of-the-road Christian Democratic Union, whose venerated leader, Konrad Adenauer, was elected chancellor. As West Germany's first leader, Adenauer managed to raise the country from an occupied zone to an independent nation accepted as an equal by its former conquerors. Attaining this goal became easier when the U.S., Britain, and France recognized that Western Europe could not withstand Soviet pressure without the aid of a strong West Germany.

European cooperation. Accordingly, by the Bonn Convention of 1952, the military occupation was ended. In 1955 the Federal Republic became completely independent and, allowed to rearm, joined the North Atlantic Treaty Organization for the defense of Europe. It also cooperated in the European Community, the European Coal and Steel Community, the European Atomic Energy Community, and the Council of Europe. As partial reparation for war crimes and out of gratitude for postwar Marshall Plan aid from the U.S., West Germany assumed the obligation to give aid to

The Kurfürstendamm, Berlin's main avenue, has theaters, fine shops, and sidewalk cafés. As the style and condition of the buildings suggest, much of Berlin has been rebuilt since World War II. J. Messerschmidt–Bruce Coleman, Inc.

On Oct. 2, 1990, French, British, and U.S. military commanders and representatives of the Berlin parliament mark the end of the allied military occupation of West Berlin. The formal unification of East and West Germany took place on the following day.
© A. Tannenbaum–Sygma

Israel and developing nations. Although not a member of the UN until 1973, the Federal Republic joined many UN agencies and made large contributions to UN projects. In 1963, reversing long-standing Franco-German hostility, Adenauer and French president Charles de Gaulle agreed on regular conferences. West Germany also improved relations with Eastern European countries. Always hoping for reunification, Adenauer encouraged trade with East Germany but steadfastly refused to recognize it as a sovereign state during his chancellorship.

Economic resurgence. In domestic affairs Adenauer and his economic minister, Ludwig Erhard, encouraged economic recovery through free enterprise aimed at the consumer market both at home and abroad. Industrial growth was aided by tax laws favoring owners, by heavy private investment, and by hardworking, relatively undemanding laborers. The work force was augmented first by a large influx of highly skilled immigrants, who were among the more than 11 million refugees from East Germany and former German areas of Europe. Later, "guest workers" (Ger. *Gastarbeiter*) were imported from Italy, Spain, and Turkey. The result was an "economic miracle," whose creation and enjoyment absorbed the energies of most West Germans. With the profits, an army was formed and the social security system was improved.

Social Democrats in Power. When Adenauer retired at the age of 87, he was succeeded by Erhard (1963–66) and Kurt Georg Kiesinger (1966–69),

head of Baden-Württemberg, both of whom were supported by coalition governments. In 1969 a Social Democratic victory brought Willy Brandt, former mayor of West Berlin, to the chancellorship. With the approval of big business, he initiated an *Ostpolitik* ("eastern policy") to improve political and trade relations with the Soviet bloc. He concluded nonaggression treaties (1970) with the USSR and Poland that confirmed existing boundaries. Overturning Adenauer's intransigent policy, he reached an accord (1972) with East Germany that eased West German access to West Berlin. In 1973 the two countries granted each other full diplomatic recognition and were admitted to the UN. Less successful in domestic affairs, Brandt resigned in 1974 and was succeeded by Helmut Schmidt.

Schmidt was faced with domestic problems that had been simmering since the late 1960s. Rapid inflation was accompanied by rising unemployment, exacerbated by the presence of 4 million guest workers and their families. The country was also troubled by student unrest and by a wave of bombings, kidnappings, and murders by terrorists such as the Baader-Meinhof group. These difficulties, however, were by and large overcome. In foreign affairs Schmidt generally continued Brandt's *Ostpolitik*. He won a renewed mandate from the voters in 1980, but two years later the Free Democratic party ended the Schmidt coalition government by crossing over to form a coalition, headed by Helmut Kohl of the Christian Democrats. The new alignment was confirmed in elections in 1983 and 1987. New financial and travel accords between the two states were reached in 1984, and East German leader Erich Honecker (1912–) paid his first official visit to West Germany in 1987.

The fall of East Germany's Communist government in 1989 profoundly altered relations between the two nations. With the opening of the Berlin Wall and the ending of other emigration barriers, more than 200,000 East Germans settled in West Germany. The West German government not only aided the new immigrants but also allocated a massive infusion of capital to shore up the ailing East German economy. West Germany and East Germany merged their financial systems in July 1990, and in October the German Democratic Republic dissolved and all its citizens became citizens of the Federal Republic of Germany. The coalition led by Kohl scored a decisive victory in all-German elections in December. The newly elected combined Bundestag named Berlin the capital of Germany on June 20, 1991. The transfer of administration from Bonn was expected to take several years.

For further information on this topic, see the Bibliography in volume 28, sections 935, 941.

GERMINATION. *See* SEED.

GERMISTON, city, NE South Africa, in Transvaal, near Johannesburg. It is an important rail hub and industrial center situated in the heart of the Witwatersrand, the country's rich gold-mining and manufacturing region. Gold is refined, and machinery, chemicals, mining explosives, fabricated steel, textiles, and railroad equipment are manufactured. Germiston grew rapidly after gold-mining operations began on the Witwatersrand in the 1880s. Pop. (1985) 116,718.

GERM WARFARE. *See* CHEMICAL AND BIOLOGICAL WARFARE.

GERONIMO (1829–1909), chief of the Chiricahua tribe of North American Apache Indians, born in present-day Clifton, Ariz. After his wife, children, and mother were killed by Mexicans in 1858, he participated in a number of raids against Mexican and American settlers, but eventually settled on a reservation. In 1876 the U.S. government attempted to move the Chiricahua from their traditional home to San Carlos, N.Mex.; Geronimo then began ten years of intermittent raids against white settlements, alternating with periods of peaceful farming on the San Carlos reservation. In March 1886, the American general George Crook (1829–90) captured Geronimo and forced a treaty under which the Chiricahua would be relocated in Florida; two days later Geronimo escaped and continued his raids. Gen. Nelson Miles (1839–1925) then took over the pursuit of

Geronimo, Chiricahua Apache Indian leader. UPI

Geronimo, who was chased into Mexico and captured the following September. The Indians were sent to Florida, Alabama, and finally to Fort Sill, Oklahoma Territory, where they settled as farmers. Geronimo eventually adopted Christianity. He took part in the inaugural procession of President Theodore Roosevelt in 1905. Geronimo dictated his memoirs, published in 1906 as *Geronimo's Story of His Life*. He died at Fort Sill on Feb. 17, 1909.

For further information on this person, see the section Biographies in the Bibliography in volume 28.

GERONTOLOGY, scientific study of old age, with emphasis on the social and behavioral aspects of aging. Although aging is a lifelong process and varies greatly in its effects on individuals, old age is commonly defined as beginning at the age of 65. Since 1920 the number of people living to old age in industrial societies has increased dramatically. In the U.S. in 1986, for example, life expectancy—that is, the average number of years that members of a society will live—was 78.9 years for white females, 72 years for white males, 75.1 years for nonwhite females, and 67.6 years for nonwhite males. As childhood diseases are eliminated and better sanitation methods are employed, life expectancy will also rise in developing nations.

Problems of the Elderly. Gerontologists study how older people are treated within a society and how the elderly deal with the inevitable problems of aging, particularly those involving health and income. Health problems include normal losses in hearing, eyesight, and memory and the increased likelihood of chronic diseases. These losses are gradual and proceed at different rates for each person. Many people do not experience declines until very old age, and the great majority of the elderly learn to adapt to the limitations imposed by health problems. In general, the health of older people today is superior to that of previous generations, a condition that is likely to improve still further as more people receive better medical care throughout their lives. In most industrial societies, the high cost of treating chronic illness has been assumed, at least partially, by national health plans such as Medicare and Medicaid in the U.S. *See* HEALTH INSURANCE.

The second major problem of the elderly involves income and economic welfare. Because most old people are no longer in the labor force, some form of income maintenance is necessary. Industrial societies are characterized by systems of pensions and benefits such as social security (q.v.) in the U.S., which presently is increased automatically as the cost of living rises, thus reducing somewhat the impact of inflation. Although the income of retired people is about half that of those who remain in the labor force, most manage to maintain themselves independently. In the U.S., however, about 20 percent of the elderly live below or slightly above the poverty level; these are predominantly women and members of minority groups for whom economic security has always been a problem. In numerous other industrialized nations, more exten-

An electrically powered duocycle makes a convenient means of transportation for this retired California couple. L.L.T. Rhodes–Taurus Photos

sive systems of social welfare have reduced the proportion of the elderly who lack adequate housing, transportation, and social services.

People age 65 and over made up less than 3 percent of the U.S. civilian labor force in the late 1980s, and the trend has been toward increasingly earlier voluntary retirement. Income needs and health are the primary considerations in the decision to retire. Eliminating the mandatory retirement age is not expected to cause many workers to stay on the job if they can afford to retire. The need to relieve strains on the Social Security system, however, has led to legislation gradually raising the age of eligibility for full benefits, which may force people to work longer in the future.

The vast majority of elderly men are married and live with their wives in homes of their own. Because of the higher death rates for men than for women, however, most older women are widowed. In the U.S. today most widowed women are able to maintain an independent one-person household. Thus, fewer than 20 percent of the elderly live in the household of an adult child, and only 5 percent are in institutions such as hospitals or nursing homes. Those who live with an adult child or who are institutionalized are typically very old or have serious health problems. Although both the elderly and their children express a strong preference for independent residence, most old people live within a few hours of one of their children. Members of different generations often visit one another and provide help in emergencies. Few elderly parents are abandoned or neglected by their children.

Social relationships may be difficult to maintain in old age because of health limitations, death of family members and friends, loss of workmates, and lack of transportation. Still, the majority of old people are deeply involved in friendships and family, and many find companionship at special senior centers.

Attitudes Toward the Elderly. In many ways, the aged are victims both of the youth orientation of modern times and of a tendency toward denial of death. In the past, old people commanded respect because they controlled the sources of power: wealth, land, political office, and information, and the fate of other family members. In most modern societies, however, young people are independent; they choose whom they will marry, and receive public education. The image of the elderly reflects this powerlessness. Groups such as the Gray Panthers, the National Coalition on Aging, and the American Association of Retired People strive to reverse this stereotype and improve the status of the aged.

Elderly persons themselves often display high levels of morale, satisfaction with life, and feelings of self-worth. The important variables are health and income. The task of modern societies is to ensure that the aged have their basic needs met and that they have the resources to continue to function in the community without becoming a burden on their own offspring.

See also AGING. B.B.H.

For further information on this topic, see the Bibliography in volume 28, sections 296, 450.

GERRY, Elbridge (1744–1814), fifth vice-president of the U.S. (1813–14), born in Marblehead, Mass., and educated at Harvard College (now Harvard University). His long political career began in 1772, when he became a member of the Massachusetts General Court, the representative body of the colony. He soon joined the revolutionary patriot Samuel Adams in opposition to the British. In 1775 Gerry introduced and secured passage of a bill to arm and equip ships to carry out aggressive acts against British maritime commerce. He was a member (1776–81) of the Continental Congress and was a signer of the Declaration of Independence. He resumed his seat in Congress in 1782, and in 1787 he represented Massachusetts at the Constitutional Convention in Philadelphia. He refused to sign the Constitution on the ground that it failed to provide sufficient protection for the liberties of the people. As an Anti-Federalist (see FEDERALIST PARTY), he represented his Massachusetts district in the U.S. House of Representatives from 1789 to 1793. In 1797, when the U.S. was involved in serious disputes with France, he was sent with the American statesmen John Marshall and Charles Cotesworth Pinckney to France to secure a treaty of settlement (see XYZ AFFAIR). In 1810 and 1811 Gerry was elected governor of Massachusetts as a Democratic-Republican; during his second term, and under his direction, the Democratic-Republican legislature passed a bill redistributing Massachusetts in such a manner as to ensure their continued control (see GERRYMANDER). From 1813 until his death, Gerry served as vice-president in the second administration of President James Madison.

For further information on this person, see the section Biographies in the Bibliography in volume 28.

GERRYMANDER, apportionment of electoral districts in such a way as to give the political party in power an advantage in electing its representatives. Gerrymandering is usually accomplished by so dividing electoral districts as to mass the voters for opposing parties into a small number of districts, while the favored party's electorate is spread out in order to win by a light majority in many districts. One result of this device is to have electoral districts of curious shapes. The term gerrymander originated in 1812, when Governor Elbridge Gerry of Massachusetts signed a bill giving his own Republican party, which had temporarily come into power, such an advantage over the Federalists. One electoral district was shaped so fantastically that it was compared by one Federalist to a salamander. "No," said another, "better call it a Gerrymander."

The first known instance in America of gerrymandering took place in 1709, when various counties in Pennsylvania tried to deprive Philadelphia of due representation. Later examples were a "shoestring" district in Mississippi, about 480 km (about 300 mi) long and 32 km (20 mi) wide, and a district in Pennsylvania shaped like a dumbbell. In 1842 Congress passed the Reapportionment Act, requiring that electoral districts for members of the House of Representatives be compact and contiguous. Even when observing the letter of the law, however, gerrymandering is still possible. Among the remedies that have been proposed for gerrymandering are the election of all representatives at large and election by the system of proportional representation. In 1962 the U.S. Supreme Court, in the first of a series of decisions about election practices, ruled that election districts in all states be apportioned according to the principle of "one man, one vote." These decisions restricted the possibility of gerrymandering. In 1985 the Court ruled unconstitutional the practice of manipulating election district lines so as to give any political party an advantage over others.

GERSHWIN, George (1898–1937), American composer, whose musicals and popular songs are among the finest in those genres and whose compositions in art-music forms are infused with the idioms of jazz and popular music.

Gershwin was born in Brooklyn, N.Y., on Sept. 26, 1898. He studied with the American composers Rubin Goldmark (1872–1936), Henry Cowell, and Wallingford Riegger and with the Russian-born composer and theorist Joseph Schillinger (1895–1943). At the age of 16 Gershwin became a pianist and song promoter for a music publishing firm, but the success of his song "Swanee" (1918) established him as a Tin Pan Alley composer. The lyrics for nearly all his songs were written by his brother Ira Gershwin (1896–1983), his collaborator in a series of revues and musical comedies that included George White's Scandals (1920–24); Lady Be Good (1924); Funny Face (1927); and the political satire Of Thee I Sing (1931), the first musical comedy to win a Pulitzer Prize.

George Gershwin   ASCAP

Gershwin's songs are marked by uncommon harmonic inventiveness, and he was one of the first to introduce into popular songs the rhythms and melodic twists of jazz. Among his best-known songs are "The Man I Love," "I Got Rhythm," and "Someone to Watch Over Me."

At the invitation of the bandleader Paul Whiteman, Gershwin wrote his *Rhapsody in Blue* (1924) for piano and jazz band, later orchestrated by the American composer Ferde Grofé. The work profoundly influenced European and American composers to use jazz-derived melodic and rhythmic patterns. Gershwin's other concert works include the Piano Concerto in F (1925), the tone poem *An American in Paris* (1928), the *Second Rhapsody* (1931) for piano and orchestra, and the opera *Porgy and Bess* (1935). Based on a novel by the American writer DuBose Heyward, *Porgy and Bess* draws on the idioms of black folk music, jazz, Tin Pan Alley, and European classical music to produce a work of unique character that is Gershwin's masterpiece. Gershwin died in Beverly Hills, Calif., on July 11, 1937.   G.V.

GERSON, Jean de (1363–1429), French churchman and theologian, remembered for his efforts to settle the Great Schism (*see* SCHISM, GREAT) and for his writings on contemplation.

Gerson was born in Gerson in the Ardennes on Dec. 13, 1363. He entered the University of Paris in 1377, and in 1395, shortly after receiving his doctorate in theology, he became chancellor of the university. The schism was then at its peak, and Gerson began his efforts to end it through a council, hoping to use the occasion for a thoroughgoing reform of the church. In 1415 he attended the Council of Constance (*see* CONSTANCE, COUNCIL OF), where he urged a moderate conciliar theory (q.v.), contended that doctors of theology as well as bishops had a right to vote, and led in the condemnation of John Huss (Jan Hus). Meanwhile he had incurred the hostility of the duke of Burgundy, which prevented him from returning to Paris. Instead, he went to Austria and later to Lyons, where he spent the last ten years of his life in writing, prayer, and ministry. He died in Lyons on July 12, 1429.

Gerson's reputation during his lifetime was so great and his interests so broad and typical of his age that historians often speak of the "century of Gerson." Besides writing on speculative and mystical theology, he was one of the greatest preachers of his day. He participated actively in the religious confraternity at the university and severely criticized religious superstition.   J.W.O.

GERSONIDES or **LEVI BEN GERSHOM** (1288–1344), French rabbi, who wrote extensively on philosophy, mathematics, astronomy, law, and biblical exegesis. He was born in Bagnols-sur-Cèze in Languedoc and lived at Orange and Avignon. As an astronomer, he invented the so-called Jacob staff (a navigational instrument) and proposed a theory to account for lunar motion that went beyond the prevailing Ptolemaic model. Many of his treatises were translated into Latin and were highly influential. He also wrote commentaries on the works of Aristotle and the Spanish-Arab Islamic philosopher Averroës. His best-known work of philosophical theology is *The Wars of the Lord* (1329), in which he proposed solutions to philosophical problems he felt had not been adequately treated by his predecessors, particularly Averroës and the Jewish philosopher Maimonides.   R.S.S.

GESELL, Arnold Lucius (1880–1961), American psychologist and pediatrician, born in Alma, Wis., and educated at the University of Wisconsin, Clark University, and Yale University. He was appointed assistant professor of education at Yale in 1911. The same year he founded and became the director of the Clinic of Child Development of the Yale School of Medicine, and in 1915 he became professor of child hygiene at the medical school. He served as research consultant at the Gesell Institute of Child Development from 1950 until his retirement in 1958. With his associates Gesell observed hundreds of children under carefully controlled conditions in his studies of infant and child behavior; he used the motion picture camera to film thousands of children in various stages of development. He theorized that the maturing of a child cannot be hastened by intensified education (*see* CHILD PSYCHOLOGY). Gesell's work, which delineates behavioral norms for successive developmental stages, was influential in childrearing practices during the 1940s and '50s.

His writings include *The First Five Years* (with others, 1940), *Infant Development* (1952), and *Youth: The Years from Ten to Sixteen* (with others, 1956). With the American educator Frances Ilg (1901–81) he also wrote *Infant and Child in the Culture of Today* (1943) and *The Child from Five to Ten* (1946).

GESNER, Konrad von (1516–65), Swiss naturalist, born in Zürich. He studied at many European universities and took his M.D. at Basel in 1541. He practiced medicine in Zürich and became a lecturer in physics in that city. He wrote 72 books on various subjects, but he is best known for his work in collecting and describing plants and animals. His most important work is *Historia Animalium* (5 vol., 1551–58 and 1587), in which he attempted to describe and systematize all the known animals; this work is considered the foundation of modern zoology.

GESTALT PSYCHOLOGY, school of psychology that deals mainly with the processes of perception. According to Gestalt psychology, images are perceived as a pattern or a whole rather than merely as a sum of distinct component parts. The context of an image plays a key role. For instance, in the context of a city silhouette the shape of a spire is perceived as a church steeple. Gestalt psychology tries to formulate the laws governing such perceptual processes.

Gestalt psychology began as a protest. At the beginning of the 20th century, associationism (q.v.) dominated psychology. The associationist view that stimuli are perceived as parts and then built into images excluded as much as it sought to explain; for instance, it allowed little room for such human concepts as meaning and value. About 1910, German researchers Max Wertheimer, Wolfgang Köhler, and Kurt Koffka rejected the prevailing order of scientific analysis in psychology. They did not, however, reject science; rather they sought a scientific approach more nearly related to the subject matter of psychology. They adopted that of field theory, newly developed in physics. This model permitted them to look at perception in terms other than the mechanistic atomism of the associationists.

Gestalt psychologists found perception to be heavily influenced by the context or configuration of the perceived elements. The word *Gestalt* can be translated from the German approximately as "configuration." The parts often derive their nature and purpose from the whole and cannot be understood apart from it. Moreover, a straightforward summation process of individual elements cannot account for the whole. Activities within the total field of the whole govern perceptual processes.

The approach of Gestalt psychology has been extended to research in areas as diverse as thinking, memory, and the nature of aesthetics. Topics in social psychology have also been studied from the structuralist Gestalt viewpoint, as in Kurt Lewin's work on group dynamics. It is in the area of perception, however, that Gestalt psychology has had its greatest influence.

In addition, several contemporary psychotherapies are termed Gestalt. These are constructed along lines similar to Gestalt psychology's approach to perception. Human beings respond holistically to experience; according to Gestalt therapists, any separation of mind and body is artificial. Accurate perception of one's own needs and of the world is vital in order to balance one's experience and achieve "good Gestalten." Movement away from awareness breaks the holistic response, or Gestalt. Gestalt therapists attempt to restore an individual's natural, harmonic balance by heightening awareness. The emphasis is on present experience, rather than on recollections of infancy and early childhood as in psychoanalysis. Direct confrontation with one's fears is encouraged.

GESTAPO (Geheime Staatspolizei, or Secret State Police), common designation of the terrorist political police of the Nazi regime in Germany from 1933 to 1945; technically, however, the term refers only to its executive branch.

The Gestapo was founded by Hermann Göring, one of Adolf Hitler's lieutenants, in April 1933. As a nucleus he used the political section of the police of the Weimar Republic, but he extended it greatly, removed from it all legal and constitutional restraints, and gave the organization its name. Its new purpose was to persecute all political opponents of the Nazi regime (including dissenting Nazis), not only defensively, in cases of oppositional acts, but also preventively, in cases of suspected or potential opposition. In this role, the Gestapo was to collaborate with the SD (Sicherheitdienst, or Security Service), an organization of the Nazi party; the SD did the intelligence work that served as the basis for Gestapo operations. Suspects were arrested and usually placed in concentration camps. It was at the Gestapo's discretion whether or not the arrested were brought to trial and whether or not they were released if acquitted.

In April 1934, Göring's rival, Heinrich Himmler, who headed the paramilitary SS (Schutzstaffel, or Defense Squads; also called Black Shirts), won control over the Gestapo, a step in his ascendancy that in June 1936 carried him to the command of all German police forces. The SS then gradually infiltrated the police, which was reorganized in two divisions: the regular and the security police. The latter, the political police—headed until 1942 by Reinhard Heydrich (1904–42) and thereafter by Ernst Kaltenbrunner (1902?–46)—then included the SD, also run by Heydrich; the Gestapo, led from 1936 to 1945 by Heinrich Müller (b. 1901?); and the Kripo (Kriminalpolizei, or Criminal Police), a detective service aimed against nonpolitical criminals, run from 1936 to 1945 by Arthur Nebe (1896?–1945).

In September 1939, after the outbreak of World War II, the security police had received a central staff, the RSHA (Reichssicherheitshauptamt, or State Security Head Office), thus preparing it to serve as a nearly omnipotent tool for Hitler's racist and terrorist plans in Nazi-controlled Europe, including extermination policies against Jews and other "undesirables." Rivalries between the various branches nonetheless continued. Thus, the concentration camps, including the death camps, were actually run by the SS, although technically they were under the control of the Gestapo. After the war, the Gestapo was dissolved and declared a criminal organization.

See also CONCENTRATION CAMP; NATIONAL SOCIALISM; SECRET POLICE. W.W.S.

GESUALDO, Don Carlo (c. 1560–1613), sometimes known as the Prince of Venosa, Italian lutenist and composer, known for the daring chromatic harmonies of his madrigals. After ordering the murder of his wife, her lover, and their infant in 1590, he traveled from his native Naples to northern Italy. In 1594 he married the Ferrarese noblewoman Eleonora d'Este and settled at the court of Ferrara. When the death of Duke Alfonso II d'Este (1533–97) marked the end of Ferrara as a cultural center, Gesualdo returned to Naples. Of his six volumes of five-part madrigals, the last two especially reveal a dramatic, highly innovative harmonic style aimed at emotional expression.

GETHSEMANE (Aram., "oil press"), in biblical times, a small olive grove situated on the Mount of Olives, just outside Jerusalem. In agony over his betrayal by Judas Iscariot, Jesus Christ withdrew with his disciples to Gethsemane (see Matt. 26:36) on the eve of his crucifixion. This "Grotto of the Agony" was identified from about the 4th century AD by a sanctuary that was later destroyed; another was constructed on the site in the 12th century, but it too was destroyed. The Franciscans acquired the site in 1681 and enclosed and landscaped a flower garden in 1848.

GETTY, Jean Paul (1892–1976), American oil executive and financier, born in Minneapolis, Minn., and educated in California and at the University of Oxford. He became an independent oil producer in 1914 and held presidential and directorial positions with several oil companies between 1930 and 1936. From 1942 to 1961 Getty was president, general manager, and principal owner of the Minnehoma Financial Corp. In 1948 he became president and principal owner of the Getty Oil Co. and in 1956 president of the Mission Corp. From World War II until his death Getty was considered one of the richest men in the world. The art collections he began to assemble in the 1930s formed the nucleus of the J. Paul Getty Museum, opened on his estate in Malibu, Calif., in 1974. Unusually well endowed, it includes a library, an archive of photographs of art works, and conservation laboratories.

GETTYSBURG, borough, seat of Adams Co., S Pennsylvania; inc. 1806. It is a tourist center and has industries manufacturing processed food, footwear, textiles, electrical equipment, and printed materials. Gettysburg is famous as the site of the decisive Battle of Gettysburg (July 1863), one of the bloodiest encounters of the American Civil War. Subsequently, President Abraham Lincoln delivered his noted speech, the Gettysburg Address, when Gettysburg National Cemetery was dedicated on Nov. 19, 1863. The battlefield and cemetery are now part of Gettysburg National Military Park (1895). Several museums and other points of interest in and near the borough are concerned with the Civil War events. Also in the borough are Gettysburg College (1832) and Lutheran Theological Seminary at Gettysburg (1826); Eisenhower National Historic Site, encompassing the home and farm of President Dwight D. Eisenhower, is nearby.

The community, laid out in the 1780s, is named for Gen. James Gettys (1758–1815), an early resident. Pop. (1980) 7194; (1990) 7025.

GETTYSBURG, BATTLE OF, battle fought on July 1–3, 1863, considered by most military historians the turning point in the American Civil War. The Army of the Potomac, under the Union general George Gordon Meade, numbered about 82,000; the Confederate army, under Gen. Robert E. Lee, numbered about 75,000. After the Battle of Chancellorsville, in which the Confederates had obtained an important victory on May 2–3, Lee divided his army into three corps, commanded by three lieutenant generals, James Longstreet,

Confederate forces engaged in hand-to-hand fighting during the Battle of Gettysburg.　　　National Park Service

Richard Stoddert Ewell, and Ambrose Powell Hill. Lee then formulated a plan for invading Pennsylvania, hoping to avert another federal offensive in Virginia and planning to fight if he could get the federal army into a vulnerable position; he also hoped that the invasion might increase Northern war-weariness and lead to Northern recognition of the independence of the Confederate States of America. In pursuance of this plan, Lee crossed the Blue Ridge Mountains, proceeded up the Shenandoah Valley, and, crossing Maryland, entered Pennsylvania, where he concentrated his whole army at Gettysburg.

The battle began on July 1 with an encounter between Hill's advance brigades and the federal cavalry division commanded by Maj. Gen. John Buford (1826–63), supported by infantry under Maj. Gen. John Fulton Reynolds (1820–63). Hill encountered stubborn resistance, and the fighting was inconclusive until Ewell, arriving from the north, forced the federal troops to retire from their forward positions to Culp's Hill and Cemetery Ridge, southeast of Gettysburg. On the following day, July 2, Meade formed his forces in the shape of a horseshoe, extending westward from Culp's Hill and southward along Cemetery Ridge to the hills of Little Round Top and Round

Top. The Confederates, on the other hand, were deployed in a long, thin concave line, with Longstreet and Ewell on the flanks and Hill in the center.

Lee, against the advice of Longstreet, resolved to attack the federal positions. Longstreet was unable to advance until late afternoon, thus allowing the federal troops to make preparations for the expected assault. The federals held Cemetery Ridge and Little Round Top but were driven from advance positions in the Peach Orchard and Devil's Den. Although Ewell won part of Culp's Hill, he was unable to break the federal line there or on the eastern part of Cemetery Ridge. On the night of July 2, Meade held a council of war in which the decision was made not to retreat; early next morning Culp's Hill was stormed and retaken from the Confederates. Maj. Gen. George Edward Pickett then led his own and parts of two other Confederate divisions, totaling fewer than 15,000 men, in a memorable charge on Cemetery Ridge, against a withering barrage of federal artillery and musket fire. Although he breached Meade's first line of defense, the strain on the Confederates proved too great, and Pickett fell back, having lost over three-fourths of his force.

Four score and seven years ago our fathers brought forth, upon this continent, a new nation, conceived in Liberty, and dedicated to the proposition

A portion of the original draft of Abraham Lincoln's Gettysburg Address.
Paul Falkenberg

With the repulse of Pickett's charge, the Battle of Gettysburg was virtually over. On the night of July 4, Lee began his retreat to Virginia. During the three days of battle, the federal army lost 3070 killed, 14,497 wounded, and 5434 captured or missing. The Confederates lost 2592 killed, 12,706 wounded, and 5150 captured or missing.

The Battle of Gettysburg was a decisive engagement in that it arrested the Confederates' second and last major invasion of the North, destroyed their offensive strategy, and forced them to fight a defensive war in which the inadequacies of their manufacturing capacity and transportation facilities doomed them to defeat. B.C.

For further information on this topic, see the Bibliography in volume 28, section 1155.

GETTYSBURG ADDRESS, famous speech delivered by President Abraham Lincoln, at the dedication of the Gettysburg National Cemetery, on Nov. 19, 1863. This brief discourse followed a two-hour oration by Edward Everett, one of the most famous speakers of the time. In the contemporary newspaper reports of the dedication ceremonies, Everett's remarks were lauded highly and given prominence on the front page, while the words of Lincoln were relegated to an inside page. Everett, however, was sufficiently moved by the simple and sincere eloquence of Lincoln to write the following note to him on the day after the dedication: "I wish that I could flatter myself that I had come as near to the central idea of the occasion in two hours as you did in two

The headquarters of the Union general George Gordon Meade during the battle.
National Park Service

Old Faithful, one of the natural phenomena at Yellowstone National Park, shoots hot water and steam about 52 m (about 170 ft) into the air, erupting on an average of about once every 65 minutes. National Park Service

minutes." Today, the Gettysburg Address is universally recognized not only as a classical model of the noblest kind of oratory but also as one of the most moving expressions of the democratic spirit ever uttered. The text follows.

"Fourscore and seven years ago our fathers brought forth on this continent, a new nation, conceived in Liberty, and dedicated to the proposition that all men are created equal.

"Now we are engaged in a great civil war, testing whether that nation or any nation so conceived and so dedicated, can long endure. We are met on a great battle-field of that war. We have come to dedicate a portion of that field as a final resting place for those who here gave their lives that that nation might live. It is altogether fitting and proper that we should do this.

"But, in a larger sense, we cannot dedicate—we cannot consecrate—we cannot hallow—this ground. The brave men, living and dead, who struggled here, have consecrated it, far above our poor power to add or detract. The world will little note, nor long remember what we say here, but it can never forget what they did here. It is for us the living, rather, to be dedicated here to the unfinished work which they who fought here have thus far so nobly advanced. It is rather for us to be here dedicated to the great task remaining before us—that from these honored dead we take increased devotion to that cause for which they gave the last full measure of devotion—that we here highly resolve that these dead shall not have died in vain—that this nation, under God, shall have a new birth of freedom—and that government of the people, by the people, for the people, shall not perish from the earth."

GEYSER, hot spring that erupts intermittently in a column of steam and hot water. Some geysers erupt at regular intervals, but the majority erupt irregularly, the intervals ranging from a matter of minutes to years. The length of time of the eruption varies with the geyser, from seconds to hours. The height of the column ranges from about 1 m (about 3 ft) to about 100 m (about 328 ft), and the amount of water ejected in a single eruption varies from a few liters to hundreds of thousands of liters.

A geyser erupts when the base of a column of water resting in the earth is vaporized by hot volcanic rock. The force with which the water column is expelled depends on its depth. The weight of the water column increases with its depth. The weight, in turn, increases the pressure exerted on the base of the column, thereby increasing the boiling point of the water there. When the water finally boils, it expands, driving some water out into the air. With the weight of

the column reduced, the pressure correspondingly drops, and the boiling point of the water remaining in the column falls below its actual temperature. Thereupon, the entire column instantly vaporizes, causing the geyser to erupt.

Almost all known geysers are located in three countries of the world—New Zealand, Iceland, and the U.S. The most famous geyser in the world is Old Faithful in Yellowstone National Park (q.v.), which expels about 38,000 to 45,000 liters (about 10,000 to 12,000 gal) at each eruption. Old Faithful erupts at intervals of between 37 and 93 min, its column rising to a height of between 38 and 52 m (125 and 170 ft). The geyser gives warning of its impending activity by ejecting jets of water 3 to 7.6 m (10 to 25 ft) high.

Eruption intervals depend on such variables as the supply of heat, the amount and rate of inflow of subsurface water, and the nature of the geyser tube and its underground connections.

See GEOTHERMICS; VOLCANO.

GHAGHARA, also Gogra, river, N India, one of the largest affluents of the Ganges R. It rises in the S slopes of the Himalaya in Tibet, at an altitude of about 3962 m (about 13,000 ft) above sea level. The river flows S through Nepal as the Karnali. In Uttar Pradesh State the Ghaghara flows in a SE direction to the town of Chapra, where, after a course of 917 km (570 mi), it joins the Ganges R. The Ghaghara is one of the most important commercial waterways of Uttar Pradesh.

GHALI, Boutros Boutros. *See* BOUTROS GHALI, BOUTROS.

GHANA, country, W Africa, bounded on the N and NW by Burkina Faso (Upper Volta), on the E by Togo, on the S by the Atlantic Ocean, and on the W by the Ivory Coast. Formerly a British colony known as the Gold Coast, Ghana was the first black nation in sub-Saharan Africa to achieve (1957) independence. The country is named for the ancient empire of Ghana, from which the ancestors of the inhabitants of the present country are thought to have migrated. The total area is 238,537 sq km (92,100 sq mi).

LAND AND RESOURCES

Ghana is a lowland country, except for a range of hills on the E border. The sandy coastline is backed by a coastal plain that is crossed by several rivers and streams, generally navigable only by canoe. In the W the terrain is broken by heavily forested hills and many streams and rivers. To the N lies an undulating savanna country that is drained by the Black and White Volta rivers, which join to form the Volta (q.v.), which then flows S to the sea through a narrow gap in the hills. Lake Volta, in the E, is one of the largest artificial lakes in the world. No natural harbors exist. Ghana's highest point, in the E hills, is about 884 m (about 2900 ft) above sea level.

Climate. The climate of Ghana is tropical, but temperatures vary with season and elevation. Except in the N two rainy seasons occur, from April to June and from September to November. In the N the rainy season begins in March and lasts until September. Annual rainfall ranges from about 1015 mm (about 40 in) in the N to about 2030 mm (about 80 in) in the SE. The harmattan, a dry desert wind, blows from the NE from December to March, lowering the humidity and creating hot days and cool nights in the N. In the S the effects of the harmattan are felt in January. In most areas the highest temperatures occur in March, the lowest in August. The average annual temperature is about 26.1° C (about 79° F).

Plants and Animals. Much of the natural vegetation of Ghana has been destroyed by land clearing for agriculture, but such trees as the giant silk cotton, African mahogany, and cedar are still prevalent in the tropical forest zone of the S. The N two-thirds of the country is covered by savanna—a grassland with scattered trees. Animal life has also been depleted, especially in the S, but it remains relatively diverse and includes leopard, hyena, lemur, buffalo, elephant, wild hog, antelope, and monkey. Many species of reptiles are found, including the cobra, python, puff adder, and horned adder.

Natural Resources. The chief mineral resources of Ghana include gold, silver, iron, manganese ore, bauxite, and diamonds. Forest resources are significant, and the offshore waters are rich in fish. Minor resources include petroleum, natural gas, beryl, tantalite-columbite, and chromite.

Energy. The first stage of the Volta R. hydroelectric project, the Volta Dam at Akosombo, was completed in 1966. Construction on a second hydroelectric dam downstream was begun in the late 1970s. Total production of electricity in Ghana in the late 1980s was approximately 4.8 billion kwh annually; almost all the power was generated in hydroelectric facilities.

POPULATION

The population of Ghana is divided into more than 50 ethnic groups. The majority of the people are agricultural workers who live on farms or in small villages.

Population Characteristics. The population of Ghana (1984 prelim.) was 12,205,574; the estimated population in 1989 was 14,566,000, giving the country an overall population density of about 61 persons per sq km (about 158 per sq mi). The most densely populated parts of the country are the coastal areas, the Ashanti region in the S cen-

Liberty Ave., a principal thoroughfare of Accra, the capital and largest city of Ghana.   John Elk III–Bruce Coleman, Inc.

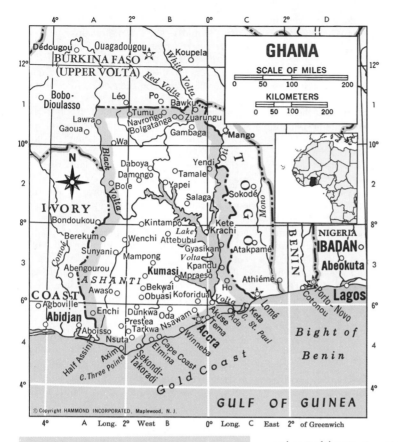

tral part of the country, and the two principal cities, Accra and Kumasi (qq.v.). Seventy percent of the total population lives in the S half of the country. The most numerous of the coastal peoples are the Fanti, who belong to the Akan family, and the Ashanti, who live in central Ghana. The Nzima and the Ahanta live in the SW. The Accra plains are inhabited by the Ga. Most of the inhabitants in the N region belong to the Moshi-Dagomba group of Volta peoples or to the Gonja group.

Political Divisions. Ghana is divided into ten administrative regions: Northern, Eastern, Western, Central, Upper East, Upper West, Volta, Ashanti, Brong-Ahafo, and Greater Accra.

Principal Cities. Accra, the capital, had a population (1984) of 964,879. Kumasi (348,880) is the capital of the Ashanti region. Sekondi-Takoradi (93,882) has an artificial harbor; it is the first modern port built in Ghana. Other major cities include Tamale (136,828), Tema (99,608), and Cape Coast (57,700).

Language and Religion. English is the official language of Ghana and is universally used in schools, but in 1962 the government selected nine Ghanaian languages, in addition to English and French, for use in educational institutions: Akuapem-Twi, Asante-Twi, Dagbani, Dangbe, Ewe, Fanti, Ga, Kasem, and Nizima.

Traditional religions, adhered to by more than one-fifth of the population, generally involve some form of animism. The Christian population, which accounts for about three-fifths of the total population and includes Roman Catholics, Anglicans, Methodists, and Presbyterians, is concentrated in the coastal region. The Muslim population (about 16% of the total) is located chiefly in the N part of the country.

Education. Six years of primary education and three years of secondary education are free and compulsory in Ghana. In the mid-1980s some 1.6 million pupils were attending about 9180 elementary schools annually, and about 5700 secondary schools had an enrollment of about 768,300. More than 130 vocational and teacher-training institutions had more than 40,000 students. Higher education is provided by the University of Ghana (1948), in Accra; the University of Science and Technology (1951), in Kumasi; and the University of Cape Coast (1962). Total university enrollment was about 8000.

ECONOMY

The economy of Ghana is based on the production of a few primary agricultural and mineral products. Despite sustained economic growth since the mid-1980s, Ghana remains one of the world's poorest countries, with a per capita income of about $400 annually. The estimated national budget in the late 1980s showed revenues of about $766.3 million and expenditures of about $737.5 million.

Agriculture. The most important export crop of Ghana is cacao, which is produced chiefly in the Ashanti region. In the late 1980s Ghana produced about 290,000 metric tons annually. Production is in the hands of small-scale farmers. Other major export commodities are coffee, palm kernels, shea nuts, coconut oil, copra, bananas, peanuts, kola nuts, palm oil, and tobacco. Plantings of rubber have been introduced in the SW. The government has initiated programs to promote the improvement of cacao cultivation and of other cash crops.

The most important agricultural products in the S are cassava, palm kernels, palm oil, corn, plantain, peanuts, and yams. Other crops include oil nuts, cotton, tobacco, and rice. The shea tree, which bears seeds yielding an edible solid fat called shea butter, is widely distributed in the N, where yams, durra, millet, and corn also are grown. Peanuts and cowpeas are grown in the NE. Coconuts, coffee, bananas, and citrus fruits are grown along the coast. Cattle, totaling

The coast of Ghana, once known as the Gold Coast, is now the focus of a thriving fishing industry under the control of the Ghana Fishing Corp.

Douglas Waugh—Peter Arnold, Inc.

GHANA

approximately 1.3 million in the late 1980s, are raised principally in the N. Other livestock include 3 million goats, 2.5 million sheep, and 12 million chickens.

Forestry and Fishing. Forests cover about 36% of Ghana's land area. Forest reserves are controlled under the 1959 Timber Lands Act to ensure that a given timber area has been fully exploited before the area is cleared for agricultural use. Through this act and by increasing the reservation and afforestation hectarage, the government is attempting to counteract the deforestation caused by farming. Most of the timber production is from areas outside the forest reserves, although production from reserves is increasing. In the late 1980s roundwood production totaled about 9.9 million cu m (about 350 million cu ft) annually.

The fishing industry has grown rapidly since the 1960s. In the late 1980s the annual catch was about 371,800 metric tons, about 10% of which came from inland waters (mainly Lake Volta). Fish markets with cold-storage facilities exist at Sekondi-Takoradi and at Tema.

Mining. In the late 1980s annual gold production was about 11,600 kg. About 230,900 metric tons of manganese and 287,300 metric tons of bauxite also were produced. Production of diamonds was about 215,900 metric carats, mostly of industrial quality.

Manufacturing. Ghana has, compared to other African countries, a relatively well-developed industrial sector. Manufacturing establishments are generally small, however. Printing and publishing plants are numerous, and the country has a number of sawmills and furniture-producing establishments. Large-scale operations are found mainly in those industries producing beer, cigarettes, soft drinks, edible oils, nails, oxygen and acetylene, and sheet aluminum. The industrial base at Tema, a port city E of Accra, includes an oil refinery. A large aluminum smelter, which utilizes energy generated by the Volta River Project, produced about 47,500 metric tons of metal per year in the mid-1980s. Other manufactures include textiles, footwear, iron and steel, sugar, flour, and glass.

Currency and Banking. The Bank of Ghana (est. 1957) is the central bank for the country and issues the national currency. Since 1967 the currency unit has been the cedi, divided into 100 pesewas (311 new cedis equal U.S.$1; 1990). The National Investment Bank makes development loans to private business and public corporations.

Foreign Trade and Labor. Generally, the annual balance of trade has shown a deficit since independence. In the late 1980s annual imports to Ghana were valued at about $952 million and exports at about $827 million. Great Britain is Ghana's leading trade partner.

Nearly 60% of Ghana's labor force is engaged in agriculture. Manufacturing employs 11% and services 29%. The minister of labor certifies unions for collective bargaining. Uncertified trade unions may not strike. Public service, municipal, and local government employees are forbidden to strike and are not entitled to arbitration.

Transportation. In the late 1980s Ghana was served by 953 km (592 mi) of railroads. The main line forms a rough triangle, connecting Sekondi-Takoradi, Accra, and Kumasi.

The country has about 28,300 km (about 17,600 mi) of roads, of which about 20% are paved. Motor vehicles in use in the mid-1980s totaled about 76,200. The country's two major ports, Tema and Sekondi-Takoradi, are both artificial.

Five major airports, located at Kotoka (near Accra), Sekondi-Takoradi, Kumasi, Sunyani, and Tamale, serve the country, together with additional airstrips for internal flights. International airlines have regular flights to Accra. Ghana Airways provides domestic and international service.

Communications. Radio, television, telegraph, and telephone services are owned and operated by the government of Ghana. Radio programs are broadcast in English and African languages. Programs in English and French are beamed to other parts of Africa as part of an international radio service. A television service was established in 1965. An estimated 2.9 million radios and 175,000 television receivers were in use in the late 1980s.

GOVERNMENT

Until the end of 1981 Ghana was governed under a constitution adopted in 1979 that provided for an executive branch headed by a president popularly elected for a term of four years. The president appointed ministers of state to form a cabinet. Legislative power was vested in the parliament, a single-chamber body of 140 popularly elected members. The president was advised by a Council of State, consisting of respected elders, former presidents, and members of major professions. The constitution also provided for an independent judiciary headed by a supreme court. Following a coup d'état on Dec. 31, 1981, the 1979 constitution was suspended and a Provisional National Defense Council, headed by a chairman, was established.

HISTORY

The earliest known states in what is now Ghana were the Dogomba and Mamprussi kingdoms in

Traditional houses of Tamale, in the rural northern region of Ghana, are constructed with round walls and thatched roofs.　　　John Elk III–Bruce Coleman, Inc.

the north, which flourished in the 12th and 13th centuries. About that time groups of Akan speakers—among them the Ashanti and the Fanti—migrated from the savanna and established their predominance below the forest line, forming a series of small states. By the early 15th century these communities carried on a lively trade with the sub-Saharan peoples to the north.

The first Europeans to visit the region, subsequently called the Gold Coast, were Portuguese explorers. In 1482 they established a trading settlement on the site of present-day Elmina, and the developing slave trade during the 16th century whetted the interest of other European nations; by 1642 the Dutch had forced the Portuguese out. The ocean-directed European trade aided the ascendancy of the Ashanti, who had gradually moved and settled at the junction of trade routes around Kumasi that enabled them to dominate commerce both north and south. By 1670 their supremacy in the Kumasi area was unchallenged, and further expansion left the Ashanti Empire unquestionably predominant among the native states by the middle of the 18th century.

British Dominance. Among the European invaders the Dutch were soon challenged by the British, who established forts at Kormantine and Cape Coast. The ensuing rivalry between the two

powers culminated in war, from which the Dutch emerged victorious. The British continued, however, to pursue their interest, developing by 1750 a flourishing slave trade. Forts were also established by the Danes at Christiansborg and elsewhere, but by the end of the 18th century the British dominated the region. In 1821, 14 years after the abolition of the slave traffic, the British settlements were taken over by the Crown. In 1850 the British purchased the Danish forts, and in 1871 the Dutch settlements were also transferred to them. The coastal area, by then entirely under British control, was designated a crown colony in 1874. British interests in the area were recognized by an international conference held in Berlin in 1884–85. The boundaries of the colony were established in 1901; at the same time the Ashanti and the northern territories were annexed to the colony. Part of the German Togoland was added in 1922. Three years later the first elections for a legislative council were held.

Rapid political development, however, began only after World War II, when the British, faced with sustained agitation for national independence, allowed increasing measures of self-government, with the object of gradually establishing an independent country. Accordingly, the British Parliament in January 1957 passed the

Ghana Independence Act, and on March 6 of that year the National Assembly of Ghana issued an independence proclamation. Two days later it joined the UN.

The Nkrumah Years. The dominant political party of the new nation was the Convention People's party (CPP), headed by Kwame Nkrumah, who was the country's first prime minister. There was, however, marked dissension between the CPP and various disaffected political groups. A prime source of resentment was Nkrumah's desire to create a centralized rather than a federated state. The government retaliated harshly against its critics, and in October 1957 six opposition groups formed a coalition known as the United party.

The Ghana Constitutional Amendment Bill of 1958 made it possible for the National Assembly to alter the constitution by a simple majority. A new republican constitution was drafted early in 1960 and approved by the electorate. At the same time, Prime Minister Nkrumah was elected the first president. The country was proclaimed a republic on July 1, 1960.

During the following years the opposition was severely limited in its freedom of action; leading members of the United party were held under the Preventive Detention Act, which provided for up to five years' imprisonment without trial, and defamation of Nkrumah was made a crime. In 1961, in order to suppress protest strikes centering in Sekondi-Takoradi, the government decreed a state of emergency. A series of assassination attempts against Nkrumah in 1962 led to another state of emergency. In late 1963 Nkrumah began to limit the freedom of the judiciary. A one-party system was introduced in 1964.

Political Instability. On Feb. 24, 1966, Nkrumah, who was on a state visit to China, was ousted in a military coup. He took refuge in Guinea, but his supporters in Ghana were arrested, and Soviet and Chinese technicians, whom Nkrumah had brought in, were expelled from the country. For the next three years Ghana was ruled by a National Liberation Council. In 1969 power was transferred, under a new constitution, to a civilian government headed by Kofi A. Busia (1913–78). Busia, however, was ousted by another army coup in 1972, this one headed by Col. Ignatius K. Acheampong (1931–79). Acheampong suspended the constitution, banned political activity, and curbed freedom of the press and union activities. Military control was relaxed slightly in 1974, and a civilian political affairs advisory council and an economic planning council were set up. Acheampong, however, was forced to resign in 1978, giving way to Gen. Frederick W. Akuffo (1936–79), who ruled for less than a year

before he was overthrown by Flight Lt. Jerry Rawlings (1947–). Dedicated to uprooting corruption, Rawlings had both Acheampong and Akuffo executed for that offense. In September 1979 Rawlings stepped down in favor of an elected civilian president, Hilla Limann (1934–). Economic conditions worsened, however, and on New Year's Eve 1981, Limann was deposed in a second coup led by Rawlings. Ruling as chief of the Provisional National Defense Council (PNDC), Rawlings imposed an austerity plan that helped control inflation and attract financial aid from the West. The PNDC regime suppressed what it claimed was a series of coup attempts throughout the 1980s.

For further information on this topic, see the Bibliography in volume 28, section 1026.

GHANA, KINGDOM OF, medieval West African state from which the modern republic of Ghana takes its name. It arose in what is now southeastern Mauritania and southwestern Mali sometime before the 8th century, when it was first mentioned by Arabic writers, and was described in some detail by the Spanish Muslim geographer al-Bakri (1040?–94). Ghana's ruling dynasty belonged to the Soninke people, but a number of other peoples in the area were subject to it. Its economy was based on a trade in gold acquired from the south, which was exchanged for products from Muslim North Africa, especially salt. Its capital was at Kumbi Saleh in what is now southeastern Mauritania. Ghana's principal enemies were the Muslim Sanhaja Berbers, who, under Almoravid leadership, overran the kingdom in 1076. It later revived but was finally destroyed when one of its former subject peoples, the Soso, captured Kumbi Saleh in 1203.

GHATS, two converging mountain ranges running along the E and W coasts of S India, called the Eastern and Western Ghats.

The Eastern Ghats parallel the Coromandel Coast. The average elevation of the range is about 457 m (about 1500 ft), but several peaks reach an altitude of about 1219 to 1524 m (about 4000 to 5000 ft) above sea level. The Eastern Ghats lie generally at a distance of about 80 to 240 km (about 50 to 150 mi) from the coast, but at Visakhapatnam they form precipitous escarpments along the Bay of Bengal. The chief rivers that cross or penetrate the mountains are the Godavari, Krishna, and Kaveri.

The Western Ghats extend from the S portion of the Tapti R. valley along the Malabar Coast to Cape Comorin. The range is divided by Palghat Gap (about 40 km/25 mi wide); the section N of the division is about 1290 km (about 800 mi) long and that S of the gap about 320 km (about 200 mi). In many sections, the range is separated from the coastline only by a narrow strip of land. The Western Ghats have an average elevation of 914 m (3000 ft), but S of Palghat Gap some peaks are as high as 2438 m (8000 ft).

GHAZALI, AL-, full name ABU HAMID MUHAMMAD IBN MUHAMMAD AT-TUSI AL-GHAZALI (1058–1111), Islamic philosopher and theologian whose Latin name is Algazel. He was born in Tus, near Meshed, Persia (now Iran). Having gained an excellent reputation as a scholar, in 1091 al-Ghazali was appointed by Nizam al-Mulk (1018–92), vizier to the Seljuk sultan, to teach at Nizamiya University in Baghdad. In 1095, following a personal crisis of faith, he relinquished his position, left his family, and became an ascetic. After ten years of wandering and meditation, he accepted another teaching position in Nishapur but left it shortly afterward and retired to Tus.

Al-Ghazali reported his internal struggle and the religious solution he finally achieved in *The Deliverance from Error,* a work that has been compared to *The Confessions of Saint Augustine.* In *The Revival of the Religious Sciences* he presented his unified view of religion incorporating elements from all three sources formerly considered contradictory: tradition, intellectualism, and mysticism. The work has been considered the greatest religious book written by a Muslim, second only to the Koran. After having mastered the methods of philosophy, al-Ghazali set out to refute the Neoplatonic theories of other Muslim philosophers, particularly those of Avicenna, which were opposed to such orthodox religious doctrines as that of the creation, the immortality of the soul, and divine providence. The resultant attack on philosophical theory and speculation, set forth in al-Ghazali's *Destruction of the Philosophers,* was in large measure responsible for the eventual decline of the element of rationalism in Islam.

GHAZNAVIDS, Turkish Muslim dynasty that ruled Afghanistan and neighboring Punjab for more than 200 years. It was founded by Alptigin (d. 963), a Samanid slave, who conquered the strategic mountain town of Ghazni in 962 and made it into an independent kingdom. The greatest of the Ghaznavids was Sultan Mahmud of Ghazni (971–1030), Alptigin's grandson, who led numerous raids into the Punjab, looting Indian cities of enormous wealth that he used to convert Ghazni into one of the great centers of Islamic culture. Before his death Mahmud annexed the Punjab to his kingdom, and in 1160 the Ghaznavid capital was moved to Lahore. Muhammad of Ghur (fl. 1174–1206) deposed the last Ghaznavid ruler in 1186.

GHAZNI, city, E Afghanistan, capital of Ghazni Province, on a plateau at an altitude of about 2220 m (about 7280 ft) above sea level. Ghazni, a market center for the cereal grains, fruit, wool, and animal skins from the surrounding region, lies on the trade route between Iran and India. A short distance NE of Ghazni are the remains of Old Ghazni, once an important city. The only ruins in Old Ghazni retaining a semblance of architectural form are two towers, about 43 m (about 140 ft) high and some 365 m (some 1200 ft) apart. According to inscriptions, the towers were constructed by the Afghan sultan Mahmud of Ghazni (971–1030) and his son. In 1842, during the First Afghan War, the present city was taken and its defenses destroyed by the British. Pop. (1982 est.) 32,000.

GHENT (Fr. *Gand;* Flemish *Gent*), city, W Belgium, capital of East Flanders Province, at the confluence of the Scheldt and Lys rivers, near Brussels. The rivers and canals traversing the city divide it into a number of small islands, which are connected by a network of about 200 bridges. Two important ship canals connect Ghent's waterways with the sea. One canal connects the Grand Basin along the N side of the city with the large harbor at Terneuzen on the Scheldt; the other connects Ghent with Bruges and Oostende. Because of these important sea outlets, Ghent is one of the foremost trading and export centers in the North Sea region. Although the city has decreased relatively in industrial importance since the 15th century, when it was one of the chief textile-producing centers in Europe, the number of its manufacturing establishments is large. The principal commodities produced include lace, woolens, leather, soap, paper, cotton and linen goods, machinery, sugar, beer, and tobacco products. Horticulture, both in Ghent and in the surrounding area, is a flourishing industry. Ghent is the site of the flower shows called *Floralies,* held every five years, which attract visitors from all over the world.

The most important educational institution in the city is the State University of Ghent (1817). The city is also the site of a noted art gallery. The Begynhof, or Béguinage, a small walled town containing numerous small houses, 18 convents, and a church, is situated in the suburbs of Saint Amandsberg. It is inhabited by 700 members of the Beguines, a lay sisterhood devoted to charitable work. The Cathedral of Saint Bavon, with a crypt dating from 941, houses the celebrated 12-paneled *Adoration of the Lamb,* painted by the Flemish artists Hubert van Eyck (c. 1370–1426) and Jan van Eyck.

Ghent is mentioned as early as the 7th century,

Historic houses along one of the many canals traversing Ghent.
Belgian Government Information Center

and in the latter half of the 9th century Baldwin I, count of Flanders (r. 864–79), known as Bras de Fer (Fr., "Iron Arm"), built a fortress in Ghent as a defense against the coastal incursions of the Norsemen. The subsequent history of the city is closely integrated with that of Flanders. Seized by France in 1792, Ghent was made part of the Netherlands in 1814. In 1830 it became part of independent Belgium. The city was occupied by German forces during World War I and for most of World War II. Pop. (1988 est.) 232,600.

GHENT, TREATY OF, agreement signed by the U.S. and Great Britain in Ghent, Belgium, on Dec. 24, 1814, concluding the War of 1812 (q.v.) between the two powers. The treaty provided for the return of all captured territory to the country in possession before the outbreak of hostilities. It did not deal with the questions that had been the chief basis of controversy, but made provision for joint commissions to determine and delimit the borders in dispute between the two countries.

GHETTO, formerly a section of a town or city within which Jews were compelled by law to reside. By extension the term came to denote any section inhabited principally or exclusively by Jews. Ghettos arose principally as the result of both the intolerance practiced by Christians and the desire on the part of Jews to maintain their unity and exclusiveness. The first legally established ghetto was set up in Rome, in 1555, by Pope Paul IV. Similar ghettos were established in most of the countries of Europe during the ensuing three centuries. The ghettos (Ger. *Judengasse*) were surrounded by walls, and the gates were locked at night. In many instances Jews were compelled to wear identifying insignia outside the ghettos. The abolition of the ghetto system was brought about largely by the French Revolution and the liberal movements of the 19th century. By 1870 the ghetto at Rome had become the last legally compulsory ghetto remaining in Europe; in that year it was abolished by Victor Emmanuel II, king of Italy. Adolf Hitler caused ghettos to be established in German-occupied countries during World War II as part of his overall plan for annihilating the Jews. In recent years the term *ghetto* has been applied, often derogatorily, to crowded urban areas, lived in primarily by nonwhites. *See also* ANTI-SEMITISM.　　　　　　　　　　　　　　　　N.N.G.

GHIBELLINES. *See* GUELPHS AND GHIBELLINES.

GHIBERTI, Lorenzo (1378–1455), one of the most important early Renaissance sculptors of Florence; his work and writings formed the basis for much of the style and aims of the later High Renaissance.

Originally named Lorenzo di Bartolo, Ghiberti was born in Florence and trained as a goldsmith; in his sculpture he showed lyrical grace and technical perfection as well as a concern for classical clarity of weight and volume. In 1403, competing against such formidable rivals as Filippo Brunelleschi and Jacopo della Quercia, Ghiberti won his first major commission, the making of the second pair of bronze doors for the baptistery of the cathedral of Florence. (The first pair had been made in the early 14th century by Andrea Pisano.) He spent more than 20 years completing them, aided by his students, who included Donatello and Paolo Uccello. Each door contains 14 quatrefoil-framed scenes from the lives of Christ, the Evangelists, and the church fathers. Installed in 1424, the doors were highly praised. Although the reliefs were mainly Gothic in style, the later ones show an increased interest in the antique and in deep pictorial space, with the figures assuming more importance than the drapery. This transition toward Renaissance style is also evident in three bronze statues of saints he made for Or San Michele (1416–24).

Ghiberti developed these ideas intensively after 1425. His reliefs for the cathedral at Siena (1417–27) and his greatest work, the third set of bronze doors for the baptistery at Florence (completed in 1452), show a development toward naturalistic movement, volume, and perspective and a greater idealization of subject. These doors, each portraying five scenes from the Old Testament, were called the "Gates of Paradise" by Michelangelo.

Ghiberti was actively involved in the dissemination of humanist ideas. In the *Commentarii* (1447–48) he gave his autobiography and expounded his views on art. He died in Florence on Dec. 1, 1455.

GHIRLANDAIO, assumed name taken by a family of Florentine painters, whose real name was Bigordi. The appellation *ghirlandaio* ("garland maker") was first applied to Tommaso Bigordi, a 15th-century goldsmith and silversmith noted for his skill in fashioning wreaths of silver for ladies' headdresses. The most important members of the family included the following.

Domenico di Tommaso Bigordi Ghirlandaio (1449–94), son of Tommaso and the outstanding member of the family, born in Florence. He studied painting and mosaic with the noted Florentine painter Alesso Baldovinetti, and his style was also influenced by the Italian Renaissance artists Giotto, Masaccio, Andrea del Castagno, and Andrea del Verrocchio. Except for a period spent in Rome by order of Pope Sixtus IV, Domenico Ghirlandaio lived in Florence, where he became one of the greatest masters of the Florentine school. He brought to its height in the 15th century the realism that is one of the dominating characteristics of that school. Domenico painted religious frescoes and easel pictures but often introduced recognizable Florentine scenery and portraits of contemporary personages attired in the costumes of the time. He is particularly distinguished for his frescoes, among which are *The Calling of Saints Peter and Andrew* (1481–82, Sistine Chapel, Vatican City); his masterpiece, scenes from the life of Saint Francis (1485, Church of Santa Trinità, Florence); and *Legend of the Virgin* and *Life of John the Baptist* (1490, choir of the Church of Santa Maria Novella, Florence). He also painted altarpieces, including *Adoration of the Shepherds* (1485, Santa Trinità) and *Virgin in Glory* (c. 1490, Pinakothek, Munich); and among his easel pictures, all painted in tempera, are *Adoration of the Kings* (1487, Uffizi Gallery, Florence) and *Old Man with His Grandson* (1480, Louvre, Paris). Among Domenico Ghirlandaio's pupils was the Italian Renaissance genius Michelangelo.

Ridolfo Ghirlandaio (1483–1561), son of Domenico. He studied with the Florentine painter Piero di Cosimo. Ridolfo's style was modeled successively after that of Leonardo da Vinci and of Raphael.

GHOSE, Sri Aurobindo (1872–1950), Indian nationalist and mystic philosopher, considered a saint by many Indians. He was born in Calcutta on Aug. 15, 1872, and was educated at the University of Cambridge. Returning to India in 1893, he became an educator and a fiery nationalist agitator. In 1908, suspected of responsibility for terrorist acts in Bengal, Ghose was arrested and prosecuted by the British; however, he was later acquitted.

While in prison, Ghose underwent a religious experience. When released, he abandoned politics, renounced violence, and retired (1910) to Pondicherry in southern India, where he studied Yoga, attracted a devoted group of disciples, and formed an ashram, or religious community, to further spiritual growth. In 1926, having achieved *Sadhana,* or the path of enlightenment, Ghose went into seclusion and gradually ceased to see his disciples. He died in Pondicherry on Dec. 5, 1950.

Ghose's teachings emphasize a two-way path to salvation. Enlightenment comes from the divinity above, but human beings possess a spiritual "supermind" that enables them to reach upward toward illumination. Spiritual perfection is achieved through Yoga practices that lead to the ultimate fusion of these two drives.

Ghose's original ashram remains active in India. His principal writings include *The Life Divine* (1940), *The Human Cycle* (1949), *The Ideal of Human Unity* (1949), and *Essays on the Gita* (1928; repr. 1950).

GHOST, nonmaterial embodiment or essence of an organism, especially of a human being. The term is sometimes used virtually as a synonym for soul or spirit, and in the Christian religion, in the form Holy Ghost (now, more often, Holy Spirit), it has a specialized meaning. More frequently, however, the term *ghost* is applied to an apparition, usually of a dead person, that varies in apparent solidity from a mere foglike mass to a perfect replica of the person. A wraith, in contrast, is the visible spirit of someone still alive. A doppelgänger is a special form of wraith that makes its appearance at a time when the physical body of the subject is observed at some distant place.

In many religions, and particularly in primitive faiths, the belief exists that the spirit wanders away from the body during periods of unconsciousness such as sleep. Such religions also teach that after death the spirit lingers near the body of the dead person. A common practice of groups holding such beliefs is to propitiate the ghosts of the dead by offerings of food, clothing, and other objects that the ghosts may find useful in the spirit world. In many primitive civilizations the personal possessions of a dead man, including his weapons, his pets, and sometimes even his wife, are buried or burned with his body. The practice of ancestor worship, as well as the mourning rites of many modern civilizations, probably originated in the belief in ghosts; *see* FUNERAL RIGHTS AND CUSTOMS.

GHOST DANCE. *See* WOVOKA.

GIACOMETTI, Alberto (1901–66), Swiss sculptor and painter, born in Stampa. After a period of study in Geneva and Rome, Giacometti settled in Paris in 1922. He established himself as one of the leading surrealist sculptors of the 1930s with work that showed a great deal of wit and imagi-

Man Pointing *(1947), sculpture in bronze, 179.1 cm (70.5 in) high, by Alberto Giacometti.*

nation. Perhaps the most outstanding of his surrealist pieces is *The Palace at 4 AM* (1932–33, Museum of Modern Art, New York City), an architectonic skeleton holding suspended figures and objects that expresses the subjectivity and the fragility of the human sense of time and space. In 1948 Giacometti exhibited his works after a 12-year lapse, during which he experimented in sculpture and painting. From his experiments Giacometti evolved a distinctive style of highly expressive, attenuated figures. Infused with a pervasive melancholy, both his paintings and sculptures convey a sense of tenuous existence, as though the figures were constantly threatened with obliteration by the surrounding space. In such paintings as *The Artist's Mother* (1950, Museum of Modern Art), the seated figure seems about to disappear in the web of lines and strokes that delineates the sitting room and its faintly ominous furnishings.

GIAMBOLOGNA (1529–1608), Flemish-Italian sculptor, one of the most influential artists of late 16th-century Mannerism. Originally named Jean Bologne, he was born in Douai, Flanders. He spent two years in Rome (c. 1554–55), where he was strongly influenced by Michelangelo's sculpture. Also called Giovanni da Bologna, Giambologna remained in Italy for the rest of his life, principally in Florence.

Pope Pius IV gave Giambologna his first major commission, for a colossal bronze *Fountain of Neptune* (1566) in Bologna. In his later work, he strove for a strong sense of movement, often based on spirals or twisting lines. A series of bronze statues of Mercury culminated in the renowned "flying" *Mercury* (1580, Bargello, Florence), outstanding for the airy elegance of its pose: the nude figure stands poised on the toes of the left foot, with the right arm raised high in a pointing gesture. *Rape of the Sabine Woman* (1583, Loggia dei Lanzi, Florence), considered his masterpiece, is a complex three-figure work in marble, a compact yet light group spiraling upward from a crouching to a standing to an airborne figure. Giambologna was the most successful sculptor of his age, creating an international Mannerist style that directly influenced succeeding baroque sculpture, particularly the work of Gian Lorenzo Bernini.

GIANNINI, Amadeo Peter (1870–1949), American banker, born in San Jose, Calif. At the age of 13 he left school and entered his stepfather's wholesale food business. He was made a partner in the firm when he was 19 years old. In 1904 he organized the Bank of Italy. Other bankers did not consider him a serious competitor until 1906, when San Francisco was devastated by a calamitous earthquake and fire. On the morning of the disaster Giannini rescued the deposits from his bank in a wagon, driving through the town with $2 million in gold and securities hidden under a load of fruits and vegetables. When the flames subsided, the Bank of Italy opened temporary offices in a waterfront shed, the only bank in the city open for business. Later Giannini began the first big branch banking program in the U.S. by buying up small banks and making them branches of the Bank of Italy. In 1928 he organized and became chairman of the board of directors of the Transamerica Corp., a holding company for all of his interests, including the Bank of Italy, which two years later became the Bank of America National Trust and Savings Association. His bank made loans on crops to California fruit growers and lent large sums to motion picture producers at a time when no other bank would finance films.

By the time of Giannini's death, the Bank of America had become the largest unincorporated bank in the world, with more than 3 million depositors and $6 billion in assets.

GIANT HOGWEED. *See* COW PARSNIP.

GIANT'S CAUSEWAY, rocky promontory on the N coast of Northern Ireland. It consists of thousands of polygonal columns of basalt, ranging to more than 6 m (20 ft) in height. It is thought by geologists to have formed when an ancient lava flow cooled and solidified. Its name is derived from a local legend that the formation was built by giants as part of a roadway to Scotland.

GIAP, Vo Nguyen (1912–   ), Vietnamese general and minister of defense (1945–80), the architect of the Communist military victory in that country. Born in the province of Quangbinh, he studied law at the University of Hanoi, receiving a doctorate in 1937. During the 1930s he joined the Indo-Chinese Communist party, and when it was outlawed in 1939, fled to China, where he became a military aide to Ho Chi Minh. He returned with a Vietnamese army in 1945 and liberated Hanoi from the Japanese. A master of guerrilla war tactics, he later planned and directed the military operations against the French that culminated in their subsequent defeat at the Battle of Dien Bien Phu in 1954. During the 1960s Giap took charge of guerrilla operations against South Vietnam and the U.S. and planned the Tet offensive of 1968, which dealt a severe psychological blow to the American forces. Giap retired from politics in 1982.

GIAUQUE, William Francis (1895–1982), American chemist and Nobel laureate, best known for discovering a method for producing temperatures approaching absolute zero (q.v.) by adiabatic demagnetization. He was a codiscoverer (1929) with Herrick L. Johnston (1898–1965) of the oxygen isotopes of mass 17 and 18. Through his research Giauque found an experimental basis for quantum statistics and the third law of thermodynamics (q.v.). For his work in chemical thermodynamics he received the 1949 Nobel Prize in chemistry.

GIBBON, common name for any of the small anthropoid apes (*see* APE) constituting the genus *Hylobates* and family Hylobatidae. Found in the subequatorial forests of India, Indochina, and the Malay Archipelago, the gibbon is a slender animal with a small, round head and soft, woolly fur. It is good-natured and easily tamed. The gibbon's most notable characteristic is its long arms, by which it swings from tree to tree with great agility, using its hands as hooks rather than grasping the limbs. A large specimen stands about 85 cm (about 33 in) high; the arm span is nearly twice as long. The gibbon is the only anthropoid ape to walk on its hind limbs only, usually raising its arms for balance. Gibbons are monogamous; the young, born singly, remain with the family group until they are five or six years old. The animals feed on birds, birds' eggs, fruit, leaves, insects, and spiders. They are quiet during the day but commonly howl at sunrise and sunset. About nine species of gibbons exist. The silver gibbon, or wou-wou, *H. moloch,* of Java, is ashy gray; the whitehanded gibbon, or lar, *H. lar,* of the Malay Peninsula, is distinguished by its white hands and feet and its musical howl.

The largest gibbon is the siamang (q.v.), *H. syndactylus,* of Malaysia and Sumatra. In 1979 the Grant Park Zoo in Atlanta, Ga., reported a four-year-old female "siabon," the hybrid offspring of a male silver gibbon and a female siamong; this was the first known mating involving different primate species.

For further information on this topic, see the Bibliography in volume 28, sections 475, 482.

GIBBON, Edward (1737–94), the greatest English historian of his time and author of *The History of the Decline and Fall of the Roman Empire.*

Gibbon was born April 27, 1737, in Putney (now part of London), the eldest of seven children in an upper-middle-class family; the other six all died in infancy. Gibbon himself was a sickly child and had almost no formal schooling. He was, however, an avid and omnivorous reader. By the time he was approaching age 15, his health suddenly improved, and his father entered him in Magdalen College, University of Oxford, for what he later called in his *Memoirs* "the most idle and unprofitable 14 months of my life." Study of early Christianity led him to embrace Roman Catholicism in June 1753, thus barring him from the university. His father swiftly packed him off to Lausanne, Switzerland, in care of a Calvinist pastor, who by Christmas, 1754, had reconciled him to Protestantism. (The *Memoirs* termed it acquiescence.)

Gibbon remained in Switzerland for nearly five years. He rounded out his classical education, adding the study of logic and Greek to his Latin. He conversed with savants, did some writing in French, and for the first and only time he fell in love. On his return to England in 1758, however, his father put an end to the engagement. By this time he had determined to devote his life to scholarship and writing. After two dreary years in the Hampshire militia, he left again for Europe, and on Oct. 15, 1764, sitting among the ruins of Rome, "the idea of writing the decline and fall of the city first started" to engage his mind. In another two years his project was clear, and he began to set down on paper 1300 years of history.

Gibbon also lived the life of an English gentleman. He was elected to Parliament in 1774, where he sat for 12 speechless years. Excessively obese, short (less than five ft), overdressed, and vain, he was often the butt of ridicule. London's intellectual circles, however, admired his clear mind and absolute control of emotion. Those qualities, plus the skill and beauty of his writing, were ac-

Edward Gibbon

claimed when the first volume of *Decline and Fall* appeared in 1776. He ignored outcries against his religious skepticism (he had dealt rather coolly with early Christianity), but he stoutly defended all attacks on his facts. The next two volumes, which bring to an end the period of the Western Empire (to about AD 480), came out in 1781. The final 1000 years of the empire in the East unfold in his last three volumes, completed in Lausanne in 1787 and published in 1788. Gibbon died Jan. 16, 1794, in London.

Despite the availability of new factual data and a recognition of Gibbon's Western bias, *Decline and Fall* is still read and enjoyed. Gibbon's verdict on the Roman historian Tacitus, whose writings, he said, "will instruct the last generation of mankind," applies equally to his own work.

GIBBONS, Grinling (1648–1720), English sculptor, best known for his superbly decorative carved woodwork in palaces, country houses, churches, and colleges (*see* WOOD CARVING). His mantels, chimneypieces, wall panels, and screens contain most of the common motifs of the time—fruit and flowers, small animals, cherubs' heads—in complex and finely carved groupings. Examples of Gibbons's work are found at Windsor Castle, Hampton Court, Trinity College (Oxford), and country mansions such as Petworth and Belton. He also produced statuary in marble and bronze, but these stiffly classical pieces fell short of the exuberant richness of his woodcarving, which set a pattern for English baroque interior decoration.

GIBBONS, James (1834–1921), American Roman Catholic prelate, born in Baltimore, Md., and educated at Saint Charles College, near Baltimore, and at Saint Mary's Seminary, in that city. He was ordained to the priesthood in 1861, and later that year he was appointed pastor of Saint Bridget's Church, in a suburb of Baltimore. In 1868 he became vicar apostolic of North Carolina, with the rank and title of bishop, and in 1877 he was appointed archbishop of Baltimore. In 1884 Pope Leo XIII made him apostolic delegate (representative of the Holy See) to the Third Plenary Council of Baltimore, a council of all the American bishops of the Roman Catholic church. In 1886 Gibbons was made a cardinal. His first important achievement in this post was the establishment of the Catholic University of America at Washington, D.C. Gibbons's writings include *The Faith of Our Fathers* (1876), a simple explanation of Catholic doctrines and practices; *Our Christian Heritage* (1889); and *The Ambassador of Christ* (1896).

GIBBONS, Orlando (1583–1625), one of the leading English composers of the late Renaissance. Born in Oxford, he became organist in the king's chapel (1604), virginalist (harpsichordist) at the royal court (1619), and organist at Westminster Abbey (1623).

Gibbons's anthems are among the glories of Anglican church music. His anthems for chorus throughout include "Hosanna to the Son of David" and "O Clap Your Hands"; those for choir and solo voices include "This Is the Record of John" and "Behold Thou Hast Made My Days." Among his madrigals are the cynical "The Silver Swan" and the somber "What Is Our Life?" His works for virginal include stylized dance pieces, such as the "Pavan Lord Salisbury," contrapuntal fantasies, and variations on popular tunes.

GIBBS, James (1682–1754), English architect, whose conservative eclectic style combined the restrained baroque tradition of Sir Christopher Wren with elements of exuberant Italian Mannerism. His best-known buildings are the Church of Saint Martin-in-the-Fields (1721–26, London), with its temple-front portico and high steeple rising from the roof line, and the Radcliffe Library (1739–49) at Oxford, with its imposing circular rotunda and high dome. His designs, extensively illustrated in his *Book of Architecture* (1728), were widely imitated in England and America, for instance, in New York City's Saint Paul's Chapel (1764–66).

GIBBS, J(osiah) Willard (1839–1903), American mathematical physicist, born in New Haven, Conn., and educated at Yale University and in Paris, Berlin, and Heidelberg. He was professor of mathematical physics at Yale from 1871 until his death. Between 1876 and 1878 Gibbs wrote a series of papers collectively entitled *On the Equi-*

librium of Heterogeneous Substances, considered one of the greatest achievements in physical science in the 19th century and the foundation of the science of physical chemistry. In these papers Gibbs applied thermodynamics to the interpretation of physiochemical phenomena and showed the explanation and interrelationship of what had been known only as isolated, inexplicable facts. The phase rule is among the theorems discussed. Gibbs's papers on thermodynamics were published in *Transactions of the Connecticut Academy,* but because of their mathematical complexity and their appearance in an obscure journal, scientists in the U.S. did not recognize their value. *On the Equilibrium of Heterogeneous Substances* was translated into German in 1891 and into French in 1899; and its theorems were developed and used in Europe some years before American chemists realized their importance. Gibbs was awarded the Copley medal of the Royal Society of London for Improving Natural Knowledge in 1901.

Gibbs also did outstanding work in statistical mechanics, in vector analysis, and in the electromagnetic theory of light. His *Scientific Papers* (1906) and *Collected Works* (1928) were assembled and published posthumously.

GIBEON (Heb., "hill city"), an ancient city in Palestine, the site of the modern village of El-Jib, northwest of Jerusalem.

According to the Bible (see Josh. 9), the Gibeonites tricked Joshua, the leader of the Hebrews, into signing a treaty with them in order to save themselves from the destruction that was the fate of Jericho. When their trickery was discovered, they were condemned to be "slaves" and "hewers of wood and drawers of water." Gibeon is best known as the place where the sun stood still at Joshua's command (see Josh. 10:12) and as the site later chosen by Solomon (see 1 Kings 3:4) as one of the "high places" where sacrifices were made. It was also at Gibeon, in an earlier time, that in an outburst of enthusiasm or patriotism Saul ordered a general massacre of the inhabitants; this deed was atoned for after Saul's death by David, who yielded seven of Saul's descendants to the Gibeonites for hanging.

G.I. BILL OF RIGHTS. *See* VETERANS ADMINISTRATION.

GIBRALTAR, British dependency, comprising the rocky promontory, called the Rock of Gibraltar (anc. Calpe), that forms the southernmost point of the Iberian Peninsula and commands the W entrance to the Mediterranean Sea. The Strait of Gibraltar (*see* GIBRALTAR, STRAIT OF) separates the Rock from the coast of North Africa. Connecting the Rock with the Spanish mainland is a narrow,

An unusual view of the Rock of Gibraltar, which stands at the southern tip of the Iberian Peninsula, dominating the Strait of Gibraltar.　　　　Ingelborg Lippman

sandy isthmus containing a neutral zone that separates the British dependency from Spain. Gibraltar has an area of 5.8 sq km (2.3 sq mi).

The Land and Population. The Rock of Gibraltar is composed of limestone. It arises abruptly from the sea in the E; its slope is more gradual on the W. The maximum elevation is 426 m (1396 ft). Aloes, cacti, capers, and asparagus grow in the crevices. Certain parts contain grassy glens, in which pigeons, partridges, woodcocks, and the Barbary ape (the only wild monkey of Europe) are found. Among the natural caves of the promontory, Saint Michael's, with an entrance 335 m (1100 ft) above the sea, is the largest. Climate is temperate, with temperatures averaging 15.6° C (60° F) in winter and 21.1° C (70° F) in summer. Average annual rainfall is 889 mm (35 in).

The population of Gibraltar (1988) was 30,127. The overall population density was 5194 persons per sq km (about 13,099 per sq mi). Most of the civilian inhabitants are of Portuguese, Italian, Maltese, English, or Spanish descent.

The official language is English, although Spanish is widely spoken. About 75% of the population is Roman Catholic, 8% is Anglican, and 9% Muslim. Education is compulsory between the ages of 5 and 15. In the late 1980s about 4680 students were attending about 18 elementary, secondary, and special schools.

Economy and Government. Because few natural resources are found, the major factors of the economy are the processing of food products, tourism, and shipping. A free port and gambling concessions attract tourists. The Admiralty harbor is an important fortress and strategic naval base. The Gibraltar pound is at par with the pound sterling.

Gibraltar is administered by a governor, who is the representative of the Crown. The governor is advised by the Gibraltar Council, which consists of five elected and four ex officio members. The Council of Ministers makes recommendations to the Gibraltar Council. Legislative powers are vested in the House of Assembly, which consists of a speaker (appointed by the governor), 15 elected members, and 2 ex officio members. About 1800 British troops were maintained in Gibraltar in the late 1980s.

History. Gibraltar and ancient Abila (now Mount Acho at Ceuta, a Spanish exclave in Morocco) form the classical Pillars of Hercules, which were crowned with silver columns by Phoenician mariners to mark the limits of safe navigation for the ancient Mediterranean peoples. The Rock of Gibraltar was named Jabal Tariq (Arab., "Mount of Tariq") in honor of the Muslim general Tariq ibn-Ziyad (d. about 720), who invaded Spain in 711. In 1309 Gibraltar was captured by the Castilians but was regained by the Moors in 1333 and held until 1462, when it finally passed from Moorish possession. In 1502, it was annexed to the Spanish crown.

After the sacking of Gibraltar by the Algerian corsair Barbarossa II (Khayr ad-Din, 1483?–1546) in 1540, the Rock was furnished with strong defenses by command of Holy Roman Emperor Charles V. On July 24, 1704, during the War of the Spanish Succession, Gibraltar was captured by combined English and Dutch forces. The English commander took possession in the name of Queen Anne. Nine years later the acquisition was formalized by the Peace of Utrecht.

During the European phase of the American War of Independence, the Spanish, who had entered the conflict against the British, imposed a stringent blockade against Gibraltar as part of an unsuccessful siege that lasted for more than three years (1779–83). On Sept. 14, 1782, the British destroyed the floating batteries of the French and Spanish besiegers. In February 1783 the signing of peace preliminaries ended the siege. In 1830, Gibraltar was named a crown colony.

Barbary apes on the Rock of Gibraltar. According to an old tradition, the British will hold the rock as long as the monkeys remain there.
Ingelborg Lippman

In World War I, the Rock served as a strategic base for Allied naval units and was used as a coaling station for transports en route to theaters of war in the eastern Mediterranean. During the Spanish civil war (1936–39), the town of Gibraltar served as a haven for large numbers of Spanish refugees.

When Great Britain gave almost complete control over internal affairs to the dependency in 1964, Spain contended that under terms of the Peace of Utrecht it should acquire sovereignty over Gibraltar. The British step led to strained relations between the two countries and economic isolation of the dependency by Spain. In a referendum held on Sept. 10, 1967, the people of Gibraltar voted overwhelmingly to remain under British rule and to reject ties with Spain. Spain, however, pursued its claim and in 1969 closed its border to the 5000 Spanish workers who crossed it daily on their way to work in Gibraltar. The dependency consequently adapted its economy, which benefited from a general diversification, increased tourism, and military spending by the British.

Toward the end of the 1970s Spain began to show more flexibility with regard to Gibraltar. In 1980 an agreement in principle was reached on the reopening of the border, but it was not implemented due to labor problems. It was further delayed in 1981, when the prince and princess of Wales selected the Rock as the first stop on their honeymoon, a choice that Spain regarded as an affront. In 1982, however, both countries again committed themselves to resolving their differences, and in February 1985, for the first time in 16 years, the border with the Spanish mainland was fully reopened.

GIBRALTAR, STRAIT OF, narrow passage connecting the Mediterranean Sea on the E with the Atlantic Ocean on the W, separating N Africa from the Rock of Gibraltar on the southernmost point of the Iberian Peninsula. The strait is about 64 km (about 40 mi) long and varies in width from about 14 to 39 km (about 9 to 24 mi). A channel 8 km (5 mi) wide, traversing the center of the strait, has a depth of about 305 m (about 1000 ft). A continuous central current enters from the Atlantic Ocean, and tidal currents ebb and flow along the European and African shores. An undercurrent flowing westerly carries off the surplus waters of the Mediterranean Sea. The eastern end of the Strait of Gibraltar is flanked by the Pillars of Hercules.

GIBSON, Althea (1927–), American athlete, born near Sumter, S.C., and educated at Florida Agricultural and Mechanical University. At the age of 15 she was New York State black girls' singles tennis champion; this was the first of many titles she would hold during the next 15 years. In 1957 she won the All-England women's singles championship at Wimbledon, the U.S. women's clay court singles championship at River Forest, Ill., and the U.S. Lawn Tennis Association national women's championship at Forest Hills in New York City. For these achievements she was named woman athlete of the year for 1957 by the Associated Press. After repeating as Wimbledon and U.S. national champion in 1958, she played professional exhibition tennis in 1959–60 and joined the Ladies Professional Golf Association in 1963. She was named in 1971 to the National Lawn Tennis Hall of Fame.

GIBSON, Charles Dana (1867–1944), American illustrator, born in Roxbury, Mass. Gibson's pen-and-ink drawings for the humor magazine *Life* and for *Scribner's, Century,* and *Harper's* made him one of the most popular U.S. illustrators in the early 20th century. His subject matter was generally the life, particularly that of women, of the wealthy classes of American society. His pictorial conception of the ideal American female, a tall, slim-waisted young woman characterized by a calm and stately bearing, became world famous as the "Gibson girl."

GIDE, André (1869–1951), French writer, whose novels, plays, and autobiographical works are distinguished for their exhaustive analysis of individual efforts at self-realization and Protestant ethical concepts; together with his critical works they had a profound influence on French writing and philosophy.

Gide was born Nov. 22, 1869, in Paris into a strict Protestant family and educated at the École Alsacienne and the Lycée Henri IV. In his first book, *Les cahiers d'Andre Walter* (The Notebooks of Andre Walter, 1891), Gide described the religious and romantic idealism of an unhappy young man. He then became associated with the Symbolists, but in 1894 began to develop an individualistic approach and style. In *Les nourritures terrestres* (The Fruits of the Earth, 1897) he preached the doctrine of active hedonism. Thereafter his works were devoted to examining the problems of individual freedom and responsibility, from many points of view. *The Immoralist* (1902; trans. 1930) and *Strait Is the Gate* (1909; trans. 1924) are studies of individual ethical concepts in conflict with conventional morality. *The Caves of the Vatican* (trans. 1927 and also published in English as *Lafcadio's Adventures*), in which Gide ridiculed the possibility of complete personal independence, appeared in 1914. The idyll *La symphonie pastorale* (The Pastoral Symphony, 1919; produced as a motion picture, 1947) dealt with love and responsibility. Gide examined the problems of middle-class families and of adolescence in *If It Die* (1920; trans. 1935) and in the popular novel of youth in Paris, *The Counterfeiters* (1925; trans. 1928).

Gide's preoccupation with individual moral responsibility led him to seek public office. After filling municipal positions in Normandy, he became a special envoy of the colonial ministry in 1925–26 and wrote two books describing conditions in the French African colonies. These reports, *Voyage au Congo* (1927) and *Retour du Tchad* (1927), were instrumental in bringing about reforms in French colonial law. They were published together in English as *Travels in the Congo* (1929). In the early 1930s Gide had expressed his admiration and hope for the "experiment" in the USSR, but after a journey in the Soviet Union he reported his disillusionment in *Return from the U.S.S.R.* (1936; trans. 1937).

Many of Gide's critical studies appeared in *La Nouvelle Revue Française,* a literary periodical that he helped to found in 1909 and that became a dominant influence in French intellectual circles. These essays are principally analyses of the psychology of creative artists.

Besides writing the verse dramas *Le roi Candaule* (The King Candaule, 1901) and *Saül* (1903), Gide translated Shakespeare's *Antony and Cleopatra* and *Hamlet* into French. He also made distinguished translations of *Marriage of Heaven and Hell* by the early 19th-century poet William Blake and of excerpts from the works of the mid–19th-century American poet Walt Whitman. The publication of Gide's *Journal* (4 vol., 1939–51), a series of literary diaries, excited worldwide critical interest. Gide received the 1947 Nobel Prize in literature. He died Feb. 19, 1951, in Paris.

GIDEON (Heb., "hewer" or "warrior"), in the Old Testament, a hero of Israel. During Gideon's youth the people of Israel were oppressed by the Midianites, nomadic people who had invaded Palestine from the Arabian Desert. Acting on a divine exhortation, Gideon summoned the Israelites and, with a small band of followers, attacked the Midianites at Mount Gilboa, pursuing them to the Jordan River. Following the victory, the Israelites offered Gideon a crown as a reward for his leadership, but he refused the symbol of power because of his belief that God was the king of Israel (see Judg. 6–8). Gideon asked only for the many golden earrings captured from the enemy. From them he made an ephod, or ceremonial garment. Under his rule Israel enjoyed 40 years of peace.

GIELGUD, Sir (Arthur) John (1904–), English actor, director, and producer. Born in London and educated at the Westminster School and the Royal Academy of Dramatic Art, Gielgud made

André Gide   Gullers, Stockholm

his stage debut in London in 1921 with the Old Vic Repertory Company. His success in the title role of Richard II in 1929 established him as a leading Shakespearean actor. He is perhaps best known for his interpretation of the title role in *Hamlet,* which he first played in 1929 and has repeated many times. Gielgud also became a director of Shakespearean and other plays. In 1959 he performed in *The Ages of Man,* a program of readings from the works of Shakespeare. Roles in contemporary drama include Edward Albee's *Tiny Alice* (1964) and *Home* (1970) by David Storey (1933–   ). He has appeared in many motion pictures, notably as Cassius in *Julius Caesar* (1952) and as the Duke of Clarence in *Richard II* (1955). Other films include *Becket* (1964), *Murder on the Orient Express* (1974), *Chariots of Fire* (1980), and *Arthur* (1981; Academy Award for best supporting actor). Notable was his role as the narrator's father, Edward Ryder, in the television series *Brideshead Revisited* (1981). His autobiography, *Early Stages,* published in 1939, was revised in 1976. He also collaborated in the writing of *Gielgud: An Actor and His Time* (1980). He was knighted in 1953.

GIEREK, Edward (1913–   ), Polish Communist party leader. Born in Będzin, near Katowice, he grew up in France, where, at the age of 13, he became a miner. He joined the French Communist party in 1931 and, during World War II, fought the Germans with the Belgian Communist underground. Returning to Poland in 1948, he obtained a degree as a mining engineer (1954) and rose through the Communist hierarchy to become party boss (1957–70) of Katowice, Poland's most important industrial region. When price increases led to riots in 1970, he replaced Władysław Gomułka as the party's first secretary. Similar unrest in 1980 forced him in turn to relinquish the post. Expelled from the party in July 1981, he was arrested the following December and "interned" for a year.

GIESEKING, Walter Wilhelm (1895–1956), German pianist, whose interpretations of classical and impressionist works were noted for their attention to detail and masterly shading and color. Born to German parents in Lyon, France, he studied in Germany, beginning his international career in 1923. After World War II his performances were controversial until he was cleared of charges of cultural collaboration with the Nazi government of Germany. Gieseking's recordings include works of the French composers Claude Debussy and Maurice Ravel and the complete piano sonatas of W. A. Mozart. He also performed 20th-century music by the Austrian-born composer Arnold Schoenberg and others.

Sir John Gielgud   Camera Press–Photo Trends

GIESSEN, city, W central Germany, in Hesse, on the Lahn R., near Frankfurt am Main. It is a transportation and manufacturing center, producing rubber and leather goods, chemicals, machinery, furniture, tobacco products, and beer. Giessen dates from about the 12th century. It is the site of Justus Liebig University (1607), at which the German chemist Justus von Liebig established (19th cent.) the first practical laboratory for the teaching of chemistry. The city suffered heavy damage during World War II. Pop. (1989 est.) 71,800.

GIFT, in law, voluntary transfer or conveyance of property made without consideration or compensation. Gifts are generally divided into two classes, *inter vivos* and *causa mortis.*

A gift *inter vivos* (between living persons who expect to continue living) must fulfill the following conditions in order to be legally binding: (1) the donor must be deemed competent, or mentally sound, to make a contract, and the donee must have legal existence to take and hold the gift; (2) the donor must act voluntarily; (3) the transfer must be complete, with nothing left undone; (4) the subject matter of the gift must be delivered by the donor to the donee during their lifetimes, and it must be accepted by the donee; certain symbolical or token deliveries, such as delivery of the key to the box containing the gift, are recognized as valid; and (5) the intent to make an immediate gift must be clear and unmistakable, and the transfer must take immediate and permanent effect.

A gift *causa mortis* (on condition of death) is one made by the donor in apprehension of death. The gift is revocable, or retrievable, by the donor during his or her lifetime, and it is revoked or defeated by the physical recovery of the donor. To be legally binding a gift *causa mortis* must fulfill the following conditions: (1) delivery must be satisfactorily proven, with intent to pass title to the donee conditionally, by a donor apprehending his or her own death; (2) the donee must accept the gift; (3) the death of the donor from the apprehended cause must occur; and (4) the donee must survive. Gifts *causa mortis* of real property are not recognized.

GIFT TAX, in tax law, federal tax levied since 1932 on transfers and conveyances of property by gift. As defined in the Internal Revenue Code, the tax applies whether the property transferred is real or personal; whether the gift is direct or indirect; and whether the transfer is in trust or otherwise. Thus a transfer subject to the gift tax may be effected by a declaration of trust, the forgiveness of a debt, the assignment of a judgment, the assignment of the benefits of a contract of insurance, or the transfer of cash or securities. The gift tax applies to all property, including federal, state, or municipal bonds that are exempted from other taxes. In the case of citizens or residents of the U.S., the tax applies to any property transferred by gift, no matter where the property may be. Gifts to charitable organizations, schools, churches, government bodies, and certain other organizations are exempt.

Payment of the tax is the responsibility of the donor, who must file a gift-tax return with the Internal Revenue Service. The gift-tax law was designed to prevent escape from transfer or estate taxes, while encouraging lifetime gifts.

The Economic Recovery Tax Act of 1981 changed many of the provisions of earlier gift-tax legislation. The new law eliminated the marital deduction; beginning in 1982, a person may make unlimited tax-free gifts to a spouse. In addition, each year a donor may give to any number of donees gifts of up to $10,000 each. These gifts are excluded from the amount subject to tax. Gifts made by a husband or wife to others may be reported as if made one-half by each spouse—that is, each tax-free gift may equal $20,000. A gift of any amount used to pay medical expenses or tuition at an educational institution is also exempt from taxation.

GIFU, city, Japan, central Honshu Island, capital of Gifu Prefecture, on the Nagara R., near Nagoya. The city is a railroad and manufacturing center. The chief industries are the manufacture of paper goods and textiles. In summer trout fishing with cormorants is popular here. Gifu was rebuilt after its destruction by an earthquake in 1891. Pop. (1988 est.) 407,800.

GIGANTISM, excessive symmetrical growth, especially of the arms and legs, accompanied by a corresponding growth in height of the entire body. In humans, when gigantism begins in childhood, before normal ossification has been completed, it is usually caused by overactivity of the anterior pituitary gland in production of the growth hormone (q.v.). Hereditary defects that prevent normal ossification at the time of puberty, and thus permit continued growth, may also cause a type of gigantism. Because the growth hormone depresses the secretory powers of the gonads, gigantism is often accompanied by weakened sexual function and is then called eunuchoid gigantism. Gigantism may occur, however, without disturbance in sex function. Individuals affected by either type of gigantism are muscularly weak.

Acromegaly (q.v.), a related condition caused by excessive production of the pituitary growth hormone, occurs in the third decade of life. It usually results in excessive growth of the hands, feet, and chin.

See ENDOCRINE SYSTEM; PITUITARY GLAND.

GIGLI, Beniamino (1890–1957), Italian tenor, regarded as the successor to the Italian tenor Enrico Caruso, because of his sweet lyric tenor voice, known for its smoothness, power, and fluency. Trained in Rome, he made his debut in 1914 and sang with the Metropolitan Opera in New York City in 1920–32. He is best known for his roles in operas of such Italian composers as Giuseppe Verdi and Giacomo Puccini; his most famous role was Faust in *Mefistofele* by Arrigo Boito (1842–1918). He was also praised in the title role of *Lohengrin,* by the German composer Richard Wagner.

GIGUE. *See* JIG.

GIJÓN, city and seaport, NW Spain, in Asturias Province, on the Bay of Biscay, near the city of Oviedo. Coal, copper, iron, zinc, and other minerals, as well as fish and agricultural products, are exported from Gijón. Industrial establishments in the city include foundries, textile and paper mills, oil and sugar refineries, and tobacco, chemical, glass, and porcelain factories. Gijón is thought to be the ancient Roman town of Gigia. It was captured by the Moors in the early 8th century; later in the same century, however, it was one of the first cities to be reconquered by Christian forces. In 1395 it was destroyed by fire. During the Spanish civil war (1936–39), the capture of the city by the Nationalists in October 1937 completed the fighting in NW Spain. Gijón has the most important roadstead on the N Spanish coast between the ports of Santander, on the E, and El Ferrol del Caudillo, on the W. The construction of the port was begun in 1480; it was fortified in the latter half of the 16th century, and in 1788 it was equipped to handle West Indian trade. Pop. (1986) 259,226.

GILA, river of the U.S., rising in the mountains of SW New Mexico and flowing westward across Arizona to join the Colorado R., near Yuma. For the greater part of its total course, which is about 1014 km (about 630 mi), the Gila flows through mountain canyons. The lower part of its course is through open and comparatively level country, where the climate of the river valley is semitropical and the land is made fertile by irrigation from the river. Coolidge Dam, on the Gila in E Arizona, impounds water for the irrigation of the Casa Grande Valley around Florence and Casa Grande. Numerous remains of prehistoric Indian dwellings, among which are those contained in the Gila Cliff Dwellings and Casa Grande national monuments, are situated along the banks of the river or of its tributaries. In addition, the river passes through the San Carlos, Gila River, and Gila Bend Indian reservations.

GILA CLIFF DWELLINGS NATIONAL MONUMENT, SW New Mexico, established in 1907. The monument preserves three groups of Indian cliff dwellings that were inhabited from about 1100 to about 1300. Located in the canyon of a tributary of the West Fork of the Gila R., the well-preserved dwellings were constructed in natural cavities in the canyon wall. Most were probably two stories high and contained about 35 rooms; the original masonry still stands in several caves. Area, 2.2 sq km (0.8 sq mi).

GILA MONSTER, common name of *Heloderma suspectum,* the only poisonous lizard in the U.S. and one of the only two known poisonous lizards in the world. It is found in desert areas of Arizona, Nevada, Utah, and New Mexico, especially around the Gila River. The adult lizard is between 46 and 61 cm (18 and 24 in) in length. The body is often strikingly colored. On a black background are numerous tubercles, or beads, usually pink, orange, yellow, or white, and the black head is marbled with pink. The tongue is forked, broad, and flat. The Gila monster is heavily built and moves slowly, on four short legs, dragging a thick, short, blunt tail, in which food is stored. It can live for months on this reserve.

Gila monsters eat small rodents, ants, and the eggs of other desert reptiles. The Gila monsters in captivity have shown a fondness for eggs of snakes and other lizard species. The females are oviparous, laying tough-shelled eggs about the size of hen eggs. A dozen or so of these eggs are laid in a wide hole in moist sand, covered, and abandoned. The young hatch in a month.

Gila monster, Heloderma suspectum   Allan D. Cruickshank–National Audubon Society

The poison of the Gila monster is secreted by glands in the lower jaw and flows out along grooves on the external surface of the teeth. The venom attacks the nerve centers controlling the heart. Gila monsters strike quickly and then hang on tenaciously, rolling over on their backs to allow the poison to flow down into the wound and chewing to inflict further lacerations. The bite is occasionally fatal to human beings.

The other poisonous lizard is the beaded lizard (q.v.), *H. horridum*, a closely related species found in Mexico and other parts of Central America. This species has a black head and a yellow and black body.

For further information on this topic, see the Bibliography in volume 28, sections 470-71.

GILBERT, Cass (1858-1934), American architect, born in Zanesville, Ohio, and educated at the Massachusetts Institute of Technology and in Europe. He entered the firm of McKim, Mead & White in New York City in 1880 and in 1882 established an independent architectural practice in St. Paul, Minn., where he designed the Roman baroque State Capitol in 1896. In 1899 he returned to New York; he submitted the winning design in a competition for the U.S. Customs Building in New York City, built in 1907. Gilbert designed distinctive structures in many American cities, the most famous being the Woolworth Building (1909-13) in New York. This 60-story building, the tallest in the world until 1930, is a triumph of Gothic Revival architecture adapted to 20th-century technology.

Gilbert's later structures, which are distinguished for their individual adaptations of eclectic architectural styles, include the Detroit Public Library (1921), the Supreme Court Building (1924-35) in Washington, D.C., and the State Capitol in Charleston, W.Va. (1924-32).

GILBERT, Sir Humphrey (1539?-83), English navigator and soldier, who annexed Newfoundland for the British crown and devised brilliant, if unsuccessful, colonization schemes.

A half brother, on his mother's side, of Sir Walter Raleigh, Gilbert was born near Dartmouth about 1539; he was educated at Eton College and the University of Oxford. His family wished him to become a lawyer, but he joined the English army instead. He saw active service (1562-64) in France during the French religious wars and in 1566 was commissioned a captain in the English army in Ireland. He was appointed governor of Munster, Ireland, in 1569 and in the following year was knighted. He served (1571) in Parliament and was sent (1572) to the Netherlands with an English force in an unsuccessful attempt to aid the Dutch Protestant revolt against Spain.

Gilbert spent the period from 1572 to 1578 in retirement, mainly engaged in writing. As early as 1566, and again a year later, he petitioned Queen Elizabeth I of England to be allowed to seek a northeast or northwest passage to the Orient. In consequence, during his period of literary activity his most important production was *A Discourse of a Discovery for a New Passage to Cataia* (1576). In 1578 his efforts were finally rewarded by a royal charter granting the privileges of exploration and colonization in North America. Gilbert and Raleigh fitted out an expedition the same year, but their ships were dispersed by the Spanish off the coast of Africa, and they were forced to return. A second expedition sailed from Plymouth in 1583 and, after a voyage of 50 days, reached Newfoundland, where Gilbert founded the first English colony in America near the present city of Saint John's. The colonists were mutinous, however, and the expedition returned to England. On the return voyage, Gilbert sailed in the small 9-metric-ton frigate, the *Squirrel*, rather than in his 36-metric-ton flagship, the *Golden Hind*. In a storm off the Azores, the *Squirrel* was lost in September 1583.

GILBERT, William (1544-1603), English physicist and physician, known primarily for his original experiments in the nature of electricity and magnetism. He was born in Colchester and educated at Saint John's College, University of Cambridge. He began to practice medicine in London in 1573 and in 1601 was appointed physician to Elizabeth I, queen of England.

Gilbert found that many substances had the power to attract light objects when rubbed, and he applied the term *electric* to the force these substances exert after being rubbed. He was the first to use the terms *electric force, electric attraction,* and *magnetic pole.* Perhaps Gilbert's most important contribution was the experimental demonstration of the magnetic nature of the earth. The unit of magnetomotive force, the gilbert, was named after him. He was also the first exponent in England of the Copernican system of celestial mechanics, and he postulated that fixed stars were not all at the same distance from the earth. His most important work was *Of Magnets, Magnetic Bodies, and the Great Magnet of the Earth* (1600; trans. 1890), probably the first great scientific work written in England.

GILBERT, Sir William Schwenck (1836-1911), English playwright, born in London, and educated principally at the University of London. Although trained as an attorney, Gilbert turned early to writing, producing humorous poetry, later published as the *Bab Ballads* (1869 and 1873), and several comedies. He is best known for his long collaboration, from 1871 to 1896, with the English composer Sir Arthur Sullivan. Their efforts resulted in the creation of 14 comic operas, which were produced by the noted theatrical manager Richard D'Oyly Carte; they rank among the best and most popular works ever written in this genre. In his librettos Gilbert created fantastically absurd characters and paradoxical stage situations and employed pointed but never bitter social and political satire. Known as the Savoy operas (after the London theater that was built to stage them), they include *Thespis* (1871), *Trial by Jury* (1875), *The Sorcerer* (1877), *H.M.S. Pinafore* (1878), *The Pirates of Penzance* (1879), *Patience* (1881), *Iolanthe* (1882), *Princess Ida* (1884), *The Mikado* (1885), *Ruddigore* (1887), *The Yeomen of the Guard* (1888), *The Gondoliers* (1889), *Utopia, Limited* (1893), and *The Grand Duke* (1896). Gilbert also collaborated with other English composers, notably with Sir Edward German (1862–1936) on the opera *Fallen Fairies, or the Wicked World* (1909).

GILBERT ISLANDS. See KIRIBATI.

GILDING. See FURNITURE.

GILEAD, name appearing more than 100 times in the Old Testament and referring to geographical sites and to the names of tribes and specific people. The most frequent mention of Gilead concerns geographical designations. It is the name of a mountainous but fertile region between the Jordan River on the west, the Arabian plateau on the east, the plateau of Moab on the south, and the Bashan region on the north; it corresponds to parts of modern Jordan. Gilead was known for its "balm" (see Gen. 37:25; Jer. 8:22, 46:11), aromatic resin with medicinal qualities, derived from plants that apparently thrived there. Gilead is also the name of a mountain (914 m/3597 ft above sea level) west of the Jordan River, in central Palestine. The grandson of Manasseh, the elder son of the Hebrew leader Joseph, was also named Gilead.

GILGAL, name of several geographical locations mentioned in the Old Testament. It was the name of the first camping site of the Israelites after their crossing of the Jordan River, near the city of Jericho. Gilgal was also the city visited by the Hebrew prophets Elisha and Elijah. It is identified with a modern village near Baitin, the biblical Bethel.

GILGAMESH EPIC, an important Middle Eastern literary work, written in cuneiform on 12 clay tablets about 2000 BC. This heroic poem is named for its hero, Gilgamesh, a tyrannical Babylonian king who ruled the city of Erech (now Warka, Iraq). According to the myth, the gods respond to the prayers of the oppressed citizenry of Erech

and send a wild, brutish man, Enkidu, to challenge Gilgamesh to a wrestling match. When the match ends with neither being a clear victor, Gilgamesh and Enkidu become close friends. They journey together and share many adventures. Accounts of their heroism and bravery in slaying dangerous beasts spread to many lands.

When the two travelers return to Erech, Ishtar (guardian deity of the city) proclaims her love for the heroic Gilgamesh. When he rejects her, she sends the Bull of Heaven to destroy the city. Gilgamesh and Enkidu kill the bull, and, as punishment for his participation, the gods doom Enkidu to die. After Enkidu's death, Gilgamesh seeks out the wise man Utnapishtim to learn the secret of immortality. The sage recounts to Gilgamesh a story of a great flood (the details of which are so remarkably similar to later biblical accounts of the flood that scholars have taken great interest in this story). After much hesitation, Utnapishtim reveals to Gilgamesh that a plant bestowing eternal youth is in the sea. Gilgamesh dives into the water and finds the plant but later loses it to a serpent, and disconsolate, returns to Erech to end his days.

This saga was widely studied and translated in ancient times. Biblical writers appear to have modeled their account of the friendship of David and Jonathan on the relationship between Gilgamesh and Enkidu. Numerous Greek writers also incorporated elements found in the Gilgamesh epic into their dragon-slaying epics and into stories concerning the close bond between Achilles and Patroclus.

GILIAK. See GILYAK.

GILL, one of the paired respiratory organs, also called branchia, in many animals that breathe air dissolved in water; also found in the embryo stage of air breathers that evolved from a marine environment. In general, gills are outgrowths of the body wall and are, characteristically, thin-walled structures plentifully supplied with blood vessels. The gill structure varies widely but is typically arranged so that it is constantly bathed in water; the oxygen in the dissolved air passes through the thin membranes of the gill and into the bloodstream of the animal. At the same time the waste carbon dioxide in the blood of the animal passes out through the gill membranes and into the water. The annelid worm, brachiopod, mollusk, echinoderm, certain arthropods, fish, and the larvae of amphibia are equipped with gills.

GILL, (Arthur) Eric Rowton (1882–1940), British sculptor, type designer, engraver, and author. Gill's stone carvings were first exhibited in London in 1911. Two years later he joined the Ro-

Eric Gill stands beside his bas-relief Creation of Adam *(1937–38), executed for the League of Nations and now in the Palais des Nations, Geneva.* British Information Services

man Catholic church and was commissioned to carve the stations of the cross in London's Westminster Cathedral, a task he completed in 1918. His relief *Christ Driving the Money-Changers Out of the Temple* was executed as a war memorial at the University of Leeds in 1922-23. His interest in lettering led him to design new typefaces for book printing; outstanding examples are the faces known as Perpetua (1925) and Gill Sans-serif (1927).

GILLESPIE, Dizzy (1917–), full name JOHN BIRKS GILLESPIE, American jazz trumpeter, one of the leading exponents of bebop, and one of the foremost jazz trumpeters through four decades. He was born in Cheraw, S.C. After playing in the big bands of such figures as Cab Calloway (1907–) and Earl "Fatha" Hines, he collaborated (1945) with saxophonist Charlie Parker to produce some of the most important recordings of the era. He was prominent as a leader of big bands as early

as 1946 and continued to perform internationally in the 1980s. His compositions include "Salt Peanuts" and "Bebop."

GILLETTE, William Hooker (1853-1937), American actor and playwright, born in Hartford, Conn. Gillette spent several years touring the U.S. with various stock companies and in 1881 produced and starred in his own play, *The Professor*. He is best known for his dramatization of *Sherlock Holmes* (1899), which he adapted from the celebrated stories of the English detective-story writer Sir Arthur Conan Doyle. He also appeared in *The Admirable Crichton,* by the British playwright Sir James Matthew Barrie, in 1903.

GILLINGHAM, borough, Kent, SE England, on the Medway R. An industrial and residential community, Gillingham has dockyards. Among its many manufactures are chemicals and electrical equipment. It was incorporated as a borough in 1903. Pop. (1981) 93,741.

GILLRAY, James (1757–1815), English caricaturist, one of the fathers of political cartooning. His satirical caricatures followed in the tradition of William Hogarth but were more overtly political than Hogarth's generalized social commentary. His cartoons—which lampooned the court, the government, and in particular the royal family—were biting, witty, and often outrageous. Characterized by pitiless exaggeration of the personalities and physical features of their subjects, they set the style for later English political cartooning.

GILLYFLOWER, common name given to several aromatic plants. The word is believed to have come from the Middle English *gilofre* ("clove"). Since the late 16th century, gillyflower has been applied to the clove pink, *Dianthus caryophyllus,* from which the cultivated carnation is derived (*see* PINK). The name gillyflower has also been applied to other pinks, and it has been applied to some species of wallflower and stock (qq.v.).

GILSON, Étienne (1884–1978), French philosopher and teacher, whose research into medieval philosophy contributed to the 20th-century revival of Thomism, the philosophical method based on the thought of Saint Thomas Aquinas, and influenced generations of scholars. Gilson was born in Paris. He studied at the Sorbonne and was professor of the history of medieval philosophy there (1921–32), then at the Collège de France. In 1929 he helped found the Pontifical Institute of Mediaeval Studies at the University of Toronto. He was admitted to the French Academy in 1947.

Besides histories of philosophy, Gilson wrote on Saint Augustine, Peter Abelard, Saint Bonaventure, John Duns Scotus, Dante, and many works on Aquinas. He insisted that the Judeo-Christian revelation of God as Creator and Existence itself profoundly affected the character of Christian philosophy. His major works include *The Philosophy of St. Thomas Aquinas* (1924), *The Spirit of Medieval Philosophy* (1936), *The Unity of Philosophical Experience* (1937), *God and Philosophy* (1941), *Being and Some Philosophers* (1949), *Painting and Reality* (1957), and the autobiographical *The Philosopher and Theology* (1962). D.J.F.

GILYAK, tribe of about 4500 persons, inhabiting a region of Russia, in southeast Siberia, near the mouth of the Amur River. Broad-headed and of moderate height, with well-proportioned bodies, the Gilyaks are of two racial types, one resembling the Ainu and the other the Tungus. The Gilyaks are primarily hunters and fishers. Their religion is a form of shamanism.

GIN, alcoholic liquor, distilled from grain, and deriving its flavor principally from an infusion of juniper berries. The name is an abbreviation of the word *geneva,* a corruption of either the French *genièvre* or the Dutch *junever,* both meaning "juniper." The two principal kinds of gin are the American or English variety, usually described as London gin or dry gin, and the Dutch type, called Geneva schnapps or Hollands. Dry gin is prepared from grain alcohol that has been purified by fractional distillation. The purified alcohol is then mixed with juniper berries and other flavoring agents, distilled once more, and diluted to approximately 80 or 90 proof. Dutch gin is prepared in much the same way as dry gin, except that the grain alcohol is less highly purified, and thus retains more of the flavor of the grain. Sugar syrup is sometimes added to the final product. Gin drinking became a social evil in Great Britain early in the 18th century, when it was so cheap that one could get "drunk for a penny, dead drunk for twopence." Increasingly heavy taxes, however, were levied on gin, beginning with the Gin Act of 1736. Gin is a popular beverage in Great Britain and the U.S.

For further information on this topic, see the Bibliography in volume 28, section 604.

GINASTERA, Alberto Evaristo (1916–83), Argentine composer, known for combining nationalistic musical idioms with 20th-century techniques. Born and trained in Buenos Aires, he taught at several Argentine conservatories and in 1971 moved to Geneva. He developed a personal synthesis of compositional procedures that draws on serial and chance methods of organization and utilizes microtones (intervals smaller than a half step), as well as using more traditional forms. His Second String Quartet, first performed at the first Interamerican Music Festival (1958), won him international stature. With his chamber opera *Bomarzo* (1967) he was recognized as a leading 20th-century composer of opera.

GINGER, common name for the plant family Zingiberaceae, the largest member of the order Zingiberales, with about 50 genera and 1300 species. It is pantropical in distribution, although mostly Far Eastern. Its complicated, irregular flowers have one fertile stamen and a usually showy labellum, formed from two or three sterile staminodes. The family is cultivated widely in the Tropics for its showy flowers and useful products, derived mostly from the rhizomes. These products include the flavoring ginger, *Zingiber officinale;* East Indian arrowroot, *Curcuma angustifolia,* a food starch; and turmeric, *C. longa,* an important ingredient in curry powder.

The order includes 8 families and some 1800 species, abundant throughout the moist Tropics. Characteristically, members of the order have

Ginger, Zingiber officinale

rhizomes, underground rootlike stems. These are often fleshy, containing large amounts of starch or other useful substances. Leaves consist of a broad blade with parallel veins running perpendicular to a thick midrib. The midrib extends into a petiole, or stalk, and a sheathing base. The bases of the leaves overlap tightly, forming a rigid pseudostem. Thus, the "trunk" of the banana (q.v.) tree is not a stem at all but many overlapping leaf bases. Stems, except those bearing the flowers, are rarely exposed in the ginger order, as they are underground or covered by leaf bases.

Flowers of the Zingiberales are usually showy, although sometimes bracts (specialized leaves) below the flowers or flower clusters are more showy than the flowers themselves. In about half the families of the order the three sepals and three petals are the conspicuous parts of the flowers. These families have five or, very rarely, six fertile stamens (male parts). The other families have only one functional stamen and two to five petallike, sterile staminodes, which are often showy; sepals and petals are less conspicuous.

The banana family, Musaceae, with 2 genera and about 40 species, typically occurs in disturbed habitats in the Old World Tropics. It has unisexual, often bat-pollinated flowers. The banana, *Musa paradisiaca,* originated in Southeast Asia, but it is now an important crop throughout the moist Tropics, both as a local food staple and as an export crop. Bananas have sterile flowers, and the fruits develop unfertilized, so bananas contain no seeds. Production of new plants is by vegetative means, and propagation is from suck-

ers that develop at the bases of the old plants.

The bird-of-paradise family, Strelitziaceae, with 3 genera and 7 species, occurs in tropical America, southern Africa, and Madagascar. The traveler's tree, *Ravenela madagascariensis,* one of the few woody members of the order, belongs to this family. *Strelitzia,* bird-of-paradise flower, and *Heliconia,* false bird-of-paradise, of the family Heliconiaceae, are cultivated for their often long-lasting flower clusters, borne in large, colorful, boat-shaped bracts.

The Marantaceae produces West Indian arrowroot, *Maranta arundinacea,* and *M. leuconeura* is cultivated as a houseplant, commonly called the prayer plant.

Plants of the order Zingiberales are members of the class Liliopsida (*see* MONOCOTS) in the division Magnoliophyta (*see* ANGIOSPERM).

See also CANNA.

For further information on this topic, see the Bibliography in volume 28, sections 451–52, 593.

GINGOOG, city, S Philippines, Mindanao Island, in Misamis Oriental Province, on Gingoog Bay, near Cagayan del Oro. It has a sawmilling industry and is an agricultural trade center for the area, which produces coconuts and corn. Pop. (1980 prelim.) 81,098.

GINKGO, genus of deciduous trees of the famly Ginkgoaceae, phylum Ginkgophyta (see GYMNOSPERM). The maidenhair tree, *Ginkgo biloba,* is the only living representative of this family and of the order Ginkgoales, although other plants of this order were abundant in the Mesozoic era. The ginkgo has been preserved as a sacred tree in Chinese temple gardens since ancient times. Botanists long believed that the species would have become extinct without this care, but wild ginkgos have been found in recent years in remote valleys of western China.

Ginkgo trees grow 12 to 37 m (40 to 120 ft) tall. The ginkgo leaf is a fan-shaped structure with veins arising from the base and branching dichotomously throughout. The common name, maidenhair tree, is derived from the resemblance in venation between the ginkgo and the maidenhair fern. Larger branches of the ginkgo are covered with dwarf branches, called spurs, which grow slowly and bear leaves yearly. The ginkgo is dioecious (male and female cones are borne on separate trees). Male cones produce pollen that is distributed by wind; female cones bear seeds that are surrounded or enclosed by a malodorous fleshy integument that makes female ginkgo trees less preferred for ornamental purposes. The seed, called the ginkgo nut, is roasted and esteemed as a delicacy in China and Japan.

The ginkgo is frequently planted in parks and

The ginkgo, or maiden-
hair tree, Ginkgo biloba
Arthur W. Ambler–National
Audubon Society

ornamental gardens. The tree is also grown on the streets in large cities, where it flourishes in spite of air pollution, low sunlight, and other urban conditions. Horticultural varieties of ginkgo have been developed as a result of such extensive use.

For further information on this topic, see the Bibliography in volume 28, sections 456, 675.

GIN RUMMY. *See* RUMMY.

GINSBERG, Allen (1926–), American poet, born in Newark, N.J. The spokesman for the Beat Generation of the 1950s, Ginsberg writes in the tradition of Walt Whitman and William Carlos Williams. His poetry is informal, discursive, even repetitive; its immediacy, honesty, and its explicit sexual subject matter often give it an improvised quality. *Howl* (1956) is an angry indictment of America's false hopes and broken promises. Other volumes of Ginsberg's poetry include *Kaddish* (1961), *Reality Sandwiches* (1963), *Planet News* (1968), and *White Shroud* (1987).

GINSENG, common name for plants of the family Araliaceae, and for one of its genera, *Panax*. The family consists of about 55 genera and 700 species of herbs, trees, and shrubs. It occurs in tropical and temperate regions, with the greatest concentration of species in the American Tropics and the Indo-Malayan region. The flowers are small and borne in dense, branched clusters called compound umbels. Each flower usually has five sepals (outer floral whorl) and five petals (inner floral whorl), which are fused to the ovary (female flower part). The stamens (male flower parts) are borne on a disk on top of the ovary. The ovary consists of five fused carpels (egg-bearing structures) that mature into a five-seeded fruit. The usually lobed or compound leaves are divided into separate leaflets.

Ginseng, *P. pseudoginseng,* is the source of a stimulant and supposed aphrodisiac, which is extracted from the roots. It is native to China, although a closely related species, American ginseng, *P. quinquifolius,* occurs in eastern North America and is sometimes substituted for the Chinese variety. Other economically important members of the family are mainly used in horticulture. English ivy, *Hedera helix,* is widely grown as an evergreen ground cover and climber. Several other species of *Hedera* are also cultivated. The genus *Aralia* contains several curiosities, including the devil's-walking-stick, *A. spinosa,* native to eastern North America; this plant is a treelike shrub with leaves and stems armed with large spines. Houseplants generally called aralia belong to other genera such as *Dizygotheca* and *Polyscias,* also members of the ginseng family.

That the ginseng family is a member of the order Apiales (*see* PARSLEY) is indicated by the small, simple flowers, with ovaries below the stamens, that are clustered into umbels, and the compound, often highly divided, leaves. M.R.C.

For further information on this topic, see the Bibliography in volume 28, sections 452, 593, 675.

GINZBERG, Asher. *See* AHAD HA-AM.

GIOLITTI, Giovanni (1842–1928), Italian liberal prime minister, known for his ability to form governments out of the numerous competing political factions of the pre-Fascist era.

Giolitti was born on Oct. 27, 1842, in Mondovì, Piedmont, and trained as a lawyer. He recognized the workers' right to strike during his first premiership (1892–93) but was forced to resign after being implicated in a banking scandal. He returned to power in 1903, this time remaining prime minister until 1905. From 1906 to 1909 and again from 1911 to 1914 he headed broad coalition governments, which he managed with great skill. In this period he was responsible for passage of a national insurance act and for the introduction of universal male suffrage. In 1911–12 he involved Italy in a war with Turkey that resulted in the annexation of Libya, Rhodes, and the Dodecanese Islands. Out of office at the beginning of World War I, Giolitti tried to keep Italy neutral; when Italy joined the war in 1915, he retired from politics. As prime minister again in the turbulent postwar years of 1920–21, he formed an alliance with Benito Mussolini. This increased Mussolini's prestige and made it easier for him to seize power in 1922. Giolitti died on July 17, 1928.

GIONO, Jean (1895–1970), French novelist, born in Manosque. At the age of 19 he was inducted into the French army and fought in World War I. Later he wrote about the horrors of war in *Le grand troupeau* (The Great Herd, 1931). His pacifist creed was expounded in *Refus d'obéissance* (Refusal to Obey, 1937). Giono used his native province as the setting for his novels, the major-

ity of which are concerned with the relationship of people to the soil, as in *Les vrais richesses* (True Riches, 1936). Among his other books are *Hill of Destiny* (1920; trans. 1929), *Harvest* (1930; trans. 1939), and *Horseman on the Roof* (1951; trans. 1954).

GIORDANO, Luca (1632–1705), Italian baroque painter, born in Naples. He was known as Fa Presto ("Hurry Up") because of the speed with which he worked. He studied with the Spanish painter Jusepe de Ribera and the Italian painter and architect Pietro da Cortona, and his style was derived from the styles of Cortona and Paolo Veronese. Giordano lived and worked mostly in Naples; he also executed commissions in Florence, and from 1692 until after 1700 resided and worked in Madrid under the patronage of King Charles II of Spain. Giordano painted numerous pictures, perhaps as many as 5000. His work is characterized by harmonious color, charm, and facile invention. Among his frescoes are those in the cupola of the Corsini Chapel, Florence; *Christ Expelling the Traders from the Temple* (Church of San Filippo da Girolami, Naples); and *Battle of Saint-Quentin* and *Taking of Montmorency* (Escorial, Madrid). His easel paintings include *Venus and Mars* (Louvre, Paris) and *Birth of John the Baptist* (Metropolitan Museum of Art, New York City).

GIORGIONE (c. 1478–1510), Italian painter, who founded the Venetian school of painting and changed the course of European art through his innovations in the portrayal of mood.

Details of Giorgione's life and career are sparse and unreliable, but it appears that he was born in Castelfranco and that he studied under the Venetian painter Giovanni Bellini. His original name was probably Giorgio Barbarelli. Only three oil paintings can be positively attributed to him—the *Castelfranco Altarpiece* (1504, San Liberale, Castelfranco), *Three Philosophers* (Kunsthistorisches Museum, Vienna), and *Tempest* (Accademia, Venice). Other works are attributed to him on the basis of indirect evidence.

Most of Giorgione's paintings consist of a figure or group of figures integrated in a broad surrounding landscape. Unlike earlier pictures in this mode, these works exhibit a new and highly lyrical use of light: The lighting is soft and hazy and is used to create mood rather than to define sharply the objects in the scene. He deliberately refused to make preparatory drawings, preferring instead to compose directly on the canvas; he felt that this led to a more atmospheric rendering and to more striking color effects.

Giorgione's innovations in subject matter were especially important in two areas: the landscape and the female nude. Prior to Giorgione, landscape scenes were taken from biblical, classical, or allegorical stories, but the *Tempest* appears to have no such source and stands on its own as a purely imaginative work. It gave birth to a revolution against the storytelling element in landscape painting and paved the way for later masters such as the French painter Claude Lorrain and the Dutch artist Rembrandt. *Sleeping Venus* (c. 1510, Gemäldegalerie, Dresden, Germany), attributed to Giorgione, pictures a reclining nude and is one of the first modern works of art in which the female figure is the principal and only subject of the picture. It inaugurated the nude as one of the great themes of European art and led directly to the work of artists such as the Venetian painter Titian and the Flemish master Peter Paul Rubens.

Giorgione died of the plague, a few years after his 30th birthday, in Venice in 1510.

GIOTTO, full name GIOTTO DI BONDONE (c. 1267–1337), the most important Italian painter of the 14th century. His conception of the human figure in broad, rounded terms—rather than in the flat, two-dimensional terms of Gothic and Byzantine styles—indicated a Concern for naturalism that was a milestone in the development of Western art.

Giotto was born in Colle di Vespignano, near Florence. Details of his early life are scarce, but it appears that he probably served an apprenticeship in Florence before embarking on a career that took him to Rome, Padua, Arezzo, Rimini, Assisi, and Naples.

Giotto's entire output consists of religious works, primarily altarpieces and church frescoes. Few remain in good condition, and most have disappeared entirely or have been almost wholly repainted. Others cannot be securely attributed to him and are more likely to be the work of followers or apprentices. His earliest attributable work is the large fresco cycle illustrating the lives of the Virgin and Christ in the Scrovegni (Arena) Chapel in Padua, painted between 1305 and 1306. Giotto's scenes break with rigid medieval stylization to present human figures in rounded sculptural forms that appear to have been based on living models rather than on idealized archetypes. He rejected the bright jewellike colors and long elegant lines of the Byzantine style in favor of a quieter, more realistic presentation. His emphasis is on the human and the real rather than on the divine and the ideal—a revolutionary development in an age dominated by religion. His settings (here as in all of his works) consist of shallow, boxlike architectural backdrops. These are somewhat more open than the flat planes of Byzantine and Gothic paintings but fall short of the full perspective of the Renaissance.

The *Ognissanti Madonna* (c. 1310, Uffizi, Flor-

The Wise Men's Adoration of the Holy Child, *a detail from the early 14th-century frescoes in the Scrovegni Chapel, (or the Arena Chapel), in Padua, Italy, by the Italian innovator Giotto.*

ence) is roughly contemporary with the Arena frescoes and is Giotto's only attributable panel painting. It shows the influence of the earlier Florentine painter Giovanni Cimabue in composition and style, but is unique in its humanization of the Madonna's face. Two fresco cycles in the Church of Santa Croce, Florence—depicting the life of St. Francis and the lives of St. John the Baptist and St. John the Evangelist—are thought to be later works. While they are extensively restored, they represent the most advanced stage of Giotto's style, showing human figures grouped in free, active poses.

Giotto was ahead of his time. Most of his followers painted in a less significant, more overtly decorative style. It remained for Masaccio, a century later, to expand upon his monumental style. Giotto's example was crucial to the development of later Florentine painting, and his preoccupation with the realities of the human figure and the visible world became the dominant concerns of the Florentine Renaissance. He died in Florence, in 1337.

GIOVANNI DI PAOLO (c. 1403–c. 1482), one of the most important painters of the 15th-century Sienese school. His early works show the influence of earlier Sienese masters, but his later style grew steadily more individualized, characterized by cold, harsh colors and elongated forms. Many of his works have an unusual dreamlike atmosphere, such as the surrealistic *Miracle of St. Nicholas of Tolentino* (c. 1455, Philadelphia Museum of Art), while his last works—particularly *Last Judgment, Heaven, and Hell* (c. 1465) and *Assumption* (1475), both at Pinacoteca, Siena— are grotesque treatments of their lofty subjects. Giovanni's reputation declined after his death but was revived in the 20th century.

GIRAFFE, common name for *Giraffa camelopardalis,* or camel-leopard, as the Romans called this spotted "camel" when it inhabited North Africa. The giraffe is the only member of its genus; it and the okapi are the only two members of the family Giraffidae. The several subspecies of giraffe now inhabit dry, tree-scattered terrain south of the Sahara. The male stands close to 5 m (16 ft) high, and with its 40-cm (15-in) tongue is able to reach high into acacia trees, the leaves of which are one of its main foods.

The giraffe, like most mammals, has only seven neck vertebrae, which are greatly elongated to support its extremely long and muscular neck. Due to the great distance between the animal's heart and head, its vascular system is equipped with valves so that sufficient blood reaches the brain. Both sexes have two or four short, blunt, skin-covered horns. The long, flexible tongue

Giraffe, Giraffa camelopardalis   South African Tourist Corp.

and long, muscular upper lip are used to rip leaves from branches. Giraffes have chestnut brown blotches against a buff background, markings that blend with the dappled shadows of tree branches. As giraffes age, their color grows a darker brown. Each animal has a unique set of markings. A giraffe's life span is 15 to 20 years.

Giraffes have a keen sense of smell and hearing and an outstanding sense of sight, which due to their height makes them the most vigilant of the African big-game species. They congregate in loosely organized herds of 12 to 15 members, with individuals often joining and leaving again. Each herd is led by an adult bull and consists of cows, calves, and sexually immature males. The females of the herd are the most alert to danger.

Giraffes gallop with the hind feet reaching in front of the fore feet and the neck swinging widely, giving the appearance of slow motion, although they can actually reach 48 km/hr (30 mph). When walking they pace, moving the two feet of one side forward simultaneously. Due to their great weight, which reaches 1800 kg (4000 lb), they are unable to traverse boggy swamps or riverbeds. On dry, hard land, however, they range widely and are found hundreds of kilometers from water. Unlike many grass-eating herbivores of Africa, giraffes do not migrate during dry seasons, because they get their food and most of their moisture from leaves. They can go for over a month without drinking, and the few times they do drink, they must spread their long forelegs widely to reach the water. For this reason giraffes rarely graze grass. When giraffes do vocalize, they emit moans or low notes. They usually sleep in standing positions. They protect themselves by kicking with their large, heavy hooves. Lions are their chief predators.

During mating season males vie for females by butting with their heavy necks and heads. After about 15 months the cow bears a single calf, 2 m (6 ft) high, which can stand 20 minutes after birth. Calves come to sexual maturity in three or four years. Once heavily hunted for their thick, leathery skins, giraffes are now protected.

For further information on this topic, see the Bibliography in volume 28, sections 475, 478.

GIRARD, Stephen (1750–1831), American businessman and philanthropist.

Girard was born in Bordeaux, France. At the age of 24 he became captain and part owner of a ship engaged in the West Indian and American coast trade. In 1776 he settled in Philadelphia and became a merchant. Two years later he resumed his trading activities with the West Indies, accumulating a sizable fortune. In 1810 he invested about $1 million in shares of the First Bank of the United States. In 1812, when the charter of the bank lapsed, he purchased a controlling interest in its stock and continued the business as the Bank of Stephen Girard. During the War of 1812 he was an important financial supporter of the U.S. government; in 1814 he subscribed for about 95 percent of the war loan of $5 million. When the Second Bank of the United States was chartered in 1816, Girard became one of its principal stockholders and was a dominant influence on its policy for many years.

The fortune that Girard left at his death was probably the largest in the U.S. up to that time, amounting to about $7,500,000, the bulk of which he designated for philanthropic purposes. His will, which made legal history, provided money for municipal improvements, especially the improvement of the Philadelphia police system, and for the establishment of a school or college for "poor, white, male orphans." In the regulations for the management of the institution, the will provided that no minister or ecclesiastic of any sect might hold office in the school or enter upon its premises, and that no teaching of religious doctrine in a denominational sense should be permitted. The heirs at law contested the will in 1836, and in 1844 the statesman and orator Daniel Webster argued for the heirs before the U.S. Supreme Court, making a famous plea for Christianity. The Court upheld the will, and the school was organized. In 1968 the Court ruled that Girard College be racially integrated.

GIRAUD, Henri Honoré (1879–1949), French general, born in Paris, and educated at the military school of Saint-Cyr. While serving in World War I, he was captured by the Germans but escaped after a short imprisonment. He fought against the Riffs in Morocco in the campaign of 1925–26. In the spring of 1940, during World War II, Giraud was in command of Allied defenses in northern France, and after the fall of Sedan he was again captured by the Germans. He escaped from Germany to unoccupied France in April 1942 and made his way to Algeria the following November, after the Allies had invaded North Africa. Upon the assassination of Adm. Jean Darlan in December 1942, Giraud was appointed high commissioner of French North and West Africa. In June 1943, he became copresident of the French Committee of National Liberation with Gen. Charles de Gaulle, and in July was named commander in chief of all French forces. In November, however, under pressure from de Gaulle, Giraud resigned his political office and in April 1944 relinquished his military command. In 1946, after the liberation of France, Giraud served briefly as a deputy in the second Provisional Assembly.

GIRAUDOUX, (Hyppolyte) Jean (1882–1944), French playwright, novelist, and diplomat, whose witty, originally expressed works in an impressionistic style helped free French theater from the restrictions of realism. Giraudoux was born in Bellac and educated at the École Normale Supérieure in Paris, the University of Munich, and Harvard University. In 1910 he entered the French foreign service. He became director of information of France in 1929 and held a similar post under the government of Marshal Henri Philippe Pétain, the so-called Vichy regime.

Giraudoux first won literary acclaim for several novels that appeared shortly after World War I, including *My Friend from Limousin* (1922; trans. 1923) and *Églantine* (1927). These were followed by such internationally successful plays as *Siegfried* (1928; trans. 1930), *Amphitryon 38* (1929; trans. 1938), *Intermezzo* (1933), *Tiger at the Gates* (1935; trans. 1955), *Électre* (1937), and *Ondine* (1939; trans. 1954). Many of these were modern treatments of ancient Greek stories. In 1943 he completed his last play, the satirical *La folle de Chaillot*, produced posthumously in 1945 and produced in the U.S. in 1947 as *The Madwo-*

man of Chaillot. A novel, *La menteuse,* was discovered in 1968 and published in English as *The Lying Woman* in 1972.

GIRL SCOUTS OF THE UNITED STATES OF AMERICA, largest voluntary organization for girls and young women in the world. It provides opportunities for members, aged 5 through 17, to develop their potential, make friends, and become a vital part of their communities.

Founded in 1912 by the American youth leader Juliette Gordon Low (1860–1927), the organization currently has more than 3 million members including adult volunteers. They participate through 335 local Girl Scout councils across the U.S. All girls, including those with physical or mental disabilities, may enter the Girl Scout program at any of five age levels: Daisy Girl Scouts, ages 5–6; Brownie Girl Scouts, 6–8; Junior Girl Scouts, 8–11; Cadette Girl Scouts, 11–14; and Senior Girl Scouts, 14–17.

Activities take place in small groups sometimes called troops, or individually under the guidance of an adult leader or adviser. Approximately 179,000 such troops are presently maintained throughout the U.S.

For girls aged 5–11, the Girl Scout program of activities is designed to help members discover and explore girl scouting's five worlds of interest: well-being, people, today and tomorrow, the arts, and the out-of-doors. They also learn about careers and can earn 88 action-oriented proficiency badges offered in such fields as sports, computers, and camping. Activities for teenagers include career exploration, international travel, community service, and special projects in the Girl Scouts' five interest areas.

The organization is part of a worldwide sisterhood—the World Association of Girl Guides and Girl Scouts—made up of 7.5 million girls and young women living in 112 countries. The World Association maintains four world centers: Olave House in England, Our Cabaña in Mexico, Sangam in India, and Our Chalet in Switzerland.

Girl Scouts of the United States of America, with national headquarters in New York City, operates three program centers for structured activities: Juliette Gordon Low Girl Scout National Center in Savannah, Ga. (birthplace of the founder); Girl Scout National Center West in Wyoming, for outdoor activities; and Edith Macy Conference Center in Westchester Co., N.Y., a training and meeting facility. Handbooks for all ages and booklets on contemporary issues such as peer pressure and family problems address the concerns of girls and offer direction. The organization also publishes a quarterly magazine, *Leader,* for adults in girl scouting.

GIRL SCOUTS OF THE UNITED STATES OF AMERICA

Scouts hiking with backpacks at the Girl Scout National Center West, Ten Sleep, Wyo.   Girl Scouts of the U.S.A.

GIRONDE, estuary, W France, in Gironde Department. The largest in France and one of the largest in W Europe, the estuary is formed by the confluence of the Garonne and Dordogne rivers near the Bay of Biscay. Its widest point, near the mouth, is about 10 km (about 6 mi). It is divided by small islands and mud banks into an E and a W channel. At the mouth of the estuary stands a famous lighthouse, the Phare de Cordouan, built in 1585 and enlarged in the 18th century.

GIRONDISTS, moderate Republican faction active in the French Revolution from 1791 to 1793. Called Girondists because many of their prominent members represented the department of Gironde, they were also named Brissotins, after Jacques Pierre Brissot, one of their leaders. The group first emerged in the Legislative Assembly elected in October 1791. It was originally identified with the Jacobins (q.v.), but the two groups split on the issue of war with Austria, which the Girondists favored, believing it would unite France behind the Revolution. Led by Brissot and Jean Marie Roland de La Platière (1734–93), they persuaded the assembly to vote for war in April 1792. After that their influence declined. Opponents of the economic controls and radical democracy favored by the Paris-based Jacobins, they tried unsuccessfully to win armed support in the provinces in October 1793. When Brissot and 30 of his followers were guillotined by the Jacobins on October 31, the power of the Girondists was destroyed.

GIRTIN, Thomas (1775–1802), English watercolorist, whose technical and artistic innovations gave birth to the distinctive English romantic manner in watercolor. His early works follow the 18th-century style of line drawings tinted with monochromatic washes. His mature works, however, particularly *White House at Chelsea* (1800, Tate Gallery, London), are freer and more intense, using strong colors unencumbered by linear outlines. They convey a unique sense of the sweep and scale of the English countryside. Their naturalistic style and sensitivity to mood prepared the way for the full-scale romanticism of later artists such as J. M. W. Turner and Richard Bonington.

GIRTY, Simon (1741–1818), American frontiersman and scout, born in what is now Dauphin Co., Pa. He was called the "Great Renegade" for turning traitor during the American Revolution. From 1759 until the outbreak of the Revolution he served as interpreter and scout at Fort Pitt (now Pittsburgh, Pa.). At the beginning of the Revolution he acted as interpreter for the Continental army. In 1778, however, he deserted to the British and was declared a traitor by the Pennsylvania legislature. During the rest of the war he led raiding parties of British and Indians along the northern and western frontiers. After the war he settled near Detroit, which remained in British hands, and continued to lead Indian raids on outposts. In 1791 he took part in the defeat of an American expedition led by Maj. Gen. Arthur St. Clair (1736–1818), first American governor of the Northwest Territory. When Detroit was ceded to the U.S. under the terms of Jay's Treaty in 1796, Girty escaped to Canada, where he lived for the rest of his life. Although the stories circulated about Girty's savagery were exaggerated, he was greatly feared in the western settlements and is known to have permitted the torture and burning of settlers by Indians.

GISCARD D'ESTAING, Valéry (1926–), president of France (1974–81), who continued the conservative policies established by his two predecessors of the Fifth Republic.

Giscard was born on Feb. 2, 1926, in Koblenz, Germany , and educated at the École Polytechnique and École Nationale d'Administration. He began his career in 1952 in the Ministry of Finance and Economic Affairs, where he served as assistant director of the minister's staff. Elected to the National Assembly in 1956 and reelected in 1958, Giscard was appointed secretary of state for finance under Charles de Gaulle in 1959; three years later he became minister of finance. His economic program lowered the rate of inflation but was also the cause of a brief recession and he was dismissed in 1966. Shortly thereafter he was returned to the National Assembly. In 1969 Giscard joined the government of President Georges Pompidou as minister of finance and economic affairs, imposing strict economic controls. After Pompidou died in April 1974, Giscard was narrowly elected president of France as an Independent Republican. He was inaugurated on May 27, 1974.

Giscard was a proponent of closer economic and political ties among European nations and soon established personal contacts with other world leaders. He also made a strong effort to improve France's recession-bound economy; in early 1976 he outlined a wide-ranging program that included reforms designed to revitalize the economy. He could not, however, halt the economic deterioration and social unrest caused by a worldwide recession, and he was defeated for reelection in 1981.

GISH, name of two pioneer American actors who were sisters: **Lillian Gish** (1896?–) and **Dorothy Gish** (1898?–1968).

The sisters, both born in Ohio, made their theatrical debuts at a very early age and by 1902 had

begun touring through the eastern U.S. and Canada. In 1912 they joined the production company of the pioneer American film director D. W. Griffith. The sisters appeared together in silent-film classics by Griffith, such as *Hearts of the World* (1917) and *Orphans of the Storm* (1921); Lillian appeared without her sister in Griffith's *The Birth of a Nation* (1915), *Broken Blossoms* (1919), and *Way Down East* (1920). Each of the actors made many more silent films; with the advent of talking pictures, they returned to the stage.

Lillian appeared in revivals of *Uncle Vanya* (1930) and *Camille* (1932). Dorothy also acted in many Broadway productions, including *The Magnificent Yankee* (1946). Both sisters appeared as Mother in *Life with Father* in 1941, Lillian in the national company in Chicago and Dorothy on tour with the road company. Dorothy did not appear on the Broadway stage after *The Man* (1950). Lillian, however, continued to make frequent appearances, among them in *All the Way Home* (1960) and *I Never Sang for My Father* (1968). Lillian appeared in many talking pictures, including *Duel in the Sun* (1946), *Night of the Hunter* (1955), and *A Wedding* (1978), but Dorothy made only three.

Lillian is coauthor of the book *Lillian Gish: The Movies, Mr. Griffith and Me* (1969).

For further information on this family, see the section Biographies in the Bibliography in volume 28.

GISLEBERTUS (fl. 12th cent.), French Romanesque sculptor, whose decoration (c. 1125–35) of the Cathedral of Saint Lazare at Autun, France—consisting of numerous doorways, tympanums, and capitals—represents some of the most original work of the period. His sculpture is unusually expressive and imaginative for its time, from the terrifying *Last Judgment* (west tympanum), with its strikingly elongated figures, to the *Eve* (north portal), the first large-scale nude in European art since antiquity and a model of sinuous grace. His influence can be traced to other French church sculpture, and his techniques helped pave the way for the Gothic style.

GISSING, George Robert (1857–1903), English novelist, born in Wakefield, and educated at Owens College, Manchester. He taught and did free-lance journalism, first in the U.S. and then in London. By such gestures as marrying a prostitute and rejecting regular employment, he seemed to invite the deprivations of poverty that supplied material for many of his works. His novels deal chiefly with the lives of lower-middle-class Londoners, and his favorite theme is the degrading and brutalizing effect of poverty on human beings. *Workers in the Dawn,* the first of his 22 novels, appeared in 1880.

Gissing did not receive any recognition until the publication of his fourth novel, *Demos* (1886), an imaginary account of the effect of socialism upon poverty-stricken people. Among his other writings are novels of contemporary life such as *Thyrza* (1887), *New Grub Street* (1891), a realistic picture of the struggles of an unsuccessful writer, and *In the Year of Jubilee* (1894); the semiautobiographical *The Private Papers of Henry Ryecroft* (1903); and *Veranilda* (posthumously pub. 1904), a novel of 6th-century Italy.

GIULIO ROMANO, real name GIULIO PIPPI (c. 1499–1546), Italian painter and architect in the Mannerist style. He was born in Rome and became the chief pupil of the Italian painter Raphael, whom he assisted in many of the latter's finest works. At Raphael's death he completed the frescoes *Battle of Constantine* and *Apparition of the Cross* in the Vatican Palace, Rome. He inherited a portion of Raphael's wealth, including his works of art, and succeeded him as head of the Roman school.

About 1524, Giulio accepted the invitation of Federigo Gonzaga (1500?–40), ruler of Mantua and patron of the arts, to carry out a series of architectural and pictorial works. The drainage of the marshes surrounding the city and its system of protection from the inundations of the Po and Mincio rivers attest to Giulio's skill as an engineer; his genius as an architect found scope in the planning and construction of the Palazzo del Te, the cathedral, the streets, and a ducal palace. Among his works of this period are the frescoes *Psyche, Icarus,* and *Titans,* in the Te palace. In Bologna, he designed the facade of the Church of San Petronio. Among the best of his works are *Martyrdom of Saint Stephen* (San Stefano, Genoa) and *Mary and Jesus* (Louvre, Paris).

GIZA, also al-Jizah, city, N Egypt, capital of Giza governorate, on the Nile R., a SW suburb of Cairo. It is the third largest city in Egypt and a leading administrative, cultural, and commercial center, with diverse manufactures that include motion pictures, chemicals, machinery, and cigarettes. The city has traditional Muslim districts, a sector of luxury apartment buildings along the river, and many foreign embassies and government offices. Educational facilities include the University of Cairo (1908), relocated here in 1924; the Academy of the Arabic Language (1932); an ophthalmic research institute; and a music institute. An important city has been on or in the vicinity of this site since the time of the 4th Dynasty (c. 2680–2544 BC) of the ancient pharaohs. Famous landmarks nearby are the Great Sphinx (2565 BC or earlier) and three of Egypt's most famous pyramids—the Great Pyramid of Khufu, or Cheops, and the Khafre and Menkaure pyramids. Pop. (1986 est.) 1,670,800.

GJELLERUP, Karl Adolph (1857–1919), Danish writer and Nobel laureate, born on the island of Sjaelland. He studied theology, but later became an atheist under the influence of the Danish literary critic Georg Morris Brandes. After 1892 Gjellerup lived in Germany; many of his writings are in German and demonstrate his admiration for the humanistic and mystical side of German culture. His last writings also show a preoccupation with Buddhism. Among his works are the novels *En ideaist* (1878), *Minna* (1889; trans. 1913), and *The Pilgrim Kamanita* (1906; trans. 1911). Gjellerup was also a poet and a playwright. He shared the 1917 Nobel Prize in literature with the Danish novelist Henrik Pontoppidan.

GLACE BAY, town, Cape Breton Co., NE Nova Scotia, a port on the Atlantic coast of E Cape Breton Island; inc. 1901. It is a coal-mining and fishing center. In the town are the Miners' Museum, with exhibits depicting the evolution of coal mining in the region, and Glace Bay Lake, a bird sanctuary. The settlement grew after large-scale coal-mining operations began here in the mid-19th century. The Italian physicist Guglielmo Marconi sent one of the first transatlantic wireless messages from a nearby transmitter in 1902. Pop. (1986) 20,467; (1991) 19,501.

GLACIAL PERIOD. *See* ICE AGES.

GLACIER, large, usually moving mass of ice formed in high mountains or in high latitudes where the rate of snowfall is greater than the melting rate of snow. Glaciers can be divided into four well-defined types—alpine, piedmont, ice cap, and continental—according to the topography and climate of the region in which the glacier was formed.

Alpine Glaciers. The snow that falls on the walls and floors of valleys in high mountain regions tends to accumulate to a great depth, because the rate of melting, particularly in wintertime, is far lower than the rate at which the snow falls. As a result, the earlier snows, compressed by later falls, are changed into a compact body of ice having a granular structure. In some areas, however, where the temperature rarely rises as high as the melting point, this accumulation of ice can be formed by the recurrent process of sublimation and recrystallization. Sublimation is a change from the solid state into vapor without an intermediate liquid stage. When the depth of the glacier reaches about 30 m (about 100 ft) the whole mass begins to creep slowly down the valley. This flow continues as long as a superabundance of snow falls at the top of the glacier. As the glacier flows down the valley to a lower altitude where it is not replenished by snowfall, it melts or wastes away, the meltwater forming the source of streams and rivers.

In cross section the structure of all glaciers is

similar. At the top is a mantle of freshly fallen snow with a very low density (q.v.) of not more than 0.1. Below this is a layer in which the snowflakes have diminished in size to become granular snow, of which the density may be 0.3 or greater. This is caused either by the influence of moisture and the pressure exerted by accumulated snow, or by sublimation and recrystallization. Further recurrent action results in névé, or firn, which approaches a density of 0.5. At the base of the glacier is a layer of clear ice that may approach a density of 0.7 to 0.8 and flows like a viscous fluid.

The lower glacial ice is under such great pressure that any cracks or separations occurring in this layer are quickly healed. The upper layers, however, may suffer tensions and strains from moving over underlying obstructions or from differential movement, in which the center of the glacier moves more rapidly than its edges. These strains produce crevasses that may be many meters deep and are frequently covered by newly fallen snow. A large crevasse known as the bergschrund is usually formed in the shape of a semicircle at the head of the glacier, between the glacier itself and the headwall of the valley in which it lies.

Glaciers are usually bordered at their sides by zones of rock debris that have fallen from the sidewalls of the valley as a result of frost-wedging action (*see* EROSION). These zones of rock fragments are called lateral moraines. At the lower end of the glacier the moraines increase in size. When two glaciers from neighboring valleys meet, the moraines at their adjoining sides coalesce to form a medial moraine in the middle of the resulting glacier. As the ice melts at the lower end of a glacier, rock and debris that have been plowed up by its progress over the valley floor, in addition to rock material that may have fallen into crevasses, are deposited in a series of semicircular hillocks called the terminal moraine.

As a glacier moves down its valley, it eventually reaches a point at which the ablation, or melting and evaporation, from the surface exceeds the amount of snow falling on it. At this

Emmons, the largest glacier in the continental U.S., with Little Tehoma Peak (left) and the summit of Mt. Rainier.
National Park Service

In 1986 an ice dam formed by Hubbard Glacier in Alaska blocked the 25-m long Russell Fjord. Behind the dam is Disenchantment Bay.
© Steve McCutcheon

point, often called the névé, or firn, line, the surface of the glacier is névé rather than snow.

The speed at which glaciers flow varies within wide limits. Most glaciers move downward at the rate of less than 1 m (less than 3 ft) per day, but observation of the Black Rapids Glacier in Alaska, during 1936–37, showed that it was moving more than 30 m (more than 100 ft) per day. This is the swiftest advance ever recorded for any glacier in the world and was probably due to the extremely heavy snowfalls that had occurred in the area some years earlier.

With variations in climate, glaciers shrink and expand to a marked extent. An excess of precipitation creates a situation analogous to a river flood and causes the glacier to increase in size. Similarly, when precipitation decreases, the glacier shrinks.

Glaciers of the alpine type are found in high mountain ranges throughout the world, even in the tropics. In the U.S., alpine, or valley, glaciers exist on the slopes of Mount Rainier, Mount Ba-

ker, and Mount Adams, in Washington, Mount Hood in Oregon, and Mount Shasta in California. The Hubbard Glacier in Alaska is one of the longest alpine glaciers in the world. Glaciers of the northwest U.S. were observed in 1955 to be advancing for the first time since the middle of the 19th century.

Piedmont Glaciers. When a number of alpine glaciers flow together in the valley at the foot of a range of mountains, they frequently form extensive glacier sheets known as piedmont glaciers. Glaciers of this type are especially common in Alaska. The largest of the piedmont glaciers in North America is the Malaspina Glacier in Alaska, which has an area of approximately 3900 sq km (approximately 1500 sq mi). The lower portion of this glacier is almost flat and is covered with so much soil and rock debris that it supports a thick forest.

Icecap Glaciers. The glacier system that covers a large portion of the Norwegian island group of Svalbard, in the Arctic Ocean, is unusual in form, being a type intermediate between the alpine glacier and the Greenland glacier described below. The entire center of each island is covered with an ice sheet that overlies a high plateau. At the edges of the plateau the sheet breaks up into a series of alpine glaciers that move down steep valleys, sometimes reaching the sea.

Continental Glaciers. Covering almost the entire extent of Greenland is a huge glacial blanket over 1.8 million sq km (over 700,000 sq mi) in area and more than 2700 m (more than 9000 ft) in maximum thickness. This gigantic glacier flows slowly outward from two centers, one on the southern part of the island and one in the north. Because of its thickness the Greenland ice sheet rises far above both the valleys and hills of the land beneath it, and the underlying rock is exposed only near the seacoast, where the glacier breaks up into tongues of ice somewhat resembling valley glaciers. From the ends of these tongues, where they reach the sea, large and small fragments of ice break off during the summer, forming icebergs. A glacier of a similar type covers the whole of the Antarctic continent and has an area of about 13 million sq km (about 5 million sq mi). Continental glaciers covered much of North America during the Pleistocene epoch of the Quaternary period (q.v.), which ended about 10,000 years ago.

Glacial Erosion. As a glacier moves down a valley, or cross-country in the case of a large ice sheet, it sculpts the land in a characteristic manner. Rocks in its path are plowed out of the way, and rocks beneath it are broken up by frost action and then carried away. The rocks embedded in the bottom of the glacier act as abrasive particles, scratching and scouring the rocks beneath.

At the head of a valley in which a glacier is formed, the headwalls are eroded into a characteristic semicircular form called a cirque. Progressive erosion of headwalls occurring simultaneously on several sides of a mountain produces what is called a horn, an example of which is the Matterhorn (q.v.). Valleys down which glaciers have traveled are eroded to a U shape rather than the V shape caused by stream erosion. Frequently the valley is excavated so deeply that the mouths of tributary valleys are left high above the new valley floor as hanging valleys. Fjords are glaciated valleys that have been partly flooded by the sea. Alaska's Columbia Glacier, near Valdez, began retreating so rapidly in the 1980s that it is expected to reveal a fjord up to 40 km (25 mi) long by the end of the next few decades.

See also GEOLOGY; ICE; ICE AGES.   D.Li.

For further information on this topic, see the Bibliography in volume 28, section 429.

GLACIER BAY NATIONAL PARK, SE Alaska, established 1925, redesignated as a national park in 1980. The park, located in the Saint Elias Mts. on Glacier Bay, is noted for its great tidewater glaciers and lofty peaks, the highest of which is Mt. Fairweather (4663 m/15,300 ft). Among the park's glaciers, which rise to about 60 m (about 200 ft) above the water's edge, is Muir Glacier. The park is important for scientific research on the formation and movement of glaciers and on the conditions existing after glacial retreat. The landscape ranges from rocky ice-swept terrain to lush forests of spruce and hemlock. Wildlife includes the black and brown bear, mountain goat, seal, sea lion, whale, puffin, eagle, and cormorant. Area, 13,052.3 sq km (5039.5 sq mi).

GLACIER NATIONAL PARK, SE British Columbia, established 1886. Located in the Selkirk and Purcell Mts., and within the N bend of the Columbia R., this park has many peaks, some over 3350 m (over 11,000 ft), and more than 100 glaciers. Avalanches are common because of heavy snowfall—often more than 12 m (more than 40 ft) a year. Below the snowline the park is heavily forested. Area, 1349 sq km (521 sq mi).

GLACIER NATIONAL PARK, NW Montana, established 1910. Straddling the Continental Divide, the park is distinguished by its extraordinary beauty. It has nearly 50 glaciers, more than 200 glacier-fed lakes, broad glacier-carved valleys, and precipitous peaks, with a maximum elevation of 3185 m (10,448 ft) atop Mt. Cleveland. The E and W sides of the park are connected by the Going-to-the-Sun Highway, which crosses the Continental Divide through Logan Pass (2031 m/6664 ft). On the E slopes of the divide are stands of spruce, fir, and lodgepole pine; the moister W slopes are thickly forested with ponderosa pine, larch, fir, hemlock, and cedar. Animal life includes grizzly bear, elk, moose, cougar, mountain caribou, bobcat, mountain goat, bald eagle, and osprey. The park is linked with the adjacent Waterton Lakes National Park in Alberta to form the Waterton-Glacier International Peace Park (est. 1932). Area, 4101.9 sq km (1583.8 sq mi).

GLACKENS, William James (1870–1938), American painter, born in Philadelphia, and educated at the Pennsylvania Academy of the Fine Arts. Starting his career as a newspaper and magazine illustrator, Glackens became a realistic painter of the group called The Eight. His dark-hued works marked a turning away from lofty academic subjects to scenes of everyday life. Later, as a result of his travels in France, Glackens's works became lighter, influenced by the impressionists, especially the French painter and sculptor Pierre Auguste Renoir. Glackens's works include *Luxembourg*

Gardens (1904, Corcoran Gallery, Washington, D.C.), *Washington Square* (1914, Museum of Modern Art, New York City), and *Promenade* (1926, Detroit Institute of Arts).

GLADDEN, Washington (1836–1918), American Congregationalist minister and journalist, known for his pragmatic social theology. After graduating from Williams College in Williamstown, Mass., he entered the ministry and served congregations in New York, Massachusetts, and Ohio. He was also the religion editor for the *New York Independent* from 1871 to 1875. Gladden linked theological liberalism with strong social concern. His attempts to apply biblical teachings to the problems of industrialization made him a leader in the Social Gospel (q.v.) movement. Gladden's more than 38 books include *Working People and Their Employers* (1876) and *Social Salvation* (1901).

GLADIATOR (Lat. *gladius,* "sword"), professional fighter who performed in spectacles of armed combat in the amphitheaters of ancient Rome. The practice of armed men fighting to the death originated in Etruria, in central Italy, probably as a funeral sacrifice. The first gladiatorial exhibition in Rome was in 264 BC, when three pairs of gladiators fought as part of a funeral celebration. By 174 BC, at a 3-day spectacle, 37 pairs participated. Julius Caesar's large-scale exhibitions (300 pairs on one occasion) prompted the Roman Senate to limit the number of contestants. The largest contest of gladiators was given by the emperor Trajan as part of a victory celebration in AD 107 and included 5000 pairs of fighters. The emperor Domitian in AD 90 presented combats between women and between dwarfs.

Mostly males, gladiators were slaves, condemned criminals, prisoners of war, and sometimes Christians. Forced to become swordsmen, they were trained in schools called *ludi,* and special measures were taken to discipline them and prevent them from committing suicide. One gladiator, Spartacus, avenged his captivity by escaping and leading an insurrection that terrorized southern Italy from 73 to 71 BC.

A successful gladiator received great acclaim; he was praised by poets, his portrait appeared on gems and vases, and patrician ladies pampered him. A gladiator who survived many combats might be relieved from further obligation. Occasionally, freedmen and Roman citizens entered the arena, as did the insane Emperor Commodus.

According to their arms and methods of fighting, gladiators were divided into various light- and heavy-armored classes. For example, the *retiarius* ("net man"), clad in a short tunic, at-

tempted to entangle his fully armed opponent, the *secutor* ("pursuer"), with a net and then to kill him with a trident. Other classes fought with different weapons, or from horseback or chariots. According to the most common tradition, when a gladiator had overpowered his opponent, he turned to the spectators. If they wished to spare the defeated man, they waved their handkerchiefs; to indicate that he should be killed, they turned down their thumbs.

Although Constantine the Great proscribed gladiatorial contests in AD 325, they continued to be held until about 500.

GLADIOLUS, genus of herbaceous flowering plants of the family Iridaceae (*see* IRIS) with sword-shaped leaves and showy flowers, widely cultivated in gardens and used as cut flowers. Some 180 species of *Gladiolus* exist, mostly native to southern Africa, but some are also found in the Mediterranean area. Modern cultivation dates from the early 19th century. Because of the ease with which gladiolus hybridize and the length of time they have been bred for color, flower size and shape, and other desirable features, it is now impossible to assign most cultivars (cultivated forms) to botanical species.

Gladiolus are generally not hardy in temperate

The funnel-shaped flowers of a member of Gladiolus, *a genus of herbaceous plants of the iris family.*

zones and are grown as annuals from corms (swollen underground stems) or cormels (small, hard structures produced at the bases of corms) after the ground has warmed. The irregular funnel-shaped flowers are borne in vertical rows on long, unbranched flower stalks.

GLADSTONE, city, Clay Co., W Missouri, near the Missouri R.; inc. 1952. It is a suburb of Kansas City; some industry is here. The settlement, established in the late 19th century, was first called Linden; its present name was adopted in 1952. Pop. (1980) 24,990; (1990) 26,243.

GLADSTONE, William Ewart (1809–98), four times prime minister of Great Britain (1868–74, 1880–85, 1886, and 1892–94), and one of the dominant political forces in Victorian England. Leader of the Liberal party after 1867, he became the symbol throughout Europe of the reforming trends of his age.

Gladstone, born in Liverpool on Dec. 29, 1809, was the son of John Gladstone (1764–1851), a prosperous merchant of Scottish origin. He was raised in a devoutly evangelical home, and religion became a dominant force in his life. Following four years at Eton, he had a distinguished university career at Christ Church, Oxford. There, after much soul-searching, he chose politics rather than the church. Because of his conservative views, he was elected to Parliament as a Tory in 1832.

Gladstone's Political Development. Throughout the 1830s the young Gladstone opposed almost all reform; his first speech was a defense of slavery in the West Indies, and he was a staunch defender of the Church of England. In 1843 he became president of the Board of Trade in the conservative (Tory) cabinet of Sir Robert Peel. Gladstone supported Peel's movement toward free trade, but when Peel rescinded (1846) the Corn Laws, which had taxed imported grain, the Tory party was shattered, and Peel's government collapsed. Between 1846 and 1859 Gladstone, a Peelite, was politically isolated, although he held some cabinet posts. During this time his views changed. He accepted the need for religious freedom, including the admission of Jews into Parliament. He also supported the cause of Italian nationalism and unity, which made him a moral force throughout Europe. In 1859 he joined the Whigs (or Liberals) as chancellor of the Exchequer (1859–66) under Lord Palmerston. His consequent acceptance of the democratic principle made him a champion of the lower classes. In 1866 he proposed successful amendments to the Reform Act, which was passed in 1867, and which extended the vote to about1 million urban workers.

Gladstone as Prime Minister. In his first and greatest ministry (1868–74) Gladstone sought to free

William Ewart Gladstone

the individual from obsolete restrictions. Entrance to the civil service was based on competition, the purchase of army commissions was ended, and the secret ballot was introduced. In addition, a system of state-supported elementary education guaranteed all children the right to schooling. Replaced by his great Conservative rival Benjamin Disraeli in 1874, Gladstone strongly condemned Disraeli's aggressive foreign and imperial policies. He appealed to the morality of the British voters during the famous Midlothian campaign and was returned to power in 1880.

Gladstone's most important reform during his second term (1880–85) was the Reform Act of 1884, which extended the vote to many rural voters. He also eliminated corruption in elections and secured for married women greater control over their property. Increasingly, however, he was forced to devote much of his time to troublesome imperial and Irish questions. His Land Act of 1881 attempted to end Irish unrest by giving Irish tenant farmers greater rights to the land they farmed, but by 1885 he accepted the necessity for Irish home rule.

Gladstone's third (1886) and fourth (1892–94) ministries were dominated by his home rule crusade. His first home rule bill of 1886 split the Liberal party, when many Liberals refused to support any reduction in British power over Ireland. In 1893 a second home rule bill passed the House of Commons, but it was rejected by the House of Lords. Gladstone, who as early as 1868 had stated that his "mission" was to "pacify Ireland," wanted to continue to fight for home rule, but his cabinet refused. He therefore resigned as prime minister in 1894 and retired. He died of cancer at Hawarden on May 19, 1898, at the age of 88. He was buried in Westminster Abbey.

Evaluation. Gladstone's importance rests in part on his reforms, which attempted to free the individual from all unnecessary restrictions—a fundamental 19th-century liberal belief. More than any other statesman of his age, he was able to mobilize the idealism of the British public. He succeeded in part because of his strong religious convictions. A daily reader of the Bible and the author of numerous books on religion, he believed that through politics religion could be reflected and made practical. His personal life supported his public life. Gladstone was a devoted husband to his wife, Catherine Glynne, whom he married in 1839; they had eight children. His family and his home at Hawarden, where he spent six months each year, were sources of rest and inspiration.

Despite Gladstone's many achievements and his idealism, most historians today argue that he never really understood the needs and aspirations of the lower classes. His insistence on economy in government, his distrust of imperialism and foreign adventure, his hatred of socialism, and his disbelief in the ability of government to solve social problems made him reluctant to accept the implications of democracy. Gladstone remains what he always was—the greatest liberal of the Victorian Age.   B.L.B.

For further information on this person, see the section Biographies in the Bibliography in volume 28.

GLÅMA, also Glomma, largest river of Norway, rising near the town of Røros, E central Norway. The river flows in a southerly direction, emptying into the Skagerrak at the city of Fredrikstad after a course of about 604 km (about 375 mi). Navigation on the Glåma is possible for 16 km (10 mi), from the mouth to a waterfall, and then for 32 km (20 mi) to a second waterfall.

GLAMORGANSHIRE, former county, S Wales; Cardiff was the county town. Glamorganshire comprised a hilly area in the N and a fertile lowland area, including the Gower Peninsula, in the S along the Bristol Channel. Glamorganshire was conquered by the Normans beginning in the late 11th century. It was made a county in 1536. The county's mineral wealth (especially coal) was exploited in the mid-19th century and was responsible for the growth of the towns of Port Talbot, Cardiff, and Swansea. In 1974 Glamorganshire was divided between the new counties of West, Mid, and South Glamorgan (qq.v.).

GLAND, any structure of animals, plants, or insects that produces chemical secretions or excretions. Glands are classified by shape, such as tubular and saccular, or saclike, and by structure, such as simple and compound. Types of the simple tubular and the simple saccular glands are, respectively, the sweat and the sebaceous glands (see SKIN). The kidney (q.v.) is a compound tubular gland, and the tear-producing glands are compound saccular (see EYE). The so-called lymph glands are erroneously named and are in reality nodes (see LYMPHATIC SYSTEM). "Swollen glands" are actually infected lymph nodes.

Glands are of two principal types: (1) those of internal secretion, called endocrine, and (2) those of external secretion, called exocrine. Some glands such as the pancreas (q.v.) produce both internal and external secretions. Because endocrine glands produce and release hormones (see HORMONE) directly into the bloodstream without passing through a canal, they are called ductless. For the functions and diseases of endocrine glands, see ENDOCRINE SYSTEM.

In animals, insects, and plants, exocrine glands secrete chemical substances for a variety of purposes. In plants, they produce water, protective sticky fluids, and nectars. The materials for the eggs of birds, the shells of mussels, the cocoons of caterpillars and silkworms, the webs of spiders, and the wax of honeycombs are other examples of exocrine secretions.

GLANDERS, highly contagious febrile disease of horses, donkeys, and mules, sometimes transmitted to other animals and humans. Glanders, also known as equinia, attacks the mucous membranes and lymphatic system in animals. The disease is characterized by ulceration of the nose, involving the cartilage and bone, with a sticky discharge. Advanced cases involve the liver, spleen, and respiratory system. Swollen lymph nodes, called farcy buds, appear beneath the skin, especially of the legs, and later ulcerate.

Public health measures have made equine glanders in humans rare in the U.S. and Canada, with nearly all cases occurring among veterinarians, farmers, and horse handlers. Glanders can be transmitted from human to human. The disease organism, *Malleomyces mallei,* usually is introduced through a break in the skin. After an incubation period of from three to five days, headache, chills, fever, and vomiting occur, and farcy buds may appear. If untreated, the disease may be fatal within two to three weeks. The disease is treated with antibiotics as well as with medications that relieve the symptoms.

For further information on this topic, see the Bibliography in volume 28, section 594.

GLANVILL, Ranulf de (d. 1190), English statesman and jurist, born in Stratford (now Stratford Saint Andrew), Suffolk. He was sheriff of Yorkshire from 1163 to 1170 and of Lancashire after 1173. In 1176 he was appointed justice of the king's court, and in 1180 he became justiciar (chief political and judicial officer) to King Henry II of England.

During Henry's frequent sojourns in France, Glanvill ruled England. He reformed the English judicial system and was responsible for the first work embodying a systematic codification of English law, *Tractatus de Legibus et Consuetudinibus Regni Angliæ* (Treatise on the Laws and Customs of the Kingdom of England). This compilation, which bears his name, is based on the common law of England as it had developed by the middle of the 12th century.

GLASGOW, city, administrative center of Strathclyde Region, W Scotland, on the Clyde R. Glasgow is the largest city and leading industrial center of Scotland. It has an excellent harbor and modern port facilities. Major imports include petroleum, grain, and timber; exports are largely manufactured goods. The city is located near important coalfields and is a major steel-producing center. Other industries include shipbuilding and printing and the manufacture of textiles, carpets, aircraft engines, electronic equipment, chemicals, alcoholic beverages, and processed foods.

Relatively few buildings in Glasgow predate the 18th century; the most prominent of these are Saint Mungo's Cathedral (begun about 1136 and completed in the mid-15th cent.) and Provand's Lordship (c. 1471), the city's oldest house. Glasgow is an educational center; the University of Glasgow (1451), the University of Strathclyde (1796), the Royal Scottish Academy of Music and Drama (1890), Glasgow School of Art (1840), and several technical colleges are located here. The extensive collections of the Glasgow Museums and Art Galleries are among the finest in Great Britain. Also of note in the city are the Hunterian Museum (1807), the botanic gardens, and a zoo.

Glasgow grew around a church built in the mid-6th century by St. Kentigern (518?–603, also called St. Mungo), apostle to the Scots. In 1116 the town's church was rebuilt for the reconstituted episcopal see of Glasgow. The great commercial growth of the community dates from the union of Scotland with England in 1707. Glasgow obtained a large share of the American commerce and soon became a center of the tobacco trade. The river was dredged to accommodate seagoing vessels. The tobacco trade ceased as a result of the American Revolution and was subsequently supplanted by cotton textile manufacture and the sugar trade with the West Indies. In the early 19th century, Glasgow began its growth as a major iron founding and shipbuilding center. During World War II the city suffered some damage from German bombing. Slum clearance and urban redevelopment projects have been undertaken since the war. Pop. (1981) 762,288.

GLASGOW, Ellen Anderson Gholson (1874–1945), American novelist, born in Richmond, Va. Although she was a member of a southern aristocratic family, in her novels she rebelled against the idealization of the genteel traditions of the South before the American Civil War. She attempted a realistic interpretation of the South and its problems, showing the contrast between the old society and the new in the period following the war. Among her most important works are *The Battle-Ground* (1902), *Virginia* (1913), *Barren Ground* (1925), *The Romantic Comedians* (1926), *They Stooped to Folly* (1929), and *Vein of Iron* (1935). She won the Pulitzer Prize for her last novel, *In This Our Life* (1941).

GLASGOW, UNIVERSITY OF, institution of higher learning, in Glasgow, Scotland, founded in 1451 under a papal bull of Pope Nicholas V. In 1460 the school was moved from its original site on Rottenrow to High Street, where it remained for four centuries. For its first 200 years the university's standing fluctuated, but it acquired a distinguished academic reputation in the 18th century. The university was moved to its present site on Gilmore Hill in 1870. The ruling body includes a chancellor, elected to a life tenure by a general council; a principal, similarly appointed; and a rector, elected for a 3-year term by the students. The university grants degrees in arts, pure and applied science, medicine, veterinary medicine, engineering, divinity, law and financial studies, and social sciences. After three years of work or a 4-year honors course of study the university awards either the master of arts or the bachelor of science degree. Both degrees are the approximate equivalent of the U.S. baccalaureate degree. As graduate degrees the university offers both the degree of master (distinct from the master of arts) and the doctorate in specific fields. In the 20th century several new chairs and lectureships in branches of medicine, chemistry, physics, history, and literature were founded. Two of the colleges, Queen Margaret and Muirhead, are for women, who were first admitted to the university in 1892. The endowments of the institution have been supplemented by grants from the Carnegie Trust and the British government. The university library has benefited from several bequests, including the collection of the 18th-century Scottish anatomist

William Hunter (1718–83), consisting of coins, medals, anatomical exhibits, and black-letter books.

GLASHOW, Sheldon Lee (1932–   ), American physicist and Nobel laureate, who helped to span what appeared to be divergent explanations of the physical world and advance physics toward a single unifying theory. Born in New York City, Glashow went to Bronx High School of Science, Cornell University, and Harvard University, where he received a Ph.D. in physics in 1958. After five years at the University of California in Berkeley, he returned to Harvard to work on a theory involving the unification of weak interactions and electromagnetism. In 1979 he shared the Nobel Prize in physics with the physicists Steven Weinberg of Harvard and Abdus Salam of the University of London for devising a theory that demonstrates the identity of electromagnetic interactions of particles and interactions caused by weak nuclear force.

GLASS, an amorphous substance made primarily of silica fused at high temperatures with borates or phosphates. Glass is also found in nature, as the volcanic material obsidian (q.v.) and as the enigmatic objects known as tektites (see TEKTITE). It is neither a solid nor a liquid but exists in a vitreous, or glassy, state in which molecular units have disordered arrangement but sufficient cohesion to produce mechanical rigidity. Glass is cooled to a rigid state without the occurrence of crystallization; heat can reconvert glass to a liquid form. Usually transparent, glass can also be translucent or opaque. Color varies with the ingredients of the batch.

Molten glass is plastic and can be shaped by means of several techniques. When cold, glass can be carved. At low temperatures glass is brittle and breaks with a shell-like fracture on the broken face. Such natural materials as obsidian and tektites (from meteors) have compositions and properties similar to those of synthetic glass.

Glass was first made before 2000 BC and has since served humans in many ways. It has been used to make useful vessels as well as decorative and ornamental objects, including jewelry. Glass also has architectural and industrial applications.

MATERIALS AND TECHNIQUES

The basic ingredient of glass compositions is silica, derived from sand, flint, or quartz.

Composition and Properties. Silica can be melted at very high temperatures to form fused silica glass. Because this glass has a high melting point and does not shrink or expand greatly with changing temperatures, it is suitable for laboratory apparatus and for such objects subject to heat shock as telescope mirrors. Glass is a poor conductor of both heat and electricity and

therefore useful for electrical and thermal insulation (q.v.). For most glass, silica is combined with other raw materials in various proportions. Alkali fluxes, commonly the carbonates of sodium or potassium, lower the fusion temperature and viscosity of silica. Limestone or dolomite (calcium and magnesium carbonates) act as stabilizers for the batch. Other ingredients such as lead and borax give to glass certain physical properties.

Water glass and soda-lime glass. Glass of high soda content can be dissolved in water as a syrupy fluid. Known as water glass, it is used commercially for fireproofing and as a sealant. Most manufactured glass is a soda-lime composition used to make bottles, tableware, lamp bulbs, and window and plate glass.

Lead glass. The fine-quality table glass known as crystal is made from potassium-silicate formulas that include lead oxide. Lead glass is heavy and has an enhanced capacity to refract light, which makes it suitable for lenses and prisms, as well as for imitation jewels. Because lead absorbs high-energy radiation, lead glasses are used in shields to protect personnel in nuclear installations.

Borosilicate glass. Borosilicate glass contains borax as a major ingredient, along with silica and alkali. Noted for its durability and resistance to chemical attack and high temperatures, it is widely employed for cooking utensils, laboratory glassware, and chemical process equipment.

Color. Impurities in the raw materials affect the color of glass. For a clear, colorless substance, glassmakers add manganese to counteract the effects of iron traces that produce greens and browns. Glass can be colored by dissolving in it metallic oxides, sulfides, or selenides. Other colorants may be dispersed as microscopic particles.

Miscellaneous ingredients. Typical glass formulas include broken waste glass of related composition (cullet), which promotes melting and homogenization of the batch. Fining agents such as arsenic or antimony are often added to cause the release of small bubbles during the melting.

Physical properties. Depending on the composition, some glass will melt at temperatures as low as 500° C (900° F); others melt only at 1650° C (3180° F). Tensile strength (q.v.), normally between 280 and 560 kg per sq cm (4000 and 8000 lb per sq in), can exceed 7000 kg per sq cm (100,000 lb per sq in) if the glass is specially treated. Specific gravity ranges from 2 to 8, or from less than that of aluminum to more than that of steel. Similarly wide variations occur in optical and electrical properties.

Mixing and Melting. After careful preparation and measurement, the raw materials are mixed

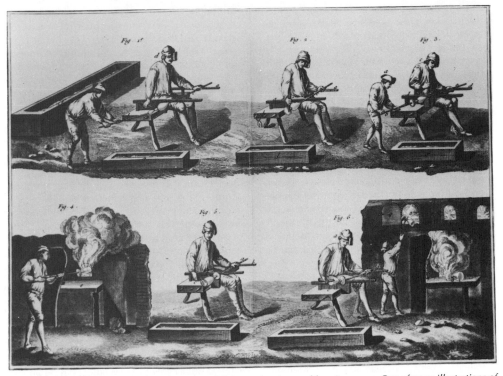

The last stages of shaping glass in wood-burning ovens. One of many illustrations of glassmaking from Denis Diderot's 18th-century encyclopedia.

and undergo initial fusion before being subjected to the full heat needed for vitrification. In the past, melting was done in clay pots heated in wood- or coal-burning furnaces. Pots of fireclay, holding from 0.5 to 1.5 metric tons of glass, are still used when relatively small amounts of glass are needed for handworking. In modern glass plants, most glass is melted in large tank furnaces; these furnaces, which were first introduced in 1872, can hold more than 1000 metric tons of glass and are heated by gas, oil, or electricity. The glass batch is fed continuously into an opening (doghouse) at one end of the tank, and the melted, refined, and conditioned glass is drawn out the other end. In long forehearths, or holding chambers, the molten glass is brought to the correct working temperature, and the vitreous mass is then delivered to the forming machines.

Shaping. When working glass in its plastic state, five basic methods are employed to produce an almost limitless variety of shapes: casting, blowing, pressing, drawing, and rolling.

Casting. In this process, known to the ancients, molten glass is simply poured into a mold and allowed to cool and solidify. In modern times centrifugal casting processes have been developed in which the glass is forced against the sides of a rapidly rotating mold. Capable of forming precise, lightweight shapes, centrifugal casting is used for the production of television-tube funnels.

Glassblowing. The revolutionary discovery that glass could be insufflated and expanded to any shape was made in the third quarter of the 1st century BC, in the Middle East along the Phoenician coast. Glassblowing soon spread and became the standard way of shaping glass vessels until the 19th century. The necessary tool is a hollow iron pipe about 1.2 m (about 4 ft) long with a mouthpiece at one end. The glassblower, or gaffer, collects a small amount of molten glass, called a gather, on the end of the blowpipe and rolls it against a paddle or metal plate to shape its exterior (marvering) and to cool it slightly. The gaffer then blows into the pipe, expanding the gather into a bubble, or parison. By constantly reheating at the furnace opening, by blowing and marvering, the gaffer controls the form and thickness. Simple hand tools such as shears, tongs (pucellas), and paddles are used to refine the form, often while the glassblower sits in the special "glassmaker's chair," one with extended arms to support the blowpipe. Blown glass can also be shaped with molds: Part-size molds pattern the gather, which is then removed and blown to the desired size. Full-size molds into which the gather is entirely blown impart size, shape, and decoration. Additional gathers may be applied and manipulated to form stems, handles, and feet, or they may be trailed on and tooled for decoration. A shaped bubble can be "flashed" with color by dipping it into molten glass of contrasting color. To make cased glass, a gather is placed within, and fused to, one or more layers of differently colored glass. For finish work and fire polishing at the mouth of the furnace, the gather is transferred to a solid iron rod called a pontil, applied opposite the blowpipe, which is then removed. When the pontil is cracked off it leaves a "pontil mark" that may be later ground or polished away.

In 1903 a fully automatic blowing machine was perfected, thereby making mechanical glass-blowing possible.

Pressing. Some pressing was involved in the production of ancient cast wares to ensure that the glass had full contact with the mold. Islamic artisans used simple handpresses to form glass weights and seals. European manufacturers rediscovered the technique in the late 18th century, using it to make decanter stoppers and the bases of stemmed tableware. In the 1820s patents were taken out, particularly in the U.S., that led to the development of fully mechanical pressing. In this process, a gather of glass is dropped into a mold, and a plunger then squeezes the glass between itself and the outer mold and forms the final shape. Both the mold and the plunger may be patterned to impart decorative design to the object being made.

Drawing. Molten glass can be drawn directly from the furnace to make tubing, sheets, fibers, and rods of glass that must have a uniform cross section. Tubing is made by drawing out a cylindrical mass of semifluid glass while a jet of air is blown down the center of the cylinder.

Rolling. Sheet glass, and plate glass in particular, was originally produced by pouring molten glass on a flat surface and, with a roller, smoothing it out prior to polishing both its surfaces. Later it came to be made by continuous rolling between double rollers.

Lampworking. Lampworking consists of the reworking of preformed and annealed glass, generally to produce scientific laboratory equipment and decorative toys and figures. Rods and cylinders are reheated by air-gas or oxygen-gas flames and refashioned by hand or machine.

Annealing. After being formed, glass objects are annealed to relieve stresses built up within the glass as it cools (see ANNEALING). In an oven called a lehr, the glass is reheated to a temperature high enough to relieve internal stresses and then slowly cooled to avoid introducing new stresses. Stresses can be added intentionally to impart strength to a glass article. Because glass breaks as a result of tensile stresses that originate across an infinitesimal surface scratch, compressing the surface increases the amount of tensile stress that can be endured before breakage occurs. A method called thermal tempering introduces surface compression by heating the glass almost to the softening point and then cooling it rapidly with an air blast or by plunging it into a liquid bath. The surface hardens quickly; the subsequent contraction of the slower-cooling interior portions of the glass pulls the surface into compression. Surface compressions approaching 2460 kg per sq cm (35,000 lb per sq in) can be obtained in thick pieces by this method. Chemical strengthening methods also have been developed in which, through an ion-exchange process, the composition or structure of the glass surface is altered and surface compression introduced. Strengths exceeding 7000 kg per sq cm (100,000 lb per sq in) can be attained by chemical strengthening.

Decoration. After annealing, a glass object may be embellished in a number of ways. Some of them are as follows:

In cutting, to produce cut glass, facets, grooves, and depressions are ground into the surface with rotating disks of various materials, sizes, and shapes and a stream of water with an abrasive. The steps are marking the pattern, rough cutting, smoothing, and polishing.

Designs are engraved by means of a diamond point or a metal needle, or with rotating wheels, generally of copper.

In the etching process intaglio decoration is achieved with acid, the results varying from a rough to mat finish.

In sandblasting, fine grains of sand, crushed flint, or powdered iron are projected at high speed onto the glass surface, leaving a design in mat finish.

In cold painting, lacquer colors or oil paints are applied to glass but are not affixed by firing.

In enamel painting, enamel colors are painted and then fused onto the surface in a low-temperature firing.

In gilding, gold leaf, gold paint, or gold dust is applied to glassware and sometimes left unfired; low-temperature firing, however, is necessary for permanency.

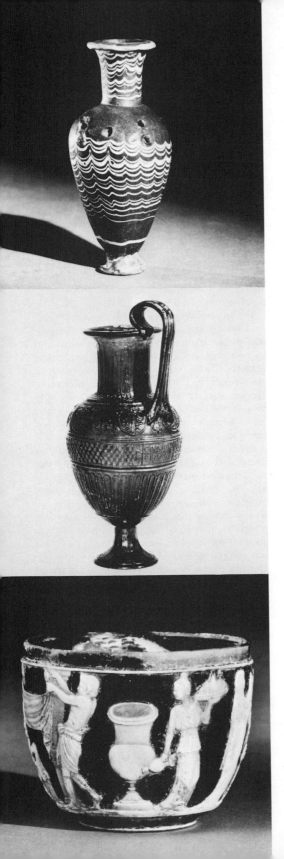

GLASS AS AN ART FORM

Archaeological evidence indicates that glass was first made in the Middle East, sometime in the 3d millennium BC.

Ancient Glass. The earliest glass objects were beads; hollow vessels do not occur before about 1500 BC. Asian artisans may have established the glass industry in Egypt, where the first vessels date from the reign (1504–1450 BC) of Thutmose III. Glass production flourished in Egypt and Mesopotamia until about 1200 BC, then virtually ceased for several hundred years. In the 9th century BC, Syria and Mesopotamia emerged as glassmaking centers, and the industry spread throughout the Mediterranean region. In the Hellenistic era, Egypt, because of the glassworks at Alexandria, assumed a leading role in supplying royal courts with luxury glass. It was on the Phoenician coast, however, that the important discovery of glassblowing occurred in the 1st century BC. In the Roman period glassmaking was undertaken in many areas of the empire, from Rome to Cologne.

Early techniques. Before the invention of the blowpipe, several methods existed for shaping and embellishing objects of colored glass, both translucent and opaque. Some articles were carved from solid blocks of glass. From potters and metalworkers glassmakers adapted casting processes, pouring molten glass into molds to produce inlays, statuettes, and open vessels such as jars and bowls. Preformed rods of glass could be heated and fused together in a mold for a "ribbon" glass. Patterns of great complexity were achieved by a mosaic technique, in which elements, fused in a rod, together made a design in cross section. Slices of such rods could be arranged in a mold to shape a vessel or plaque and then heated to fusion. "Gold band" glasses featured irregular bands of different colored glass, with gold leaf embedded in one translucent band.

The majority of pre-Roman glasswares were fashioned by the core technique. A mixture of clay and dung was fixed to a metal rod and given the internal shape of the desired vessel. It was dipped into a crucible of molten glass or was wound with threads of glass. The object was constantly reheated and smoothed on a flat stone. Threads of different colored glass were trailed on and combed, creating striking feather

Top: Amphoriskos, or small vase, core formed, with embedded trailed thread decoration, from Egypt (16th Dynasty). Center: Ewer of mold-blown amber glass, from the Roman Empire (1st cent. AD). Bottom: Cup, carved in the cameo technique from the Roman Empire (c. 1st cent. AD). The Corning Museum of Glass

patterns, as seen on Egyptian glass of the 18th and 19th dynasties. Handles, feet, and the neck were added and the object cooled. The rod was withdrawn and the core material picked out. Only vessels of limited size, such as cosmetic containers and small vases, could be made this way. Later core-formed articles from the 6th century BC closely followed the forms of Greek pottery (*see* POTTERY).

Roman glass. Glassblowing, a less expensive and time-consuming method of manufacture, spread from Syria to Italy and other parts of the Roman Empire, gradually superseding the old techniques. A new taste in glass styles developed: The earlier manufacturing processes emphasized color and pattern; blowing enhanced the thin, translucent qualities of the material. Also, by the end of the 1st century AD, colorless glass supplanted colored glass as the most fashionable sort. Glassblowing made large-scale production possible and changed the status of glassware to an everyday material, used for windows, drinking vessels, and containers of all kinds.

The structure of the empire doubtless fostered the extraordinary developments in glassmaking that occurred in this period. Most of the known decorative techniques were invented by artisans of the Roman era. Blown glasswares were patterned in part and full-size molds. Such molds enabled novelty items such as head-shaped flasks to be produced in quantity. A delicately patterned ewer (1st century AD) in the Corning Museum of Glass, Corning, N.Y., is one of a remarkable group of mold-blown objects that bear the names of their makers. Some Roman glass has elaborately threaded and tooled decoration. Glasswares could be painted with religious and historical scenes, or could feature designs in gold leaf pressed between two layers of clear glass. Ancient glassmakers adapted lapidary skills to make lathe-cut, carved, and engraved glass of considerable beauty. In cameo glass, layers of different colored glass were fused together and then carved so as to leave contrasting motifs in relief. Best known of Roman cameo glass is the Portland Vase (1st century AD, British Museum, London), which depicts the myth of Peleus and Thetis. Delicate effects were achieved in the *diatreta,* or caged cups, in which great portions of the outer surface were cut away, leaving an intricate openwork frame that appears to stand almost free of the vessel within. The famous Lycurgus Cup (4th century AD, British Museum) epitomizes this practice.

Western Glass. The manufacture of household glass suffered a general decline in the West with the fall of the Roman Empire.

Medieval glass. Under Frankish influence glassmakers in northern Europe and Britain continued to produce utilitarian vessels, some of new, robust forms. The decoration of these objects was limited to simple molded patterns, threading, and applied ornaments such as prunts (blobs of glass). Mostly green in color, the glass was at first a soda-glass composition made with ashes of marine plants imported from the Mediterranean, as they had been during Roman times. By the late Middle Ages, however, soda was no longer available, and northern glassmakers turned to the wood ash from their own wood-fired furnaces as a flux, for a potash-lime glass. Because the glasshouses were situated in the forests that provided fuel and ash, the glass made was called forest glass, waldglas. Common glass in the waldglas style continued to be made in the lesser European factories until modern times.

The glory of Western glassmaking in the medieval period, through patronage of the church, was mosaic glass in Mediterranean Europe and stained-glass windows in the north (*see* MOSAIC; STAINED GLASS). Mosaics were made of small glass cubes, or tesserae, embedded in cement. The tesserae, cut from solid cakes of glass, could be extremely elaborate, with gold and silver lead inlaid. Little is known of the production of mosaic glass before the 14th century.

Glass windows in churches are mentioned in documents as early as the 6th century, but the earliest extant examples date from the 11th century. The finest windows are considered those from the 13th and 14th centuries, primarily in France and England. Glasshouses in Lorraine and Normandy may have provided much of the flat glass for medieval cathedral windows. The glass was colored, or flashed with color, and then cut into the shapes required by the design. Details were painted into the glass, often with a brownish enamel. The pieces were fitted into lead strips and set in an iron framework. The art declined in the late Renaissance but was revived in the 19th century.

Renaissance to the 18th century. Although glassmaking was practiced in Venice from the 10th century on, the earliest known Venetian glassware dates from the 15th century. Concentrated on the island of Murano, the Venetian industry dominated the European market until 1700. The major contribution of the Venetians was the development of a highly refined, hard-soda glass of great ductility. Colorless and highly transparent, the glass resembled rock crystal and was known as *cristallo.*

The first *cristallo* wares were simple forms, often embellished with jewellike enamel designs.

Objects were also blown of colored and opaque glass. By the late 16th century, forms became lighter and more delicate. The blowers exploited the workable nature of their material to produce fanciful tours de force. A type of filigree glass was developed in Venice and widely imitated. With lacelike effect, opaque white threads were incorporated in the glass and worked into intricate patterns. Some vessels were blown entirely of opaque white glass and painted with enamels in the manner of Chinese porcelain. Novelties made of lampworked glass were made at Murano, but Nevers, France, became most famous for this type of ware by the 17th century. Particularly suited to soda glass was the practice of diamond-point engraving, a technique favored in the 17th century by Dutch artisans. By hammering the diamond-point stylus for a stippled effect, they created ambitious pictorial designs.

Glass manufacturers throughout Europe tried to copy the Venetians in their production methods, materials, and decorative vocabulary. Knowledge was spread through the glasswares themselves, through the *Art of Glass* (1612) by Antonio Neri (1576–1614), and through Venetian glassblowers. Although forbidden by law to leave Venice and to divulge the secrets of their craft, many Murano glassmakers left Italy to set up glasshouses elsewhere in Europe. Each country developed its own *façon de Venise,* as nationalistic preferences for certain forms or decorations tempered the Venetian model. Italy's influence was ultimately weakened in the 17th century by the development of new glass recipes in Germany and England.

Germany's potash-lime glass, thicker and harder than *cristallo,* was well suited to wheel-engraved decoration. Caspar Lehmann (c. 1565–1622), at the court of Holy Roman Emperor Rudolf II in Prague, was largely responsible for the development of engraving in the early 1600s. Glass cutters and engravers in Nuremberg and Potsdam became famous for skillfully executed designs in the baroque manner. At the same time, the Germanic glasshouses continued their tradition of enameled and cold-painted glass.

The other improvement in glass that served to diminish Europe's reliance on Venice was the lead-oxide glass formulated (c. 1676) by George Ravenscroft (1618–81) in England. Softer, more brilliant, and more durable than the brittle *cris-*

Top: Goblet of blown, colorless glass, enameled, from Venice, Italy (16th cent.). Center: Beaker of blown green glass with applied looped prunts (glass ornaments fused on) from Germany (c. 16th cent.). Bottom: Goblet, blown, diamond-point engraved with a peasant scene, from the Netherlands (17th cent.). The Corning Museum of Glass

A wine fountain of lead glass, made toward the end of the 18th century, possibly in Ireland. After 1780, taxation of the materials used by English glassmakers induced many to transfer their operations to Ireland. Here lead glass, in which lead was an important ingredient, was extensively produced until about 1830. Lead glass possesses a special softness and brilliance that make it particularly suitable for cut glass.

The Henry Francis du Pont Winterthur Museum

tallo, English lead glass was considered the finest glass of the 18th century. English table glass dominated the European and colonial markets and became a model for Continental production. English innovations of the mid-18th century were glasses with air or opaque-enamel twists encased in the stems. Among the most prestigious forms of the period was the English cut-glass chandelier. Lead glass, especially suited to cutting, reached its full potential in the neoclassical wares of the Anglo-Irish period (1780–1830).

American glass. Glassmaking was the first manufacture undertaken in America, with a glasshouse built at Jamestown, Va., in 1608. The first commercially successful glassworks was that of Caspar Wistar (1696–1752) in Salem Co., N.J., between 1739 and 1777. Immigrant German artisans there and at other factories produced bottles, windowpanes, and some table glass in Germanic styles. Henry William Stiegel (1729–85) sought to imitate English imported lead glass at his factory in Lancaster Co., Pa., from 1763 to 1774. The most important glassworks built after the American Revolution was that of John Frederick Amelung (1741–98) in Frederick Co., Md., which was in operation from 1784 to 1795.

19th and 20th centuries. The stylistic history of glass in the 19th century is dominated by rapid advances in glass technology and by the rediscovery and adaptation of older methods.

Mechanical pressing, introduced in the U.S., was a cheap, fast means of production that greatly expanded the role of glass in the home and in industry. Before 1850, wares were pressed in intricate lacy designs that offset a cloudiness in the glass caused by contact with the cooler mold. Simpler designs popular from the 1840s on, known as pressed pattern glass, were available in many forms. The more expensive cut glass declined in favor because of the competition from pressed glass. Only about 1880 did cut glass regain some of its earlier popularity with the elaborate "brilliant" patterns, examples of great technical virtuosity that exploited the refractive properties of quality glass.

Beginning in the late 18th century, a number of Roman glassmaking techniques were revived and modified to suit neoclassical taste. Continental glass factories made a version of laminated gold-leaf glass, called *zwischengoldglas.* Cameolike effects were attained with encrusted sulphides, and actual cameo engraving and cutting were practiced by artisans beginning in midcentury, culminating in the work of Thomas Webb and Sons (founded 1837), a glasshouse in Stourbridge, England. Paperweights, popular from about 1845, were often made in a millefiori (thousand flowers) design recalling the mosaic glass of ancient times. Renaissance rock crystal inspired a technique of polished engraved glass in the late 19th century.

Bohemia continued to excel in wheel-engraved decoration with the work of such artisans as Dominik Biemann (1800–57). Other methods, such as cased glass, were practiced in Bohemian factories and copied throughout Europe and the U.S. Chemical advancements led to new opaque colored glass such as lithyalin, which resembled semiprecious stones. Transparent enamels and stains were applied to vessels, paralleling the revival of stained-glass windows.

Inspired by the revivals of historical glassworking methods and spurred by the capabilities of improved chemical technology, glassmakers by 1880 were creating new styles of handworked glass, generally called art glass. These were mostly decorative and novelty forms, made in reaction to mass-produced wares. Between 1890 and 1910 the most fashionable styles reflected the international Art Nouveau (q.v.) movement. Louis Comfort Tiffany in the U.S., and Émile Gallé (1846–1904) and the firm of Daum Frères (founded 1889) in France, were the leading proponents of the style. They produced glasses of naturalistic shapes, sinuous lines, exotic colors,

A vase of iridescent glass from the studios of Louis C. Tiffany. Metropolitan Museum of Art– Gift of the Louis Comfort Tiffany Foundation, 1951

English millefiori paperweight, magnum-size mushroom, by George Bacchus & Sons of Birmingham (mid-19th cent.). New-York Historical Society

and unusual surface effects, such as Tiffany's iridescent Favrile glass.

After World War I new interests in texture and formalized decoration emerged, seen in the designs of René Lalique and Maurice Marinot (1882–1960). Beginning in the 1930s, exquisitely clear, colorless lead glass, often engraved, was popularized by several Scandinavian and American firms.

A new era in glassmaking began in the early 1960s with the studio glass movement, led by the Americans Harvey Littleton (1922–   ) and Dominick Labino (1910–87). With small tank furnaces in studio settings, artisans explore glass as an artistic medium. Innovative sculptural forms and decorative techniques are being developed at workshops in the U.S. and around the world.

Non-Western Glass. Glassmaking was not as strong a tradition in Islamic and Far Eastern countries as it was in the West. Forms and techniques developed that closely reflected their individual cultures; these, in turn, influenced Western forms.

Islamic glass. The history of glass from the 8th through the 14th century focuses on the Islamic world of the Middle East. Earlier Sassanian traditions of carved glass were continued by Muslim artisans, who made high-relief cut (*hochschnitt*) vessels, many with animal subjects. Quality colorless glass with fine wheel-engraved designs was also produced. The possibilities for decoration were expanded with the introduction of fired-on enamel colors and gilding, techniques for which the glasshouses at Aleppo and Damascus were famous. From Egypt came the discovery of luster stains, which created lustrous metallic effects in browns, yellows, and reds on both pottery and glass. Mosque lamps, bowls, beakers, and bottles were painted in the rhythmic, geometric patterns of Islam. Their shapes and decorations influenced later Western production, particularly in Venice and Spain.

Islamic mosque lamp decorated with enamel and gilding, from Syria (c. 1350).
The Corning Museum of Glass

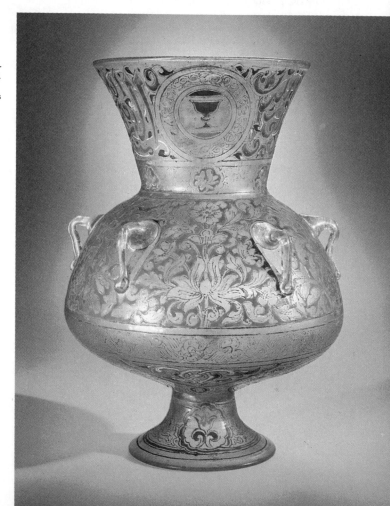

Indian glass. Glass was made in India as early as the 5th century BC, but the industry was not established until the Mughal period, and particularly in the 17th century. Forms included hookah bases, sprinklers, and dishes, usually gilded or enameled in floral patterns. In the 18th century the British East India Co. sold quantities of English glass to the Indian market, some of which was then wheel-engraved by Indian artisans.

Far Eastern glass. Chinese-made glassware in the distinctive "eye bead" form, with inlays resembling eyes, has been excavated from Chou dynasty sites (c. 1027–256 BC). Early glass objects, often melted from imported preformed glass cakes, were small and were carved in close imitation of gemstones. The use of glass to simulate semiprecious stones for jewelry and later for snuff bottles is a recurring theme in Chinese glass. Few vessels of glass are known before the glassworks at the Peking Imperial Palace was erected in 1680. Under the influence of the Jesuits at the Peking court, blown glass vessels in Western European styles were produced. Glass in the Chinese idiom dominated 18th- and 19th-century production, however, featuring richly colored objects with carved and enameled decoration. The Chinese mastered the art of cameo cutting in glass. Chinese glass vessels are characteristically of simple, porcelain-inspired shapes, with thick, often multilayered walls and a waxy surface sheen.

No evidence exists of glass made in Japan before 200 BC. Some glass vessels in the forms of Buddhist relic bottles and cinerary urns are believed to date from the Asuka/Nara periods (AD 552–784), but glassmaking apparently ceased in the 13th century. The craft was revived about 1750.

TYPES OF COMMERCIAL GLASS

The wide range of uses of the material has resulted in the development of a number of different types of glass.

Window Glass. Window glass, in use since the 1st century AD, was orginally made by casting, or by blowing hollow cylinders that were slit and flattened into sheets. The crown process was a later technique, in which a gather of glass was blown and shaped into a flattened globe or crown. The pontil rod was attached to the flat side, the blowpipe removed. By spinning the reheated crown on the rod, the hole left by the blowpipe enlarged, and eventually the disk, through centrifugal force, flapped out in a large circular sheet. The pontil rod was cracked off, leaving a scar, or bull's-eye. Today, nearly all window glass is made mechanically by drawing glass upward from a molten pool fed from a tank furnace. In the Fourcault process the glass sheet is drawn through a slotted refractory block submerged in the surface of the glass pool, into a vertical annealing furnace from which it emerges to be cut into sheets.

Plate Glass. Ordinary drawn window glass is not entirely uniform in thickness because of the nature of the process by which it is made. The variations in thickness distort the appearance of objects viewed through panes of the glass.

The traditional method of overcoming such defects has been the use of ground and polished plate glass. Plate glass was first produced at Saint Gobain, France, in 1668, by pouring glass into an iron table and rolling it flat with a roller. After annealing, the plate was ground and polished on both sides. Plate glass is now made by rolling the glass continuously between double rollers located at the end of a forehearth. After the rough sheet has been annealed, both sides of it are finished continuously and simultaneously.

Grinding and polishing are now being supplanted by the cheaper float-glass process. In this process flat surfaces are formed on both sides by floating a continuous sheet of glass on a bath of molten tin. The temperature is high enough to allow the surface imperfections to be removed by fluid flow of the glass. The temperature is gradually lowered as the glass moves along the tin bath, and the glass passes through a long annealing oven at the end.

Unpolished rolled glass, often with figured surfaces produced by designs incised in the rolls, is used architecturally. Wire glass, made by introducing wire mesh into the molten glass before it passes between the rollers, is used to prevent the glass from shattering if it is struck. Safety glass, for automobile windshields, is made by laminating a sheet of transparent polyvinyl butyral plastic between two sheets of thin plate glass. The plastic adheres tightly to the glass and holds the broken shards in place even after hard blows.

Bottles and Containers. Bottles, cosmetic jars, and other glass containers are produced by an automatic process that combines pressing (to form the open end of the container) and blowing (to form the hollow body of the container). In a typical automatic bottle-blowing machine, a gob of molten glass is dropped in a narrow, inverted mold and forced down by an air blast into the lower portion of the mold, which corresponds to the neck of the finished bottle. A baffle then drops over the top of the mold, and a blast from the bottom, up through the neck, partly forms the bottle. The half-formed bottle, called a parison, is held by the neck, inverted, and then lowered into a second finishing mold, in which

A sheet of glass takes form as molten glass is forced between double rollers. Next the sheet is annealed in an oven. PPG Industries, Inc.

another air blast blows it out to its finished dimensions. In another type of machine, used for large-mouthed containers, the parison is simply pressed in a mold by a plunger before being blown in a finishing mold. Shallow jars, such as those used for cosmetics, are merely pressed.

Optical Glass. Most lenses used in eyeglasses, microscopes, telescopes, cameras, and certain other optical instruments are made from optical glass (*see* Lens; Optics). Optical glass differs from other glass in the way in which it bends, or refracts, light. The manufacture of optical glass is a delicate and exacting operation. The raw materials must be of the highest purity, and great care must be taken so that no imperfections are introduced in the manufacturing process. Small air bubbles and inclusions of unvitrified matter will cause distortion on the surface of the lens. Striae, the streaks caused by incomplete chemical homogeneity in the glass, will also cause serious distortion, and strains in glass caused by improper annealing will further impair optical qualities.

Optical glass was originally melted in pots for prolonged periods, during which it was constantly stirred by a refractory rod. After a lengthy annealing, the glass was broken into pieces. The best fragments were further reduced, reheated, and pressed into the desired forms. In recent years a method has been adopted for the con-tinuous manufacture of glass in platinum-lined tanks, using platinum-lined stirrers in the cylindrical end chambers (or homogenizers). This process produces greater quantities of optical glass that are cheaper and superior to glass produced by the earlier method. (Plastics are increasingly used in place of optical glass for simple lenses: Although not as durable and scratch resistant as glass, they are strong and lightweight and can absorb dyes.)

Photosensitive Glass. Photosensitive glass is similar to photographic film in that gold or silver ions in the material will respond to the action of light. This glass is used in printing and reproducing processes. Heat treatment following an exposure to light produces permanent changes in photosensitive glass.

Photochromic glass darkens when exposed to light but fades to its original clear state when the light is removed. This behavior is achieved by the action of light on extremely small silver chloride or silver bromide crystals distributed throughout the glass. Photochromic glass finds a natural use in spectacle lenses that darken into sunglasses when in the sun and lighten again when removed from sunlight. The field of electronics also finds uses for this kind of glass.

Glass Ceramics. Glass containing certain metals will form a localized crystallization when exposed to ultraviolet radiation. If heated to high temperatures, the glass will convert to crystalline ceramics with mechanical strength and electrical insulating properties greater than that of ordinary glass. Such ceramics (q.v.) are now made for such uses as cookware, rocket nose-cones, and space-shuttle tiles. Other metallic glasses—including alloys of pure metals—can be magnetized, are strong and flexible, and prove very useful in high-efficiency electrical transformers.

Glass Fibers. It is possible to produce fibers that can be woven or felted like textile fiber by drawing out molten glass to diameters of a few ten-thousandths of an inch. Both long, continuous multifilament yarns and short-staple fibers 25 to 30 cm (10 to 12 in) long may be produced.

Woven into textile fabrics, glass fibers make excellent drapery and upholstery materials because of their chemical stability, strength, and resistance to fire and water. Glass fabrics alone, or in combination with resins, make excellent electrical insulation. By impregnating glass fibers with plastics, a composite fiberglass is formed that combines the strength and inertness of glass with the impact resistance of the plastic.

Miscellaneous Types of Glass. Glass bricks are hollow construction blocks with ribbed or patterned sides that can be laid in mortar and used for exterior walls or interior partitions.

Foam glass, used in floats or as insulation, is made by adding a foaming agent to finely ground glass and heating the mixture to the softening point. At that point the foaming agent releases a gas that produces a multitude of small bubbles within the glass.

In the 1950s glass optical fibers (see FIBER OPTICS) were developed that have many uses in science, medicine, and industry. High-refractive-index glass fibers, laid parallel to one another and separated by thin layers of low-refractive-index glass, can be optically worked as a lens. Fiberscopes incorporating such bundles can transmit an image through acute angles, thus easing the examination of normally inaccessible sites. Such solid fiber-optics applications as magnifiers, minifiers, and faceplates also improve viewing. When used in conjunction with lasers, optical fibers are also proving important in the development of various communications systems (see TELEPHONE). A new kind of glass called halide glass, discovered in the 1970s, may prove especially useful for this application. It is made of a halide, such as fluorine, combined with a heavy metal, such as zirconium, barium, or hafnium.

Laser glass is doped, or mixed, with several percent of neodymium oxide and is capable of emitting laser light if the glass is pumped and assembled in the proper device. It is considered a good laser source because of the relative ease with which large, homogenous specimens of the glass can be obtained for extremely high-powered generation.

Double-glazing cells are units in which two sheets of plate or window glass are sealed together at their edges, leaving an air space between. Various types of seals and spacing materials may be used in their construction. As windows they provide superior heat insulation and will not cloud over in moist air.

A method for making large glass structures without using high temperatures was developed in the 1980s at the University of Florida. Called the sol-gel technique, it mixes water with a chemical such as tetramethoxysilane to produce a silicon oxide polymer; a chemical additive slows down the condensation process and allows the polymer to build up uniformly. The method may prove useful for making large, complex shapes with specific properties.   A.P.S.

For further information on this topic, see the Bibliography in volume 28, sections 625, 709.

GLASS, Carter (1858–1946), American congressman and senator, who was responsible for major banking reforms. From Virginia, he served in the U.S. House of Representatives from 1902 to 1918 and, as chairman of the House Committee on Banking and Currency, was the chief author of the Federal Reserve Act in 1913. In 1918 he became secretary of the treasury in the cabinet of President Woodrow Wilson. Two years later Glass resigned the secretaryship to fill a vacancy in the U.S. Senate. He was elected senator in 1924 and was subsequently reelected three times. He was cosponsor of the Banking Act of 1933, which established the Federal Deposit Insurance Corporation (q.v.).

GLASS, Philip (1937–), American composer and performer, born in Chicago, Ill. He was educated at the Juilliard School and studied with Nadia Boulanger in Paris. He was greatly influenced by Indian sitar player and composer Ravi Shankar. Glass's music, which he often performs with his own ensemble, is built around a very few musical phrases that are repeated over and over with slight changes in pattern and rhythm. His best-known works are the operas *Einstein on the Beach* (1976); *Satyagraha* (1980), about Mahatma Gandhi; *Akhnaten* (1984); and *The Voyage* (1992), about Christopher Columbus.

GLASSBORO, borough, Gloucester Co., S New Jersey; inc. 1920. Manufactures include cocoa, bottle closures, and precision instruments. A glass museum is here. The community was settled in the 1770s by glassmakers and was an important glass-bottle manufacturing center for 150 years, from which its name is derived. In 1967 a meeting between President Lyndon B.

Johnson and Soviet premier Aleksey N. Kosygin took place here at Glassboro State College, now Rowan College (1923). Pop. (1980) 14,574; (1990) 15,614.

GLASS SNAKE, common name for any lizard of the genus *Ophisaurus,* of the family Anguidae, characterized by the absence of limbs and by smooth, hard, highly polished, shinglelike scales that ring the body. The glass-snake lizard moves in the manner of snakes, but is less graceful, being restricted by its hard scales. This genus, like other lizards of the same family (*see* BLIND-WORM), has a fragile tail; the tail is twice as long as the body and breaks off readily when handled. The posterior portion of the tongue is thick and fleshy; the anterior portion is thin and forked and retracts into the posterior portion. A deep fold runs along each side of the body.

The American glass-snake lizard, *O. ventralis,* is found from North Carolina and southern Illinois to southern Mexico. The color varies among members of the species: Some are black with a green spot on each scale; others are olive-colored with clusters of yellowish dots on each scale. In some specimens the dots coalesce and form a longitudinal stripe. It may reach a length of 91 cm (36 in); and mainly lives on insects. The largest species of glass snake is the Old World scheltopusik, *O. apodus,* which reaches a length of 1 m (4 ft).

GLASTONBURY, town, Hartford Co., central Connecticut, on the Connecticut R., near Hartford; inc. 1693. It is situated in a farming region, and some manufacturing industries are here. It has a number of fine homes dating from the 18th century. Settled in 1650 as part of Wethersfield, the community became a separate town in the 1690s and was named for Glastonbury, England. Pop. (1980) 24,327; (1990) 27,901.

GLASTONBURY, town, in Mendip District, Somerset, SW England. It has a livestock market and manufactures that include footwear and leather articles. Glastonbury is famous as a historical religious center and for the many legends associated with it. A Celtic monastery existed on the site as early as the 4th century. By the 10th century the abbey here was one of the most important in England. The town declined after the dissolution of the monasteries in the 1530s. Legends assert that the first English Christian church was founded here in the 1st century AD by Joseph of Arimathea. Glastonbury is also identified with the Island of Avalon, of Arthurian legend. Nearby are the remains of an Iron Age lake village. The village, which flourished from the 1st century BC to the 1st century AD, was built over a swamp on timber piles. Pop. (Mendip District, 1981) 87,030.

GLAUBER, Johann Rudolph (1604–70), major German-Dutch chemist, born in Karlstadt, Germany, who foresaw the importance of chemistry in industry. He developed several techniques, including flame and bead tests, still used in the field of inorganic chemistry called qualitative analysis. He also developed the distillatory furnace and prepared several salts for the first time, including hydrated sodium sulfate, called Glauber's salt, used as a flux in metallurgy (q.v.).

GLAUCOMA, a family of diseases, characterized by abnormal pressure within the eyeball (*see* EYE) leading to loss of visual field and declining vision. Approximately one-eighth of all blindness in the U.S. is due to glaucoma.

The most common glaucomas, called primary, consist of two types: open angle (chronic simple) and narrow angle (acute). Secondary glaucomas may be caused by infections, tumors, or injuries. A third group, congenital glaucomas, are largely due to developmental abnormalities.

The pressure of the fluid contents of the eyeball serves to maintain its shape for optical purposes. Intraocular pressure, which normally varies between 15 and 20 mm of mercury, is regulated by a balance between aqueous humor production and outflow. In glaucoma the outflow of aqueous fluid is obstructed at the angle of the anterior chamber, and pressure within the eyeball increases. Glaucoma usually develops in middle age or later.

Patients with chronic simple glaucoma often have a family history of the disease, in which insidious damage, with loss of field, occurs even though pressure elevation is modest and no symptoms are exhibited. Acute narrow-angle glaucoma, on the other hand, causes pain, redness, pupil dilation, and severe vision loss. The cornea becomes cloudy and intraocular pressure is high. The field of vision is reduced increasingly as the disease progresses, a phenomenon that is demonstrated with an ophthalmic instrument called a perimeter. Because pressure within the eyeball increases with fluid intake, open-angle glaucoma can be verified by having the patient drink water and recording the intraocular pressure before and after with an instrument called a tonometer. In narrow-angle glaucoma, pressure measurements before and after dilating the pupil may provide a positive diagnosis.

Chronic simple glaucoma usually responds well to local medication to increase outflow. Systemic medications may be used to decrease aqueous production. If the disease does not respond to medical treatment, laser or mechanical surgery to create a new channel for outflow of intraocular fluid may be indicated. Acute glaucoma represents an emergency situation. Unless pressure within the eyeball is lowered within 24 hours, permanent damage may occur. Both medical and surgical intervention may be needed.

Formerly, glaucoma patients were told to avoid stimulants and spices. Little evidence exists to support such restrictions; however, avoiding large fluid intakes in short time periods is advisable.

REV. BY I.S.J.

For further information on this topic, see the Bibliography in volume 28, sections 487, 516.

GLAUCUS. *See* BELLEROPHON.

GLAZE. *See* PAINTING: *Renaissance Painting;* POTTERY.

GLAZUNOV, Aleksandr Konstantinovich (1865–1936), Russian composer, born in Saint Petersburg. Glazunov studied with the eminent Russian composer Nikolay Rimsky-Korsakov. Glazunov was the last important composer of the Russian national school founded by Mikhail Glinka; his work also shows the influence of the Hungarian composer Franz Liszt and the German composer Richard Wagner. In 1889, together with Rimsky-Korsakov, he completed the opera *Prince Igor,* left unfinished by the Russian composer Aleksandr Borodin on his death (1887). Glazunov taught at the St. Petersburg Conservatory between the years 1900 and 1906 and was its director from 1906 to 1917. He left the Soviet Union in 1928 and lived in Paris. His compositions include eight symphonies, the symphonic poems *Stenka Razin* and *The Kremlin* (1892), the ballets *Raymonda* (1898) and *The Seasons* (1901), the Violin Concerto op. 82 (1904), chamber music, and music for piano and for voice.

GLEE (from A.S. *gligge*, "music"), piece of unaccompanied vocal music for at least three voices, usually male. A glee may be either sprightly or melancholy and contains a number of harmonically supported musical themes. An English musical form, the glee was popular chiefly between 1700 and 1825. The most important composer of glees was Samuel Webbe (1740–1816). One purpose of the London Glee Club (1783–1857) was the encouragement of glee writing. In the U.S., *glee club* refers to choral groups that perform a popular style of music.

GLEN COVE, city, Nassau Co., SE New York, on the N shore of Long Island, at the entrance to Hempstead Harbor; inc. 1918. A residential community popular for recreational boating, it is the site of the Webb Institute of Naval Architecture (1889) and a Friends meeting house (1725). Settled in 1668, it was called Muskuito Cove until 1834. Pop. (1980) 24,618; (1990) 24,149.

GLENDALE, city, Maricopa Co., central Arizona, near Phoenix; settled 1892, inc. 1910. It is an important shipping point for fruit, vegetables, and cotton grown in the irrigated Salt R. valley. Clothing and paper products are manufactured in the city. The American Graduate School of International Management (1946) is here, and Luke Air Force Base is important to the local economy. The city was named for a community in Pennsylvania by settlers belonging to the Church of the Brethren. Pop. (1980) 96,988; (1990) 148,134.

GLENDALE, city, Los Angeles Co., SW California, a commercial and residential suburb of Los Angeles, at the junction of the San Gabriel and San Fernando valleys; platted 1887, inc. 1906. The city is a financial center and includes publishing firms and some light industry. A community college and the well-known Forest Lawn Memorial Park are here. Glendale is the site of the first Spanish land grant (Rancho San Rafael, 1784) in California. Pop. (1980) 139,060; (1990) 180,038.

GLENDORA, city, Los Angeles Co., SW California, at the foot of the San Gabriel Mts.; inc. as a city 1911. Irrigation systems, pumps, dental equipment, and strawberries are produced in the city. A community college is here. A ranch was established here in 1844 but permanent settlement did not begin until 1874. The community was a citrus-growing center until large-scale residential growth began in the late 1940s. Pop. (1980) 38,654; (1990) 47,828.

GLENDOWER, Owen (Welsh *Owain ab Gruffydd*) (1359?–1416?), lord of Glyndwr, in Wales, and the last Welsh chief to claim the title of independent prince of Wales. He is a Welsh national hero and historically famous as the leader of a major revolt for Welsh independence from English domination during the reign of King Henry IV of England. Henry retaliated in 1400 and 1401, but his campaigns were ineffectual. Glendower, gaining control of most of Wales, negotiated for aid with the Irish, the Scots, and the French, all enemies of England, and intrigued also with prominent English lords. The Welsh chief began to style himself prince of Wales; he called a parliament, established his own government for Wales, and entered a formal alliance with France in 1404. A year later, an English army under Prince Henry, later Henry V, defeated Glendower's forces in three successive battles. He was pardoned by Henry V in 1415; nothing is known of him after that date.

Glendower was the last great champion of Welsh independence. The Welsh have invested him with a mythology that has obscured historical fact. Shakespeare's *Henry IV, Part I,* presents Glendower as this idealized hero.

GLEN ELLYN, village, Du Page Co., NE Illinois, on the Du Page R., a residential suburb of Chicago;

settled 1830s, inc. 1892. It has a community college. In 1891 a developer created a lake here by damming a brook; he named it for his wife Ellen (Welsh, Ellyn), and the village, which had had several previous names, became known as Glen Ellyn. Pop. (1980) 23,649; (1990) 24,944.

GLENN, John Herschell, Jr. (1921–   ), American senator and former astronaut, born in Cambridge, Ohio. He entered Muskingum College, Ohio, in 1939, and left in his junior year to take preflight training in the Naval Aviation Cadet Program. As a pilot in the U.S. Marine Corps, he flew 149 combat missions in World War II and the Korean War. As a test pilot, in 1957, he became the first person to make a nonstop supersonic transcontinental flight, from Los Angeles to New York City, setting a speed record of 3 hr 23 min 8.4 sec. On Feb. 20, 1962, Glenn became the first American to orbit the earth in space, in the Project Mercury Gemini capsule *Friendship 7.* The three-orbit flight covered approximately 130,000 km (approximately 81,000 mi) in 4 hr 55 min. *See* SPACE EXPLORATION.

Glenn retired from the Marine Corps in 1965 and became a business executive and consultant to the National Aeronautics and Space Administration. His many awards and honors include the Distinguished Flying Cross (five times) and the Air Medal with 18 clusters. In 1974 Glenn was elected to the U.S. Senate as a Democrat from Ohio; he was reelected in 1980, 1986, and 1992. Glenn unsuccessfully contended for the 1984 Democratic presidential nomination.

GLENS FALLS, city, Warren Co., E New York, at falls on the Hudson R., near Lake George and in the foothills of the Adirondack Mts.; inc. as a city 1908. It is a manufacturing center situated in an agricultural and resort area; major products include pulp and paper, electrical equipment, clothing, machinery, chemicals, textiles, cement, and surgical instruments. Glens Falls is the site of the Hyde Collection, a museum containing European and American art; the Chapman Historical Museum; and a community college. Settled in the 1760s, the community, then known as Wing's Falls, was destroyed by British forces in 1780. The settlement was rebuilt in 1788 and named for Col. Johannes Glen (1735–1828). Cooper's Cave and other places in the area are described in *The Last of the Mohicans* (1826) by the American writer James Fenimore Cooper. Pop. (1980) 15,897; (1990) 15,023.

GLENVIEW, village, Cook Co., NE Illinois, on the Chicago R., near Lake Michigan and Chicago; settled 1833, inc. 1899. Major products include steel, machinery, printing equipment, and printed materials. A U.S. naval air station and the Grove

John H. Glenn, Jr., preparing for his historic earth-orbiting flight in the spacecraft Friendship 7 *in 1962.*   UPI

National Historical Landmark, a nature preserve with three historic homes, are located in the village. After a succession of names, the villagers selected the name Glenview in 1895. Pop. (1980) 32,060; (1990) 37,093.

GLIDER, heavier-than-air craft that has no engine, deriving its motive power from the aerodynamic forces acting upon it. In form, gliders resemble ordinary airplanes, but are characterized by extreme lightness, by low wing loading (the ratio of weight to wing area), and by high aspect ratio (the ratio of the wingspan to the wing width). Glider wings are much longer and narrower than those of powered aircraft. A good modern glider of the sailplane type (see below), when flying level in still air, sinks at a rate less than 90 cm (36 in) per sec, and therefore is able to climb in an air current that is rising at the rate of about 3 km/hr (about 2 mph).

Experiments with gliders laid the foundations for the design of the first powered aircraft. Beginning in the 1870s a number of pioneer aeronauts built gliders that made successful flights and provided much information regarding the efficient design of wings and control systems. Among these pioneers were the German inventor Otto Lilienthal and the American inventor Octave Chanute (1832-1910), Orville and Wilbur Wright, and John Joseph Montgomery (1858-1911). The first powered airplane to fly successfully was designed by the Wrights as a direct result of their earlier work with gliders. *See* AIRPLANE; AVIATION.

The chief impetus to the modern development of gliders, and the art of flying them, came from the Germans. In the years following World War I, Germany, which was forbidden by the Versailles Treaty to manufacture powered airplanes suitable for military use for the training of pilots, turned to the building of gliders and to research in glider flight. German aeronautical engineers discovered the great efficiency of light craft with long, birdlike wings and the meteorological conditions under which soaring flight could be successful.

Glider Flight. Upcurrents in the atmosphere, on which the glider pilot depends for motive power, are principally of two kinds: ridge currents and thermal currents. Ridge currents are formed when a steady wind blows against the side of a ridge or a range of hills. Such currents can be quite strong but are limited to an area relatively close to the windward edge of the ridge. Thermal currents are formed by heat rising from the ground, as, for example, over a bare field on a hot day. These currents are always present under cumulus clouds and to a dangerous extent under and in the towering, anvil-shaped clouds of thunderstorms.

In gliding flight, the craft must be launched from the ground by some exterior force. In practice this launching is usually accomplished by catapulting the glider by means of long elastic cords or by towing it aloft by means of a winch, an automobile, or a powered airplane. When a glider is launched by a tow, the pilot cuts loose the towline after reaching the desired altitude. Once in the air the pilot directs the glider in search of upcurrents. If simply wishing to remain in the air, the pilot may fly back and forth along a ridge where a suitable current exists. If making a cross-country flight, however, the pilot flies by "cloud chasing" or "thermal sniffing," searching for thermal currents that will give the glider lift. When such a current is found, the pilot will spiral the craft to remain within the current while gaining altitude. After reaching the maximum altitude to which the current will lift the glider, the pilot glides away to find another current. High-performance gliders can glide 20 km horizontally for every kilometer of altitude they have attained. Such flights are generally restricted to daylight hours, because of meterological conditions as well as lack of visibility.

Glider Types. In general, gliders are of three types. Primary gliders, used entirely for instruction purposes, consist of little more than a girder

The third glider of Wilbur and Orville Wright is launched from the top of Kill Devil Hill near Kitty Hawk, N.C., in 1902. This glider served as a model for the airplane they built the following year.　　　Smithsonian Institution

443

A modern single-space secondary glider, or sailplane, soars over the countryside, kept aloft by upcurrents.

framework to which the wings and control and stabilizing surfaces are attached. In them the pilot sits on an open seat at the front of the framework. Secondary gliders, or sailplanes, are built like ordinary airplanes with a fuselage and an enclosed cockpit seating one or two persons. They are designed for the maximum of aerodynamic efficiency. Gliders of the third type, cargo gliders, are used for military or peacetime purposes and are large craft designed to carry heavy loads. They are built not to soar but to be towed in groups behind a powered plane to increase the payload of the plane. The chief advantages of the cargo glider are its carrying capacity and its low landing speed, which make possible the landing of a heavy payload in a space too restricted for the operation of conventional planes.

Lifting Bodies. Experimental craft called lifting bodies were under investigation in the late 1960s as potential space vehicles that would allow astronauts to glide in from outer space. The U.S. Air Force and the National Aeronautics and Space Administration (NASA) were studying designs for a space vehicle that would acquire lift as it hurtled into the atmosphere of the earth and would then be maneuverable to a desired landing zone. Because conventional wings would snap off such a craft as it entered the atmosphere

at high speed, the entire undersurface of the craft had to function as a lifting surface. This is the source of the term *lifting bodies*. See SPACE EXPLORATION.

The lifting body program was started in the late 1950s. At that time NASA started experimenting with the M-2 and later with the HL-10 lifting bodies. These vehicles were dropped from B-52 bombers at high altitudes, and they glided to earth without power but with aerodynamic control. In the late 1960s the air force tested the X-24 lifting body. Rocket engines on this craft pushed its speed up to about 2200 km/hr (about 1350 mph). At that speed, the descent of the X-24 simulated a gliding reentry from space.

Other Glider Uses. Before World War II gliding was regarded largely as a sport. Annual glider meets at Elmira, N.Y., and elsewhere attracted hundreds of participants and thousands of spectators. During the war, however, gliders were put to extensive logistic use for carrying supplies and airborne troops. Notable glider operations were the German invasion of Crete and the Allied attack on Myitkyina in Burma. In the same period the technique of glider pickups was developed, in which a plane in flight hooks onto the tow-rope of a glider on the ground and lifts it into the air. Glider pickups have been successfully employed for the rescue of fliers forced down on terrain on which conventional craft could not be landed.

See also SOARING AND GLIDING.

For further information on this topic, see the Bibliography in volume 28, section 810.

GLIÈRE, Reinhold Moritzevich (1875–1956), Russian composer, one of the most facile and popular of the country's modern composers. Born in Kiev, Ukraine, he studied under the Russian composers Anton Arensky (1861–1906), Sergey Taneyev (1856–1914), and Mikhail Ippolitov-Ivanov (1859–1935). His early music followed styles of the Russian nationalist school, with elements of late romanticism and impressionism, and he later became a successful composer on revolutionary and folk themes, following the Soviet government dictum of "socialist realism" in the arts. His best-known works are his Symphony No. 3, titled *Ilya Murometz* (1911), based on the tale of a legendary Russian hero; and the ballet *Red Poppy* (1927). His other works include the opera *Shakh-Senem* (1925), based on Azerbaijani folk music; and orchestral and chamber works.

GLINKA, Mikhail Ivanovich (1804–57), Russian composer, born in Novospasskoye, and educated in Saint Petersburg. Glinka studied with various teachers in Russia, Italy, and Germany. Until 1835 his compositions consisted mainly of songs. His opera *A Life for the Tsar* (1836), which drew its story and music from Russian folktales and folk songs, was the first Russian opera of a national character. The music of his second opera, *Russlan and Ludmilla* (1842), based on a poem by the Russian poet Aleksandr Pushkin, was also drawn largely from Russian folk music. Glinka established himself as the founder of the Russian national school of music, which was subsequently carried on by such composers as Aleksandr Borodin, Modest Mussorgsky, and Nikolay Rimsky-Korsakov. Glinka was also interested in the popular music and dance of Spain, where he lived from 1845 to 1847, which inspired the overtures *Jota Aragonesa* and *Night in Madrid* (1851). His other works include the orchestral fantasia *Kamarinskaya* (1848), chamber music, piano pieces, and songs.

GLIWICE, city, S Poland, in Katowice Province, on the Klodnica R., at the E end of the Gliwice Canal near Katowice. A river port, road and rail hub, and coal-mining center, Gliwice has industries producing steel, machinery, chemicals, food products, cement, and bricks. Iron foundries were established in the 18th century. Gliwice is the site of the Silesia Technical University (1945) and several mining-research institutes. Chartered in 1276, the city has a rebuilt 13th-century church, a museum, and Chopin Park. Gli-

wice was called Gleiwitz when it belonged to Prussia and Germany (1742–1945). Pop. (1985 est.) 209,700.

GLOBE, in cartography, a spherical map of the earth (terrestrial globe) or the sky (celestial globe). The terrestrial globe is the only true cartographic representation of the earth and possesses several advantages over flat maps: Distances, directions, and areas are shown without distortion. Although the earth is not a perfect sphere (having a larger diameter at the equator than at the poles), the deviation is negligible at the scale of most globes. A celestial globe takes the earth as its imaginary center in showing the positions of the stars. The German geographer Martin Behaim constructed one of the first terrestrial globes in 1492. *See* MAP.

GLOBEFLOWER, common name for the perennial genus *Trollius*, of the family Ranunculaceae (*see* BUTTERCUP). Flowers of this genus, born in globe-shaped clusters, have large, yellow, petallike sepals and small, linear petals. Globeflowers are native to the colder parts of the northern hemisphere. The common globeflower, *T. europaeus,* called *lucken gowan* in Great Britain, is cultivated in flower gardens in the U.S. and Europe. It reaches a height of 60 cm (24 in). The spreading globeflower, *T. laxus,* somewhat smaller, grows in swampy areas of the northeastern U.S. and the Rocky Mountain region. It is now rare. An unrelated plant, a double-flowered variety of *Kerria japonica,* family Rosaceae (*see* ROSE), is called the Japanese globeflower. It grows to 2 m (6 ft).

GLOBE THEATRE, 17th-century English theater in Southwark, London, notable for the initial and contemporaneous productions of Shakespeare's plays and of the dramatic works of Ben Jonson, Beaumont and Fletcher, and others. The Globe was constructed in 1599 by the famous English actor Richard Burbage in partnership with Shakespeare and others. The octagonally shaped outer wall of the theater enclosed a roofless inner pit into which the stage projected; around the pit were three galleries one above the other, the topmost of which was roofed with thatch. In 1613 a cannon, discharged during a performance of Shakespeare's *Henry VIII,* set fire to the thatched roof and destroyed the building. The theater was rebuilt in 1614 but 30 years later was razed by the Puritans. A brewery now stands on its site.

For further information on this topic, see the Bibliography in volume 28, section 839.

GLOCKENSPIEL, percussion musical instrument, consisting of a series of metal bars tuned to a chromatic scale and mounted in two rows. It is played by a pair of knobbed beaters and produces a high-pitched, bell-like sound. Its range is two and a half to three octaves, extending up to the fourth C above middle C and notated two octaves lower. Military and marching bands use a portable form called a bell lyre, in which the bars are mounted on an upright lyre-shaped frame. The orchestral glockenspiel is played horizontally and sometimes is equipped with a keyboard, allowing the player to produce chords. Orchestral glockenspiel parts occur in *The Magic Flute* (1791), by Wolfgang Amadeus Mozart, and in *Die Walküre* (1870; The Valkyrie), by the German composer Richard Wagner. An offshoot of the glockenspiel is the celesta, in which metal bars, suspended over wooden resonators, are sounded by keyboard-controlled piano hammers and provided with a pianolike damper pedal. Patented in 1886 by the French builder Auguste Mustel (1842–1919), it was first used orchestrally in *The Nutcracker* (1892), by the Russian composer Peter Ilich Tchaikovsky. Both the glockenspiel and the celesta are metallophones (like a xylophone but with metal, not wooden, bars).

GLORIOUS REVOLUTION, name applied to the English Revolution of 1688. *See* ENGLAND: *History.*

GLOSSOLALIA (Gr. *glossa*, "tongue"; *lalein*, "to speak"), religious term for the ancient, and modern, practice of speaking in a state of ecstasy and thus in a pattern of speech different from normally intelligible patterns.

Two New Testament authors, Paul and Luke, indicate that speaking in tongues was a notable part of early Christian church life. The descent of the Holy Spirit at the festival of Pentecost (q.v.) that followed the first Easter marked the first exercise of this gift of speech (see Acts 2:1–42) in the church. Members of the church founded by Paul in Corinth spoke in tongues and valued the practice more highly than did Paul himself (see 1 Cor. 12–14). That members of Paul's other churches experienced glossolalia is suggested in Acts 19:2–7. Moreover, passages in the Old Testament such as 1 Sam. 19:20–21 and 1 Kings 18:28–29 tell of prophecy among the ancient Israelites that may parallel New Testament practices.

Luke says that the tongues in which the believers spoke at Pentecost were foreign languages; doubtless this was intended to prefigure the intelligible preaching of the gospel to people of all nations. The glossolalia practiced in Paul's churches, on the other hand, was unintelligible speech, uttered to God and of use to the assembled congregation only if interpreted by someone other than the ecstatic speaker.

The consistent element in the New Testament references to glossolalia is the belief that the Holy Spirit causes Christians to speak in tongues and that the practice is one of the Spirit's gifts. Speaking in tongues is thus considered a manifestation of one's being under the direction of the Spirit rather than of one's own rational faculty or of, for example, an administrative hierarchy. Accordingly, glossolalia has repeatedly emerged in Christian history, notably in groups reacting to what they perceive to be an overemphasis on rationality and a corresponding failure to celebrate adequately the role of the Holy Spirit.

See also CHARISMATIC MOVEMENT. J.L.Ma.

For further information on this topic, see the Bibliography in volume 28, section 108.

GLOUCESTER (anc. *Glevum*), city, administrative center of Gloucestershire, W England, on the Severn R. Gloucester is an inland port, connected by a deepwater canal (completed 1827) to docks on the Severn estuary. Harbor traffic consists chiefly of petroleum imports. Manufactures include aircraft parts, agricultural machinery, railroad equipment, and food products. Gloucester's cathedral is essentially a Norman (11th cent.) structure with Gothic additions. Edward II, who was murdered nearby, is buried in the cathedral. Also here are a historical museum, an art gallery, and a college of art. Gloucester was founded by the Romans about AD 97. Development was spurred after 681 when the Abbey of Saint Peter was built here. The town became the capital of Mercia, and by the early 11th century it had a royal residence and a mint. It was made the seat of an episcopal see in 1541. Pop. (1981) 92,133.

GLOUCESTER, city, Essex Co., NE Massachusetts, on Cape Ann; settled 1623, inc. as a city 1873. It is a port of entry, with a fine protected harbor on Gloucester Bay, an inlet of the Atlantic Ocean. One of the oldest cities in Massachusetts, Gloucester has been a famous fishing center for more than 300 years. The major industries remain fishing and fish processing, although electronic equipment, clothing, and leather items are also produced. The picturesque narrow streets, old fishing wharves, and historic buildings attract many tourists. The city has an art colony and is the hub of a large summer resort area known for its scenic rocky coast and whale-watching opportunities. Museums of interest include Hammond Castle (1928), which houses an art collection; the Beauport Sleeper-McCann House, featuring exhibits of colonial furnishings; and the Cape Ann Historical Association, with exhibitions of paintings, furniture, and maritime history. A bronze statue of a fisherman, dedicated to the thousands of Gloucester men lost at sea, is the focal point of an annual memorial

The cloister of the cathedral at Gloucester, the earliest example of English Gothic fan vaulting. British Information Services

service for those lost during the year. The French explorer Samuel de Champlain sailed past the site in 1605 and mapped the harbor in 1606. The community was settled by English fishermen and was a shipbuilding center in the 17th and 18th centuries. It is named for Gloucester, England. Pop. (1980) 27,768; (1990) 28,716.

GLOUCESTERSHIRE, county, W England; Gloucester is the administrative center. Gloucestershire is roughly divided by the Cotswold Hills. In the W is the valley of the Severn R. and near the border with Wales is the Forest of Dean, where coal is mined. The county is predominantly agricultural, dairying being especially important. Crops include grains and fruit. Diversified light manufacturing is located in the larger towns, including Gloucester, Cheltenham, and Tewkesbury. The county is rich in evidence of prehistoric habitation. Roman settlements here include Gloucester and Cirencester. An important wool trade developed in the Cotswolds in the late Middle Ages. Area, 2643 sq km (1020 sq mi); pop. (1981) 499,351.

GLOVE, covering for the hand. In modern usage a glove has a separate sheath for each finger; a mitten has a separate division only for the thumb. The wearing of gloves is generally believed to date from prehistoric times. The earliest examples come from a royal Egyptian tomb of about 1350 BC. Gloves are mentioned by such ancient Greek authors as Homer and Xenophon. The Greeks and Romans, living in comparatively mild climates, used gloves chiefly to protect the wearer doing heavy work. By the 8th and 9th centuries AD, gloves were in general use in the British Isles, Germany, and Scandinavia.

In the Middle Ages, richly jeweled and embroidered gloves were commonly worn by mon-

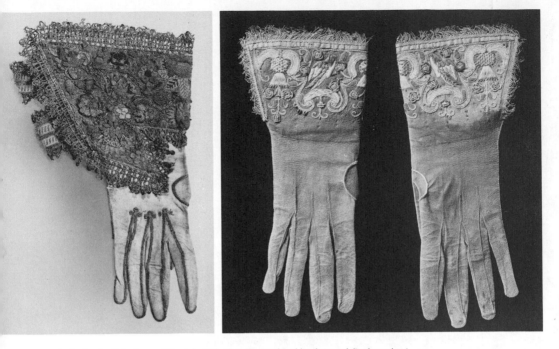

Left: An English glove of the late 16th century, made of leather and finely embroidered. Right: A pair of English buff leather gauntlets with cuffs embroidered in metal thread and silk.   Metropolitan Museum of Art—Rogers Fund

archs, noblemen, and high ecclesiastical officials; such gloves were also made a part of the papal vestments. Armored gloves, or gauntlets, were worn in hunting and in battle. Ornamental, elbow-length gloves became fashionable for ladies in the 13th century. Gloves acquired symbolic importance. A folded glove was commonly presented as a token of intent to carry out a contract in good faith. A glove was thrown down as a challenge to battle and picked up to indicate acceptance of the challenge. A lady's glove was often given as a love token.

During the 16th, 17th, and 18th centuries, fashionable men and women wore gloves of silk, velvet, and kid, often richly embroidered. Later,

gloves were also made of other woven or knitted fabric and of heavier leather. Once required for formal occasions, gloves are less frequently worn for such occasions today.

Various specialized types of gloves are used in modern scientific and industrial establishments. Among these are the fine-textured rubber gloves used by surgeons and nurses to preserve antiseptic conditions during operations, and the heavy rubber gloves worn by electrical workers, the leaded rubber gloves worn by X-ray technicians, and the asbestos-covered gloves worn by workers in steel mills, all as insulation.

For further information on this topic, see the Bibliography in volume 28, section 341.